Shakespeare's Europe

SHAKESPEARE'S
EUROPE:

A Survey of the Condition of Europe at the end of the 16th century

Being unpublished chapters of

FYNES MORYSON'S

ITINERARY (1617)

With an Introduction and an Account of
Fynes Moryson's Career by Charles Hughes

Second edition, with a new index

Benjamin Blom
New York

First published London 1903
Reissued 1967 by
Benjamin Blom, Inc. New York 10452

Second edition, with new Index
© Copyright 1967 by
Benjamin Blom, Inc.

L. C. Cat. Card No. 66-12287

Printed in U.S.A. by
NOBLE OFFSET PRINTERS, INC.
NEW YORK 3, N. Y.

These Writings of
FYNES MORYSON
Now for the first time printed
and completing his Itinerary published in 1617
are dedicated by
CHARLES HUGHES
Yarn Agent, of Manchester
to
his old friend and teacher

ADOLPHUS WILLIAM WARD, Litt.D.,

Master of Peterhouse, Cambridge
[of which College the said Fynes Moryson was a Fellow]
and formerly
Principal of Owens College, Manchester
[of which College the said Charles Hughes is an Associate]
February, 1903

INTRODUCTION.

FYNES MORYSON was born in 1566, two years after the birth of
Shakespeare.   He was the third son of Thomas Moryson, of
Cadeby, Lincolnshire, who held the lucrative office of Clerk of
the Pipe,[1] and was M.P. for Great Grimsby in the Parliaments of
1572, 1584, 1586, 1588-9.   Thomas Moryson's father was George
Moryson, of Waltham, Lincolnshire, who is said, in the
Visitation of Lincolnshire, 1592,[2] to be "descended out
of Northumberland."   The Morysons[3] were not therefore an
old Lincolnshire family, but Thomas Moryson's marriage
connected them with the oldest and best families of the county.
Fynes Moryson's mother was the daughter and one of the
co-heirs of Thomas Moyne (or Moigne) by Bridget, daughter
of Sir William Hansard, of North Kelsey.   This Thomas
Moigne, whose family had been among the gentry of Lincolnshire from the 13th century, took an important part in the
rising at the time of the Pilgrimage of Grace.   He was tried
by Sir William Parr, at Lincoln, in 1537, with the Abbot of
Kirksted and others, and the Lincoln jury sympathised with
the prisoners.   Moigne spoke in his own defence for three
hours so skilfully that "but for the diligence of the King's
serjeant" he and all the rest would have been acquitted.
"Ultimately the Crown secured their verdict.   The Abbot,
Moigne, and another were hanged on the following day at

1. The Pipe Roll was the register of the ancient revenues of the Crown,
so that Thomas Moryson's office was probably equivalent to Chief Registrar of
the Land Tax.   The persons connected with this office must have had ample
opportunities, more or less legitimate, of enriching themselves, and Thomas
Moryson became very wealthy.

2. The Visitation of Lincolnshire, 1592, edited by W. C. Metcalfe.   London :
Geo. Bell & Son, 1882.   Taken from Harl. MS., 1550.

3. I have not found any connection of this family with Sir Richard
Moryson (or Morisson) the Ambassador of Henry VIII.   He commenced the
building of Cassiobury House, near Watford, which has descended (by the
marriage of a Moryson heiress to Arthur, Lord Capel) to the present Earl of
Essex.

Lincoln, and four others a day or two later at Louth and Horncastle." [1] The Moigne family seems never to have quite recovered from this blow.

Thomas Moryson's eldest son, Edward, married Elizabeth, daughter of Robert Wingfield, of Upton, co. Northampton, Esquire. The second son, Thomas, seems to have married well, as he is described in the Visitation of 1592 as " of Sandon, co. Herts, married Ellen, daughter of Edward Powlter, of Hertford." The third and fourth sons, Fynes [2] and Henry, were sent to Cambridge; and the youngest son, Richard, went into the army. Fynes Moryson, being a student of Peterhouse, took his Bachelor's Degree at the age of 18—about the time when Shakespeare first arrived in London—and afterwards was chosen Fellow of that College. [3] The actual entry in the books of Peterhouse shows that he took the usual oath on March 13th, 1586, or, as we should say 1587, for in England at that time the new year commenced on March 25th. [4] He was expecting to be made Master of Arts, when he had a dream of his mother's death. "My brother Henry lying with me early in the morning, I dreamed that my mother passed by with a sad countenance, and

1. Froude's History with reference to Sir William Parr's letters to the King and Council. Thomas Moigne's widow married Vincent Grantham.

2. Otherwise Fines, Fiennes, and (Latinized) Fyneus. He was, no doubt, called after Edward Fiennes de Clinton, Lord Clinton and Saye, who was Lord Lieutenant of Lincolnshire at the time of Moryson's birth. This nobleman was created Earl of Lincoln in 1572, and was Lord High Admiral of England. He is said to have been a great tyrant among the gentlemen of Lincolnshire, but the Dymokes of Scrivelsby disputed his pre-eminence.

3. Itinerary, Pt. I., Page 1. The references to the Itinerary are to the Folio of 1617.

4. The entry is as follows—as supplied by Dr. T. A. Walker through the Master of Peterhouse : Anno Domini millesimo quingentessimo octuagessimo sexto decimo tertio Marti, Fyneus Moryson loco Thomae Dixy a venerabilibus viris Johano Bell in theologia et Richö Bridgwater in jure civili Doctoribus et spiritualitatis Eliens' sede vacante custod' delegat' in perpetuum socius hujus Collegii sancti Petri admissus fuit ; et eodem die ejusdem anni coram sociis dicti Collegii personaliter constitutus juramentum corporaliter præstitit quod singulis ordinationibus et statutis dicti Collegii quantum in ipso est reverenter obediret et specialiter praeter hoc de non appellando contra amotionem suam secundum modum et formam statutorum prædictorum, et de salvando cistam magistrorum Thomae de Castro Bernardi et Johannis Holbroke quantum in ipso est indemnem.

per me Fyneü Morison Lincolniensem.

told me that shee could not come to my commencement; I being within five months to proceed Master of Arts and shee having promised at that time to come to Cambridge: And when I related this dreame to my brother, both of us awaking together in a sweat, he protested to me that he had dreamed the very same, and when we had not the least knowledge of our mother's sickenesse neither in our youthfull affections were any whit affected with the strangenesse of this dreame, yet the next Carrier brought us word of our mothers death." [1] Moryson had for some years had an ambition to be a traveller, and the statutes of Peterhouse permitted two of the Fellows to travel. [2] His parents had given their consent, and he deliberately prepared himself for the task of surveying the different countries of Europe. Many young Englishmen of good family had a craving for travel, and it was especially their custom to visit the Italian Universities. [3] Moryson, however, seems from the first to have had special aims, and to have resolved to write an account of Europe, to make, in fact, a sociological survey of the civilised world of his time. Before he went abroad he was admitted to an *ad eundem* M.A. degree at Oxford. [4] This was an honour frequently given to graduates of Cambridge, Leyden, and other Universities. There is little doubt that his reason for desiring an

1. Itinerary, Pt. I., Page 19.

2. The Peterhouse records have a memorandum of a grant on August 3rd, 1590, to Fynes Moryson of "leave to discontinue," by request of his Grace of Canterbury, (Queen Elizabeth's "little black husband," Whitgift, a Lincolnshire man, born at Grimsby); the term was for five years from the Feast of All Saints' next ensuing. The records also shew entries on August 3rd, 1590, June 17, 1594, and Oct. 27, 1595, giving Fynes Moryson extra leave to travel beyond the seas.

3. For example, George Cranmer and Edwin Sandys, the friends and pupils of Richard Hooker, spent three years travelling and studying in France, Germany, and Italy.

4. According to Wood's Athenae, Moryson was "incorporated" M.A. on March 22, 1590 (this is probably a mistake for 1591). In the same year five other Cambridge men were incorporated M.A., and Saravia (afterwards the dear friend of Richard Hooker, and a graduate of Leyden) was "incorporated" as D.D. In no case is there mention of any of these persons being attached to an Oxford College—the conferring of *ad eundem* degrees being apparently a purely University function. I have consulted the volumes of the Oxford Historical Society, which contain, as Mr. Madan of the Bodleian informs me, all that is known on this subject. The Peterhouse records, however, mention a special allowance made to Fynes Moryson so long as he was on the buttery-books of an Oxford College.

Oxford degree was that the fame of Oxford in other countries was greater than that of Cambridge.

During his absence abroad he left a power of attorney with his relative Thomas Moigne, also a Fellow of Peterhouse, to receive all money due to him from that college. Thomas Moigne was the son of Moryson's mother's cousin, Francis Moigne, who left his children under the guardianship of Moryson's father.

I have prepared the following Abstract of Moryson's journeys abroad, and have printed in small capitals the places where he made a long stay.

ABSTRACT OF MORYSON'S TRAVELS.

FIRST JOURNEY.

1591.   May 1st.   Sailed from mouth of Thames, passing Heligoland to Stode (Stade), then by land to Hamburg, Lübeck, Luneburg, back to Hamburg, and thence by Magdeburg to Leipzig.

WITTEBERG (Wittenberg). "Lived there the rest of the summer," to Friburg (Freiburg), Misen (Meissen), Dresden, back to

LEIPZIG. "Stayed all winter."

1592.   Early spring, by Dresden to Prage (Prague).

PRAGUE. Stayed two months; 6 days' journey to Nürnberg, then by Augsburg, Ulm, Lindau, Schaffhausen, Zurich, Baden, to Bazill (Bâle), Strassburg and Heidelberg.

HEIDELBERG. "Lived there the rest of the summer." While there visited Spires and Worms. On leaving went by Frankfurt, Cassel, Brunswick, Luneburg, Hamburg to Stade, Oct. 1st., and travelling in disguise of a servant[1] arrived, Oct. 21st, at Emden, thence to Dockam (Dokkum), Lewerdan (Leeuwarden), Froniken, Harlingen, and over the Zuider Zee to Amsterdam. After visiting Haarlem settled in

LEYDEN for the winter.

---

1. He was passing through a country infested by Spanish troops of the worst type.

1593. [The year of the publication of Shakespeare's "Venus and Adonis"]. In the spring made a tour through the States; "Delph," "Sluse," Brill (in English occupation), "Roterodam," Dort, to "Count Maurice his camp," besieging Gertruydenberg. Then to Middleberg, Bergen-op-Zoom, Vlishing (Flushing), and by Rotterdam, Delft, and the Hague back to Leyden.

JUNE. To Utrecht and Amsterdam.

JULY. By land to Emden, then to Stade, Hamburg and Lübeck. Sailed to Denmark, "Coppenhagen," "Roschild," and Elsinore.

Aug. 26th. Sailed from Elsinore to "Dantzk," landing at Melvin (Elbing).

Sept. 9th. (old style). Coach to Cracow. From here on horseback through Vienna into Italy, and arrived end of October.

PADUA. Stayed the winter in Padua and VENICE.

1594. [The year of the publication of Shakespeare's "Lucrece"]. Feb. 3rd (new style). Ferrara, Bologna, Imola, Ravenna, Rimini, Pesaro, Ancona, Loreto, Spoleto.

March 12th. Rome, whence he immediately set out for Naples by Velletri, Ferrocina, Nola, and Capua. Travelled about Naples and Baiae for a few days, returned to Rome. "Did" the sights of Rome in four days, and departed the Tuesday before Easter, reaching Sienna on Friday.[1]

Spent the summer "in the state of FLORENCE, chiefly at San Casciano, visiting Pisa and Leghorn, and again Sienna.

Nov. 18th. Sienna to Lucca and Pisa, Carrara, Lirigi, sailed to Genoa, then to Pavia and Milan, Cremona, Mantua.[2]

PADUA. Arrived Dec. 14th (new style); visits to Arqua, etc.

1595. Left 3rd March (new style). Vicenza, Verona, Peschiera, Brescia, Bergamo, and over to Chur, Zurich, Solo-

---

1. On looking up Easter, 1594, in "L'Art de vérifier les dates," I find it quite impossible to make all the dates given by Moryson harmonize with one another.

2. Here Moryson saw the Duke of Mantua who, in his youth, had murdered his tutor, the admirable Crichton.

thurn, Losanna (Lausanne), Geneva, Berne, Strassburg, Saverne, Nanzi (Nancy), Metz, Chalons, Paris, Fontainebleau. Then by Roanne (Rouen) and Dieppe to Dover and London. Arrived May 13th (old style).

SECOND JOURNEY.

November 29th (old style). Moryson and his brother Henry left London to take ship at Gravesend, and after waiting for a wind at Margate till Dec. 7th, arrived Dec. 9th at Vlishing; arrived Dec. 16th at the Hague and then to Amsterdam, and after a hard journey through West Friesland came to

1596. Emden and by Oldenburg and "Breme" to "Stoade." Then by Oldenburg and Brunswick, Mansfeld, Erfurt, Coburg to Nürnberg and Augsburg. Then by carrier through Innspruck, Bolzena (Bozen), Trent to Venice.

April 21st. Left Venice and sailed down the Adriatic and through the Ionian Islands to Cyprus, where landed at Larnaca. Hired a ship to take seven passengers to Joppa, wait 15 days for them to go to Jerusalem, and then take them to Tripoli.

June 14th (new style) went up to Jerusalem; sailed to Tripoli and went by land to "Haleppo." June 30th (old style) left Aleppo and came to Antioch, near which Henry died. July 4th (old style), after severe illness sailed from Scanderoon (Alexandretta) to Crete, Oct. 10th (new style). Landed on the south shore of Crete and passed right across to Candia. Sailed Dec. 20th, calling at Naxos, landed on Christmas eve at Gallipoli, and thence to Constantinople.

1597. [In this year were published the quarto editions of "Richard II." and "Richard III."] CONSTANTINOPLE. Left on the last day of February.

April 30th (new style), Venice. Rode on horseback direct to Stade, July 4th (old style). Landed at Gravesend (July

9th) and arrived at 4 o'clock in the morning, July 10th, at the Cock, Aldersgate Street.

It must be remembered that the reason the dates are given sometimes "old style" and sometimes "new style" is that, speaking generally, the Gregorian Calendar of 1582 was only adopted in Roman Catholic countries. Protestant Europe was ten days behind—*i.e.*, October 4th in England was October 14th in Rome or Venice. I call attention to the places where Moryson settled down, and took up his residence because his descriptions of their social life are much more valuable than his discourses of countries where he merely passed through as an intelligent tourist and note-taker. It is true that a traveller on horseback or in posting-wagons sees much more of the country and people than a man who is whisked through on a railway; but the personal touch shows very differently after a long residence. Thus Moryson writes of Germany and its people with much more life and interest than about France and the French, and his words are more valuable about Venice and Florence than about Rome and Naples.

Moryson's plans were changed on his first journey by the death of his father. "Whilst I lived at Prage and one night had set up very late drinking at a feast, early in the morning the Sunne beames glancing on my face, as I lay in bed, I dreamed that a shadow passing by told me that my father was dead; at which awaking all in a sweat and affected with this dreame, I rose and wrote the day and houre and all circumstances thereof in a paper booke, which Booke, with many other things I put into a barrel and sent it from Prage to Stode thence to be conveied into England. And now being at Nurnberg, a Merchant of a noble family, well acquainted with me and my friends arrived there, who told me that my father died some two months past. I list not write any lies but that which I write is as true as strange. When I returned into England some four yeeres after, I would not open the barrell I sent from Prage nor looke on the paper Booke in which I had written this dreame, till I had called my sisters and some friends to be witnesses, where myself and they were astonished to see my written dreame answere the very day of my father's death." [1] Moryson arranged, while in the Low Countries, to realise his small patrimony (" for in England gentlemen give their younger sons lesse, than in forraine parts they give to their bastards "), and this must have required much correspondence with his father's executors in England.

I have been able to obtain a copy of Thomas Moryson's will which was registered in the Prerogative Court of Canterbury and is preserved in Somerset House. [2] It is a formal and carefully drawn document, the will of an energetic man who had been successful in his life and desired to order things, so far as might be, after his death.   The following passages relate to his third son. " Item I give and bequeath to my sonn ffines Morison three hundred pounds of good and lawfull money of Englande, To be paide unto him when he shall come and be of the age of twentie eighte yeeres.   And in the meane time I will that my Exequutors shall paie unto him Tenn poundes yeerelie unto suche time as he shall come and be of the age of twenty eighte yeeres.   Item I giue unto my said son ffines Morison the advouson of the nexte gifte of the prebende or rectorie of Louthe in the said countie. The which I and my son [3] George Alington have of the gifte and graunte of Mr. Devereux and Mr. Cave esquiere. . . . . Item I giue and bequeathe to my sonns ffynes Morison, Henrie Morison, Richarde Morison And to my daughters Jane Allington and ffaithe Massenden all my plate nowe in my house in London, not bequeathed in this my laste will and testamente, to be divided amongste them by the discrecion of my Exequutors or anie two of them." It does not seem too fanciful to read into these bequests that Thomas

---

1. Itinerary, Pt. I., Page 19.

2. The reference to this will was found in Vol. IV. of the Prerogative Court of Canterbury Wills, 1584—1604, issued by the British Record Society, Ltd.

3. Son-in-law.

Moryson had intended his son Fynes for the Church.   Probably he had sent him to Cambridge with that intent, and had secured the next presentation to Louth Church for a very definite purpose.   The son's yearning to see the world had spoiled his father's plans, and the bequest of the advowson may have been intended as a hint to the wanderer that he might yet reconsider his career.   Louth Church is an exceptionally imposing and beautiful building even for Lincolnshire, than which, according to Thomas Fuller, no county affords worse houses or better churches.   So Fynes Moryson may be considered to have sacrificed a comfortable and dignified position in the Church to his passion for travel.   No doubt he got a fair price for his advowson, and probably realised altogether about £500 from his father's bequests.

It must be noted that the starting point of Moryson's Continental journey was Stade,[1] near the mouth of the Elbe, the reason being that the English merchants had recently removed their traffic from Hamburg to Stade, and thus infused fresh life into this once important town.   From Stade ships were constantly sailing between the Elbe and the Thames, and therefore when Moryson hastened home from his second journey he rode on horseback from the mainland near Venice to Stade, as along the great trade route, to a place where he was sure of a speedy crossing to London.   In this case Moryson bought two horses for himself and his servant, and sold them without loss at Stade.   In his early journey he bought a horse at Cracow, and rode it to Padua, and this method seems to have been the swiftest and safest for long journeys.   Often travellers joined at a carriage, and often the carriers' carts offered a convenient, though leisurely, conveyance.   In Italy the vetturino system was in force—that is, a personally conducted tour, the traveller being relieved from all haggling with natives.   By this predecessor of the Cook system Moryson travelled from Rome to Naples and back.   In Italy he sometimes tried

---

1. Moryson spells it Stode or Stoade.

walking, and seems to have enjoyed it,[1] but does not recommend it for Germany or other countries. It must be remembered that Moryson took great trouble to learn the German,[2] Italian and French languages, that he could not only speak but write them, and that he also spoke and wrote Latin with facility. Indeed, all the accounts of his travels were written in Latin as he records on the title-page of his printed volume, and he evidently hoped to publish his book in the universal language. He is very reticent as to the names of the Englishmen whom he met when abroad;[3] for example, in Holland he notes that Brill was in English occupation, Bergen-op-Zoom held by English in States' pay, and Flushing garrisoned by ten companies of English, under Sir Robert Sidney; yet he makes no mention of any conversation with individual Englishmen. In Rome he called on Cardinal Allen to ask his "protection," but carefully avoided association with English Papists, lest he should be drawn into religious discussions. Before his departure from Rome he "interviewed" Cardinal Bellarmine, waiting for him at the Jesuits' College. "I followed him into the Colledge (being attired like an Italian and carefull not to use any strange gestures; yea, forbearing to view the Colledge or to looke upon any man fully, lest I should draw his eyes upon me). Thus I came to Bellarmine's chamber, that I might see this man so famous for his learning and so great a Champion of the Popes: who seemed to me not above forty yeeres old, being leane of body, and something low of stature with a long visage and a little sharpe beard upon the chin, of a broune colour,

1. He walked three days from Genoa into Milanese territory, and afterwards from Pavia to Milan.

2. He frequently passed himself as a German (Dutchman) in Italy. He commonly speaks of the Germans as Dutchmen, and of the Dutch as Netherlanders. The descendants of those fellow-countrymen of Moryson and Shakespeare, who emigrated to New England and to Virginia, have continued to speak of Germans as Dutchmen until the last few years.

3. Exception must be made of Francis Markham, "an English gentleman whom I left at Heidelberg," and the Davers or Danvers brothers hereafter mentioned. Francis Markham was brother to Gervase Markham. He was studying law at Heidelberg, after a period of soldiering in the Low Countries. He afterwards served as a Captain under Essex, in France and Ireland. In later life he became muster-master at Nottingham, where he wrote "The Booke of Honour," published in 1625.

and a countenance not very graue, and for his middle age,
wanting the authority of grey heires. Being come into his
chamber and having made profession of my great respect to
him, I told him that I was a Frenchman and came to Rome for
performance of some religious vowes, and to see the monuments,
especially those which were living, and among them himselfe
most especially, earnestly intreating, to the end I might from
his side returne better instructed into my Countrey, that he
would admit me at vacant houres to enjoy his graue conversation.   He gently answering, and with grauity not so much
swallowing the praises I gaue him, as shewing that my company
should be most pleasing to him, commanded his Novice, that he
should presently bring me in when I should come to visit him,
and so after some speeches of curtesie, he dismissed me who
meant nothing less than to come again to him." [1]   It must not
be supposed that he indulged in these mystifications without
very good reason.   He was willing to take a little risk for
the pleasure of coming into personal contact with a great
man, but as an English Protestant he was in constant peril of
the clutches of the Inquisition.   The protection of Cardinal
Allen might have been of small avail, and he informs us that
it was only since the defeat of the Spanish Armada that Allen
himself had ceased to persecute Protestants.   As an antidote
against his conversation with Bellarmine, Moryson took the
opportunity, when he reached Geneva on his way home, to visit
Beza, the head of the Calvinist Church.   "Here I had great
contentement to speake and converse with the reuerent Father
Theodore Beza who was of stature something tall, and corpulent,
or big boned and had a long thicke beard as white as snow.
He had a graue Senatours countenance and was broad-faced but
not fat, and in generall by his comely person, sweet affabilitie,
and gravitie he would have extorted reuerence from those that
least loued him.   I walked with him to the Church, and giving
attention to his speech, it happened that in the Church porch
I touched the poore man's box with my fingers and this reuerend

1. Itin., Part I., Page 142.

man soone perceived my errour, who hauing used in Italy to dip my fingers towards the holy water (according to the manner of the Papists, lest the omitting of so small a matter generally used, might make me suspected of my Religion and bring me into dangers of greater consequence) did now in like sort touch this poore man's box mistaking it for the Font of holy water. I say, hee did soone perceiue my errour, and taking me by the hand, advised me hereafter to eschew these ill customes, which were so hardly forgotten."[1] In Moryson's accounts of Rome and other Italian cities he shows little or no knowledge of architecture or appreciation of art. Of St. Peter's Church he remarks " They say it was built by Constantine the Great." He gives absolutely no indication that what he saw was partly the present St. Peter's and partly the old basilica of Constantine, the eastern portion of which was not pulled down till 1606.[2] This certainly seems to show a want of intelligent observation, though we have no right to expect much accuracy of detail from a traveller who saw all the sights of Rome in four days. His account of this four days' sight-seeing fills twenty large folio pages containing as much matter as fifty pages of this volume.[3]

In passing through France on his way to England Moryson incurred much danger, as the country was full of disbanded soldiers returning to their homes, the Civil War between Henri IV. and the League having come to an end. Though he sold his horse and went on foot with an appearance of poverty, this did not save him, for he was robbed of his " inward doublet wherein I had quilted the gold," and of his "sword, cloake and shirtes." The soldiers left him the rest of his " apparell, wherein I doe acknowledge their courtesie since theeues give all they doe not take." His elaborate precautions, however, saved him from absolute destitution. "One thing in this miserie made me glad.

1. Itinerary, Part I., Page 181.

2. Lanciani, The Destruction of Rome, Page 253.

3. It was probably largely based on the guide-book printed in Venice entitled " Le Cose Maravigliose della Città di Roma." A copy of the appendix to this book, called " La Guida Romana," printed in Rome in 1562, has recently been discovered by Mr. W. M. Voynich, with a preface shewing that the author was an Englishman named Shakerley.

I formerly said that I sold my horse for 16 French Crownes at Metz, which Crownes I put in the bottome of a wooden box and covered them with a stinking ointment for scabs. Sixe other French Crownes for the worst event I lapped in cloth, and thereupon did wind divers colored threads, wherein I sticked needles, as if I had been so good a husband as to mend my own clothes. This box, and this ball of thread I had put in my hose as things of no worth; and when in spoiling me they had searched my pockets they first tooke the boxe and smelling the stinke of the ointment they cast it away on the ground; neither were they so frugall to take my bal of thread to mend their hose, but did tread it likewise under their feet. Then they rode swiftly to their companions, and I with some sparke of joy in my greater losse tooke up the box and ball of thread, thinking myself lesse miserable, that by the Grace of God I had some money left to keepe me from begging in a strange Countrey." In Paris he had some difficulty in raising money, but was assisted by two English brethren,[1] " namely Sir Charles and Sir Henry Davers who for an ill accident[2] liued there as banished men," and whose remittances had been confiscated by Queen Elizabeth. " Yet did they not cast off all care to provide for me but with great importunitie perswaded a starueling Merchant to furnish me with ten French Crownes." Before leaving for England Moryson journeyed to Fontainebleau to see Henri IV., a sight well worth seeing, no doubt, and very sugges-tive to such a sturdy Protestant as Moryson. Though he had

1. Itinerary, Part I., Page 186.

2. They had killed in a quarrel a Wiltshire gentleman named Long, of the same family as the present President of the Local Government Board. They were not pardoned till 1598. Charles Davers (or Danvers) was indebted for his escape from England to Shakespeare's patron the Earl of Southampton, through whom he was afterwards involved in the Essex conspiracy. He was executed on Tower Hill, March 18, 1600—1601. His estates were confiscated, but after the accession of James I. were restored to his brother Henry Danvers, who afterwards became Earl of Danby and lived till 1644. Another brother, John Danvers, when a youth of twenty, married Magdalen Herbert, the widowed mother of Lord Herbert of Cherbury, and of George Herbert. This lady was twice as old as her husband and had been the mother of ten children, yet, according to their friend Dr. John Donne, they were a happy couple. John Danvers lived to sign the death warrant of Charles I.

taken some trouble to see the King he says absolutely nothing about him. Probably he thought the more.

So Moryson returned home from his first journey after four years' absence, and came to the London house of his sister Jane, wife of George Alington.[1] " It happened that (in regard of my robbing in France) when I entered my sister's house in poore habit, a servant of the house upon my demand answered that my sister was at home; but when he did see me goe up the staires too boldly (as he thought) without a guide, hee not knowing me in respect of my long absence did furiously and with threatning words call me backe, and surely would have been rude with me had I not gone up faster than he could follow me, and just as I entred my sisters chamber he had taken hold on my old cloake which I willingly flung of, to be rid of him. Then by my sisters imbraces he perceived who I was, and stole backe as if he had trodden upon a Snake." [2]

Before the end of the year Moryson started again, taking with him his younger brother Henry, who also had a longing for foreign travel. Moryson felt that he had seen most of Europe, for Spain was practically sealed to him owing to the continued war, " Yet I had an itching desire to see Jerusalem the fountaine of Religion and Constantinople of old the seate of Christian Emperors, and now the seate of the Turkish Ottoman." Henry Moryson " put out some four hundred pounds, to be repaied twelve hundred pounds upon his returne from those two Cities, and to lose it if he died in the journey." [3] This method of insuring the costs of a journey in the event of a safe return was not uncommon, and is mentioned in Shakespeare's

---

1. George Alington, of Swinhope, of whom some account is given on Page xxii.

2. Itinerary, Part I., Page 197.

3. Moryson takes another opportunity of reprehending "the English Law most unmeasurably favouring elder brothers," and " the ignorant pride of fathers," by which younger sons "rush into all vices," and makes the singularly false statement "all wise men confesse that nothing is more contrary to good-nesse than poverty."

"Tempest." [1] Moryson followed his brother's example, "Onely I gave out one hundred pound to receiue three hundred at my return among my brethren and some few kinsmen and dearest friends of whom I would not shame to confesse that I had received so much of gift. And lest by spending upon [2] the stocke my patrimony should be wasted, I moreover gave to fiue friends one hundred pounds with condition they should have it if I died, or after three yeeres should repay it with one hundred and fifty pound gaine if I returned; which I hold a disadvantageous adventure to the giver of the money. Neither did I exact this money of any man by sute of Law after my returne which they willingly and presently paid me only some few excepted, who retaining the very money I gave them, dealt not therein so gentleman-like with me as I did with them. And by the great expences of my journey much increased by the ill accidents of my brother's death, and my owne sicknesse, the three hundred fifty pounds I was to receive of gain after my return and the one hundred pounds which my brother and I carried in our purses, would not satisfie the five hundred pounds we had spent, (though my brother died within the compasse of the first yeare) but I was forced to pay the rest out of my owne patrimony." [3] It is clear that Moryson adopts a tone of apology in speaking of their financial methods, and he explains this by showing that times had changed and that customs once favoured by gentlemen of good position were no longer considered creditable. They had been adopted by a lower class of society. [4] " Now in this

1. Actus Tertius, Scena Tertia—
   Gonzalo.—Faith Sir you neede not feare : when wee were Boyes
   Who would beleeve that there were Mountayneers,
   Dew-lapt, like Buls, whose throats had hanging at 'em
   Wallets of flesh? or that there were such men
   Whose heads stood in their brests? which now we finde
   Each putter-out of five for one, will bring us
   Good warrant of.
I quote from the First Folio as the spelling is similar to Moryson's.

2. That is " out of "

3. Itin., Part I., Page 199.

4. William Kemp in the curious account of his Morrice-dancing from London to Norwich, which he dedicated to Mistress Anne Fitton, and published in 1600, under the title " Kemp's nine daies wonder," says, " I put out some money to have three-fold gaine at my returne." We should now speak of this financial method simply as betting.

age, if bankerouts, Stage-players, and men of base condition
have drawne this custome into contempt : I grant that Courtiers
and Gentlemen have reason to forbeare it; yet know not why
they should be blamed who have thus put out their mony in
another age,[1] when this custom was approved."

So Fynes and Henry Moryson arrived at Venice and
prepared for their journey to the Turkish Empire; " Our swords,
daggers and European garments we left in our chests with a
Flemmish Merchant lying at Venice, to be kept against our
returne; and howsoever he, falling banckerout, left the City
before that time, yet our goods were by the publike officer laid
apart and readily deliuered to us at our [2] returne." Travel in
Turkish territory was humiliating to Elizabethan Englishmen.
Not only could they carry no arms, but they dared not look a
Turk straight in the face, and, unless they hired a Janizary to
protect them, were obliged to submit patiently to all insults and
injuries.   To draw a sword or a knife upon a Turk would
involve "an ill death by public justice," and the travellers bore
with outward meekness a treatment " which notwithstanding I
know not how any man carrying Armes could have the patience
to endure."   When they landed at Joppa, Henry, who had been
noted on shipboard for his " fast walking and melancholy
humour," leaped upon land " and, according to the manner, bent
down to kisse it; by chance he fell, and voided much blood at
the nose: and howsoever this be a superstitious sign of ill,
yet the event was to us tragicall, by his death shortly after
happening."   Moryson's description of Jerusalem is very full
and interesting, but as he reports much which was told him
by the Italian Friars at the Latin Monastery he is careful to
say : " Yet doe I not myselfe beleeue all the particulars I write
upon their report, neither do I perswade any man to beleeue
them."   He was himself deeply impressed, and confesses " that
(through the grace of God) the very places struck me with a

---

1. When Moryson published his book in 1617 it must indeed have seemed
'another age' compared with the times when his continental journeys were
made, with great Elizabeth in all her glory.

2. He means " my " returne, for Henry had died in Asia Minor.

religious horrour, and filled my mind prepared to devotion with holy motions." Moryson confesses that they incurred much needless danger in the Holy Land through want of experience. If they had gone first to Constantinople and there hired a Janizary through the medium of the English Ambassador, they would have been quite safe at Jerusalem and independent of the help of the Italian priests, at whose convent they stayed. Towards these Friars he conducted himself with great carefulness and dissimulation, disguising the fact that he was a "heretic." In the previous year two Englishmen, Henry Bacon and Andrew Verseline, had died under suspicious circumstances. Their names were written on the walls of the chambers where the Moryson brothers lodged, and our author thinks the friars quite capable of having poisoned them. Moryson believed that a friendly French friar who was travelling with them detected their heretical characters, and making a pun on Moryson's Christian name, said to him : " En verité vous estes fin." The pretence of being "Catholiques" was, however, kept up to the end, and the Franciscan Friars gave them "freely and unasked as it seems of custome a testimony under the seale of the Monastery, that we had beene at Jerusalem, and for better credit, they expressed therein some markable signes of our faces and bodies." After this "there remained nothing but the Epilogue of the Comedy, that we should make some fit present to the Guardian of the Monastery."[1]

On returning to Joppa the Morysons sailed in their Cyprus ship[2] to " Tripoli of Syria so-called for difference from Tripoli in Africke." "A Christian who useth to entertaine the French did very well entreat us here : and when I did see a bed made for me and my brother, with cleane sheetes, I could scarcely containe myself from going to bed before supper, because I had never lien in naked bed since I came from Venice to this day, having alwaies slept by sea and lande in my doublet, with

1. Page 235, Part I.
2. The Captain was not to be paid till he returned to Cyprus with a letter from Moryson that he had been landed at Tripoli—the money being left for him with merchants at Larnaca.

linnen breeches and stockings, upon a mattrasse, and between couerlets or quilts, with my breeches under my head. But after supper all this joy vanished by an euent least expected. For in this part of Asia great store of Cotten growes (as it were) upon stalkes like Cabbage; and these sheetes being made thereof, did so increase the perpetuall heat of this countrey, now most unsupportable in the summer time, as I was forced to leape out of my bed, and sleepe as I had formerly done." [1]　From Tripoli the travellers proceeded by land to " Haleppo," where the English merchants, living in three houses " as it were in Colledges," entertained them very courteously, and they were especially indebted to the English Consul, George Dorington, for much kindness. They departed thence with a merchant's caravan, but soon after passing Antioch, Henry Moryson was taken ill of a flux.[2] He was much shaken on the back of a Camel and died in his brother's arms " after many loving speeches, and the expressing of great comfort in his Divine meditations." It is clear that Moryson was deeply attached to his younger brother thus cut off in the twenty-seventh year of his age. The circumstances were such as to drive him nearly distracted. " While myself and my brother were in our last imbraces, and mournefull speeches, the rascall multitude of Turkes and Moores ceased not to girde and laugh at our sighes and teares; neither know I why my heart-strings brake not in these desperate afflictions; but I am sure from that day to this I neuer enjoied my former health, and that this houre was the first of my old age." [3] Moryson returned from Scanderoon to protect his brother's grave by a large pile of stones from the jackals,[4] who had nearly uncovered it. On returning he tells us that " the greefe of my mind cast me into a great sicknesse, so as I, who in perfect health had passed so many kingdoms of Europe, at this time

1. Part I., Page 242. That Moryson should be unacquainted with cotton sheets seems at first sight rather strange, since Manchester "Cottons" had been renowned for a hundred years. These were all, however, made of wool.

2. Dysentery.

3. Part I., Page 249. He was in his thirty-first year.

4. " A kind of beast a little bigger than a Foxe and ingendered between Foxes and Wolues, vulgarly called Jagale."

in the very flower of my age, first began to wax old. This sicknesse brought the first weaknesse to my body, and the second, proceeding of another greife after my returne into England,[1] tooke from me all thoughts of youthful pleasures, and demonstratively taught me that the Poet most truly said *Cura facit canos*, that is, Care maketh gray-headed." His weak state of health made his journey across Crete[2] (then under the rule of the Venetians) very arduous to him. Of his visit to Constantinople[3] the fruits are seen in the brilliant and vivid account of the Turkish empire now first printed in this volume. He came home as swiftly as possible, and on his arrival at the Cock in Aldersgate Street, in July, 1597, closed his long course of Continental travel.

The following year, in April, he "tooke a journey" to Berwick-on-Tweed upon "occasion of businesse" as to the nature of which he leaves us in the dark. He found Berwick "abounding with all things necessary for food, yea with many dainties as Salmons and all kinds of shell fish, soe plentifully as they were sold for very small prices. And here I found that for the lending of sixtie pounds there wanted not good Citizens who would give the lender a faire Chamber and good dyet as long as he would lend them the money." He seems to have remained at Berwick till September, and before returning made a journey to see the King of Scots' Court. "So from hence I rode in one day fortie miles to Edenborrow the chiefe Citie of that Kingdom." This was a good day's ride, for the distance by Moryson's route, through Dunbar, Haddington and Mussel-burgh, is 58 English miles.[4] Moryson does not treat the

1. As Moryson makes no reference to the death of any near relative soon after his return to England, he possibly refers to a disappointment in love.

2. He speaks of passing near to the "Laberinth" and the cave of Minos "which the Candians call the sepulcher of Jupiter."

3. Here he saw a Giraffe "newly brought out of Affricke (the mother of monsters), which beast is altogether unknowne in our parts . . . the picture whereof I remember to have seen in the Mappes of Mercator."

4. Staying in Northumberland last summer, I had the curiosity to follow this ride of Moryson's from Berwick to Edinburgh on my bicycle, only diverging from his route to pass through the demesne of Whittinghame, the seat of our present Prime Minister, who is a descendant of Lord Burleigh and Robert Cecil. The fortifications of Berwick, erected in the time of Queen Elizabeth, are still almost intact.

"mile" as a fixed measure of length, but says: "A common English Mile makes one and a halfe Italian but towards the North and in some particular places of England the miles are longer among which the Kentish mile (being a Southerne county) is proverbially held to be extrordinarily long." King James was hunting at Falkland, and Moryson crossed the Firth of Forth from "Lethe" to Kinghorn and rode ten very long miles to this "Pallace of old building and almost ready to fall." He had intended to go to Stirling and St. Andrews, but "some occasions of unexpected businesse recalled me speedily into England." It seems highly probable that Moryson was at Berwick as a channel of communication with the future King of England from some of the many English noblemen and statesmen who were preparing for what must follow on Elizabeth's death.[1] It is extremely likely, as will be seen from what follows, that he was employed by the Essex faction, and his sudden journey and rapid return to England probably meant that he was entrusted with verbal communications too dangerous to be put in writing. At this time negotiations were going on for sending Essex to Ireland to put down Tyrone's rebellion, then in the height of its success, and to restore order. The Queen's warrant for the "establishment" of the Earl of Essex in Ireland was signed on the 24th of March, 1599 (or on the last day of 1598 according to the English reckoning at that time), and comprised provision for an army of 16,000 foot and 1,300 horse. Included in this army were two fine regiments of tried soldiers from the Low Countries, in one of which Richard Moryson, the younger brother of Fynes, was a captain. Fynes Moryson himself, however, had a period of rest and quiet in his native Lincolnshire. He did not reside with his elder brother

1. There is ample evidence of the general uneasiness that was felt as to what would happen on the death of Elizabeth. The fear of a Civil War about the succession to the throne had never entirely disappeared, from the time when Henry VIII. had his difficulties about getting a male heir. It had commenced when old people could remember the Wars of the Roses, and in Elizabeth's old age the uncertainty was beginning to get on people's nerves. The peaceful accession of James in 1603 does not prove that Englishmen's fears were ground-less. There was no precedent to guide them as to what might happen.

at Cadeby, but with his married sisters, Jane, the wife of George Alington, of Swinhope, and Faith, the wife of Francis Mussenden (or Massendeene, or Missenden),[1] of Healing.   Each of these places is within a few miles of Cadeby, and it seems reasonable to suppose that Fynes had no great affection for his brother Edward, as he never mentions him (while speaking of his "deare" sisters), and often makes bitter remarks about eldest sons.   The old Roman road, called Barton Street, passes near Cadeby, which is almost midway between Louth and Great Grimsby, and it also passes near Healing, which is not far from the south bank of the Humber.   At Healing " whilest I passed an idle yeere I had a pleasing opportunitie to gather into some order out of confused and torne writings the particular observations of my former travels to be after more deliberately digested at leisure."   As a matter of fact, he had nearly two years of this restful time before he departed for active service in Ireland.   I have visited all these places, Cadeby, Healing and Swinhope, riding a bicycle, where Fynes Moryson used to ride on horseback.[2] Cadeby is in a very secluded situation under a small range of wolds.   The present house is comparatively new, probably built after the Civil Wars, when the Moryson family had

---

1. The Mussendens came to Lincolnshire in the fourteenth century, bringing the name from the Buckinghamshire village of Missenden, known in connection with John Hampden.   The main branch of this family became extinct on the death of Fynes Moryson's brother-in-law.   The Rector of Healing sends me the following extract from the Parish Register of 1612, " Francis Massenden, Esq., was buried the 13th day of November."

2. Moryson's elder brother, however, was probably able to go to London in his own coach, for about this time the gentlemen of Lincolnshire began to keep carriages or coaches, not merely in and about Lincoln, but also in the manor-houses situated near small villages. This shows not only an increase of wealth and luxury, but also an improvement in the roads.   For example, Sir John Langton, of Langton, near Spilsby, who died in 1616, left to his wife " my Charoch, three Coche horses, with all furniture to eche of them belonging."   Readers of Boswell may be interested to hear that the Langtons are the oldest family in Lincolnshire.   The present Langton of Langton has a continuous descent in the male line from the 13th Century in occupation of the land from which the family takes its name, and one of the links in this chain of long descent is Johnson's friend, Bennet Langton.   I take this opportunity of expressing my great indebtedness to the two admirable volumes of " Lincolnshire Wills " published by the Revd. A. R. Maddison, F.S.A., Priest-Vicar of Lincoln Cathedral.—(Lincoln, 1888, 1891).

disappeared from Lincolnshire.[1]   The situation is just such as
would have been chosen for a religious house.   There is also an
underground passage leading to two vaulted larders that have
no connection with the present building, and a fine system of
brick drainage belonging to an older period.   Moreover the
fish-ponds are said by local tradition to have belonged to the
monks.   One of them is, curiously enough, called the Monk's
bath.   When we remember that Fynes Moryson's grandfather
came from Northumberland about 1540, it seems very likely
that he obtained the property of some religious house.[2]

Swinhope is about four miles west of Cadeby on the other
side of the small range of wolds which extend southward, increasing in height.   It lies rather low, and is a little village
with an exceedingly small church,[3] the chancel perhaps of a
larger fabric.   The Swinhope estate,[4] comprising nearly the
whole parish of Swinhope, was bought about the year 1580 by
George Alington or Allington, who married Jane Moryson.
This George Alington became a very wealthy man.   He was
born in 1550, being the second son of Giles Alington, of Rus-
ford, Norfolk, who married the sister of Sir John Cheke.   He
obtained, quite early in life the office of Master of Escheats for
Lincolnshire,[5] and accumulated a very large fortune.   Swinhope
was only a small part of the land which he bought in the
county.   He also had estates in Kent, and property in London.
This large fortune was evidently the result of his offices which

1. What the Wars of the Roses were to the mediæval Nobility, the Great
Rebellion was to the Gentry of Lincolnshire.   The majority were on the King's
side ; and fines for 'malignancy' completed the ruin of those whose ancestral acres
were already heavily mortgaged.—*Maddison.*

2. This is of course a matter of conjecture.   The local traditions cannot
be absolutely trusted, and Dugdale's Monasticon has no mention of a religious
house at Cadeby.

3. Only in a few out-of-the-way villages of Cumberland have I seen smaller
Churches.

4. The Alingtons' house at Swinhope was burnt by the Roundheads in the
Civil War.

5. Probably also for other counties, as these offices were in the gift of the
Lord Treasurer.   George Alington seems also to have had some position in the
Pipe Office.   See Add. MS. 32472, f. 196 v. British Museum.   My friend,
Mr. Joseph Hall, the editor of "King Horn," has searched on my behalf the
collections of papers relating to Lincolnshire in the British Museum for references
to the Morysons and Alingtons.

gave him opportunities of buying land when sales were forced. There is not much mystery as to how he obtained these posts when we remember that the first wife of William Cecil, Lord Burleigh, was a sister of Sir John Cheke, and therefore aunt to George Alington. Sir John Cheke himself, who was tutor to Edward VI. obtained priory lands at Spalding in Lincolnshire, and Burleigh's connection with that county was very close. His mother was daughter and heiress of a Lincolnshire man, and he received part of his education at Grantham grammar-school. When we remember how the Lincolnshire gentry were intermarried,[1] and how people from all parts of the county would meet at Lincoln, it is not very far-fetched to suppose that Fynes Moryson's father may have owed his office of Clerk of the Pipe to the connection of Cecil and Cheke with his native county. George Alington lived to be 82 and his son and grandson died before him. His lands, therefore, went to his great-nephew, from whom the present owner of Swinhope, Admiral Alington, is descended. I am indebted to Admiral Alington[2] for a sight of the family pedigree, drawn out by W. Darel in 1639, and showing after the fashion of those times, the descent of the family from a follower of William the Conquerer. I looked, of course, for the connection with the Morysons, and found it duly recorded. He also showed me a contemporary—and well painted—portrait of Fynes Moryson's brother-in-law, and his will, drawn up by himself in his 82nd year. George Alington left £50 to the poor of St. Botolph's,[3] Aldersgate Street, and a similar sum to the poor of Clerkenwell. He mentions by name all his relatives and

1. A network of relationships was spread throughout the county. It is not too much to say that every gentleman of good descent and estate was related, either more or less nearly, to his neighbours of the same degree. Exclusiveness in the modern sense of the term did not exist and the Civil War had not yet come to sever friendship.—*Maddison's Lincolnshire Wills.*

2. Admiral Alington commanded the gunboats on the Canadian lakes at the time of the Fenian raids into Canada.

3. St. Botolph lived in the fens of Lincolnshire. According to Thomas Fuller the town of Boston derived its name from this seventh century saint. As, however, there were other churches of St. Botolph in London, we must not assume that the Lincolnshire Saint attracted Lincolnshire people to this parish.

connexions, including several of the Morysons, and leaves them
each a ring of Angell Gold, value two pounds, with the inscription G.A., and a death's head, with the motto : " *Sum Quod
eris.*" From one of his dispositions we learn that he expected
an investment of £1,600 in land to bring in £100 per annum.
These facts about George Alington [1] will serve to show that
Fynes Moryson had the advantage of a very rich brother-in-law,
to whose house in Aldersgate Street he could go when he pleased,
and who had the inestimable advantage of a connexion with the
Cecils.

After resting with his relatives in Lincolnshire and putting
his papers into order, Fynes Moryson prepared for a new
career in the public service, to which he was called by the
presence of his younger brother with the English army in
Ireland.[2] Essex had failed deplorably to understand the situation, and returned to England without permission, leaving
affairs in a most critical condition. Charles Blount, Lord
Mountjoy, was appointed to succeed him. Moryson applied to
be one of his Secretaries. Mountjoy was already provided, but
wrote that if Moryson would come out, he would find him some
fit and good employment. Before setting out for Ireland, he
visited Cambridge, to bring his long and pleasant association
with Peterhouse to a close. " The Master and Fellowes by
speciall indulgence had continued unto mee my place with
leaue to trauell from the yeere 1589 to this present July in the
yeere 1600. At which time being modest further to importune
so loving friends, and having the foresaid assurance of preferment in Ireland, I yeelded up my Fellowship which in my
former absence had yeelded me some twenty pounds yeerely.
And the society (to knit up their loving course towards me) gave
me aforehand the profit of my place for two yeeres to come.
For which curtesie and for my education there, I must euer

1. The present Lord Alington (Sturt) is descended from the Alingtons of
Swinhope in the female line through the Napiers.

2. Moryson's brother was knighted by Essex, in Dublin, in August, 1599,
and is henceforth called Sir Richard Moryson.

acknowledge a strict bond of loue and seruice to each of them in particular and to the whole body jointly." [1]

Fynes Moryson was now about to enter the service of Lord Mountjoy, one of the greatest Englishmen of his time, whom Camden describes as " so eminent for virtue and learning that in those respects he hath no superior and but few equals." He was born in 1563 and shewed the combination of studiousness with military adventure that characterised so many of the Elizabethans. When a young man he had a duel with Essex, who afterwards became his friend and ally. While serving in the Low Countries he was present at the Zutphen skirmish, in which Sir Philip Sidney met his death. Sidney had been the lover of Penelope, wife of Lord Rich, and sister of Essex. She was the Stella of his poems, and had been married to Lord Rich against her inclination, as she had been promised to Sidney. She never professed any affection for her husband, though she bore him a large family, and some years after the death of Sidney, Mountjoy succeeded him in her affections. It was one of those *liaisons* which, from the celebrity and high rank of the persons concerned and its long duration, became recognised by Society and by the Court. Lord Rich shewed no resentment during the lifetime of his wife's brother the Earl of Essex. Mountjoy had been with Essex to the Azores in 1597, and was certainly involved in that nobleman's correspondence with King James of Scotland.

While Fynes Moryson was waiting at Chester—which he calls Westchester—for a passage to Ireland, he received a letter from Mountjoy, " by which I did gather that his Lordship purposed to imploy me in the writing of the History or Journall of Irish affairs. But it pleased God in his gracious providence (which I may never leave unmentioned) to dispose better of me. For staying for a wind till the end of September, one of his Lordships three Secretaries (either to avoid the trouble and danger of the warres, or for other reasons best knowne to him)

1. The Peterhouse records say that it was on August 7th, 1600, that he relinquished his fellowship and was pronounced *non-socius*.

came over, and told me that he had left his Lordships service.
Thus with better hopes of preferment I crossed the seas in very
tempestuous weather.   After a few days spent in Dublin I tooke
my journey to Dundalke on the Northerne borders, where my
brother Sir Richard Moryson was then Governour, and there I
lodged till the Lord Deputies returne with the Army.   And the
thirteenth of November being the day of Carlingford fight,
whilest I walked in my brothers garden, I sensibly heard by
reverberation of the wall, the sound of the vollies of shot in
that skirmish, though the place were at least six miles distant.
In this fight the Lord Deputy his chiefe Secretary George
Cranmer was killed, and his Lordship having now only one
Secretary did receive me the next day at Dundalke into Cranmers
place."

This George Cranmer—whose career was cut short so
opportunely for Fynes Moryson—was the grand-nephew of
Archbishop Cranmer, and the pupil and intimate friend of
Richard Hooker.   The account in Izaak Walton's "Life of
Hooker," of the visit of George Cranmer and Edwin Sandys to
their old tutor's country parsonage at Drayton-Beauchamp, in
Buckinghamshire, is one of the most charming passages of a
charming writer.[1]   As Moryson now became a "servant" of
Mountjoy, and until the death of that nobleman remained in his
service, it may be well to quote here a portion of the elaborate
description by our author of his patron:—" He was of stature
tall, and of very comely proportion, his skin faire with little
haire on his body, which haire was of colour blackish (or
inclining to blacke), and thin on his head where he wore it
short, except a locke under his left eare, which he nourished
the time of this warre, and being woven up, hid it in his necke
under his ruffe.   The crown of his head was in latter days
somthing bald as the forepart naturally curled; he onely used

---

1. Walton says of Cranmer, in his Life of Hooker, " I shall refer my
Reader to the printed testimonials of our learned Mr. Camden, Fynes Moryson,
and others."   A long letter of George Cranmer to Hooker is printed in the
Appendix to the Life.   It may be noted that Izaak Walton's first wife was
George Cranmer's niece.

the Barber for his head, for the haire on his chin (growing slowly) and that on his cheekes and throat he used almost daily to cut it with his sizers, keeping it so low with his owne hand, that it could scarce be discerned as likewise himselfe kept the haire of his upper lippe somewhat short, only suffering that under his nether lip to grow at length and full; yet some two or three yeeres before his death, he nourished a sharpe and short pikedevant on his chin. His forehead was broad and high; his eyes great, blacke, and lovely; his nose somethink low and short and a little blunt in the end; his cheekes full, sound, and ruddy, his countenance cheerefull, and as amiable as ever I beheld of any man, onely some two yeeres before his death upon discon-tentement his face grew thinne, his ruddy colour failed, growing somewhat swarthy, and his countenance was sad and dejected. His armes were long and of proportionable bignes, his hands long and white, his fingers great in the ende and his leggs somewhat little which he gartered ever above the knee, wearing the Garter of Saint Georges order under the left knee, except when he was booted and so wore not that Garter, but a blew ribbon instead thereof aboue his knee, and hanging over his boote.[1] . . . For his diet he used to fare plentifully and of the best, and as his meanes increased so his Table was better served, so that in his latter time no Lord in England might compare with him in that kind of bountie. Before these warres, he used to have nourishing brackefasts, as panadoes, and broths; but in the time of the warre, he used commonly to breake his fast with a drie crust of bread and in the Spring time with butter and sage with a cup of stale beer wherewith sometimes in Winter he would have suger and Nutmeg mixed. He fed plentifully both at dinner, and supper, having the choicest and

---

1. Moryson apologises for the elaborate particulars which he gives of Mountjoy's dress (I omit these from considerations of space)—but remarks that "the wise man hath taught us that the apparell in some sort shewes the man." Moryson was not quoting from Polonius in Hamlet,
 "For the apparell oft proclaimes the man,"
for he would never have mentioned Shakespeare as the "Wise Man," and indeed he might have quoted from "Measure for Measure,"
 "Everie true man's apparell fits your Theefe"
to the very opposite effect.

most nourishing meates, with the best wines which he drunk
plentifully but never in great excesse; and in his latter yeeres
(especially in the time of the warre, aswell when his night
sleepes were broken, as at other time upon full diet) he used to
sleepe in the afternoones and that long, and upon his bed.   He
tooke Tobacco abundantly, and of the best, which I think
preserved him from sicknes (especially in Ireland where the
Foggy aire of the bogs, and waterish foule, plentie of fish,
generally all meates with the common sort alwaies unsalted and
greene rosted doe most prejudice the health), for he was very
seldom sicke, onely he was troubled with the head-ach which
duly and constantly like an ague for many yeeres till his
death, tooke him once every three months, and vehemently held
him some three daies, and himselfe in good part attributed,
as well the reducing of this paine to these certaine and distant
times, as the ease he therein found to the virtues of this
herbe.[1] . . . Touching his affecting honour and glorie, I may
not omit that his most familiar friends must needes obserue, the
discourses of his Irish actions to have been extraordinarily
pleasing to him: so that, howsoever hee was not prone to hold
discourses with Ladies, yet I have observed him more willingly
drawne to those of this nature with the Irish Ladies entertaining
him, then into any other. . . . Touching his studies or Bookish-
nesse (by some imputed to him in detraction of his fitnes to
imbrace an active imployment) he came young and not well
grounded from Oxford University; but in his youth at London
he so spent his vacant houres with schollers best able to direct
him, as besides his reading in Histories, skill in tongues (so
farre as he could read and understand the Italian and French
though he durst not adventure to speak them), and so much
knowledge (at least in Cosmography and the Mathematics) as
might serue his owne ends, he had taken such paines in the
search of naturall Phylosophy, as in divers arguments of that

1. Sir Walter Raleigh with whose name tobacco is inseparably connected—
as also potatoes—was at this time Captain of the Queen's Guard and Lord
Warden of the Stanneries.   He was, however, distrusted and disliked as being
hostile to the King of Scots, Elizabeth's probable successor.

nature held by him with schollers, I have often heard him (not without marvelling at his memory and judgement) to re-member of himselfe the most materiall points, the subtilest objections, and the soundest answers. But his chiefe delight was in the study of Divinity, and more especially in reading of the Fathers and Schoolemen; for I have heard himselfe professe that being in his youth addicted to Popery, so much as through prejudicate opinion no Writer of our time could have conuerted him from it, yet by observing the Fathers consent, and the Schoolemens idle and absurd distinctions he began first to distaste many of their opinions, and then by reading our Authours to be confirmed in the reformed doctrine which I am confident he professed and beleeued from the heart, though in his innated temper he was not factious against the Papists but was gentle towards them, both in conversation and in all occasions of disputation. And I will be bold to say, that of a Lay-man he was (in my judgement) the best Divine I ever heard argue, especially for disputing against all the Papists, out of the Fathers, Schoolemen, and aboue all out of the written Word whereof some Chapters were each night read to him, besides his never intermitted prayers at morning and night."[1]

This was the man who subdued Ireland, which he found at the height of its greatest revolt against England, and brought to absolute submission and subjection. By constant activity summer and winter, by keeping his plans secret, and by the establishment of strong posts,[2] he was able to crush the Irish chieftains, sweep off the cattle and starve out the people. Nor were the Irish the only enemy. A large Spanish force landed in Ireland to assist the rebels. Mountjoy besieged them in Kinsale, routed with enormous loss the Irish army which tried to relieve them, and forced them to an honourable capitulation.

1. These portions of the character of Mountjoy are taken from pages 45—47 of Part II.—the Irish portion of the 1617 Itinerary. The "character" is evidently modelled on those of Plutarch.

2. Roughly speaking Mountjoy instituted a block-house system without any concentration camps, the country being swept of food. The destitution caused revolting cases of cannibalism. In those days nobody dreamed of housing and feeding a hostile population.

During the war Fynes Moryson was slightly wounded while the Lord Deputy was attacking Brian MacGahagan's castle in West Meath. As they approached the castle which was " compassed with bogges," the horsemen being within shot moved about continually, " but myself being a raw soldier, stood still, and because I had a white horse I gaue the Rebels a faire marke, so as the first shot flew close by my head, and when I, apprehending my danger, turned my horse, the second flew through my cloake, and light in my padde saddle (which saued my life) and brused my thigh." Moryson was also affected by what he very properly calls the Essex tragedy. The arrest of Essex for an attempt at armed insurrection in London caused the utmost danger and confusion to all friends of that rash and reckless nobleman. Mountjoy himself had been so closely allied with Essex that he was stricken with uneasiness and distrust. He could not be sure how much of his correspondence was in the hands of " Master Secretary " the vigilant Robert Cecil. His real security lay in the fact that his services were absolutely indispensable; but he could not be sure how far even these great services would protect him at this time of suspicion. According to Moryson he had made all preparations, in case of a recall to England, to fly to France. Mountjoy adopted the policy of subserviency to Cecil for his own protection. " Whereas before he stood upon terms of honour with the Secretary, now he fell flat to the ground, and insinuated himselfe into inward love, and to an absolute dependancy with the Secretary." He could not in this crisis overlook the fact that his secretary had been introduced to him by a protégé of Essex, Sir Richard Moryson.[1] " It is not credible that the influence of the Earles malignant star should work upon so poor a snake as myselfe, being almost a stranger to him yet my neerenesse in bloud to one of his Lordship's above named friends, made it perhaps seeme to his Lordship improper, to use my service in such

1. One of the accusations against Essex at his trial was that he had made so many knights. Essex said in his speech that "he made but two of his servants, and those men of special desert and good ability." One of these was Sir Richard Moryson.

neerenesse as his Lordship had promised and begun to doe. So as the next day he tooke his most secret papers out of my hand yet giving them to no other, but keeping them in his own cabinet; and this blow I never fully recovered while I staied in Ireland." [1]

Mountjoy had the proud satisfaction of receiving Tyrone's complete submission to Queen Elizabeth before that arch-rebel had received news of the great Queen's death. Fynes Moryson is not a little proud of his own share in this transaction. Elizabeth died on March 24th, 1603.[2] The Lord Deputy, with his staff, was occupying Sir Garret Moore's [3] house at Mellifant. A gentleman, who was very ambitious to be knighted by the Lord Deputy,[4] received the news from London on the evening of March 27th, (" a servant of his posting from London and getting a happy passage by sea "), and took the all-important news to Moryson. "Whereupon I required his servant not to speak a word thereof to any man, threatening him with the Lord Deputies displeasure and severe punishment if any such rumour were spread by him. Then I was bold to giue his Master confidence of receiuing the honour he desired, if he would follow my advise which was this; that he should goe to the Lord Deputy and tell him this report of the Queenes death, brought by his servant, and the strict charge he had giuen unto him for the concealing thereof, till his Lordship should think fit to make it known and withall to make tender of himselfe and all his meanes to followe his Lordships fortune in this doubtful time (for such it was in expectation, though most happy in euent). This Gentleman did as I aduised him." [5] Mountjoy hurried on

1. When they came to England James I. was on the throne, and it was no disadvantage to have been a friend of Essex, but quite the contrary. Many readers will remember the case of Sir Henry Wotton, who was in Ireland with Essex, and on that nobleman's recall had the discretion to proceed to the Continent.

2. Or on the last day of 1602, according to the English reckoning of that time.

3. Sir Garret Moore was ancestor of the present Earl of Drogheda.

4. Even in those days private secretaries were the channels for receiving confidences as to hopes of preferment and titles of honour.

5. Itinerary, Part II., Page 277.

the submission of Tyrone, and on March 30th the Irish leader
" kneeled at the doore humbly on his knees for a long space
making his penitent submission to her Majesty and after being
required to come neerer to the Lord Deputie, performed the
ceremony in all humblenesse, the space of one houre or there-
abouts." The next day he presented his submission in writing
—drawn up doubtless by the hand of Fynes Moryson—
" kneeling on his knees before the Lord Deputy and Counsell
and in the presence of a great assembly." Then Mountjoy
brought Tyrone [1] with him to Dublin, where an English ship
brought " Sir Henrie Davers " [2] with the official announcement
from London of the proclamation of James I., and also " Master
Liegh, kinsman to the Lord Deputy, who brought his Lordship
a favourable letter from the King out of Scotland." So " cozen
Leigh " was knighted, and also the gentleman whose servant
brought the early tidings of the Queen's death. Moryson
does not mention his name, nor does he state whether the new
knight gave him a handsome present for his sage advice.

After settling some further troubles in Ireland, Mountjoy
" was chosen to be one of his Majesties Priuie Counsell in
England, and being made Lord Lieutenant of Ireland with
two-thirds part of the Deputies allowance assigned to him was
licensed to come over into England." [3] So bringing with him
his prisoner Tyrone and his secretary Fynes Moryson, the man
who had reconquered Ireland set sail for home, and after
narrowly escaping shipwreck on the Skerries, landed in
Beaumaris Bay. On the road to London there was some
difficulty in protecting Tyrone from the attacks of women " who
had lost Husbands and Children in the Irish Warres."

1. When Tyrone heard of Elizabeth's death he shed tears " in such quantity
as it could not well be concealed." It was a bitter reflection that, if he had
only held out a few days longer, he might have curried favour with James by
" freely submitting to his mercy." Tyrone might well weep. Irish leaders are
always beaten but seldom outwitted.—See Itinerary, Part II., Page 281.

2. Moryson's old acquaintance, who had helped him in Paris.

3. Itinerary, Part II., Page 296.

Mountjoy was received with the utmost honour by King James, and was created Earl of Devonshire.

Moryson is very properly reticent as to Mountjoy's private life. He never mentions Lady Rich, and needed not to do so for the readers of his own time, because the affair was only too notorious. After the death of Essex, in 1601, Lord Rich and his lady separated, probably by mutual consent, though, according to her statement, her husband abandoned her. It is significant, however, to learn that negotiations were taking place in Ireland for the marriage of Mountjoy with the only daughter of the Earl of Ormonde. It is easy to imagine the rage of Lady Rich when she heard the rumour of this marriage.[1] She let it be openly known that Mountjoy was the father of her five youngest children.[2] Mountjoy's marriage with the heiress of the Butlers[3] did not take place. Moryson makes the extremely significant remark, " Griefe of unsuccessful love brought him to his last end." What is certain is that the Earl of Devonshire and Lady Rich lived together openly, and that they were received with the highest favour at Court—the lady being granted a special precedence, and taking her part as one of the most prominent figures in Court festivities. All the Irish business passed through Devonshire's hands and those of his secretary, Fynes Moryson, who remained in his office until the Earl's death. It must have been a pleasant and profitable service, the Earl and his brilliant lady receiving the best society of the time,[4] both in London and at the Wanstead mansion, which Mountjoy had bought from Essex before he went to Ireland. The young Earl

1. One naturally thinks of the great scene when Cleopatra hears of Antony's marriage to Octavia.

2. Dr. Gardiner says that this declaration was made on Mountjoy's return to England, but it seems probable that the separation occurred earlier, and had some connection with the failure of the Irish marriage.

3. She inherited ultimately a large part of her father's land, as many of her male relatives were attainted.

4. The Earl of Southampton, Shakespeare's friend and patron (released by James from the long imprisonment he had incurred for his share in the Essex rising), was doubtless on specially friendly terms with Devonshire, as they were joint Lords Lieutenant of Hampshire. One of the first Acts of Southampton's freedom was to produce Shakespeare's " Love's Labour's Lost " for the Court.

of Pembroke [1] was a frequent visitor, as we learn from Moryson's dedication to him of his 1617 volume : " I had the happiness to stand sometimes before you, an eye and eare witness of your Noble conversation with the worthy Earle of Devonshire." The chaplain was no less a person than William Laud—afterwards Archbishop of Canterbury—persecutor and martyr. A fool— that is, a Shakespearian fool—was also an inmate of this great household. " My honored lord the late Earle of Devonshire till his dyeing day kept an Irishman in foole's Apparell and commonly called his lordships foole, but wee found him to have craft of humoring every man to attain his owne endes, and to have nothing of a naturall foole." [2] We can imagine that an Irishman playing such a congenial part would break many jests on the private secretary, and especially upon his fashion of walking with downcast eyes looking upon the ground. Moryson had acquired this habit in Turkey and the Holy Land when it was dangerous to look a Turk in the face, and he could never entirely break himself of it. The secretary was not forgotten in Mountjoy's prosperity, but received a pension sufficient to keep a bachelor of studious habits in comfort.[3]

At the production of Ben Jonson's " Masque of Blackness," by the Queen at Whitehall, on Twelfth Night, 1604—5, which

1. The lover of Mistress Fitton, and many other gay ladies. His statue stands in the picture gallery of the Bodleian, and his numerous other honours are dwarfed by his receiving (with his brother Montgomery) the dedication of the First Folio Shakespeare. He was the nephew of Sir Philip Sidney.

> Thou art thy mothers glasse and she in thee
> Calls backe the louely Aprill of her prime.
> *Shakespeare's Sonnet*, No. III.

2. Twelfth Night Actus Tertius—Scæna prima.
> This fellow is wise enough to play the foole
> And to do that well craues a kind of wit,
> He must observe their mood on whom he jests
> The quality of persons and the time.

3. Calendar State Papers, Dom. Add. 1580—1625. Page 445. Warrant of June 19th, 1604, the King to Lord Treasurer Buckhurst. In consideration of the surrender of a pension of 4s. a day granted by us to Sir John Skinner, and of another pension of 2s. per day to Clement Turner, we grant to Fras Morison, at suit of Sir John Skinner and Clement Turner, a pension of 6s. a day, provided Fras Morison bring a certificate from time to time from the paymaster of Berwick that neither of the said pensions of 4s. and 2s. granted to Skinner and Turner have been paid [1¼ pages draft. The docquet of this grant gives the name as Fynes Morison].

cost £3,000, the twelve nymphs were impersonated by the Queen herself and the noblest ladies in the land, including the Countesses of Suffolk, Derby and Bedford, and Lady Rich. Lord Rich, however, grew tired of his false position, and in 1605 obtained a divorce, *a mensa et thoro*, and immediately married again. On December 20th, 1605, William Laud celebrated a private marriage at Wanstead between the Earl of Devonshire and Lady Rich. This created an enormous scandal. The Earl and Countess were forbidden to appear at Court, and were practically disgraced. It was one thing to condone and recognise a *liaison* sanctified by time, but the line had to be drawn somewhere. The marriage was opposed to the canon law, and Laud bitterly repented of his share in it, which delayed his promotion in the church. Probably Lady Rich insisted on the marriage, knowing that she had lost Devonshire's heart, and determined to prevent the possibility of his marrying elsewhere. Neither of them can possibly have expected that such a storm of indignation would be aroused by the legitimation of their ties. Devonshire did not long survive his disgrace. He died at Savoy House in the Strand on April 3rd, 1606. " He was surprised with a burning fever, whereof the first fit being very violent he collected to him his most familiar friends, and telling them that he had ever by experience and by presaging mind been taught to repute a burning Feuer his fatall enemy desired them (upon instructions then given them) to make his will and then he said, Let death look never so ugly he would meet him smiling, which he nobly performed for I neuer saw a braue spirit part more mildly from the old mansion, then his did, departing most peaceably after nine daies sickenesse." [1] His Countess, stricken by his loss and the feeling that she had ruined the man whom she loved, did not survive him many months. His title became extinct. [2] He had attained wealth, honour and

1. Itinerary, Part II., Page 296.

2. In 1618 Lord Cavendish paid £10,000 for the title of Earl of Devonshire, and from him the present Lord President of the Council derives his title. At the same time Lord Rich, Lady Penelope's ex-husband, paid £10,000 to be made Earl of Warwick. These large sums of money were not bribes to James I. but honest payments into the Exchequer for value received.

glory, but his youthful ambition to refound his ancient house "*ad re-aedificandam antiquam domum*" was foiled when success was within his grasp.   He was only 43 years of age.

And now Fynes Moryson settled down to the fulfilment of his original ambition—the writing of a *magnum opus*—giving a survey of Europe and of the peoples of Europe.   He commenced by wasting three years labour.   "I abstracted the Histories of these 12 Dominions thorow which I passed with purpose to joyne them to the Discourses of the seuerall Commonwealths for illustration and ornament, but when the worke was done and I found the bulke thereof to swel, then I chose rather to suppresse them than to make my gate bigger than my Citie."   Judging by the historical introductions which Moryson has given to the Chapters in this volume[1] we may thank him for this heroic suppression.   He was a painstaking but uncritical historian, and in compiling from books he loses his Elizabethan freedom and force of style.   These three lost years bring him to 1609, the year of the first edition of Shakespeare's Sonnets.   Then he settles down to his final scheme which is as follows :—

PART I. Containeth a Journall through all the said twelve Dominions—*i.e.*, Germany, Bohmerland, Sweitzerland, Netherland, Denmarke, Poland, Italy, Turky, France, England, Scotland, and Ireland—Shewing particularly the number of miles, the soyle of the Country, the situation of Cities, the descriptions of them with all Monuments in each place worth the seeing, as also the rates of hiring Coaches or Horses from place to place, with each daies expences for diet, horse-meate and the like.

PART II. Containeth the Rebellion of Hugh, Earle of Tyrone, and the appeasing thereof : written also in forme of a Journall.

1. The first few pages of the Chapter on the Commonwealth of Poland will serve as a specimen.   I did not suppress them as we need to be reminded to-day of the nationality of Poland.

Part III. Containeth a Discourse upon severall Heads through all the said seuerall Dominions.

It will be gathered from this that Part I. contains a straightforward and minute account of his European travels, arranged with but little art. He follows his notes and diaries and gives at full length letters which he had written to foreigners, and of which he had kept copies. His details of expenses leave no obscurity whatever as to the methods of travel, and he also goes fully into the questions of letters of credit, and the transmission of money from place to place. It is probably more interesting now than it was to Moryson's contemporaries, but they must have found parts of it useful when preparing for a Continental journey. Thomas Fuller says that he "printed his observations in a large book which for the truth thereof is in good reputation. For if so great a *Traveller* he had nothing of a *Traveller* in him as to stretch in his reports."

Part II. is practically an independent work. It is an important chapter in the history of Ireland, told in great detail by an official who was behind the scenes, and who is able to quote at length confidential letters and official documents. It is as long as Part I., and to sandwich it between Part I. and Part III., as Moryson does, is thoroughly inartistic.[1]

Part III. opens with an elaborate discourse on travel in general, with precepts for travellers and a collection of proverbs "which I observed in forraigne parts by reading or discourse to be used either of Travellers themselves or of divers Nations and Provinces." Moryson then commences the most interesting and valuable portion of his work—viz., a series of discourses about the different countries under the following heads : —

1. Geographical description, situation, fertility, trafficke and diet.

1. It was republished separately at Dublin in 1735, with the description of Ireland from Part III. The latter was printed in Mr. Henry Morley's Carisbrooke Library. These are the only portions of Moryson's work that have ever been reprinted. Spedding frequently quotes from Part II. in his Life of Bacon. There is a good summary of facts about the Itinerary in Notes and Queries, 2nd Series, Vol. XI., page 321.

2. Apparell.

3. The Commonwealth, " under which title I containe an historical introduction, the Princes Pedegrees and Courts, the present state of things, the Tributes and Revenewes, the military state for Horse, Foot, and Navy, the Courts of Justice, rare Lawes, more specially the Lawes of Inheritance and of womens Dowries, the Capitall Judgements, and the diversitie of degrees in Families, and in the Commonwealth."

This proceeded as far as Germany, Switzerland and the Netherlands. . . . Here the printed portion of Fynes Moryson's Itinerary, published in 1617, the year after Shakespeare's death, comes to an abrupt end, and we read in the Table of Contents : — " The Rest of this Worke, not as yet fully finished treateth of the following heads," and the matter of the " Rest of this Worke " may be read in the present volume, and is summarised in its Table of Contents. Technically, this is the completion of Part III., but in preparing it for the press, for which it has had to wait nearly 300 years, Moryson called it Part IV.[1]

From 1609 to 1617, when the Itinerary appeared, Moryson tells us : " I wrote at leasure giving (like a free and unhired workman) much time to pleasure, to necessary affaires, and to diuers and long distractions. If you consider this, and withall remember that the work is first written in Latine, then translated into English, and that in diuers Copies, no man being able by the first Copie to put so large a worke in good fashion. And if you will please also take knowledge from me that to saue expences, I wrote the greatest part with my owne hand, and almost all the rest with the slowe pen of my servant: then I hope the loss of time shall not be imputed to me." [2]

1. I found the reference to the MS. continuation in the Dictionary of National Biography, to which great work I have to acknowledge many obligations. The MS. was not permitted by the authorities of C.C.C. to leave Oxford, and it was copied for me by Miss E. G. Parker in the Bodleian library. I am indebted to the Rev. C. Plummer, M.A., Librarian of C.C.C., for obtaining for me the permission of the President and Fellows to publish their MS. Nothing is known as to how the MS. came to C.C.C., but it was catalogued there under the same number in 1697.

2. In the Hist. Man. Commission Reports there is catalogued among the Crowcombe Court MSS. a letter from Fynes Moryson to Pembroke, asking him to accept the dedication of the work. After many efforts to obtain a sight of it I learn through a friend of the present owner that this interesting document has been lost.

On the 26th of February,[1] 1611—12, Fynes Moryson attended the funeral of his dear sister Jane Alington at St. Botolph's Church, Aldersgate Street. A full account of the order of this funeral has been preserved. It was drawn up by the "Wyndsor Herald for Henry St. George, Blewmantel." Thirty-six poor women walked two and two. The male relations wore black cloaks. The chief mourner was Lady Guevara (wife of Sir John Guevara[2]) a connection of the Moryson brothers through the second marriage of their grandmother, the widow of Thomas Moigne. Lady Guevara was no doubt a close personal friend of the deceased. Behind the clergyman, walked Fynes Moryson, carrying a pennon.[3]

In the year 1613 he had a rather long "distraction." "By the entreaty of my brother, Sir Richard Moryson (Vice-President of Munster), and out of my desire to see his children God had giuen him in Ireland (besides some occasions of my private estate), I was drawne over again into Ireland, where we landed the ninth of September miraculously preserved from shipwreck."[4] Moryson was not favourably impressed by the prospects of Ireland, for he thought that much stronger measures should be taken for the suppression of "Poperie" and the Popish priests. Sir Richard Moryson, whose stay in Ireland had been so long and honourable, returned to England in 1615 and settled at Tooley Park, Leicestershire. He was appointed Lieutenant General of Ordnance, and in 1620 became M.P. for Leicester. He died in 1628. His son Henry, a young man of great promise, became the intimate friend of Sir Lucius Cary, afterwards Viscount Falkland. Ben Jonson addressed his

1. A few months after Shakespeare's retirement to Stratford.

2. The Guevaras, Spaniards from the Basque Provinces, settled in Lincolnshire in the early part of the reign of Henry VIII. They probably belonged to the same family as Anton de Guevara, Bishop of "Guadix" and counsellor of Charles V., whose "Diall of Princes" was translated into English by Thomas North, and published in the last year of Queen Mary. The last of the Lincolnshire Guevaras was a barber at Market Rasen, whose will was proved in 1697.

3. "Collectanea Topographica et Genealogica," Vol. IV., London, 1837.

4. In Youghall harbour.

Pindaric Ode on the death of Sir H. Moryson[1] to his sorrowing friend. It was a surprise to me to find that the well-known Strophe, commencing

> " It is not growing like a tree
> In bulk, doth make man better be "

commemorates the untimely death of Fynes Moryson's nephew. I quote a less known antistrophe:

> " Alas! but Morison fell young;
> He never fell—thou fall'st my tongue.
> He stood a soldier to the last right end,
> A perfect patriot, and a noble friend;
> But most a virtuous son.
> All offices were done
> By him, so ample, full, and round,
> In weight, in measure, number, sound
> As, though his age imperfect might appear,
> His life was of humanity the sphere."

The year after young Moryson's death his sister Lettice married Sir Lucius Cary. It was purely a love match, and he was much blamed by judicious friends, for she had no fortune. Lord Clarendon says of her: " She was a lady of a most extraordinary wit and judgment, and of the most signal virtue, and exemplary life, that the age produced, and who brought him many hopeful children, in whom he took great delight."

I give these facts about Fynes Moryson's nephew and niece to cover up to a certain extent my ignorance as to the later portion of my author's life. There can be no doubt that after the publication of his 1617[2] folio he prepared the MS. from

---

1. He died in 1629, at the age of twenty. We know that his mother Lady Moryson was still living in 1632, as George Alington left her a gold ring in his will—one of the " Sum quod eris " rings.

2. Extract from the Register of the Stationers Co., Arber's Edition III., 606, under date 4 April, 1617. "John Beale—Entred for his Copie under the handes of Master Docter Westfield and both Wardens. An Itinerary written by Fines Morison Gent. contayning his Travailes through divers dominions, vizt Germany Bohmerland &c.—vjd." In the previous year Shakespeare died. In the following year Raleigh was executed.

which the present volume is printed, and that a portion of it is in his own hand-writing. At the end of the MS. is written :

"14 Junii, 1626.

Imprimatur.—Tho. Wilson.

Internal evidence shows that it was finished by 1619 or 1620 at the latest, and much of it was probably already sketched out in 1617.

We may therefore conclude that after keeping the MS. by him until 1626 (three years after the publication of the First Folio of Shakespeare), Moryson got his book licensed for publication by the head of the State Paper Office, Sir Thos. Wilson.[1] After obtaining the license, however, there must have been difficulty with the publisher. Probably the 1617 folio had not been a great pecuniary success, and possibly Mr. John Beale, or any other expert who was consulted in the matter suggested that large omissions or excisions were desirable. Moryson was in his sixtieth year and belonged to a past age. Perhaps he felt that the Germany, which he had so sympathetically described, was passing away in the welter of frightful wars from which it has only really recovered in our own times. At all events, the MS. has waited till now.

During the later years of his life Moryson no doubt employed himself by working upon the treatise "Of the Commonwealth of England," which he had planned as an addendum to his survey of Europe. Of this work nothing is known. Probably it was never finished. Possibly he realised that under the Stuart Kings there was no fixity in the state of England. Certainly he could not have foreseen that the word Commonwealth would soon acquire a new significance in the History of England.

1. Acting under the Archbishop of Canterbury, who had a general power of licensing books. Sir Thos. Wilson had been at Cambridge with Fynes Moryson, and also was in Italy in 1596, when he translated from the Spanish (and dedicated to Southampton) the play "Diana," the plot of which is considered to be the source of "The Two Gentlemen of Verona." Wilson was one of Cecil's most trusted foreign agents, and, as Keeper of the Records he rendered great public services. He was knighted in 1618 and died in 1629.

I am now able to publish Fynes Moryson's will as recorded in the Probate Act Books.[1]

> Mr. Fines Morison his last will and testament
> bearinge date 15 Sept. 1629.

To Mrs. Elizabeth Dynne his pictures. To George Allington Esqr. his best night Capp and hand kercheife. To Mr. ffrancis Dynne his bookes and Cabonett. To Mr. William Ireland his guilded halberd. To Mris Susan Ireland his wife all his lynnen and the trunck wherein it lyeth. To Sarah Ireland two redd chaires and two redd stooles both of cloth. To Mr. Edward Waterhouse twentie shillings. To his servant Isaack Pywall all his wearinge apparell except his best cloke alsoe his bed wherein he lay with all the furniture belonginge to it and the bedd wherein his servant Isaack Pywall lay with the furniture belonging thereunto. As alsoe the hanginge of his Chamber. And of this his last will he makes Mr. ffrancis Dynne Executor. This is the effect of the will of Mr ffynes Moryson who died the twelveth of ffebr last.

Witnes ffra Dynne Isaak Pywall, Susan Ireland Probatum fuit Testamentum suprascript, apud London. . . .
decimo octavo die mensis Martii Anno Domini Millimo sexcentesimo vicesimo nono Juramento ffrancisei Dynne Executoris.

This document fixes the date of Moryson's death as Feb. 12th, 1630,[2] or as it is usually printed 1629—30. He was in his sixty-fourth year. His old friend and brother-in-law, George Allington, to whom he leaves his best night-cap, was then in his

---

1. Year Books of Probate from 1630, Vol. I., Part I., 1630-1634. Edited by John Mathews and George F. Mathews, B.A., 93, Chancery Lane, London, W.C. Page 38 Morison Fines of p. St. Botolph, London (27 Scroope). This list was only printed in March, 1902. I am indebted for the reference to Mr. W. R. Credland, of the Manchester Free Reference Library.

2. Some of the old Biographical Dictionaries give the date of Moryson's death as 1614. This is repeated in one of the latest publications of the Harleian Society, "Musgrave's Fragmenta Genealogica," 1900. It originated from Thomas Fuller in his Worthies of England. Mr. Sidney Lee, in the Dictionary of National Biography, supposes, in the absence of information, that Moryson died soon after the publication of his 1617 volume. I take this opportunity of acknowledging the kind assistance given to me by the officials of the Rylands Library and the Manchester Free Reference Library, and also for references given by Mr. Goulding, librarian to the Duke of Portland, and by Mr. J. S. Bogg, of Altrincham.

eightieth year. It is clear that Fynes Moryson lived the later years of his life with every reasonable comfort that a studious gentleman of his age would require. If he left no money it was probably because he had sunk his small patrimony in an annuity which, added to his pension, enabled him to support a servant and rent suitable rooms. We may assume that the Irelands were the people in whose house he made his home, and that Francis Dynne was a congenial friend who would appreciate his library. Sir Richard Moryson and his promising son were both dead. William Laud had arrived at the bishopric of London on his road to Canterbury and the block. Charles I. had been five years on the throne. Buckingham had been assassinated, the Petition of Right had been passed. The prologue of the great Civil War tragedy was being played, and Wentworth, Pym and Eliot were the chief performers on the political stage. It was time for a man who had been elected a Fellow of Peterhouse before the defeat of the Spanish Armada to leave the world. Fynes Moryson's body was buried, we may be sure, enfolded in the " beste cloke " which he had excepted in his bequest to Isaac Pywall.

As for the MS. of the present work, no information is obtainable as to how it came into the Library of Corpus Christi College, Oxford. It contains three handwritings, which are no doubt those of (1) Moryson himself, (2) his regular assistant, who wrote from dictation, and (3) a less skilful assistant, whose spelling is much more free and easy than his employer's, and who sometimes indicates, by spelling a difficult word correctly, that he has asked how to spell it. Occasionally this third writer makes faults in dictation which show that Moryson has not given extreme care to the revision of the MS., as when for " a Navy " he writes " an Avay." [1] The first paragraph of the

1. There are also a few lines in a fourth handwriting. These four hand-writings are in the old English script used by Shakespeare. The Latin and Italian quotations are in the Roman hand in which Moryson wrote his original Latin work (see facsimile). As Malvolio says : " I think we do know that fine Roman hand." I may here thank Miss A. Montgomerie Martin for her careful work in the correction of proofs.

Chapter on Turkey shows that the author has listened to critic-isms, not in all respects laudatory of his 1617 volume.[1]

With regard to the merit of Moryson's work in the present volume, its readers can judge for themselves. In undertaking its publication I was fortified by the favourable opinions of Dr. Ward and Mr. Sidney Lee, to whom I forwarded a portion of my copy of the MS. At the same time, I must accept the entire responsibility as being, like Mr. W. H. in Mr. Lee's inter-pretation of the dedication of Shakespeare's Sonnets, "the onlie begetter of these insuing" chapters, and also for the omissions. My intention at first was to publish the whole MS., but I came to recognise that it was not of equal value through-out, and that a selection must be made. The following passage from the prospectus of this book will explain my course of action : —

"Unfortunately Moryson, the historical compiler, is a much inferior person to Moryson the social historian; he is laborious and widely read but quite uncritical. Moreover his style, which is vivacious and masculine when he is writing from his own knowledge, often becomes flat and commonplace when he is working from other men's books. To have printed the whole of the MS. would have needed 1,200 pages, and would have weighted down the valuable cargo with useless ballast. Perhaps those who would have blamed me for publishing useless matter may now complain that the work is incomplete. . . . . In printing this book, the aim will be to reproduce the author's MS., only correcting obvious slips of the pen. In cases of doubt, as to whether there is a slip of the pen or a blunder of the author, the MS. will be followed. Nor will there be any expurgations.

1. Mr. E. Gordon Duff has sent me an account of an interesting copy of the 1617 Itinerary in the Cambridge University Library. It is in handsome contemporary binding, having on both backs Fynes Moryson's arms. "Or, on a cross sable, five fleurs de lis of the field. Crest: Out of a coronet Or an eagle's head between two wings Argent," and the inscription "THE GIFTE OF THE AUCHTER FYNES MORISON." Mr. Sayle, of the C.U. Library, informs me that there is no writing whatever on the volume to indicate its past ownership. Probably it was a present to the Earl of Pembroke. I owe to Mr. Gordon Duff—who was formerly librarian of the Rylands Library— my first introduction to Fynes Moryson.

Moryson is very plain-spoken, and in discussing social questions is sometimes more free in his language than is usual to-day in books intended for the general reader, and sometimes he himself apologises for using a coarse word. This book, now published nearly 300 years after its due date, will have the same varied spelling as 'The Itinerary' published in 1617."

I cannot admit that it is any reflection upon Moryson to omit those portions of his work which are not of permanent interest. The fondest lovers of a great writer are readiest to admit that their hero is not always at his best, and would often be glad to throw away the worser part of him. While I would not speak of Fynes Moryson as my " hero," yet he has been my companion for two years, and a very pleasant and profitable companion I have found him. He had seen the world and mixed with all sorts and conditions of men. He was enterprising, studious, and discreet. He had a sturdy hatred of " Poperie;" but, as Rosalind says, " I'll pardon him for that." He was intensely proud of his own country and his own countrymen, yet he judged the people of the countries where he sojourned with appreciative commonsense. He had a sane charity for all men, except Turks and Irish priests. He thought English stage-players the best in the world, but despised them personally. He shows no sign whatever that he recognised the greatness of the pieces these stage-players performed. Not a word of Shake-speare, Spenser, Marlowe, or Jonson in all his records of the time—which, taken together would occupy about 3,000 pages like these. In modern phrase we must say that Fynes Moryson was lacking in poetic and artistic sensibility. But his own prose style, when he is writing from personal knowledge and observation, has the freedom and picturesqueness of North or Philemon Holland, as unconfined as his spelling, and as refreshing. It seems to me that few can fail to find in this volume some new impressions of Europe as it was before the Thirty Years' War desolated Germany, of the time between the defeat of the Spanish Armada and the sailing of the Mayflower, in fact, of " Shakespeare's Europe."

It is unfortunate that no portrait of Fynes Moryson is known, as it would have been a great satisfaction to the editor to prefix his likeness to this volume.

" But, since he cannot, Reader, looke
Not on his picture, but his booke."

CHARLES HUGHES.

Kersal, Manchester, February 1903.

Fynes Moryson
Itinerary

WITH King James his Maiesties full and sole Priuiledge to the Author Fynes Morison gent. his Executors Administratours Assignes and deputyes for xxj yeares next ensuing from the graunt thereof, to cause to be imprinted, and to sell assigne or dispose to his or their best benefitts, the former parts and this fourth Part of this booke entitled An Itinerary &c. as well in the English as in the latine tongue; straitly forbidding any other during the said yeares to imprint or cause to be imprinted to import vtter or sell or cause to be imported vttered or sold, the said Booke or Bookes or any part thereof within any of his Maiesties dominions, vppon payne of his Maiesties high displeasure, and to forfeit Three pounds lawfull English money for euery such Booke printed imported vttered or sold contrary to the meaning of this Priuiledge, besides the forfeyture of the said Bookes &c. As appeareth by his Maiesties lettres Pattents dated the xxvth of Aprill, the Fifteenth yeare of his Maiesties Raigne of England Fraunce and Ireland. And of Scotland the Fiftieth.

A TABLE OF THE CONTENTS OF THE SEUERALL CHAPTERS IN THIS FOURTH PART.

The first Booke.

The second Booke.

CHAPTER i. Of the Commonwealth of Fraunce according to the seuerall heads contayned in the tytle of the first Chapter of the former Booke.

CHAPTER ii. Of the Commonwealth of Denmarke according to the seuerall heads contayned in the tytle of the first Chapter of the former Booke.

CHAPTER iii. Of the Commonwealth of England according to the seuerall heads contayned in the tytle of the first Chapter of the former Booke.

CHAPTER iiii. Of the Commonwealth of Scotland according to the seuerall heads contayned in the title of the first Chapter of the former Booke.

CHAPTER v. Of the Commonwealth of Ireland according to the seuerall heads contayned in the tytle of the first Chapter of the former Booke.

The third Booke.

CHAPTER i. Of Germany touching Religion.

CHAPTER ii. Of Bohemia touching Religion.

CHAPTER iii. Of the Sweitzers, the Netherlanders, the Danes, and the Polonians touching Religion.

CHAPTER iiii. Of the Turkes Religion.

CHAPTER v. Of the Italians or rather Romans touching Religion.

CHAPTER vj. Of Fraunce, England, Scotland, and Ireland touching Religion.

The fourth Booke.

CHAPTER i. Of the Germans nature, and Manners, strength of Body, and Witt, Manuall Arts, Sciences, Vniuersityes, Language, Pompe of Ceremonyes, especially in mariages, Childbearings,

Christnings and Funeralls as also of their diuerse Customes, Sports, exercises, and particulerly of hunting, hawking, Fowling, Birding, and Fishing.

CHAPTER ii.   Of Sweitzerland touching the heads of the first Chapter.

CHAPTER iii.   Of the Vnited Prouinces of Netherland touching the heads of the first Chapter.

CHAPTER iiii.   Of Denmarke touching the heads of the first Chapter.

CHAPTER v.   Of Bohemia touching the heads of the first Chapter.

CHAPTER vj.   Of Poland touching the heads of the first Chapter.

CHAPTER vii.   Of Turky touching the heads of the first Chapter.

The fifth Booke.

CHAPTER i.   Of the Italians nature and manners, Bodyes, and Witts, manuall Arts, Sciences, Vniuersityes, Language Ceremonyes, particulerly in marriages, Childbearings, Christnings and funeralls, as also of their diuerse Customes, Pastimes, exercises, particulerly hunting, hawking, fouling, Birding, and Fishing.

CHAPTER ii.   Of the Frenchmen touching the heads of the first Chapter.

CHAPTER iii.   Of England touching the heads of the first Chapter.

CHAPTER iiii.   Of Scotland touching the heads of the first Chapter.

CHAPTER v.   Of Ireland touching the heads of the first Chapter.

CHAPTER vj.   A generall and breife discourse of the Jewes, and of the Greekes.

The first Booke.

CHAP: i.

Of the Turkes Comonwealth, vnder which tytle I contayne the historicall Introduction, the kings Pedegrees, and Courts, the present State of publique affayres, the Tributes, and Revenues, the military power for Horse, Foote, and Navye, the Courts of Justice, rare lawes, more specially those of Inheritance, and contracts of mariage, the Criminall Judgments, and the diuersitye of degrees in Family and Comonwealth.

Noe man can iustly expect from me a full, and exact discourse vppon the heads aboue written, which few men, (and that with extraordinary Labour and practice) can write of their owne Country that should be best knowne to euery man, But it ought to suffice, that I make such obseruations as a Passenger can make in a Cursory Journey of a straunge Country, by reading Conference, and like obiects of the sence. And because as many hearers of sermons come from Church well satisfyed, if they haue obserued two, or three witty exceptions against the Preacher; so in our age (as experience hath taught me) there be some Readers of the same Condition, with whome (among some other exceptions) my large Writing in the former parts, hath turned to my reproofe, I will in this part write breifely, collecting myselfe from all excursions, as being drawne to the writing hereof, rather out of a naturall affection to giue all the members to this my vnlicked whelpe, then out of any desyre or hope fully to satisfy the curious readers of our Crittick age.

The Historical Introduction.

Thus I fall to the purpose, beginning with the historicall introduction of Turkye. Wicked Mahomett, were he an Arabian or Persian, was borne in the yeare of our lord 597, and wrote the Alcoran of his new religion about the yeare 622, whome his followers saluted king, and the Saracens (more truely called Agarines) leaving the pay of the Christian Emperor of the East, ioyned their armes to his forces, against whome the Persian king drew to his ayde the Turquestans inhabiting Turquemania or Turkye lying vppon the Confines of Parthia. The said Persian king being ouercome in the yeare 640, by the Mahometan Saracens, the Turquestans (vulgerly called Turkes) yeilded themselues tributory to these Saracens, and withall tooke their Mahometan Religion which to this day they hold; But a difference of this religion falling among the Saracens, deuided their Empire, part following the Caliph of Persia and part the Sultan of Egipt. The Turkes about the yeare 1040 casting of the yoke of the Saracens, made themselues a king, and increased their kingdome with the fall of the Saracen Empire about the yeare 1080. The Tartars about the yeare 1258 cast the Turkes out of Persia where they planted Christian Religion and after subdued Syria, but the Sultan of Egipt droue them out of Syria about the year 1268. At last the Turquemans or Turkes seated in Asia the lesser, swallowed the Saracens Empire in the East. These Turkes had then fower Familyes, which like the Cantons of Sweitzerland gouerned their Commonwealth till Ottaman of the Ogusian family, suppressing the other three, and getting the whole Empire of the Turkes about the yeare 1300, left the name of Ottoman hereditary to the kings of the Turkes, as that of Cæsar, was left to the Romane Emperors. Orcanes the sonne of Ottoman seated himselfe at Prusa or Bursia in the lesser Asia. The Christian Emperor of the East required ayde against the Bulgarians of Amurath sonne to Orcanes, who inticed by the pleasant fertilitye of Greece passed the Hellespont with an huge army, and openly affecting the Empire of the East, in the yeare 1363, stayed in Thrace with his army. Cyrisceobes (or as others write Calapin) being king of the Turkes in the yeare 1397, left his sonnes to be his heyres, but his brother Moses caused them all to be killed, whome his third brother Mahomett slewe with like trecherie, and became the first king of that name, from which tyme the manner of the Turkish kings to beginn their Tyrannicall gouernment with the cruell strangling of all their brothers first grew into Custome, and after was established for a lawe. This Mahomett the first, seated himselfe at Adrianopolis in Thrace, and subdued Macedonia. Amurath called vulgarly Morat-Beg in the yeare 1419. subdued Seruia, and gaue the Hungarians a wofull ouer-throw at Varna, and first instituted the famous military footmen called Janizares. Mahomett the second vtterly extinguished the Christian Empire of the East, taking the head Citty thereof Constantinople in the yeare of our lord 1453. so first deseruing to be stiled the Emperor of the Turkes. In the meane tyme the Mahometan Parthians about the yeare 1350, had driuen the Christian Tartars out of the kingdome of Persia, and the Scithian Tamberlane in the yeare 1400, driuing out them, had possessed himselfe of that kingdome. After Constantinople was taken by the Turkes, Assimbeius discending of the Turkes did againe driue the Scithians out of the Persian kingdome in the yeare 1470. Baiazet the second possessed the Turkish Empire at Constantinople in the yeare 1481. and in the tyme of his Empire, Ismael Sophus king of Persia, reputed by his [sic] for a Prophet, became the Author of a new Mahometan sect, differing from that of the Turkes, as pretending a more pure reformacion thereof, and thereby sowed a successiue and deadly hatred, rising from the said difference of religion, and to this day remayning betweene the Persian sect of the Persians, and the Arabian sect of the Turkes. Selimus Emperor of the Turkes subdued the Empire of the Saracen Sultan of Egipt, with his order of knights called Mamalukes vtterly extinguishing them both in the yeare 1517, Amurath (vulgarly Moratt) the sonne of Selime succeeded Emperor in the yeare 1574. and was living, in the yeare, when I began my iourney towards Turky. He was said to have liued with his Sultana (or Empresse) 32 yeares, and to have had no Concubine for the first 20 yeares, but the people murmuring, that contrary to the Custome of his Ancestors, he suffered the succession of his Empire to depend vppon one sonne, therevppon to haue taken some Concubines, and his obseruance of Chastity once broken, to haue had so many as they could hardly be numbred. He was of a meane stature, of a cleare complexion white and ruddy, a chearefull Countenance, and corpulent or fatt in the body. He greatly delighted in Jewells which he bought at high rates, and wore rich apparrell. He was of a merry disposition and hated crueltie, which his dying mother as it were by her last Testament (nothing being more religiously obserued by the Turkes then their parents last Will) charged him to avoyd. He loued peace, yet with good successe made warr against the Persians, not in person, but by his Generalls, which kinde of making warr is more commodious for these Emperors, then if in person they should lead their Armyes, since their Confines are farr distant from Constantinople where they alwayes winter, so as great part of the sommer is spent in leading forth and bringing back their Army. Howsoeuer he was of a soft nature, and giuen to pleasure, yet in Affrick he subdued the kingdome of Tunis and razed Goleta to the ground, and in Hungarie he tooke Chiauerin and left the Hungarian warr hereditary to his sonne, who pursued the same with great earnestnes. He did willingly read histories, causing some to be translated into the vulgar tongue, and was said to be an excellent Poett, inviting his Courtiers by rewards to that study. He greedily affected Noueltie, and built the greatest part of his Imperiall Serraglio or Pallace. He loued Musick, but had not the patience to attend the tuning of instruments, so as the Venetians sending him a Consort which he desyred to heare, they could not be so ready after they had long expected him, but that vppon his sodeine Coming they were forced to spend a little tyme in tuning their instruments, whereat he grew so impatient, as he went away in anger, and would neuer come againe to heare them. Indeed I could neuer obserue that the Turkes haue any skill in musick, only I haue heard them play with a strong hand vppon a poore litle fidle nothing lesse then delightfully to the eare.

He was by nature carryed to extremes, seldome holding the

meane, and easily beleeued the first information without due examination thereof, but he was said to be more courteous and mercifull, and to haue gathered more treasure than any of his Ancestors. He admitted his sonne Mahomet to Circumcision the fifteenth yeare of his age in the yeare 1580. which was performed in great Pompe with the presence of many Princes Ambassadors. To his Sultana, namely the mother of his eldest sonne, he would neuer giue a letter of dowry vulgarly called Chebin, which only makes her his wife, and without which she is esteemed a Concubine and slaue, and cannot be buryed by the syde of the Emperor. And this he refused by the example of his father, and some of his late Ancestors, thincking he should not long liue after he had done it, which suspition was not without iust cause, since the mother of the eldest sonne while the father liueth, is in seruile subiection to him, but when her sonne raigneth, out of his religious duty to her, vseth to haue great authority and liberty to liue at her pleasure. He raigned 19 yeares 26 dayes and liued 51 yeares, and dyed the second hower of the night vppon the 6 day of January after the old style in the yeare 1595, while I was yet in my Journey to Constantinople. He left two daughters maryed, one to Ibrahim cheife Bashawe (or Visere) the other to Halil Basha, and besides 25 daughters kept in the old Serraglio to be marryed to like great Subiects by the Emperor their brother, and also he left 19 male children, besides the eldest succeeding him and three of his Concubines great with Childe.

The Emperor then liuing.

Amurath being dead the Admirall presently sailed to Bursia in Magnesia that he might bring from thence to Constantinople Mahomet the third heyre of the Empire who publiquely and by day entred the Citty contrary to the Custome of his Ancestors who vsed to come by night, and to conceale the death of their fathers for feare lest the Citty might be sacked, by some mutiny of the Janizaries. Yea he spent eleuen dayes in this iourney

of his retorne and at last arriued at Constantinople the 27th of
January in the morning at the stayres of his Serraglio, after he
had bene 12 yeares absent, wherein (according to their Custome)
he had neither seene father nor mother. Then (according to
the Custome) he gaue a boone or guift to the Admirall vppon his
petition, and comaunded his fathers dead body to be carryed to
the graue with great pompe vppon the palmes of Eunuches who
were clothed in black, yet wore their white heads, or Turbents
ouer a black rap. The same evening his 19 brothers were
brought to kisse his hands, at which tyme, he was said to have
wept, and in detestation of the horrible lawe to beginn their
raigne with the cruell murther of their brothers, was said to
haue sworne neuer to take any Concubine, nor to know any
other woman then his owne Sultana, yet after few dayes he
receiued 50 virgins presented to him, and within few moneths,
by that tyme I came to Constantinople, had 500. Concubines
for his owne saddle, whereof that somer going to the warr in
Hungary, he was said to leaue 40 great with childe. His said
brothers having done reuerence vnto him, vnder pretence to be
circumcised were led into the next chamber, where that
Ceremony being performed to them, (whereby a Turke is called
Musulman that is admitted into their Church), they were
presently strangled by dumbmen, and so laid in Coffins of
Cypres, with their faces open, that the Emperor (after the
Custome) passing through that chamber to visitt his mother,
might see their faces, and with his eyes behold them both living
and dead, lest any one should be preserued. The same brothers
were thence carryed, and presently laid by their father in the
same Coffines and in a stately Sepulcher built by Amurath of
purpose for himselfe and them. Then the Emperour went to
doe reuerence to his mother in her lodgings; for as I formerly
said, the Emperors make great religion to obserue their dead
parents last Testament, and to giue their liuing mother great
respect and power in state matters, wherevppon I said the late
Emperors were afraid to giue the mother of their eldest sonne
(though neuer so deare to them) a letter of dowry lest she being

thereby made Sultana, for hope of power in her sonnes tyme, should practice their death. And so great is this power of the mother in state matters, as the king of Persia not long before sent a woman to this Court for his Ambassador, as most fitt to treat with the Sultana and her women.

When the Emperor had done reuerence to his mother, he presently putt out of his Pallace his fathers cheife Concubines, and sent them to the old Pallace or Serraglio, to be kept their by Eunuches apart with the rest of his fathers Concubines, and thence to be giuen in mariage by the Emperor to his greatest Subiects. Likewise he sent out his fathers Sodomieticall boyes. But the three Concubines left with childe by his father were left to the speciall charge of trusty Eunuches that the Children at the birth might be strangled if they proued male Children. Also he sent out of his Pallace the dumbmen and dwarfes, in whome he tooke noe such delight as his father did. The said Concubines while the Emperor liueth, are for the most part kept in the old Serraglio with his sonnes and daughters, but in seuerall parts of the house onely the eldest sonne with his mother and some few Concubines in whose more frequent Conversation the Emperor is delighted, vse to be kept in the Emperors owne Serraglio. Ordinarily each hath 15 Aspers a day for mantenance and is apparrelled twice euery yeare at the end of their two lents. Certaine old women are sett ouer them, but the whole Serraglio is gouerned by an Agha with Porters, and other officers being all gelded men. When it pleaseth the Emperor to take viewe of them they are all sett in order, and as he passeth by he casts his handkercher to her whome he will haue brought to his bed, and she is presently carryed to the Bath, where she is anoynted with balme and precious oyntments, and washed, and then richly apparrelled, is brought to the Emperors bed who giues her presently tenn thousand Aspers, and besides if she please him, vseth to graunt her a boone, or request for some brother, kinsman, or freind of hers to be preferred to some gouernment, and from that tyme she is separated from the other virgins, having a greater stipend for mantenance, and living with greater respect then formerly she did, especially if she proue with Childe. When any of them become 25 yeares old (at which age the Turks repute women past the best) they are maryed to officers in the Court, or Commaunders in the Army, except they haue either borne children, or otherwise gotten fauour with the Emperor by wanton daliance, and young virgins are placed in their roomes.

This Emperor Mahomett the third living at the tyme I came to Constantinople, was borne in the yeare 1564. the moneth of August and began to raigne in the yeare 1595. being about 31 yeares of age. His eldest sonne was called Selim being about 14 yeares of age but vncircumcised, and it was expected, that with great pompe and Concurse of Princes Ambassadors, he should be circumcised in the moneth of August following at the end of Lent, and the Feast of Beyram (as our Easter) which they keepe twice each yeare. And after that he was presently to be sent (according to the old Custome) to Bursia, of old called Prusa the ancient seat of the kings of Bithinia and after they were conquered made the seat of the Turkish Sultanes till they tooke Constantinople. And that Citty and Prouince he was to governe, and neuer more to see the face of his living father, nor of his mother, till his father should dye, in regard of the great ielousye attending the throne of kings, which among the Turkes is so excessiue, as it takes away all naturall loue betweene fathers children and brethren. The Emperors second sonne was called Solyman. This Mahomett began his Empire with a guift to the Army of three millions of gold Sultanons, for the number of the soldiers was greatly increased, so as besides other orders, there were then at Constantinople more then 24000 Janizaries. Then he caused his fathers debts and all mony due for any soldiers stipends to be fully paid. Having a Janizarie for my guide in spite of a great Chiaass offering by force to repell me (as I shall shew in the following discourse of the Janizaries power) I did see this Emperor when he came riding to St. Sophy the chiefe Mosche or church ioyning close to his Pallace, at which tyme all the Commaunders

and officers on horseback, or on foote according to their place,
came in the morning to the Emperors Serraglio and sett themselues in rancks, from the dore of his Chamber in the third
inner Court to the very dore of the Church on both sydes the
way to guarde his person, who at last came riding on horseback
with diuers horses richly furnished, and led empty by him,
having many great men walking before him, and many footemen
running by, vulgarly called Pykes, carrying short bowes and
arrowes, and wearing a Cap of mingled Coulors in the forme
of a suger loafe with white shirts hanging out ouer their
breeches, and when the people cryed Alla Hough (as we say
long liue the king) the Emperor bowed downe his body. He
had a round face which was faire and ruddy, but somewhat
frowning, or austere, and he nourished a broad and long black
beard, but was very Corpulent or fatt, and seemed on horseback
to be of somewhat a low stature. He was said to delight in the
exercise of shooting, and to haue skill in the trade of a Fletcher,
vsing to make many arrowes with his owne hand, and to giue
them to his great Subiects for a present of no small importance,
(as indeed all the Turkish Emperors vse to haue, and professe
skill in one manuall trade or other). For his exercise of
shooting, he had a paire of Butts in a priuate Chamber, and the
first sommer within few monethes after his coming to the
Empire, being to lead his Army into Hungary, for prosecution
of that warr which his father left him with the Emperor of
Germany, and his great Commaunders being loth he should
take that iourney, yet not daring to disswade him themselues,
and so inticing a Concubine in greatest grace with him to goe
into him while he was shooting, and by her best skill to diuert
him from that enterprise, he scorning that boldnes in a woman,
did in a rage putt her from him, and while she trembling euery
ioynt hasted out of his Chamber, shott her in the back with
an arrow, and so basely killed her, for whose death he did after
more basely lament. He was reputed obstinate in his purposes,
and of a great Courage, and surely he gaue good testimony of
his Courage in the said expedition into Hungary, when all his

men flying, he alone catching the gowne of his Prophett Mahomett in his hand as a holy Relick, stood boldly at his tent dore, except you will rather call it pride then Courage, he being taught to thinck himselfe deare to God and greater, then whome fortune could hurt. Of this Emperors death hapning within few yeares and of his young sonne succeeding him, and of some great Commaunders therevppon raising Ciuill warr, together with the Janizaries insolent mutiny and other passages of that State falling out since my being there, the French history compendiously treateth.

I shall not need to add any Geneologye of the Emperors, since they vsing to strangle all their brothers, and not only the daughters but the male children borne of them, being excluded from succession in the Empire, that Family of the Ottoman hath noe collaterall lynes, neither can any man be said to be of the bloud Royall, but only the Emperors sonnes, kept for the like butcherie of their elder brother. Only the common voyce was, That the Emperor of Turky and the king of the Tartars were to succeed one another vppon defect of heyres males on either side.

The Turkish state.

The Turkish Empire in our tyme is more vast and ample then euer it was formerly contayning most large prouinces. In Africk it beginnes from the straight of Gibralter and so con- taines Mauritania, Barbaria, Egipt, and all the Coasts of the Mediterranean sea. The cheife Citty of Egipt Al=caiero hath rich traffick, and yeildes exceeding great Revenues to the Emperor though no doubt much lesse since the Portugalls sailing by the South coast of Affrick and planting themselves in the East, brought all the Commodityes thereof into Portugall, from thence distributing them through Europe, which voyage in our dayes, is yearely made by the English and Flemings. From Egipt it contaynes in Asia the three Prouinces of Arabia, all Palestina, Syria, Mesopotamia, the many and large

Prouinces of Natolia or Asia the lesser, and both the Prouinces of Armenia to the very confines of Persia (in these tymes much more straightned then in former ages) herein the famous Citty of Haleppo, whether all the precious wares of the East are brought by great Riuers and vppon the backs of Camells, yeildeth huge Reuenues to the Emperor. In Europe it containes all Greece and the innumerable Ilands of the Mediterranean sea, some few excepted, (as Malta fortifyed by an order of Christian knights, Sicilye and Sardinia subiect to the king of Spaine, and Corsica subiect to the Citty of Genoa, and the two Ilands of Cephalonia, that of Corfu, of Zante and of Candia with some few other small Ilands, subiect to the Venetians). Also it contaynes Thracia, Bulgaria, Valachia, almost all Hungary, Albania, Slauonia, part of Dalmatia and other large Prouinces to the Confines of the Germane Emperor, and king of Poland.

The forme of the Ottoman Empire is meerely absolute, and in the highest degree Tyrannicall vsing all his Subiects as borne-slaves.

No man hath any free Inheritance from his father, but mangled if any at all, since all vnmouable goods belong to the Emperor, and for moueable goods, they either haue litle, or dare not freely vse them in life, or otherwise dispose them at death then by a secrett guift, as I shall shew in his place. Yea the Children of the very Bashawes and cheife Subiects, though equall to their fathers in military vertues (since there is no way to avoide contempt or liue in estimation but the profession of Armes), yet seldome rise to any place of gouernment. For this Tyrant indeed vseth to preferr no borne Turke to any high place, but they who sitt at the Sterne of the State, or haue any great Commaund either in the Army, or in Ciuill gouernment are for the most part Christians of ripe yeares, either taken Captiues or voluntarily subiecting themselues, and so leaving the profession of Christianity to become Mahometans, or els they be the Tributory Children of Christian Subiects gathered euery fifth yeare or oftner if occasion requires, and carried farr from their parents while they are young to be brought vpp in the Turkish religion and military exercises; So as when they come to age, they neither know their Country nor parents, nor kinsmen so much as by name. But of those after, I shall speake more in the due place.

All that liue vnder this Tyrant, are vsed like spunges to be squeased when they are full. All the Turkes, yea the basest sort, spoile and make a pray of the Frankes (so they call Christians that are straungers, vppon the old league they haue with the French) and in like sort they spoile Christian Subiects. The soldiers and officers seeking all occasions of oppression, spoile the Common Turkes, and all Christians. The Gouernors and greatest Commaunders make a pray of the very souldiers, and of the Common Turkes, and of all Christians, and the superiors among them vse like extortion vppon the Inferiors, and when these great men are growne rich, the Emperor strangles them to haue their treasure. So as the Turkes hide their riches and many tymes bury them vnder ground, and because nothing is so dangerous as to be reputed rich, they dare neither fare well, not build faire houses, nor haue any rich household stuffe. The Emperor seldome speakes or writes to any, no not to his cheife Visers but by the name of slaues, and so miserable is their seruitude, so base their obedience, as if he send a poore Chiaass or messenger to take the head of the greatest Subiect, he though riding in the head of his troopes, yet presently submitts himselfe to the execution. Neither indeed hath he any hope in resistance, since his equalls are his enemyes in hope to rise by his fall, his felow soldiers forsake him as invred to absolute obedience, and he not knowing his parents, kinsmen or any freindes, is left alone to stand or fall by him-selfe. Yea such is the pride of this tyrant, as the Emperor of Germany paying him some tribute for peace in Hungarie, he did not long before this tyme write letters to him with the style of his slaue, had not the Emperors Ambassador refused to receive the letters till the superscription thereof was altered. Like is his pride toward all Confederate Princes, neuer seeking the freindshipp of any by first sending Ambassadors to them, but only accepting such as he liketh, vppon their offer and desyre of amity, and league with him. If he admitt any Ambassadors to his presence, he giues them no answer, or at most in a word referres them to the cheife Visere, not thincking it for his dignity to haue any particuler conference with them, only he vouchsafeth to behold their presents or guiftes to the end they may become more large and rich, neither is any admitted to him without bringing a present. The Turkes in generall scorning all busines that brings not profitt, and makes not entrance with a present. This Tyrant seldome speakes to any of his subiects, but wil be vnderstood by his lookes, having many dumb men about his person, who will speake by signes among themselues as fast as we doe by wordes, and these men together with some boyes prostituted to his lust, and some of his dearest Concubines, are only admitted to be continually nere his person. The cheife Visere only receiues his Commaundements and his mouth giues lawe to all vnder him, being of incredible power and authority by reason of this pride and retyrednes of the Tyrant, were not this high estate of his very slipperye, and subiect to sodaine destruction. They who are admitted to the Tyrants presence, must not looke him in the face, and having kist the hemm of his garment, when they rise from adoring him, must retorne with their eyes cast on the ground, and their faces towards him, not turning their backs till they be out of his sight.

Captiues or Slaues.

Nothing can be imagined more miserable then a Towne taken by the Turkes, for they demolish all monuments sacred and prophane, and spare not the life of any one whose age or lamenes makes him worthy litle mony to be sold for a slaue, and they who scape the sword, are yet more miserable, reserued as slaues for base seruice and filthy Lusts, yea the young men are most miserable who forsweare Christ and become Mahometans to avoyd slavery of men, so becoming slaues to the divell.

The Marchants or bawdes following the Camp, to buy slaues, sell them againe to any buyer whatsoever, at great prices, vsing no Compassion to noble, or aged persons, or to tender wemen, and children, neither doth nobility make any man worth a peny more then an other, nor learning, or wisdome, or witt, which the buyers value not, but only respect beuty in women, or strength in men, except they have skill in some manuall art, being Smiths or Sadlers (of whome they haue great vse for their horses) or Jewellers (whome they esteeme desyring to haue all their riches portable and easy to be hidden) or be skilfull in nauigation, for at this tyme they greatly wanted Saylors. And these kindes of Captiues, as they are better vsed then others, so are they more warily kept, and more hardly redeemed. Thus a Princesse or lady, if her maydseruant be fayrer then shee, and a Prince or lord if his manseruant be stronger then hee, shall in this Captiuity be forced to serue them in the most base offices can be imagined. The faire women and boyes suffer fowle prostitutions, the strong men are vsed to grinde in mills, to beare heauy burthens and to doe all base and laborious woorkes. And if these who promise gaine in the selling are thus vsed, what thinck you becomes of those, who are lesse esteemed. The Marchants or Bawdes buying these Captiues, lead them bound one to another in Chaynes, forcing the sick and weake with whips to march as fast as the rest, or els cutt their throates if they be not able to goe, and at night when they are brought into a stable, and might hope for rest, then they suffer hunger, the men are scourged with whips, the women and boyes are so prostituted to lust, as their miserable outcryes yeild a wofull sound to all that are neere them. While myselfe was at Constantinople, I wente to view the Besestein or Exchaunge, where I did see Captiues to be sold and the buyers had as much freedome to take the virgins aside to see and feele the parts of their body, as if they had bene to buy a beast. For a woman not very faire, I heard the Bawde demaund three thowsand Aspers and the buyer to offer eight hundred. The Janizary who conducted me by the Commaund of our

Ambassador, told me at the same tyme, that the sommer past, when the Army was in Hungarie, himselfe bought a Captiue virgin, whome he had no sooner led to his Tent, but he found about her (hidden as priuily as can be imagined) more gold then he had paid for her. And while we walked together from the Besestein to the parts of the Citty farther remoued, an old woman meeting vs, and taking vs for Christian Captiues, asked our price of the Janizarie who telling me merrily thereof, I wished him to treat with her about buying vs, and for myselfe being leane and weake after a long sicknes, she could not be induced to giue any more then an hundred Aspers, that is some eight shillings fower pence English, but for one of our Ambassadors seruants that walked with me, being of a strong able body, she offered fower hundred Aspers at the first word, though I had better worldly meanes to redeeme my head then he had, who was beside young having small experience or skill in arts, all which the Turkes despise in respect of their man slaues strength. The cheife slaues of the greatest men liue in some good fashion, and as all degrees in Turky are knowne by their heads, so they did weare redd veluett bonnetts raised in the Crowne of the head. The lord hath absolute power of the goods, yea body and life of his Captiue or slaue, whereof they geld many, that they may be fitt to attend their Concubines and daughters. Yet I haue heard, and read of great lords killed by their slaues, when they had foreknowledge that they should be gelded by them.

Touching the Emperors reuenues and Tributes, some say that the ordinary revenues amount yearely to eight some say to twelue millions of Sultanons, besides the pay of the Army; others affirme that they are fifteene millions yearely ordinary and extraordinary. Namely five brought in treasure, and tenn disbursed to pay the Army. But the stipends and payments for the Forces and the officers in that vast Empire being excessiue great, it seemes not probable to me, that so much treasure should remayne, and yet for that huge Empire these Reuenues seeme small, saue that in respect of the Soldiers Tyranny, all arts, traffique, and husbandry are generally neglected, besides that the subiects liues being prodigally wasted in warr, many large feildes and Countries lye wast without Inhabitants or tillage. But howsoeuer the ordinary reuenues are great, surely the extraordinary are much greater. Such are the Confiscations of goods where all manner of Subiects by many frauds and extortions, frequent in that Empire, haue meanes to gather much treasure, and as euery superiour spoyles his inferiour, so the great Tyrant wants not occasion at his pleasure to take the heads, and goods of the greatest when they are full of riches. Such are likewise the guifts and presents of vnspeakable number and value, since noe man hath any gouernment without buying it, the same being oft sold to diuers men at one tyme, besides that they are scarce warme in their seats before they are recalled by a Successor sent from Constantinople: So as they must vse great speed and cruell extortion to scrape together so much mony in short tyme, as will not only satisfy themselues but also afford them guiftes to be presented to the Emperor, and their cheife superiors, without which they can neuer make a good accompt of their imployment. Besides no Ambassador hath audience before he hath giuen his present; neither can any Weaker Princes bordering vppon the Empire treat about their affayres without like presents, or haue peace, truce or immunityes without buying them. Such also are the goods of straungers dying in his Empire, to whome the Emperor is heyre, vppon which accidents of Christians dying besides taking their owne goods, many fraudes are putt vppon the rich as if their goods belonged to the dying men. In which kinde my brother dying by the way betweene Haleppo and Constantinople the Turkes pretending the Tynne and Cloth of English marchants to belong to my brother, and vppon his death to be due to the Emperor, extorted much mony of the Marchants before the goods could be released.

The Customes for marchandize are excessiue great at Haleppo (a famous Citty of traffique) of 80 Chests of Indico eleuen were giuen to the Emperor for Custome, and of all other goods he had for custome generally five in the hundred; only the English nation had the fauor to pay three in the hundred; But these Customes are vncertaine, being increased or decreased at pleasure.

For reuenues of Land, The Tymars giuen in farme only for life, (besides the horse and foote they are bound to finde, as a horse for each 60 Sultanons rent; whereof I shall speake in due place) pay tythes and other duties to the Emperor. Thus the tythes and Tributes of the playne of Tripoly alone (by which the rest may be coniectured) were said to passe 200th thousand French Crownes yearely : For the Turkes pay the Emperor the tenth part of all their fruites and Cattell. The Christianes not only pay the fourth part thereof, and of all gaine by manuall trades, but also being numbered by pole in their Familyes, each one payes yearely a Sultanon or more for his head, if he be aboue fifteene yeares old, and if he haue no meanes to pay it, he must begg it from dore to dore of other Christians, and if he cannot so gett it, shall for want thereof be made the Emperors slaue. Besides that the Christians Children are exacted for Tribute, whereof I shall speake in his place.

Among many particulers wherein myselfe had experience of their extortion towards Christians, I remember that when wee sailed vppon the Coast in vnarmed Barques, wee were advised to avoyd putting into any harbour, as much as we could, and especially not to goe on land, because the Gouernors of such Townes vse to exact from Christians so driuen in, a Zechine by the pole. And a kinsman of myne driuen into Tripoli Port, about this tyme, hardly escaped the trecherie of a Janizarie who purposed to sell him for a slaue to the Turkes dwelling within land, to be imployed in seruice of husbandry, whence he should haue had small hope to be redeemed, since Christians traffique only in places neere the sea, and the Turkes within land carefully keep their slaues vsing (besides many other meanes) the help of witchcraft, to bring them back when they runn away towards the sea. When we ariued in the Hauen of Joppa, any Turke would take from vs what he list, especially victualls, and when wee landed, having a safe Conduct to Hierusalem, from the Sobasha of Ramma, for which euery man paid six Zechines by the pole, yet wee were not free from the rapine of Mores, and Arabians all the way, flying vppon vs for vndue tributes or extortions by way of guift. These Arabians partly subiect to the Turkes, partly to the Persian, yet liue as outlawes, spoiling all men that are not in pention to some great Family among them, in which case they will protect any Marchant, and reueng his wrongs against all other men, euen of their owne nation. Neither can they be pursued by any Army, because at such tymes, they withdraw themselues into such places where an Army cannot follow them for want of water, the trouble of passing mountaines, and the huge aboundance of sand, which is carried with the windes like the flouds of the Sea, and ouerwhelmeth all, who haue not the skill to void them by obseruing the windes. When we entred Hierusalem wee paid each man two Zechines for tribute, and when wee entred the church built ouer the Sepulcher of Christ, wee paid each man nine Zechines for tribute. So as the Emperors exactions vppon Turkes and Christians may appeare to be vnsupportable.

Constantinople the seat of the Empire is by the Greekes called Stamboll and more commonly by the Turkes Capy, that is the Port gate or Hauen and the Emperors Court is called Saray, which the Italians call Serraglio.

The court and cheife officers of State.

Touching the officers of the Court, first vnderstand that as well they as the officers of the State are military men, since only soldiers beare sway in this Empire and all the officers of Court follow the Emperor in the Army. Six young men or Pages, attend the Emperors person, two each day by course who pull of his Clothes at night, and putt them on in the morning, and watch all night at his Chamber dore, putting into his pockett each morning on the one syde a thousand Aspers, on the other syde twenty Sultanons, whereof what remaynes at night falls to them by course for their availes. The first of them called Odabassi hath thirty Aspers, the rest twenty, or twenty five each day for their fee. The Capabassi or Captaine of the Court, an Eunuch and the Casnadarbassi cheife of the Treasures, had each of them 60 Aspers by the day. The Chilergibassi cheefe of the dispensors or Pantlers, and the Sarandarbassi, or Saraybassi keeper of the Serraglio in the Emperors absence had each 50 Aspers by the day. And these fower officers of Court had 12 Eunuches vnder them. Of the tributary sonnes of Christians (hereafter to be discoursed of in due place) 500 are brought vpp in the Emperors Serraglio, from the age of 8 yeares to 20 being the choyse of those Children, whereof many are deare to the Emperor in a most sinfull kinde. These are instructed in reading, writing, the study of the lawe (so much as to be able to read it in the Arabian tongue wherein it is written), but they medle with no higher misteries, saue only horsmanshipp and vse of their Armes. In the first they are instructed by old Talismans called Cozza, as it were doctors of the law, and twice in the yeare at each Beyram (so they call the Feast succeeding lent) they are apparrelled in Cloth, neuer going out of the Serraglio till they be come to ripe age and are preferred to bee Spacoglans or Silichstars. In the meane tyme they liue in Chambers as in our Hospitalls divided into tenns, an Eunuch being sett ouer each tenn, who is called Capoglan (oglan signifying a boy). The Serraglio or Pallace is some two myles in Circuit, having a spacious Garden kept by 35 Gardiners vulgarly called Bostangi, being Janizarrotti or inferiour Janizaries, who haue for stipend 3 or 5 Aspers the day, and are yearely apparrelled in sky-coloured cloth whose hope of preferment is to become Janizaries, Solacchs or Capigies. The cheife ouer them is called Bostangibassi, and hath 50 Aspers the day for fee, with many availes belonging to his office, neither doth he goe out of the Serraglio, but only to looke to the Emperors gardens out of the Citty, in which they vse to take much pleasure, having alwayes two boates at the stayres of this garden, by which the Emperor may passe to other gardens, or rowe vppon the water for his pleasure, being rowed only by these gardeners, the cheife whereof is commonly in good reputacion with him by the often vse of his seruice. The cheife of the Cookes in Court, is called Assibassi, who hath 50 Cookes vnder him (Assi signifying a Cooke) and this cheife hath 40 or 50 Aspers, whereas the rest haue only from 4 to 8 Aspers by the day each man. Among other ministers of the Court (who cannot without tœdiousnesse be all named), one hundred Janizarotts bring wood by Cartloads, and haue each man three or five Aspers by the day, besides apparrell. The Casnegirbassi that is Sewer or cheife of them that bring vpp the Emperors meat, hath 80 Aspers by the day, and vnder him one hundred Casnegirs, haue some 40 some 60 Aspers by the day. The charge of diett for the Emperor and all his Court was then said to be some 5000 Aspers by the day, by which small expence the temperance of the Turkish diett may appeare. Three cheefe Porters called Capigibassi had each one hundred Aspers by the day, and one of them stands alwayes at the Emperors dore, having vnder them 250 Porters called Capigi, whereof each hath 5. or 7. Aspers by the day. Some write that each of these three cheife Porters hath 250 vnder them, surely there be many in number, and no Ambassador, or other having busines in Court, doth enter the gates without giuing them a large reward. They are often sent abroad with the Emperors Mandates for the strangling of great men, and to see the execution done. There be many Eunuches in the Court, aswell blackmoores, as other with white skinnes, but all with black harts, hauing forsaken the faith of Christ, to become Mahometans, and these haue the charge of keeping the treasure, and the women.

The Musteraga is cheife of the Musteraes or Squiers of the body and these goe often to the tables of the great Turkish Commaunders, and of all Ambassadors, being then reputed as Spyes, making relation of their actions to the Emperor. Some 30. or 40. Footemen called Peychs liue in Court, who having (as they said) taken out their splene, or milt, were of wonderfull swiftnes in running, alwayes attending the Emperors stirropp.

The Court Drogoman, or Interpreter of tongues, had some 500 Aspers by the day, and asmuch more by Timar, besides great guiftes from Ambassadors, and other men vsing his seruice.

The Visers or Viceroyes residing in Constantinople being 4. of old, were 7 at this tyme. These together with the Mofty (that is the cheefe Interpreter of the law) may be said to be the Emperors Counsell of State. The cheefe of them is next to the Emperors person in dignity, by whome all his Commaunds are executed with absolute power, but a slippery estate to whome the rest are joyned for assistance, but farr inferiour to him in power, and one of these alwayes leades the Army when the Emperor goes not in person. The cheefe had 24,000 Sultanons each of the rest about 16000 yearely fee with thrice asmuch by Timar, besides their robes, and large guifts from Ambassadors, and all men preferred to any dignity yeilding an incredible reuenue. These reside in Constantinople, saue when they follow the Emperor in the Army, and keepe Royall Courts and traynes some one of them having some 600 slaues following them. They distribute all offices and gouernments, preferring none, nor yet speaking with any man, who hath not first giuen them a present, or bribe. And the dignityes of Viseres are for life. Next to these out of the Citty are the two Beglerbegs (or lords of lords) the one of Greece, or Romagna lying at Sophia in Bulgaria, or more comonly at the Emperors Court commaunding in cheefe all the Prouinces of Europe: the other Natolia, or Asia the lesse, commaunding all the Provinces thereof yet vnder him of Romagna being present. These are next the Generall in commaunding the Army in sommer seruice, and commaund it absolutely at other tymes, and haue vnder them the inferior Bassaes not Visers and the Sangiachs or Sangiglens (Sangis signifying a Standard) and all inferior Gouernors of Prouinces, Townes, and Castles. He of Greece hath 10000 Sultanons yearely by Timar and was said to haue then vnder him 37 Sangiacchi, 400 Sobbassi 50000 Spachi and Timaristi (who are not called Spachi, because they possesse a small Timar about the yearely value of 100 Sultanons) and 60,000 Achengi, or Adventurers who serue without stipend to be free of Tribute. And all these are horsemen not to speake of two or three other Bassaes or Beggs in Hungarie, and those Confines with the Zangiacchs and horsemen vnder them. The other of Natolia having 4000 Sultanons yearely by Timar, was said to Commaund 12 Sangiacchi, and 30000 Spachi and Timariotts. The Bassa sett ouer Damascus, Syria, and Judea having 24000 Sultanons yearely by Timar was said to haue 2000 slaues, and to commaund 12 Sangiacchi having 7000 Sultanons by Timar, and 20000 Spachi, and Timariots, not to speake of some 30 Bassaes, or Begs in diuers Countries of Asia the greater, with the Zangiachs and horsemen vnder them. The Bassa of Cayro, Egipt, Africk and Arabia having 30000 Sultanons yearely by Timar was said to haue an infinite number of Slaues, and to commaund 16 Sangiacchi, and 160000 Spachi and Timariotts not to speake of two or three inferior Bassaes or Begs in Africk. Those Beglerbegs commaund but for some yeares and the rest are often changed. In generall vnderstand that these reuenues of those great Commaunders by Timar, and stipend, are nothing to them in respect of the treasure they gett by extortion, for which they are neuer questioned, so they be able to bribe the Emperor, and Viseres by presents at their retorne.

I retorne to the Commaunders that reside at Constantinople, or follow the Army, marching thence. The Bassa of the Sea or Admirall commaunds all the Gallies and of old, this place belonged to the Sangiacch of Gallipolis till the great Pyrat called Barbarossa some 100 yeares past, had that place giuen him, from which tyme also this officer hath the title and dignity of a Visere Bassa, and hath yearely 14000 Sultanons by Timar out of three Ilands, being absolute Commaunder at Sea, but having the cheife Viseres Commission to direct and warrant his actions. He hath 14 Zangiachs or Gouernors of Citties vppon the Sea vnder him. The Janizar-Agar or cheife of the Janizaries is an office of great authority as shal be shewed, and he hath one 1000 Aspers stipend by the day, and 6000 Sultanons yearely by Timar. The Chiause-Aga or cheife of the Chiauses

(400 horsemen in number) is of so great authority, as being sent to any great man to see him putt to death, he is obeyed by word of mouth, though he haue no mandate to that purpose. He and all vnder him, are like our Gentlemen Pentioners, and bearing a mace on horsback, ride before, and about the Emperors person, and are sent abroad vppon the foresaid or any other messages, and many of them attend at the Cheife Viseres Pallace to execute his Commaunds, and also in Courts of Justice, and some of them follow the Beglerbegs in the feild. Two Solachbassi commaund 150 of the strongest Janizaries chosen out for the Emperors guard, and called Solacchi, and the Commaunders ride on horsback neere the Emperors person, wearing long feathers, but they and their men are vnder the Commaund of the Janizar-Aga, whome I did see riding by the Emperors side (as he vseth to doe) wearing a great plume of feathers, and being a goodly tall man. The Spacchoglan-Aga is a great office, and he hath 10 Sultanons each day in mony, and by Timar. I passe ouer the Silichtar-Aga, two Olifagibassi cheefes of their orders, and the Mechterbassi who hath 40. Aspers by the day and Commaundes 60 Mechteri, who have the charge to carry the Emperors Tents and Carpetts and to sett vpp and spread them : and the Sechmembassi having one 100 Aspers by the day with charge of the hunting doggs and having vnder him some 2000 Janizaries. I passe ouer the Zagarzibassi having of a speciall kinde of hunting doggs and the Zachengi-bassi, having charge of some 100 Falcons : and the Imralem-Aga who caryes the Emperors Standard, having 200 Aspers by the day : with many other like officers. Certaine swift horsmen called Vlacchi alwayes attend the Pallaces of the Emperor, and cheife Visere to carry letters, and woe be to those who furnish them not presently with horses.

Besides these officers in Court and Commaunders of the Army, they haue Judges who are skilfull in the Mahometan lawe, for they haue aswell humane as diuine lawes from Mahomett. The cheife Interpreters of these lawes called Mofty, is had in exceeding great honor, whose voice is held for an

oracle, and the Emperor consults with him in the most difficult
matters, and vseth him with great respect. Next to him, is the
Hosi, or Hogsi, who was schoolemaster to the Emperor in his
youth. Two Cadilisquieri (others write Lischieri) are Talismani
as it were doctors of the lawe, and they are the cheife Judges,
one for Europe, the other for Asia, to whome all appeales are
made, each having seuen 1000 Sultanons yearely by Timar,
besides that the Emperor payes tenn Clarkes for each of them,
and each of them hath some 200 or 300 slaues. At Constantinople they assist the cheife Visere, who committs civill causes
to them, reseruing Criminall to himselfe. They take place
before the Visere, but are farr inferior to him in power; with
his consent they place or displace all inferior Judges, as those
called Cadi, who are Judges of Citties or Townes, and haue a
kinde of Episcopall authority, and the Judges vnder them,
aswell in Citties and Townes as in villages, called Percadi, and
Nuipi, as also those that are called Sobassi. And vppon these
depend the Muctari or Sergeants, who apprehend guilty men,
and execute Judgments, rewarded out of the malefactors goods.
All these exercise horrible extortions vppon all Turkes and
vppon christians, especially those that are Subiects.

Among officers of State the Nisangibassi like the Chancelor
of the Empire, keepes the Imperiall Seale taking place next the
Beglerbegs, and having yearely by Timar 8000 Sultanons, and
said to have some 300 slaues bought with his mony, who (as all
other Judges) followes the beck of the cheife Visere. Of two
Isnadicbassi or Defterdari (that is Treasorers) the one receiues
the reuenue of Europe, having 6000 Sultanons yearely by Timar
and when the Emperor goes out of Constantinople (as sometymes he doth with the Army) he is left to gouerne the Citty
in his absence: the other receiues the reuenues of Asia and
Africk, having yearely 10000 Sultanons by Tymar, but the
availes of these offices are of farr greater moment. They haue
vnder them 50 Clerkes, and to each of them the Emperor giues
30 or 40 Aspers by the day, besides many other helpers to cast
vpp the accompts of the Casna or Treasure. They send their

deputies into all Prouinces, Cittyes,and Townes, who committ
vnspeakable extortions, especially vppon strangers, Widowes,
Orphanes, Christians and the heyres of such as be dead.   Two
Rosunamegi, or cheife Clerkes, and 25 inferior Clerkes, receiue
and disburse the mony, and each of the cheife hath 40 Aspers,
each of the other hath 8 or 10 Aspers by the day.   Two
Desnedari waigh the Aspers each having 30 Aspers by the day.
One Casnadarbassi or Thresorer out of the Citty of Constantinople had 50 Aspers by the day, and had vnder him 10 others
having each 10 or 15 Aspers by the day.   One Deftermine kept
the Register of the Timars and had 40 Aspers by the day, and
he had vnder him 10 Clerkes, each having 10 or 15 Aspers by
the day.   The cheife Visere is as the Secretary of State, and he
had vnder him two Riscatapi or Secretaries, who presented all
petitions to him, and gaue his answer in writing.

Of the Cheife Visere then gouerning the State.

When I was at Constantinople the cheife Visere was called
Ibraym Bassa, who had maryed one of the sisters of the Emperor
(for the sisters are neuer putt to death with the brothers, but
are maried to the greatest Subiects the Emperor hath).   He
gouerned the Empire with absolute power, but was ruled and
supported by the Sultana the Emperors mother.   It was told me
by men of Creditt, that he neuer lay with his wife without first
asking her leaue, and when he came to her bed, he entred not
at the side, but crept in at the feete, and if this be the Condition
of them, that marry the sisters of the Emperor, they are more
like their slaues then their husbands.   And while I was yet at
Constantinople one was apprehended, who attempted to kill this
Visere with a knife, and he fayned himselfe madd and though
he was cruelly tormented, yet would not confess why he had
attempted it, nor any one that was priuy to his purpose.   But
the ruine of this Visere shortly following, shewed how slippery
these high dignityes are, euen in respect of the Envie among
equalls, when the Emperor is not offended; For in October last

past, some three monethes before I came to this Citty, the
Emperor, retorned from the Hungarian warr, and having bene
offended with Ibraym for some thing had happened that Somer
in the said warr, had taken from him the dignity of cheife
Visere, while he was yet in Hungarie and giuen the same to
Sigala Ogly an Italian Reneagate of Genoa, but receiuing
letters from his mother at Adrianopolis on the behalfe of
Ibraym, whome she supported, they preuailed somuch with
him, as he had presently restored Ibraym to his former dignity,
and before the Emperor came to Constantinople, his mother and
Ibraym had so incensed him against Sigala, as he was forbidden
to enter Constantinople, the cheife pretended cause of which
offence was that Sigala had perswaded the Emperor in the
choice of the king of the Tartarians to fauour a younger brother
who then followed him in the Army, wherevppon the elder
brother getting the victory and kingdome, was much alienated
from the Emperor.   This Sigala was preferred to the dignity of
a Bassa by the Hogsi (others write Hogsialer) the schoolemaster
of the Emperor in his youth, and lest he should vse meanes to
restore him to the Emperors fauor, his mother and Ibraym,
vnder pretence of honor, but indeed to send the Hogsi so farr
of as by reason of his old age he should not be likely to retorne,
procured the Emperor to make him Gouernor of Meccha, so
as all men reputed Sigala for a dead man.   But myselfe in the
springtyme retorning into Italy, there heard by credible
relation, that Sigala was receiued to the Emperors fauour.
When I was at Constantinople, Halil Bassa, who had maryed
another of the Emperors sisters, succeeded the Admirall Vccelli
an Italian Renagate of Calabria, being dead, but he began the
exercise of that office with ill fortune, For myselfe in my
retorne before I came to the straight of the Castles, being driuen
by a storme into the Iland Aloni, not far distant from
Constantinople, there heard that seuen of the Emperors Gallies
were lost in that storme.

Princes Ambassadors.

Touching Princes Ambassadors. The Persian and other like Potentates, vppon particuler occasions send Ambassadors to Constantinople, but I did not heare at my being there, of any such continually residing in the Citty. Among the Christian Princes, I may say the like of the king of Poland. Of the rest only three had leiger Ambassadors at my being there, Namely Elizabeth Queene of England, vppon amity contracted in her Raigne only for traffique of Marchants. And the French King vppon a league made by Francis the first extending further then traffique as may appeare by some events of his tyme, and from this league all the Christians of our parts are called Francks in Turky. The third from the State of Venice vppon the necessity of many differences happening betweene that State and the Turkes, but he hath only the title of Bailye giuen him from his owne Nation. These three had houses in the Citty of Persa, or Galata, being as it were a Subvrbe of Constantinople, seated on the north syde of a very narrow sea like a Riuer. And they Liued in great freedome having Janizaries allowed to guard their persons, and houses, which were as Sanctuaries, no officer daring to enter them in making any search, and they as freinds had liberty to weare the apparrell of their nations only when they went abroad, instead of Clokes, they wore a loose Turkish garment with sleeues to putt out their armes. The Emperor of Germany had his leiger Ambassador in tyme of peace, but he as Tributary wore Turkish apparrell, and had his house in Constantinople, that they might more narrowly obserue his actions. Myselfe being at Constantinople, lodged in the house of Mr. Edward Barton Ambassador for England, by his fauour, having also my diett at his Table, and one of his Janizaries allowed him by the Emperor, daily conducted and guarded me, when I went abroad. Of whome for his great Worth, and my loue towards him, I must add something to preserue his memory as much as I can. He was no more learned then the Grammer schoole and his priuate studyes in Turkye could make him, but he had good skill in languages, especially that of the Turkes.

He was courteous and affable, of a good stature, corpulent, faire
Complexion and a free chearefull Countenance, which last, made
him acceptable to the Turkes, as likewise his person, (for they
loue not a sadd Countenance, and much regard a comely
person) but especially his skill in their language made him
respected of them, so as I thinck no Christian euer had greater
power with any Emperor of Turkye or the officers of his state,
and Court, then he had in his tyme.   When Amurath father to
Mahomett the third began the Hungarian Warr, with the
Emperor of Germanye, he cast his Ambassador into prison with
sixteene seruants, and some Barons and gentlemen of Germany
(who at that tyme had the ill hap to be lodged in his house)
and after many yeares, when the Emperor resolued to sett them
at liberty, and the French Ambassador made great means, and
gaue large guifts to haue the honor to send them back, the
Emperor of his free will said, he would giue them to the
Lutheran Elshi (so they call the English Ambassador) and this
shortly after he performed, deliuering all those prisoners to his
hands, and Mr. Barton as freely sent them into Germany.   But
I haue heard him complaine with greife, that for his Courtesy,
he neuer receiued so much as thancks from the Emperor, but
rather heard that some imputations were laid vppon him in the
Emperors Court, who therevppon incensed the Queen his
mistres against him.   The most proud Turkish Tyrant, as he
disdaynes to speake to his owne Subiects, so when he admitts
any Ambassador, he only adores his person, but seldome or
neuer speakes with the Emperor, or at least neuer receiues any
answer to his speach, whatsoeuer some may report to the
Contrary.   Yet hath this master Barton our Ambassador
receiued many tokens of speciall fauour in this Court.   He had
the Emperors graunt that the Flemings and other christians not
being in league with him might enter his Havens vnder the
Protection of the English flag.   For which and some other
causes, he was much envied by some Christians espetially by the
French Ambassador who formerly had enioyed that priuiledge.
Myselfe being at Constantinople, waited vppon Mr. Barton to

the Serraglio, where he was told he should be admitted to speake
with the Emperor. In which case all his attendants should
haue kissed the hem of his garment, and each one should haue
receiued a Cloth of gold gowne (for they according to the old
fashion of the East, still giue rayments for rewards, and tokens
of favour) but after long attendance, the Emperor sent him the
graunt of his petition, and a gowne of cloth of gold for himselfe,
and so we were dismissed. When this Emperor Mahomett the
third led his Army to the seige of Agria, in Hungarie, among
the Christian Ambassadors he chose Mr. Barton to goe with
him, and when he retorned to Constantinople, Mr. Barton being
to goe to his house, the Emperor stayd on horsback till he came
to kisse the hem of his garment, and till he retorned to his horse,
and was mounted, at which tyme he answered his wonted
reuerence with bowing of his body, and so roade into the Citty,
not without the wonder of all his Army, that he should doe
such honor to a dog (for so they call and esteeme all christians).
But howsoeuer leiger Ambassadors vse not to refuse their
attendance to the Princes with whome they reside, and howsoeuer Mr. Barton followed his Camp without bearing Armes; yet
this his iourney into Hungary, made the Queene of England
much offended with him, for that he had borne the English
Armes vppon his Tent, whereof the French Ambassador accused
him to the Emperor, and the French King, who expostulated
with the Queene that her Armes should be borne in the Turkes
Campe against christians, though indeed in that iourney, he
intended and might haue had many occasions to doe good vnto
the christians; but had neither will, nor meanes to doe them
hurt. But the truth is, that howsoeuer Mr. Barton had strong
parts of nature, and knew well how to manage great Affaires in
the Turkes Court; yet he coming yong to serue our first
Ambassador there, and being left to succeed him, could not
know the English Court, nor the best wayes there to make good
his actions. Besides that the English Marchants were ready to
accuse rather then excuse his actions in Court, being displeased
with him for medling in State matters, whereby their goods in

Turky might vppon some ill accident be confiscated : for howsoeuer he bore the name of the Queenes Ambassador, yet he lay there only for matter of traffique, and had his stipend of some 1500 Zechines by the yeare paid from the Marchants. By the way giue me leaue to add that not only he, but all Christian Ambassadors, haue as great allowance as that before named from the Emperor of Turkye, though not in ready mony yet in mutton, Beefe, hay, oates, and like prouisions, saue that they spend halfe thereof in bribes or presents to the officers of whome they are receiued. Nothing is more hatefull to the Turkes then pouerty, who doe nothing without guifts, yet this our Ambassador notwithstanding he was poore, had power in his tyme both to treate and depose Princes vnder that State. The Emperor Amurath made a King of Bulgarie at his request, and vppon his word giuen for payment of his great tributes, which that king failing to pay, and falling to the Christians party in open Rebellion, yet the Emperor not only forgaue Mr. Barton that ingagement, but in his last testament (never disobeyed) commaunded Mahomett the third to remitt the same vnto him. And this Mahomett likewise did so much esteeme him, as he had power with him to preferr a friend of his to be Patriarke of the Greekes (a place of so high dignity with the Greekes as the Papall seate with the Papists). And when Mahometts Army was ready to march against the king of Poland, he had power to diuert him from that warr, and to make peace betweene them, for which good office the king of Poland retorned thankes to the Queene of England. Besides that in discourse with myselfe, I found him confident, that he should be the meanes to make peace betweene the Turke[s] and the Emperor of Germany, but his vntymely death prevented that his hope. By these and other his like actions, it may appeare that they did him wrong, who did attribute his greatnes in the Turkish Court, to his betraying the Counsells of Popish christian Princes, especially such as were enemyes to the State of England. For as he was a man of good life and constant in the profession of the reformed religion, so he protested to abhorr

from furthering the Turkes designes against any the greatest
enemy of his profession and Country, further then to diuert
them for the tyme from some malicious attempt.

Forrayne Princes. The Queene of England.

Touching forrayne Princes, England was so farr remoued
from Turkye as from the forces thereof the Turkes could expect
neither good nor ill, and when the Emperor beheld England in
a Mapp, he wondred that the king of Spaine did not digg it
with mattocks, and cast it into the Sea. But the heroick vertues
of Queene Elizabeth, her great actions in Christendome, and
especially her preuailing against the Pope and king of Spaine,
her professed enemyes, made her much admired of the Emperor,
of his mother, and of all the great men of that Court, which did
appeare by the letters and guiftes sent to her Maiestie from
thence, and by the consent of all strangers that liued in that
tyme at Constantinople.

The Persian King.

For the Persian king; The Turkes hold their strength to
be farr greater then his in the bands of foote, and aswell in
the quantity as the vse of Artillery. But the power of the
Persian is in his troopes of horse, to which he only trusts, and
howsoeuer by the same he hath often giuen great ouerthrowes
to the Turkes; yet at the same tyme they gott Prouinces from
him, and held them by strength of their Foote, and plenty of
Artillery both which the Persian wants. And by Sea the
Persian then could doe him no hurt, being hindred from
building Gallies, or attempting any thing at Sea, by the forces
which the Portugalles held aswell in the Persian as in the redd
Sea.

Preste Jean or Gianni. Seriffus.

In Africk Preianes commonly called Prester Gianni ruling
the south parts towards the redd Sea is freed from the feare

of the Turkes, not so much by Armes as by the high mountaynes of the moone and the mountaines of Sand carryed with the wynds like the Waues of the Sea, yet have they taken from him all his cheife places vppon the red-sea. The Seriffus his kingdome lyes from thence towards the West, not so large but more fertile then the other, and he doth no way acknowledge the Turkes, but is a free Prince, yet they are both kept from acts of hostility by their mutuall feare of the Spaniards lying vppon them.

The Kingdome of Poland.

The Turkes doe not willingly prouoke but rather seeme to feare the Polonians, as very strong in braue troopes of horse, and no way yeilding to them in their body of Footemen. No doubt the Turkes haue for a long tyme passed ouer without any reuenge diuerse incursions and spoyles made by the Polonian Cosacchi, and of late haue for their owne purpose wincked at great iniuryes offered by them. In the yeare 1597 when Mahomett the third beseiged Agrea in Hungarie and great troopes of Tartarians coming to his ayde, were to passe the Confines of Poland, they were ouerthrowne with a great prey taken from them by the Polonian horsemen called Cosacchi, about which action two Polonian messengers came in one and the same day to the Turkes Campe, whereof the first advised the Turkish Emperor that the Tartarians might be ledd an other way, lest they falling vppon the Cosacchi guarding the Confines, and they being both furious and prone to Armes, it should not be in the power of the Captaines of either syde to keepe them from mutuall iniuryes, but was rather to be feared that they would ioyne in battell together. The second Messenger brought Newes, that they had fought, and the Tartarians were ouerthrowne; yet the Turkish Emperor with a chearefull Countenance was content to vnderstand this act as hapning by chaunce, not of purpose according to the messengers relation, tho he could not but thinck it as manifest an iniurye as any open enemy could have done him.   Notwithstanding it cannot be denied, that for the Common sloth of all christians, or the priuate Want of mony, Artillery and all munitions, the Polonians have not only not bene able to free the Moldauians and the Walachians their Confederates from the slauery of the Turkes, but have themselves lost to the Turkes a Territory lying vppon the black or Euxine Sea.

The State of Venice.

On the Contrary the Turkes seemed of purpose to prouoke the Venetians with continuall iniuries, and they taught by experience to be ielous of the Spaniards ayde vppon any league, and themselues wanting Victualls and soldiers, and equall strength of any forces to make warr without ayde against the great power of the Turkes, were content to stopp their fury by strong fortes, till by peaceable arts and guiftes, they might have tyme to appease the Turkish Emperor, and make their peace with him, in which kinde they had vnfaithfull peace with him, troubled with many iniuries, and yet were said to pay him the yearely Tribute of 18000 duccatts, for enioying the Ilands and Townes they possessed in the mediterranean sea, whereof notwithstanding he hath taken many from them at diuers breaches of peace.   While myselfe was in Turkye, certaine Turkish Pyratts of the South West part of Morea or Greece, spoyling the Christians with a few small barques, had the Courage to assaile a Venetian Shipp of 700 Tonns burthen, and well furnished with brasse ordinance, which they tooke and loaded all their Barques with the most precious Commodityes thereof. Vppon Complaint of which hostile act made to the Emperor of Constantinople by the Balye of Venice for a shewe of Justice he obtayned that a Chiauss was sent thither to apprehend the Pyrats but they withdrawing themselues into other Havens, and vsing meanes by large presents to make the Chiauss their freind for the present, and after in like sort to make their peace with the Emperor, the cheife Visere and the Admirall they so handled the matter as first the Chiauss retorned back with answer, that they could not be found, and after the Venetians were so tyred with delayes of Justice, in that Court, as they were forced in the end to desist from following the cause, without having any restitution.

The King of Spaine.

The king of Spaine, being of the elder house of Austria had no league nor Ambassador with the Turkish Emperor, and howsoeuer about this tyme vppon a peace made, the king of Spaine had sent an Ambassador to Constantinople, yet Mr. Barton the English Ambassador professed, that he had caused him to be stayd by the way and forbidden to come to Court, with absolute denyall of his residence in that Citty. The Spaniards and Turkes at that tyme did some hostile acts one against the other at Sea, and on both sides the Captiues were made Gally slaues, but they had no open Warr, because the Territoryes of the king of Spaine lay so farr of, as the Turkes could not assaile him without a strong Navy at Sea. In which Sea-fights, the Turkes had no confidence in their strength and much more feared to ingage themselves in such a kinde of warr since they receiued the great ouerthrow at Corsolari neare the Gulfe of Lepanto, by the Confederate forces of the king of Spaine the Pope and the Venetians vnder the generall Conduct of Don John of Austria. And the Turkes more feare the Spaniards at Sea, because they haue bene heretofore fouly defeated by the Portugalls, having Forts in the Red-sea; yet the king of Spaine in regard of his dispersed dominions and distracted forces, hath neuer alone attempted the Turkes. It is very probable especially in respect of the infinite number of Christians groning vnder the Turkish Tyrannye, that the king of Spaine might with lesse charge and efusion of blood, have conquered all Greece, and Palestine itselfe, then he [sic] made warr in those dayes with Christians, and howsoeuer his iust anger, and good reason, might moue him rather to subdue his rebelling Subiects; yet all men would have iudged this a more honourable and religious Warr, then that he made with England and France, except the Pope, with his votaries, who as he thought it for his greatnes to suffer the Greeke church at first to be subdued by the Turkes : so in our tyme he had rather see all Christendome turned vpsyde downe, then himselfe to fall from his Antichristian tyranny to the iust dignity of a Christian Bishopp.

The Emperor of Germanye.

The Emperor of Germany being of the younger house of Austria, hath in our tyme continually borne an vnsupportable warr in Hungarye against the powerfull forces of the Turkish Emperor, and with losse of great part of that kingdome; which ill successe Botero the Romane attributes to a false cause, as if the Germans had lost the glory of Warr together with the puritie of Religion. For not to dispute of the Romane Religion to be nothing lesse then pure, no doubt the Warr of Hungarie hath bene made by those Germanes who still remayne Papists, Wherein the auxiliarye bands of the very Italians haue as litle preuailed against the Turkes, as any other. And if euer the Germanes resume their old Customes to visitt and reforme the Romane Church, I doubt not but the Italians shall finde them no lesse equall in the glory of warr, then they passe them in the truth of religion. But indeed the difference of religion betweene the Emperor and the Princes of Germany, and the advantage of the Turkes horse swift to pursue, or saue themselues ouer the horse of Germany, howsoever able to endure assault, yet vppon any disaster vnfitt to escape by flight and other like advantages of warr, on the Turkes part many and easy to be named haue made the Germanes vnable to withstand the great power of the Turkes. And God graunt that the Princes of Germanye through their dissention, doe so not lay open that easy way to the Turkes inuasion as all christian Princes when they most would, shall hardly be able to stopp the same.

The foundations of the State and Army.

I haue formerly shewed that they which gouerne the Turkish tyranny, are not Turkes borne, but voluntary or Captiue Christians torning Mahometans, and the Children of Christian subiects exacted for tribute and trayned vpp in the Turkes Religion and discipline, in parts so farr remoued from their natiue Country and freinds, as they forgetting both become most deadly enemyes to all christians. Each fifth yeare (or oftner as need requires), the Turkes Emperor sends officers into Greece and Natolia (the lesser Asia) and to his Prouinces in Asia the greater (excepting some priuiledged places) to exact the tribute Children choosing in each family the children they iudge most strong, and of best Capacity for witt, of which they bring away tenn or twelue thousand at one tyme, and howsoeuer by old custome, they should only take the third sonne of a Family, yet now they spare not to take a mans only childe. The poorest of these may rise to the highest places of that State, if they can make their way by valour and Wisdome. They are disposed by phisiognomy selecting the most Witty to learne the Lawe, the most beutifull to be brought vpp in the Emperors Serraglio, the strongest (according to their age and strength) to learne the vse of bowes and arrowes, whipping them so oft as they misse the marke, who are promoted to be Solacchi (which are choice Janizaries appointed for the Emperors guard) or els learne the vse of the sword and the peece, and then are made ordinary Janizaries. But many of them especially those which are to make Solacchi and Janizaries are first brought vpp for fower Yeares in Caramania and Bursia vnder husbandmen who for their labour during those yeares mantaine them without any charge to the Emperor, in which tyme they learne the Turkes Language and religion, and are invred to learne labour, hunger and thirst. After with the rest, they are distributed into Colledges, where they liue together in large Chambers. Of these 500. chosen for beauty are brought vpp in like Chambers within the Walles of the Emperors Serraglio. The like number of a second sort is brought vpp in the Colledge of Pera or Galata (being as it were a Svbvrbe of Constantinople beyond the Water). Of a third sort 300. are brought vpp in a Colledge of Adrianopolis in Hungarie, out of these and some other Colledges, the troopes of horses are supplyed, namely the Spachi, the Silichtari, and the like. The rest of the tributary Children are called Azimoglani, and Janizarotti, that is rude Janizaries, and they are brought vpp in diuerse Colledges of Bursia (or Bithinia) of Constantinople, and of Adrianopolis out of which ye Janizaries come being the strength of the footebands, and therefore chosen of the strongest Children in Europe, not of those in Asia, who haue euer bene reputed effeminate.

The second foundation of the Army is the Timariotti: For when the Emperor takes any Prouince, he retaynes to himself the Inheritance of the land, dividing it into Timares or Farmes which he giues only for life to his great vassals with Condition, besides the tythes and tributes, to finde him a certaine number of horse after 60. Sultanons yearely Rent for a horse, whereby he not only supplyes his troopes of horse, but in some sort establisheth husbandry, which being neglected by other Subiects in regard of the soldiers tyranny (the people having a prouerbe, that no fruit will grow where the Emperors horse hath once sett his feete) by the giving Commodity of husbandry to the soldiers themselues, it is for their owne profitt in some sort mantayned by them. Europe hath of old had some lands possessed by like tenure in Fee for life only, namely to serue the Lord in his Warres, and howsoeuer Emperors and Kings haue made these Lands to be hereditary, yet still the owners are bound to some military duties, the difference only is, that these lands at the first and the Worst, had vnder christian Princes light military duties imposed on them, whereas the Turkish Tyrant, according to his absolute Will and pleasure exacteth almost to the highest value of the Land. These Tymariotts are horsemen, and are of an vnspeakable number, being thought to be some 250 thousand in Europe and almost 500 thousand in

Asia the lesser, and the greater, and in Africk.   They keepe in
awfull subiection all the Christian Subiects vnder the Yoke of
extreme Tyranny, being sodenly ready, and sufficiently able to
suppresse any the greatest sedition may be stirred vpp.   Yet
indeed the Christians, there borne and bred in slauery
especially having neuer tasted the sweetnes of liberty, are of
such abiect myndes, as with the Israelites, they seeme to preferr
an Egiptian bondage with slothfull ease, before most sweet
Christian liberty, with some danger and hazard.   Howsoeuer
the number of these horsemen is so great, as two third parts
being left at home for these and like ends; yet the Turkish
Emperor can lead forth in his Army, for any sommers seruice
some 200th thousand of them.

These foundations of the Army being laid, the Turkish
Emperors not without cause vse to vaunt, that they care not for
the defeate, no nor yet the destruction of an Army, so their
christian mares (so they call the wemen their Subiects) liue and
be fruitfull, and so they leese no Prouince, for these preserued,
they doubt not in short tyme to strengthen or renewe their
Army.   And this makes them so prodigall of their subiects
bloud, filling ditches with their bodyes in warr, so they may
gett a Towne and Territory, and many other wayes destroying
them, as only fatted for slaughter.

Warfare in generall.

Certaine positions of religion and the due conferring of
rewards and punishments make the Turkes bold adventure their
persons and carefully performe all duties in Warr.   By blinde
religion they are taught, that they mount to heauen without any
impediment, who dye fighting for their Country and the Law of
Mahomet.   And that a Stoicall Fate or destiny gouernes all
humane affaires, so as if the tyme of death be not come, a man
is no lesse safe in the Campe then in a Castle, if it be come, he
can be preserued in neither of them, and this makes them like
beasts to rush vppon all daungers euen without Armes to defend

or offend, and to fill the ditches with their dead Carkases, thincking to ouercome by number alone, without military art. Againe all rewards as the highest dignityes, and the like giuen continually by the Emperor to the most valiant and best deseruing, make them apt to dare any thing. And in like sort seuere punishments neuer failing to be inflicted on all offendors, more specially on such as brawle and fight among themselues, who are punished according to the quality of the offence, sometymes with death, and also such as breake martiall discipline, sometymes punishing him with death that pulls but a bunch of grapes in a Vineyard. I say these punishments neuer failing to be inflicted vppon offendors, make the soldiers formerly incouraged by rewards no lesse to feare base Cowardise, brawling, fighting or any breach of discipline, and keepe them in awe, as they keepe all other Subiects and enemyes vnder feare of their sword hanging ouer them. And the forme of this State being absolute tyranny, since all things must be kept by the same meanes they are gotten, the State gotten and mantayned by the sword, must needs giue exorbitant Priuiledges or rather meanes of oppression to all the Soldiers who (as I formerly haue shewed) are not themselues free from the yoke of the same Tyranny which they exercise ouer others, while the superiors oppressing their inferiors are themselues grinded to dust by greater men, and the greatest of all hold life and goods at the Emperors pleasure, vppon an howers warning, among whome happy are the leane, for the fatt are still drawne to the shambles. The poorest man may aspire to the highest dignityes, if his mynde and fortune will serue him, but vppon those high pinnacles, there is no firme abiding, and the same Vertue and Starr, that made him rise, cannot preserue him long from falling. The great men most rauenously gape for treasure, and by rapine gett aboundance, but when they haue it, all that cannot be made portable, must be hidden or buryed, for to build a fairer house, to haue rich household stuff, or to keepe a good table, doth but make the Puttock a prey to the Eagle. Thus the Emperor nourishing poore men to strangle

them when they are rich, seemes not vnlike the Seriffo in
Africk, whom Boterus the Romane writes gladly to giue large
pentions and stipends to rich men, that he may gett their wealth
by the Law that makes him heyre to all his Pensioners, so as for
feare of this fraudulent bounty, the richest men liue as farr as
possibly they can from his Courts.

Our Ambassador told me, that the Turkish Emperor giues
daily stipend to some Eighteene hundred thousand persons, and
that as well in peace, as in Warr. The number seemed incredible vnto me though great part thereof should be of Women
and children having small stipends, except all that serue the
Timariotts in tillage may iustly be said to liue of the Emperors
purse. But no doubt his Army is mantayned as well in peace
as warr, so as it seemes Warr is litle more chargable vnto him
then peace, yea more profitable by the gayning of Townes and
Territories, saue that it consumes his Subiects. The foresaid
incredible number receiuing stipend from the Emperor, makes
me lesse wonder at the French gentleman Villamount, who
writes that all the Turkes Subiects haue some pay from him,
tho it is most certaine that most Turkes borne, living as Pleibeans
vppon manuall Arts, and tillage, not only haue no pay, but are
much oppressed by the soldiers. Men of experience in Turkish
affayres agree that the Emperor cannot gather all his forces
into one Army, no Country being able to feed them, besides
that the Christian Subiects living vnder great tyranny might
haue meanes to rebell by such remote absence of the soldiers.
But many of them thinck that the Emperor can make an Army
of five or sixe hundred thousand, as he hath often led forth more
than halfe the number Which I dare not attribute, with Boterus
the Romane to the plenty of Victualls in the Easterne parts,
since of old, the Hunns Gothes and Vandalls in diuerse
Countries of Europe, and the dukes of Muscouy of late in the
Northern parts, haue led forth like huge Armyes. But giue me
leaue to say, besides vulgar opinion, that the invention of Gunns
and Gunpowder was not diuelish and bloudy, but profitable to
all mankinde, since histories Witnes, that when battells were

fought by hand strokes, then huge Armies were Levyed, and the part defeated euer lost great numbers, Whereas since that invention, Armyes haue not bene greater then some 20000, and the part defeated seldome lost the fourth part, the rest retyring to safe Forts. As also experience teacheth that the invention of dangerous fights, as Rapiars, pistolls and the like, hath caused fewer quarrells and lesse bloodshedd, then the old vse of swords and bucklers. Therefore I thinck that the great Armyes of the Turkes may be attributed to their small skill, and rare vse of fighting with gunns, which only some part of the Janizaries vseth, tho they haue great store of Artillery, which in like sort they cannot generally so Well manage as the Christians. Or els lett these great Armyes of the Turke and Moscouite, be attributed to their tyrannicall gouernments making all Subiects ready to follow them, and all officers rather comitt any rapine, and not to spare their owne goodds, then the Army should be vnfurnished with victualls to the hazard of their owne heads. But especially the Turke may lead great Armyes, by reason of his subiects singuler temperance in diett. For they vse no wyne nor any kinde of drinck, but only water in the Campe, being also forbidden wine at home in peace by their lawe if they would obserue it. Euery man can carry his owne prouision of meat being only Rice and hony, except sometymes they gett mutton, and their Cariages are not great, having in Campe as at home only a small pott to seeth Rice or Mutton, and vsing no Corsletts or other Armor for defence. Only they vse not to ly in Townes or Villages but in the open feild, so as all sleeping vnder Tents, that Kinde of baggage is great. For offensiue Weapons, they carry store of Artillery, but for great part in rude matter to be cast in the feild. Of their Armes, I shall speake in due place, only I will say that all in generall are furnished with excellent short swords whereof they haue great store, those of Damascus being famous for the mettall, but they seeme not much to delight in musketts, nor to haue such ready vse of them as the Christians. Whereas our Christian Soldiers are in tyme of peace cast out of pay, and exposed to

perish by want, The Turkes have asmuch pay in peace, as in
Warr, and so are more ready and willing to spend their life
for the Emperor, and againe the Emperor receiuing no lesse
Revenues in Warr then in peace, Yea rather more by selling
Captiues at high rates, by turning subdued places into Timars,
and by making good vse of Victories in all parts, is thereby
enabled at all tymes to make quarterly payment to his soldiers,
wherein he neuer faileth. The Sangacchi going to or coming
from their gouerments, ride in tyme of peace (as I thinck they
march in the Armyes) with drumms and Hoboyes, or such lowde
instruments as we in our Citties vse by night, but they haue two
drums, one litle one to be beaten at one end, which they vse
by the way, and a great one to be beaten at both ends, not
wearing it about the neck when they beat it, but setting it
downe vppon the ground, and with that they sett their Watches.
All degrees among them are knowne by their heads; For as all
Turkes in generall weare white heads, (as the Persians weare
greene) called by some Tsalma by others Tolopa, and vulgarly
Tulbent; so all degrees are distinguished by the same either
by feathers and Jewells, or by the forme, lesse or more rounde
or Long. This Tulbent is made of twenty or more ells of most
fine linnen, and very white, only the Christians wearing Shasses
of mingled Coulors, and it is folded into a rounde or long forme,
the Emperor, the Viseres and some cheife degrees putting out
of the top, a peece of red-velvet, vppon which they fasten
Jewells, and other things to distinguish their degrees.   The
Janizaries, being in the house weare such a Tulbent without
any red velvett, but when they goe abroad in the Citty, and in
the Campe, or before any Magistrate, they weare a Capp proper
to their order, made of cloth standing vpp from the head, with
very small brimmes and a guilded horne of brasse standing vpp
before, and a flapp like that of a French hood falling behinde,
some having plumes of the Ostridge fastned to the guilded
horne, falling backward downe to the very leggs, which feathers
they only weare who are of the guard to the Emperor, to the
Viseires and some great persons. In like sort the Azimoglani

weare Piramidall-capps Like our suger loaues made of a mingled coulored stuffe. The Turkes have no fortifyed Townes or Castles, in the hart of the Empire, excepting only the two Castles of Hellespont, and the two Castles of the black-sea, guarding the passages by Sea to Constantinople, neither haue they any vppon the Persians, who make Warr after their owne manner, but vppon the Confines of Christians, they are forced to keepe the places, as they tooke them fortifyed from the Christians, namely Famogosta in the Iland of Cyprus, and another in the Iland of Rhodes, and diurse Townes in Hungarie, yet they keepe them rather with strong Garrisons, lying vppon the Frontiers ready to be drawne into the feild vppon all occasions, then with small numbers resolued to indure any long seige without present succour as Christians vse to keepe them.

Their discipline of warr.

For their discipline of warres. They haue small art in ranging battells, especially in small numbers fitting them to the advantages of the place, and howsoeuer they haue officers for each tenn men, Whome they readily obey, yet priuate men runn after a tumultuarye fashion to fight, and they are often beaten out of their Tents to fight as in like sort Without discharge they leaue the place, and retorne from fighting. In which respect, and because they haue no Corsletts, or other Armor of defence, it is no Wonder that a small number of Christians in a strong Fort, or vppon advantage of straights, and skill to chuse places' to fight fitt for their number, hath bene able to resist, and sometymes to defeat their huge Armyes. But their discipline is singuler in duely giuing rewards, and punishments. Whosoeuer disobeyes his Commaunder or neglects his charge, may himselfe goe to the gallowes, for he shall neuer escape it, and he that fights or performes his charge brauely, may of a poore tribute childe become the cheife Visere of that Empire. They keepe Wonderfull silence in the Army, speaking with becks, and signes, so as they will rather lett a Captiue escape by flight, then they will make the least noyse to stopp him. In their huge Armyes there is not one woman to be found; The entring a Vineyard or an orchard to steale anything, is a Capitall offence. But aboue all things they are to be praysed aboue Christians, and to be imitated by them, that single fights are forbidden them by the law of Mahomett, and by military discipline, vppon paine of death, so as they neuer happen among them, as also that all brawles are seuerely punished as if such were vnworthy to eat the Emperors bread, who fall out with their Felowes, whome the lawe teacheth to ioyne in brotherly loue, and to vent all their anger and rage vppon the Common Enemyes of their Country and the law of Mahomett.

Of the Seige of Agria.

Some three monethes before my coming to Constantinople, Mahomet the third retorned thether from the seige of Agria in Hungary, and because our Ambassador and his gentlemen attended that Emperor in this Sommers Warr, I thinck it not amisse to relate some things which I vnderstood from them by discourse. The Army began to march at Midnight, and satt downe the next day about noone. The Emperor rode in the midst of the Army, with two Viseres, one on the right, the other on the left hand, and before him certaine Janizaries of his guard carryed torches lighted in the darke of the night, and likewise certaine horsmen called chiausslari bearing maces of yron in their hands kept the press from him. On both his sydes rode the horsemen called Spachi and Silichtari (of whome we haue spoken, and shall treat more particulerly) being chosen men for the guard of his person. . . . The Emperor had two suites of Tents, whereof one was pitched in the present Campe, the other carryed before him to the next quarter. And when his Tents were once pitched, then all the Army according to their place and order pitched their Tents or Tabernacles about him, in a huge Circuite of ground, few or none sleeping in the open ayre. The discipline is so rigorous and seuere against those that take any thing by force, as litle boyes brought all things to be sold in the Campe, and no soldier (as I have said) durst spoile meadow corne, Vineyard, or Orchard vppon paine of death. The Beglerbey of Greece, and the Sangiacchs vnder him did in their seuerall gouernments furnish the Armies with muttons, and necessary prouisions, which they might easely doe for that huge Army, their diett (as I haue said) being very simple, with small or no Variety or Change of meats, and did neuer faile in performance, such negligence neuer being passed ouer without seuere punishments euen to death. The Turkish Army thus marching forward, daily expected the coming of the auxiliary Troopes of the Tarters of Circassia, vsing continually to serue the Turke, when he leades forth his Army to any sommer seruice, Who within few dayes ariued and ioyned with the Turkes, but their troopes had bene broken by the way and in great part defeated by the Polonian horsemen called Cosacchi, Who lay to guard the Frontiers of Poland, for they both being feirce nations, could not be restrayned from incountring one an other by any Commaund of their Captaines tho the king of Poland, and the Turkish Emperor, were then in league of peace. These Tartars were said to eat the flesh of horses and Camells, not otherwise roasted then by putting it vnder their sadles, and riding vppon it. They serue altogether on horsback, and when they come to any great riuer, the horses swimm ouer, and great part of the men passe by holding fast by the tailes of the horses, but the best sort carry boates of leather for that purpose. And the Turke vseth them only to forrage for his Campe, which they doe each man having some five spare horses tyed one to the taile of the other, still changing his horses as they grow weary, so as they being swift and thus often changed, these Tartars in short tyme range ouer large Compass of ground. The Turkish Emperor ariued with his Army at Buda in Hungarie vppon the second of September, and part of the Army begann the seige of Agria the xxjth of the same moneth, and after six dayes the beseiged Christians burnt the Citty being a Bishopps seat, which the Turkes tooke at the first assault with losse of 800 men,

but the Christians retyred into the Castle, and held out some
20 dayes seige, and then yeilded vppon composition, which the
Turkes kept not but killed them all. The christian Army consisting of Thirty two Thousand horse, and Twenty eight
thowsand foote, and having 120 peeces of Artillery, began to
skirmish with the Turkes, vppon the 23th of October. Mahomett
the Turkish Emperor himselfe arriued not till the xxiiijth of
October at night. Whose Army was thought to exceed three
hundred Thowsand fighting men, besides halfe as many more
Camell driuers, and like base people. The 25th both Armyes
skirmished, and the next day both were ranged in battell, but
they Were diuided by a Riuer and a marrish ground. The
Turkish history writes at large, how the Christians passed ouer
the Riuer, tooke the Turkes Artillerye, and defeated the Army,
which with the Emperor Mahomett retyred to Agria for safety.
Only Sigala a Renegate of Genoa, and one of the Viseres retyred
with some tenn thousand horse, and the troopes of Tartars vnto
places of safety neere hand, whence beholding the Christians,
not somuch as turning the Turkes Artillery for their owne
defence, to fall negligently vppon the tents for pillage, he fell
vppon them thus scattered, and vtterly defeated them, who had
gotten the Victory, but could not vse it. The Prince of Transiluania made a good retrait of his men with litle or no losse,
but the Hungarians greedy of spoile, and the slow horsmen of
Germany, and most of the Christian Army vnder the Emperors
brother were killed to the number of some Twenty Thowsand;
Yet was the Victory bloudy to the Turkes, who had some sixty
Thousand men killed, and were putt in such feare, as for three
dayes they durst not retorne to their Artillery and Tents, lest
the Transiluanians should retorne and fall vppon them againe.
Then about the end of October, the Turkish Emperor left tenn
Thousand in Garrison of Agria, and distributed halfe his Army
to Winter in the Country of Belgrado, and with the rest retorned
to Constantinople, and the last day of his iourney incamped a
myle without the Citty, which he entred the next day with great
triumph as I haue formerly shewed.

Thus farr I haue digressed to make a breife relation of that I heard from our Ambassador and his gentlemen who followed the Turkes Army in that sommers seruice; Now I retorne to follow the generall discourse of the Turkes forces and Common Wealth.

Of their great ordinance.

The Turkes haue in former Victoryes taken great store of brass ordinance from the Christians, in Hungary, Cyprus and in Galetta, and it is manifest by all seiges and assaults made by them often, and with much fury, that either at home or brought by Marchants, they haue great plenty of Artillery, Bulletts and Gunpowder.

Of their horse and horsmen.

Their horse are very beautiful having their skinns shining which is caused by the horsedung, which they lay vnder them first dryed into powder, for I neuer saw any of them lye vppon any other litter, or soft thing vnder them, either in Asia subiect to heat, or the more cold parts about Constantinople. They are very swift, and vsed by their Riders either to galloping or a foote pace, but not taught to amble or putt to a trott or managed by Ryders as our great horses are, for indeed they are but of a midle stature the best of them, And thus vntaught they generally hold vpp their nose with vncomelines. For this swiftnes rather then strength they are preferred before the heauy horse of Germany, the shock whereof they cannot beare, but they soone ouertake the horse of Germany flying, and easily scape from them being chased. They are not fitt for long iourneys, but soone tyred if they be putt to gallop, and no lesse tyre the Ryder, when they goe a foot pace. In warr they are only fitt for light horse, neither vse the Turkes any great horse armed, Nor themselues (either horsmen or Footmen) weare any defensive Armor, but only for offence carry Lances and sheilds and

good short swords. They haue no Racks nor Mangers, but feed
their horses on the ground. Their sadles are litle, and hard in
the seate, for they vse no Warr sadles which their horses cannot
beare, and the Crooper is comonly Wrought like a Caparison,
and the stirrops are vnder the foot long, and sharpe beyond
the heele of the Rider seruing them for spurrs, which I neuer
saw vsed of any horsemen nor yet boots, all riding in their cloth
stockings close to their breeches, and their bridles are like our
snafles but commonly sett with Copper studds guilded, yea
sometyme sett with glistering if not precious stones, For the
Turkes are proud, as of their swords (in like sort adorned with
stones) so no lesse of their horses, for which they will giue great
prices. The horsemen for the most part are mantayned by the
Timarrs as I have formerly shewed, which are called Timariotts,
and I haue likewise spoken of their incredible number, and how
they are distributed vnder the two cheefe Beglerbegs, and inferior Bassaes or Beggs. These liue all vppon Timars or
Farmes, tilling their grounds by Christians, or Mores, or their
owne bought slaues, and many of them mantaine more horses
then one for themselues, and they are of a mingled sort of
people. But the cheife strength of the Turkish horse is of them
which were tributary Children or Captiues or Renegates and are
paid partly in mony, partly by Timar, being in number aboue
Thirty thousand generally called Spachi and out of them some
troopes are chosen to guard the Emperors person. The first of
them in dignity are the Spachoglani (Spachi signifying an
horseman, and Oglan a Youth) who being tributary Children
brought vpp in the Emperors Court, (except some Captiues and
Renegates) attaine this degree while they are young, and from
thence are promoted to the highest degrees as Sangiachs,
Beglerbeges, Bassaes and Visiers. Of them 3000 guard the
Emperors person riding on his right hand, and each hath some
Twenty, some Forty Aspers by the day, and each mantaynes
fower or five slaues and horses for them. Their Aga hath 500
Aspers, or as others say tenn Sultanons by the day. His
Checaya or lieuftenant hath a hundred Aspers by the day. But

of the Cheife Officers stipends I haue formerly written, and
will hereafter omitt them. The Silichtari are in the second
ranck being of tributary Children, having the same stipends,
and the same hopes of preferment to the highest places, only
they differ in the Coulor of their pendants and in that they
ride on the left hand of the Emperor, three thousand of them
being likewise chosen to guarde his person. Next to them two
thowsand Olefagi (that is Stipendiaries) guard the Emperors
person on both hands, and eighty Muteferachi beare long lances
before him, whereof the least hath tenn, the Cheife Eighty
Aspers by the day. The Chiausalari, are horsemen, that beare
sheilds and lances, and having broken their launces, they fight
with their Simiters or short swords, holding it disgracefull to
thrust and kill with the point of the sword, or to kill an Enemyes
horse, and having no other Armes of defence. Of these horsmen I did meet diuerse Troopes in the way sent out by the
Sangiachs to cleare the high way of Theeues, And they seemed
to me so many Amades of Gaule. The horsmen in generall are
armed with a Simiter or short sword, a weake launce and a
round buckler or sheild, and some of them also carry short
bowes and arrowes. They haue an other sort of horsmen,
which wee call Adventurers, (they call Vlacchi if I be not
deceiued) having no stipend, but the hope of preferment and
freedome of tribute, being said to be sixty Thousand, only when
they are in the Army they are allowed victualls. Also I haue
heard them called Achengi and by others Delli, but this last
name I thinck to be giuen them in scorne as seeming madd;
for so the Turkes call those that shew to be lightheaded by
Countenance, apparrell or gestures, as if they were madd men.
And indeed these are in those kindes ridiculous, wearing a
Gippo or Jackett, and breeches of the skinns of lyons and beares,
with the hayre outward, and Capps of the skinns of ownees, and
leopards couered with an Eagles Wing, Which wings they also
fasten to their bucklers and the hinder parts of their horses are
couered with skinns of lyons and wilde beasts, affecting thereby
to seeme terrible to their Enemyes. They are light horsmen

and are armed with a Simiter or short sword, and a short weapon
of yron hanging at their Saddles, bearing a long dart or short
horsmans staffe in the right hand. I passe ouer the horsmen
vppon the Confines, who make excursions into the Enemeyes
Country, and haue no pay but the booty they can gett, as also
those that haue pay only in the tyme of warr, and serue for the
baser Imployments. Neither will I speake of the great auxiliary
troopes of the Tartars, comonly some 50 or 60 thousand, nor
those of Walachia and Moldauia. Only I will add that the
Turkish Emperor having these great numbers of horsmen, yet
placeth small trust in them, being excellent in nothing but in
swiftnes to pursue and fly, For the Timariotts and Spachi are
corrupted with rurall sloth, or by living in Citties waxing
Couetous, and louers of peace. And the very Spachoglans and
Silichters are in like sort corrupted by living in Court, and howsoeuer they rise to the highest dignityes, yet for the most part
having bene prostitute to lust in their youth, this suffering like
Women must needs make them effeminate, and they being after
vsed to liue in the Court, cannot but loue ease and freedome
from the labours and dangers of Warr. Yet no doubt the huge
nomber of them keepes the great multitudes of Christian
Subiects in awfull slauery, and were they not disioyned by
imployment in vast Prouinces farr remoued one from the other,
were they not of necessity to be best in great numbers to keepe
the Christian subiects in awe, so as they cannot be gathered
together, without great difficulty, long tyme, and apparent
dangers of rebellion, their huge number might iustly seeme
fearefull to all Christians that ly nere their Confines.

Of the footemen.

The cheife strength of the Army consists in the Footemen
called Janizaries (as a new order of Soldiers), who like the
Roman Triarij, come last to fighting, when others haue prepared
the Way and filled the ditches with their bodyes, and they
consist of Captiues and voluntary men of ripe yeares forsaking

the Christian faith and of the Azimoglans, so called as boyes of tribute; yet all tributary children are not so called as those who are brought up in the Emperors Serraglio and other Colledges, whence they are made horsmen, and preferred to the highest places of the State but only those Children which are seuerely brought vpp vnder husbandmen, and after in Colledges for this purpose, and are of the strongest children, and of the most Warlick nations, for the greatest part of Europe, those of Asia, being reiected as of more soft and peaceable natures at least by old Custome for of late, this and all the austere institutions are neglected and infringed. These are first circumcised then instructed in the Mahometan Law and that in places farr distant from their Parents and Country, so as they easily forgett both, only calling and reputing the Emperor their father, and they are taken so young as they cannot remember anything of Christian Religion, but are trayned vpp, and easily made deadly haters of all christians. After they haue bene fower yeares vnder husbandmen, they are brought to Constantinople and there receiued by the Azimoglan-Aga who distributes them into Colledges there, and in other parts to be trayned as a Seminary of the Janizaries. These Janizaries were first instituted by Amurath the second in number sixteene thousand, and Amurath the third added two thousand to that number, Which since hath bene much increased, and cannot be lesse then Forty thousand. Howsoeuer Sansonime and Botero Italians writt them to be no more then 12 or at most 14 thousand: For I haue formerly said that when Mahomet the third began his Raigne, there were 24 thousand Janizaries at Constantinople which receiued his larges, and nothing was more generally knowne at Constantinople then that 12 thousand of them lye continually there in tymes of peace and the Common Voice was that the Beglerbeg of Asia had 12 thousand vnder him, besides those in Egipt and them that lye vppon the Persians And a farr greater number in all proba[bi]lity lying vppon the Confines of Hungary, Where they haue strong enemyes bordering vppon them. Yet doe I not thinck them to be 60. thousand as our Ambassadors men at Constantinople affirmed to me. The Janizar-Aga or Captaine of them is one of the greatest dignities in that Empire, to whome the Emperor doth often giue a sister to wife, but no man is had in such ielousy, the loue of the Janizaries being Capitall to him, so as he seemes to walke vppon Thornes and bryers while he neither dares gaine their loue for feare of the Emperor, nor vse them roughly for feare of their insolencye. And such is this ielousy, as he may not (according to the Custome) appoint his owne Checaya or leiuftenant, but the Emperor names him and giues him 200 Aspers by the day, as each Odebassi sett ouer tenn hath 40 Aspers, and each Boluibassi or Bolichbassi that is Captaine of one hundred hath 60 Aspers by the day. These may ride, and these Commaunds, and to be Solacchi, are the highest preferments a Janizary can expect. For I haue formerly spoken of the Solachbassi having 300 Aspers by the day, sett ouer the Solachters or Solacchi, Which are some of the strongest Janizaries chosen to guard the Emperors person, and armed with bowes and Arrowes, besides their swords wearing a Capp differing from the Janizaries and having a larger stipend each man 20 Aspers by the day. All the male Children of Janizaries (some say only the Eldest) as soone as they are borne, haue three or fower Aspers by the day, the yonger Janizaries haue noe more, but the rest haue eight Aspers by the day, and each new Emperor besides his largesse or donatiue adds an Asper by the day or some like increase to each mans pay. Three of them in the Campe haue a horse allowed to carry their baggage, and to each hundred a Tent is allowed. At the ends of two lents or tymes of fasting, the Emperor apparrells them, and all without difference weare large Trowses with stockings vndiuided from them, and a long gowne or vpper garment both of violett coulored cloth. Some of them have Wiues contrary to their old institution or Custome, and these liue scattered through the Citty in litle houses, but the rest, by eights, by tenns and by twelues as it were in brotherhoods, liue in Colledges or houses appointed for them, wherein they haue a Cooke, (tho lesse needfull since in their temperate diett each man may soone haue skill inough in that art) and Contributing their mony, they haue a Cater to buy their meat, and the younger having lesse stipend bring in their meat, which is soone done, they having but one dish of meat, and a Cruse of water betweene three or fower. When they are past seruice of Warr, they are putt to guard Castles, and keepe Watches by night, and their Captaines likewise being old, haue the gouernments of those Castles. Some of them are armed with Halberts, some with musketts, but their muskets are not very good; neither are they actiue or skilfull in vsing them, and some only carry Semiters or swords. They who commend the Janizaries that warr being ended they willingly retorne to enioy peace, doe not consider that they haue the same stipend in peace as in warr, For if our men had the same, without doubt they would be no lesse glad of peace. In like sort they who praise them for laying downe Armes in tyme of peace, and not so much as wearing a sword, seeme not to haue obserued that they neuer haue any single fights, and very seldome any quarrells among themselues. Whereas our soldiers are forced in peace to weare swords for their owne defence. Besides that our men haue no such authority ouer men of peace as they haue, who are more feared bearing no weapons, then our men should be with swords and Pistolls. For as a Christian is most seuerely punished if he draw a knife against a Musulman, (that is a circumcised Turke) or strike him with the hand; so is it a greater offence for any Common Turke to resist a Soldier, who aboue all tremble for feare of the Janizaries, so as I haue seene one of them having no Armes but only bearing in his hand (as their manner is) a Cudgell of an hard reed, more then an Ell long, not only beat many Citizens in Townes and Cittyes, but also a whole Caravan in the high way, of two or three hundred men armed with musketts and swords till they obeyed all his Commaundements and kissed his feet for mercy. Of the last kinde myselfe did see a straunge example in my iourney from Tripoly to Haleppo. Aboue all Soldiers the Janizaryes are

insolent aswell for priuiledges, as because they take part one
with another in all tumults. When myselfe went to see the
Emperor, and standing next to him, did fully behold him a
Chiauss on horsback, bearing a mace, offered to thrust me back,
and to strike me, but a Janizary that our Ambassador had sent
to conduct me, putt him back, and when he would not admitt
his excuse for me, but said it might not be indured that a
Christian dogg should come so neare to the Emperor, presently
other Janizaries whome I had neuer seene, ioyned with my
guide, and threatned the Chiauss, so as in spite of his teeth, he
was forced to lett me stand. No maruell then that these men
willingly lay downe their Armes, being without them as terrible
as feirce mastyes to all inferiors they meet, for they are knowne
by the Caps peculiar to their order, and if they be offended so
much as with a looke, vpp goes their long Cudgell (Which they
call Mutcher) and they will giue him that offends them,
according to their pleasure hundreths of blowes vppon the belly,
or the back, or the soles of his feet, and that without any
sentence or condemnation of a Judge, and not only for offences
against themselues, but for mony giuen them by an enemy,
so as being protectors of Christians, they will vppon their
Complaints beate any other Christian or Plebean Turke, till
they craue mercy of him for whose sake they are beaten,
except they haue also a Janizarie to protect them, in which Case
they vse not to fight, nor yet striue one with an other. And
one Janizarye of the least, is sufficient to guard a man against
a thousand Mores, or Arabians or Plebean Turkes in respect of
his awfull authority ouer them, as also against all other Soldiers
or Janizaries in respect of their brotherly agreement, and feare
to breake their law by fighting or quarrelling among themselues.
Therefore the Christian Ambassadors at Constantinople haue
assigned to each of them, fower or six Janizaries, and the
Consulls of Christian nations lying in other Citties and Townes,
haue one or two of them to guard their houses and persons
from all Wrongs, neither will any Christian having meanes to
spend, goe abroad in Cittyes and Townes or take a iourney

without a Janizarie to guard him.   And it is wonderfull, how
faithfull and affable, they wilbe to a Christian thus hyring them
for hyring them for some viij Aspers by the day, yea how
readily they will serue him, doing his busines, buying, and (if
need be) dressing his meat, especially if they haue taken this
charge from any Ambassador or Consul, to whome they must
giue accompt of his safety, and bring back letters, without
which charge out of meere rules of their law or nature, myselfe
haue by experience found them faithfull, courteous and faire
Companions.   And by these seruices to Christians many of
them gett Crownes, and lead faire liues.   Myself not well
knowing the Turkish fashions, and taking iourneyes without any
Janizarie to protect me, did often by the way meet spachies and
Janizaries, who would take away my wine and prouisions of
Victualls, as if they had bene their owne, and once being
to take a Journey with some of them, our Muccaro (that is he
who letts horses and Asses) hearing them inquire after our
Condition, advised each of vs to giue them halfe a Piastro or
siluer Crowne, wherevppon they vndertooke to protect vs, who
otherwise were like to haue plotted some mischeife against vs as
at Tripoli some Janizaries had almost betrayed about this tyme
an English gentleman, by selling him to husbandmen, within
land for a slaue.   An other tyme having a Janizary to protect
me, and landing in a Greeke Iland, the wemen hidd all their
bedding, bread and meat, lest he should force them to intertaine
vs for litle or nothing, since they vse to take any thing from
them, and going iourneys in tymes of peace to extort victualls
from them for litle or nothing, but when one of our Company
being a Christian, and speaking the Greeke tongue, told them
we would pay a iust and honest price for anything we tooke,
they presently receiued vs into their houses, and furnished vs
with all necessaries for meat and lodging.   An other tyme
landing at an Iland of Greece without any Janizarie to protect
me, and walking abroad, a Plebean Turke mett me, and taking
my hatt in his hand first desyred to borrow it for a base vse
(for the forme not vnlike the pann of a Closestoole) and after

flung it into the durt. For a Christian having no Janizarie
With him cannot avoyde many such insolencyes, though
myselfe had the happ to meet with very few like affronts, and
neuer to receiue blow from Janizarie or other, which notwithstanding are no rare accidents vnto Christians.

Of the Janizaries it is vulgarly sayd they haue all skill in
one manuall trade or other (as the very Emperor hath), but as
all Turkes are idle, and very slow woorkmen for gaine, which
they cannot enioy further then from hand to mouth, so I did
neuer see any Janizarie woorking at his manuall trade. To
conclude the insolency of the Janizaries cannot well be imagined
much lesse described, by whome the Ottoman Empire seemes to
stand, and the Emperors first to enter. For the heyre of the
Emperor assoone as he is circumcised, vnder pretence to gouerne
a Prouince, is sent away to be hidden from the Janizaries lest
they should cast their eyes vppon him, or he insinuated
himselfe into their loue, and while in that Prouince he expects
his fathers death, nothing is more dangerous for him, then to
affect to be esteemed and renowned of them. The new Emperor
thinkes not himselfe safe till he be saluted by them, beginning
his Raigne with their ioyfull shouts, and a largesse or donatiue
giuen to them, besides the foresaid small increase of each mans
pay. So as they are and still grow more and more like the
Pretorian bands in the State of Rome, who being at hand nere
the Citty, at first strengthned the choice of the Emperors, but
at last named and deposed them at pleasure. No doubt the
Janizaries want little of their power, and pride, for in the life
of Amurath father to Mahomett the third living at the tyme
of my being at Constantinople, they made a tumult, requiring
the head of the cheife Visere much esteemed of the Emperor,
only because he had putt a Janizarie to death by due forme of
Justice, and the Emperor was forced to giue them his head
before they would be appeased. And because they will not be
Judged but by their owne Agha, nor can without tumult indure
any of their number to be putt to death, the Custome was then
priuately to strangle such of them, as had deserued to dye.

At my being there I remember that walking in the streets, I did see a dead Carkasse that had bene cast out, which being naked the person and quality of the dead man could not be knowne, but the vulgar opinion was, that he should be a Janizarie so strangled, because no man durst proceed against him by publick iustice. Many tumults like to the former haue bene raised by them, wherein they haue driuen the Emperors into great straights, but none more famous then that which hapned there shortly after my retorne vppon the death of the Emperor then being, which the French history relates at large, and to the same I referr the Reader. Finally howsoeuer the wicked practice of killing the Emperors brothers, takes away all likely good of any great Ciuill warr among them (by which Commonly all kingdomes and Empires haue bene ouerthrowne) yet Christians haue one probable hope, that as the Pretorian bands of Rome at last vsurping the power to name, and depose Emperors, without any decree of the Senate, and often contrary to the same, did first wound and by degrees weaken the Maiesty thereof, till it was transplanted into Germany, whereat this day it languisheth so the Janizaries by like insolency, if not presently, yet in short tyme, will breake the power of the Turkish tyranny.

The Army hath other footmen but of small reputations being neither tributary children, nor trayned vpp in that discipline. Such are the Azapli, Whome the Italians call Asappi, having no stipend in peace, but only in warr, being otherwise imployed about the Navye. And these are the sonnes of Turkes knowne from others by their fowre Cornered Capp of red cloth, vulgarly called Tachia. Also they haue an other kinde of Footemen like to the former called Voinichlar, raised out of Walachia, who have no stipend at all, but serue in the Campe only to be free from Tributes. And both these kindes of Footemen are only vsed as Pyoners and for all base seruices. They only are beaten to the first assault of beseiged Castles, and exposed by the Turkes like so many beasts to be murthered, and fill the ditches, that vppon their dead bodyes, the Janizaries may by the breaches enter the Castles and Townes.

Of their nauall Power.

Touching their Nauall power, I haue spoken of the Admirall among the cheife Comaunders. The Emperor cannot want matter to build Shipps, having most large Coasts of the Sea shadowed with vast Woods, but his cheife woodds most vast, and most fitt to make tymber for this purpose, are said to be in Albania, Carimania, Trapezuntium, and most aboundantly in Nicodemia, all Prouinces lying close vppon the Sea. At this tyme whereof I write they had of their owne few and vnskilful woorkmen to build shipps; only there wanted not Couetous Christians, who for large stipends wrought with them, and taught their art vnto them, so as after the Navall defeate of the Turkes at Corzolari (called the defeate of Lepanto) they could the next yeare bring forth a Navye, which seemed able and willing to fight with the christians. But no doubt the Gallies of the Turkes are neither so well built, nor so swift in saile, nor so fitt to fight, nor so strong, nor built of so durable Timber, as those of the Spaniards, Venetians and other Christians their enemyes. And howsoeuer the Gallies, some Fifty in number, yearely wont to be sent out, to cleare the Sea of Pyrats, and diuerse lesse Gallies and small Barques armed by priuate Turkes to robb Christians (many times not sparing those that were in league with them) gaue some good meanes to furnish the Turkes Nauie with Marriners; yet since the Jewes and Christians had all traffique in their hands, so as nothing was exported by Turkish Shipps, (excepting some twelve great Shipps each of seauen hundreth or a Thousand Tonns, built rather for burthen then Warr, which the Emperor had to bring necessaryes yearely from Egipt, to Constantinople), and since all Turkes and Christian subiects are by nature slothfull, which kinde of men loue not the trouble and danger of the Sea, the Emperor was forced to vse Cow heards and Shepheards to fitt the sailes, and row in the Gallies, and howsoeuer the Greekes had some practice at Sea, to sayle by the Coast rather then by Compasse; yet they being slaues and Christians,

the Turkes could promise themselues no faithfull seruice from
them especially in tymes of danger. So as I dare be bold to
say the Turkish Mariners were partly vnskilfull in the art,
partly vnfaithfull to them, and generally all dasterly in
Courage. They consisted of Christians taken Captiues, most
comonly in places farr distant from the Sea, and of condemned
men, all chayned to the oares, except cases of necessity forced
them to vse christian Greekes and Country people, and this
made them gently to vse all Captiues and to preferr all voluntary
forsakers of the Christian faith, who were skilfull Seamen, or
Carpenters to build shipps (as also Sadlers for their horses and
Juellers to make their treasure portable) and much to esteeme
the said Captiues, if they would torne Mahometans. Barbarossa
the famous Pyratt of the mediterranean sea, in the tyme of
Charles the fifth Emperor of Germany, forsaking the Christian
faith and becoming Mahometan, was made Admirall of the
Turkish Nauye, who subdued the kingdome of Tunis in Africk
and made the Turkes somewhat better Seamen then they had
formerly bene, but nothing equall to the Christians. Their
Navall power in those days was seene at Goletta, at Cyprus, at
Malta, and at their great defeat at the Corsalari, since which
ouerthrowe to the tymes whereof I write, they neuer drew forth
their full forces to fight at Sea. They had at this tyme a place
in Pera or Galata beyond the water from Constantinople walled
in for building and wintering of Gallies, Which the Christians
call Arsenale, the Turkes Terferate, And without the Walles it
had Thirty two vaults, but within, it was narrow, and of small
Compasse. They said that two hundredth woorkemen did daily
labour therein and two hundreth Masters or cheife Mariners,
had each man tenn Aspers by the day, and that Fifty Carpenters,
and Artificers had each man twelue Aspers by the day when
they wrought, and sixe Aspers when they had no woorke. That
they had a thousand Asappi (vsed also for footemen in the Army
as I formerly shewed) which did woorke about the Gallies, and
had each man fower Aspers by the day. That in this Arsenale
at that tyme were two hundred Gallies, and twelue Gallions, but

that the Emperor could in short space for his full force send three hundred Gallies to Sea, besides some of fewer oares and small Barques to victle and attend them.

Within some sixteene yeares last past, the generall peace of Christendome made our soldiers, for want of meanes to liue, turne Pyratts, who having no safety in the Ports of christian Princes, retyred themselues to Algier in Barbary, the people whereof and of the parts adioyning, are most daring of all the Turkes (except those perhapps vppon the Confines of Hungarie). They gladly intertayned these Pyratts, and were content at first to haue share of the spoyles and to goe with them to Sea, but of late they haue gotten some 60 or 80 good shipps of warr from the Christians by their meanes, and from them haue learned such skill to saile by the Compasse, as they haue bene able to man these Shipps with Turkes, and haue had the dareing to rob vppon the Ocean, which they neuer knew, nor durst behold in any former age. And of what consequence this may proue after ages shall finde (I feare me) by wofull experience.

Of their ciuill iustice.

I haue formerly spoken of Judges and Magistrates, and the stipends they haue from the Emperor. Now it remaynes to add something of Ciuill Justice. The strict obseruance of lawes among the Turkes is worthely called Tyranny, as I haue formerly shewed, since that which is iust must be done iustly. Whereof there is no practice in this Empire. I formerly said that ·there be two supreme Judges called Cadilischieri which reside at Constantinople, the one sett ouer the Causes of Asia, the other ouer those of Europe, both vnder the Mofti with absolute authority. These two appoint all inferior Judges of the Law, as those called Cadi, which are magistrates sett ouer Prouinces and Cittyes, with a mixed authority of our Bishopps, and lay Judges, for the Law of Mahomett is obserued aswell in administration of iustice, as in matters of religion. Each Citty and Towne hath military magistrates, as Sangiachi, who are like

the Captaines of Garrisons, and Gouernors of Townes, and if
there be any Castle or Fort, it hath also an Agha to commaund
it. And as with vs in tyme of war the Ciuill Judges giue place
to Marshalls having martiall law in their hands; so among the
Turkes living with the same discipline at home as in the Campe,
(the Common Wealth being as it were gouerned by the sword).
These Cadies are vnder the authority of the Sangiachs in each
Citty or Towne. And from them there is appeale graunted to
the Diuan or Court of the Basha gouerning diuerse Prouinces
and from those Courts to that of the Visyeres in the Emperors
Serraglio at Constantinople as from it to the Mafti the oracle of
the Mahometan Lawe, from whose sentence there is no appeale.
One thing causeth great oppression to the Christian subiects
that howsoeuer they are more in number then the Turkes; yet
they haue no peculiar Judges, but haue their causes tryed vnder
Turkish magistrates, where the witnes of a Turke is taken
against a Christian, but not of a Christian against a Turke.
What Justice can be expected where a Common soldier for
mony without any triall at law, or priuate examination of the
cause, will beat with Cudgells a Christian, or common Turke,
euen accused by a Christian, till he craue mercy of his enemy.
When wee being Christian straungers retorned from Hierusalem
to Joppa, and there found an Arabian Turke, who had done vs
wrong by the way, vppon our guides accusation, and three
Meideines giuen to a Janizarie, he was beaten till he kissed our
feete, And if they dare doe this to the Turkes, how may you
thinck Christians are vsed. The false accusations and frauds,
which daily they lay vppon Christians espetially vppon
straungers (whome they call Francks of their league with
Fraunce) are vulgarly called Vaines. Such was that which
Villamont a french gentleman relates of the Sangiach of
Hierusalem, who cast the Guardian of the latin monastery into
prison, pretending that a Spanish old Woman coming with him,
had brought the dead body of the King of Spaynes sonne to be
buryed there, and howsoeuer the fraude was manifest; yet the
Guardian vnderstanding that it was a mony matter, offered

Thirty Crownes and the Sangiach demaunding five hundred, at last he paid Fifty to haue his freedome. The like is that which he also relates of the Christians at Tripoli, who being accused by the Turkes for killing a More, whose dead body was cast among their dwellings, were forced to pay one hundred Crownes to be acquitted. Like fraudes they continually practice against Christian societyes, and priuate men by casting a dead body before their dores of burying it nere them, and as it were casually finding it out, or by like fraudes drawing them into suspition of Crimes, from all which notwithstanding they are redeemed with mony except they be accused to haue done or spoken any thing against Mahometts Religion or be intangled in like netts, from which there is no redemption but death or turning Mahometans. When myselfe and my brother tooke our iourney from Haleppo towards Constantinople, an English Marchant Factor to Sir John Spencer Alderman of London sent diuers Camells loaded with his masters goods, as Kerseyes and Tinne, which were to passe in the same Carauan with vs, and howsoeuer the Camel-driuers, and many Turkes knew them to be his goods, and he not without a present or guift commended both vs and these his goods to the protection of a cheife Magistrate passing along with vs; yet my brother dying by the Way, all these goods were seized vppon for the Emperor, only to putt a Vaina vppon the Marchant, who not without trouble and bribes long after recouered them againe. It cannot be expressed, what great iniuryes the Turkes will doe vnto Christians vppon the lightest causes. When we came neere vnto Hierusalem, a horseman of the Army crossing our way, rann a full course at one of our Company with his Launce, in rest, who only escaped killing, by the slipping of the Launce into the pannell of the Asse wherevppon he rode, and with like force he was ready to assaile each man of vs, and that only (as our Interpreter told vs) because wee did him no reuerence as he passed, so that we were glad to tumble off from our Asses, and bend our bodyes to him, which done, he rode away with a sterne proud looke. For a Turke will not abide any Christian to looke him full in

the face without striking him, so as I then vsing to walke with
my eyes cast on the ground, as going about some busines, tooke
that ill custome which I could neuer leaue, though I haue often
bene reproued by freinds for the same. Neither may a Christian
carry Armes, yea Woe to him that drawes a knife against a
Turke; so as we hearing what Asses patience wee must haue,
except we would perish in the iourney, by our freinds advice,
left our Rapiers in a Chest at Venice trauelling through all
Turky with our hands in our hose. At Hierusalem wee were
forced to beare a thousand iniuries, hardly keeping the very
boyes from leaping vppon our shoulders from the Shopps and
higher parts of the way while their Parents looked on, and
commended them for so doing, besides many wrongs done vs
in the way by Mores and Arabians, who mixed with some other
nations, inhabit that Country (the Jewes only living scattered
vppon the Sea Coasts and in Citties of traffique) and a more
wicked people cannot be imagined, so as the Duke of Normandie
being carryed on some of their backs towards Hierusalem, and
meeting a freind retorning into Fraunce, did pleasantly and
in that part iustly desyre him to tell his freinds there, that he
saw him carryed into heauen (meaning Hierusalem) vppon
diuells backs, for litle better they were that carryed him. In
our Journey from Tripoli to Haleppo, when our whole Carauan
was in danger, for a fyre casually burning the Feilds howsoeuer
my brother and myselfe were free from causing, yet we knowing
how the magistrate would woorke vppon vs more than the rest,
thought good to giue the Janizarie that droue vs a large bribe
to dismisse vs, and not to bring vs before him. And howsoeuer
we were not altogether vnskilfull in the fashions of Turky, and
did warily obserue the Customes, so as we neuer came within
iust danger, nor prouoked any Turke to strike vs (which kind of
Wronge they are easily moued to offer any Christian) yet
myselfe landing in the Iland Aloni had my hatt taken from my
head (as I formerly said) and with Words of scorne cast into
the durt by a plebean Turke which I was glad to take vpp
without repining. And when I landed at Constantinople in a

Greeke Shipp of Candia, assoone as our Anchor was cast, many plebean Turkes came aboard and the shipp being laded with Muskedines, they drunck as freely as if they had bene Owners, and the basest of them hardly held their hands from beating the best of the Greeke Mariners, whereof some were graue men, and well skilde in languages, though they neuer forbadd them to drinck. But within a short space, when a Janizarie came to protect the Shipp sent from the Balye of Venice, it was no lesse straunge to see him alone beat out all the Turkes like so many doggs. To conclude it may appeare what iustice Christians may expect in this Empire by one example of the Venetians, who were in league with the Emperor, yet having a very rich Shipp robbed by Turkish Pyratts withdrawing themselues, and bribing the cheife Visere, after long delayes, were forced to sett downe by the losse.

In generall howsoeuer the Turkes are seuere in punishing offendors, seldome vsing mercy, yet the administration of iustice both towards Christians and Turkes, is made infamous by tyranny For first all Gouernors and Judges buy their offices and are often chaunged, so as they that buy being forced to sell, and hunger-starued flyes sucking more then those that are gorged, these Gouernors paying dearely for their places, and from the first entrance daily expecting a successor to recall them, are in rapine not vnlike the diuell, roaring like a lyon, because he knowes he hath but a short tyme. Againe no magistrate, nor yet a priuate man, will doe anything for an other without a present or guift; yea the Courts of iustice are so corrupted with briberie, as the best cause is in danger to be lost, if mony be wanting, and where that is, an ill cause may pass and the woorst shalbe excused. The most Commendable thing is that generally causes, are summarily decided and soone ended (excepting such Cases as that of the Venetians foresaid shipp robbed, which they seeme to mingle with State matters). And this expedition is the greater, because they haue no multiplicity of Lawes, or Pleaders, holding themselues to some morall rules left them by Mahomett. But especially because the

Magistrate is loth to leaue any cause to his Successor, that will yeild mony. Yea such is the Corruption of bribery and so generall, as when the Emperors mother sent a present of a whole linnen attyre richly wrought, to Elizabeth Queene of England, many peeces thereof were detayned by her women, to the vtter disgrace of the present, till our Ambassador redeemed them with more mony then they were woorth. And as I formerly said the Emperors large allowance to the Christian Ambassadors, vsed to be more then halfe purloyned by the officers. Nether is the Emperors person free from this Corruption, no Ambassador or other great suiters being admitted to his presence without larg presents. So as the office of the Capagi or Porters, keeping the gates of the Emperor, and other magistrates, is most gainefull for they will thrust Homer himselfe out of dores if he bring nothing.

Of the lawes of inheritance.

Touching the lawes of inheritance. The Emperor is heyre to all strangers dying in the hideous Gulfe of this Vast Empire, be they neuer so rich Marchants; yet their goods are commonly by freinds sequestred before their death, as belonging to them and so kept for the heyres or owners according to euery mans faith and honesty, which in so remote parts is not alwayes sound. And often the goods are secretly purloyned and more commonly stollen by them that are present at the partyes death. But the goods that remayne, and cannot well be hidden, are swallowed by this Gulfe. When my brother dyed in Asia, the Turkes of our Carravan not only snatched his goods, but myne also, and the magistrate (as I formerly sayd) seased the rich goods of Sir John Spencer, Alderman of London, in the Emperors Right, as if they had belonged to my brother. In like sort while I was at Scanderoon, Mr. Saunders coming from Constantinople to be Consul of the English Marchants at Haleppo, and dying by the way in Natolia, the Turkes tooke not only all his goods, but those also that belonged to his poore seruants and followers. For this cause, myselfe being sick in Turkye, and fearing that my host hoped to haue my Crownes at my death, thought to publish what mony I had about me, and so taking away all hope of gaine by my death from my Host and those of his house, from that tyme I found myselfe better vsed and better attended by them.

The Condition of Subiects in Turkey is not much better. For vnmoueable goods : The Emperors soldiers haue none, nor yet his great Officers, being all Captiues or tributarye Children. And howsoeuer the Emperor subduing any Prouince divided it into Timars or Farmes giuing them vppon the foresaid Conditions to the cheife men of his Army, yet they hold them only for life, or at his pleasure. In other parts, and perhaps in these subdued Prouinces, some say that priuate Turkes and christians haue inheritance of houses and lands, but surely they are not great for I did neuer see any Subiect that was reputed to haue such inheritances, but all looked like poore slaues, nothing being more dangerous to any man then the reputation of rents or of mouable wealth. And the same men told me, that as the Turkes haue few lawes and short pleading, so for these Lands (whatsoeuer they be) their euidences are not great nor many having only a small paper subscribed by the Cady to witnes the emption or the discent.

For moueable goods. The great men of the Army gather huge treasure by extortion but the Emperor comonly strangles them, and takes all their goods, if they doe not convey them to some Childe or freind being most in Jewells and portable things. And for the rest of the great men he taketh their goods and giues their sonnes stipends for life. Some say that other Subiects make last Wills and Testaments to giue their goods, whereof a third part belongs to the Emperor, but I rather thinck these goods are priuately conveyed to the heyre. For I am sure they are not possessed without much feare and danger, nor can be transmitted by publique act to the heyres without vnavoydable oppressions. To conclude if any Turkes haue vnmouable inheritances, they for these causes care not to

increase them, and all their riches comonly consisting in moueable goods, they hide or bury them in life, and convey them
secretly at death.

Judgments corporall and capitall.

Touching their Corporall and Capitall Judgments.   For
small offences they are beaten with Cudgles on the soles of the
feete, the bellyes and backs, the strokes being many and paynefull according to the offence, or the anger of him that inflicts
them.   Myselfe did see some hanging and rotting in Chaynes
vppon the Gallowes.

Also I did see one that had bene impaled (vulgarly Casuckde)
an horrible kinde of death. The malefactor carryes the
woodden stake vppon which he is to dye, being eight foot long
and sharpe towards one end, and when he comes into the place
of execution, he is stripped into his shirt, and laid vppon the
ground with his face downeward, then the sharpe end of the
stake is thrust into his fundament, and beaten with beetles vpp
into his body, till it come out, at or about his Wast, then the
blunt end is fastened in the ground, and so he setts at litle ease,
till he dye, which may be soone if the stake be driuen with
fauour, otherwise, he may languish two or three dayes in payne
and hunger; if torment will permitt him in that tyme to feele
hunger, for no man dares giue him meat.

They haue an other terrible kinde of death vulgarly called
Gaucher. The malefactor hath a rope or Chaine fastned about
his body, whereof the other end is made fast to the topp of a
Tower or of a Gibbett made high of purpose, and so this rope
or chaine being of fitt length, his body is cast downe to pitch
vppon a hooke of Iron, where he hangs till he dyes, with horror
of the hight of payne, and of hunger. For howsoeuer he may
dye presently if any vitall part pitch vppon the hooke, yet
hanging by the shoulder or thigh he may liue long. And if
any men giue these executed men, meat, or helpe to prolong
their miserable life, he shall dye the same death; Mores and

christians and they that are not of the Army, are often putt
to this death, yea the Beglerbegs sometymes putt Gouernors to
this death for extortions or Cruelties committed by them, or
rather to gett their wealth. They haue an other terrible kinde
of death to flea the skinn of from the living body, and thus they
cruelly putt to death Bragadino a Venetian Gouernor of
Famagosta in Cyprus, after he had yeilded the Citty vppon
Composition for life to him and his soldiers.

A Turke forsaking his fayth and a christian doing or
speaking any thing against the law of Mahomett are burned
with fyer. Traytors or those whome the Emperor so calles, are
tortured vnder the nayles and with diuerse torments, but the
great men of the Army are only strangled.

A murtherer is putt to some of the former cruell deathes. A
theefe is hanged, and I haue read of a soldier that had stollen
milke and denyed the fact, who was hanged vpp by the heeles,
till he vomitted the milke, and after was strangled. The
Adulterer is imprisoned for some Moneths, and after redeemed
with mony, but the Adultresse is sett naked vppon an Asse with
the bowells of an oxe about her neck, and so she is whipped
about the streetes having stones and durt cast at her. If a
Christian man committ fornication with a Turkish woman both
are putt to death, and this Common danger to both, makes them
more wary of others, and more confident to trust one an other,
but the sinne is Common, and at Constantinople the houses of
Ambassadors being free from the search of magistrates very
Turkes, yea the Janizaries guarding the persons and howses of
these Ambassadors, will not stick to play the bawdes for a small
reward. In case of this offence nothing frees a Christian from
death, but his turning Mahometan. Yet I remember that I
saw a Tower at Tripoli called the tower of Loue, built·by a
rich Christian to redeeme his life being condemned for this
Crime. But if a Turke lye with a Christian woman, he is not
putt to death, but sett vppon an Asse with his face towards the
tayle, which he holds in his hand, and hath the bowells of an
oxe cast about his neck, and so is ledd through the streetes in

scorne. If a Christian lye with a Christian woman, the fault
is punished with paying of mony. All harlotts write their
names in the booke of the Cady or the Sobbassa, and not only
the Turkes but euen the Janizaries are permitted to haue
acquaintance with them so it be not in the two lents, wherein
they yearely fast, For in that Case, while I was in Turkye many
women were sewed in sacks, and so drowned in the Sea at
Constantinople. Generally for greater Crymes, the Judge of
the Turkes deuiseth and imposeth a death with greater torment
especially for reproching their law or Prophett, which a
Christian cannot redeeme, but by turning Turke.

Of degrees in the common wealth and Family.

Touching degrees in the Commonwealth, and Family, I haue
spoken of the former particulerly in this Chapter, and haue
shewed that they are all knowne by their heads, I will only
add that there be not any noble Familyes in this Empire,
excepting that of the Emperors, who are called Ottomans, of the
first of that Family Founder of the Turkish Empire. There be
no dukes, Earles, Barons, knights nor gentlemen, neither can
any vertue bring a man to such dignityes, the greatest men
being slaues howsoeuer with military titles and gouerments.
Like players on a Stage they carry themselues like Princes for
the short and slippery tearme of life. A man most basely borne
may attaine the highest places vnder the Emperor, So he will
turne Mahometan and be strong valiant and actiue of body and
mynde. Neither doth the Valor or greatnes of the father
anything profitt, but rather hurt the sonne, all authority in the
Empire being putt in the hands of new men, that are Captiues
or tributary Children or such as turne Mahometans at ripe
Yeares. They haue no Gentry nor high nobility by discent,
nor Armes belonging to seuerall Familyes. Only the Emperor
to leade his Army, hath a Standard, and therein beares a new
moone. For the Turkes when they first see a newe moone, fall
to their prayers, and thanck God they haue liued to see it.

Of the miserable state of Captiues whose buyers haue power ouer their goods, and ouer their bodyes to prostitute them to lust, to make them Eunuches; and to dispose of them at leasure, I haue formerly spoken, as likewise I haue shewed, that the Condition of borne Turkes, and of Christian Subiects, is in many thinges litle better then that of slaues.

For the priuate Family each man may haue as many Wiues as he is able to feede so he take a letter of permission from the Cady, and some of them keepe their wives in diuerse Cittyes to auoyd the strife of women; yet if they liue both in one house with him, they seldome disagree, being not preferred one aboue another. The Turkes vse not to take a dowrye but as they buy captiue women, (whome they may sell againe or keepe for Concubines or for any other seruice); so they also buy Free women to be their wiues, so as the father is inriched by having many and fayre Daughters. Diuorce is permitted for peruerse manners, for barrennes or like faults allowed by the Cady. As they buy Captiue Women, so may they buy any other for Concubines so they write their names in the booke of the Cady. For as Christians are maryed by Preists in the Church; so Turkes are maryed by taking a letter, or bill from the Cady (who is their spirituall Judge) and writing the mariage in his booke at his priuate house. But at the day of mariage, they also vse to bathe, and to pray in their Moschees.

Lastly it is no disgrace to be borne of a Captiue Woman, or out of mariage, for that is the Condition, of the very Emperors, Whose mothers are Captiues, and before the birth of their first sonne, neuer haue a letter of dowry to make them free women and wiues, which after they haue a sonne was of old wont to be graunted them, but the Emperors of late tymes seldome giue that letter to them, for ielousy lest they should practice their deathes to haue power in the raigne of their succeeding sonne.

To conclude howsoeuer this power of the Turkish Empire may seeme dreadfull to all Christendome; yet the Emperors of late being giuen to pleasure and nothing Warlike, the whole force being not possibly to be vnited for feare of Christians, and

other subiects rebelling, the greatest part of the Army
consisting of baser kindes, of horsmen and footemen, the best
horsemen generally being corrupted with rurall sloth and
dilicate liuing in Cittyes, the best footemen the Janizaries
having lost the old seuerity of manners, and therewith the old
valor of their Predecessors, many of them being now marryed,
and all prone to insolent mutinyes, the soldiers generally
wanting defensiue Armes, and for offence having few musketts
or shott (great part of the Foote vsing bowes and Arrowes
insteed thereof, as the horsmen haue no Carbines, but staues or
speares), the particuler soldiers of Asia being more effeminate
then the rest, the iustice of State being growne to the hight of
extortion, and oppression, the zeale of their religion being
generally in all degrees abated, and the great Commaunders
having of late made strong rebellions against the Emperors,
For these reasons, and because no Tyranny (especially so great
as this) hath euer bene durable, and lastly because the Empire
is so great, as by his owne weight it seemes to threaten ruine,
Christians may well hope, that the power of this great enemy
is declining, if not sodeinely falling, which God in his mercy
graunt.

[The silver crowne or Piastro worth fiue shillings English is given
heere for 70 there for 80 or more Aspers—an Asper is some three farthings
English.—Moryson.]

CHAP: ii.

Of the commonwealth of Poland according to the seuerall heads conteyned in the title of the first Chapter.

The historicall Introduction.

FOR the Historicall Introduction, know that the Polakes or Polonians are discended of the old Sarmatians or Slauonians, of which nation Zechus a young Prince, to avoid factious sedition at home, ledd forth a Colony in the yeare of our lord 550, and planted himselfe in a Country full of thick woods, which since hath bene called Poland of the plaine ground. The Family of Zechus being extinguished, twelue Palatines gouerned the Common Wealth, called Vuoyuodes to this day, and next to the king in authority, not hereditary, but chosen by the king for life. But after twenty yeares these Palatines disagreeing, Cracus nephew to the king of Bohemia was chosen Prince about the yeare 700, who built the Cittye Crakaw, at this day the seate of the kings. His Family being extinguished, in the yeare 730, the Common wealth was againe gouerned by twelue Palatines to the yeare 750, at which tyme the people growing weary of many Gouernors, againe chose them a Prince. About the yeare 842 (others write 806), Piasti was chosen Prince, whose Family ruled to the yeare 1370, as it were by hereditary succession, but so as euery Prince was chosen to succeed the other. Myesco a Prince of that Family became Christian with all the nation in the yeare 965, whose sonne Boleslaus had the title of king and a Crowne giuen him in the yeare 1000, by the Germane Emperor, Otho the third with freedome from all tributes and homage to the Emperor. Cassimere a Prince of the said Family being a Monck the Polonians obtayned of Pope Benedict in the yeare 1041. to haue him freed of his vowe, and to be their king, vppon three Conditions, first that each man of that kingdome by the pole should yearely pay an halfpenny to the Bishopp of Rome (called St. Peters due) secondly that all the men should shaue the haire of the head vpward aboue the eares (which most of them vse to this day). Thirdly that vppon holydayes all the men should weare white linnen Cloth for girdles. About the yeare 1124 the Palatine of Crakawe forsaking the king in a battell for shame hanged himselfe, since which tyme the Castellan of Crakaw (contrary to the manner of Poland) is preferred before the Palatine in dignitye and authority. King Cassimere not long after dying, the kingdome was long divided betweene that kings sonnes till by their death it was againe vnited vnder one king. About the yeare 1370. king Cassimere in his life tyme appointed Lodwike his sisters sonne by the king of Hungary to succeed him, and so the kingdome of Poland came to a straunger, which had bene to this tyme gouerned by naturall Polonians. But Lodwick being dead the Polonians gaue a yonger daughter of the foresaid extinct Family (not respecting any right of the Eldest sister) to Jagellan duke of Lituania and ehose him king in the yeare 1386. Albrecht master of the Knights of the Teutonick order in Prussen did in the yeare 1521. make agreement with the king of Poland that the order being extinct, the king should presently haue part of Prussen and part should remayne to him and his heyres males with the title of duke, and for want of such heyres fall to the king of Poland. The foresaid Family of Jagellon beginning to raigne 1386. by continuall discent succeeded in that kingdome to the yeare 1572, as if it had bene by right of inheritance, yet not one of them being Crowned that was not first chosen in a solemne and free Assembly by the Palatines and gentlemen of Poland. At that tyme the heyres males of that Family failing, Henry of Valois brother to the French king was chosen king, and he within few yeares retorning to inherrit the kingdome of Fraunce the Polonians in the yeare 1575, chose for their king Stephen of the Family of Bathori, Prince of Transiluania, and howsoeuer part of the Polonians at the same tyme chose Maxmilian brother to the Emperor of Germany, yet he made no warr for that right, after Stephen was possessed of the kingdome.

The king then liuing.

Stephen being dead some of the Polonians in the yeare 1587. chose Sigismund the third who liued and raigned at the tyme of my being there, and was sonne and heyre to the king of Suecia [Sweden] and by the mothers syde of the foresaid Family of Jagellon. But an other part did againe choose the said Maximilian who beseiging Crakawe was opposed, and putt to the worst by Zamoski the Archchancelor of Poland and so he retorning into Germany to reinforce his Army, Sigismund was crowned the same yeare at Crakawe. Zamosky followed Maximilian and defeating his forces tooke him prisoner in the moneth of January 1588. and kept him in Poland till the moneth of September in the yeare 1589, at which tyme he freed himselfe (as the Germans write) in the manner following. A place in Silesia was appointed for treaty of peace, whether the Polonians brought Maximilian, and the Silesians at the same tyme levying forces for Hungarie, Maximilian by that meanes finding his party strongest, the Polonians being farr inferior in number refused to retorne with them into Poland. At last Sigismund marrying the daughter of the Archduke of Gratz vncle to Maximilian, he yeilded his right to Sigismund. The Tartarians in the yeare 1589 prouoked by the Cosacchi Polonian horsmen vppon the borders, did invade Podolia with a great Army, but were defeated by the Polonians and lost 25000 men in that battell wherevppon they craued ayde of the Turkish Emperor, so as the Cosacchi also prouoking the Turkes by many skirmishes vppon the Confines of Walachia and the Cheife Gouernor of the Turks demaunding of Zamoski to haue the breakers of peace deliuered to his hands to be punished and Zamoski referring the matter to the king, and the king referring it to the Generall Assembly of the Nobles, the Turkes in the yeare 1590 prepared for open Warr, and were ready to invade Poland, had not the English Ambassador at Constantinople made peace betweene them as the Common voyce was, and as himselfe avowed to me.

The Common wealth.

It appeared by the history of Poland that the kingdome is electiue and so limited as it rather seemes a Common Wealth then a kingdome, yet that the Polonians alwayes vsed such Constancye in publick Counsells, as not only they chuse the heyres males (except sometymes the affayres of the State being turbulent) but also reputed the kings widowes and daughters to pertaine to the Care of the State (as hath bene seene by many examples for many ages, while the two Familyes of Pyastus and Jagellon raigned) so as they often imposed vppon the newe Chosen king the Condition, to marry the widow or daughter of the deceased king, (whereof the historyes yeild many examples) and had great respect for want of heyres males to the Father to chuse the male childe on the mothers syde of the blood Royall if he were Capable of that dignity, (for which respect Sigismund the king then living was chosen by them).   In the tymes betweene the death of the king, and the Choyce of the new king, by an old lawe the Arch-Bishopp of Gesna hath the priuiledge to call the Assemblyes, and to publish the choyce of the king, who is chosen by the Palatines, Bishopps, Castellanes, deputies of Townes and Cittyes, and by all the gentlemen.   For euen those gentlemen haue voyces who are become so poore, as they are forced to attend on other gentlemen as likewise those who come from holding the plowgh, barefooted without hose or shooes, haue asmuch freedome in their voices as any other. At this election to auoid confusion, they chuse Certaine gentlemen who like Tribunes pronounce the voyces, and these in latter ages haue vsurped so great authority to the preiudice of the kings (whome they daily restraine within stricter limits) as therein they passe the Bishoppe of Leopolis and' his Suffragane yea the very Palatines, and Castelanes.   Their History sheweth that some Prouinces of Germany belonged of old to Poland, which in process of tyme by Contracts of mariage, by diuisions of Prouinces among brothers, and by warr especially Ciuill, became alienated from Poland which notwithstanding hath in the meane tyme vnited to itselfe many other Prouinces no lesse then the former in greatnes, riches and power. The heyres males of the dukes of Masouia failing, that dukedome was vnited to Poland. The large dukedome of Lituania was vnited to the same by duke Jagello when he was Chosen king of Poland vppon his mariage to a daughter of the last kings bloud, and howsoeuer the Princes of Lituania being of the dukes Family long deferred the vniting of that Prouince to Poland, lest they should loose an hereditary Dukedome for an electiue kingdome, yet their heyres males failing, it was at last fully vnited to the same. The Prouince of Liuonia was wonn by Armes from the order of the Teutonick Knights and from the Dukes of Moscouy. After warr betweene the Polonians and the said order of knights, at last agreement was made, that the Polonians should presently possess great part of the dukedome of Prussen, and the said order being then extinguished, the rest should remayne to the master thereof with title of Duke, and to his heyres males, he being a Germane Prince of the Family of Brandeburge, yet so as for want of heyres Males that part also should be vnited to the kingdome of Poland. This Prouince is more ample and rich then almost any other of the Germans, whose language they speake. The Citizens and Marchants are most rich and magnificall, and the husbandmen are very rich and next to the English of any I haue seene in forayne parts. The Cittyes are many and stately as Konigsberg the seate of the duke, as Mariemburg a Fort and Cheife Citty of the Polonians part, as the free Citty Danzk, sumptuous in buildings and famous for Traffique, and the litle but most pleasant Citty Meluin, and more pleasant for the Ciuill Inhabitants, where the English Marchants had their Staple, which is of no small moment to inrich any Citty. The two Cittyes last named are free and gouerned by their owne Magistrates, yet acknowledge the king of Poland, who hath an officer in each of them to gather his tributes, but they will not receiue his forces, nor himselfe without a limitted trayne. And the king is content with this their subiection, lest they should refuse to pay his tributes, and they being Germans, and the Citties well fortifyed, and bordering vppon the Sea, should seeke meanes to vnite themselues to the Empire, and the free Cittyes thereof. King Sigismund at this tyme raigning, was also by Inheritance king of Suetia, but that kingdome was not otherwise vnited to Poland. If a man consider the large Circuit of the vast Prouinces and the vnited power of the king, the Palatines and the gentlemen to resist Common enemyes, he will say this kingdome is most ample and powerfull. But if withall he obserue the many and vast deserts and woods, the moderate riches of priuate men, rather seruing to liue plentifully at home, then sufficient for the vndertaking of any great actions abroad, the former amplitude and power, will seeme much extenuated. And lastly if he consider the kings limitted power often subiect to the constraint of the Palatines in publique Counsells, and the Palatines, Castellanes and Gentlemens immunity from lawes and liberty in generall, and absolute Comaund with power of life and death in their owne Territories and lands, the said amplitude and power of the kingdome will appeare to be vanished into smoke; yet euery king hath more or lesse authority, and respect, as he is more or lesse Wise, and valiant. For in the age past Stephen Bathori Prince of Transiluania being Chosen king of Poland, was said vppon pretence of publick occasions to haue raised an Army, and still keeping himselfe armed and strengthned therewith to haue abated the pride of the Palatines & Gentlemen, and then ioyning himselfe with Zamosky Chauncellor of the kingdome, and his faction, to haue preuailed so farr against the Contrary faction as he banished, yea putt to death (a thing neuer heard of in Polonia) some of the Sborosky a cheefe Family on that part. It belongs to the king to appoint publick assemblyes and with consent of the same to make peace and warr, and to giue for terme of life, the places and dignityes of Counsellors, Bishopps, Palatines and Castellanes; For these dignityes are not hereditary, but only giuen for life by the king, who is also the head of these Assemblyes, and the supreme Judge of all Causes euen

concerning gentlemen whose pride, and liberty is such as he
cannot well moderate, and suppress, so [id est, howsoeuer] great
is this authority and power of the king. Breifely I say that
Poland is divided into the greater, whereof the cheife Citty and
seat is Guesna, and the lesser Poland, whereof the Cheife Citty
and seate of the kings is Crakawe, besides the vnited Prouinces,
All which are gouerned by Palatines, Castellanes, Captaines,
Judges, Senators or the kings Counsellors.

The Palatines vulgarly wawoedes are in seuerall principali-
tyes. The Castellanes their leiutenants, are leaders of the
gentlemen. The Captaines are Gouernors of Forts, and Castles.
The Judges or Burgraues determine Criminall, and Ciuill
Causes. The Bishopps of old 9. be many in number by annexed
Prouinces, the Palatines of old Fifteene now 26. The Castellanes are about sixty fiue, and the number of the rest is farr
greater. Besides they haue great Ciuill and martiall Officers,
Ciuill, as two Chauncellors that haue the great Seale, and two
Vicechancelors having a lesse Seale, two Secretaryes having no
voyce in the Senate. Martiall, as two Marshalls, two Generalls
of Armyes. 91. Colonells Chosen by the king. In generall
obserue that only the Castellane of Crakawe hath place of the
Palatine thereof, as I shewed in the History, and so of all other
Palatines, vppon the Cause therein mentioned. The Historyes
often make mention of two noble Familyes, the Zborowski
seated neare the Confines of Prussen, and the Zamoisky of
greater power seated vppon the Confines of Transiluania.

The King and his Court.

Myselfe did see Sigismund the third and his Queene at the
Port of Dantzt, a free Citty of Prussen, where 30 shipps of
Swecia, and one of Holland (in which shipp the king and
Queene passed) were ready to conduct him into his hereditary
kingdóme of Suecia, expecting nothing but a faire Wynde. He
made this voyage to take possession of his Fathers kingdome
lately dead, which in the meane tyme was gouerned by his

Vncle Charles, not without the suspected fauour of the people, he being of the reformed Religion as they were, but the king being brought vpp by his mother in the Roman Religion. The king was tall of stature, somewhat leane of body, with a long visage and browne Complexion, and the hayre of his head was black and short, with a thinn, short, and sharpe pointed beard of a Yelowish Coulor. He wore a litle black silck bonnett hanging downe about his neck, and plaine black garments, he then mourning for his father. The Queene of the Family of Austria and the house of Gratz, was of a low stature, a full face, and sanguine Complexion. When the Gentlemen brought vpp meat for the king, one went before with a short white staffe in his hand, and three gentlemen carryed vpp each of them three Couered dishes with a white Napkin betweene euery dish, and each of them had a Page to beare vpp the trayne of his gowne, for they did weare two long Garments, the Inner hanging to the knees, the other to the Anckles. They who kept the dore of the Chamber, wherein the king and the Queene did eat were base Groomes, and they admitted any man to enter, so as the roome was full with people of all Conditions, and those that stood somewhat distant from the Table, putt on their hatts, only when the king did drincke, the Queene herselfe, and they that satt at the Table rose vpp, and all that were in the Chamber putt of their hatts. They seemed not to know any such reuerence, as kneeling to the king, or putting of the hatt to the Chaire of estate. The king came to this Port, an english myle distant from Dantzt, Where there was only one house, and that very vnfitt to receiue a King with his trayne, because some few dayes before, a tumult had happened at Dantzt, betweene the Polonians and the Citizens which Credible men thus related to me. A Porter of the Citty being loded, and passing by a Polonian, first hurt him with his burthen, then bad him take heed, wherevppon he (as all Polonians are soone stirred vpp, and prone to quarrells) drew his short sword or Semiter, and therewith almost cutt of the poore Germans Arme, who running through the streets, bewayled his mayme, and so stirred vpp

the Citizens, as they killed Fifteene Polonians, and among
them, a boy that carryed meat to his master, these being all
they could meet, For there were no other Polonians in the
Towne, but only those of the kings Court. Of the Germans no
more then fower were killed, but the king had fower hundred
footemen of his Guarde called Haiducs, who were lodged in the
Suburbs, and vppon this Tumult marched with banner dis-
played towards the Citty, and had not the Gates bene shutt
vppon them in fitt tyme, no doubt there had bene farr greater
slaughter. The king was most offended at the shewting of a
peece, the bullett whereof came in at his Chamber window. At
last the Magistrates with great difficulty appeased the multitude, For the Germans having the advantage doe not willingly
forbeare, neither can the Polonians though vppon disadvantage,
easily sett downe by the losse. The tumult being appeased, the
Magistrates made a Proclamation to haue him made knowne
that shott into the kings Chamber, and (as it seemed for forme)
promised an hundred Guldens to any man should bring him
forth, but neither could he be found, nor were the Polonians
herewith satisfyed. The king had come from Crakaw to Danzt
in boates vppon the Riuer Vistula, vulgarly Wexel. Crakaw is
the seat of his Court, and I vnderstood by some Polonian
Gentlemen, that he there mantayned for his guard 60 horsmen
called Hascheri, whereof each man had fowerteene Guldens by
the moneth, and 400 Footemen called Haiducs, whereof each
man had fower Guldens by the moneth. And that his Courtiers
kept 2000 horses, some one officer keeping eight horses with the
monethly stipend of Thirty Guldens. But that these stipends
were slowly payd, the king being alwayes in their debt, and
hardly making full payment once in fower yeares. Neither did
these Courtiers or officers eat in the Court, there being no Table
kept but the kings, the reuersion whereof serued the Queenes
Women. So as howsoeuer the king might be well attended
riding abroad, yet within dores his Court seemed to haue small
magnificence.

The King's reuenues and tributes.

Indeed the Kings Reuenues are small, For the Mynes of siluer belonging to him are few, and yeild not great profitt, and the Citties of traffique being few, and the exactions not great, his Customes also are small. The mynes of salt also belong to the king, and yeild him greatest profitt, but the Gentlemen haue a portion thereof at a moderate price, whereof they sell, what they cannot spend themselues. And this salt is partly decocted of water, but most growes in pitts, and is digged vpp in black and great peeces like stones. The king hath also certaine Territories of land proper to himselfe, wherein he hath absolute power, the husbandmen being his slaues, as particuler Gentlemen haue in their owne Territories And all things being very cheape in Poland, excepting forayne Cloathes, Stuffes, wynes and spices, these Reuenues may well answer the kings expences, but for publike vses, I could neuer heare nor read that the kingdome had any great Treasure. Diuerse affirme, that the mynes of siluer and salt, yeild the king sixe hundred thousands Crownes yearely, yet vnderstand that part thereof was ingaged by Sigismund Augustus, and that almost halfe was alienated by Henry of Valois to diuerse gentlemen for gayning their loue. They said also that Lituania and other Prouinces giue the king all necessaries for food, while he keepes his Court among them. And that in publike Causes of Warr, and necessityes of State, Subsidies are imposed by consent of the generall assembly, aswell vppon lands, as beare, and all things to be sold. The dukes part of Prussen yeildes him yearely twenty thousand Crownes and the king of Polands part thereof being as great and as fruitfull, cannot but yeild him like profitt. It is most certaine that the king hath also many meanes of great moment to gratify his subiects as the appointing of his Cownsellors and great Officers, the keeping of Castles and Territories, which he giues to gentlemen for life, and if he would make profitt thereof, he might very much increase his Reuenues, but in that case he should offend the Gentlemen, whose loue the kings are so carefull to preserue, as they not only bestow these guiftes freely among them, but comonly graunt to the Palatines and Castellanes, such rights as belong to the king in their seuerall Territories.   But it is a matter of no small moment, that vppon any inuasion of enemyes, or vppon offensiue warr decreed by common Consent in publique assemblyes, the Gentlemen are bound to assemble, and serue vppon their owne Cost and Charges, in whome is all the strength of the kingdome, so as no great Treasure is required for defending the same, or for making offensiue warr decreed by publike Consent.

The horse and horsmen.

The Polonians are a warlike nation, valiant, and actiue, but all their strength consists in their horse, whereof they haue so great number, as some affirme they can bring a hundred thousand horse into the feild, and one Prouince of Lituania, can bring 70 thousand, and king Stephen in the last age had 40. thousand in his Army.   Of these horsmen, some are called Hussari, who are armed with long speares, a sheild, a Carbine or short gunn, and two short swords, one by the horsmans syde, the other fastned vnder the left syde of his sadle.   The light horsmen called Cosachi are armed with short swords, Jauelin, bowes and arrowes, and a Coat of maile and the whole Country of Poland being playne, this great body of horsmen must needs be a powerfull strength to the kingdome.   The horses are of small stature, but of no lesse agility, then those of the Turkes and singuler in boldnes for any seruice of warr.   Yet are they all made Gueldens; And the gentlemen are not prouder of any thing, then of their horses and horsmanshipp professing to weare long garments, as Commodious for horsmen, that they may cast their vpper garment vppon their horses when they are heated with running.   And for this Cause many haue their bridles (Which are alwayes snafles by Which the horses are easily turned) sett with studds of gold or siluer, sometymes having gold Chaynes, and like ornaments at the eares of their horses, and Commonly paynting the mayne and taile yea the whole body, excepting the back of their horses with light Coulors, as Carnation and the like, therein seeming ridiculous, that whereas art imitates nature, these Coulors are such as are most vnnaturall for horses. They haue guilded stirropps as also spurrs which are some handfull long at the heele. Not only soldiers but Ambassadors and their gentlemen, haue the hinder part of their horse couered with the wings of an Eagle, or skinn of a Tyger, or leopard or some like ornament, either for beauty, or to seeme more terrible, as in generall all haue them couered, some lesse, some more richly. The Polonian horsmen restraine the incursions of the feirce Tartars, and seeme so bold to the Turkes, as they haue no hart to invade Poland; Neither can the Moscouites indure their assault, howsoeuer for feare of their Tyrant, they must be prodigall of their bloud. The Polonians haue no care to fortify Cittyes professing nothing more to be disgracefull then to fly from their enemyes, and vaunting to defend their Country with their owne brests, not with walled Townes which they lesse desyre to fortify lest their kings should vsurpe power ouer them by giving the keeping of such places to their deuoted seruants.

The footemen.

The Germans inhabiting strong Cityes haue no cause to feare the Polonians, having no strong body of Footemen to force them. For those that dwell in the Cittyes of Poland, are Marchiants or Tradesmen, both enemyes to Warr, and the Country people are all slaues, a generation not capable of military glory. And of these should the bands of Foote consist; For the gentlemen are all horsmen, and the strength of horse being only in the playne Feild, strong Townes need not feare them. Thus whiles the kings authority is limitted so as he cannot make warr of himselfe, nor force his subiects to take Armes with him, and while they want treasure the sinew of Warr, except the warr and the meanes to raise mony be decreed

in the generall Assembly, it falles out, that as in the Comunion
of Plato, what all men care for, each man neglects; so many
tymes a Senate of many heads, is either diuerted from the best
Counsells by Confusion of opinions, or letts the best occasion
slipp by slow and too late resolutions.   For which Causes, and
for the foresaid want of Footmen, the Polonians, howsoeuer in a
Common danger they readily concurr to stopp any inuasion; yet
seeme vnfitt to inlarge their kingdome by Conquering new
Prouinces.   The strength of their Warfare consisting in their
horse, and their slaues seruing only for Pioners, or like oxen
to draw Artillerie, and for like vses, whensoeuer they raise an
Army the Footmen are mercenary straungers, commonly
Germans, Hungarians, and Slauonians (whereof king Stephen
had sixteene thousand in his Army).   But the king mantaynes
a certaine number of Hungarian and Slauonian Footmen, not
sufficient to serue in the Army, but only to guard his owne
person, and these being commonly taken for Polonians are called
Haiducs, and are most bold in fighting and vndanted in
receiuing vgly wounds, and maymes made by the Simeters or
short swords they vse.

Their nauall power.

All parts of Poland lying within land excepting Prussen and
part of Liuonia, which are subiect to the king vnder a free yoke,
and haue few shipps of their owne, most commonly vsing those
of strangers for trafficke, the Polonians may be sayd to be
altogether ignorant in Nauigation.   So as when king Stephen
had beseiged Danzt, and the Citizens had hyrdd a Flemish
shipp to cutt downe a Bridge of Wood, by which the Polonians
passed ouer the Riuer, the Dantzkers at this day tell for a Ieast,
that the Polonian Footmen stood vppon the bridge to defend it
thincking with their Pikes to stopp the shipp vnder all sailes
with a strong gaile of Winde, till the shipp cutting the bridge
with an instrument in the Prowe, these ignorant men were all
drowned in the Riuer.

Warfare in generall.

In generall the warfare of Poland hath three impediments one of wanting mony and power in the Kings to make peace and Warr, both these being raised and determined in Parliaments and againe the want of Footmen for which they vse strangers, but (as I formerly sayd) it hath more or lesse reputation and power according to the kings person.   For the histories shew that some vnwarlike kings haue suffered Losses, and indignitye without reuenge or repayre of them, but their Successors being valiant, and of warlike myndes haue not only recouered and repayred those losses and wrongs, but haue at home kept the proude Gentlemen in awe, and haue abroad mantayned their owne and their kingdomes reputation against all their powerfull neighbors.   The Polonians suffer the present vsurpation of the king of Suecia confining vppon Liuonia because they haue not power at Sea, and cannot lead an Army against him by land without great difficultyes, neither doth he offend them being restrayned by iust feare of the Danes and Moscouites, continuall enemyes to that kingdome, and bordering it on all sydes.   The Duke of Moscouye, in the Warr for Liuonia, with Stephen king of Poland, did by his victorys finde him so powerfull, as he was content to haue peace with him. The Moscouite hath his subiects more at Commaund and more vnited vnder tiranicall obedience, but the Polonians are more valiant, more bold and apt to dare any thing in a iust warr decreed by publike Consent. The Moscouites are more fitt to defend fortifyed places, the Polonians invincible in the playne Feild.   The Moscouites lesse feare hunger and want of necessaryes, the Polonians more despise the sword and death. The neighbor Germans feare not the power of the Polonians, wanting footmen (as I sayd) to force their strong Cittyes, and the Polonians doe nothing lesse then feare the Germans in the playne Feild since in such fights the Polonians, though farr inferior in number boast themselues to haue often prevailed against the Germans, as namely of late in the Warr of Prussen, and likewise when Maximilian the Emperors brother, was taken prisoner in the Feild. The Tartarians haue often made incursions into Poland, but rather as Robbers then Invaders, wasting the Country for the tyme, but neuer planting themselues therein, and this they haue done in tymes betweene the death and choyce of kings, when the Polonians wanted their head to lead them, yet euen then haue they often (of old and lately in the age past, and this present) bene beaten back with such ouerthrowes as they had litle cause to bragg of their booty. The Turkes haue subdued the Prouince of Walachia, the Prince whereof did homage to the king of Poland, and haue bene bold to prouoke the Polonians in tymes betweene the death and Choyce of Kings, or when they had vnwarlike kings. Againe the Polonians remembring the great defeat of king Ladislaus by the Turkes and being compassed on all sydes with the aboue named powerfull neighbors, and warily obseruing the disvnited myndes of Christian Princes, are not willing to make any Warr against the Turkes. But no doubt the Turkes had rather make any warr then against the Polonians, in regard of their strength in horse, wherein the Turkes ouertopp all other enemyes fearing to be forced by them to fight a battell with all forces. And for this Cause they haue of late borne with the Polonians seruing against them in Valachia, and with many incursions made by their Cosacchi that is light horsmen into the Confines of Turkye. As also when the Tartarians passed the Confines of Poland to ayd the Turkish Emperor, at the seige of Agria in Hungary, and were vtterly ouerthrowne by the Polonian Cosacchi, the Turkish Emperor was Content to dissemble as if he thought this hostile act to haue happened by Casualty, though the same day the Polonian Ambassador came to the Turkish Court to excuse the king in Case they should fight, a messenger within few howers after arriued there, who related the defeat and ouerthrow of the Tartarians.

Ciuill iustice.

The Polonians owe their lawes aswell martiall as Ciuill, which at this day remayne in force to Cassimere the great

Crowned in the yeare 1333. But besides these Prouinciall lawes or Statutes, the Ciuill Causes of debts of Inheritances, and the like as also cases belonging to our spirituall Courts, about dowries, divorces, last Testaments, and the like are determined by the Ciuill and Common lawes there in Common vse, the sonnes of Gentlemen and of Citizens studying those lawes in the vniversityes, and many of them taking the degree of doctors. In Cittyes they haue two Courts of Justice, the inferior of certaine Richters or Judges from whome the greiued party may appeale to the superior Court of the Senators. And from both these if the cause be of a certaine value, or aboue one hundred pounds, the greiued party may appeale to the kings Courts of Justice, which are likewise two, the one of Judges, called Assessors from whome appeale is likewise admitted to the highest Court where the king setts in person, attended by his Lords spirituall and temporall, not vnlike our Starr Chamber. And these Courts are in the place where the king resides for the present, be it at Crakawe, or at Warsawe, where he commonly abides, or otherwhere. The causes of dowrye and inheritance are determined by the Ciuill and Comon lawes. The daughters and sonnes have equall portions. If the husband outliue the wife, he hath halfe the goodds, and the other halfe is divided among the Children, as likewise if the wife outliue the husband, and when the longer living Parent dyes, that halfe also is divided among the Children. Among gentlemen the eldest sonne may haue the Cheife house, and lordshipp, but if the value exceed the portions of his brothers and sisters, he must pay them that proportion in mony. For our strange lawe of giving all the land to the eldest sonne, is not pratized among them.

Capitall Judgments.

Touching Capitall Judgments. The gentlemen, trusting to their exorbitant priuiledges, often comitt murthers against strangers or any other prouoking them to anger; For they cannot be iudged but in a generall assembly which is comonly called at Warsaw where also the Kings are chosen, and that but once in two yeares (except the Kings death, or some like great occasion of meeting happen) and then they are tryed by the most voyces of gentlemen, who are thought partiall Judges in a Common Cause, which may concerne any of them vppon the like euent; yet men of Creditt report that they proceed directly in this manner. The dead Corpes of the murthered is imbalmed and brought to that assembly, whether the murtherer is cited, and not appearing is banished, looseth his goods, his howses being pulled downe, and the very trees being turned vpp by the rootes, and his person made infamous, but appearing as commonly they doe, he must either purge himselfe by the law or sometymes by the fauour of great freinds by voyces finding him not guilty of murther, (but neuer by any pardon which the king neither doth nor can graunt) or els must dye, but in that case his goods goe to his Children or heyres. And the gentlemen for murther are beheaded, whereas others haue their bones broken vppon a wheele. Of late a slaue, that had killed his master (as I vnderstood by credible report) had first one hand and foot cut of in the place where he did the fact, and after in the place of execution had first the other hand and foote cutt of, then had a large thong of his skinne fleaed round about his body, and lastly being yet aliue, had his body cutt into fower quarters. Coyners of mony by the lawe are to be burned, but sometymes in mercy are only beheaded. They that sett houses on fyre are fastned to a Gibbett and smoked to death. He that deflowres a virgine of noble Parentage, must dye by the law, and generally he that Comitts a rape is burned. Adulterers by the law are beheaded, if they be accused; but I heard that gentlemen maryed, did many tymes keepe Concubines, seldome questioned, neuer condemned to death for it, being (as I haue formerly sayd) only to be tryed in cases of life by gentlemen in the said generall assemblyes.

Degrees of Common wealth and Family.

Touching the degrees in Common wealth and Family, the
Archbishopp of Guesna is primate and legate to the Pope,
and crowneth the kings. The Archbishopp of Lempurg and
diurse Bishopps haue priuiledges as Princes. I did only heare
of two Earles of Osterloch, but I neuer heard nor read of any
more Earles nor any Barrons among them. The highest
secular dignityes are these of the Palatines and Castellanes,
Marshalls Chauncellors Vicechauncellors Generalls and
Colonells, which are only for life. The next and cheife for
number and power is that of the gentlemen who haue very great
priuiledges aswell in the choyce of the kings as in all things
iudged by the publike assembly (wherein as I sayd Crymes
Comitted by themselues are iudged by themselues) and also in
the absolute Commaund of their owne Territories, wherein they
haue power of life and death ouer their owne slaues, and all
Confiscated goods and tributes, as the king hath in his
territories. These priuiledges were first graunted them by
Cassimere the great Crowned in the yeare 1333 and since by
other kings haue bene increased, alwayes with so much
diminution of the kings power. And the priuiledges of the
nobility are comunicated to the nobles of Conquered, and vnited
Prouinces. Euery king at the end of his Coronation doth with
solemne Ceremony knight some Counsellors and gentlemen.
And some two or three dayes after, coming into the markett
place of Crakawe to take the oath of the Citizens and their
guifts presented him, he doth againe draw the sword, and
knight some men of best meritt. But they are not dubbed after
the manner of our knights nor haue any adition to their names
as Sir with vs, and if perhapps they add the title of knight to
their written stile, yet are they not vulgarly named by it. All
these haue moderate riches scarce sufficient to buy forayne
Commodityes, farr brought and much vsed by them as Spanish
wynes and spices and stuffes of silk and English Cloth, the
greatest not having aboue 5000li. yearely Rent, excepting the

Duke of Prussen, of Brandeburg house, and the duke of Curland of Denmark Family, nor were they subiect.

The marchants and Artisans in Cittyes are not many in number, there being few Cittyes for so great a kingdome, neither are they rich dwelling farr from the Sea, so as straungers fetch their Commodityes, and they are subiect to the gentlemen in whose Territories they dwell as they are subiect to the king that liue in his Territoryes. The rest are meere slaues, (as in Bohemia) the Lord hauing power ouer their bodyes and goods, and ouer their Children to make them seruants in their houshold, and if they haue skill in any art to make them woorke for their Lordes profitt, for they cannot woorke for themselues, nor haue any proper goodds, all belonging to the lord; Yea the Germans affirme and write that in Lituania, the lord will cutt of his slaues foote, lest he should runn away. But their seruants attending their persons, are comonly poore Gentlemen: For many Gentlemen are so poore as they drinck water, and follow the plough bare-footed, yet loose they not their right to be gentlemen, nor their voyces in generall assemblyes, as in choyce of the King, and like occasions. These gentlemen seruants waite with their hatts on, and sett at their masters table, both at home and abroad where their masters are invited: For they account it a disgrace to haue slaues wait on them, yet some will apparrell their slaues as Gentlemen to attend on them to the Court, or to Cittyes, and when they retorne take this apparrell from them. The Polonians are Courteous and kinde hearted, and so vse their wiues with much loue and respect, as also these Gentlemen seruants with mildnes and affability. In generall a gentleman will not marry a marchants daughter, nor any ignoble woman, for any riches whatsoeuer, and if any should so mary, his Kinsmen would force him to be diuorced. For they are Carefull not to stayne their nobility, insomuch as a gentleman will not buy or sell anything, but his owne Corne and Catle.

CHAP: iii.

Of the Common wealth of Italy according to the several heads contayned in the title of the first Chapter and the severall absolute Princes thereof. But in this Chapter only of the Historicall Introduction in generall for all the Dominions.

CHAP: iiii.

Of the Common wealth of Italy namely the Pedegrees of the Princes, and the Papall dominion, and the new power of the kings of Spaine in Italy; Of these I say touching some of the heads contayned in the title of the first Chapter.

THE Popes of Rome and the Dukes of Venice haue no hereditary succession, but are chosen for life, so as I omit their private Pedegrees.

V. CHAP.

Of the Common wealth of Venice in particular touching some of the heads conteyned in the title of the first Chapter.

[I have decided to omit the whole of these three Chapters which extend from Page 56 to Page 135 of the original MS. They are laborious compilations and are enlivened with very few personal Touches. The first sentence of Chapter III. has an unconscious humour of its own. "Italy was inhabited at first by the Ligurians and Iletrurians, then by the Galles who called the lower part thereof Gallia Cisalpina that is on this syde the Alps." C. H.]

CHAP: vi.

Of the Commonwealth of the Dukedome of Florence intermixed wlth that of the Free Citty Lucca; of both touching some of the Heads contayned in the tytle of the first Chapter.

FLORENCE is sayd to haue beene inhabited some yeares before the birth of Christ, and to haue bene destroyed by Totilus king of the Goathes, or as others write by the Frisolanes, a people of that Territory, at this day subiect to the Florentines, and that the Emperor Charles the great after that he had ouercome the Lombards, retorning from Rome that way tooke such delight in the pleasantnes of the Seate, as he caused the Citty to be built againe in the yeare 802 from which tyme it was vnder the Emperor, and other Princes, till the yeare 1287, when the Cittyzens bought their liberty for 6000 Crownes from Rodulphus Emperor of Germany, which liberty they enioyed many yeares, till the Family de Medicis growing great brought them in subiection, Which Familye beares fiue Pills, gules, and one Azure in a feilde ore, for their Coate of Armes. Cosmo de Medicis was the first of that Family, that grew eminent in the Citty, who had such power as he might easely haue disposed of that Common Wealth, but for the publike good he attempted no change, and dyed in the yeare 1464. His sonne Peter the first kept his fathers authority, and the loue of the Citizens, wisely gouerning the Common Wealth, rather as a priuate Citizen then as a Prince. The Pedigree of this Family inserted in the beginning of the fourth Chapter of this booke, among other Princes of Italy, doth giue light to that I now write. The said Peter left two sonnes Lorenzo called the Great, and Juliano. By a Conspiracye of the Familyes de Paccij, and de Saluiati, the yonger Juliano was killed, but Lorenzo keeping his old authority, demeaned himselfe so modestly and so wisely, as he seemed not only to gouerne the Citty, but all Italy, the

Princes thereof reuerencing him, and seeking Counsell of him as from an Oracle. But he dying in the yeare 1492, his sonne Peter the second, seeking to rule as absolute Prince, when Lewes the french King entred Italy, with an Army, was banished with his brothers Giouanni and Juliano. At which tyme Pope Alexander the sixth sought to bring that State subiect to his sonne Cæsar Borgias, who to that end, Peter being dead, laboured to bring back his two brothers from banishment, but their reuocation was effected in the yeare 1512, by Ramondo Generall of the Army of Ferdinand king of Naples, yet still the Cittizens had theire wonted Magistrate called Gonfaloniere, and theire Priour of Justice, and howsoeuer the Commonwealth was gouerned at the becke of the Pope Leo the tenth, and Pope Clement the seuenth, both of the Family De Medici, and by theyre fauorites, yet the sayde Magistrates were yearely chosen, till Pope Clement the seuenth being besidged by the Emporour Charles the fyfth, the Florintynes resolued in the yeare 1527 to take Armes for the recovery of theire liberty. Wherevpon the Pope after obtayned of the Emperour desirious to regaine his fauour, to send the Prince of Orange with his Army to Florence, who droue the Cittizens to such want of Vittles as they were forced to obey the Pope in receauing his kinsman Alexander sonne to Lawrence, and in electing him perpetuall Priour, whome shortely after in the yeare 1535. the sayd Emperour created Duke of Florence, giuing him his base Daughter to wife. Alexander was killed by one of his kinsmen in the yeare 1537. And Cosmo sonne to John succeeded him first stiled great Duke from which tyme to this day, that family by right of inheritance succeedes in that Dukedome, as absolute Princes. The sayd Pope Clement the seuenth was a bastard, and historyes record with what art he proued himselfe legitimate, for bastardes are not capable of the Papall seate. Now the family de Medici begann to be in great estimation, hauing had diuers Popes and Cardinalls, and the French King Henry the second hauing marryed one of that family namely Queene Catherine that so wonderfully in our age troubled Fraunce by factions, which she raysed, and so tempered, as the strongest still had neede of her helpe (but vnderstand that Henry the second was a younger brother when he maryed her and by the death of his elder brother came to that Crowne) yea Pope Leo the tenth Chusing 30 Cardinalls together of his owne faction, left the Papall Sea as it were intaled to his Family, for by them Julio de Medici was likewise chosen Pope who wrote himselfe Clement the seuenth. Fraunces the last deceased Duke before my being at Florence, had to wife Joane of the house of Austria, and by her had a sonne who dyed yong, and two daughters Leonora then maryed to the Duke of Mantua, and Māria then a Virgin and a most fayre lady, of whose marryage I shall hereafter speake. His wife Joane being dead, he liued long vnmaryed, and it was vulgarly spoken aswell among his subiects as strangers, and a thing sowell knowne in Italy as I thincke it fitt for good vses to be here mentioned, that during the tyme of his single life a Floryntine marchant intangled in his loue a Venetian gentlewoman called la Signora Bianca di Capelli, so as shee stole from her frendes, and being his Concubyne came with him to Florence, where he hauing wasted his estate in shorte tyme, shee was thought a fitt pray for a better man. Wherevpon Duke Fraunces, after the manner of Italy, in the tyme of Carnovall or shrouetyde going masked through the streetes with a little basked of egges filled with Rose water, passed by her windowe and threwe vp an egge, which shee caught and retorned it broken into his bosome, and so modestly played the wanton with gracefullnes, as the Duke inamored brought her to his Palice, where shee being his Concubyne, first brought him a sonne called Antonio, then seeming to make conscience to liue a Concubyne, at last shee had the power to make him to take her to wife, which donne shee bent all her witts to haue her sonne legitimate, and admitted to succeede in the Dukedome, and while Cardinall Ferdinand brother to Duke Fraunces opposed this her desseigne, it happened that he came to Florence to passe some dayes merrily with the Duke, and

they being to goe out hunting earely in a morning, the
Duchesse sent the Cardinall a March payne for his breakfast,
which he retorned with due Ceremony saying that he did eate
nothing but that was dressed by his owne Cooke, but the Duke
by ill happ meeting the messenger, did eate a peece thereof,
and when the Duchesse sawe it broken, shee smiled and spake
some wordes of Joy, but the messenger telling her the
Cardinalls Answer, and that the Duke had eaten that peece,
shee with an vnchanged Countenance tooke another peece, and
hauing eaten it, locked herselfe in a clossett, and herevpon the
Duke and shee dyed in one hower, and the Cardinall Ferdinand
succeeded in the Dukedome, who liued at the tyme when I
was at Florence. Duke Fraunces (as I heard from Credible
men) was of a meane stature, black hayre, nothing curious or
sumptious in Apparell, not delighting in hunting or any
laborious exercises, but giuen much to his studdyes, hauing
invented the melting of Cristall of the mountayne, and
delighting to make Porcellana d' India which wee call China
dishes, and to Cutt Jewells, and sett the false to make them
appeare true, to norish silke wormes, to distill many waters,
for which he had many fornaces, to make bulletts to breake and
murther. He was sayd to be of good and sounde Judgement,
warye in speech, eloquent to discourse of the Mathematiques or
such thinges wherein he was more Conversent, faythfull in his
promises, a louer of peace, frugall, popular, and so confident as
by night he would walke out alone. The noble Familyes of
Pulci and Caponi are sayd to haue Conspired to kill him, and
his two brothers Cardinall Ferdinand and Don Petro, but that
one of the consperitours made knowne theire purpose,
wherevpon they were all put to death, yet the Duke vsed such
moderation therein, as he scarcely confiscated 3000 Crownes of
their goods, and put the Judgement of them to the publike
magistrates, who had not yet forgotten the loue of theire owne
liberty, nether did he after the manner of the Italian factions
punish any of theire Familyes that were Innocent, but still held
in his seruice with good estimation the brother of a Cardinall

one of the Consperitours.   Don Petro yongest brother to Duke
Frances marryed the daughter of Don Garzia di Toledo a
Spaniard brother to his mother, so as his wife was his cosen
germane, of whome he had a sonne, yet because he liued in
Spayne, he was sayd to be lesse loved of Duke Frances, so as he
perswaded Cardinall Ferdinand his brother not to be a Cardinall
Priest, that he might succeede him hauing no sonnes, and
might be free to marrye.   This Ferdinand hauing giuen vp his
Cardinalls hatt, possessed the Dukedome when I was in
Florence, being of a meane stature, Corpulent and fatt with
great leggs, one eye a litle squinting or some such way
blemished, his visage broode and full with a great Chinn and
a browne bearde, not thicke of hayre and kept short.   He
seemed to mee to haue nothinge in his apparell furniture or
trayne to drawe mens eyes vpon him.   His Cloke was of blacke
Cloth with one silke lace, his breeches were rownd of black
velvett without any the least ornament, he wore lether stockings
and a lether sheath to his sworde, his Coach was lyned with
greene velvett, but worne till it was thredbare, nether was it
drawne with braue horses but such as seemed to come from the
Plough, and those that went on foote by his coach spake to him
with theire heades Covered, only the Bishop of Pisa satt in the
Coach with him on the same syde, and on his right hand, who
was his cheefe fauorite.   He was sayde to be of good and sounde
Judgment, affable, and mercifully disposed, and in matters of
loue to desyre the first gathering of the Rose, but neuer after
to care for the tree.   At the same tyme when I did see him
passing the streetes of Florence, his Duchesse was in his
Company carryed in a litter vppon mens shoulders, for that she
was great with Childe; she was daughter to the Duke of
Loraine whome the Duke had wooed with rich Jewells and
presents, and not long before at her entry into Florence
intertayned her with great pompe and magnificence.   I did see
her apparrelled once in a Tuft taffety gowne and an other tyme
in a purple Taffety gowne, then and alwayes attyred after the
French fashion, her visage was long and pale with a short nose.

The second tyme when she came from her Pallace to the Church, she had none in her trayne but a wayting mayde and two dwarffs, only the Princesse Maria, daughter to the late Duke Francis by his wife of the howse of Austria, went before the Dutchess, being a Lady of excellent beauty, and in all things of princely Port, tall in stature, her face gracefully mixed with white and redd, so as a straunger by her sanguine complexion might know her to be of the German bloud, the hayre of her head hunge downe Knotted in curious wreaths, Her gowne was of Cloth of siluer, loose yet not hanging only at the back, but like our ladyes night gownes with larg hanging sleeues, and buttoned close vpp from the brest to the Chinn, and she wore a thick short Ruffe altogether of the Italian fashion, and she was ledd by a man on each hand.

This Dukedome contaynes three famous Common Wealthes, that of Florence, that of Pisa (first bought by the Florentines, and after in tyme of their liberty vppon a long rebellion reduced againe to subiection), and that of Sienna, added by Duke Cosmo to this dominion, and these with their territories contayne the greatest part of old Hetruria, being compassed on three sydes with the Mount Apennine, and open on the fourth syde in a playne towards the Sea, and to the Roman Confines being said to haue in length some two hundreth and in breadth one Hundred Italian myles. The State of Florence hath one Archbishopp, and xviij bishopps vnder him. The State of Pisa hath one Archbishopp, and two Bishopps vnder him, and the State of Sienna hath likewise one Archbishopp, and three bishopps vnder him.

The Duke had no Counsell of State, but gouerned the Common Wealth by publique Magistrates, and his secrett affayres by the advice of some fauourites, among which the Arch-Bishopp of Pisa was sayd to be in greatest grace with him whome commonly he carryed with him in his Coache, and in his Company wheresoeuer he went. Formerly I haue shewed that this Dukedome was setled by Spanish forces vnder the Family of Medici, in fauour of some Popes of that Family, but at this

tyme the Duke of Florence no lesse then all other Princes of
Italy, suspected and maligned the greatnes of Spayne as ready
to swallow vpp their Principalityes, and oppresse the liberty of
all Italy, howsoeuer for the present they were not disturbed
while the king of Spayne was busy about his ambitious
dissignes of subduing Fraunce, Netherland and England. In
which warrs, he had great vse of the Popes fauourable
authority, which once ended Italy was so intangled on all sydes
with his netts, as the Conquest thereof seemed not difficult.
The Dukes at the first setling of their State by Spanish forces,
either to shew their Confidence in Spayne, or because they had
neede of forrayne succors to keepe their new Subiects in
obedience, did receiue and pay Spanish Garrisons in two Forts
of Florence and in three Ports vppon the Sea, called Telamone
Pentevole, and Orbetello, but they soone groned vnder their
suspected support, and ceased not till by petition, mony and all
like meanes, they had freed themselues of that burthen, so as at
this tyme Ferdinand the present Duke had only one Spanish
Garrison in a Towne vppon the Seacoast called Porto d' Ercole.
Francisco his brother and Predecessor, in the life of his father
Cosmo, was brought vpp in the Court of Spaine, and being there
when his Father dyed, did not without some difficulty gett the
possession of his Dukedome; For while he liued in Spayne, he
had by diuerse accidents, alienated the Spaniards myndes from
his affayres.   And after he did more prouoke them against him,
by releeuing the Citty of Genoa with victualls, and their
fauourers abroad by all other meanes, when Don Jean base
brother to the king of Spaine sought to bring that Citty vnder
his subiection, whome thereby he also made his open Enemy,
yet in the midst of these Jelousyes, he was strengthned by his
mothers being of the Family of Toledo most powerfull in
Spaine. As he was likewise strengthned by his Consanguinity
with Catherine Queene of Fraunce, and by the fauour of the
Pope, and the Colledge of the Cardinalls, by which meanes he
kept his State in peace.   No doubt while the kingdomes of
Fraunce and Spaine were equally ballanced, the french were

a strong support to preserue the Italian Princes from the yoke
of Spaine, so as the Dukes of Florence had great strength by
Catherine de Medici, then Queene of Fraunce. But this Queene
had borrowed great sommes of mony of Duke Francisco her
kinsman vppon her Jewells laid in pawne to him, and before
a third part of the debt was paid, she desyred the vse of her
Jewells, which the Duke to witnes his loue and Confidence
easily restored to her, yet he after finding that not only the
mony was kept from him, but that also the Queene pretended
right to some of her Fathers goods that the Duke had in his
possession, he did not only euer after forbeare like offices of
Loue, but diuerse ielousyes therevppon grew betweene them.

Touching Ferdinand the present Duke at this tyme whereof
I write, he had none of his brothers Jealousyes with the Court
of Spaine, he had the same mother of the Spanish Family of
Toledo, and the same or greater grace with the Pope Clement
the Eight, being a Florentine gentleman borne, and with the
Colledge of the Cardinalls, whereof himselfe had bene a
member, but he could haue no Confidence in any support from
the kings of Fraunce, that kingdome being then rent and
wasted with strong factions of the league, the Royalists and the
party of the good Patriotts, as also the party of the Protestants
betwene whome three Ciuill warrs had long continued. Only
in this Dukes latter tyme, those Ciuill warrs being composed,
the Duke much strengthned himselfe and his Successors, by
giuing the Lady Mary his deceased brothers daughter in
mariage to the famous french king Henry the fourth. And no
doubt he did nothing lesse then fauour the growing power of
Spayne. For howsoeuer that kings warrs with England and
Fraunce for his mayne proiect of obtayning the Westerne
Empire, kept him for the present from attempting anything in
Italy, yet the greatnes of his power, could not but be fearefull
to all the Princes thereof. And that this Duke feared the king
of Spaine appeared by many infallible arguments, and not to
insist vppon all, in particular, namely by his deliuering the
miserable Captiue bearing himselfe for the king of Portugall

into the hands of the Viceroy of Naples; whome men feare, they also hate, and as all the people subiect to him manifestly shewed at this tyme great hatred of the Spanish nation, so no doubt the Duke, howsoeuer he in policy obserued the king of Spaine by outward offices, yet he was farr from wishing well to the successe of his ambitious affayres, and earnestly laboured by all meanes to haue the foresaid Spanishe Garison in Port Ercole drawne out of his Country. For his mariage, he sought not a wife in Spaine, though his mother were a Spaniard; but as I formerly sayd, he maryed a french lady daughter to the Duke of Loraine, which Family then pretended to be of the Spanish faction, and the Ciuill warrs being ended (as I sayd) gaue his neece to the french king, vppon whome himselfe and the other Princes of Italy then cast their eyes for protection against the power of Spaine. The last Duke his brother had much depended on the Emperor of Germany, in regard his first wife was of the house of Austria, and with the expence of mony mantayned freindshipp with him, and the Princes of Germany, more specially the Duke of Bauaria, aswell to gett a more full investiture of his Dukedome from the Emperor, as in hope to haue aydes from them in any tyme of danger. But this Duke Ferdinand litle inclined to the declining Empire, but rather nourished amity with the Protestant Princes especially after the appeasing of the Ciuill Warrs in Fraunce. He had long tyme kept the picture of Elizabeth Queene of England and expressed asmuch reuerence and loue towards her as he might well doe towards the Popes professed Enemy, and not only he but the State of Venice had for many yeares admitted the said Queenes priuate Agents, as they and the Duke of Sauoy haue since receiued the publike Ambassadors of our Soueraigne king James to be resident with them, and haue openly shewed much to depend vppon his Royall ayde and protection.

For the Citty of Genoa I formerly shewed that Duke Francisco ayded them against Spaine, but this could not take away the hereditary quarrells betweene that Citty, and the Dukes of Florence, in regard that Genoa still keepeth the Forte of Sorezana of old belonging to the Citty of Florence and the Iland Corsica of old subiect to the Citty of Pisa.

It is manifest that the Princes of Italy depend vppon the fauour of the Popes, and Cardinalls, aboue all others. And I haue shewed that this Duke and his deceased brother especially affected and euer had great power in the Court of Rome. For no State is more able to anoy them, then the Popes, Rome lying on the Eastsyde, and the Popes State of Bologna on the Westsyde of them. From which parts their State can only be entred, being otherwise compassed with the Sea, and vnpassable mountaynes. Besides that a great Army of Enemyes cannot finde victualls in the State of Florence, being all layd vpp in Cittyes, which only the Pope can supply having aboundance thereof. And this they haue found by wofull experience in that two Popes had the power to oppresse the liberty of that State, and bring it in subiection to the Family of Medici. Thus say the Florentines, but for my part I thinck aboue all they feare the Thunderbolts of his Ecclesiasticall Censures, which no mountaynes can resist, though our ages contemning them, and the frequencye thereof, hath much blunted and abated their force, and terror; Neither doe I reade that the Popes temporall power hath euer done great hurt to any State, and howsoeuer two Popes haue of late oppressed and subdued the liberty of Toscanye; yet it was effected by the Army of the Emperor Charles the Fifth for their sakes, not by their owne forces. The Commodityes are of no lesse importance which this Duke findes in the freindshipp of the Popes and Cardinalls, as the reputation he thereby gayneth among all Princes of the Roman Religion, together with his safety from any their purposes against his State, and the true intelligence thereof from Rome, where by Confession and all other meanes they best know all such Princes most secrett Counsells, yea euen by their owne communicating of them to the Pope for his approbation thereof: As also by the benefitt the Duke reapes of Ecclesiasticall livings, which by the Popes fauor, he hath liberty oftentymes to bestow on his seruants and Followers.

For howsoeuer the Popes for some 400th yeares past, haue made a new heresye and Simony for laymen to dispose of Ecclesiasticall Benefices, tho neuer so freely bestowed without any the least bribery, yet they approue laymens disposing of them with their Consent and indulgence first obteyned.   Not to speake of the supply of Victualls from the States vnder the Pope, and many like Commodityes.   To conclude howsoeuer the Popes are not in these dayes as of old, the Arbiters of all Christian affayres; Yet the Vnion of the Pope, the State of Venice, and the great Duke of Florence, is the cheife foundation and strength of the peace of all the small Principalityes of Italy.   For the Venetians since their State was almost ruined by the french king Lewes the xijth seeme to haue cast of all ambition to invade their neighbors, and are not as before they were suspected in that kinde of the Italian Princes, but are honoured by them as defenders of the Common liberty.

The commonwealth of Lucca.

The Citizens of Lucca are afrayd of this great Duke as Partridges of an hawke, being compassed with his territories on all sydes, and furnished with Corne from the Maremme of Sienna, with flesh and oyle from the Territory of Florence, and with all kindes of victualls from other parts of his dominion, and if they haue any victualls from any other places; yet the same as all other goods of Marchants or Citizens whatsoeuer, can passe no other way to Lucca, then through some part of the Dukes dominion, and with his safe conduct, so as it is apparent the Duke might with ease subdue that Citty were it not that he forbeares to disturbe the peace of Italy, which warr would soone bring in confusion, Italy consisting of many petty principalityes gouerned by many heads.   All which the beginner of any Warr should make his enemyes, and so the Duke in stead of gayning a Citty, might leese or disturbe his owne Dominion.   And besides that Lucca in this Case is like to receiue strong aydes from Genoa which of old in like sort so supported Pisa rebelling against the Florentines, as also from other Cittyes, and States of Italy, who making the Case their owne, would in all probability assist any member in Italy invaded by an other, no doubt Lucca relyeth vppon forraine succours, which the Emperor Charles the fifth and after his sonne Phillip in their tymes professed to haue in protection. Againe the Duke suffers Lucca to rest in peace, because the Citizens wealth consists litle of stable inheritance, and almost altogether of ready mony and moueable goods, who finding their liberty in danger, would no doubt remoue their estates and dwellings to some other free Citty, and so the Duke should haue lesse profitt in taking the Citty thus vninhabited, then now he hath by their respect and feare of him in regard whereof vppon his occasions he may commaund the loane of any mony he needeth, and all like offices from them, who seldome refuse him any request, being in name free, and yet in some manner subiect to him. Lucca is a small Citty lesse then two myles Compasse, and hath a small territorye, as I haue shewed in my Journall of Italy, but is Compassed on all sydes by States of farr greater power. It is gouerned in cheife by the great Counsell consisting of 150 Citizens, and the Citty is diuided into three parts, and of each part three Senators are chosen, and in course of each part the cheife magistrate called Gonfaloniere is chosen, which tenn men inioy this dignity for three yeares, and representing the Dominion, are vulgarly called La Seignoria. This Senate heares Petitions, giues all graunts, administreth Justice, and to these ends alwayes remayneth in the publike Pallace, whence none of them may goe forth vppon payne of death, but they are there mantayned out of the publique Treasure. These tenn men chuse one among them who is called Commandator, and for three dayes comaundes all the rest, euen the Gonfaloniere himselfe, and for those three dayes, he receiues all Petitions, which he must notwithstanding (howsoeuer contrary to his liking) comunicate to all the rest, and can doe nothing without their Consent, and whatsoeuer is agreed by them with seauen voyces, the Gonfaloniere propounds

it in the great Counsell to be approued or reiected. This Senate
of Tenne men hath absolute authority ouer strangers, but not
so ouer Citizens, whose causes, and all other matters they
cannot fully determine, but must propound them in the great
Counsell. Three Secretaries are absolute Judges of Treasons,
and therein are aboue the Gonfaloniere, yet he must necessarily
be present at those Judgments, and howsoeuer they must
comunicate such causes to the great Counsell, yet often it
happens, that after the execution of the iudgment, they giue
accompt thereof to the great Counsell, as in cases dangerous to
be deferred till the Counsell can be assembled. They haue a
second Counsell of 18 Citizens chosen by the great Counsell to
determine doubtfull Causes. And a third Councell of six men,
that hath care of the receipt and expence of the publique
Treasure, chosen likewise by the great Counsell, as all other
magistrates are. They haue a body of Judges called La Rota,
namely three Doctors of the Ciuill Lawe, whose place of birth
must be fiftye myles distant from Lucca, and one of them hath
the title of Podesta, the other Judgeth Crymes, and the third
Ciuill Causes, and these places by course they chaunge euery
halfe yeare. If any Citizen be accused before the Podesta, he
only formes the processe, and subscribeth his opinion, but the
Judgment is referred to the great Counsell to be approued,
reiected or moderated, only in the Causes of Straungers this
Podesta hath absolute power. They haue a Court of nyne
Marchants assisted with one Doctor of the Ciuill Lawe being
a straunger borne, who iudge the Causes concerning Marchants,
and in those Cases also may condemne to death. In like sort
they haue nyne men sett ouer the office called Abundanza,
namely three of each third part of the Citty, and the office hath
that name, because their duty is to furnish the Citty with
victualls in aboundance, and to see that the Citty neuer want
three yeares prouision of Corne before hand. They haue a like
Counsell of men sett ouer the Ordinance and munitions of
Warr. Many Citizens inroll themselues soldiers, and six
Commissaries are sett ouer them. Three Officers haue the Care

of health, whose duty is to looke that no musty or rotten thing be sold, that no filthines be suffered in the Citty, and that no goods or persons be admitted into the Citty coming from places suspected to be infected with the plague.   Besides they haue a Counsell called de Discoli, most woorthy of obseruation and imitation, and their duty is once in the yeare some fewe weekes before Easter to assemble together, at which meetings any one of them may putt into a Chest the names of such persons as with vs are called of the Damned crue or roaring boyes, and these names being after read in the great Counsell, if two or more of those Counsellors haue concurred in any one mans name, he is called in question by voyces in the great Counsell (the voyces being dumbe, not by mouth, but by litle balls putt into diuerse vessells) and if he be iudged such a person by the voyces of two third parts of that Councell, then he is banished for three yeares, so as he may not for that tyme dwell within 50 myles of the Citty, wherein if he fayleth, he is in absence condemned to death, and a reward of mony sett vppon his head is proclaymed to be giuen to any man who shall kill him, which is the highest prosecution in Italy against banished men; and after sentence is pronounced against him, he must goe out of the Citty before night, and after three yeares he may retorne agayne to dwell in Lucca, but shall euery yeare be subiect to this tryall, if he mend not his manners. Thus the Athenians banished their Citizens by Ostracisme, but they bannished for tenne yeares, and not Wicked persons as these of Lucca doe, but eminent persons in power or riches, being therby like to inuade their liberty.   The Judges called vulgarly de La Loggia, inquire what buisinesse Strangers haue in the Citty, and finding suspicious persons, examine them by the Tortor of the Strappa di corda, which wee call Strappado, and all that keepe Inns must giue to these Judges the names of all strangers they receaue, and must aduertise what buisines they haue in the towne, and that dayly, so as it may appeare to them how long they stay.   Thus doe they with great warines and feare watch to preserue theire Liberty, but for trayned soldiers, they haue only some hundreth in the Pallace, whose places of birth must be fifty myles distant from Lucca, and out of these are chosen Captaines to leade theire soldiers in tyme of warr, but they are punnished no lesse then with death, if in the night time any of them alone or accompanied goe to the walls of the Citty, for only the Artisans of the Citty (hauing good wiues and children there) watch vpon the walls in the night, and two Cittisens with a Commissary, keepe each Gate therof in the day time. And the sayd hundreth soldiers haue each of them three gold Crownes stipend by the moneth.

The Court of the great Duke of Florence.

After this excursion, I retourne to speake of the great Duke of Florence. The Italians write and speake of the Dukes Court, as if it were magnificall, aboue the degree of a Duke yet somthing vnder that of a King, and that he hath a great number of Gentlemen attending him, whereof some only haue a stipend, others both dyett apparrell and stipend. But in my opinion strangers, be they English or French, will hardly say that they haue obserued any such magnificence therein. For howsoeuer wee may yeald the Italians some preheminence of glory in Fountaynes, Aqueducts, Gardens, Jewells, and some such permanent goods, yea somtimes likewise in theire Feasts, which being rare, and the people being as proud as rich, may often tymes exceede like Niggards Feasts. Yet no doubt they of all Nations can worst iudge what it is to keepe a plentifull house, or a Princes Court and trayne. The Duke was sayd to haue sixty young gentlemen for his Pages, whome he trayned vpp in exercises fitt for them. He had 100 Dutchmen for his guardd, for the Italians trust not their owne Countrymen for the guarding of their bodyes but commonly vse Dutchmen whome they esteeme most faithfull and each of them had fiue Guldens of Germany by the moneth, finding themselues apparrell and dyett. Perhapps formerly they had somewhat more allowed for apparrell or dyett, for themselues told me, that this Duke had abated their intertainment. Thirty of them by course each day and night attend at Court, be it held in the Citty or in the Dukes Pallaces, not farr distant, and that day they haue 14 loaues of bread and two Flagons of wyne allowed them by the Duke, but otherwise I haue seene them vppon high dayes haue homely fayre, as Cabages and Colewoorts, only they haue great releife by wayting on their owne Countrymen and other straungers that come to the Cittye. He had 30 Footmen which by course wayted and followed his Coaches; And they said that the Dutchess had not more then some 12. women in her seruice. For my part, I saw nothing in the trayne, or Tables of the Court, wherein many of our Earles and Barons doe not equall it, and I dare boldly say, that very few, and I dare boldly say, that very few, and I thinck not aboue 30 persons haue their diett allowed. The Italians that magnify this Court, say that the Duke spends some fiue hundreth thousand ducates yearely in his Court, his priuate delights, his pleasures and the keeping of his houses, Gardens, Aquaducts, in repayre. For his Stable they report, that he had 150 Coursers of Naples and Gianetts of Spayne, besydes choyce horses of his owne Races. For my part, I could only see in Florence two Stables, each having some 32 horses, which seemed to me of his owne Races, and not of any extraordinary woorth, and twice or thrice I saw his Coaches drawne with very ordinary horses, and I conceiue that the Italians reckon the expence of his Stable in the estimate of all his like expences formerly made. Of the Dukes forces, Tributes, Lawes, and Justice, I shall speake in the following Eight Chapter of this Booke.

The Citty of Pisa.

The Citty Pisa with the Territory is the second principall member of this Dukes State, first subdued by the Florentines, and after rebelling by the aydes of the french king Charles the Eight, when he entred Italy to conquer Naples, againe subdued by the Florentines while they yet enioyed their old liberty, and free Common Wealth, which the Family of Medici shortly after invaded. And for the manner of the second subduing of Pisa, Guicciardine in his history hath fully described it.

It is a pleasant Citty, and an vniversity, and the Duke hath there an Arsenall, or Storehouse for his Gallyes, in which respect the knights of St. Stephen imployed to goe to Sea with them, haue their residence in that Citty where also the great Duke was wont to hold his Court, Some three monethes in the yeare, aswell to shew his loue to the Citizens, as by his presence to incite them to more diligence in drying vpp the adioyning Fenns, not only for profitt, but also to make the ayre more pure and free from the wonted infection.

Sienna.

Sienna is the third principall member of this Dukedome, having a shadow but not altogether so true fruition of the old libertye as Florence itselfe hath in the Continuance of the wonted magistrates. For it was a free Common Wealth; First subdued by Duke Cosmo, by whose institution they haue still their wonted Magistrates, and the wonted authority of the Pallace, where they liue to iudge causes; yet the Duke setts his Gouernor called Podesta to represent his person, without whose approbation the said Senate determines nothing of importance. The Senators office lasteth for two monethes, and they are said vppon payne of death to be tyed not to goe out of the Pallace by day during that tyme, but with their faces couered, perhapps lest the people should be incited by them to mutinyes for recouery of their old liberty, and myselfe haue seene diuerse of them goe abroad thus masked; yet I thinck they are allowed some pompe vppon some festiuall dayes, for myselfe haue seene these Senators vppon such occasion come in solemne pompe from the Church of St. Katherine cloathed in gownes of Redd silke, and square Caps of redd veluett with two banners, and

two maces before them.　But howsoeuer these Senators liue in
the publique Pallace of the Citty and there assemble to iudge
causes, no doubt the Dukes Gouernor hath absolute power in all
affayres, and vseth their helpe rather to dispatch, then to
determine them.　Also the Duke hath a Fort in the Citty
where he mantaynes Soldiers to keepe the Citizens in due
obedience, and hath a Captayne ouer them chosen by himselfe
as an officer of great trust.

CHAP: vii.

Of the free Citty Genoa and of the Dukes of Mantua, and of Vrbine touching some of the heads conteyned in the title of the first Chapter.

The Citty of Genoa.

GENOA is an ancient Citty whereof the Romans make mention some 300 yeares before Christs birth, and when the Empire of Rome declyned, it became a free State, and was of old powerfull at Sea, having vnder it all Liguria in Italy, and diuerse Ilands adioyning, besides sondry dominions vppon the Sea Coasts of the Easterne Parts. And at this day it possesseth Liguria, a large and though mountanous and rocky, yet pleasant and fruitfull Prouince of Italy, and the Isle of Corsica not farr distant. But by the factions of the Citizens, betweene the Guelphs and Gibellines, one of the Popes, the other of the Emperors syde, and the Familyes Adorni and Fregosi, as also other noble and popular Familyes, the Common Wealth hath bene subiect to many hazards, and sometymes oppressed, and subiected to the french, sometymes to the Dukes of Milan. At last when it was subiect to the french, Andrea d' Auria a cheife Citizen of Genoa, being Admirall to the french king, and having by Sea gotten a victory against the Spaniards, refused to send his Captiues taken into Fraunce, desyrous to keepe their Ransomes to himselfe, and so combined with the Marquis of Vasto alluring him to the Spanish party, and not only opened the first advantage to the Spaniards of casting the french out of the kingdome of Naples, but practised by all meanes to free Genoa from subiection to the french from which party himselfe was fallen, and this he easily effected by the vnion of the factions newly made, whereof the frenche Gouernor had improuidently bene the cheife Author, whereas wise men thought he should rather haue nourished some dissention among them. This Prince d' Auria (after the manner of the

Italian Princes and States often to chaunge their protecting
Patrons to better their estate vnder others) thus falling from
the Frenche to the Spaniards, animated the Genoesi to expell the
french, and to institute that forme of gouernment, which they
haue at this day. The said vnion of the factions was made in
the yeare 1527, and the yeare following the said Prince d' Auria
fell from the french to the Spanish party. And for the making
of the said vnion twelue Reformers were chosen, who made a
lawe to abolish all faction, and reduced all the nobles into
28 cheife Familyes, all other inferior being inserted into them,
so as to auoyde factions, no Nobleman might signe any other
Sirname then one of them, and to the hands of these 28
Familyes, the Stern of the Commonwealth was committed, all
Plebeans being excluded from the same, yet so as by a lawe
then made tenn of the richest, or best deseruing Citizens might
euery yeare be receiued into the number of these noble
Familyes. And thus all factions haue from that tyme ceased
from any fact, but to this day they are iealous one of an other,
and haue certaine fashions of attyre, of wearing Roses in their
Capps, and sondry manners of drincking, and like signes
whereby they are easily distinguished and knowne among
themselues. The said Andrea d' Auria is much praysed of the
Italians, that he not only freed his Country from all subiection,
but also hauing that power yet forbore to invade the liberty
thereof himselfe. But no doubt, if he had not had the
protection of Spaine in such measure as he could not probably
haue had in any action of his priuate ambition, he could not
haue expelled the french or resisted their powerfull forces,
neither would the Citizens haue bene so constant to him, but
for the loue of Common liberty. The Genoesi are generally
reputed to be of a wauering disposition, affecting chaunge. Wee
reade that their estate hath bene much troubled with factions
and innouations among themselues, and when for the miseryes
thereof they haue bene forced to cast themselues into the
subiection of forrayne Princes for present protection, wee finde
that assoone as they could in any reasonable manner allay these

troubles, their first endeuours were to practise for recouery of
liberty, yea since their state setled by Andrea d' Auria in the
forme of gouernment it now hath, Conte Gio: Luigi Fiesco
wanted litle of oppressing their liberty, and making himselfe
Lord of Genoa, by a tumult he raysed in the night, if in his
first attempt to surprise the Gallies, while he leaped from one
Gally to another, he had not bene drowned by a casuall fall into
the water. Touching the Kings of Spaine by whose aydes the
french were cast out of Genoa, they haue searched all Counsells
to finde the best course to subdue this Citty, and at first builded
a Fort, kept it with a strong garison, and probably thought to
keepe the Citizens in awe of them possessing great part of Italy
and adioyning Lombardy, but in the end considering that they
could not be subdued without disturbing the peace of Italy with
Common preiudice of all, and as the affayres stood no lesse of
Spayne in priuate, that the Citizens vsed to subiection of
forayne Princes were dead, all now liuing having beene borne
in the tyme of sweet liberty : That the cheife riches of the
Citizens are in mouables and huge Treasures of ready mony :
That they are like Froggs coming to Land for pleasure, but
vppon the least feare ready to leape back into the water, and
having bene of old antiquity a nation powerfull at Sea,
are not only like to flye with their Wealth vppon danger to be
subiected, but also to surprise the Spanish Gallies harbouring
in their Port, and vse them for their defence, I say considering
these and like reasons, they haue not thought good to hazard
the certaine power they presently haue in the Citty for the
vncertaine hope absolutely to subdue it. Spaine presently hath
full vse of their Commodious Port for harbouring and building
of Gallies and of the Citizens bodyes and Treasures aswell in
warr as peace. The cheife Princes or Nobles of Genoa, haue
Commaunds in the Spanish Army and Navye (as the aboue
named Andrea d' Auria was Admirall of the Spanish Gallyes
in Italy), and aswell the Noble as popular Familyes are great
Marchants and sayd to be the richest in ready mony of any
Citizens in the world, and this Treasure the Kings of Spayne

may not only commaund at all occasions to their great
advantage, but also they inthrall the priuate men and the
publick liberty by having it in their hands: For as we reade
that the french king Charles the viijth after the example of
his Progenitors, had and held the Florentines in awe and
dutifull respect to his Commaund by their couetousnes of gayne
in the traffick of Lyons; so the kings of Spayne by the same art
but a stronger bayte haue the Genoesi at their Commaund.
For they continually borrow great sommes of those marchants
giuing them for assurance of repayment, the Tolls and
Customes of Maritime Ports and Cittyes and diuerse Monopolies
of traffique yeilding great gayne for the vse of those monyes,
and the same being not halfe repayd still renewe the debt,
and so having alwayes in their hands the Citizens Treasure,
and the hart being where the Treasure is (as of all men so more
specially of the Genoesi noted aboue others with the vice of
vnsatiable Couetousnes) they haue the Citty more in their
power, then if they had a Fort and strong Garison therein.
Lett a Citty be neuer so strong, yet if the Enemy beseiging it,
can cutt of the Conduicts of Water seruing it, he shall soone be
master thereof, and in like sort if the King of Spayne not
paying his debt to the Genoesi, or stopping the payments Course
for a tyme, can make all them and their bancks breake and
faile in Creditt, I may boldly say he hath them fast bound
in Fetters of gold. And that Genoa hangeth in this sort vppon
Spaine as a dore vpon the Hinges, experience sheweth
plainely to the world at this tyme of my being in Italy, when
the King of Spaine having besides his exhausted Cofers
contracted great summes of debt, and so not being able for
the present to giue his wonted Assignments of Customes, and
the like for payment of his debt, the cheife Marchants and
bancks of Genoa were forced to breake with their Creditors, and
the Contagion of this mischeife soone had spread itselfe to
Venice and Florence, and other Cittyes after a straunge
manner. Yet howsoeuer this Comon Wealth is thus at the beck
of the kings of Spaine, it hath the name and reputation of a

Free State gouerned by the Nobles, that is gentlemen of 28 Familyes. The magistrates are not chosen (as of old) so many of one faction, so many of another, neither (as of old) are the Gentlemen excluded from being Dukes, but these and like nourishments of factions are abolished, and at this day out of the body of the said 28 Familyes, 400 Senators are chosen, Which Senate is called the great Counsell, and chuseth the Duke and 8 Gouernors, which nine persons represent the Dominion, and are vulgarly called la Signoria. The Duke, the 8 Gouernors, and the great Counsell, gouerne the affayres of State but they chuse by dumb voyces, that is with diuerse balls, out of the body of the great Counsell, 100 gentlemen called the lesser Counsell, which dispatcheth other things of lesse importance. The Duke being head of the Common Wealth is chosen for two yeares, during which tyme he liues in the publike Palace, and hath 300th Dutchmen for the guarde of his body; when he enters this dignitye for the first two dayes he weares the Ducall habitt, but after vseth an other habitt, comonly a gowne of Veluett, or Satten of Crimson, or Peacocks blewe Coulor, and a Corner Capp of the same Coulor, as myselfe haue seene him attyred, and the 8 Gouernors weare black gownes and Capps. The Duke hath great authority, since no man besides himselfe can propound any thing in the great Counsell, so as nothing can be confirmed therein, which he doth not first allow. The two yeares ended, vppon the first day of January he becomes a priuate person, and goes to dwell in his owne house, but euer after he hath the dignitye of a Procurator during his life. Then (as he formerly was) a newe Duke is chosen after the manner following. The third day of January the lesser Counsell, and the Eight Gouernors chuse 28 gentlemen, namely one of every Family and these chuse the like number who in like sort chuse 28 gentlemen, and these last chosen, with the Senators who for age or other cause are not capable of the Ducall dignity, choose 4 gentlemen whose names are propounded in the great Counsell, and he that hath most voyces is chosen Duke for the next two yeares.

The foresaid Eight Gouernors (who with the Duke represent
the Dominion, yet can determine nothing without the Consent
of the great Counsell) are chosen in like manner for two yeares,
yet not all at one tyme, but two each third moneth in manner
following. The Duke, the Gouernors, and the lesser Counsell,
chuse 28 gentlemen who chuse 12 gentlemen, and propound
their names to the great Counsell, out of which number the
Duke, the Gouernors and the great Counsell chuse one
day one, and the next day an other to succeede in the
place of two Gouernors whose tyme is ended. And of these
Gouernors being like Counselors, two dwell for three monethes
by course, with the Duke in the Pallace, and the other sixe
dwell in theire owne howses. The Gouernors having ended
that office, are chosen Procurators for two yeares. And these
Procurators namely the old Dukes chosen for life, and the old
Gouernors chosen for two yeares, haue Care of the Treasure,
and other publique affayres, and are of great reputation. The
magistrates of St. George are eminent in this Citty, instituted
in the yeare 1407, who haue long preserued this Commonwealth.
These officers first setled the meanes to raise mony sodenly for
publique vses, in any doubtfull occasion of the Commonwealth,
taking it vpp of priuate men, were they willing or vnwilling,
yet so as the State, according to the variety of tymes, allowed
sometymes 10. 9. or 8, sometymes but seauen in the hundreth,
for vse of the mony, lest priuate men should suffer losse by
promoting the publike good, besides that they gaue them
security for repayment by ingaging to them some publike
reuenewes, or by selling to them some Tolls or Customes of the
Citty for a certayne tyme. By this institution Eight men were
yearely chosen to be sett ouer this busines to prouide for the
satisfaction of publike Creditors. The charge of this office
daily increased, by many villages and Communityes subiected
to the gouernment thereof, and many large Priuiledges were
granted to this office in process of tyme, aswell by the State
of Genoa, as by diuerse Popes and Emperors, and all men
coming to any place of gouernment in the State, must take an

oath not to infringe these Priuiledges of the office of St. George, which is not subiect to the power of any other magistrate. At this day more exact courses are taken in these affayres, and the Creditours haue not the same gayne at all tymes for vse of theire mony, but more or lesse according to the increasing or decreasing of the publike Rents, Tolls, and customes. And this office in tyme hath apropriated to itselfe diuers large revenuewes. So as this one Citty may be sayd to contayne two Commonwelths, the greater of the Pallace, administring Justice to all the Citty, which hath often bene oppressed with tyranny, and the lesser of St. George sett over publike Creditours, which hath allwayes beene free without suffering any such oppression, so as the same Citty within the same walls and at the same tyme might be sayde to haue lost liberty and to inioye it. The foure sayd eight Magistrates of this office, are called the protectors of St. George, and are chosen for a yeare in this manner. All the Creditors in the Citty of what condition soeuer, chuse by lott among themsellues 80. persons out of which nomber agayne 24 are by lott selected, who being shutt vp in a chamber, may not depart till by dumb voyces, that is by diuers litle balls, they haue chosen eight Protectours, and each one that is chosen must haue 16. voyces of the 24. Electors. This office increasing, so as the eight protectors in one yeare could not dispatch all the affayres thereof, the Creditors in the year 1444. instituted the choyse of 24 men, who should dispose the remayning Reuenewes (which is the sinewe of the publike Treasure) for the Common good of the Citty, and that most secretly, lest any Tyrant might take occasion to lay violent hands on the Treasure. The Iland Corsica, and other places of no small importance, are vnder the gouernment of this office, which is bound to preserue them aswell in warr as peaee. Touching the forces of Genoa, the munitions for warr, the difference of degrees in the State, the iustice and Judgments, both Capitall and Ciuill, I shall speake in the following Eight Chapter of this Booke.

The Duke of Mantua.

Vincenzo Duke of Mantua, (at this tyme whereof I write) was a young man, having a redd bearde, a full visage, a chearefull ruddy Complexion like the Germans of whome he discends, and of somewhat a low stature, and mourning then for his dead mother, he was apparrelled in black Freesado. His Court was after the Italian manner, faire for building but solitarye for trayne of Courtiers; yet he was sayd to giue pay to Gentlemen for 200th horses after six Crownes the moneth for each horse, and when these gentlemen vppon occasion iourney with him, they also haue diett in Court, but not otherwise. In his Stable, neare his Pallace in the Citty, I numbred 114 horses (whereof many were Coursers of Naples, the rest of Italian races, and most of his owne races, which are accounted more generous then any other in Italy) and two Camells, beside a like number of horses, Which they said were kept in an other stable for Coaches and other seruices, and a stable without the Citty, wherein were some sixty faire Colts all bredd of Neapolitan horses and Mares with that Dutchye. The Duke had 50 Germans for his guarde, hauing each man 4 Crownes stipend by the moneth, without any diett, except each Eight day when it comes to euery mans Course to waite, vppon which day they haue diett in Court. I was credibly informed that the Duke gaue pay to 500th soldiers in tyme of peace, kept for defence of his Dominion, and that his yearely reuenue amounted to some 350 thowsand Crownes by the yeare, yet that he was greatly in debt. Of tributes exacted by him is to be spoken in the following Eight Chapter of this Booke. This Dukes honor was much scandaled among the Italians, because in his youth while his father liued, he had in following manner killed a Scottish gentleman reported to haue bene indued with extraordinary vertues. This Prince one night walked the streets with his followers but vnknowne, and by ill adventure meeting the said Scottish gentleman well reputed in his fathers Court, took a fancye to trye his valor, and to that end commaunded one of his familiar freinds to assault him with his drawne sword, whome he taking for an enemy, in good earnest resisted valiantly, and at the first encounter hapned to giue him a deadly wounde, wherevppon the Prince much lamented, and the Scottish gentleman knowing him by his voyce, and so humbling himselfe at his feete, with tender of His Rapier the point towards himselfe, the Prince in rage killed him with his owne Weapon.

Inferior Princes.

For the Duke of Vrbine, I passed through some part of his Territory, but did not see his person, or Court, and of the tributes exacted by him I shall speake something in the following Eight Chapter of this Booke.

Of the Neapolitan Princes subiect to the King of Spaine and others not having absolute power, I haue no purpose to write. Passing from Pisa to Lirigi, by chaunce at Masso lying vppon the Confines of Toscany, I did see the Prince of that Towne and small Territory, wherein he hath absolute power, and is of the Family Malaspina being a goodly gentleman of a good stature, comely person, and manly Countenance, with a black pointed bearde. Besides this small Territory, whereof he was absolute Prince, they said he had great Inheritance in the kingdome of Naples vnder the King of Spaine. Here I heard that the Count Stentafiori was absolute Prince of a Territory not farr distant, but I did neither see him nor his Court. These are petty Princes of small power to defend their States, only subsisting by the equall ballance of Italy, and protection from Spaine, or Fraunce, or other States of power, and more specially by the Common ayme of all States in Italy, to preserue it in peace; For as a Crased shipp may be safe in a calme Sea, but lyes open to the waues vppon any storme, so the small States of Italy haue safety in peace, but fewe of them may iustly haue confidence to stand vnshaken vppon troubles of Warr.

CHAP: viii.

Of the Common wealth of Italy in generall and of some of
the greater States thereof in particular touching the
remayning Heades conteyned in the tytle of the first
Chapter.

Tributes in generall.

The Princes of Italy aboue all others in the world impose not
only vppon their Subiects but vppon all strangers passing
through their Territories great and many Tolls, Customes, and
like exactions. All gates of Cittyes and Townes swarme with
searchers, who if the passengers haue any thing that payes
custome search narrowly to finde it, and if they haue nothing,
yet will ransack the smallest things they haue, except they will
giue them some reward. The Cittyes, and Townes and newe
Territoryes of petty Princes, are very frequent, so as a Traueller
passeth in any of them in one dayes iourney, and he cannot
passe a Towne or a bridge, but he shall pay for his person, at
euery bridge two or three Quatrines, at some Gates six at some
Eight Solde of Venice, besides that he payes for his baggage.
He that carryes Jewells or any thing of Gold or siluer or
pretious thing of small weight easy to be hidden, if he conceale
it, and pay not Custome for it till he haue passed a certaine
stone or marke, then the same found by the searchers is
confiscated to the Prince, and if he shewe them to paye
Custome, he runnes no lesse danger of his life by being knowne
to haue such things about him. For any thing almost that
he carryes through Italy, he shall pay asmuch as the thing is
worth. In some places it is vnlawfull to carry a sword, in some
to carry a dagger, and at these Gates men attend to offer their
seruice to carry the Passengers sword to the Inn, whome he
must pay, and these places being frequent, he shall pay the
worth of his sword before he haue passed through Italy, paying
for carrying of it in each Citty at the entring and going out of

the Towne, and many tymes in one dayes iourney.   A poore woman that carryes twelue Eggs to the markett, must giue one at the Gate for Custome, and if she buy a payre of shooes in the Towne, or spice, or any like thing, tribute must be paid going out of the Gate.   If a poore body gett his living by a wheele, to spinn, by Carding or by a Weauers Loome, he must pay yearely tribute to his Prince for licence to vse that trade.   And all Inkeepers and those that sell any thing to eat or drinck, pay so great yearely Tributes to the Prince (as likewise the Poast-masters and those that haue horses to hyre) as they must needs vse great extortion vppon all Passengers, and vppon subiects that haue occasion to vse them, for such licences are sold to them as it were at the outcrye, to him that will giue most for them.

The Tributes in the Popes State.

The Pope is more mylde to his Subiects in this kinde then any other Prince in Italy.   And no doubt the fame of this gentlenes auayled him more then his excommunications to gayne the Peoples harts, when he tooke into his possession the Dukedome of Ferrara, the Dukes whereof had formerly oppressed their Subiects with great exactions; so as all other Princes haue iust cause to feare this Foxes practises, lest he conuert this fame of his gentlenes to their preiudice by like vsurpations.   Yet the Popes themselues lay vppon their Subiects many and heauy exactions, so farr as they make filthy yet great yearely gayne of the Harlotts in the Stewes, who haue for theire Judge the Marshall of the Court Sauella, and he also for himselfe makes no small yearely Rent of them.   As also for gayne they allowe the Jewes a place in Rome for theire habitation, wherein they haue theire Synagoges, which priuiledge they would not permitt to any Christians differing from them in poynts of Religion, and (after the manner of Italyan Princes) suffer the Jewes to grynde the faces of theire subiectes, so they may extorte large tributes from them,

and haue the commaund of theire treasure to vse vpon all
occasions. Besydes the Popes governours and Magistrates sett
ouer theire Provinces and townes, are more often changed then
by any other Prince of Italy, and as hungry flyes sucke more
greedily than those that are full, so these gouernors often
changed must needes be a greater burthen to theire subiects
then if they continued long in office. Of the Papall exactions
by spirituall Power, as Indulgences Pardons and the like, I
haue formerly spocken in the fourth chapter of this booke. I
will only add in generall, that a learned historiographer of
Germany, after theire manner of Computation of Treasure,
writes the yearely Reuenewe of them to haue exceeded one
hundreth Tunns of Gould Guldens, but in oure age to be much
abated by the defection of many Dominions from the Popes
obedience. In the same chapter I haue spocken of exactions by
the Popes temporall power and State, and the yearely Reuenewe
of all his tributes, I will only add that passengers going through
the Papall State, in all his Portes, Frountyer townes, the
Citty of Rome, and all passages where tribuites are frequently
imposed, not only pay Customes for all Marchantdize, but for
every litle Portmanteau to carry daly necessaryes pay one Julio,
yet haue not the same ransacked as in other places.

The tributes in the Dukedome of Florence.

They who will learne the Art to spend treasure sparingly
and to exact it cruelly from theire Subiects, lett them Imitate
the Italian Princes, among whome the Dukes of Florence excell
in both kyndes, of whose frugality I haue formerly spoken, and
now will perticularly sett downe some exactions in that State.
For each measure of land vulgarly called Stoara contayning
60. Perches euery way, the owner payes yearely to the Duke
(if the land be most barren) tenn Julij, if it be firtile thirty
Julij yea more, not only according to the firtelity of the land,
but also vpon any extraordinary increase of the yeare. For an
asses loade vulgarly called Soma of wyne they pay 32. Quatrines,

For a bottle of some three quartes of wyne two Quatrines, For the like measure of oyle three Quatrines, For an asses loade of oyle 4 Julij. For a Barrell of wyne one Julio. For the grynding of a Sacke of Corne 12. Quatrines, and for a note of license to grynde it 6. Creizers (very Monkes and Religious Fryers paying this trybuite for grynding of Corne). The Country people to the age of 60. yeares pay each man for his head a Crowne yearely : For euery beast or any head of Cattle 20. Soldi, and asmuch for euery horse, Asse, or like Beast solde from man to man, how often soeuer the property is altered, but the worth of the beast allters the payment after the rate of one Julio in two Ducates. He that will keepe a shop to sell warres payes at the entrance 50. lire, and yearely one Crowne. The Duke sells all Salt as his owne, and the Country people are bound to carrye it, hauing in that respect the priuiledge to buye a measure theireof for foure Quatrines, which is soulde to others for 12. but they must buye no more then serues theire priuate vse, for if it be knowne they sell any, they are condemned for a tyme to serue in the Gallyes, or in like sorte punished. The Duke Commandes the very Snowe to be gathered and layde vp in the winter, which he sells in the Sommer to be mingled with wyne, and for like vses. Whosoeuer brings the least thing into the Citty to be solde, or Carryes out the least thing bought, payes tribuite at the gate. For Jewells or any thinge of gould or siluer according to the worth they pay a Gross for each Crowne : For a payre of new shooes foure Quatrines. An old woman that hath a Cerchio of eggs, that is 12. eggs to sell, payes two Quatrines, or giues one of the eggs to the officers at the gate. Flesh sold in the markett payes a quatrine the pound that is some iiid. [?iiijd.] of our English mony in the stone, For a liuing hogg solde, they pay to the Duke 4. Julij, one for each foote : And the like trybute the poore people pay for Cherryes, Rootes, and the least thinge they haue to sell, yea a dead body carryed in or out of the Citty to be buryed, payes a Piastro or Crowne to the Duke. And least any fraude should be vsed by those that are poore or crafty, the officers search not

only the Carryage but the very Apparrell of the people, and
sometymes the secrett parts of the body, and there is a place at
each gate with a marke which if any haue passed without
paying of tribuite, those goods are forfeited to the Duke. Yet
they report of many that haue plesantly and coningly deceaved
the Crafty and Crewell searchers. As of an old woman, that
tooke a gold Chayne her master had bought, and foulding it
vnder the Flax of her Distaffe, passed the gate without paying
tribuite. And of an other old woman, who carryed a Gammon
of Bacon to sell, and being demaunded at the gate if shee had
any thinge that payed tribuite, scoffengly yet truely answered
that shee had Vna coscia secca a dry thigh, and they thincking
her to speake of her owne body, with laughter dismissed her
free of tribuite. And of a Country Clowne, who hauing bought
Cherries for which they demaunded tribute, at the Gate, did
rather eat them vpp in their presence, then he would pay ought
for them. And of an other that having bought a Crucifixe of
siluer, for which like things being newe, and vnvsed, tribute
is payd, hung it vpp at the gate, and falling vppon his knees,
mumbled prayers to it, by that vse to saue the tribute; And of a
soldier who having bought a gold Chayne putt it into the hollow
handle of his horsemans speare, so as the Searchers could not
finde it, tho by spyes they knew he bought it. And of a
pleasant Monke, who having bought spice, and sewing it in the
hinder part of the Cusheon, which the Italians vse ouer their
sadles, and being demaunded what he had to pay tribute,
answered scoffingly yet truely, Ho del specie al culo, I haue
spice at my backsyde, and so passed for a rude, or merry Felowe
and paid no Tribute, without danger to forfeit the confessed
spice, if they had after found it. But to omitt Jeasts, I retorne
to the serious purpose. In the dowryes of women to be
marryed, and all bargaynes, the Duke hath seauen (others say
eight) Crownes in euery hundreth Crownes. In hyring of
houses he hath the tenth part of the yearely Rent and a like
Tribute out of the last Wills and Testaments of his subiects.
And one tribute I wish all Princes would imitate and exact the

like, that no man goes to Lawe, but he payes tribute, according
to his cause before he can enter his suite.   When the Duke
foresees a dearth of Corne, he makes search what Corne priuate
men haue, and leaving them as much as will serue their owne
Familyes, he buyes the rest at a reasonable price, and layes it
vpp in the office of Aboundance, as they vulgarly call it, vsing
equalitye towards all, in that he spares no man more then
another, but when Corne growes scant, it is sold to the people
with great gayne.   In like sort to preuent famine, the Duke
buyes sheepe, comonly each yeare three thousand, and more if
need seeme to require, out of Lombardye the only Prouince of
Italy yeilding plenty of grasse to feede Catle, and these sheepe
he distributes amongst the Butchers of his Dominion at such
rates, as howsoeuer he pretend the releife of the publique want,
yet those Butchers thinck themselues most fauoured who haue
fewest of his sheepe allotted to them.   The State of Florence
aboundeth with wyne and flesh for foode, and the Fenns of
Sienna called la maremme yeild such plenty of Corne as from
thence great quantity vseth to be transported for the releife of
neighbors as Lucca, and Genoa, yet often it happens that when
corne beares a good price in Italy, shipps fraught therewith
ariue in the havens of this State, in which Cases priuate
Marchants buy not this Corne according to the Custome with
vs, but the Duke himselfe buyes it, and sells it by small
measures in the markett with good gayne, and with such
priuiledge, as the Dukes corne must be sold before any priuate
man may expose his in the Markett.   And if by any accident
the foresaid Office of Aboundance (as they call it) suffer losse in
buying any prouision, a taxe is allotted vppon euery Family for
repayre of that losse, yea euen vppon those that were no way
releiued by that prouision, In which case I haue seene my host
a poore Inkeeper pay three lire at one taxe, and his brother a
poore Artisan pay halfe asmuch, having had no whitt of the
Corne for which it was imposed.   If an extraordinary Death
happen the Duke hath vsed to make an Edict, that all men shall
haue a quantity of brann mixed with theire meale, and

howsoeuer the very meanest Italians vse to feede of pure
wheaten bread, wherewith and a poore rootte, or apple, they
will make a good meale, so their bread be pure, and so greatly
abhorr this mixture, yet for feare of spyes (neuer wanting) the
richest dare no more breake this Edict then the poorest.
Besides ordinary Tributes, many extraordinary taxes are
imposed vppon diuerse accidents, as when the Duke is maryed,
when his Children are baptised, when his daughters are maryed,
when any bridges are broken by the ouerflowing of the Riuer
Arno, or like accident, and vppon many such casuall events.
Yea the Statua of Duke Cosmo, newly then sett vpp in the
markett place, was erected at the charge of the people, by a
generall taxation.   And in generall, since in all publique
Collections more is gathered comonly then laid out, the Prince
himselfe gaynes by the very mischeifes, and burthens of the
Common Wealth. The Ditches of Cittyes and Townes and
Wast places of highwayes belong to the Duke, and in them he
planted mulbery trees, whereof he sold the leaues for feeding of
silke Woormes with great profitt, no man daring to breake a
leafe from them.   Myselfe in heat of Sommer breaking a small
branche to carry for shade, a gentleman meeting me and
obseruing me thereby to be a stranger, advised me nobly to cast
the bough away before I passed by any house or village, for
otherwise the breaking thereof would cost me many Crownes,
besides imprisonment.   Aboue all other things the Duke makes
excessiue profitt by Innes and victualing howses, which
sometymes he builds and letts the houses at high rates.   Againe
those that haue houses of their owne or hyred, that are fitt to
be made Inns, yet pay excessiuely yearely tribute for license to
keepe them, so as it makes litle difference, whether the house be
publike or priuate, and since he that buyes must needs sell,
the Florentines otherwise courteous to strangers by their
Princes auarice, are forced to oppresse them.   When any Inne
(I meane not the house but the license to keepe an Inne) is to be
lett (for the Custome is to lett them at first for one, and then
for sixe yeares, and those ended againe for one and then for

six yeares, and so euerlastingly in that order) I say when such Inns falling voyd are to be lett, it is done by the Outcrye, a Candle being lighted, where the people are called together, and he that offers most before the Candle is burnt out, shall keepe that Inn during the foresayd tyme, and many tymes Citizens of noble Familyes harken, and beare out poore men in taking these high rented Farmes, to the end themselues may vtter in those Inns more easily at an high rate, the increase of theire owne Wynes, oyle and fruites which they haue to sell. Myselfe for learning of the Language did lodge for some moneths in two Inns, whereof the first was in the high way to Rome, yet in a village, about eight myle distant from Florence, and the Hostesse being an old widow, and paying 23 Crownes yearely to a gentleman for the Rent of her howse, did also pay to the Duke 56 Crownes yearely for license to keepe that Inn, wherein she sold no wyne but such as she fetched from an other man, that had license to sell it. The other was kept by a shooemaker out of the high way to Rome, in a village, whose house was his owne Worth six Crownes by the yeare to be lett, and he paid to the Duke yearely 20 Crownes for license to keepe this Inn and sell wyne, and a Julio and a halfe to exercise his poore trade. For the poorest old woman may not keepe a wheele to spinn, without paying tribute and each weauer payes a Crowne or more yearely to the Duke for his Loome. Most Inns pay the Duke yearely one hundreth or a hundreth Fifty, some few pay fiue hundreth or six hundreth Crownes yearely, as I remember the Inn vppon the Confines of Toscany in the way to the Sea-syde of Liguria paid six hundreth Crownes yearely to the Duke. Whensoeuer the Duke wants mony, he takes a list of his Subiects able to lend it, and diuides the same among them according to their ability giuing them assurance for repayment by assignments out of his Customes, which payments are alwayes duly made to them. The Siennesi are rich in yearely Rents of Lands, but the Florentines having a more barren soyle are rich by arts & traffique. For Sattens they pay to the Duke 50. in the hundreth and the very traffique of Sattens in the

Citty of Florence amounted in one extraordinary yeare, to two millions of gold.   The Reuenues of the Duke were said ordinarily to exceede a Million and a hundreth thousand ducates, others said one million and a halfe.   The very Citty of Florence was said to yeild fiue hundred thousand Ducates.   The Port of Ligorno one hundreth thousand yearely.   The other Portes in generall one hundreth Fifty thousand.   The Tribute of flesh one hundred forty thowsand.   The mynes of salt and of yron, and the Tribute for siluer a like somme.   The Toll of milstones (besyde the State of Sienna) was said to yeild yearely one hundreth sixty thousand Ducates, And the sole Tribute for Inns was said yearely to amount at least to two hundreth thousand Crownes.   Besides that the Duke makes great gayne by the bankes of Exchaunge wherein he hath much mony espetially in Banco de Rizzi whereof himselfe is the Cheife.   If we consider the Continuall peace of Italy wherein the Duke was thought to lay vpp yearely at least halfe a milion of gold, no doubt he must be powerfull in Treasure.   And as I dare boldly say that no Christian Prince euer did or can exact more of his Subiects, so I reade in a late writer that this Duke Ferdinand left to his sonne and successor ten millions of gold in ready mony, and two millions in Jewells.

No Prince of Italy exacts much lesse of his subiects, and for the Dukes of Ferrara of the Family of Este, before that Dukedome fell to the Pope as Lord of the Fee for want of heyres males, I did not obserue more exactions in any place then in the Citty of Ferrara.   Each straunger paid a Gagetta to the Duke at the Gate for his head where the searchers rifeled all parts, Carriages, and the least Portmanteau, to finde out things for which Tribute was to be paid, and if they founde any such thing, as gold Chaynes spoones any thing of gold or siluer (which as I sayd in Italy can neither be hidd without danger, nor shewed without as great daunger of spoyling), nor any new apparrell, or any thing newe or not vsed, so as it may be fitt to be sold, all these things if they had not paid tribute for them, were confiscated to the Duke.   The searcher followed vs to our Inn, there to search the small things we carryed with vs, and for this office of Respect that he did not stay vs and search vs at the gate, he extorted a reward from each one of vs, and those straungers who gaue them not rewards aswell as Dutyes, were sure to be molested by them many wayes, as by keeping their mayles or other Cariage at the gate with them, to be searched at their leysure, in which meane tyme they would not suffer him to take out a shirt to chaunge or any other necessarye for daily vse.   The Dukes territory was small, yet this one Citty lying in the beaten way to Rome, by like exactions yeilded large yearely Reuenues.   The very fishing of Eeles in the lakes of Comaccio where the Riuer Po enters the Sea, or rather ends in standing waters, was said to yeilde to the Duke 150 thousand Crownes Yearely.

The tributes in the state of Venice.

The State of Venice in imitation of the Pope, calling his Rents the Patrimony of St. Peter, doe also call their tributes the Reuenues of St. Marke the protecting Saint of the Citty. Of Stable Rents, not such as are Casuall and gotten by industry, each man payes tenn Crownes to St. Marke in the hundreth.   Each measure of wyne called Botta vulgarly, payes fiue Ducates, and each Secchio of wyne payes tenn Soldi.   Each measure of Corne called Staio vulgarly payes 48 Soldi.   But the shopkeepers pay no such Tributes as are exacted in Florence, exercising their trade freely.   The Magazines of Wyne only in the Citty of Venice, were said yearely to yeild three hundreth thousand Ducates, for those that sell wyne by small measures, paid each man some thousand Crownes for his License, after which rate the Inkeepers also paid for their licenses.   Many houses kept Chambers to be lett, and suppose the house be hyred for some hundreth Crownes the yeare, or being theire owne be valued at so much, they pay halfe the Rent, namely Fifty Crownes to St. Marke.   The very boyes and men wayting in the marketts, like our Porters with basketts to carry home things bought, and vulgarly called Cisterolli, doe pay each moneth Fiftye Soldi each one for his License. In diuerse written relations I finde the generall Reuenue of this State valued at two millions of gold yearely though Monsr. Villamont attributes so much to the Citty of Venice alone. And for seuerall tributes of the State, I finde them thus valued in generall. The wyne yearely at one hundreth sixteene thousand Ducates; The oyle at fower Thousand; Marchandize imported at Thirty thousand, and exported asmuch. Corne at fowerteene: Flesh at seauenteene thousand. The fatt vulgarly Il Grasso, as butter, suett, and the like, Fourteene thousand. The Iron seauen thousand. The fruites foure thousand: The wood six thousand. And for particular Cittyes, these relations record, that Padoa brings yearely into the Treasure of Venice thirteene thousand Ducates. Vicenza thirtye two thousand: Verona nyntye thousand: Brescia (besydes many extraordinary Subsidyes) one hundreth thousand foure hundreth and fyfty: Bergamo fyfty thousand: Vdane twenty fyue thousand: Treuigi foureskore thousand. Not to speake of the Ilandes of Istria, and Dalmatia Cittyes, Cataro and Zara, and other places of small importance, this sufficing for probable coniecture of theire Reuenues, which may satisfye a stranger, who can hardly and needeth not for his owne vse search the perfect knowledge thereof. My selfe retorning from Padoa towardes England, and hauing the testimony of the vniuersity (vulgarly called Matricola) that I was Student thereof was thereby freed from many small payments in that State, as six Soldi demaunded at the Gate of Padoa, and eight Soldi at the gate of Verona, and some Quatrines for the passing of bridges, and the like, which I mention only to shewe that these payments were due to St. Marke only for my person, since I carryed nothing with me but some two or three shirts, and that the same payments being exacted of euery Passenger for his head, in such a beaten waye from Fraunce, Germany and many kingdomes to Rome, must needes amount to a great somm yearely. I haue omitted to speake of the Tribute raysed by

Harlotts, called Cortisane, which must needs be great in that State, neither haue I spoken of extraordinary Tributes, as in tyme of warr, wherein the Tenths for Land, and in like sort the Customes are doubled or trebled, and priuate men not only with Chearefulnes lend, but also giue great sommes of mony and the women haue not spared to giue their Jewells, so as it may be sayd that the publique treasure is neuer poore, so long as priuate men be rich.   Neither haue I spoken of the depost payd by gentlemen when they are admitted capable to beare office, nor of many like Reuenues.   Giue me leaue to add that a late writer hath published in print, that the generall Reuenue of Venice amounts yearely to two millions of gold Crownes. That the Townes yeild yearely eight hundreth thousand Crownes, of which summ Bergamo and Brescia yeild three hundreth thousand; That the Imposts of Venice amount to 700 thousand, wyne alone in the State to 130 thousand, and salt alone to 500 thousand Crownes.

Tributes in the Dukedome of Mantuoa.

The Duke of Mantua maketh no lesse exactions vppon his subiects and all straungers, then other Princes of Italy, but hath one thing singular, that to the preiudice of his subiects he intertaynes the Jewes with greater priuiledges then they haue in other parts of Italy, so as in Mantua they keepe the cheefe shops, and are not easily knowne from Cittizens, carying only a marke in obscure places, as vnder theire Clokes, whereas all Jewes in other parts of Italy ether weare yellow hatts, or haue other notorious markes by which they are very aparently knowne.

Tributes in the Dukedom of Vrbin.

The Reuenues of the Duke of Vrbin were sayd to amount yearely to one hundreth thousand crownes, yet his territory was small, and he thought to be a gentle exactor in comparison of others, wherevpon he was sayd to be much beloued of his subiects. Notwithstanding passing by Senogallia (which towne belongs to the Pope, but it seemed the Dukes territory came to the gate therof, for the Inn without the gate lodging all passengers belonged to the Duke) I say passing by Senogallia and lodging in the Inn without the gate, I vnderstood that the Innkeeper payd yearely 500th Crownes to the Duke of Vrbin, for keeping that Inn, and his being Postmaster, so as I nothing marueiled to be abused in our supper and the hyring of horses, but rather wondred at the auorice of the Italian Princes, who by these immoderate exactions not only oppresse theire subiects, but force them to grinde the Faces of all strangers passing through theire territories.

Tributes in the kingdome of Naples.

The tributes of the kingdome of Naples are no lesse rather more excessiue, for not only marchants pay them, but gentlemen buying silkestockings and like smale thinges, pay tribute, except they were them once, and so likewise for chaynes and Jewells of gold except they be openly worne about the neck or handwrests. And if any haue passed Naples gate without paying tribute and taking a testimony therof, his goods shalbe forfeyted when the Searchers at Sportelle vpon the Frontiers fynde them. Yet all these caterpillers will also extort somthing of guift. And great tributes are payd for horses which cannot goe out of the kingdome without license from Naples, searchers attending at Fondi and other places otherwise to forbid theire passage. Yea the Searchers will not only rifle a strangers portmanteau, but will see what mony he hath in his purse, and those who lett horses & Mules, must haue a pasport for passing of theire beasts. To conclude this point too perticularly handled already. I will only add that the Catholike king of Spayne imitates his holy Father the Pope in the tribute exacted for harlotts, wherof 60. thousand were sayd to be in the Citty of Naples, and of them the poorest payd two Carlini the month, but the proudest and fayrest not only payd much more to the kings treasure, but allso were subiect to many extortions of diuers magistrates sett ouer them. So as the Pope and these Papal Princes seeme to haue learned of the heathen Emperour of Rome, that the smell of gayne is sweete though it come of Dung, who exacting mony of vrine sold, and taxed by his owne sonne for the basenes of the gayne, putt to his nose a peece of mony of that tribute, and another of a sweete Commodity (as spice or the like) and asked him what difference there was betweene the smell of them.

Of the power of Italy in warr generally.

The Princes of Italy placing all the hope of preseruing theire States in the greatnes of theire treasure, not in the loue of theire subiectes, which they loose by the foresayd cruell exactions (vnder which they grone as vnder the bondage of Egipt) and so hold theire faythfulnes suspected, for that cause keepe them from any the least experience in military seruice, or somuch as the vse of the wearing of the sword desyring to haue them as base & fearefull as men may be. And for this Cause in their warrs, they vse auxiliary soldiers, and especially Generalls of other Nations. Yet I confesse that the State of Venice being a free State, vnder the which the people are not so much oppressed as vnder other Princes of Italy, raise part of their foote of their owne Peasants, but the strength thereof is in straungers, as likewise they imploy some gentlemen of the Cittyes subiect to the State to comaund some troopes of men at Armes or Armed horses. But howsoeuer they make gentlemen of Venice Gouernors and Generalls of their Navye, yet they neuer imploy them to commaund their Land forces, having alwayes a Straunger to their Generall. But this they doe, not that they suspect their faith, but lest any gentleman gayning great reputation in Armes, and the loue of the soldiers, should haue power at any tyme to vsurpe vppon the Freedome of their State. Againe I will boldly say that the Italians generally haue so litle Confidence in the hopes of the life to come, and

finde such sweetnes in the possession of their earthly Paradice,
as they care not to hazard Certayne things, for those that they
hold vncertaine, and so howsoeuer they are more proude then
valiant in reuenging priuate wrongs with base advantages,
which pride may also make them braue in warr, when they are
forced to that Course, yet I thinck they are not willingly bold
adventurers of their persons in any action that presents death to
their eyes. And for this Cause in the great warrs of Europe, in
forrayne parts, and particularly in the long Warr of our tyme
betweene England, Fraunce, Spayne, and Netherland, wee
neither reade, nor heare of any great voluntary troopes or bands
of Italians carryed to that seruice with Loue of that profession.
For those few Italians which haue serued in Netherland, were
for the most part Neapolitans, pressed by the king of Spayne,
or banished men, or such whose fortunes permitted them not to
liue in Italy. For the Foote of Italy the Marchians subiect to
the Popes of Rome, are most commended and I know not how
good soldiers they are abroad but surely straungers finde them
at home rude, and feirce towards them. But the woorthy
Historiographer Guiccerdine, being himselfe an Italian
confesseth in the warr of the French king Lewes the twelueth
in Italy, that the Italian foote were base, and litle to be
esteemed, and that the Italian horsemen could not sustayne or
beare the strength and the force of the french horsemen
charging them. And he that reades his Historye, shall finde
in the warr at that tyme, aswell in the kingdome of Naples, as
in the State of Pisa & Dukedome of Milan that the Italian
Troopes and bands deserued small or no prayse, and sometyme
much blame. I will not dispute whether the old Romans
conquered the world by their owne wisdome which they still
retayne, or by the valour of forrayne Legions, made free of the
Citty and so called Romans, or whether the old Romans were
indeed braue soldiers while they beleeued that all men dying
for their country went directly to the Elisian Feildes, rather then
now, when they haue woorse Maximes of Religion, but Historyes
warrant me to say, that after the declining of the Roman

Empire, the barbarous people neuer made inuasion, nor the
Emperors of Germany any expedition with Armyes into Italy,
wherein the Italians did make any braue resistance for life
liberty and goods, but rather did not basely yeilde themselues
to the invading power.   And that in the last age, when Fraunce
and Spaine stroue for the dominion ouer Italy, the Italians euer
subiected themselues to the invading Armye, yea that all the
forces of the States and Princes of Italye combyned and assisted
by the power of Ferdinande king of Arragon were all straungly
beaten by the French alone.   And for the ill successe of the
french in the kingdome of Naples, Guiccardine himselfe
attributes it in no part to the Italians, but altogether to the
Valour of the Spaniards.   About the tyme when I was in Italy,
one of the brothers to the Duke of Florence ledd some Italian
bands of Foote and troopes of horse to assist the Emperor in
Hungarie against the Turkes, but after a yeare they retorned,
having done no memorable seruice.   For the horse of Italy, the
race of the kingdome of Naples is much prised, being vulgarly
called Corsers of their swiftnes, wherein notwithstanding the
Giannetts of Spaine excell them.   And that kingdome also
yeildes strong and great mules.   Otherwise in Lombardy they
vse litle naggs, and comonly Mares for cariage & riding, and
oxen to drawe euen in Coaches; sometymes as in Toscany and
the mountanous vpper parts of Italy, they vse Asses and litle
mules, neither haue any good races of horses, saue that
some few Princes breede a small number of the Race of Naples.
Yet some Princes and especially the State of Venice in tyme
of peace mantayne some troopes of Armed horse, which I haue
seene mustered in very braue equipage, the horses being
well armed and beautifull, and the horsemen attyred in Coates
of blewe Veluett or like Coulor, whereof I shall speake in the
particular discourse following. The Foote Captaynes especially
of the State of Venice, are to be commended that they liue not
luxuriously and prodigally, but content with their pay of
Twentye five Crownes the moneth, liue modestly both for diett
and apparrell, as the Common Soldiers likewise liue of the pay

of some three or fower Crownes the moneth, the Pioners
having only 12 Soldi of Venice by the day. Nether doe the
Captaynes make any extraordinary advantages by their
Companyes, either in deficiency of numbers or in victualls or
Apparrell for them, only Guiccardine writes that the Popes vse
to be much cosened in those kindes.

The nauall power in generall.

For the Nauall power of Italy in generall. The Italians the
old Conquerors of the world, are at this day so effeminate and so
inamored of their Paradice of Italy, as nothinge but desperate
fortune can make them vndertake any voyages by Sea, or Land
(great part of them having neuer seene the villages and Townes
within fiue or tenn myles of their natiue soyle), or any warfare
by Sea, or Land, or any hard Course of life. And as generally
they are reputed not very confident in Gods protection by land,
so they lesse trust him at Sea, thincking that man to haue had
a hart of Oake and brasse who first dared to make furrowes
vppon the waues of the Sea, having nothing but a boarde
betweene him and ougly death. To which purpose they haue a
Prouerbe, Loda il mar', sta su la terra. That is, Praise the
Sea-tyde, on Land abide. So as they seldome proue expert,
neuer bold marriners. And howsoeuer some venture to sayle
along the Coast at home, fewe, or none professe to be marriners
at Sea, having their shipps for the most part (or altogether)
furnished with Comaunders and Common Saylers of the
Greekes, and Ilanders about them. These Greeke Marriners I
haue found by experience to be very superstitious for ominous
tokens of Shipwrack, and they sayling only in the narrow
Mediterranean sea, if once they haue lost the sight of the Loued
shore by any mist vppon the least ill weather, most of them
soone leese the knowledge where they are, and if any storme
arise, they make such a fearefull noyse, and by confusion shew
such ignorance, and want of Courage, as would make a man
afrayd where no feare is. In my Journall of my retorne

from Constantinople & landing at Zante, I haue shewed that
with great wonder I vnderstood a Venetian Shipp of fiue
hundreth Tonnes well armed, to be taken by a fewe small
Frigatts of Turkes, being themselues neither good Seamen, nor
bold soldiers, but only Pyratts hartned to Rapine where they
finde small resistance.   Neither durst any Italian Shipp in that
Port, for feare of these Pyrates goe forth to fetch Corne for
the necessarye foode of the Iland, but were forced to compell an
English Shipp to wast their Corne from Morea into the Port of
Zante.   Likewise I obserued English Shipps going forth from
Venice with Italian Shipps to haue sayled into Syria and
retorned to Venice twice, before the Italian Shipps made one
retorne, whereof two reasons may be giuen, one that the Italians
pay their Marriners by the day, how long soeuer the voyage
lasteth, which makes them vppon the least storme, putt into
harbors, whence only fewe wyndes can bring them out, whereas
the English are payde by the voyage, and so beate out stormes
at Sea, and are ready to take the first wynde any thing
fauourable vnto them.   The other that Italian Shipps are
heauy in sayling, and great of burthen, and the Gouernors &
Mariners not very expert, nor bold, and so are lesse fitt in
that narrow Sea full of Ilands, to beate out stormes at Sea,
whereas the English Shipps are swift in sayling, and light of
burthen, and the marriners excellent both in knowledge and
Courage, and so more fitt to beat out all weathers at Sea.
Insomuch as I haue obserued the Italians with astonishment
and admiration stand vppon the shore beholding an English
Shipp woorke into the harbor with a very slant, and boysterous
gayle of wynde while their Shipps lay abroade and neither
durst nor could come in.   In generall the shipps of Italy
trading in forrayne parts, are of great burthen From fiue
hundreth to twelue hundreth Tonne, and howsoeuer they are
well furnished with great peeces of brasse ordinance; yet in
regard of this greatnes, being slowe to vse their sailes,
and being built large in the Wast and Keele for Capacitye of
Marchandize, they are vnfitt to fight at Sea, howsoeuer they

may serue like Castles to defend a Port or the entrance of a
Riuer lying at Anchor. The lesse Barques seruing to vnlade
these shipps, and for passage vppon the Coasts, are altogether
vnarmed. For in Warr vppon that Calme Sea, they altogether
vse Gallyes, whereof the greatest are called Gallyons, the Midle
Gallies and the least Galliasses and Frigotts. And only the
king of Spaine, at Naples, and in the Hauens of that kingdome
and in the Port of Genoa (as likewise that Citty in the same
Port, and the Venetians in the Port of Venice) may be said able
to arme a Navye of Gallyes: For otherwise the Ports of Italy
are fewe, as Ligorno subiect to the Duke of Florence and Ciuita
Vecchia on the one syde, and Ancona on the other syde vppon
the Sea subiect to the Pope, which Ports also are not open
and secure Rodes for great Shipps, but shutt and fortifyed for
security of Gallyes, and that in no great number. And
howsoeuer the Pope hath some fewe Gallyes, and the Duke of
Florence, and the Knights of Malta, haue likewise some fewe
Gallyes, whereof they arme some part yearely to spoyle the
Turkes vppon that Sea, yet the number of them is so small as
they deserue not to be called a Nauy. More miserable
men cannot be found than those who are condemned to Rowe
chayned in the Gallyes. Some of these for Capitall Crimes are
condemned to this slauerye for life, others guilty of lesse Crimes
are condemned to this seruice for certayne yeares, and some are
so foolish as to sell their liberty for mony to vndergo this
bondage, till the mony be repayd. As at Naples they haue a
stone where vnthrifts play at dice, and the Commaunders of
Gallies are alwayes ready there to lend them mony, who will
take it vppon this slauish Condition, and if they haue ill luck
to leese those fewe Crownes, they are presently carryed into the
Gallyes, and they are chayned, whence they are seldome or
neuer redeemed. For their allowance of victualls being scant,
and the victualers in the Gally giving them Creditt, their debt
monethly increaseth, till it be so great as fewe or none can
fynde freinds to pay it. And this their misery proues more
intollerable by the extreme Cruelty of the Commaunders who

beat them with Cudgells and whipps for slacknes in rowing, and when they fall downe for faintnes they lift them vpp with a Rope, and beat them still to their woorke, yea after the manner of Turkye when they committ any fault, they are terribly beaten with Cudgells vppon the back, the bellye, and the soles of the feete.

The power of the State of Venice in warr.

The State of Venice is more powerfull in warr then any other State, or Prince of Italy.   And this power made them suspected in the last age to affect the subduing of all Italy, where vppon the Pope of that tyme, the Emperor Maximilian, the french King Lewes the twelueth, and Ferdinand the king of Arragon made a league at Cameracum to ioyne all their forces for suppressing the power of this State, which with great Courage defended itselfe against these strong vnited forces, and being beaten by the French alone, yet the wise Senators thereof applyed themselues first to appease the Pope by yeilding to his demaunds, who combined the rest of the league in that great action almost to the fatall ruine of this state.   And the Pope being once satisfyed, by his inconstant leaving of his Confederates, and their mutuall ielousyes among themselues, the Venetians having lost all their dominion on firme land soone recouered the same, excepting the Townes yeilded to the Pope (from whose possession as from Hell there is no redemption) and the Townes of the kingdome of Naples which the King of Arragon had ingaged for mony to the State of Venice, and now during this league had by Armes extorted out of that States possession.   From which tyme the Venetians haue only laboured to preserue their owne, and seeme to haue cast of all proiects to vsurping vppon their neighbors.   The written relations of this State taxe the Nobles (so their gentlemen are called) with want of Courage, whereby they abhorr from any Warr, and more spetially against the Turkes daily prouoking them with many iniuryes, to whose Sultans (or

Emperors) they not only pay yearely tribute for the peaceable possession of some Ilands they hold in the Mediterranean Sea, but also vppon all occasions when the Sultanes are incensed against their State, spare not by large bribes, and like meanes to appease them. And indeed the Gentlemen of Venice are trayned vpp in pleasure and wantonnes, which must needes abase and effeminate their myndes. Besides that this State is not sufficiently furnished with men and more specially with natiue Commaunders and Generalls, nor yet with victualls, to vndertake (of their owne power without assistance) a warr against the Sultane of Turky. This want of Courage, & especially the feare lest any Citizen becoming a great and popular Commaunder in the Warrs, might thereby haue meanes to vsurpe vppon the liberty of their State, seeme to be the Causes that for their Land forces they seldome haue any natiue Comaunders, and alwayes vse a forrayne Generall. Yet we reade that Gentlemen of Venice haue brauely commaunded their Navye euen in cheefe. In tyme of peace, they vse to giue a great yearely stipend to some Prince or great Commaunder to be generall of their land forces in tyme of warr.

The Fortes.

This State hath many and strong Forts well furnished with Artillery, munition and victualls vppon all their Confines being many and dangerous as before I haue shewed.

The horse.

The written Relations of this tyme testifye that in tyme of peace they mantayned in pay 600th men at Armes, or Armed horse, of their owne Subiects being gentlemen of their Territoryes vppon firme Land, each one of these 600th mustering three horses with their Riders all armed, and each one having yearely 120 Ducates, And that they can rayse 1000 or 1500 vppon necessity. They were diuided into twelue

Companyes or Troopes, and made a generall Muster euery Sommer. Two of these Troopes were of the Citty of Paduoa, which myselfe did see mustered making a glorious shewe, the horse being beautifull and well armed, and the horsemen in like sort armed & Wearing Coates of blewe veluett, with great plumes aswell for the men as horse. Of old they also mantayned one thousand light horse, but of late had none such in pay vsing for that purpose the Stradiotti of Dalmatia, whence they say 3000 may be drawne vppon occasion to vse them.

The foote.

They doe not altogether distrust their owne subiects to whome they are (after the manner of Common Wealthes) more milde and gentle in exactions, then the Princes of Italy. So as according to the number of Fyers the Subiects are to mantayne soldiers aswell for land as Sea seruice, and the Captaynes haue the names of all Subiects written for the one, or the other seruice.

They mustered 25 thousand Foote of their Peasants, seruing both in Gallyes and Land Armyes, at least for baser vses, but for foote they generally vse and haue the strength thereof of Grisons and Sweitzers, and to this end some Commaunders among them haue stipends euen in tyme of peace, but in warr each man hath 3 Crownes for 45 dayes while they were imployed, and in cases of necessity they haue giuen each man 5 Crownes the moneth. The Gentlemen of Venice serue freely without pay.

The Nauye.

For their Navall power, in the last preceding generall discourse, I haue sayd that the Italians or rather Greekes vsed by them, are neither expert nor bold Mariners, and that the great shipps are slowe in sayling, and vnfitt for fight at Sea, and that the lesser Barques are vnarmed, and that vppon the Calme Mediterranean Sea, all nauall fights vse to be made with

Gallyes whereof the greatest are called Galeoni the midle
sort Galee and the lesser Galeasses and Fregates. And therein
I spoke of the miserable Gally-slaues. All this spoken in
generall belongs to Venice as a principall part of Italy. The
Venetians haue a lawe that each marchants shipp of 500
Tonnes, must carry in the voyage it maketh, a young
gentleman of Venice, giuing him sixe Crownes stipend by the
moneth, and must bring vpp two boyes of Venice to breede
them Mariners. But this wisdome of their Progenitors hath
bene made vayne by the sluggish disposition of their posterity,
for neither haue the gentlemen any skill thereby in nauigation
or commaunding at Sea, since the young gentlemen chuse
rather to stay at home, so they may haue the stipend and value
of their diett for the voyage, neither are the shipps thereby
furnished with natiue mariners, since (as I formerly sayd) the
Italians in their nature abhorr from that or any like hard
Course of life, tho otherwise they are so proude, as they will
doe any seruice at home rather then basely to begg. They who
serue in the Gallies of Venice, are partly Freemen, as the
Gondelieri or watermen of Venice which for the Tragetto or
passage where they haue priuiledge to plye, or transport, are
bound vppon extraordinary occasions to serue in the Gallyes to
rowe, as likewise the Soldiers are free, aswell the natiue
Peasants aboue mentioned as straungers, and of them that are
free some haue stipend and victualls from this or that Citty
setting them forth, others haue the same from the Treasure of
St. Marke (so they call the Exchequer) as the Pope calles all
he hath St. Peters, and at Genoa the publique Treasure is called
the treasure of St. George (their protecting Saint). Others
that serue in the Gallyes are slaues, vppon Crimes condemned
to the Gallyes for life or certaine yeares, and St. Marke giues
them raggs to couer their shame, and victualls in scant
measure, but the victualer giues them Creditt that are
condemned for yeares, by which growing debt they are made
perpetuall slaues, and both sorts of Condemned slaues are
chayned by the legg to the place where they rowe, which their

Gouernor vnlocks at one end when he sends them forth for fresh water or wood bearing still their Chaynes on their leggs. The Gallyes are commonly called after the names of their Cheefe Gouernor. Myselfe did enter one of the Gallyes, and the Castle in the Prowe was some twelue of my paces, and the bodye with the Poope some fifty of my paces long, and the master commaunded from the Castle to the great mast, as the Comito (or mate) commaunds the rest. In the poope satt the cheefe Gouernor, vnder hoopes couered with a fayre Cloath, and beyond the sterne was a litle Gallery, and vnder the deck his Cabbin, and aboue the poope hung the cheefe banner of St. Marke, the Gally being grauen on all sydes with white lyons for the image of St. Marke. The Gally bore fower great peices in the Castle (where the Trompetters sounde) and Thirty more on the sydes, and in the poope twelue whereof two great lay aboue directly layd out vppon the sterne, and two of like greatnes vnder them, and two of like greatnes some 22 spanns long were turned towards the Gallye to shoote sydewayes, the other were lesse, but all of brasse.

The Gallye had 25 oares on each syde, and seauen men to rowe each oare, and when they are in Port two sleepe vppon the benche where they vse to sett, two in the place which is vnder their thighes, and two where they setle their feete, when they rowe, and the seauenth slept vppon the Oare, and vppon a litle boarde betweene each Oare three soldiers vsed to sleepe. So as their being in the Gallye is nothing commodious, but straight, vneasy, and subiect to contagion. The State or Citty of Venice continually vsed to arme Fifty Gallyes, whereof 25 were called of the Schooles or Companyes of Arts, arming and paying them, and 25 Palatines, Armed and payd by St. Marke in which the foresaid Watermen are bound to serue when they goe forth. In each Gallye the Cheefe Commaunder is a gentleman of Venice, and the next Commaund is likewise committed to two gentlemen, and they are called Sopracomiti as aboue the mate, and they which commaund in the Palatine Gallies are of greater estimation then the other. And I finde in written Relations, that these Commaunders haue each of them 1600 Crownes yearely stipend, for which it is expected from them, they should giue some releife to the Soldiers, and specially to the slaues, having a slender diet allowed, and so being forced to runn in the Victualers debt. They write of twelue Gallies armed by subiect Cittyes of the firme land towards the Sea Coast. This Navye they are forced to arme against the Turkish Pyrates vsing to spoyle their Shipps in the tyme of peace, and in Winter tyme, it commonly lyes in the haven of Corfu having a strong Fort, and sometymes in the havens of Candia. And hereof some five Gallyes, and some small Barques armed, lye vppon the Gulfe of Venice to purge the same of Pyrates, more specially the Vscocchi, who liuing on the Coast of Dalmatia in Signi vppon the Confines of the Empire, Turkey, and the State of Venice, and being Christians, yet liue as outlawes, neither subiect to the Turkes nor to any Christian Prince, and robb all men especially the Italian Shipps at Sea.

In the Citty of Venice, they haue a fayre and large Arcenal compassed with walls, wherein they keepe all munitions for Warr, and haue a secure Station for their Gallyes, where likewise they build their shipps and Gallyes, to which purpose they haue much timber on the Sea coast of their dominion. The walles are some three myles Compasse, and the officers shewe the same Courteously to straungers. The Maestranza consists of some 2,200 woorkemen, weekely paid by St. Marke, whereof 300 are expert men in building of Shipps and Gallyes. They shewed me fower vpper Chambers, wherein Sayles were made and layd vpp, and therein some 20 or 30 woorke continually, and each of them hath a portion of wyne, Bisquitt and Soldi by the day. In fower low roomes are layd the Cordage and Cables sufficient to furnish more then 300 Gallyes, besides an infinite number of Oares, each woorth fiue ducates, and Costing the State more then fower Ducates. They shewed mee five Magasines vppon one syde. In the first were great peeces of Artillery, disposed in 24 Rowes. In the second were peeces

for 50 Gallyes, besides 150 peeces, some greater, some lesser.
In the third were great peeces for five great Gallyes, Forty for
each one, besides 250 other ordinary peeces. In the fourth
vppon the right hand were 72 small peeces for the Feilde, and
vppon the left hand 356 peeces of battery and some 100th
Instruments called Trombi for fyre woorkes. In the fifth were
laid vpp such peeces, as at diuerse tymes were taken from the
Turkes, whereof many had bene and were daily melted and newe
cast. They told me they had in all some 2000 great peeces,
the bulletts whereof were some 70, some 100, some 200, some
300 pounds weight, and myselfe did see one great peece of
12400 poundes, and the Bullett 120 pounds. In diuerse other
roomes they layed musketts and all Armes for Soldiers at Sea.
They shewed me many Gallyes newe built, and some 100th old,
but strong, lying at Anchor, and together with the Navye they
haue alwayes abroad, this State can Arme 1200th, other say
1300th Gallies, and of late in tenn dayes they had armed 30
great Gallyes ready for a Seafight; Besides that they haue many
litle Barques and fregates. They shewed me a litle Gallye called
Bucentoro because it beareth 200th men D. by corruption of
speach being changed into B. and therein I had seene the Duke
with the Senators goe forth in pompe especially at Whitsontyde
when the Duke vseth to marry the Sea by casting a Ring into
it. Vppon this Gally is a Chamber some 38 of my paces long,
which is all guilded and couered with a rich Cloath when the
Duke and Senators goe forth in it, and vnder the Chamber sett
150 mariners to Rowe it, and it is then hung with many
banners taken from the Turkes, and the image of Justice is
grauen at the Prowe.

The Duke of Mantuoa hath the like and so called, to rowe
for pleasure, and for iourneys vppon the Riuer Po. The keele
thereof is flatt bottomed, and the Prowe and sterne are voyde
for mariners to rowe, only the sterne is couered as in Gallyes,
ouer the rest of the Gally is a litle house contayning fower
Chambers belowe, the one of 15 paces the second of 8, the other
two each 5 paces, and aboue them a gallery some 40 paces long,

having stayres at each end to ascend it, and all furnished round about with seates.

The Arcenall of Venice hath moreouer many roomes furnished with all munitions, Armes and necessaryes for an Armye at land, sufficient for 70 thousand Foote, and 2000 horse, Besides many Armes now growne out of vse, and layd vpp apart from the rest at the gate of the Armorye. To conclude they haue aboundance of all necessaryes for warr by Land and Sea, so that howsoeuer this State wants victualls for an Army, and numbers of men answerable to the furniture, and haue the defect to vse straungers for Soldiers, and euen for their Generalls by land; yet since they want not Treasure the sinewe of Warr, and the Sea is open to bring victualls which is commaunded by their Navye, and they haue orderly Officers appointed in peace and warr, and euer carefull to prouide victualls, and since the straungers are so duely paid by them, as they haue no cause to mutinye or be discontented, no doubt this State were able to vndertake and preuaile in any great attempt in Italy and vppon their neighbors at Sea, had they not the vast power of the Turkish Empire lying heauy on their shoulders.

The power of the Duke of Florence in warr.

The Duke of Florence vsed to giue large yearely stipends euen in tyme of peace, to forraine Princes and noblemen (I meane Italians but not borne vnder his Dominion) to some 1500 to some 2000 or 3000 Crownes according to their quality, that he might ingage them to his seruice in tyme of Warr. They said the Duke had some 150 peeces of Artillery in the Castle of Florence with a due proportion of powder match and bulletts. And to the same Castle, as also into the strong Cittyes, they sayd the Duke vsed yearely to haue brought and layd vpp all the Corne and victualls of his Territoryes, aswell ordinarily thereby to releiue and serue the necessityes of the Countrye and villages as in tyme of warr to mantayne soldiers.

So as for that reason, and because his Territory is all compassed with high mountaynes except the part that lyeth towardes the Sea, and towardes Rome, an Army of enemyes entring the same, can fynde no victualls in the open Country, if the number were great, and so would either be driuen out with ease, or doe litle harme, if the number were small. Only because the Popes Territories are plentifull in victualls whereby they are able, aswell to furnish the Dukes subiects therewith as to detayne it from them and releiue their enemyes, for this and many other reasons before alledged, the Dukes neuer faile by all meanes to keepe the Popes and Cardinalls fauour. Againe the Duke vsed to trayne his subiects of diuerse Townes and Territories (but not the Florentines, for suspition of Revolt), and of these he was sayd to haue inrolled some 35 thousand Foote, some 100th men at Armes or horse armed (having seauen Crownes the moneth pay), and some 400th light horse, having each man three Crownes the moneth, besides that in tyme of Warr, the horsmen haue a proportion of Victualls allowed them. All these haue many immunityes and priuiledges, as to weare swords, not only abroad, but euen in the Citty of Florence, and to be free from imprisonment for debt (which doth not a litle increase the number of them), and diuerse like. And all these may be drawne to Florence in eight dayes, as they say, but the Territory is of so small Circuite, as me thinkes they might be drawne thether in much shorter tyme. In tyme of peace, the Duke sometymes vsed these men to keepe watche vppon the Sea Coast for feare of African Pyratts, whome the Duke yearely prouoked by the Gallyes he sett out to spoyle the Turkes. The Duke hath a Commodious hauen at Ligorno a Citty newly built and fortifyed, but the Florentines haue no Traffick at Sea, but haue their goods exported by forraine marchants, who likewise bring them victualls, and other necessaryes, and the Duke made much of the Captaynes and owners of these shipps espetially bringing victualls, whereof he made no small profitt. He had no league with the Turkes, but yearely sent out Gallies to spoyle them at Sea, and euen in their hauens, and by landing sometymes on their Coast. To which end there was an Arcenall in the Citty of Pisa for building and keeping of Gallyes, and munitions to furnish them, and tymber and hempe.

They said that Duke Francis mantayned 12 gallies, but this Duke Ferdinand at this tyme whereof I write, had only seuen, whereof he vsed to arme euery sommer three or fower to ioyne with the knights of Malta, in spoyling the Turkes. But some write that now the present Duke hath two Gallions, twelue gallies, and five galliaces. And for the reputation of this Navall power, Duke Cosmo instituted an order of Knights of St. Stephen, who haue their residence in the Citty of Pisa, where I said the Duke hath his Arcenall, and that Duke obteyned priuiledges for this Order of Pope Pius the Fifth, namely to haue each man two hundreth Crownes yearly pention of ecclesiasticall benefices, yet so as none of them can haue a Commendum or beare any office in the Gallies, till he haue serued three yeares therein, and likewise priuiledge or freedome to haue wiues (as Relations tstifye, tho contrary to all other military orders that I remember). Of this Order Duke Cosmo was himselfe cheife master, in which title his sonne succeeded him, as other Dukes since that tyme. Lastly the Duke was serued for Marriners, by Greekes, Ilanders of Corsica, and french men.

Of Genoa for warr.

The State of Genoa is gouerned (as I sayd) by the gentlemen, and of that body of the Nobility (So they, the Germans and French call the Gentrye) forty Captaynes are yearely chosen and changed, who commaund each a Company of one hundreth Citizens, and these 4000 soldiers the Cittye vseth for defence in tymes of vprore, or other danger, to keepe, watch, and to guarde the State. And these 40 Captaynes, are attyred in veluett Coates, the honorable habitt of the Senators, and so attend the Duke, and the Gouernors, when they come out of the publike

Pallace. Besides the rest of the Citizens, and the Inhabitants of the Territory, from 20 to 60 yeares of age, are inrolled vnder other Captaynes to serue vppon occasion for defence of the Country. Also the State in tyme of peace giues an honorable pay to a Generall of their Army, which place is giuen by them to some Citizen most eminent in military experience, as to the D'Auriæ, Spinolæ or the like. The Port of Genoa is a secure Station for Gallyes, and Commodious to build them, being large, and Compassed with a wall, and having a Mola or banck for defence, reaching into the Sea, most fayre, and some 600th of my paces in length. And for this harbors sake the Dukes of Milan, and after them the Kings of Fraunce & Spaine contending for that Dukedome, haue much laboured to haue that Citty in subiection, or in some sort at their Comaund. This Citty of old, and till after the fall of the Christian Empire in Constantinople, was famous in Nauall power. At this day it hath good shipps for traffique and a number of armed Gallies sufficient to defend their liberty, at lest from any sodeine attempt. But the king of Spaine for the reasons aboue mentioned is much respected of the Senators, and hath free vse of the Port for his Gallies. Myself did enter one of the cheefe Gallies of Genoa called la Reale, fayre, and strongly built, being some 75 of my paces in length, and having 400 Mariners to rowe it. Their shipps beare St. George (the English Tutelar Saint) in their flaggs.

Of inferior Princes for warr.

For the Duke of Mantua I formerly sayd that he mantayned 500 soldiers to defend his State, and keepe his Forts, and as I passed by Senogallia, I heard that the Duke of Vrbin then trayned some 1200 Foote of his owne subiects. But it were superfluous to speake particularly of the inferior Princes, since all the power of Italy is in the States of the Pope, the King of Spaine, the Venetians, and the Dukes of Florence, since the Dukedome of Ferrara is fallen into the Popes hands.

The difference of degrees in generall for the Common wealth.

In generall all Italians desyre to liue of their owne and generously thinck nothing more abiect then to depend vppon others for meate or any mantenance.   They which are not absolute Lordes are litle esteemed among them.   Yet the Familyes of Colonna and Vrsini being Princes subiect to the Pope were reputed then to haue great Reuenues and power, and were much esteemed as braue Captaines, by the Princes and States of Italy.   The Cardinall Colonna alone was said to haue 300 Townes and villages in the Territory of Rome, besides great inheritance in the kingdome of Naples.   And the Vrsini were sayd to haue some 100 Townes and villages vnder the Pope, besides some inheritance vnder the king of Spaine in the kingdome of Naples.   Myselfe at Sienna did see a Countesse passe the streets attended with poore maydes not any one gentlewoman, litle or nothing respected by those that mett her, and as litle in the Church, where she could hardly gett a seate. I should first haue spoken of the Clergie, Cardinalls and Bishopps, whereof are no lesse proude in their degree then the Pope, and the Cardinalls haue great Reuenues, but the ordinary Bishopps, howsoeuer they be infinite number (the Popes for voyces in Councells having made many Italian Bishopps, so as euery small towne is a small Bishopprick) yet our Bishopps in England haue much greater reuenues yearely then most of them.   In all Italy I neuer heard of any Barron, only in reproch they call Barrons such as begg and keepe dicing houses. They haue no such degree of Knights as we haue, nor any military orders of Knighthood in Italy except that of St. Stephen which I haue said to be instituted by Cosmo Duke of Florence to commaund his Gallyes armed to spoyle the Turkes. For the Nobility, whereas we call our Lords Noblemen, and the inferior Nobility Generosi, that is Gentlemen, the Germans and many forraine nations giue the title of Generosi to Princes and Lords, and call the gentlemen Nobles.   In Italy the Gentlemen of Venice in singular pride wilbe called Nobles, whereas the rich ancient Familyes of Florence, and other Italians are called Gentilhuomini Gentlemen. In generall the Italian Gentrie vseth litle, or no pride in diett, or apparrell, and disdayne not to be Marchants, yea in Florence and other Cittyes to be weauers of silke, and since the riches of Italy lye therein, by this gayne and generall frugality the gentlemen haue much Treasure in Jewells, ready mony, and rich household stuffe, and haue all pleasant Gardens, with carued fountaynes of stone, and stately Pallaces, the Chymneis whereof are litle anoyed with smoke. The husbandmen and Country people liue poorely and basely, whome the Italians vse and hyre like oxen and Asses for their Woorke, and at the yeares end turne them out of dores, not giuing them Leases or accounting them seruants belonging to the Family, as we vse them. Thus oppressed and after haruesttyme commonly turned out of seruice, they neuer grow rich, nor study to advance their masters profitt further then themselues prouide for it, and hate their masters for exactions, so as whiles I was in the State of Florence, a gentlewoman being a Widowe was found killed by one of her husbandmen. The Landlords take no rent of them, but a proportion of Corne and all things they haue, euen of their very Chickens, and Eggs, in such hard measure, as they haue not to eate or Cloth themselues in any convenient sort.

Degrees of Familyes in generall.

Husbands take straunge liberty in the vse of Courtezans (so their Harlotts are called) who liue a merry life courted and Feasted at home by their Louers, and honoured by all men with respectfull salutations, when they pass the streets so long as they are yong, and sound. I say straunge liberty to all forreinors but so generally vsed in Italye as no man doth otherwise; neither doe the wiues marry with any hope to enioy their husbands alone, but are content if they may haue the tythe of their loue. They marrye vpon agreement of Parents without having seene one an other, and the husband takes a

noble wife only with purpose to haue Children by her litle
caring that her person may content him, since he is free with
strange women to satisfy his desyres which are Comonly in high
degrees of wantonnes, while the poore wife sitts alone at home,
locked vpp and kept by old women, not having liberty to looke
out of the windowe, especially if it be towards the streete. And
if they goe to Church which liberty is rarely graunted, their
faces are couered with a vaile and they are attended with the
old women their keepers. Yea many are so cruell that they
keepe them in awe with beating, and if the husband bring home
a Courtezan (which he doe not generally having libertye inough
abroad) the wife dares not in word or deede shewe dislike. Yet
by corruption of the old wemen, and by any occasion of having
Conuersation, though it be with meane men, this strict keeping
makes them thinck it simplicitye not to take the reuenge their
husbands most feare, euen with hazard of their honors and liues.
And mariage is reputed such a yoke as brothers living with
goods in Common (whereof I shall speake in the lawes of
inheritance) thinck themselues much bound to that brother who
will marry for procreation and leaue them free, in which Case
they will mantayne him and his wife with their goods in
Common and much respect her and be as ielous of her honor
as they would be of their owne wiues. In like sort they keepe
the Chastity of their daughters and sisters at home, or for more
safety putt them into Nunneries to be kept either till they may
be perswaded to become Nunnes, or at ripe yeares may be taken
out and maryed. To the sonnes and kinsmen vnder their charge
they giue great liberty and good maintenance. And myselfe
heard two gentlemen, who asked why they were so indulgent,
the one to his sonne, the other to his Kinsman of ripe yeares
and challenging right to the inheritance he enioyed, did answer
playnely for their particular, that if they should doe otherwise,
they feared practising of their Deathes, as themselues should
doe in like Case. I haue not obserued Italians to keepe
menseruants in their houses, but to be serued altogether by
Women except in Courts of Princes, where they dyett and liue

apart from the women. For as they are viciously frugall in
housekeeping, so they dare not trust men seruants with their
wiues and daughters. Neither haue I obserued that the
Italians make it an ordinary Course of life to serue in other
mens Familyes.

Of Venice in perticular.

In my Journall describing Venice I haue sayd that they
numbred 3000 Familyes of Gentlemen in that one Citty, and
among the famous men of former ages, I haue named the
Justiniani, Contarini, Grimani, Morosyni, Dandoli, Barbarigi
and others.

The Gentlemen of Venice in singularity wilbe called
Nobles, and appropriate to themselues the title of Clarissimo,
for which and their generall insolencye, they are reproued and
condemned, not only by strangers (who may as safely stumble
vppon a Bull as vppon one of these gentlemen, so as when one
of them passed by, I haue heard men say Guarda il toro, Looke,
or take heed to the Bull, as they crye when a Bull is bayted
in the streets) but also by other Italian gentlemen who by
writings in the vulgar tongue taxe them of vnsupportable pride
insomuch as (to vse their owne words) they dreame themselues
to be Dukes and Marquises, while they are indeed couetous,
miserable, breakers of faith & hatefull to all men for their
pride, vayne glory and ambition, yea in the very Citty they
haue a Prouerb D'vna pietra bianca d'vn Nobile Venetiano,
et d'vna Cortigiana ch' abbia madre Dio ci guarda, from a
white stone (because it is slipperie) from a gentleman of Venice
(for their pride) from a Cortisan that hath a mother (to teach
her to spoile her louers), God deliuer vs. No doubt the
Senators are most graue iust reverent and comely persons, and
generally they are all rich, and many abound in Treasure.
In Poduoa, Il signor Pio obici, was sayd to haue 12000 Crownes
yearely Rent, and I was credibly informed that in Brescia

diuerse gentlemen had from tenn to thirty thousand Crownes
yearely Rent.   And the estates of the Gentlemen of Venice
must in all probabilitye be much greater.

Of Florence in Particular.

The Courtesye of the Florentine Gentlemen was by all men
highly praysed at my being in Italy.   Of old in tyme of their
freedome they had powerfull Familyes, then diuided into
factions.   We read of the Agli, Ariqui, Adimati, Grandonici,
Ardinghelli, Bardi, Gualterosi, Importuni, Boun-del-monti,
Sucardetti, Mozzicerchi, Caualcanti, Merli, Pulci, Donati, Fresco-
baldi, Tebaldi, and other powerfull Familyes of the Guelphes
faction, and the Ammidei Giuochi, Amirci Galli, Agolauri,
Abbati, Tudi, Vberti Bruneldeschi, Vbriacchi, Capiardi,
Lamberti, Capriarni, Castigliani, Malespini, Capon Sacchi,
Palermini, Scolari, and others of the Gibelline faction.   These
deadly hated each other, yet at last agreed with singular vnity to
defend the liberty of their free State against the house of Medici
invading it, but Pope Clement the seauenth of the house of
Medici preuailed against them not without the slaughter of
many and totall ruine of diuerse familyes before he could make
his kinsmen absolute Dukes.   So as at this day the number and
riches of the gentry are much decreased, but they which now
liue being borne vnder absolute Dukes, with ease beare that
yoke, hauing not theire Progenitors loue of lost liberty, nor
theire feruent desyre to recover it.   And as all gentlemen of
Italy so those of old and to this day exercyse Marchandice and
the trade of weaving silkes, though not laboring with theire
owne handes therein.

Of the gentlemen of Genoa.

The Genoesi haue euer beene much deuided in factions but
howsoeuer one faction had the name of Nobles the other of
popullar, yet no doubt the latter was so called because the people
tooke parte with them, being otherwise as noble as the other.
For among them some are called Marquises some Earles some

Vice Royes, not that they are such indeede, but that vpon diuers
occasions such names haue beene vulgarly giuen them.   And in
the most Factious Citty of Pistoia (now subiect to the Dukes of
Florence who lately forbad vpon payne of death the wearing of
Roses or like signes of Faction) wee reade that the sonne of the
Chancelor and the sonne of Signor Petruccio being both kinsmen of one Family, when contending together the sonne of
the Chancelor gaue a blow on the eare to the other, the Chancelor
sent his sonne to Petruccio to craue pardon on his knees, who
cruelly cutt of his right hand, wherevppon all the Citty was
diuided into a long lasting faction, and because the Chancelors
wife was named Bianca that faction tooke the name of Bianchi
that is the white, and the other tooke the name of Neri that is
the Black.   In Genoa they are Gentlemen who haue their names
written in the booke of Ciuilta (Civilitye) and some of them
are saluted with the titles of Marquis and others aboue-named
and are stiled illustrious by the Genoesi howsoeuer they exercise
marchandise and cannot challenge those titles abroad.   No man
of the highest degree in Genoa disdayneth to be a marchant and
to haue mony at vse vppon the bankes of Exchange.   And many
of them were sayd to haue at home and in Spaine Fifty thousand Crownes.   The Marquis of Spinola was said to haue one
hundredth thirty six thousand Crownes yearely Reuenue.   Howsoeuer the Fuggari of Augspurg in Germany are famous for
their great Treasure, no doubt Genoa hath a farr greater masse
of ready mony then any other Citty of the world wherein many
Citizens were sayd by expert men to haue 500 thousand ducates,
and some one or two to haue a Milion in ready mony, and that
it was common among them for Marchants to haue Cabbines of
5 foote long, parted into diuerse boxes, all filled and piled vpp
with diuerse Coynes of Gold.

Of Italian lawes in generall.

Sigonius shewes that when the Westerne Empire was
reuiued, the Italians chose whether they would liue after the
Roman or Salique lawe.   Now Italy is gouerned generally by

the Ciuill lawe of the old Emperors, and the Cannon lawes of
the Pope, and diuerse municipall lawes of seuerall States and
Cittyes.   Before I speake of the iustice and iudgments, I will
in a word sett downe some Common lawes of Inheritance.

In the seuerall Common Wealths of Italy the father dying
intestate, the brothers diuide his mouable and vnmouable
goods, yet in the kingdome of Naples and in the Fees of
absolute Princes the eldest brother succeeds and the Care to
mantayne their sisters, and to dispose them in mariage lyes
vppon the brothers Inheritance, the magistrate of Pupills inter-
posing his authority, and forcing them to equity if need be.
And Comonly these young virgins are putt into Nunneries for
education, where they are by all Cunning intisements allured
to become Nunns by vowe, in which Case the brothers saue
their Dowrye, but if they will not take that profession vppon
them, the brothers and the said Magistrates may take them out
of the Cloisters when they will, or when they are to be disposed
in mariage.   Sonnes may not be disinherited but for iust and
lawfull causes, as for striking their Parents, for not having
releiued them in any distresse or like Crimes, I meane for lands
discending from their Ancestors, yet euen for those it is in the
fathers power to charge them with legacyes, and the bestowing
of such goods as the father hath gotten is altogether in his
power.   A notary, and fower legall witnesses are required in a
mans last Will, or els they must be sealed in a monasterye, in
which Case the Fryers vppon payne of Excommunication must
keepe the same secrett.   The Sonne who in tyme of his fathers
life. wilbe emancipated (that is made free from the Fathers
Family to liue of himselfe) may challeng his portion of his
Fathers goods, and after that tyme all that he getts by his owne
industry is proper to himselfe, but while he remaynes in the
Family vnder his Father all the chilldren and the Father haue
equall share in all goods gotten by any of them, as all are lyable
to the debts of any of them for theire goods.   And for this
cause many Fathers emancipate prodigall Children, that they
may not be lyable to pay any debts they may after contract.

Neuer did I obserue brothers to liue in such vnity as in Italy, so as the Father being dead, many of them ordinaryly liue in one house together, not deuiding theire patrimony, but hauing all goods in common or as they call it in brotherhood (vulgarly fratellanza) and perswading one to mary for procreation, the rest liuing vnmarryed, and much respecting theire brothers wife and her honour as theire owne. And while they liue in this sorte, if any one spend wastfully, or giue his daughters in marryage, all is supplyed of the common charge, and if at any tyme after by consent, or by desyre of any one to leaue that course and liue of his owne, they will deuide theire patrimony, that brother shall not haue a penny lesse then any of the rest for hauing formerly spent more. And it is strange but most true, that the Italians in common practise make the inheritance of mony as firme and stable to the heyres as of land. As the sayd brothers by theire Fathers will or owne consent liuing in fratellanza, haue only in theire owne priuate power to dispose of the yearely increase of the mony (by what meanes soeuer), and the Creditours of any of the brothers growing in debt, haue right to recover that his part of increase, but the principall or stock is common to all, so as any one of them cannot deminish it, nether can any priuate Creditors sease therevpon, for any one brothers debt or bargayne, but only for the Common debt or contract of all the brothers ioyntly. If any mans wife dy without children, the husband keepes halfe her dowry, and restores the other halfe to her next kindred, but if shee haue children he retaynes all her portion for them. If a husband dye, his widowe leaues his Family, and taking her portion retornes to her owne kindred, whether her portion were in land or mony and mouable goods, and if she marry agayne, the second husband hath that portion, saue that the Magistrate of the Pupills interposeth his authority for due respect to be had of her children by the first husband when shee marryeth agayne, as likewise when shee dyes a widow in the house of her next kinsman.

Of Justice in generall.

The Italyans in generall are most strict in the courses of Justice, without which care they could not possiblie keepe in due order and awe the exorbitant dispositions of that nation, and the discontented myndes of theire subiects. Yet because only the Sergiants and such ministers of Justice are bound to apprehend Malefactours, or at least will doe that office (which they repute a shame and reproch), and because the absolute Principalities are very many and of little circuite, the malefactors may easily flye out of the confines, where in respect of mutuall ielosies betweene the Princes, and of theire booty in parte giuen to those who should prosecute them, they finde safe retrayt. In the meane tyme where the Fact was donne, they are prescribed and by publike Proclamations made knowne to be banished men vulgarly called Banditi. And where the ruine is haynous besydes the bannishment rewardes are sett vpon theire heades to him that shall kill them or bring them in to the tryall of Justice, yea to theire fellow banished men not only those rewardes but releases of theire owne banishments are promised by the word of the State vpon that condition, which proclamation vpon the head is vulgarly called Bando della Testa, These banished men are only found vpon confines hauing mountaynes and espetiall woods which are very rare in Italy. But because the confines of Naples kingdome vpon the State of Rome are both mountanous and also woody, they abound more spetially there, and (as in all places) committ robberies and murthers with strang examples of cruelty. For which cause Pope Sixtus Quintus first by the sayd Bando delle Teste : that is rewardes and impunityes and releases to like malefactors, sett vpon the heades of the most wicked outlawes, did free in great part those confines and all passengers from those great dangers, yet to this day the carriour of Rome or Naples dares not passe weekely from either Citty without a guarde of soldiers appointed for the guard of them, and all strangers and Passengers vsing to passe in their Company with

their loaded mules. And the very weeke before I passed that
way, I remember a gentleman banished by Pope Clement the
eight (if I be not deceiued the Nephewe of the Cardinall of
Caieta) hearing that one of the Popes minions passed that way,
did assault the Carryer of Rome, his guarde and all his
Company, with hope to take him prisoner, whereby he thought
to make his owne peace vppon good Conditions, but vnderstanding vppon the first assault that the said minion was escaped
to the next towne, he presently did withdrawe himselfe and his
men, without offering any more violence to the Company. And
perhapps these Outlawes fynde more safe being in those parts,
by the wickednes of the people commonly incident to all
borderers, and more spetially proper to the Inhabitants thereof.
But these rewards, and impunityes promised to outlawes for
bringing in the heads or persons of other outlawes hath broken
their fraternity. So as hauing found that their owne Consorts
haue sometymes betrayed others to capitall Judgment or themselues killed them, they are so ielous one of an other, and so
affrighted with the horror of their owne Consciences, as they
both eat and sleep armed, and vppon the least noyse or shaking
of a leafe, haue their hands vppon their Armes, ready to
defend themselues from assault. They haue many other
meanes also to redeeme themselues from banishment, as for
murthers by intercession of freinds at home, vppon agreement
made with the next freinds of the party murthered. And
myselfe at Loretto did see some of these outlawes ready to passe
to Sea towards Hungary, who looked like Cutthroats, and were
armed (as the Italians prouerbially say) Dal capo fin' al buco
del culo, from the head to the very backsyde, and these all had
their pardons vppon Condition to serue the Emperor in
Hungarie two yeares against the Turkes. But in Crimes
extraordinarily haynous, the Princes and States are so seuere,
as in their publique Edict of banishment, besides rewards sett
vppon their heads, great punishments and Fynes according to
the qualityes of offence and person are denounced against them
who at home shall make petition or vse other meanes at any

tyme to haue them restored to their Countryes Lands and livings.

Of Judgments in generall.

No doubt all Italy is more free from Robberies and more happy in trades and Arts by the nature of that nation, abhorring from living vppon others, and from not having meanes to liue in some free sort, by their owne industry, as likewise by the Comendable Course to condemne vagrant, idle and wicked persons to rowe in their Gallies. They haue no single Combatts, which are forbidden by the Councell of Trent, to which the Italians yeild obedience, because it is consonant to their disposition; For indeed you shall seldome or neuer heare of any mans slaughter vppon heat of bloud, but if any man be killed, it is commonly premeditated murther, vppon all advantages of Armes and otherwise, as many armed sodenly assayling one vnarmed, whether it be by theeues in woods or by murtherers in Cittyes. Of which bloudy act some are knowne to make profession to be hyred therevnto, and many are knowne to be likely men for that imployment, so that he who hath malice and mony, cannot want a man to doe the mischeife. These murthers are most common in places lying most open for escape, where banishment is the highest punishment, And are most committed in the tyme of the Bachinall Feasts of Shroue-tyde, lasting with them from after Christmasse to Lent, and vulgarly called, Il Carnoual' that is the farewell to flesh. And they are most frequent in the lower parts of Italy, more spetially in Lombardy, where many carry long peeces (the short gunns being forbidden for feare of sodeine treasons) and goe daily armed from the head to the foote, so as myselfe haue seene young Gentlemen, for feare of those with whome they had some quarrells, weare continually an yron Coate of male of 30 pounds weight, next aboue their shirts. The murtherers that cannot escape, but are taken by the officers, are putt to death by beheading.

Adulteries (as all furyes of Jelousy, or signes of making loue, to wiues, daughters and sisters) are commonly prosecuted by priuate reuenge, and by murther, and the Princes and Judges, measuring their iust reuenge by their owne passions proper to that nation, make no great inquiry after such murthers besides that the reuenging party is wise inough to doe them secretly, or at least in disguised habitts. The frequent punishment for common breaches of the Lawe, is the Corde called Strappado, or strappa di corda, where the delinquent is cast downe with Cords fastned to his Armes running in a pully, so as at the fall the ioynts at the shoulder turne rounde about, except he haue agilitye to saue himselfe, which some practise, and haue, so as they dare take the Jerke of the Corde for a small reward. For vsury five in the hundreth is allowed in the mounts of piety, which are bankes of mony to be lent to the poore, but in Common Contracts it is not limitted, so as they may take as they can agree. The very name of the hangman, and of his seruants and officers belonging to him in Criminall Justice are odious, as in Germany. About this tyme whereof I write, a Foraine gentleman lying in Rome, and being in some grace with one of the Cheefe Cardinalls had license from him to weare his sworde, but it happened that he becoming Rivall to the Cardinalls Nephew (so their bastards are called) and by free spending of his mony getting the Cortizans grace, so much as she excluded the other, he for reuenge plotted with the Serieants to take the gentleman going thether by night with his sword when he had not his License about him to shewe, and to giue him a touche of the Strappado who did accordingly, and when they had apprehended him, and he avowed his License, and offered mony to send to the Cardinalls house, they suffered him to send a messenger, but in the meanetyme putt him to the Corde, and gaue him a little Jerke, when presently the same Nephewe of the Cardinall, and some of his other gentlemen came in, and freed him, after they had attayned their end, For in reguarde the officer of Criminall Justice had but giuen the gentleman that litle touche of their hands, the

Cortisan would neuer after admitt his loue or Company, but gaue herselfe wholy to the sayd Cardinalls Nephewe. The like thing happened about that time in Vicenza a Citty vnder the Venetians; where a yong Cortisan arriuing, and setting a very high price vppon herselfe, such as the gentlemen of the Citty, howsoeuer desyrous of new game, would not giue, after they had in vayne tryed all meanes to make her fall in the price, they called the hangman, and one gaue him a dublett, an other a hatt, and so for all gentleman like attyre, and all ioyntly furnishing him with the mony she demaunded, they sent him to her that night, and the next morning all coming to her Chamber, the one cast his dublett, the other his hatt, and so the rest of the attyre into the fyer, and then the hangmans man bringing him his apparrell, after their departure, the miserable Cortisan perceiuing how she was skorned, fledd secretly out of the Citty, and was neuer more seene there.

The Justice, Lawes, and Judgments in the Popes State.

At Rome, the Lawes are with much seuerity putt in exequution, and namely the Lawes of Pope Sixtus Quintus against outlawes, Cortisans, quarrells, and the like. And it is peculiar (as I was informed) to the State of the Church, that a murtherer escaped out of an other Princes Territory, where he committed the fact, shalbe executed for the same in the Popes State, if he be there apprehended and accused thereof. It is Capitall to challenge, or answer a Challenge of Combatt, and in quarrells he that first drawes his sword, shall dye or be condemned to the Gallies or in some such sort punished. And it is not only vnlawfull to weare swords in that State without license, but the wearing of daggers openly is forbidd, and the Carrying a pistoll secretly or like pockett weapons for feare of sodeine murthers, is capitally forbidden. And at Rome, more then in any other Citty of Italy, the Strappado is giuen for euery small offence. Monsieur Villamont writes of a principall gentleman of Bologna about this tyme executed by

strangling in his Chamber at Rome, only for having receiued
an outlawe into his house: And of an other who was hanged
on the bridge of St. Angelo for having giuen a blowe to a
Sweitzer of the Popes guard. If a man be cast into prison for
debt, the Judges after the manner visitting frequently those
prisons, finding him to be poore, will impose vppon the Creditor
a mitigation of the debt, or tyme of forbearance, as they iudge
the equitye of the Case to require, or if by good witnesses they
finde the party so poore as really he hath not wherewith to pay
the debt, they will accept a release or assignement of his goods
to the Creditor, and whether he consent or no, will free the
debters body out of prison. At Rome the least idle word of
the Pope, the Church, or Religion, will drawe a man into the
Inquisition, where he may lye long tyme close prisoner (not
somuch as a keeper comming to him, but his meat being giuen
out at an hole in the dore, and he making his owne bedd),
before he shall know who hurt him, or why he is imprisoned,
and if he be found of the reformed religion (whome they call
heretiques) of old he was soone brought to the stake, but the
constant death of some, having (as they found) done hurt, since
they are kept in perpetuall prison, and a credible Convert
deceiues vs, if by the Jesuits they be not many tymes strangly
affrighted, and euen secretly putt to death in close prisons
vnder the ground. Pope Sixtus Quintus made a lawe, that no
Cortisan should ride in a Coache vnder paine to pay a 100
Crownes, and the Coachman to haue the Strappado for the first
tyme, and death for the second tyme, but they weare Clothe of
gold, and liue in all excesse for meate, and all things, and haue
incredible respect shewed them in salutations, only they are
knowne by going on foote so richly attyred. Yet I am deceiued
if knowne mistresses of great Clergymen, tho no professed
Cortisans, passe not Rome in as great pompe and pride as any.
Speaking of Justice in generall, I haue shewed the late Popes
Justice against Outlawes, whereby their strong partyes vppon
the Confines of Naples haue bene in tyme broken, and are now
weake, and almost destroyed.

The Justice, Lawes, and Judgments in the State of Venice.

The Senate of Venice is most reuerent for the gray heads, grauity and Comelynes of their persons, and their stately habitts but for nothing more then their strict obseruing of Justice. They haue a lawe that in tyme of Carnauall or Shrouetyde, no man that is masked may weare a sword, because being vnknowne, he might thereby haue meanes to kill his enemy on the sodeine, and while I was in Italy a forayne gentleman vppon a fancy to mock the officers of Justice, being masked wore a woodden lathe like a sword. The officers apprehended him, and finding it to be a lath, yet carryed him to the magistrate, who with a graue Countenance said to him, Non burlar' con la Giustitia, Veh: Jeast not with the Justice, marke me. And he found that he had mocked himselfe more then the officers, for he payd not a few Crownes before he could be freed by mediation of great freinds. But since the Citty of Venice lyes open without any walls, so as malefactors may easily escape, and the Citty lyes vppon Lombardye where murthers are frequent, this Citty especially in the tyme of Carnouall is much subiect to murthers, and like outrages. And so is the next Citty Padoa, vppon priuiledges of the Vniuersity, whereby murther in schollers is punished only by banishment. And that the rather, because in the State of Venice (for the great Confluence of strangers) it is free for all men to weare Armes by the day, excepting Pistolls, which no man may haue without the Locks taken of, and also because they who haue ill purposes, will aduenture and vse to weare these Armes by night also, I say for these reasons, murthers (especially in the libertine tyme of Carnouall) are frequent in this Citty, from which also the lesser Cittyes of that State are not free. Murther was punished by hanging till death, till Duke Michaele Morosino created in the yeare 1381, made a law that murtherers should be beheaded. But most comonly they escape by flight, and so are banished till they can make peace with the freinds of the murthered, and so obtayne liberty to retorne into their Country. Adulterers are punished (as other like Crymes) according to the Ciuill and Cannon lawes, but the Italians impatient to bring their honor vnder publique tryalls dispatch the punishment of all Jelousyes by priuate reuenge, killing not only the men so prouoking them, but their wiues sisters or daughters dishonouring themselues in those kindes. Yea brothers knowing their sisters to be vnchast when they are maryed, and out of their owne house, yet will make this offence knowne to their husbands, that they may kill them. Whereof Examples are frequent, as namely of a Florentine gentleman, who vnderstanding from his wiues brother that she had dishonoured them by adulterye, tooke her forth in a Coache having only a Preist with them, and when they came to a fitt place gaue her a short tyme to confesse her sinnes to the Preist, and then killed her with his owne hands. And howsoeuer in this Case, it is like she Confessed the Cryme, yet in this and like Cases the Magistrate vseth not to inquire after these reuenges, which the Italians nature hath drawne into Custome, besides that many are done secretly without danger to be reuealed.

Among other high Crymes it is not rare to heare blasphemous speeches in Italy, and the State of Venice is much to be praysed for the most seuere Justice they vse against such offendors, having a lawe to cutt out their tongues. Yea while I liued there, some roaring boyes one night went out vppon a Wager who should doe the greatest villany, and when they had done most wicked things, at last they came all to the windowe of the Popes Nuntio, where they song horrible blasphemyes against our Lord, his blessed mother, and the Apostle St. Peter. The next morning all these Rascalls (so I call them, whereof most notwithstanding were gentlemen) had escaped out of the Citty, only two were taken whome I did see executed in this manner, their hands were cutt of in fower places where they did the greatest villanyes, their tongues were cutt out vnder the windowe of the Popes Nuntio, and so they were brought into the markett place of St. Marke, where vppon a Scaffold they were beheaded with an axe falling by a Pully,

which done the Scaffold and their bodyes were burnt, and the
Ashes throwne into the Sea.

Ciuill Judgments in the State of Venice.

For Ciuill Judgments I remember a stone at Paduoa called
lapis turpitudinis (that is the stone of filthines) because
vppon markett dayes such were sett vppon it with naked
backsydes, as had runn into debt having no meanes to repay it.
The lawes of Venice in generall were reputed so iust by the
Senate of Nurenberg in Germany as in the yeare 1508, by
Ambassadors sent to this State they obteyned a Copy of them.
Among other Ciuill Judgments they giue singular Justice in
Cases of debt and haue particular Judges ouer Marchants
banckrowting, who giue the Creditors security to keepe them
from prison, and cite such banckrowtes as fly, selling their
goods and dividing them equally among the Creditors and
preuenting all fraudes may be vsed. So as if they finde other
mens goods deposited in their hands they keepe them for the
Owners.   In which Case myselfe when I passed from thence
into Turkye, and also my brother leauing our Chests with our
apparrell & bookes in the hands of a marchant, who shortly
after proued banckrowte, the magistrate kept our goods safe,
and when I retorned, did restore to me without any Charge,
not only my owne goods, but also my brothers who dyed in
the Journey.

I haue formerly sayd that all the Venetian lawes are made
in the Counsell called Pregadi, for when any Magistrate
iudgeth it profitable for the Comonwealth to haue any new
lawe made for any thing concerning his office and Charge, he
propounds his reasons in the Colledge of the Sauij, and they
being there approued, the lawe is propounded, enacted, and
published by the Councell di Pregadi. So the Magistrate of
the Pomps (or Ceremonies) caused certaine sumptuary Lawes
for diett and apparrell to be made in this Councell which are
in force to this day. Yet sometymes the law is made in the
Great Counsell, if the magistrate thinke that it will receiue

more life and force by being confirmed therein. So the
Censors in the last age past desyring a lawe should be made
against making any Congratulations with any man that had
obteyned an Office or magistracye, the same was first approued
in the Counsell of Pregadi, and then with generall Consent
confirmed in the great Counsell.

Of the iustice in Genoa.

I haue formerly spoken of the gouernment and magistrates
in the free Citty of Genoa; Now it remaynes in a word to speake
of their Judges. A doctor of the Ciuill Lawe borne out of the
State, hath a great yearely stipend, and is vulgarly called the
Podesta. He dwells in a Pallace adioyning to the Dukes, and
iudges all Criminall Causes, but no Capitall sentence is
executed without the Consent of the Senate, neither can he
otherwise commaund it. He hath two doctors to be his
Assistants, and one is his Vicar, who also medles in some Ciuill
Causes. Five Doctors of the Ciuill Lawe borne out of the
State, are likewise hyred for two yeares to iudge Ciuill Causes,
the body of which Doctors or Judges is vulgarly called La Rota.
Also of the Citizens the Magistrates called the seuen men extraordinary, are chosen for six monethes to represent the Dukes
person as busyed with higher affayres, in hearing of differences
betweene men, and in appointing Tutors for Pupills. And
because the lawe forbiddes a rich man to goe to lawe with a
poore man, or one kinsman with an other (a lawe in my opinion
most woorthy to be imitated), these seuen men in such cases
appoint Judges, who as Arbiters end their differences. Fiue
men called the supreme Sindici may and vse to call in question
the Duke and the Gouernors after the tyme of their magistracye
ended, and vppon iust causes to punish them, liberty being
giuen by publique proclamation for eight dayes to all men, that
they may accuse them, or any of them, for any fault done in
their magistracye, after which eight dayes, these fiue men giue
them letters Pattents to testifye their innocencye, without

which letters they cannot be admitted to the dignity of
Procurators belonging to their places, as I haue formerly
shewed. These fiue also heare many appeales being men of
great estimation, and they are chosen by the lesser Counsell.
All arts haue their Censors, who sett the price of things sold,
and prouide no deceite be vsed in weights or measures. Besides
all seuerall Arts haue their owne Magistrates chosen by the
Artisans themselues, and called Consulls, all which haue
authority ouer those of their owne Art or trade. Among them
the Consulls of the silke weauers haue the greatest authoritye,
for they may putt any of that art to the Strapado, yea
condemne them to banishment, or to be slaues in the Gallies,
and to like high punishments.

The Justice, Judgments and lawes, in the state of Florence.

I haue formerly shewed that the Duke of Florence is an
absolute Prince, and hath no priuy Counsell of State, but
comunicateth his most secrett affayres to the aduise of his
Fauorites,.whereof the Archbishopp of Pisa was reputed cheefe,
and gouerneth the Commonwealth by publique Magistrates.
For the magistrates and Tribunalls of Justice remayne still the
same they were in the tyme of the free State. Ciuill Causes (as
in other Cittyes of Italy) are iudged by a certaine number of
Doctors in the Ciuill Lawe (whose body is called La Rota), And
criminall Causes are iudged by the magistrates of Florence, in
nothing changed, but that the cheefe of old called Gonfaloniere
is now called Lieuftenant. All other magistrates as the old
Counsellors, eight men &c. and the Vicars and Gouernors of
Townes and Jurisdictions (vulgarly called Podesta) are now
chosen as in tyme of the free State, saue that the Gouernors of
the cheefe Cittyes, as Sienna and Pisa and the keepers of Forts,
are appointed sent and reuoked at the Dukes pleasure. The
said Magistrates are in this sort chosen. The gentlemens
names of the first Ranck, and so of the second and third are
putt into three vessells and the cheefe magistrates are chosen

out of the first, the inferior out of the second, and the lowest out of the third, by drawing out for each Magistrates place five names of whome he [who] hath most voyces in the Counsell is chosen. And the gentlemens names are yearely altered in the vessells, & changed out of one into the other. These Elections are confirmed by the Duke, but otherwise he medles not with their choise or Judgments, only he hath his Secretary vulgarly called Del criminale who sees the Processes of Criminall Judgments, aswell in the Citty as in the Territory, and acquaintes the Duke with those of greatest moment, and no doubt from him directs the Judges proceedings, which makes them more vigilant in doing Justice. One thing I cannot omitt, which I wondred to see in the Citty of Florence, namely a Court of Justice, whose title is written vppon the gates, La corte de l' honestà, the Court of honesty, and wherein Judges sett in Scarlett Robes to doe right to Cortisans or Harlotts if any wrong them therein. For howsoeuer the Stews be restrayned to certaine streets, no Harlott being permitted to dwell among the houses of the Matrons, if she be but seene at a window; yet it hath such priuiledges, as if a mans wife flying from him can come into the Stewes before he lay hold on her, he cannot bring her back, nor haue her punished. The very Duke passing the streete will in honor putt of his hatt to some of them, and at publique Comedies Cortisans and Torchbearers enter freely, and pay nothing. The State of the Duke of Florence is to be praysed aboue all other parts of Italy for Justice, where strangers liue more safely then any where els, so they bring not themselues in danger by foolish shewing of their mony, and may safely passe in the Citties and highwayes by day or night with their pocketts full of gold. Besides that Strangers haue more priuiledge then Natiues in wearing their swords, which is only granted to some gentlemen of Florence, but other Natiues hardly obtayne license to weare them which is easily graunted to all straungers. Nether doe any in this State (as in Lombardy) carry Gunns or goe armed from head to foote, For no man in Citty or Country may weare or haue in their howses

other Armes then Rapiers and daggers vppon great penalty.
Yet cannot I commend the Citty Ligorno for this Ciuility, nor
the Inhabitants for honest men. And no maruell for howsoeuer
it hath of old bene a place of dwelling; yet Duke Cosmo first
compassed the place with walls, Duke Francis caused many
howses to be built there, and Duke Ferdinand (living when I
was in Italy) first brought it into the forme of a Fayre and well
fortifyed Citty. And these Dukes, with lesse charge to furnish
it with buildings & inhabitants, as Rome at the first was made
a Sanctuary to malefactors, so they imposed punishments on
malefactors in lesser Crimes, according to the quality of their
offence, to build one or more howses in this Citty, and to dwell
there for yeares, or for life, so as the Inhabitants were not like
to be of the most peaceable and best sort of men.

Booke II.

CHAP: I.

Of the commonwealth of Fraunce according to the seuerall heads conteyned in the title of the first Chapter of the former booke.

[I was tempted to omit the whole of this long Chapter, for Moryson's work here is what critics sometimes call "conscientious." However, the passage on "The Tributes and Revenues," commencing on Page 207 of the MS., is such an extremely favourable specimen of it, that I quote it in full. It has a special interest for the general reader from its bearing on later French history. The Chapter extends from Page 188 of the MS. to Page 231.—C.H.]

The Tributes and Reuenues.

THE Tribute and Reuenues of this large kingdome are manifold and great, and howsoeuer it be charged in high measure with a multitude of great Stipends, since the very Counsellors attend not the publike affayres without reward of large pensions, and the officers of the Exchequer so exceede in number as they must needs wast the same Treasure they gather (of whose multitude, reformation hath bene often intended and attempted, but by their art was euer frustrated). And howsoeuer it be charged with the maintenance of many Troopes of horse and bands of Foote continually in the kings pay, and of diuerse Fortes and Garrisons vppon the Confines for defence of the kingdome; yet would it aboundantly suffice the priuate and publike vses, were it not that in the last Ciuill Warrs, not only many Customes, and Tributes were ingaged, but euen great part of the kings Domaine or land of Inheritance (which should not be ingaged

vppon any other Cause then for the necessity of warr and of
Apennages of kings yonger sonnes). But the king then
raigning, Henry the fourth, no lesse famous for policye in
peace, then for the military Art, began to drawe all expences
to the wonted limitts, and not only something too much (as the
french confesse) restrayning his bounty in guifts, but also
gouerning all things with more then kingly frugality, gaue the
french hope to restore the wonted plenty of publike Treasure.
Of the Impositions in Fraunce, some were of old graunted,
others haue bene lately extorted by the necessity of the
kingdome, and long Ciuill Warrs to which the french haue in
the last age bene easily drawne), and for other causes partly
true, partly pretended. In which exactions not only the
french, but most kings of the world make vayne the Maxime
of Logick, that the Causes being taken away the effects cease,
easily learning to raise Tributes but not knowing how to
abate them. For in Fraunce the exactions raysed in the fury
of warr, continued in the fayrest tyme of peace. Tributes
willingly offered to avoyde the spoyle of Soldiers, still
remayned, and that without restraint of their insolencyes, and
tributes allowed in tymes of publike danger by consent of the
three estates, were in peace as it were by prescribed Custome
made the Kings annuall Rents. Yea exactions made by the
Princes of the league taking Armes against the king were after
in tyme of peace taken for the king, in iust punishment of those
who supported Rebells by them. Popular seditions for like
exactions haue no where bene more frequent then in Fraunce
(tho Italy be farr more oppressed therewith) and that not only
of old, but euen of late since the Ciuill Warrs appeased, and in
all these tumults, as dogs bite the stone in steed of the Caster,
so the fury of the people fell not vppon the Imposers, but vppon
the Exactors. The Nobility high and lowe, I meane lordes and
gentlemen, are altogether free from Impositions or Tributes
because they serue the king in his Warrs (aswell in person as
with a certaine number of horsemen according to their quality)
without taking any pay. And this Immunity litle diminisheth

the kings profitt, because the Nobility scornes to be Marchants, thincking such traffique ignoble, according to the Heraults rules, howsoeuer the Italians even the very Princes disdayne not traffique by the great, leaving only the gayne of Retayling to the people, and wisely thinck it madnes to inrich the people with the cheife Commoditye of the land and to inable them to buy their lands, which idlenes must needs force them to wast and sell. As the Nobles are free from all exactions, so some fall only on the Common people, from which the Citties, and all the kings officers and ministers are exempted, but they are likewise charged with some, as with mantayning the ordinary troopes and bands of horse and foote, and for the Tenthes the very Clergie is not spared. It is a great mischeife in Fraunce that all offices vppon the necessity of the State, euen the iudiciall offices, have of old beene vsed to be sold by the king, which out of ill Custome continewes till this day, all offices being sold at high rates, and (which is more straunge) the sales thereof among priuate men being of force, as if they were graunted vnder the kings Seale, so the seller thereof liue a moneth or two after the sealing to take away all suspition of open fraude. For howsoeuer this Custome may be profitable to the king, it makes vnwoorthy men come to high offices, and since he that buyes must needs sell, it makes the king for his iudiciall places author of selling Justice. All Writers obserue that Fraunce hath fowre loadstones to drawe Treasure, namely Corne, Wyne, Salt, and linnen Cloth, and no doubt the Tribute or Impost of wyne is great, and that of Salt greater, which in many places is proper to the king, and generally payes him Tribute especially baysalt whereof plenty is made in Fraunce especially in some Ilands, and in many places the selling of white salt is forbidden, that the bay Salt may be sold for the kings better profitt, but this Reuenue of Salt was said to be then ingaged to priuate men. And since I heare from french men that the king vseth commonly to Farme out this and other Gabels (or Impositions), and that Salt alone at this tyme is farmed out to Marchants at some six hundreth thousand

pounds sterling yearely, and that the king particularly for each
mued of Salt receiueth fower pounds tenn shillings sterling to
make vpp the foresaid Rent, and that twelue Lettiers make a
Mued, and each Lettier is about a quarter of our measure, And
the french Marchants say that each Mued of wheate yeildeth
the King three pounds sterling for Gabell or Impost.   And that
each Mued of Wyne commonly yeildes the king Eighteene
Shillings of our mony, three Mueds being about a Tonn.
Considering the multitude of all exactions and the power the
king assumeth to impose them at pleasure, that which Lewes
the Eleuenth said merily wilbe found true, that Fraunce is a
pleasant Meadowe of a rich soile which the King moweth as
often as it pleaseth him.   But he that clenseth the bodye too
much shall at last fetche bloud.   For the last kings of the
house of Valois drew drye the brookes and Channells of this
pleasant Meadowe, and that when the Sunne in the Lyon (I
meane the Ciuill Warrs) most parched the same, and so
dissipated the Mowen grasse thereof, as they left all in ruine to
the succeeding house of Bourbon.

CHAPTER ii.

Of the Common wealth of Denmarke.

[This chapter on Denmark extends from Page 231 of the
M.S. to Page 243.   My first quotation commences in Page 234
and terminates Page 238, while the passage on " The Forces by
Sea " concludes the chapter.—C.H.]

The Kinge.

King Christiern or Christian the fourth then living, was yet
vnder age, being the seuenth king of the Oldenburg Family,
and in generall the hundreth seuenth king of the Danes, who
was borne in the yeare 1577, and when his Father dyed was not
fully aeleuen yeares old.   The king of Swetia John the third,
some twoe yeares before my passing this way, had vndertaken
warr against the Moscovites, to recover Naroua and other Citties
and teritoryes they had taken from him in Liuonia, in which
warr he made his brother Charles the Generall of his Army, and
this John the third about this tyme dying, the sayde Charles
gouerned the kingdome in the right of his absent Nephewe
Sigismund king of Polonia (whereof in the treaty of the
Commonwealth of Poland, I haue written somethinge more at
large).   And in this warre the English marchants furnishing
the Moscouites with Armes and Munitions, did there obtayne
great priuiledges of traffique.   But I retorne to speake of
Christiene the fourth king of Denmarke, whome I did see at
Roschild, to which towne or Citty he came, attended with tenn
Coaches, and a Courtier satt by the kings syde in his owne
Coache, which was drawne with three horses, and these Coaches
were like those are vsed in Germany, couered with black coarse
Cloth lyned with Canves or Course Cloth, and borne vpp with
litle rounde hoopes of wood fastned with hookes of yron, so as
the Couer falles backward if they will ride in open ayre, or may
be pulled ouer their heads at both ends and buckled in the

midst, if the weather be rayny or cold. He was of a fayre Complexion and bigg sett, and about some fifteene yeares of age, and they said he could speake the Dutch, French, and Italian tongues, and was delighted with shooting in a muskett, with musick and with reading of historyes, and spent two howers in the morning and as many after dinner at his booke, and passed the rest of the day in diuerse exercises, attended by his Hoffmeister (that is master of his Court) then called Hockholgersen a gentleman who had beene generall of the Army in the last Warr with Suetia. When he vouchsafed to salute any man, he gaue them his hand, not to kisse but to take in his hand, neither doe any vse to kneele to him except they answer before him accused of Capitall Crimes, but the Courtiers stood bareheaded to him in great distance. His yongest brother John followed the Court at that tyme, but Vlricus the second brother was then Student at Wittenberge in Germany who besides his Inheritance in Holsatia, had the administration of a Bishopprick in the Dukedome of Mecleburg and of an other nere Lubeck and a Channons place in a Cathedrall Church. The king was then on his iourney to Flansburg, where an extraordinary Parliament was called, For his Subiects of Holsatia to sweare him homage, which they had refused to yeilde at Copenhagen in Denmarke, where an ordinary Parliament is yearely held, the next day after Trinity Sonday. Of old 24 Counsellors or Senators did gouerne the Common Wealth vnder the king, but at this tyme twelue gentlemen chosen of the Kings Counsell for life, did gouerne the same, the generall States of the Church and nobility being assembled only for some greatest affayres. The yong kings Father by his last will and Testament appointed him six Tutors, the Threasorer, the Admirall, the Arch Marshall, the Chauncelor and two others, but some of them by the Assembly of the States were deposed, as namely the Treasorer for having beheaded one Hainson a Citizen, of which act the Danes said he should be called in question when the king should be Eighteene yeares of age, and by the same Assembly fower Tutors were confirmed, namely

Nicholas (vulgarly Nelse) Case the Chancelor, George Rosen-krantz a grayheaded old Senator, Peter Munck Admirall, and Hackwolfstand, the two last being so aged, as they could not follow the Court. The young king is called Prince by the Danes while he is vnder age gouerned by Tutors.

The Court.

The king had 70 Trabantoes for guarde of his person, and each of them had for his diett monethly five Dollers, and for wages yearely 24 dollers, and twice in the yeare they were apparrelled. And he had tenn horsemen called Hascheri, whereof each man had 20 dollers monethly for keeping of two horses, and yearely wages 20 dollers, and apparrell twice in the yeare. Some thirty gentlemen following the Court at that tyme had each man Fifty dollers monethly to keepe five horses. The Cuppbearer had asmuch to keepe so many horses, and moreouer 300 dollers yearely for wages or pention. The like intertainment had the cheefe Cooke and the gentlemen Sewers who carryed vpp the meat, and one of them supplyed the place of Caruer, but no man tasted the meat, which Ceremonye I heard was not in vse with them. Of these some haue allowance in mony for diett, others eate in the Court, but they haue no tables for Counsellors or Cheefe Officers, and they which eat not in the Court, goe thether but once in three or fower dayes. Neither did any great traine follow the Court. The king did eat alone, with the dores open for any man to enter. When they haue a Queene she dwells in a seuerall syde of the Pallace, and hath her owne officers, and her table apart from the king.

The Reuenues and Tributes.

Touching the Reuenues and Tributes; Denmarke hath no Mynes of gold or siluer (for Suetia hauing some fewe or poore Mynes hath not in these last ages bene vnited to that king-dome). The fishing of Herrings Codd and like fishes to be dryed, and the exportation of masts for shipps, and of great

quantity of deale boardes out of Norway, and of Brimstone from
the Mountayne Hecla in Iseland and some like Commodityes
yeilde a good reuenue to the Crowne. Giue me leaue to mention
the fishing which the English haue in a place called Wardhouse
to which they saile about the North syde of Norway once in the
yeare for that purpose, the Inhabitants thereof are subiect to
the King of Denmarke, and were said to liue vnder the earth,
feeding altogether vppon dryed fishes, and for the continuall
snow seldome or neuer coming out of their Caues, and therevppon having a drye complection infected with a kinde of
leprousy. And these English Marchants or Fishermen, though
they neuer enter the Sounde, yet for secure passage and leaue
to fish there, payd the king of Denmarke yearely one hundreth
Rose Nobles of gold. But these Reuenewes are of small moment
compared with two Tributes wherein the Treasure of that kingdome consists. For the first an incredible tribute is raysed of
the Shipps passing the Narrow Sea called the Sounde, dividing
Denmarke and Norway, and so leading into the Baltick Sea,
which shipps paid tribute aswell at the entrance as the retourne
out of the Sounde. For the Danes had two strong Forts built
in the narrowest mouthe of the Sounde (at the entrance into the
Hauen of Elsenure, whence the passage lyes open into the
Baltick Sea) and one of the Forts is called Chronoburg seated in
the village of Elsenure and the Cheefe Iland of Denmarke called
Sealand and the other Fort is called Elzburg seated in the
kingdome of Norway, and these Forts are so neere one to the
other, as no shipp can safely passe them without leaue, besides
that if any shipps should passe either by force, or some other
way by stealth which might easily be done, those shipps and
goods should be confiscated whensoeuer they are forced againe
to passe that sounde. So as this tribute must needes be exceeding great. For euery shipp entring vnladen (as the hollanders
doe for the most part) payeth for the ship a Rosse noble of gold,
and for beacon gelt a Doller. But those that are loden pay of
old for last gelt the hundreth penny of the goods, and a Rosse
noble of gold for the ship, yea two or three Rosse nobles if

diuers partners were owners of the ship, and halfe a dollour for beacon gelt (or mony).   Only those shipps whose burthen is not aboue forty last, pay nothinge for the shipp, as others doe (euen those that are vnladen, after the rate I formerly named, but only for the Marchandise they beare after the rate of theire burthen.   An English shipp lately returning from Dantzke laden with wax (a light commodity) had payde 900th Dollers at the Sound for tribute.   And while myselfe was at Elsenure, another English shipp of 140 Tunns burthen, being scarcely halfe laden, payd there 312 Dollers and an halfe for tribute. The kings of Denmarke by the Commaund of that narrowe sea, shutting vp the trade at Dantzke and those partes (whence all partes of Europe are furnished with precious marchandise, as Corne, wax, hony, hemp, Cables Masts, Deale boardes, sope ashes, and many like) may easily reueng any wrongs done to them by neighbor Princes, or at pleasure may doe wrong to them in theire subiectes.   For Christian the second (whome I formerly sayd to haue bene hated of his Subiects and his neighbors, and cast out of his kingdome for his Tyrannye) having warr with Suetia did at his pleasure for supporting that warr impose vppon Lubeck and the Neighbor Cittyes of Germany bordering within the Baltick Sea two guldens vppon euery last (twelue Tonnes making a Last) aboue the accustomed Tribute, and vppon all other straungers trading that way the last gelt was highly raysed, so as the English paid a dollor for eight Clothes and a dollor for each last of Flaxe, of Waxe, of wheate, and like Commodityes, and a quarter of a dollor for each Last of Pitche, of Tarr, of Rye Corne, and of like Commodityes, and if any entred Wheate for Rye, or vsed like fraude, the goods were confiscated.   And howsoeuer Lubeck and the other Cittyes by grace obteyned or by Warr extorted freedome for great part of the Imposition thus layd vppon them, and likewise the Hollanders were sayd to be then freed of the said new Imposition, yet at this very tyme whereof I write, the English and Scotts only (no other Nation that I heard) did still pay the new Imposition for all goods, wherewith they were laden aboue the old tribute. Yea the late deceased King (as I heard) being not long before offended with the States of the Vnited Prouinces, for having opened certaine letters directed to his Ambassador, did suffer their shipps to enter the Baltick-Sea (as they vse) vnladen, but when they retorned laden in a great Fleete, he made stay of them all, till they had satisfyed him for that wrong. Besides, this tribute must needs be exceeding great, since often 100 and sometymes 500 shipps lye at one tyme in that harbour, (myselfe having numbred more then 100 Sayle going forth in one morning, and the like number coming in another day in one Fleete). But that which makes the tribute greatest is that these Shipps are comonly laden inward with Sacks, Suger, Spices, and Woollen Clothes, all sold deare in those North East parts, and are laden outward with honye, Waxe, rich Furres, and Corne (wherewith all Europe is supplyed thence) being all rich and light Wares, whereof great value is carryed in small roome. So as I haue heard Danes of good sort esteeme this yearely tribute at six Tonns of gold or five at the least, reckoning one hundreth thousand dollors for a Tonne of gold. And the same Danes assured me that this Treasure was laid vpp for the extraordinary vses of the kingdome, the ordinary charge for the kings Court and all expences in tyme of peace being borne by a second great Tribute formerly mentioned, namely the Tribute of horses oxen and Calues passing the Confines of Halsatia to be sold in the lower parts of Germany towards Netherland. Otherwise small Tributes are raysed of the Subiects from which the gentlemen are free, only in tyme of warr they contribute mony and serue in person, and the Citizens are poore not able to beare them, and the Country people are base, and slaues to the king or to priuate gentlemen, and so not to be taxed in that kinde.

Therefore the Subiects pay no Tribute for flesh, bread or Danish beare (which is very small) but for beare brought out of Germany (which they drinck as largly as the Germans); for each Tonne whereof costing about seuen markes, they payd two markes to the king.

Lawes and Judgments.

Denmarke is gouerned by a peculiar lawe of the kingdome, but Holsatia of old inhabited by Saxons hath the Saxon lawe, whereof I haue spoken in the discourse of Germany. For Ciuill Causes my stay in that kingdome was so short, as I will only say that the tryalls are much agreeable to those in England.

In Capitall Judgments they doe not as the Germans extort confessions by torment, but the accused are tryed and pronounced guilty or not guilty by a Quest of sixteene men, as in England they are tryed by twelve men. King Christiern the second of Condemned men in Suetia for treason beheaded some, broke others vppon the Wheele, hanged others, and drowned some. Christiern the third beseiging Copenhaggen beheaded Meierus for Treason, and after his fower quarters were sett vppon a wheele to rott. But these things may seeme to tast more of Martiall lawe then the setled lawes of the kingdome. Therefore I will breifely add that by the lawe the Condemned, for Parracide, and for premeditated wilfull murther, haue their bones broken vppon the wheele, for manslaughter are beheaded, for theft or Robberies are hanged in Chaynes till they rott, For witchcraft are burned, for coyning and clipping mony haue their bones broken on the wheele, and then quartered are layd vppon the wheele to rott, for defiling Noble Virgins are beheaded, For adultery are putt in perpetuall prison at Dracholme a Castle of Holsatia. The goods of all (excepting Gentlemen) condemned to death, are confiscated to the king. For gentlemen are not condemned to death, but only by the publique assembly of the States, and forfeite not their goods; and for mutuall wrongs and manslaughters among themselues, commonly they pursue them by priuate reueng, in which quarrélls notwithstanding they (as the Germans) are of a placable nature.

In generall none but the Sargeants will apprehend murtherers or Traytors (as all men are bound to doe in England) for that office is held to belong to the hangman and his Sergeants or seruants (for such they are), which office is ab-

horred as in Germany. The king neuer pardons any murther
or Capitall Crime. Robbing by the high way is very rare, and
only happens sometymes to Footemen, so as Trauellers passe
safely for their bodyes, and for their goodes, so they take heede
of Pilferers.

.   .   .   .

Their forces by Sea.

Touching their forces by Sea: The old Invasions of the
Danes vppon our Coasts of England, serue nothing to proue
their strength at Sea, since they preuailed not by Sea-fights
but by landing in diuerse places, and flitting from one place to
an other, but especially since Navall fights and strength at Sea
cannot be measured by those tymes, being long before the Invention of Artillery. From which tyme to this day, the Danes
did no exployte by Sea saue in Warrs they haue had within the
Baltick Sea in manner aforesayd. But to giue some guesse to
their forces at Sea in our age. First I haue shewed in the
former Chapter of their traffique, that their marchants vse not
to export or fetch Commodityes by any long Navigation into
forrayne parts, because the Shipps of all nations passing the
sounde supply their wants, and export their dryed fish and like
Commodityes they can spare. So as the Marchants haue no
strength of well armed shipping. But I did see the Kings
Navye wintering in the haven of Copenhagen, then consisting
of some tenn great and well-armed Shipps, which for building
or sayling of all other Shipps in Europe came neerest to the
English, saue that they last not so long by tenne yeares at the
least. For I vnderstood from good Seamen, that their Shipps
built of the Oakes in Norway last not aboue twenty yeares.
And it seemes they haue no very good Shipwrights, for the
cheife Shipwright who then built the kings Shipps was an
English man named Matson, to whome the king gaue one
hundreth Fifty dollors yearely pention, besides a house, fuell,
Corne, and other necessaryes of asmuch more value. The said
English Shipwright, howsoeuer the Danes doe not without

suspition shewe their Forts or Shipps to straungers, yet perswaded me in his Companye to enter some of the kings Shipps.
Among the rest I entred a great Shipp newly built, and at first
called Dauid, but after Fortune, the burthen whereof was 1400
Tonns, the very ballast being 700th Tonns, and to man and
furnish the same, were required 400 Mariners, 300 Gunners,
and 700 soldiers, as he told me, and the breadth was 25 Ells the
length of the keele 67 and aboue the Hatches 108 Ells, the
depth of the holde was Eleuen Ells and a halfe, and it bore in
the lower Orlob 22 Cannons, in the midle 22 Culverins, and in
the vpper Orlob 24 Sakers; the mast was 37 fadoms long, and
36 Palmes thick, and it cast out seuen Ankers lying in the
Haven. Vppon the Poope these great letters were written,
M.H.z.G.A.* (For the Danes as the Germans vse to expresse
the Mott of an Embleme by great letters for wordes) and
this sentence was likewise written, Regna Firmat Pietas,
that is, Piety makes Kingdomes firme, and the yeare of our
Lord 1592 was vnderwritten in which the Shipp was built,
which the best Seamen iudged more fitt to serue as a Fort in a
Riuer then to fight at Sea where lesse and swifter Shipps would
haue great advantage of it. Also I did enter other of the Kings
Shipps in his Company, namely the Raphaell reputed very swift
and said to haue runn with a fayre Wynde in 33 howers from
Dantzke to Elsenure. And an other called the Gedeon, and
a third called the Jehosaphatt which some few moneths before
had bene admirall of three men of warr wafting the Danish
Ambassador into England, Each whereof was of some 400
Tonnes burthen, and all were strong, swift, and well armed.
Besides I did see some old shipps, as the Sampson that could
not last aboue nyne yeares, the Josuah built before the former,
the Drake built 16 yeares past, and the Wolhiere, or rather the
Carkas thereof, all being tall shipps of like burthen, and of the

---

* I learn from Copenhagen, through Mr. C. Collman, German Consul in
Manchester, that Frederick II., King of Denmark (1559-1588), had a favourite
Motto "Mein Hoffnung zu Gott Allein"—and that several of his portraits
bear it.—C.H.

kings Navye. In the same Haven were fower other men of
warr not of halfe that burthen, whereof one was English lately
taken by the Danes in the more northern parts beyond Norway
for some offence in Fishing. And before my going out of Denmarke, I did heare that two other English Fishermen but well
armed and furnished with Artillery were in the same parts
seased by the Danes for the king vppon the occasion and in
manner following. The Danes gaue freedome of fishing to
straungers in all the Hauens and Coasts thereof, excepting one
which they reserued for themselues, And these English Shipps
fishing at the mouth of this forbidden Hauen, and driuen in
by Tempest, presented the Gouernor with a Tonne of English
beare for liberty to Anchor in that Hauen till the storme was
ouer, who receiued the present, but while the master and Cheife
Marriners were drincking with him, sent soldiers to seaze the
Shipps and possess them for the king, and they said the Shipps
with the masters and Maryners being in the way to be brought
into Denmarke one of the English masters walking aboue the
Hatches and lamenting his estate with his Countrymen, as
having small hope to finde mercy in Denmarke, and doubting
that the Queene of England having her hands full with warr
on all sydes against the Spaniard, would not easely be induced
to write earnestly to the king of Denmarke on their behalfe,
did vppon the sodeine desperately cast himselfe ouer board,
and so perished.

CHAP: iii.

Of the comonwealth of England according to all the particular Subiects mentioned in the Title of the first Chapter and first Booke of the Part.

BEING to write more exactly of the Common Wealth of England, then of others, lest while I seeme to affect knowledge of other kingdomes, I should bewray my ignorance in the State of my owne Country, I haue thought good to referr the same to a Treatise to be written of purpose, and with deliberation vppon that nice Subiect; which Treatise I haue begunn, but it will require tyme and leysure to perfect it, And so for this tyme I passe it ouer vntouched.

CHAP: iiii.

Of the common wealth of Scotland according to all the particular Subiects mentioned in the Title of the first Chapter and first Booke of this Part.

FOR the like reasons I haue thought good likewise to referr this discourse to the said intended Treatise to be Written more exactly and at large, And so for this tyme passe it ouer vntouched.

CHAP: v.

Of the common wealth of Ireland according to all the particular Subiects mentioned in the Title of the first Chapter and first Booke of this Part.

[I omit the historical introduction for which Moryson acknowledges his indebtedness to our "worthy antiquary Camden" (page 244 to 250). The history of the last few years of Queen Elizabeth's reign had been written by Moryson himself with extreme completeness in Part II. of his 1617 volume.—C. H.]

Now briefely I will write of the Irish commonwealth wherein it shall suffice with a finger to point at the fountaynes of past mischeifes.

The lord Deputy and Counsell.

It is gouerned by a lord deputy and Counsell of State resident at Dublin, and the Counsellors are made by the kings letters, and continue in that place during their life, yet at the kings pleasure to recall, or remoue them, whereof notwithstanding we haue few or none examples, and at the end of the Warr, they were not many, only consisting of the lord chancelor the lord high Treasorer, the master of the Rolls, the Marshall of Ireland, the master of the Ordinance, the Treasorer at Warrs, the Bishopp of Meath, the Secretary and some fewe Cheife Colonells of the Army, but since that tyme there haue bene two Secretaries of State, and the number hath bene much increased by the lord Cheife Baron and many other gentlemen both of the Army and otherwise. Besides that the lords Presidents of Prouinces are alwayes vnderstood to be of this Counsell when they come to Dublin or any place where the lord Deputy resides. As for the lord Deputy he is made by the kings letters Pattents during pleasure, and commonly hath continued some three yeares, but sometymes fewer, or many more yeares at the kings pleasure. Sometymes he hath the title of Lord Leifetenant for greater honor, as the Earle of Essex lately had, and sometymes for diminution is stiled lord Justice, as more spetially when vppon the death of the lord Deputy one or more Lordes Justices are Chosen to gouerne till a new lord Deputy be appointed. Yet of old when our kings were stiled lords of Ireland, this cheife Gouernor vnder them, was commonly styled lord Justice. But howsoeuer the titles differ, the power is all one. Sometymes of old, kings brothers, and sonnes (as John sonne to Henry the second and Leonell Duke of Clarence son to Edward the third and George Duke of Clarence brother to Edward the fourth) haue gouerned this kingdome with title of Lord Leiuftenant, and with power to leaue their owne Deputy to gouerne it, when at any tyme themselues retorned into England, which Deputy gaue them at the Court an Accompt of the Irish affayres, where they gaue the like accompt thereof to the king and his Counsell of State. In our tyme Charles Blount Lord Mountioy for his great deserts in subduing Tyrones Rebellion was by our Soueraigne king James created Earle of Deuonshire, and besides rich rewards of Inheritance in England was made Lord Leiuftenant of Ireland, with two parts of the Lord Deputies intertainment, who had the other third part with his owne Commaunds in the Army and kingdome, and gaue like accompt of the Irish affayres to this noble Earle living at Court, only he was not the Earles, but the kings Deputy. And this Earle during his life, not only swayed all Irish suits at the Court, but all other cheife affayres in Ireland, his letters of direction being as Commaunds to the Deputy. But after his death the intertainement, and full power retorned to the lord Deputy, the Commaund of Lord Leiuftenant ceasing from that tyme to this day, which dignity indeed seems more fitt for the sonnes or brothers of kings then for any Subiect. It is enacted by Statute of Parliament in the 33th yeare of king Henry the Eight, that vppon the death of the lord Deputy or like vacancy of that gouernment the Lord Chancelor and Counsell there may chuse one or two to supply the place of lord Justice, till the king may be advertised of that vacancy, and appoint an other gouernment Prouided that they chuse no Churchman, nor any but an English man.   The foresaid lord Leiuftenant deputy or Justice (be they one or more) haue ample power litle differing from Regall, yet alwayes limitted according to the kings letters Pattents, which doe very rarely inlarge or restrayne the same to one more then the other, and that power also is countermaunded many tymes by Instructions from the State, and by letters from the kings of England.   The lord Deputy by his letters Pattents vnder the great Seale of Ireland, may graunt Pardon of life, lands and goods, to any guilty or condemned men, euen to Traitors, only spetiall treasons against the kings person are commonly excepted, as likewise wilfull murthers, which the kings themselues professe not to pardon. And to these men he may likewise giue the kings Protection for a tyme, when they liue in the woodes as outlawes or Rebells. And in like sorte he may giue the landes and goods of Fellons and Traytors Convicted, to any of his servants or frends, or to whome he will ether English or Irish.   The king commonly reserues to his owne guift some Eight cheefe places, as of the lords Presidents the lord high Treasurer, the lord Chancelor, the master of the Rowlles, the Secretary, the Cheefe Justice, and cheefe Barron, and likewise some cheefe places of the Army, as of the Marshall, the master of the Ordinance, and the master Treasurer at warrs.   For all other places, the lord Deputy graunts them vnder the great Seale of Ireland (as the former also when he is first warrented by letters out of England) and these he disposeth, not only for his owne tyme, but for the life of the Possessors.   The king reserues to himselfe the choyse of Bishopps, but all other Church liuings are in the lord Deputies guift.   The king reserues to himselfe the Puples of Earles and Barrons, but the rest are in the lord Deputies guift, who likewise desposeth to his servants frendes and followers all intrusians, Allinations, Fynes, and like thinges of great moment.   And howsoeuer by inferiour Commissions some of the Counsell are

ioyned to assist the Deputy in disposall of these thinges, yet
that was wont to be only for forme, these Counselors very rarely
apposing themselues to his pleasure. Yea the guifts of the
higher places in the State and Army, Of Bishoprickes, of Earles
and Barrons Pupills, tho reserued to the king, were wont
seldome to be granted in England but vpon the lord Deputies
letters of recommendation sent out of Ireland. Fynally the
lord Deputy may leiue Forces, and doe all thinges of Regall
authority, saue Coyning of mony, which was allwayes Coyned
at London, and sent into Ireland: True it is, that in those
thinges which are putt in his meere power by his letters Pattens,
he hath allwayes subiected himselfe to instructions and letters
sent out of England, which notwithstanding seldome haue
crossed his Free disposall of all thinges in his power, since he
vsed to graunt them presently, before any can passe into
England and retorne hauing obtayned them there, notwithstanding in thinges putt in his meere power, the most wise
and moderate Deputyes, foreseeing the shorte tyme of theire
gouernement, and knowing that the Counselors of State haue
theire places for life, and obseruing that most Deputies retorned
into England laden with Complayntes, aswell of Counselors as
many priuate men, so as after good seruice they haue beene
glad to receave the Pa[r]don of theire errors for theire deserued
rewarde, for these causes haue beene so warye, as in many
thinges of theire absolute power they vsed to referr the Consideration of them to one or two of the Counsell, by that art
drawing theire Consent, and yet still hauing theire owne in-
tentians, seldome or neuer apposed by those Counselors, who
founde those referments gracefull and profitable to them, and
so willingly seconded the lords Deputyes pleasure.

In my opinion nothinge is so contrary to the affections of
the Irish to which the kings personall presence might not
easily leade or drawe them, more then his sworde in his Deputies
hand can force them, but the dangerous passages of the Sea and
the generall affayres of State giuing the Irish small hope of
their kings frequent presence, no doubt in his absence they

more reverence a lord Deputy that is by degree a Duke Earle
or Barron, then any knight though he be of any like great
Family, and such a Deputy shall by the Authority of his degree,
more easily suppresse theire rebellious spirittes against the
State, and tyranny towardes theire tennants, then any Deputy
of inferiour degree can doe, by greater vallour and wisdome.
And since the Irish are most prone to tumults and Commotions,
theire nature in generall rather requires a valiant Actiue
Deputy, then one that is wise and politicke if withall he be slowe
and fayntharted.

But it may well be doubted whether the shorte gouernment
Commonly allotted to the Deputies be profitable to our State or
no : For Magistrates often changed like hungry flyes sucke
more blood, and as the Deuill rageth more because his tyme is
shorte, so these Magestrates feareing soone to be recalled, are
not so much bent to reforme the Commonwelth, the fruite
whereof should be reaped by the successor, as they are vigilent
to inrich themselues and theire Followers. Nether indeede can
that Crafty and subtile nation be well knowne to any governnour
by fewe yeares experience, so as the Irish, hopeing the Magistrate shalbe recalled before he be skillfull of theire affayres,
and that another farr more vnskilfull shalbe sent ouer in his
place, vse nothinge more then delatorye temporising in theire
obedience to the kings Commaundes or lawes, hopeing that newe
magistrates will giue newe lawes, and so if they can putt off
any buisinesse for the present if it be but for a day, thincking
with Crafty Davus that in the meane tyme some chance may
happen to theire advantage, dayly gapeing for such changes
and inquiring after nothinge more. Yea many tymes they are
not deceaved in this hope, but flocking to the newe Deputy at
his first arivall, with theire causes formerly determined though
not to theire mynde and likeing, they many tymes extorte from
these Deputies wanting experience newe determinations dis-
agreeable and perhapps contrary to the former, with great hurt
to the Commonwealth, and disgrace to the government. It may
be obiected that it may proue dangerous to giue a great man

the absolute Commaunde of a kingdome for many yeares. No doubt, as barbarous Nations, not knowing God whome they see not, worship his Creatures by which immediately he conferrs ill or good vpon them, so the Irish in the first place obey theire landlordes, as neerest benifactors or oppressors, and in the next place the lord Deputy, whose person they see and whose power they feele, yet so, as keeping Fayth promised to the present Deputy, they thincke themselues Free from keeping the same to his successours, and for the king, he as vnknowne and farthest from revenge, hath euer beene lesse feared by them. But the State may allwayes be confident of a lord Deputy, whose fayth-fullnes and endes free from ambition, are well knowne to them. And lett him be neuer so fitt to imbrace newe and dangerous Counsells, yet if he haue a good estate of landes in England there is no danger of his attempts For a wise man would not change that Certayne estate for any hopes of Ireland, which will allwayes be most vncertayne, as well because the kingdome can-not subsist without the support of some powerfull king, as because the myndes of the Irish are instable, and as the Common people euery where, so they in a Farr greater measure haue most inconstant affections. Besydes that such ambitious designes cannot by any man be resolued in Counsell, much lesse putt in execution, before the State of England may haue meanes to knowe and prevent them. Theire obiection is of greater force who thincke it fitt these governments be often changed that many of the English may knowe the affayres of that kingdome, which otherwise wilbe knowne to fewe. But what if three yeares will not suffice to vnderstand howe to governe that crafty nation, suerly at least after these yeares of Contemplation, me thinckes some tyme should be giuen to the gouernour to bring his Counsells and experience into actuall reformation. For as heretofore they haue beene often changed, so the Deputies haue labored more to compose tumults and disorders for the tyme, then to take away the causes, and to make the peace permanent, lest theire successor should enter vpon theire haruest imputing the troubles to them, and arrogating the appeasing thereof to himselfe. Wherevpon sharpe emulation or rather bitter malice hath Commonly beene betweene the Deputyes neerest foregoing and succeeding. So as the newe Deputy affecting priuate fame rather then publike good, hath seldome or never troden the steps of his predicessor, but rather insisted vpon his owne maximes of government, espetially careing that his actions be not obscured by those of his predicesser, And this Babilonian confusion of distracted and contrary motians in the Cheefe governours, hath made the Irish, like wilde Coltes hauing vnskillfull Riders, to learne all theire Jadish trickes, whereas if the gouernment were continued till the magistrate might knowe the nature of the people, with the secrets of that State, and apply the remedyes proper therevnto : If after theire government, (according to the Custome of the State of Venice) each Deputy should giue in writing to the State in England a full relation of his gouernment and the State of that kingdome, so as his successour might weaue the same webb he had begunn, and not make a newe frame of his owne : If in reguard the kings presence in Ireland may rather be wished then hoped, some spetiall Commissioners, sworne to Faithfull relation, were chosen in England once in two or three yeares, and sent ouer to visitt the affayres of that kingdome, and to make like relation thereof at theire returne. No doubt that kingdome might in shorte tyme be reformed, and the kings Reuenues might be so increased, as Ireland might not only mantayne it selfe in peace, but restore parte of the Treasure it hath formerly exhausted in England, and lay vp meanes to supply future necessityes of that State, Since the sayde Deputies and commissionours would euery one be ashamed not to add somthinge to the Publike good of theire owne, and much more to doe that was allready done, or rather to destroy it, by theire imployment. And the Irish would thereby be putt from theire shifting hopes gapeing for newe vnskillfull and diuersely affected Magestrates, which haue allwayes annimated them to delatorye obedience and Rebellious Courses.

By the Complaynt of former ages rather then experience in

our tyme, I haue obserued, that the Lord Deputyes a[u]thority
in Ireland hath beene much weakened, by the graunting of
suites and rewardes in England to many of the Irish, without
hauing any recommendations from theire Deputy, and much
more because the Judiciall causes of the Irish haue beene
determined in England without the lord Deputyes priuity, or
hauing beene formerly determined in Ireland, were sent backe
to be agayne examined and determined, according to letters of
fauour obtayned by the Plantiues in England, which made the
subiect prowde, and to triumphe vpon the ouerruled
Magistrate, who no doubt is ether vnfitt to gouerne a kingdome,
or ought best to knowe who deserue punishment, who reward,
and the most fitt wayes to determine iudiciall causes. Wherein
I dare boldly say the contrary proceedinges of our tyme, giuing
that magistrate his due honour, hath much aduansed the
publike good.

Some doe not approue the residence of the lord Deputy at
Dublin, and would haue it rather at Athlone, vppon the edge of
Connaght and Vlster, where he should haue those seditious
Prouinces before him, and might easily fall with his forces into
Mounster, and so should be nearer hand to preuent Tumults
with his presence and compose them with his power, and
likewise should haue at his back the Pale (contayning five
shires, and so called because they euer were most quiett and
subiect to the English) and so might stopp all Rebells from
disturbing the Pale which would not only yeild supplyes of
necessaries to his Trayne and Soldiers, but also giue safe
passage for transporting munition and victualls to Athlone from
the Stoare houses at Dublin. And this Counsell was so much
vrged to Queene Elizabeth as these reasons together with the
saving of the Charge to mantayne a Gouernor in Connaght with
Counsellors to assist him, and the like charge then intended
for Vlster moued her to referr the determination thereof to the
Lo: Mountioy then Deputy and the Counsell of State, who
altered nothing because that course would haue ruined or
decayed the Citty of Dublin, and espetially because the

Rebellion was soone after appeased, and our State hath commonly vsed, like Marriners to be secure in faire weather, and neuer fly to the tacklings till a storme come.

The Meere Irish.

Touching the meere Irish before I speake of them, giue me leaue to remember fowre verses expressing fowre mischeifes afflicting them, as fruites of their idlenes, slouenlynes, and superstition.

> Quatuor hybernos vexant animalia, turpes
> Corpora vermiculi, sorices per tecta rapaces,
> Carniuori vastantque lupi crudeliter agros,
> Hæc tria nequitia superas Romane sacerdos.

> For foure vile beasts Ireland hath no fence,
> their bodyes lice, their houses Ratts possesse.
> Most wicked Preists gouerne their conscience,
> and rauening Woolues do wast their feilds no lesse.

That may well be said of the Irish which Cæsar in his Commentaries writes of the old Germans; like beasts they doe all things by force and Armes, after a slauish manner. The Magistrate doth nothing publiquely or priuately without Armes. They reuenge iniuryes seldome by lawe, but rather by the sword and rapine, neither are they ashamed of stealth or taking prayes or spoyles. Formerly I haue shewed that the Englishmen who subdued Ireland, and long mantayned the Conquest thereof, did flock into England vppon the Ciuill warrs betweene the houses of Yorke, and Lancaster aswell to beare vpp the factions as to inherritt their kinsmens Lands in England and so left wast their possessions in Ireland. At that tyme the meere Irish rushed into those vacant possessions, and the better to keepe them, from that tyme were ever prounce to rebelions, that the course of lawe might cease while they were in Armes, and from that tyme resumed olde barbarous lawes and Customes which had beene long abolished, and by withdrawing themselues from obedience to our lawes, became powerfull tyrants in all Countryes. From that tyme they did euer putt forth and secreetely mantayne vpon all fitt occations some outlawes to disturbe peace (like our Roben Hud and litle John in the tymes of Richard the First and John kings of England) growing to that Impudency, as these outlawes are not by them termed Rebles, but men in Action, liuing in the woodes and Boggy places. Among them (and many of the English Irish by theire example) those that became lords of Countryes were euer as many heades so many monstrous tyrants. These haue not their landes deuided in many Countryes, as our noblemen in England (whereby they are lesse powerfull to disturbe peace) but possesse whole Countryes together, whereof notwithstanding great partes lye wast, only for want of Tennants. And because they haue an ill Custome, that Tennants are reputed proper to those lands on which they dwell, without liberty to remoue theire dwelling vnder an other landlord, they still desyre more land, rather to haue the Tennants then the land, whereas if they could furnish theire old landes with Tennants (as perhapps they haue in some sorte donne since the last Rebellion, of which and former tymes I wryte) they would much exceede our greatest lords in yearely Reuenues.

It is a great mischeefe, that among them, all of one name or Sept and kindred, dwell not (as in England) dispersed in many shyres, but all liue together in one village, Lordshipp, and County ready and apt to conspire together in any mischeife. And by an old lawe, which they call of themistry, vulgarly called Tanistry by many of our lawes abolished, yet still in force among themselues, euery Sept chuseth their cheife head or Captaine, not the eldest sonne of the eldest Family but the oldest or rather the most daring man, (whereby they alwayes vnderstand the most licentious swordsman) as most fitt to defend them. And this Cheefe they not only chuse among themselues, but of Corrupt Custome impudently challenged to be confirmed by the Lord Deputyes producing many like graunts of that dignity made of old by the Lord Deputyes vnder their hands and seales, then which nothing can be more fitt to mantayne Factions and tumults and to hinder the Course of the kings lawes. By the same lawe often abolished by vs but still retayned in vse among them, they will needs haue the choyse of him that shall inheritt the land of the last Cheefe of any Sept, or name, not respecting therein the eldest sonne, according to our lawes but him that most pleaseth their turbulent humors, whence flowes a plentifull spring of Murthers Parracides and Conspiracyes against the kings and their lawes. For first hereby they professed to liue after their owne lawes, and openly denyed obedience to the kings lawes, and againe to giue an instance of one mischeife, passing ouer many other of no lesse moment, when any of these Cheefes or Lords of Countryes vppon submission to the States hath surrendred his lands to the king, and taken a new graunt of them by the kings letters Pattents with Conditions fitt for publique good, they boldly say that he held his Lands by the tenure of Thanistrye only for his life, and so will not be tyed to any of his Acts. And it is no matter what they professe, why should we heare their words, when wee see their deeds. I doe not thinck but know that they will neuer be reformed in Religion, manners, and constant obedience, to our lawes, but by the awe of the sword, and by a strong hand at least for a tyme bridling them.

By these and like corrupt Customes, neglecting our lawes, they become disturbers of the peace, and after a barbarous manner, for terror or in pride, add to their names O (noting the cheife or head) and Mac (noting the sonne of such a one), and thus they are called Oneales, O Donnells, mac Mahownes with a rable of like names, some rather seeming the names of Devowring Giants then Christian Subiects, yea some of old English Familyes degenerating into this Barbarisme, haue changed their names after the Irish tongue, as the Vrslyes are called Mahownes taking the notation from the name of a Beare; yea some of the most licentious take to themselues Nicknames suitable to their wicked dispositions, as one of the O Donnells was called Garne that is a Cholerick strong (or lusty) Gallant, and such he was indeede. And some as if they were knights of Amadis of Gaule, and had the valor of those errant knights, were called the knight of the valley, the white knight, and the like. And withall they despise our titles of Earles and lords, which so weakens the great mens estimation among them, as they must cast them away, and assume their old barbarous names whensoeuer they will haue the power to lead the people, to any rebellious action. For in those barbarous names, and nick names, the Irish are proude to haue the rebellious acts of their forefathers sung by their Bards or Poetts, at their Feasts and publique meetings. Againe they haue a Corrupt Custome to increase their power by fostering their Children, with the most valiant rich and powerfull neighbors, since that people beares such straunge reuerence to this bond and pledge of loue, as they commonly loue their Foster Children more than their owne. The events of which Custome forced our Progenitors to make seuere lawes against the same, which notwithstanding, howsoeuer restrayned for the tyme, grew againe to be of force among them in our age.

They haue likewise a ridiculous Custome, that maryed wemen giue Fathers to their Children when they are at the point of death. Insomuch as they haue a pleasant tale, that a younger sonne hearing his mother giue base Fathers to some of his brethren, besought her with teares to giue him a good father. But commonly they giue them fathers of the Oneales, O Donnells or such great men, or at least those that are most famous for licentious boldnes. And these bastard Children euer after follow these fathers, and thincking themselues to descend of them, wilbe called swordmen, and scorning husbandrye, and manuall Arts liue only of rapine and spoyle.

These foresaid meere Irish lords of Countryes gouerne the people vnder them with such tyranny, as they know no king in respect of them, who challenge all their goods and Cattell to be theirs saying, that their Progenitors did not only giue them lands to till, but also Cowes and other goods to possesse at the lords will and disposall. Neither take they any rent of them

for their Lands, but at pleasure impose mony vppon them, vppon
all occasions of spending, as Journeyes to Dublin, or into
England, paying their debts, intertayning of the lord Deputy,
or Judges, and like occasions, sometymes true, sometymes
fayned, taking a great or small portion of their goods, according
to the quality of the Cause, and these exactions they doe well
call Cuttings, wherewith they doe not only cutt, but deuoure
the people. And it litle auayleth these poore Tenants, though
some of them can proue by Indentures that they are Freeholders, and not Tenants at will, for of old to the end of the
last warr (of which tyme I write and desyre to be vnderstood)
the lords by tyrannicall Custome still ouerswayed the peoples
right in these Courses. And this Custome was the fountayne of
many evills, more specially of one mischeife, that if the Tenant
by any Cryme forfeited his goods, the lord denyed him to haue
any proprierty therein and yet if the same goods were seazed
by the Sheriffe for any Fynes for the king, or debts of the lord,
to priuate men, the tenants forthwith exclaymed of iniustice to
punish them for the lords offences With this (as it were)
Dilemna still deluding the execution of Justice. Yea these
lords challenged right of Inheritance in their Tenants persons,
as if by old Couenants they were borne slaues to till their
grounde, and doe them all like seruices, and howsoeuer they
were oppressed might not leaue their land to dwell vnder any
other landlord. And these suites betweene the lords for right
in Tenants, were then most frequent. Thus I remember the
sonne of Henry Oge to be killed in the Country of Mac Mahowne
while he went thither to bring back by force a fugitiue Tenant
(as they terme them). Like suits for Tenants were frequent at
this tyme betweene the new created Earle of Tirconnell, and
Sr. Neale Garne, and at first the magistrate commaunded the
Earle to restore to Sir Neale his old Tenants, but when peace
was more setled, the Itinerant Judges going into Vlster, added a
generall Caution in this case, that the Tenants should not be
forced to retorne, except they were willing, professing at
publique meetings with great applause of the people, that it was

most uniust the kings Subiects borne in a free Common wealth
should be vsed like slaues. Againe these lordes challenging all
their Tenants goods, thinck scorne to haue any Cowes or herdes
of Cattell of their owne, tho sometymes they permitt their wiues
to haue some like propriety. They distribute their lands among
their Tenants to be tilled only for one, two, or three yeares, and
so the people build no houses but like Nomades living in Cabins,
remoue from one place to an other with their Cowes, and
commonly retyre them within thick woods not to be entred
without a guide delighting in this Rogish life, as more free
from the hand of Justice, and more fitt to committ rapines.
Thus the Country people living vnder the lordes absolute power
as slaues, and howsoeuer they haue plenty of Corne, milke, and
Cattell; yet having no propriety in any thing, obey their lordes
in right and wrong, and being all of the Roman church, and
being taught that [it] is no sinn to breake faith with vs, and
so litle regarding an oath taken before our Magistrates, the
king was often defrauded of his right by the falsehood of Juryes,
in his Inheritance, Wardes Attaindors, Escheates intrusions,
Alienations, and all Pleas of the Crowne. At the end of the
warr among infinite examples, this was well seene in the Case
of Meade the Recorder of Corke, who having committed open
treason, was quitted by an Irish Jurye, himselfe craftily
hastning his tryall for feare he should be tryed in England.
The Court of the Starr chamber, shortly after established
seuerely punished Juryes for abuses of this last kinde but with
what effect, is besydes my purpose to write. These Irish lordes
in the last warr, had a cunning trick, that howsoeuer the father
possessing the land, bore himselfe outwardly as a Subiect, yet
his sonnes having no lands in possession, should liue with the
Rebells, and keepe him in good tearmes with them, and his
goods from present spoyling. The lords of Ireland, at this tyme
whereof I write, nourished theeues, as we doe Hawkes, openly
boasting among themselues, who had the best theeues. Neighbors intertayning these men into their Familyes, for mutuall
preiudices, was a secrett fewell of the Ciuill warr, they being

prone to rebellion, and in peace not forbearing to steale at home, and to spoyle all passengers neere their abode.

The wilde or meere Irish haue a generation of Poets, or rather Rymers vulgarly called Bardes, who in their songs vsed to extoll the most bloudy licentious men, and no others, and to allure the hearers, not to the loue of religion and Ciuill manners, but to outrages Robberies living as outlawes, and Contempt of the Magistrates and the kings lawes. Alas how vnlike vnto Orpheus, who with his sweete harpe and wholesome precepts of Poetry laboured to reduce the rude and barbarous people from liuing in woods, to dwell Ciuilly in Townes and Cittyes, and from wilde ryott to morall Conuersation. All goodmen wished these knaues to be strictly curbed, and seuerely punished. For the meere Irish, howsoeuer they vnderstood not what was truely honourable, yet out of barbarous ignorance are so affected to vayne glory, as they nothing so much feared the lord Deputys anger, as the least song or Balladd these Rascalls might make against them, the singing whereof to their reproch, would more haue daunted them, then if a Judge had doomed them to the Gallowes.

They had also an other Rabble of Jeasters which vsed to frequent the Tables of lordes and Gentlemen continuall tellers of newes which comonly they reduced to the preiudice of the publike good.

Againe the Irish in generall more specially the meere Irish, being sloathfull and giuen to nothing more then base Idlenes, they nourished a third generation of vipers vulgarly called Carowes, professing (forsooth) the noble science of playing at Cards and dice, which so infected the publique meetings of the people, and the priuate houses of lordes, as no adventure was too hard in shifting for meanes to mantayne these sports. And indeed the wilde Irish doe madly affect them, so as they will not only play and leese their mony and mouable goods, but also ingage their lands, yea their owne persons to be ledd as Prisoners by the winner, till he be paid the mony, for which they are ingaged. It is a shame to speake, but I heard by

credible relation, that some were found so impudent, as they
had suffered themselues so to be ledd as Captiues tyed by the
parts of their body which I will not name, till they had mony
to redeeme themselues. Could a Prouost Marshall be better
imployed then in hanging vpp such Raskalls and like vagabond
persons. For howsoeuer none could better doe it then the
Sheriffes; yet because the Irish frequently and in part iustly
complayned of their extortions (as I shall after shewe), I dare
not say that Marshall lawe might well be committed to them.

The Irish thus giuen to Idlenes, naturally abhorr from
Manuall Artes, and Ciuill trades to gaine their owne bread, and
the basest of them wilbe reputed gentlemen and sword men, for
so they are termed who professe to liue by their swordes, and
haue bene alwayes apt to raise Ciuill warrs, and euer most
hardly drawne to lay downe Armes, by which they had liberty
to liue in riott. Many examples might be giuen in the highest
kinde of mischeife produced by this idlenes, but that the vice
is most naturall to the Irish; I will only giue one example
which myselfe obserued of Fishermen in the Cittyes of
Mounster, who being no swordmen, yet were generally so
sloathfull, as in the Calmest weather, and the greatest
Concourse of noblemen, when they had no feare of daunger,
and great hope of gayne, though the Seas abound with excellent
fish and the Prouince with frequent Ports, and bayes most fitt
for fishing; yet so long as they had bread to eate, would not putt
to sea, no not commaunded by the lord Deputy, till they were
beaten by force out of their houses. And in my opinion this
idlenes hath bene nourished by nothing more (as I haue
formerly shewed vppon other occasions) then by the plenty of
the land, and great housekeeping, drawing the people from
trades, while they can be fedd by others without labour. This
experience hath shewed of old, aswell in England, where the
greatest Robberies were comonly done, by idle seruingmen
swarming in great houses, as in the more northern parts, and in
Ireland, where they multitude of loose Followers hath of old
bene prone to fight their Lords quarrells, yea to rebell with

them. Whereas no doubt the exercise of trades, and the Custome of industrye to liue euery man of his owne, are a strong establishment of any Comon Wealth. The mere Irish giuen to sloath are also most luxurious. And not to speake of the aboundance of all meates, they are excessiuely giuen to drunkennes. For howsoeuer, whyle they liued in woodes and in Cabbines with theire Catle, they could be content with water and milke, yet when they came to Townes nothing was more frequent then to tye theire Cowes at the dores, and neuer parte from the taverns till they had druncke them out in Sacke and strong water, which they call vsquebagh, and this did not only the lords, but the Common people, tho halfe naked for want of Cloathes to cover them. No man may iustly maruell, if among such people dissolute hucksters apt to rayse seditions and liue like outlawes, be frequently founde. Therefore at the end of the last warr, it was wished and expected, that this luxury should be suppressed at least from generall excesse, that all vagabond persons should be seuerely punished, that the people should be allured and drawne to loue manuall arts and trades, more spetially husbandry of tillage. For whereas all, yea the most strong and able bodyes, and men giuen to spoyles and Robberyes in all tymes gladly imployed themselues in feeding of Cowes, that Course of life was imbraced by them as suitable to theire innated slothe, and as most fitt to elude or protract all execution of Justice against them, while they commonly liued in thick woods abounding with grasse. But no doubt it were much better if Ireland should be reduced to lesse grasing and more tillage by the distribution of lands among Tenants in such sort, as euer after it should (as in England) be vnlawfull to chaunge any tillage into Pasture.

The English Irish.

Touching the English Irish namely such as discend of the first English conquering that Country, or since in diuerse ages, and tymes to this day transplanted out of England, into Ireland. It is wonderfull yet most true, that for some later ages they

haue beene (some in high some in lesse measure,) infected with
the barbarous Customes of the meere Irish and with the Roman
Religion so as they grewe not only as aduerse to the Reformation
of Ciuill policye and religion, as the meere Irish but euen
combyned with them, and shewed such malice to the English
nation, as if they were ashamed to haue any Community with
it, of Country, bloud, religion, language apparrell, or any such
generall bond of amity. And for this alienation, they did not
shame in the last Ciuill warr to alledge reasons to iustify their
so doing, namely that they whose Progenitours had conquered
that kingdome, and were at First thought most worthy to
gouerne the same vnder our kings, were by a new lawe excluded
from being deputyes, and had otherwise small or no power in
the State. Agayne that after they were broken, and worne out
in the Ciuill warr of England, betweene the houses of Yorke and
Lancaster, they were not strengthned with newe Colonyes out of
England, and so being weaker then the mere Irish, were forced
to apply themselues to the stronger, by contracting affinity with
them, and vsing their language and apparrell. These and like
reasons they pretended, which I will first answer and then shewe
the true causes thereof. It cannot be denyed but the English
Irish After the first Conquest were by our Kings made cheefe
Gouernors of that kingdome, yea and many ages after were
sometymes lord deputyes, and were alwayes Capable of that
place, till the tyme of king Henry the Eight, but neuer without
detriment of the Common Wealth and danger from them that
possessed it. To the first English Irish borne of noble Familyes
in England, our kings gaue large patrimonyes and great
priuiledges making them sometymes Gouernors of the State but
in processe of tyme, some of them forgetting their Country,
bloud and all pledges of loue towards the English, not only
became Rebells but by degrees grewe like the meere Irish in
all things euen in hating the English, and becoming cheefe
leaders to all seditions growing at last to such pride in the last
Ciuill warr, as if they had not rewards when they deserued
punishments, or could not obtayne pentions to serue the State,

they were more ready to rebell, then the meere Irish themselues. Among these some in hatred to the English changed
their English names into Irish, yet retayning the old notation,
as the Vrselyes called them selues Mac Mahownes, some in
Vlster of the Family of Veres, called themselues Macrones,
others of the Family of great Mortimer, called themselues
Macmarrs. These and some others, as Breningham discended
of old English Barons, and the lord Curcy whose Progenitors of
the English Nobility were among the Cheife, and first
Conquerors of the kingdome, grewe so degenerate, as in the last
rebellion, they could not be distinguished from meere Irish.
The rest retayning their old names, and in good measure the
English manners, as Tyrrell, Lacey, many of the Bourkes, and
Geraldines, and some of the Nugents, yet became cheefe leaders
in the late rebellion. These men no man will iudge capable of
the cheife gouernments in that kingdome. But lett them passe,
and lett vs consider, if the English Irish that in the Rebellion
remayned Subiects, and will not be stayned with the name of
Rebells, haue any iust cause to complayne that they are
excluded from the gouernment, because the lawe forbidds them
to be deputyes. They are in England free Denizens, having
equall right with the English to inherritt lands, and beare
offices, and obtayne any dignity whereof their merritt, or the
kings fauour may make them Capable. Lett them remember
that the Earle of Strangbowe being the leader of the English,
that first conquered Ireland, when the king would haue
committed to him the gouernment thereof, did modestly refuse
the same, except the king would ioyne some assistants with him,
not ignorant what daunger that magistracye would bring to him
more then to any other.   Lett them remember, that among
other noble Familyes of the Englishe Conquerors, first Lacy,
then Curcy, had the cheife gouernment of that kingdome, but
the first was recalled into England to giue accompt of his
gouernment, not without danger, of leesing his head, the other
was long cast into prison. Lett them remember that the lord
Deputyes place did weaken and almost destroy the Family of

the Geraldines, after which tyme king Henry the Eight by Act
of Parliament first excluded the English Irish from being cheife
Gouernors of that kingdome, as Common experience made all
men finde, that gouernment not only dangerous to themselues
aduanced to it, but also more displeasing to the people, who
least like the Commaund of their owne Countrymen and were
most ready to loade them with Complaynts in England, as also
their owne Countrymen being Counsellors of State, whose
oppressions they most felt, and greiued at. Yet many English
Irish continued Counsellors of State all the tyme of Queene
Elizabeth and the last Rebellion whereof I write. For my part
if the English Irish had English affections, I would thinck no
difference should be made betweene them and the English.
But in the last Rebellion nothing was more euident then that
our secrett Counsells were continually made knowne to Tyrone
and other Rebells, and lett men iudge vnpartially, who could
more iustly be suspected of this falshood, then the Counsellors
of State, borne in that kingdome. Many Counsells were
propounded for reforming the State, for banishing Jesuites and
other troublers of the State, and lett themselues vnpartially
speake, who did more frustrate those designes, then the
Counsellors, of that tyme borne in that kingdome. Were not
the cheife Justice and the Cheife Baron of that tyme both borne
and bredd in Ireland? Lett them say truely for what good
seruice of theirs, Queene Elizabeth appointed ouerseers to looke
into their actions and make them knowne to her deputy. No
doubt that wise Queene either thought the Counsells of Sir
Robert Dillon knight, and the said cheife Justice of Ireland
contrary to the publique good, or vppon better aduise, she would
neuer haue remoued him from that place, which her gracious
fauour had first conferred vppon him. What neede we vse
circumstances, the generall opinion of that tyme was, that the
English Irish made Counsellors of State, and Judges of Courts
did euidently hurt the publike good, and that their falseharted
helpe, did more hinder reformation, then the open Acts of the
Rebells. Generally before this tyme they were Papists, and

if some of them, vppon hypocriticall dispensation went to Church Commonly their Parents, children kinsmen and seruants, were open and obstinate Papists in profession. Tell me any one of them who did according to the duty of their place, publikely commend or Commaund to the people the vse of the Common prayer booke, and the frequenting of our Churches. Why doe they glory of their gouerning the Common Wealth, if they cannot shewe one good act of Reformation perswaded, and perfected by them.

In the Raigne of king Edward the third, when the king found the Pope obstinate for vsurping the hereditary right of him and his Subiects, in bestowing Church livings vnder their Patronage, and valiantly opposed himselfe to this and other oppressions of the Pope, obseruing that his Counsells were no way more crossed, then by Italians and French men, whome the Pope, had Cunningly preferred to Bishoppricks and Benefices, yea to be of the kings Councell of State, whereby they had meanes to betray the secretts of the State, he wisely made an Act of Parliament in the 25 yeare of his Raigne, whereby he prouided remidy against these vnfaithfull Counsellors and Churchmen. That which king Edward might doe in this Case, may not his Successors doe the same in Ireland vppon like danger, sequestring any suspected persons from places in Counsell and Judgment. When magistrates themselues vse only Connivencye in punishing disobedience to the lawes, and Sects in Religion, doth not their example confirme the people in disobedience to their king? But you shall know the lyon by his Pawe (as the Proverb saith) lett vs further see, how the English Irish in those tymes caryed themselues in military commaunds committed to them. Queene Elizabeth finding that the lord Deputies from the first beginning of the last Rebellion, had made a great error, in levying Companyes of the English Irish, to suppresse the meere Irish, so having trayned them vpp as the very horseboyes of them following our Armye were proued good shott, was at last forced to intertaine of them many Companyes of Foote, and Troopes of horse in her pay, lest

they should fall to the Rebells party. Of these some woorthy
Commaunders did good seruice, and all in generall, so long as
they were imployed in our Army, serued brauely, so as the lord
Deputy was often bold to take the feilde when halfe his forces
consisted of them.   But when they were left in Garrison,
especially in their owne Countryes, it was obserued that
generally they did no seruice, but lying still, wasted the
Queenes Treasure, and lest they should leese their pay, which
they esteemed a Reuenewe, or religion should be reformed in
tyme of peace, (which they most feared), they did make our
Counsells knowne to the Rebells, did vnderhand releiue them,
and vsed all meanes to nourish and strengthen the Rebellion.
It is straunge but most true, that aswell to merritt the Rebells
fauour, as to haue the goods of their Countrye safe from
spoyling, the very Subiects gaue large Contributions to the
Rebells, insomuch as one Country, (whereby an Estimate of
the rest may be made,) did pay the Rebells three hundreth
pounds yearely, vsing this art to auoide the danger of the lawe,
that when they made a cutting vppon Cowes for this purpose,
they pretended to make this exaction for the lords vse, vnder
hand sending the Rebells word thereof that they might by
force surprise those Cowes which indeede were leuyed for them.
And besides all or most of them had Children, brothers or
kinsmen ioyned with the Rebells, as hostages of their loue, and
pledges of reconcilement vppon all events.   Againe, I said
formerly that the Septs or men of one name and bloud, liued
together in one Towne and Country, each Sept having a
Captaine or cheife of that name. Now this point is a great
mistery, that they could giue no more certaine pledge of faith
to vs, then to drawe bloud of any of these Septs.   But the lord
Deputy making it a cheife proiect to make them drawe bloud in
this kinde vppon their neighbors, founde it a most hard thing to
effect with any of the English Irish, yea with those that were in
the Queenes pay; yet the English Irish being in the States pay,
lest they should be held altogether vnprofitable, and to purchase
reward of seruice, would sometymes kill a poore Rebell, or bring

him aliue to the State, whose reuenge they feared not, yea
perhapps a Rebell of note to whome the cheife Neighbor Rebells
bore malice, and so cast him into their hands. And this done
they vsed to triumphe as though they had done a masterpeece
of seruice, and could hardly haue the patience to expect a
Shipp to carry them into England that in Court they might
importune extraordinary reward besides their ordinary pay.
To be briefe, the Queenes letters shall beare me witnesse that
the English Irish placed in Garrisons at theire owne home lyved
idlie without doinge any seruice exhausted the publique
Treasure and by all meanes nourished the Rebellioun,
especiallie by plottes laid at priuate parlyes and at publique
meetinges vppon hills (Called Rathes) where many treacherous
Conspiraces weare made. Would any equall man blame a
Prince for puttinge such Souldgers out of pay, for prohibittinge
such partyes, and for Carefull wacchinge ouer such meetings?
Great priuiledges weare worthely graunted at first to the great
Lordes of English race for theire Conquest, and great power
over the people was wisely giuen them at first both for Reward
and for power to keepe the meere Irish in Subieccion : But if
theise Lordes vse theire priuilidges and power to Contrary
endes, spoilinge the subiectes and wastinge the Countrey by
theire sword men when the Cause Ceased, shall not the effect
cease? When theire vertue is Changed and theire endes
Corrupted, may not a wise Prince abridge theire priuilidges and
power? The same is the reason of the law forbiddinge any of
the English Irish to be Lord deputy : The famous Queene
Elizabeth findinge the ill Event of theise ill Causes became
Jealous of the English Irish Counsellours of State and Judges
and vsed the aforesaid Remedyes against a Cheeffe Justice and
a Cheffe Barroun of that tyme. Formerly I acknowledge that
the English Irish serued brauely in our Army, while they weare
vnder the Lord deputyes eic, and some worthie Commaunders
of them shewed great faithfullnes, and did speciall seruices,
yet this most wise Queene found theire defectes, and that the
strength of hir affaires Consisted in breedinge English

Souldgiers, soe as shee commaunded the other Companyes to be no more supplied, but to be Cast by degrees, as they grew defectiue, and in the meane tyme to be ymploied out of theire owne Countryes, where they might not feare to draw blood of the borderinge Septes.   The Earle of Clanricard serued the said Queene soe well, as he cannot be to much Commended for the same, and was also highly in hir Fauour; yet when the Earle of Essex had left him Gouernour of his owne Countrey, howsoeuer shee would not openly displace him, yet shee Ceased not till by hir direccions hee was induced to a voluntary Resignacioun therof into hir handes : For indeed the English Irish and meere Irish of that tyme weare generally soe humorous, as their fathers or brothers that dyed having any gouernment of the Country or commaund in the Army, they esteemed the same as due to them by Inheritance, or at least if they were not conferred on them, grew discontented and prone to any mischeuious Course.   To conclude, the English Irish of that tyme (few or none excepted) were obstinate and most superstitious Papists, and what our State might haue hoped from such men in high places of gouernment lett wise men iudge.

The second excuse of the English Irish for applying them- selues to the meere Irish in manners Lawes and Customes, and so growing strangers (if not Enemyes) to the English, hath some Coulor of truth, but can neuer iustify this action.   Namely that the Colonyes of the first English conquering Ireland, being broken and wasted in the Ciuill warr of England betweene the houses of Yorke and Lancaster, were neuer supplied, but left so weake as they were forced to apply themselues to the meere Irish as the stronger.   Since the noble Familyes of England were much wasted in the same warr, no maruell if at the end thereof, our kings first intended the restoring of England to the former vigor, before they could cast their eyes vppon Ireland, and in this meane tyme the meere Irish had taken such roote, and so ouertopped the English Irish, as the sending of English Colonyes thether so long as the meere Irish remayned good Subiects, would rather haue disturbed then established peace. The first fayre occasion of planting newe English Colonyes there, was giuen in the Raigne of Queene Elizabeth by two Rebellions, the first of the English Irish Geraldines, who had the Earle of Desmond for their head, the second of the meere Irish, and many English Irish, having the Earle of Tyrone for their head. Touching the first, when the Earle of Desmond was subdued, and that Rebellion appeased, the said Queene (of happy memory) intended great Reformation by planting new English Familyes vppon the forfeited lands of the Earle of Desmond, in Mounster. But this good intention was made voyde by a great error of that tyme, in that those lands were graunted, partly to obstinate Papists, partly to Courtiers, who sold their shares to like obstinate Papists, as men that would giue most for them. Whereof two great mischeifes grewe. First that these Papists being more obstinate then others, and therevppon choosing to leaue their dwelling in England, where the seuerity of the lawes bridled them, and to remoue into Ireland, where they might be more remote, and so haue greater liberty, shewed the old prouerbe to be true,

Cælum non animum mutant, qui trans mare currunt.

Passing the sea with a swift wynde, doth change the aire but not the mynde.

For they not only remayned Papists, but grew more and more obstinate with liberty, and by their example confirmed both the English Irish and meere Irish in that superstition. Secondly, these new planted English (commonly called vndertakers) being thus ill affected, did not performe the Couenants imposed in their graunts, for establishing peace in that Prouince; For they nether built Castles, to strengthen them against tymes of Rebellion, neither did they plant their lands with well affected Tenants out of England, giuing them Freeholds, Coppy holds and leases, and tying them to serue on Foote, or horseback vppon all occasions of tumult or warr, which would much haue

strengthned the English against the meere Irish and all
Invasions. But they tooke a Contrary Course, not only planting
their lands with meere Irish Tenants, (to whome they gaue no
such tenor of Freehold Copyhold or lease, and who serued them
vppon base abiect Conditions, whereby they made great profitt
for the present) but also intertayning them for seruants in their
Familyes, for the same reason of present profitt. And this
made their great profitt of small continuance, and their
dwellings of lesse strength and safety. For in the first troubles
of the next Rebellion of Tyrone, themselues and the State
founde by wofull experience, that they had no way strengthned
the Prouince, but only dispeopled and wasted other lands to
bring Tenants vppon their owne, so as the kings other Rents
were thereby as much diminished as increased by their Rents,
and the number of horse or foote to defend the Prouince, were
nothing increased by them; neither had they made any greater
number of English to passe in Juryes betweene the king and the
Subiects, so as the lord President had not power to suppresse the
first Rebells, and the Judges in all tryalls were forced to vse the
Irish, who made no conscience of doing wrong to the king, and
the English Subiects. Againe theire Irish Tennants ether rann
away, or turning Rebells spoyled them, and the Irish in theire
houses were ready to betray them, and open theire dores to the
Rebells. So as some of those vndertakers were in the first
tumult killed, some taken prisoners were cruelly handled, and
had theire wiues and daughters shamefully abused, great part
rann out of the kingdome, and yet shamed not to clayme and
proffesse in the ende of the Rebelion these landes, the defence
whereof they had so basely forsaken. Some few kept theire old
Reuenued Castles, but with great charg to the State in
mantayning warders to defend them, which warders were so
many, as they greatly deminished the force of our Army in the
fielde. Thus were the good purposes of that first plantation
made frustrate by ill disposed vndertakers. Touching the other
Rebelion of Tyrone, the appeasing thereof concurred at one
instant with the death of our sayd Queene, beyond which tyme

my purpose is not to write, and therefore it should be imperti-
nent for me, worthily to magnifye the Plantation in the North,
established by king James our gracious Soouerayne. Only I will
say for the want of former Colonies planting, whereof the
English Irish complayne, that as the Plantation after Desmonds
Rebellion was made frustrate by ill disposed vndertakers, so
from the foresayd Ciuill warrs betweene the houses of Yorke
and Lancaster to the end of Tyrones Rebellion, all the English
in generall that voluntarily left England to plant themselues
in Ireland, ether vnder the sayd Vndertakers of Mounster, or
vpon the landes of any other English Irish throughout Ireland,
or to liue in Cittyes and townes, were generally obserued to haue
beene ether Papists, men of disordered life, banckrots, or very
poore (not speaking of those of the Army remayning there after
the Rebellion, who are of another tyme succeeding that whereof
I write, and well knowne to be of good condition). By which
course Ireland as the heele of the body was made the sincke of
England, the stench whereof had almost annoyed very Cheap-
side the hart of the body in Tyrons pestilent Rebellion. To
conclude, I deny not but the excuse of weaknes in the English
Irish Colonies, forcing them to apply to the meere Irish as
stronger, hath in part a true ground, though it cannot Justifye
the act. And if I should perswade the planting of Ireland with
newe Colonies, I should now speake out of tyme, when that
profitable and necessary action is in great measure performed
by the prouidence of our dread Souraigne. If I should commend
and extoll the Act, I feare I should therein be reputed as foolish
as the Sophister, who in a publike assembly made a long oration
in prayse of Herculus, whome no man at that tyme or formerly
euer dispraysed. But I will passe from theire alledged excuses
to the true causes of theire Alienation from vs and application
to the meere Irish. The grand cause is theire firme consent
with them in the Roman Religion, whereof I shall speake at
larg in the next Booke of this part. The second cause also
prædominant, though in a lower degree, is the profitt they haue
long tyme found in the barbarous lawes and Customes of the

Irish, by tyrannicall oppression of the poore people vnder them, of which point I haue formerly spoken in this Chapter. The third cause is theire Contracting affinity with them by marriage, and amitye by mutuall fostering of Chilldren. The fourth is community of apparrell. The fifth Community of language. Of which three last causes I will now speake breifly.

The power of these three last causes to corrupt the manners and Fayth of any nation, being well knowne, the Progenitors of our kings with consent of the States of that kingdome in Parlament, did of old make many Actes against them, which sometymes wrought reformation, but without any during effect.

For contrary to these lawes, the English Irish haue for many ages, almost from the first conquest, contracted Mariages with the meere Irish, whose children of mingled race could not but degenerate from theire English Parents, and allso mutually fostered each others Children, which bond of loue the Irish generally somuch esteeme, as they will giue theire Foster Children a parte of theire goods with theire owne Children, and the very Children fostered together loue one another as naturall brothers and sisters, yea theire Foster brothers or sisters better then theire owne. Only I must say for the English Irish Cittisens, espetially those of Corck, that they haue euer so much avoyded these Mariages with the meere Irish, as for want of others commonly marying among themselues, all the men and wemen of the Cittie had for many ages beene of kindred in neere degree one with the other.

Agayne contrary to the sayd lawes, the English Irish for the most part haue for many ages had the same attyre and apparrell with the meere Irish, namely the nourishing of long hare (vulgarly called glibs) which hanges downe to the shoulders, hidinge the face, so as a malefactor may easily escape with his face covered theire with, or by collering his hayre, and much more by cutting it off, may so alter his countenance as those of his acquaintance shall not knowe him, and this hayre being exceeding long, they haue no vse of Capp or hatt. Also they weare strayte Breeches, called Trowses, uery close to the body

and loose Coates like large waskotes, and mantells in steede of
Clokes, which Mantells are as a Cabinn for an outlawe in the
woods, a bedd for a Rebell, and a Cloke for a theefe, and being
worne over the head and eares, and hanging downe to the heeles,
a notorious Villane lapt in them may passe any towne or
Company without being knowne.   Yet I must likewise confesse
that the best part of the Cittizens did not then vse this Irish
apparrell.

Agayne Contrary to the sayd lawes, the Irish English altogether vsed the Irish tounge, forgetting or neuer learning the
English.   And this communion or difference of language, hath
allwayes beene obserued, a spetiall motiue to vnite or allienate
the myndes of all nations, so as the wise Romans as they
inlarged theire Conquests, so they did spreade theire language,
with theire lawes, and the diuine seruice all in the lattene
tounge, and by rewardes and preferments inuited men to speake
it, As also the Normans in England brought in the vse of the
French tounge, in our Common lawe, and all wordes of art in
hawking, hunting, and like pastymes.   And in generall all
nations haue thought nothing more powerfull to vnite myndes
then the Community of language.   But the lawe to spreade the
English tounge in Ireland, was euer interrupted by Rebellions,
and much more by ill affected subiectes, so as at this tyme
whereof I write, the meere Irish disdayned to learne or speake
the English tounge, yea the English Irish and the very Cittizens
(excepting those of Dublin where the lord Deputy resides)
though they could speake English as well as wee, yet Commonly
speake Irish among themselues, and were hardly induced by our
familiar Conuersation to speake English with vs, yea Common
experience shewed, and my selfe and others often obserued, the
Cittizens of Watterford and Corcke hauing wyues that could
speake English as well as wee, bitterly to chyde them when they
speake English with vs, Insomuch as after the Rebellion ended,
when the Itinerant Judges went theire Circutes through the
kingdome each alfe yeare to keepe assises, fewe of the people
no not the very Jurymen could speake English, and at like

Sessions in Vlster, all the gentlemen and common people (excepting only the Judges trayne) and the very Jurimen putt vpon life and death and all tryalls in lawe, commonly spake Irish, many Spanish, and fewe or none could or would speake English. These outward signes being the tuchstones of the inward affection, manifestly showed that the English Irish helde it a reproch among themselues, to apply themselues any way to the English, or not to followe the Irish in all thinges. In somuch as I haue heard twenty absurd thinges practised by them, only because they would be contrary to vs, wherof I will only name some fewe for instances. Our wemen riding on horsebacke behynde men, sett with theire faces towardes the left Arme of the man, but the Irish weomen sett on the Contrary syde, with theire faces to the right Arme. Our horses drawe Cartes and like thinges with traces of Ropes or leather, or with Iron Chaynes, but they fasten them by a wyth to the tayles of theire horses, and to the Rompts when the tayles be puld off, which had beene forbidden by lawes yet could neuer be altered. Wee liue in Clenly houses, they in Cabinns or smoaky Cottages. Our cheefe husbandry is in Tillage, they dispise the Plough, and where they are forced to vse it for necessity, doe all thinges about it cleane contrary to vs. To conclude they abhorr from all thinges that agree with English Ciuility. Would any man Judge these to be borne of English Parents: or will any man blame vs for not esteeming or imploying them as English, who scorne to be so reputed. The penall lawes against abuses had often bene putt in execution, but as the Popes by theire booke taxing all sinnes with a penaltye, did rather sett sinne at a price, then abolish it, so they who had letters Pattens to execute these penall lawes did not somuch seeke reformation, as by a moderate agreement for the penalltyes to rayse a yearely Rent to themselues, and so making the fault more Common, did eate the sinnes of the people.

The Citties.

The fayre Cittyes of Ireland require somethinge to be sayd

of them. They were at first all peopled with English men, and
had large priuiledges, but in tyme became wonderfully
degenerate, and peruerted all these priuiledges to pernicious
vses, As they were degenerated from the English to the Irish
manners, Customes, Dyett, apparrell (in some measure) language
and generally all affections, so besydes the vniversall inclination of Marchants no swordmen more norished the last
Rebellion, then they did by all meanes in theire power. First
they did so for feare lest vpon peace established they might be
inquired into for theire Religion, being all obstinate Papists,
abhorring from entring a Church, as the beasts tremble to enter
the Lyons denn, and where they were forced to goe to church
(as the Maior and Aldermen of Dublin to attend the lord
Deputy) there vsing to stopp theire eares with woll or some like
matter, so as they could not heare a worde the Preacher spake
(a strange obstinacy since fayth comes by heareing, to resolue
not to heare the Charmer charme he neuer so wisely). Secondly
for Covetousnes, since during the Rebellion great treasure was
yearely sent out of England, whereof no small part came to
theire handes from the Army for vittles, apparrell, and like
necessaryes. Yea not content with this no small inriching of
theire estate, to nourish the warr and thereby continue this
inriching, as also for priuate gayne from the Rebells, they furnished them continually with all necessaries, neuer wanting
crafty euasions from the Capitall daunger of the lawe in such
cases, For among other subtileties, were obserued some of them
to lade great quantity of English wollen cloth and like
necessaries vpon Cartes and horses, as if they would send them
to some of our neighbor garrisons, but wee founde manifest
probabilities yea certayne proofes, that in the meane tyme
they advertised some Rebells of this transportation, who
meeting the goods intercepted the same as it were by force, and
theire seruants retorned home with a great outcry of this
surprisall, but nether wounded nor somuch as sadd in Countenance, as theire masters proued neuer the poorer, for no doubt
those Rebells payd them largely for those goods, who without

warme clothes should haue suffered a hard life in the woods. Nay more, they furnished them euen with swords with gunnes and with Gunpowder and all our armes, by which abhominable act they made excessiue profitt, the Rebells being sometymes in such want of munition, as they would giue whole heardes of Cowes for a small quantity of munition, for they could easily recouer Cowes againe by rapine, but most hardly gett supplyes of Armes and munition. And these Armes the Citizens vsed to buy of our Cast Captaines, as powder from our soldiers having a surplusage of that which was allowed them for exercise of their peeces, and also vnderhand of trayterous vnderministers in our office of the Ordinance residing in their Cittyes. And in like sort they furnished the Rebells with our best victualls. For the ministers of our victualers vnder pretence of leaue to sell victualls to the Citizens if they feared it would grow musty did often sell our best biskett and victualls to the Citizens who secretly sold it to the Rebells. These their abhominable practises were well seene and greatly Detested, but could not easily be remedyed, the delinquents euer having coulorable evasions, and especially because there was no forbidding the emption of munition to Marchants vppon payne of death (which was thought most necessarye), except our stores of munition had then beene, and had had sure hope to be fully supplyed, in regard that the wyndes are there so vncertaine, as the publique stores not being continually furnished, an Army might runn great hazard before new supplyes came, if the marchants could no way releiue it. And this necessity of supplying our stores, we found apparently at Kinsale, where assoone as our Shipps with men and munition were arriued, the wynde turned, and still continued contrary till we tooke the Towne by Composition, being more then six weekes. Againe for the great priuiledges graunted to the first English Ancestors of these Cittyes, more specially in all this discourse meaning Waterford, Cork and Lymbrick, For Dublin was in part ouerawed by the lord Deputies residencye, and Galloway gaue some good testimonyes of fidelity in those dangerous tymes I will shew by one or two instances, how the degenerate Citizens of that tyme peruerted the same to pernitious vses.   Waterford had a Priuiledge by Charter from king John that they should not at any tyme be forced to receiue any of the kings forces into the Citty.   And when vppon their manifest rebellion at the very end of the last Rebellion, the lord Mountioy then lord Deputy bringing to their Citty the forces of our Soueraigne king James, therewith to conforme them to his Majesties lawes, they alledging this Charter, refused to receiue any of the said forces into their Citty, his lordshipp vowed to cutt king Johns charter (as not grauntable to such preiudice of his Successors) with king James his sword, and to sowe salt vppon the soyle of their destroyed Citty, if they obeyed him not, and with much disputation and power hardly drewe them from the ridiculous Plea of the said Charter.   Secondly all Fynes for violating penall Statutes of the Admiralty and all others, were by an old Charter graunted to the Citizens, And in these days whereof I write, the Citizens degenerated from English to Irish (or rather to Spanish) if our Magistrates imposed any Fynes vppon delinquents, especially in Cases for reformation of religion, and the like, would priuately remitt those mulcts falling to the treasure of the Citty, which impunity made them offend the lawe without feare, as this and like immunityes, made them without danger of the lawe, to transport prohibited wares, to parlye with Rebells, to export and import traiterous Jesuites in their Shipps, and to doe manifold insolencies, while it was in the hand of the Maior and his brethren freely to remitt all penalties imposed on delinquents.   These and like priuiledges were in those dayes iudged too great for any Marchants, and most vnfitt for marchants of suspected fidelity (to say no woorse).   To conclude, these Citizens were for the most part in those dayes no lesse alienated from the English, then the very meere Irish, vppon the same forealledged causes, as in one particular Case of their Community of language with the Irish I haue shewed, and could many wayes illustrate, if I tooke any pleasure to insist vppon that subiect.

Errors imputed to the state by the English Irish.

The English Irish thus affected did generally in these tymes impute some errors to the State. First that when any dissolute swordman, for want, or for meanes to support his luxury, began to robb, and spoyle and so to liue in the woods for safety from the lawe, and there neuer wanted some like affected persons, ready vppon the first rumor thereof, to flye vnto the woods, and liue like outlawes with him, which small number the State might easily haue prosecuted to death, for example and terror to others, yet when these men had spoyled the Country, and all Passengers, experience taught that the State, for feare of a small expence in prosecuting them, vsed vppon their first submission to graunt them protections to come in, and then not only to pardon them, but to free them from restitution of that they had robbed, so as good and quiett Subiects might see their goods possessed by them, and yet could not recouer them. Yea nothing was more frequent then for the State to giue rewards and yearely pentions to like seditious knaues, in policy (forsooth) lest they should trouble the peace, and putt the State to charge in prosecuting them. So as quiett and good Subiects being daily wronged without redresse, and seditious knaues being rewarded for not doing ill, and as it were hyred to liue as Subiects, they said it was no maruell that so many dissolute persons swarmed in all parts of that kingdome. Galba the Roman Emperor in his oration to his Soldiers expecting and murmuring for a largesse or free guift at his election, said brauely that he did inroll, and not hire his Subiects to serue in the warr, but this free speech to a dissolute Army, cost him his life and Empire; And such was then the miserable State of Ireland, as these Corruptions could not altogether be avoyded, though they sauoured rather of a precarium Imperium, that is, a ruling by intreaty and by rewards, then absolute commaund ouer Subiects.

But they further vrged, that these abuses grew from the Corruption of the cheefe Magistrates, for as he said well, that no Citty was impregnable, that would open their gates to giue entrance to an Enemyes Asse laden with gold; so Ireland could not haue firme peace, while no man was so wicked, who for a bribe of Cowes (such and no other are the bribes of the Irish) found not the lord Deputies followers, and seruants, yea Counsellors of State, and (I shame to speake it), the very wiues and children of the lord Deputy ready to begg his Pardon, who seldome or neuer missed to obtayne it.

They further vrged, that not only armed Rebells were in this kinde pardoned, but also that those taken, and putt in our prisons, were comonly by like Corruption freely pardoned, or suffered vnder hand to breake Prison, and then pardoned vnder pretence of the publike good to saue charges in prosecuting them, whereof they gaue instances of O Donell breaking prison in the beginning, and Cormoc mac Barons eldest sonne in the end of the Rebellion, and of many like Rebells of note. So as nothing was more vulgarly said among the Rebells themselues, then that they could haue pardon whensoeuer they listed, according to the Poett.

Crede mihi res est ingeniosa, dare.

Beleeue, T'is a most witty course, to giue and bribe with open purse.

And touching the Prisons, they said, that the Jailors of Prouinciall and other Prisons, seldome brought their Prisoners to be tryed before Judges, but some were executed by Marshall lawé, contrary to the dignity of Ciuill Justice, Others they would affirme to be dead, vppon their bare word without testimony of the Crowner, or any like proceeding necessary in that case. Others they would affirme to have bene freed by the commaund of Prouinciall Gouernors auaileable rather by Custome then lawe. Yea they would not shame to confesse some to haue escaped by breaking prison, as if they were not to be punished for so grosse negligence, admitting no excuse.

Touching the sacred power of Pardons and Protections they

confessed that it was fitt to giue power of Protection to military
Gouernors, that they might bring Rebells in to the state, but
they alledged many corrupt abuses committed in that Case,
whereby not only Armed Rebells, but many taken Prisoners,
having once their Protection, had meanes with safety of their
persons to importune the State for obtayning their Pardon, in
which kinde Mac Carthen notorious for many murthers, and
many like notable villanyes, had lately beene freed from the
hand of Justice.   Againe, they confessed that the generall
giving of Protection and Pardons by the lord Deputy, was
necessary after the Rebellion was growne strong, and generall,
when it behoued the State (as a mother) with open Armes to
receiue her disobedient Children to mercy, lest they should be
driuen to desperate Courses especially since the punishment of
all was vnpossible in such a strong Combination, of the cheife
was difficult for their strong factions, and of particuler and
inferior offenders was somewhat vnequall, if not vniust.   But
they freely sayd that our State had greatly erred in not making
strong and sharpe vpposition to the first eruption of that
Rebellion before they were vnited, yea rather dallying with
them till by mutuall Combinations they were growne to a strong
body, and that for saving of Charges, without which it was
hoped they might by fayre treatyes be reclaymed, which foolish
frugality in the end caused an huge exhausting of the publique
Treasure, and which vayne hope had no probable ground, since
the Irish attributed our moderate Courses in reducing, rather
then conquering them, to our feare, rather then our wisdome,
waxing proude when they were fairely handled and gently
perswaded to their dutyes, as no nation yeildes more abiect
obedience when they are curbed with a churlish and seuere
hand.   How much better (said they) had our State done to
haue giuen no protection or pardon in the beginning, but to
haue seuerely putt to death all that fell into our hands (which
examples of terror were as necessary in Ireland as they euer had
bene rare) or if pitty and mercy had bene iudged fitt to be
extended to any, surely not to those, who after malicious and

bloudy Acts of hostilitye were at last broken, and vnable longer
to subsist much lesse without some pecuniary Mulct or Fyne
towards the publique charge, or with freedome from making
restitituion to priuate men, and least of all with rewards and
pentions bestowed on them for a vaine hope of future seruice.
In all which kindes they gaue many instances, that our State
had often erred.

To conclude they said that sharpe, and speedy prosecution in
the beginning had bene most easy (scattered troopes being soone
suppressed with small forces) and no lesse advantagious and
profitable to the State (aswell by the confiscation of their lands
and goods, as by long and firme peace likely to follow such
terrifying examples of Justice).

Againe they bitterly imputed this error to our State, proued
by many notable instances, that Irish and English Irish, who
had forsaken their lordes in Rebellion, to serue in our Army,
after when their lordes were receiued to mercy, with free pardon,
and restoring of honor and lands, had beene quitted and left by
vs to liue againe vnder the same lords highly offended with
them, and so neuer ceasing till they had brought them to
beggery, if not to the gallowes, which proceeding of ours in
their opinion argued, that so wee could keepe the great lords
in good termes, we cared not to forsake the weaker, and leaue
them to the tyranny of the other. Yea that to these great
lordes that of Rebells were become Subiects, our State granted
warrants to execute Marshall lawe against vagabond and
seditious persons, who vppon the same pretences had often
executed these men retorning to them from the seruice of the
State, and more specially those who had faithfully serued vs
in the warr for spyes, and for guides to conduct our forces
through their boggs and woods and fortifyed places, or if they
had not dared so to execute those men, yet by violent oppressions
had brought them to beggery, and sometymes by secrett plotts
had caused them to be killed. In this case if I may boldly
speake my opinion, I should thinck it were impossible so to
protect inferior persons of best desert in tyme of peace, from

the tyranny of great lordes, as they should no way oppress or hurt them, either by their power, which is transcendent or by their Craft wherein no people may compare with them.   And as formerly I haue spoken at large of oppressions done by their power; so I will giue one notable instance of their Tyranny by Craft.   The famous Traytor Hugh late Earle of Tyrone vsed in his Cupps to bragg, that by one Trick he had destroyed many faithfull seruants to the State, namely by causing them vnder-hand to be brought in question for their life, and then earnestly intreating the lord deputy, and the Judges to pardon them, who neuer fayled to execute them whose pardon he craued.   But why we should subiect the seruants of the State to the oppression of great lords that had bene Rebells, or why the State should vppon any pretence graunt them Marshall lawe (the examples of both which I confesse were frequent and pregnant), I thinck no coulorable reason can be giuen.

   To be short among many other errors, they did much insist vppon this.   That our State contrary to our lawe of England, yearely made such men Sheriffs of the Countyes, as had not one foote of land in the Countyes, and that they bought those places of the lord Deputies seruants on whome he vsed yearely to bestow them, which made great Corruption, since they who buy, must sell.   Yea that these Sheriffs were commonly litigious men of the County, who having many suits in lawe, bought those places to haue power in protracting or peruerting the Justice of their owne (as also their freinds) causes, especially by making Juryes serue their turne.   And most of all that these Sheriffs, as having ill conscience of their owne oppressions, vsed yearely after the expiring of their offices, to sue out and obtayne the kings generall Pardon vnder the great Seale of Ireland, the bare seeking whereof implyed guiltines, so as the Ministers of the State aboue all other men should be excluded from being capable to haue these Pardons who ought to be free of all dangerous Crimes.   Hereof my selfe can only say, that in England these Pardons are not obtayned without great difficulty: and that the Irish lordes in and before the last rebellion, complayned of nothing more then the extortions and oppressions of these Sheriffs, and their numerous traynes and dependants, yet pretended the same for a cheife Cause of their taking Armes.

The generall Justice.

Touching the generall Justice of Ireland howsoeuer it was in the last Rebellion tyed hand and foote, yet of the former establishment thereof and the hopefull beginning to flourish at the end of the Rebellion, something must be said, And first in generall the English haue alwayes gouerned Ireland, not as a conquered people by the sword and the Conquerers lawe, but as a Prouince vnited vppon mariage or like peaceable transactions, and by lawes established in their Parliaments with consent of the three estates. The supreame magistrate is the lord Deputy (of whose power I haue spoken) with the Counsell of State named and appoynted in England, and these haue theire residence at Dublin. The next is the lord Presedent of Mounster, with Counselors or Prouinciall assistants, named and apoynted by the lord Deputy, with a cheefe Justice and the kings attorney for the Prouince, not hauing any Courtes of Justice, but only assisting the lord Presedent at the Counsell table, where, and likewise at Dublin, causes are Judged by the lord Deputy and the lord President, as at the Counsell table in England, according to æquitie with respect to the right of the lawe. The Province of Connaght was in like sort governed by a governour (after styled lord President) with Counsellors to assist him, and among them a cheefe Justice and the kinges attornny, as in Mounster, both governing in cheefe aswell for millitary as Ciuill matters, according to theire instructions out of England, and the directions and commandes from the lord Deputy. The State purposed in like sort to establish the Province of Vlster, but at the ende of the Rebellion the Earle of Tyrone labored ernestly not to be subiect to any authority but that of the lord Deputy, so as there only some governours of Fortes and Countyes (as in other partes of

Ireland) had authority to compose differences betweene inferiour Subiectes. The Cittyes and townes had their subordinate magistrates, as Maiors and Souranes, to governe them. But the Courtes for the Common lawe for all Ireland were only at Dublin, as the kings Bench, the Common pleas, and the Exchecquer, as likewise the Chancery for equity. And there the kings Records were kept by a master of the Roulls. And all causes in these seuerall Courtes were pleaded in the English tounge, and after the manner of the Courtes in London, saue that Ireland of old tymes had made such frequent relapses to the sworde, as the practise of the lawe was often discontinued, and the Customes of the Courtes by Intermission were many tymes forgotten, and the places being then of small profitt were often supplyed by vnlearned and vnpractised men. And there also at the ende of the warr was erected the Court of the Starr Chamber. And there resided the cheefe Judges of the whole kingdom, as the lord chauncelour, mr. Cheefe Justice, the cheefe Justice of the Common Pleas, and the cheefe Barron of the Exchecquer, who had not formerly the style of lords nor scarlett habitts, both which were graunted them after the Rebellion ended, to giue more dignity to the lawe. All the Countyes had sheriffes for execution of Justice, yearely appoynted by the lord Deputy, only Vlster was not then deuided into Countyes, as now it is, and hath the same officers.

The lawes.

Touching the lawes. The meere Irish from old to the very ende of the warr, had certayne Judges among themselues, who determened theire causes by an vnwritten lawe, only retayned by tradition, which in some thinges had a smacke of right and equity, and in some others was contrary to all diuine and humane lawes. These Judges were called Brehownes, all-together vnlearned, and great swillers of Spanish sacke (which the Irish merily called the king of Spaynes Daughter). Before these Judges no probable or certayne Arguments were avayle-able to condemne the accused, but only manifest apprehensions in the fact. A murther being committed, these Judges tooke vpon them to be intercessours to reconcyle the murtherer with the frendes of the murthered, by a guift vulgarly called Iriesh. They did extorte vnreasonable rewardes for theire Judgment, as the eleuenth part of euery particular thinge brought in question before them. For the case of Incontinencye, they exacted a certayne number of Cowes (which are the Irish rewardes and bribes) from the maryed and vnmaryed, tho they liued chastely (which indeede was rare among them), yet more for the maryed and vnchast then from others. My selfe spake with a gentleman then liuing, who affirmed that he had payde seauen Cowes to these Judges, because he could not bring wittnesses of his maryage, when he had beene maryed fyfty yeares. Among other theire barbarous Lawes, or rather Customes and traditions, I haue formerly spoken of theire tennure of land, vulgarly called Themistry, or Tanistry, whereby not the eldest sonne but the elder vncle, or the most valliant (by which they vnderstand the most dissolute sword-man) of the Family, succeeded the diseased by the election of the people, whereof came many murthers and parricides and Rebelions, besydes great wronges done to the State, as in this perticular case. If the predecessor of free will or constrayned by armes had surrendred his inheritance to the king, and had taken it backe from the kings graunt by letters Pattents, vpon Rent and other conditions for the publike good, they at his death made this act voyde, because he had no right but for life. By these Judges and by these and like lawes were the meere Irish Judged to the ende of the last Rebellion, tho the English lawes had long before beene Receaued in Ireland by consent of the three States in Parlament.

For in the tenth yeare of king Henry the seuenth, by the consent of the three States in Parlament, the barbarous Bre-howne Judges and lawes, and this perticuler lawe of Themistrey by name, were all obrogated, and the Common lawe and Statutes of Parlament made to that day in England, were all established in Ireland. And from the first Conquest to that tyme and long after, the States of Ireland were called to the Parlament by the kings writts and the lawes there made were sent into England, and there allowed or deaded in silence by the king, and so the approued were sent backe to the lord Deputy, who accordingly confirmed them for acts of that Parlament, and reiected the other by the kings authority, by which also the lord Deputy, according to his instructions from the king, proroged or dissolued the Parlaments, But if the worthy Progenitors of our late kings should reuiue, and see the face of these Parlaments changed, and the very English Irish backward to make lawes of Reformation, they would no doubt repent their wonted lenity in making them lawgiuers to themselues, and freeing them from constraynt in that kynde. Att first this government was fatherly to subiects being as Children, but if they were now degenerated, should not the Course of government be made suitable to theire changed affections. No doubt if the king of Spayne (whome then they adored as preseruer of their liberty, and whose yoake then they seemed glad to vndergoe) had once had the power to make them his subiects, they should haue learned by woefull experience, that he would by the same power haue imposed such lawes on them as he thought fitt, withuut expecting any consent of theires in Parlament, and would quickly haue taught them what difference euer was betweene the Spanish and English yoke. But if this course might in vs seeme tyrannicall, the Statesmen of that tyme iudged it easy by a fayrer meanes to bring them to conformity in a Parlament. Namely by a newe plantation of English well affected in Religion, (who after the warr might be sent in great numbers, and fynde great quantities of land to inhabite) out of which men the lord Deputy by the Sheriffes and other assistance, might easily cause the greatest parte of the knights of the shire and Burgesses to be chosen for the swaying of the lower house. As likewise by sending ouer wise and graue Judges and Bishops, and if neede were by creating or citing newe Barons by writts (in imitation of king Edward the third) being men well affected to Religion and the State, so to sway the vpper house.

The generall peace after the Rebellion (when Ireland was left as a payre of cleane tables, wherein the State might write lawes at pleasure) gaue all men great hope, that the lawe should receaue newe life and vigor. Hetherto the barbarous lords at hand, had beene more feared and obeyed then the king afarr of, and though they had large teritoryes, yet nether themselues had raysed answerable profitt (at least by way of Rent) nor the kings Cofers had euer swelled with the fattnes of peace. But the end of the warr was the tyme (if euer) to stretch the kings power to the vttermost North, to bring the lordes to Ciuill obedience, to inrich them by orderly Rents, and to fill the kings Cofers out of theire aboundance. And indeede the Courtes of Justice at Dublin, began to be much frequented before our Comming from thence, and shortly after each halfe yeare Itenerant Judges began to ryde theire Circuites through all the partes of Ireland, and those who had passed through all Vlster to keepe assisses there, made hopefull relation of theire proceeding to the Earle of Deuonshyre lord leftenant of Ireland residing in the English Courte, advertising him, that in those sessions they had perswaded the lords to graunt theire Tennants theire land, by freehoolds, Coppihoolds, and leases, that they might builde houses, and cleare the paces of theire woods, to make free passage from towne to towne and likewise to giue the king a yearely Composition of Rents and seruices, and themselues abolishing the old tyrannicall exactions called Cuttings, to establish theire yearely Reuenues by certayne Rents, which would be more profitable to them. That the lords seemed gladly to yealde to these perswasions, and to establish certayne Rents to themselues, so they might be permitted after the old mannor to make only one Cutting, vpon theire tenants for the payment of theire debts. That they the Judges had taught the inferiour gentlemen and all the Common people, that they were not slaues but free men, owing only Rents to theire lords, without other subiection, since theire lordes as themselues were subiect to a Just and powerfull king, whose sacred Majestie at his great charg mantayned them his Judges to giue equall Justice to them both, with equall

respect to the lordes and to them for matters of right. That a
great lord of Vlster named O Cane, hauing imprisoned a tennant
without legall course, they had not only rebuked him for
vsvrping that power ouer the kings subiectes, but howsoeuer
he confessed his errour publikely, and desyred pardon for it,
yet for example they had allso imposed a fyne vpon him for the
same. And that the inferiour Gentlemen and all the Common
people, gladly imbraced this liberty from the yoke of the great
lords, and much applauded this act of Justice vpon O Cane,
promising with ioyfull acclamations a large Composition of
Rents and seruices to the king, so this Justice might be mantayned to them, and they be freed from the tyranny of theire
lords. So as it seemed to the Judges there remayned nothinge
to content the people, but a constant administration of this
Justice, with some patience vsed towardes the people at first,
in beareing with theire humours, amonge which they more
spetially noted these. That they not only expected easye accesse
to the lord Deputy, the Judges, and the inferior magistrates, but
were generally so litigious and so tedious in Complaynts, as they
could not be contented without singular patience. And that
from the lordes to the inferior sorte, they had a ridiculous
fashion, neuer to be content without the magistrates hand
vnder their Petitians, and therewith to be content were it neuer
so delatorye yea flatt contrary to theire request, which hand
they vsed to signe tho they knewe the ill and Crafty vses the
Irish made of it, who comming home would shewe this hand to
theire Tenaunts and adversaryes, without reading the wordes to
which it was sett, and so pretending the magistrates Consent to
theire request, many tymes obtayned from ignorant people
theire owne vniust endes, Yet had not the lawe as yet that
generall and full course in Ireland, which after it had, by continuance of peace, and by that dignity which the kings Majestie gaue to the lawe, in graunting the title of lordes to the
cheefe Judges, and scarlett Robes to them all.

It remaynes to say somethinge of the handes whereby the
lawe was to be putt in practise, namely the lawyers. They were

ether English, sent or willingly comming out of England more
spetially at the ende of the Rebellion, of whose concurring in
the reformation of Ireland I make no doubt, or English Irish,
who of old and nowe after the Rebellion in greater numbers
pleaded most of the causes in the Courtes of Justice.   These
English Irish lawyers were allwayes wont to study the Common
lawes of England in the Inns of Court at London, and being
all of the Roman Religion (as the rest in Ireland), did so lurke
in those Inns of Courte, as they neuer came to our Churches, nor
any of them had beene obserued to be taught the points of our
Religion there, but hauing gott a smacke of the grownds of our
lawe, and retayning theire old superstition in Religion, they
retorned to practise the lawe in Ireland, where they indeuored
nothinge more, then to giue the subiects Counsell howe they
might defraude the king of his rightes, and fynd euasians from
penaltyes of the Lawe, more spetially in matters of Religion, the
reformation whereof they no lesse feared then the rest, and
therefore Contrary to theire profession norished all barbarous
Customes and lawes, being the seedes of rebelion, and sought
out all evasions to frustrate our Statutes abrogating them, and
tending to the reformation of Ciuill pollicye and Religion.   For
preuention of which mischeefe, many thought in those tymes it
were fitt to exclude them from practise at the barrs of Justice,
but since experience hath taught vs how weake this remedy is,
while the Priests swarme there, Combining the people,
according to the rule of St. Paule not to goe to lawe vnder
heathen magistrates, for such or no better they esteemed ours,
and so reducing all suites of lawe, and the profitt thereby
arisinge, to the hands of the same lawyers in priuate
determinations, whome the State excluded from publike
pleading at our barrs.   So as there is no way better to remedye
this mischeefe, then during theire education at our Innes of
Courte in England, to bring them to church, and teach them
our Religion, and after to punish some particular men, that are
of greatest practise and most refractary, by which examples and
the strict eye and hand of our Magistrates seene to hang ouer

them, this mischeife might in tyme either be taken away, or be made lesse generall. These lawyers taught the proude and barbarous Lordes of Ireland, how they might keepe the people of their Countryes in absolute subiection and make them not only obey for feare of their power daily hovering ouer their heads, but also to thinck that their lords by right of lawe or equivalent Custome, had absolute Commaund of their goods and bodyes. By which and like meanes they not only gaue strength to rebellious affections, but also made open resistance to all intended reformations to their vttermost power seeking to roote out the wise foundations to that end carefully layd by former ages, or at least to shake them and still keepe them from any firme establishment. In this kynde I will only giue one instance. When Rory Odonnell at the end of the Rebellion, was come ouer into England with the lord Mountioy (after created Earle of Deuonshire), there to obtayne the Confirmation from the kings Majestie, of that Pardon and graunt of his brothers land (the second Arch Rebell) which the said lord had promised him at his submission, while he was yet in England, and all that depended formerly on his brother, houered betweene hope and feare, how they and that Country should be established, one of these lawyers imployed there by the said Rory, perswaded mac Swyne, and O Boyle, and other gentlemen of old Freeholders in Tirconnell vnder the O Donnells, that they had no other right in their lands, but only the meere pleasure and will of Odonnell. This the said gentlemen, though rude, and in truth barbarous, and altogether ignorant in our lawes, not only denyed, but offered to produce old writings to proue the Contrary. When that Fox perceiued their Confidence, and after heard that the said Rory had his Pardon, and lands confirmed in England, and was moreover created Earle of Tirconnell he assayed these gentlemen another way, telling them that the king having graunted pardon, and all his brothers land to this new Earle of Tirconnell they having yet no pardon, had lost all their old right in their lands, were it Freehold or at the lordes pleasure,

or what other right soeuer, and so could now haue no
dependencye but on the Earles fauour.   Herein he told
a triple lye, First that he denyed their right of Freehold, which
was held to be most certaine, though it had bene abolished by
long tyranny of the cheife lord, and perhapps at first ought him
some limitted seruices, as Tirlogh mac Henry for the Fewes,
and Henry Oge for his Country, did both owe to the Earle of
Tyrone, and all vnder lordes in England owe to the lord
Paramount.   Secondly that he affirmed the whole Prouince to
be giuen to the Earle by the king, whereas it was graunted in
these expresse words, to hold of his Majesties spetiall grace in as
ample manner as his brother held it before the Rebellion, (in
which he was as farr ingaged as his brother) which graunt tooke
not away the former right of Freehold or other that any Subiect
might pretend.   Thirdly that he restrayned the kings gracious
Pardon as if it extended only to the Earle, when it was
generall to all the Inhabitants of Tirconnell, restoring them
all to their former rights.   Yet by this shamefull lye, he
obtayned the vniust end he sought, to the great preiudice of
the kings Majesties seruice, and of his Subiects in Tirconnell.
For these gentlemen and the rest of the people in that Prouince
being ignorant of the Lawe, and afrayd of euery rumor, vppon
a guilty conscience of deserued punishment in their Rebellion,
and the new chaunge of the State in England, were easily
induced to renounce all their rights to the sayd Earle, (tho
with great preiudice to themselues and ignominy to the Justice
of the State) and to receiue their Lands by new graunts from
the Earle, as of his meere grace and fauour.   And howsoeuer
the Itinerant Judges did after make knowne their error to them,
and gaue them hope this act would be reuersed vppon their
Complaint, Yet they chose rather to enioy their estates in this
seruile kinde with the said Earles fauour, then to recouer their
rights and freedomes by course of lawe with his displeasure.
Againe these Lawyers in all parts of Ireland, taught the
people artificiall practises to defraude the king of his rights, in
seruices due to the lordes of their Fees, in his Court of Wardes,

and liueryes, Intrusions Alienations, yea in very Confiscations of goods and Lands, the preseruation whereof to the heyres, will alwayes make the possessor more prone to treasons and all wickednes. For the truth whereof I appeale to all freinds and seruants of former lords Deputyes, who haue obtayned any such guifts of wardes, Intrusions Alienations and Confiscations, for they well know, what tædious suites, crafty Circumventions, and small profitt they haue found thereby. And I appeale to the manifold Conveyances of landes by Feoffyes of trust, and all Crafty deuises, nowhere so much vsed as in Ireland. Insomuch as nothing was more frequent, then for Irishmen, in the tyme of our warr with Spayne, to liue in Spayne, in Rome, and in their very Seminaryes, and yet by these and like Crafty Conveyances to preserue to them and their heyres, their goods, and lands in Ireland, yea very spirituall livings for life, not rarely graunted to children for their maintenance in that superstitious education, most dangerous to the State.

Ciuill and capitall Judgments and lawes of Inheritance.

I formerly shewed that king Henry the seuenth established the English lawes in Ireland, yet the Common law having not his due course in the tyme of the Rebellion, most ciuill Causes were iudged according to equity, at the Counsell tables, aswell at Dublin, as in the Prouinces of Mounster and Connaght and by military Gouernors in seuerall Countyes And for these lawes of England, the most remarkable of them shalbe explaned in the discourse before promised of the Commonwealth of England.

In like sort these lawes of England were for Capitall matters established in Ireland, but during the Rebellion, and at the end thereof the Marshall lawe was generally vsed, hanging vpp Malefactors by withs insteed of Ropes vppon their first apprehention. In cases of Treason, the great lords of the kingdome were of old iudged by the Assembly of the three States in Parliament, but since Henry the seauenths tyme, they are tryed as in England, the lords being beheaded, and others hanged,

drawne and quartered. As in England so there, not only
Treasons but wilfull murthers and Felonyes are punished, by
death and Confiscation of Lands, and goods.

By the lawe in England, so in Ireland the Accessary cannot
be tryed before the principall be apprehended and brought
to his tryall, so as the principall escaping, the Receiuers cannot
be iudged. And so for other Capitall Lawes of England, which
shalbe at large set downe in the foresaid Treatise.

The English Lawes of Inheritance are likewise of force in
Ireland, the Elder brother having right to the lands of discent,
and the fathers last will disposing purchased lands, and goods,
among his wife and Children, and the wife being widow, besides
her part that may be giuen her by her husbands last will, having
the Joyncture giuen her before mariage, and if none such
were giuen her, then having right to the third part of his Lands
for her life.

The degrees in the Commonwealth.

Touching the degrees in the Common Wealth; not to speake
of the offices of the lord Chancelor, and the lord high Tresorer
giuing place aboue all degrees of Nobility, the highest degree
is that of Earles. And the Earle of Ormond in this tyme whereof I write, was lord high Tresorer of Ireland, and knight of the
noble order of the Garter in England.

The next degree is that of Barons. And in generall, as the
degrees of the Irish Nobility in England giue place to all the
English of the same degree, so doe the English to the Irish in
Ireland. But howsoeuer the Irish Lordes to make their power
greater in peace, are content to haue the titles of Earles and
Barons, yet they most esteeme the titles of O, and Mac, sett
before their Sirnames, after their barbarous manner (importing
the cheife of that Sept or name), as Oneale O Donnell, mac
Carthy, and the like. And these names they vsed to resume
when they would leade the people into Rebellion. The title of
knights Barronetts, was not then knowne in Ireland. They

haue no order of knighthood like that of the order of the Garter
in England, and the like in other kingdomes, but only as in
England, such knights as are made by the sword of the king,
or of the lord Deputy there, who alwayes had the power by his
Commission from the king to make any man knight, whome he
iudgeth worthy of that dignity.   The poorest of any great Sept,
or name, repute themselues gentlemen, and so wilbe swordmen
despising all Arts and trades to mantayne them, yet such is the
oppression of the great lordes towardes the inferior sorte, the
gentlemen and freeholders, as I haue seene the cheefe of a Sept
ryde, with a gentleman of his owne name (and so learned as he
spake good lattin) running barefooted by his stirrop.   The
husbandmen were then as slaues, and most exercised grasing,
as the most idle life, vsing tyllage only for necessitye.

The degrees in the Family.

Touching the degrees in the Family.   The Cittisens of
Munster, as in Waterford, Limricke, and more spetially in
Corke, and they of Galloway in Connaght, vpon the lawe
forbidding mariage with the meere Irish, and espetially to keepe
the wealth of the Cittyes within the walles thereof, haue of old
Custome vsed to marye with theire owne Cittisens, whereby
most of the Familyes and priuate branches of them, were in
neere degree of consanguinity one with another, frequently
marying within the degrees forbidden by the lawe of God.   And
the maryed wemen of Ireland still retayne theire owne sirnames,
whereas the English leesing them vtterly, doe all take the
sirname of theire husbandes.   The men hold it disgracefull to
walke with theire owne wiues abroade, or to ryde with theire
wiues behinde them.   The meere Irish diuorced wiues and with
theire consent tooke them agayne frequently, and for small yea
ridiculous causes, allwayes paying a bribe of Cowes to the
Brehowne Judges, and sending the wife away with some fewe
Cowes more then shee brought.   And I could name a great
lord among them, who was credibly reported to haue putt away

his wife of a good family and beautifull only for a fault as light
as wynde (which the Irish in genrall abhorr) but I dare not
name it, lest I offend the perfumed sences, of some whose
censure I haue incurred in that kynde.   The more Ciuill sorte
were not ashamed, and the meere Irish much lesse, to owne
theire bastards, and to giue them legacies by that name.
Insomuch as they haue pleasant fables, of a mother who vpon
her death bedd (according to their aboue mentioned Custome)
giuing true Fathers to her chilldren, and fynding her husband
offended therewith, bad him hold his peace, or ells she would
giue away all his Children.   As also of a boy, who seeing his
mother giue base Fathers to some of his bretheren, prayed her
with teares to giue him a good father.*   The Children of the
English Irish, and much more of the meere Irish, are brought
vp with small or no austerity, rather with great liberty yea
licentiousnes.   And when you reade of the foresayde frequent
diuorces, and generally of the wemens immoderate drincking,
you may well iudge that incontinency is not rare among them,
yea euen in that licentiousnes they hold the generall ill affection
to the English, sooner yealding those ill fruites of loue to an
Irish horsboy, then to any English of better condition, but howe
theire Priests triumph in this luxurious field, lett them tell who
haue seene theire practise.

Of their military affaires.

It remaynes to speake something of their military affayres.
Their horsemen are all gentlemen, I meane of great Septs or
names, how base soeuer otherwise, and generally the Irish
abhorr from vsing mares for their Sadle, and indeed they vse
no sadles, but either long narrow pillions bumbasted, or bare
boardes of that fashion.   So as they may easily be cast of from
their horses, yet being very nimble doe as easily mount them
againe, leaping vpp without any helpe of stirropps, which they
neither vse nor haue, as likewise they vse no bootes nor spurres.

*This story must have impressed Moryson ; he tell it here for the second
time.—Ed.

They carry waightye speares not with points vpward resting them on their sides or thighes, but holding them in their hands with the poynts downewards, and striking with them as with darts, which darts they also vse to carry, and to cast them after their enemyes when they wheele about. These speares they vse to shake ouer their heads, and by their sydes carry long swords, and haue no defensiue Armor, but only a Morion on their heads. They are more fitt to make a brauado, and to offer light skirmishes then for a sound incounter. Neither did I euer see them performe any thing with bold resolution. They assaile not in a ioynt body but scattered, and are cruell Executioners vppon flying enemyes, but otherwise, howsoeuer, they make a great noyse, and Clamor in the assault, yet when they come neere, they sodenly and ridiculously wheele about, neuer daring to abide the shock. So as howsoeuer the troopes of English horse by their strong second giue Courage and strength to their Foote Companyes, yet these Irish horsemen basely withdrawing themselues from daunger, are of small or no vse, and all the strength of the Irish consists of their Foote, since they dare not stand in a playne feilde, but alwayes fight vppon boggs, and paces or skirts of woods, where the Foote being very nimble, come of and on at pleasure, and if the Enemyes be fearefull vppon the deformity and strength of their bodyes, or barbarous Cryes they make in the assault, or vppon any ill accident shew feare and begin to flye, the Irish Foote without any helpe of horse are exceeding swift and terrible Executioners, in which Case only of flying or fearing, they haue at any tyme preuailed against the English. And how vnprofitable their horse are, and of what small moment to helpe their foote, that one battell at Kinsall did aboundantly shewe, where the Irish horse and Foote being incouraged by the Spaniards to stand in the Playne feild, the horse were so farr from giuing the Foote any courage or second, as for feare they brake first through their owne bodyes of Foote, and after withdrawing themselues to a hill distant from the Foote, as if they intended rather to behold the battell then to fight themselues, by this forsaking of their Foote, they might iustly be said to be the cheife Cause of their ouerthrowe. Their horses are of a small stature, excellent Amblers, but of litle or no boldnes, and small strength either for battell or long Marches, fitt and vsed only for short excursions in fighting, and short Journeyes and being fedd vppon boggs, and soft ground, are tender houed and soone grow lame, vsed vppon hard ground. So as our English horsemen having deepe warr sadles and vsing pistolls aswell as Speares and swords, and many of them having Corsletts, and like defensiue Armes, and being bold and strong for incounters and long marches, and of greater stature then the Irish, our Troopes must needs haue great advantages ouer theirs.

Touching their Foote, he that had seene them in the beginning of the Rebellion so rude, as being to shoote off a muskett, one had it laid on his shoulders, an other aymed it at the marke, and a third gaue fyer, and that not without feare and trembling, would haue wondered in short tyme after to see them most bold and ready in the vse of their peeces, and would haue sayd that the Spartaynes, had great reason who made a lawe, neuer to make long warr with any of their neighbors, but after they had giuen them one or two foyles for strengthning of their subiection, to giue them peace, and lead their forces against some other, so keeping their men well trayned, and their neighbors rude in the Feates of Warr. But when the Earle of Tyrone first intended to rebell, he vsed two Crafty practises. The first to pretend a purpose of building a fayre house, (which we hold a sure argument of faithfull hartes to the State) and to couer it with leade, whereby he gott license to transport a great quantity of leade out of England, which after he converted to make bulletts. The second to pretend to ioyne his forces in Ayde of the Englishe against the first Rebells, which himselfe had putt forth, whereby he gott our Captaines with license of the State to trayne his men, who were after called Butter Captaines, because they and their men liued vppon Sesse in his Country, having only victualls for their reward. And surely howsoeuer some of the English State, lightly reguarded the frequent Rebellions of the Irish, thincking them rather profitable to exercise the English in Armes, then dangerous to disturbe the State; yet wofull experience taught vs that the last Rebellion wanted very litle of loosing that kingdome. The Irish foote in generall are such, as I thinck men of more actiue bodyes, more able to suffer Cold, heat hunger, and thirst, and whose myndes are more voyde of feare, can hardly be founde. It is true that they rather know not then despise the rules of honor, obserued by other nations, That they are desyrous of vayne glory, and fearefull of infany, appeares by their estimation of these Bards or Poetts, whome they gladly heare sing of their prayse, as they feare nothing more then Rymes made in their reproche. Yet because they are onely trayned to skirmish vppon Boggs, and difficult paces or passages of woods, and not to stand and fight in a firme body vppon the playnes, they thinck it no shame to flye, or runn off from fighting, as they finde advantage, (and indeede at Kinsale, when they were drawne by the Spaniards to stand in firme bodyes, vppon the playne, they were easily defeated). And because they are not trayned to keepe or take strong places, they are easily beaten out of any Fortes or Trenches, and a weake house or Forte may easily be defended with a few shott against their rude multitude. Diuerse kyndes of Foote, vse diuerse kyndes of Armes. First the Galliglasses are armed with Moryons, and Halberts, Secondly the Kerne, and some of their Footemen, are armed with waighty Iron males, and Jacks, and assayle horsemen aloofe with casting darts and at hand with the sword. Thirdly their shott, which I said to be so rude in the beginning of the Rebellion, as three men were vsed to shoote off one peece not without feare, became in fewe yeares most actiue, bold, and expert in the vse of their peeces. All these Foote assayle the Enemy with rude barbarous Cryes, and hope to make them afrayd therewith, as also with their nakednes, and barbarous lookes, in which case they insist violently, being terrible Executioners by their swiftnes of Foote vppon flying Enemyes, neuer sparing any that yeild to mercy, yea being most bloudy and

cruell towards their Captiues vppon cold blood, contrary to the
practise of all noble enemyes, and not only mangling the bodyes
of their dead Enemyes, but neuer beleeuing them to be fully
dead till they haue cutt of their heads.   But after the English
had learned to abide their first assault firmely, and without
feare, notwithstanding their boldnes, and actiuity, they found
them faintly to assayle, and easily to giue ground, when they
were assayled, yet neuer could doe any great execution on them
vppon the Boggs and in woods where they were nimble to flye,
and skilfull in all passages, especially our horse there not being
able to serue vppon them.   To conclude, as they beginn to fight
with barbarous Cryes, so it is ridiculous and most true, that
when they beginn to retyre from the skirmish, some runn out
to braule and scowlde like women with the next Enemyes, which
signe of their skirmish ending and their retyring into the thick
woods neuer fayled vs.

Of their Shipping.

Touching the Shipps in Ireland, they had then no men of
warr, nor marchants Shipps armed, only some three or fower
trading for Spaine, and Fraunce, carryed a fewe Iron peeces for
defence against Pyratts in our Channell, that might assayle
them in boates, and they were all vnder one hundreth Tonnes
burthen.   The rest of their Shipps were all of much lesse
burthen seruing only to transport passengers to and fro, and
horses and merchandize out of England litle or nothing being
carryed out of Ireland in tyme of the Rebellion.   And these
were not many in number, the English shipps, most commonly
seruing for those purposes.   So as litle can be said of their
Marriners for Navigation, only by the generall nature of the
people, I suppose, that they being witty, bold and slouggish,
if they had liberty to build great Shipps for trade, they were like
to proue skilfull and bold in nauigation, but neuer industrious
in traffique.   It is true, that the Arch Traytor Tyrone vppon
his good successes grewe at last so proude, as in a Treaty of

peace he propounded an Article, that it might be lawfull for the Irish to builde great armed Shipps for trade, and men of warr for the defence of the Coast, but it was with skorne reiected by the Queenes Commissioners. Lastly I thinck I may boldly say, that no Iland in the world hath more large and Commodious Hauens for the greatest shipps and whole Fleetes of them, then Ireland hath on all sydes, excepting St. Georges Channell, which hath many Flatts, and the havens there be fewe, small and barred or vnsafe to enter; For otherwise in one third part of Ireland from Galloway to Calebeg in the North, it hath 14 large hauens, whereof some may receiue 200th, some 300th, some 400th great Shipps, and only two or three, are barred, and shallowe, besides diuerse large and Commodious Hauens in Mounster.

In generall of the Irish warrs.

Having spoken particularly of their horse and Foote and shipping, I will add something in generall of the Irish Warrs. It hath beene obserued that euery Rebellion in Ireland, hath growne more dangerous then the former, and though Maryners are industrious, and vigilant in a Tempest; yet the English haue euer bene slowe in resisting the beginnings of sedition, but as Maryners sleepe securely in Calmes, so the English having appeased any Rebellion, euer became secure without taking any constant Course to preuent future dangers in that kinde. In this last Rebellion, I am afrayd to remember how litle that kingdome wanted of being lost and rent from the English gouernment for it was not a small disturbance of peace or a light trouble to the State, but the very foundations of the English power in that kingdome, were shaken and fearefully tottered, and were preserued from ruyne more by the prouidence of God out of his great mercye, (as may appeare by the particular affayres at the seige of Kinsale) then by our Counsells and Remidyes (which were in the beginning full of negligence in the Progresse distracted with strong factions, and to the

end, slowe and sparing in all Supplyes), so as if the Irish
Soldiers which were at first vnskilfull (and ought to haue bene
so kept in true policye of State) as in short tyme they grew
skilfull and ready in the vse of the peece, the sword and other
Armes, and very actiue and valiant in light skirmishes, had
likewise attayned the discipline of warr to marche orderly, and
fight vppon the playne to assault and keepe Fortes, and to
manage great Ordinance, (which they neither had nor knew
to vse). If the barbarous lordes, as they were full of pride,
some vaunting themselues to bee descended from the old kings
of Ireland so had not nourished factions among themselues, but
had consented to chuse a king ouer them, after their many good
successes, more specially after the defeate of Blackwater, (when
it was truely said of the Earle of Tyrone, that the Romans said
of Hanniball after the defeate of Cannas, thou knowest to ouercome, but knowest not to make vse of thy victory). Not to
speake of the prouidence of God euen miraculously protecting
our Religion against the Papists. No doubt in humane
wisdome, that Rebellion would haue had an other end then by
the grace of God it had. And it was iustly feared, that if
constant serious remedyes were not vsed to preuent future erup-
tions, the next Rebellion might proue fatall to the English
State.

Now that I may not seeme forward to reproue others, but
negligent in obseruing our owne errors, giue me leaue to say
boldly, and to shewe particularly, that the following and no
other causes brought vppon vs all the mischeifes to which the
last rebellion, made vs subiect. When any Rebell troubled the
State, our Custome was, for sauing of Charges, not to suppresse
him with our owne Armes, but to rayse vpp some of his
Neighbors against him, supporting him with meanes to annoy
him, and promoting him to greater dignityes and possessions
of land, and if he were of his owne bloud, then making him
cheefe of the name, (which dignity wee should constantly haue
extinguished, since nothing could more disturbe peace then to
haue all Septs combyned vnder one head). And these Neighbor

lordes thus raysed neuer fayled to proue more pernitious
Rebells, then they against whome they were supported by vs.
One instance shall serue for proofe of the Earle of Tyrone raysed
by our State from the lowest degree, against his kinsman
Tirlogh Linnaghe, whome the Queene too long supported, euen
till his men were expert in Armes, and too highly exalted, euen
till he had all his opposites power in his hand, which he vsed
farr woorse then the other, or any of the Oneales before him.
In our State parcatur sumptui; lett cost be spared, were euer
two most fatall wordes to our gouernment in Ireland, as by this
and that which followes, shall playnely appeare.   When the
Rebellion first began we to saue charges not only vsed the Irish
one against the other, but long forbore to levye English Soldiers
vaynely thinccking to reduce them by Treatyes.   When the
Rebellion was increased, wee to saue charge in transporting
English Soldiers, raysed whole Companyes of the English Irish,
and as our Captaynes had trayned Tyrones men while he
pretended seruice to the State, so now wee trayned in our Army
all the English Irish, giuing them free vse of Armes, which
should be kept only in the hands of faithfull Subiects.   This
raysing of whole Companyes of Foote and Troopes of horse
among them, was a great error, For they once having gotten
the vse of Armes, wee durst not Cast them, lest they should fall
to the Rebells party.   Perhapps their sociall Armes might haue
bene vsefull, if wee had mixed them in our companyes, and that
in small limitted numbers, but wee not only raysed whole bands
of them, and all of one Sept, or name, (easily conspiring in
mischeife,) and vsed their seruice at home, (where they would
not drawe bloud vppon any Neighbor Sept, and liued idly vppon
their owne prouisions, putting all the Queenes pay into their
purses, which might haue beene preuented by imploying them
in remote places), but sometymes trusted them with keeping
of Forts, for which seruice they are most vnfitt, though we
doubted not of their faithfulnes, iustly then suspected, yea
further weakned all our owne bands and troopes by intertayning
them.   For an English Troope of horse sent out of England

commonly in a yeares space, was turned halfe into Irish (having woorse horses and Armes and no sadle, besides the losse of the English horsemen) only because the Irish would serue with their owne horses, and could make better shift with lesse pay. And in like sort our English bands of Foote were in short tyme filled with English Irish, because they could make better shift for Clothes and meate, with lesse pay from their Captaynes.

In all the warr we only vsed the English Irish for horseboyes, who were slothfull in our seruice, and litle loued vs, but having learned our vse of Armes, and growing of ripe yeares often proued stout Rebells. To conclude these errors, I confesse that the English Irish serued valiantly and honestly in our Army, whereof many tymes a third part consisted of them, but many particular events taught vs, that these our Counsells were dangerous, and made vs wish they had beene preuented at first, though in the end for necessity we made the best vse we could of the woorst.

Other great abuses though lesse concerning the Irish in particular, were committed in our Army. The munitions in great part was of sale wares, as namély the tooles for Pyoners, and Musketts slightly made to gayne by the emption which our Officers might haue shamed to see compared with those the Spaniards brought to Kinsale. Our Powder and all munitions were daily sold to the Rebells by diuerse practises, For sometymes the vnder officers of the Ordinance there would sell some proportions of diuerse kindes of munition to Citizens or ill affected Subiects, and sometymes the Cast Captaynes commonly vsing to appropriate to themselues the Armes of their Cast Soldiers, did sell them to the Citizens, and sometymes the Common soldier, having a proportion of Powder allowed him for exercise of his peece, sold to the Citizens whatsoeuer he could spare thereof, or of the powder left him after skirmishes, and all these munitions sold to the Citizens, were by them vnderhand conveyed to the Rebells, who would giue more for them then they were woorth. In like sort the Contractors seruing the Army with victualls, having obtayned from the

Counsell in England liberty to sell to the Citizens and poore Subiects such victualls as were like to grow mowldye, their seruants in Ireland many tymes, whiles they serued the Army with mouldye biskett, and cheefe, did vnderhand sell the best to such Citizens and Subiects by whome it was conveyed to the Rebells. For reforming of which abuses, Commaund was giuen out of England, that some offendors should be detected, and seuerely punished for example, and that the Citizens should be forbidden vppon great penalty to buy any munition vppon pretence to sell it to Subiects, who should rather be serued out of the publike Stores, and that the victualers should be restrayned from selling any victualls, or because that could not be without great losse to the publike State in allowing great wast, that faithfull ouerseers at least might be appointed to veiwe what was mouldye, and to whome it was sold. But these abuses were not detected till towards the end of the Rebellion, so as the Remidyes too late prescribed, were neuer putt in execution.

Againe one great mischeife did great preiudice to vs, that our stores were not alwayes furnished aforehand, so as the mouing of our Army was often stayed till the munition and victualls ariued which is most dangerous especially in Ireland, where wyndes out of England, are very rare, and sometymes their musters, who should haue nothing to doe with Armes; blowe contrary halfe a yeare together, whereof we had experience at Kinsale, where assoone as our soldiers, munition and victualls, were happily ariued, the wynde turned presently to the West, and blew no more out of England till the Spaniards had yeilded vppon Composition.

Agayne our Prouant masters for apparrelling the soldier, dealt as corruptly as the rest, not sending halfe the proportion of Apparrell due to the Soldier, but compounding for great part thereof with the Captaines in ready mony, they having many Irish soldiers, who were content to serue without any Clothes, so good, as the allowed price required. The Prouant Masters thus compounding with the Captaynes they contented the

Soldiers, with a litle drincking mony which the Irish desyred rather then Clothes, not caring to goe halfe naked, by whose example, some of the English were drawne to like barbarous basenes. So as in a hard winter seige, as at Kinsale (and likewise at other tymes) they dyed for colde in great numbers, to the greife of all beholders.

Agayne wee had no hospitalls to releiue the sick and hurt soldiers, so as they dyed vppon a small Colde taken, or a prick of the finger, for want of Convenient releife for fewe dayes till they might recouer.

Thus howsoeuer they wanted not excellent Chirurgeons and carefull of them, yet particularly at the seige of Kinsale, they dyed by dozens on a heape, for want of litle cherishing with hott meat, and warme lodging, Notwithstanding the lord Deputyes care, who had imposed on his Chapleine the Taske to be as it were the sick Soldiers Steward to dispence a good proportion of victualls ready dressed for comfort of the sick, and hurt soldiers, at the Charitable Almes of the Captaines aboue the Soldiers pay. Where a king fights in the head of his Army, such braue Soldiers as ours were could not haue suffered want, but deputies and Generalls though honourable and Charitable persons, cannot goe much beyond their tedder. To conclude, nothing hath more preserued the Army of the vnited Netherlanders, then such publique houses, where great numbers haue bene recouered, that without them must needs haue perished.

Lastly Guicciardine writes that the Popes are more abused in their musters of Soldiers then any other Prince; which may be true compared with the frugall Venetians, and States of the lowe Countryes, and with Armyes where the Prince is in person. But I will boldly say that Queene Elizabeth of happy memory, fighting by her Generalls, was incredibly abused in the musters of her Army, both in the low Countryes and Fraunce, and especially in Ireland, where the strongest bands of one hundreth Fiftye by List, neuer exceeded 120 by Pole at the taking of the Feilde, vppon pretence of tenn dead payes allowed the Captayne for his seruants wayting on him, and for extraordinary payes, he might giue some gentlemen of his Company, as also for sick soldiers left in his Garrison, besydes that many tymes the strongest bands were much weaker, by wanting of supplyes of English men to fill them. But they were farr more weake at pretence of men dead in the sommer seruice, yet were the the Coming out of the Feilde and retyring to Garrisons vppon Checks nothing answerable to the deficient numbers, wherein the Queene was much wronged, paying more then she had, and her Generall serued with great disadvantages, being reputed to fight with greater numbers in List, when he had not two third parts of them by Pole, yet scarce halfe of them, considering the men taken out of the Army, for warders in Castles, and Fortes. It is pitty the Popes should not be much more abused in but temporall Princes, to whome the mistery of Armes properly belongeth, ought carefully to preuent this mischeife, to pay men in list, who are not to be found by Pole when they should fight. And more specially in Fortes, where the Couetous Captaines abating their numbers, and passing their false musters by bribery, lye open to the Enemyes surprisall, as besides many other examples, we founde by the destruction of our Garrison at the Derry in Odogherties Rebellion, where the Captaine wanted many of his number, and of those he had many were English Irish, seruing for small paye, to whome the keeping of Fortes should not be committed. The Queene to preuent this mischeife, increased her number of Commissaryes, but that was found only to increase the Captaynes bribes, not the number of his men. Therefore some thought the best reformation would be, if the pay formerly made to the Captayne for his whole band, were payd by a sworne Commissary to the soldiers by Pole, and those Commissaryes exemplarily punished vppon any deceite, whose punishment the Soldier would not only well besides that the apparrell prouided by them was nothing neere induce, but ioyfully applaude. Others thought the Pay should still be made to the Captaynes as honourable persons, so their deceipt were punished by note of infamy, and Cashering out of

imployment, in which Case their honor being deare to them,
they would either not offend, or few examples of punishment
would reduce all to good order in short tyme.

Reformation intended at the end of the last Rebellion.

Having largly written of all mischeifes growne in the
gouernment of Ireland, I will add something of the Reformation
intended at the end of the last Rebellion.   The worthy lord
Mountioy (as I haue mentioned in the end of the second part of
this woorke) having reduced Ireland from the most desperate
estate, in which it had euer beene since the Conquest, to the
most absolute subiection, being made as a fayre payre of Tables
wherein our State might write, what lawes best fitted it; yet
knowing that he left that great woorke vnperfect, and subiect
to relapse, except his Successors should finish the building,
whereof he had layd the foundation, and should polish the
stones, which he had only rough hewed.   And fynding euery
Rebellion in Ireland to haue beene more dangerous then the
former, and the last to haue wanted litle of Casting the English
out of that kingdome, was most carefull to preuent all future
mischeefes.   To which end (howsoeuer his diseignes were
diuerted) I dare boldly say, both from his discourse with nearest
frends, and from the papers he left, that he proiected many good
poynts of Reformation, wherof these fewe that followe are
worthy to be remembred.

First to establish the mantenance of some necessary Forts
planted within land remote from Seas and Riuers, the warders
whereof might cleare all paces (or passages of Bogges and
woodes) and might not only keepe the Irish in awe, but be to the
State as it were spyes to advertise all mutinous and seditious
inclinations.   Also to plant like Garrysons vpon such hauens,
as be easy and commodious for the discent of forayne enemyes.
And because the Cittyes (espetially of Mounster) hauing large
priuiledges graunted to the first English inhabitants (as namely
the Profitt of Fynes and penall Statutes) had many wayes

abused them in the last Rebellion to the preiudice of the
Commonwealth (as namely in remitting to the delinquents all
Fynes and penaltyes imposed on them, for transporting and
importing Jesuits and Priests and prohibeted wares) and also
because these Cittyes in the Rebellion had nourished the same
by secreet practises, and in the ende thereof, had by open
sedition in the cause of Religion forfeited theire Charteres, his
lordship purposed to procure the Cutting off many exorbitant
priuiledges in the renewing of theire Charters, and likewise
the establishing of Forts with strong garrysons vpon those
Cittyes which had shewed themselues most false harted and
Mutinus, more spetially Corke and Watterford, who had denyed
entrance to the kings Forces, and were only reduced by a strong
hand from theire obstinate sedition, without which Fortes he
thought the Cittyes would nether be kept in obedience for
the safetie of the Army, nor be brought to any due reformation
in Religion.   But howsoeuer Dublin was no lesse ill affected in
the cause of Religion then the rest, yet he thought it sufficently
restrayned by the residency of the Lord Deputy in the Castle,
and great numbers of English that lodged in the Citty attending
upon the State.   For the Fortes within land, he hoped they
would in shorte tyme become townes well inhabited, as was
founde by experience in the old Fortes of Lease and Ophalia,
and in some newe Fortes in Vlster, and that they would much
strengthen the State, so great Caution were had that only
English soldyers shoulde keepe them, and that by faythfull
Musters they were kept strong, so as the covetousnes of
Captaynes might not lay them open to surprisall, ether by
taking Irish soldyers seruing for lesse pay, or by wanting theire
full numbere of warders, and that, as the garrysons were to haue
land allotted and many priuiledges graunted to them so constant
care were taken to kepe them from spoyling the Countrye by
seuere disciplyne.   Agayne for the Fortes, because he feared
the soldyers could not be kept from making affinity by maryage
with the neighboring Irish, and for that the Captaynes and
officers were likely to intertayne the Irish for Soldyers and

seruants as content with small or no wages, whereby the Fortes could not but be subiect to betraying, as likewise for that the Captaynes were likely in tyme by letters Pattens from the State to apropriate to themselues the land allotted to each Forte for the publike vse of the garrysons, and for diuers like reasons, more spetially for that the Continuall sound of Drommes and Trumpitts was dissonant from a Commonwealth peaceably governed : His lordship thought these Fortes were not like to yeald such strength to the State as the planting of Faythfull Colonyes. And so his lordshipp in the second place purposed to perswade the Reformation of the old Colonyes, and the leading of newe into that kingdome, both to be planted vpon the Sea Coasts, and vpon Riuers and Nauigable lakes lying vpon the Sea, Forsing the Irish to inhabitt the Countryes within land, whereby these Colonyes might be free or more safe from theire assaultes, and not only be easely releeued out of England, but growe rich with forrayne traffique. And to this purpose to exchange inland possessions pertayning to the old Colonyes or belonging to the king, with such Irish as then had theire lands vpon the Sea Coasts, Riuers, and lakes, giuing them greater proportions of ground, to make them better content with this exchange. Some aduised in this exchange, to giue the Irish also those spirituall liuings which they helde by Custody as vacant at that tyme, but this course was thought to ouerthrowe the foundation of all good reformation, that must beginn with Religion, which could not be established without settling a learned and honest Cleargy, nor they be mantayned without these liuinges. But because the Irish and English Irish were obstinate in Popish superstition, great care was thought fitt to be taken, that these newe Colonyes should consist of such men, as were most vnlike to fall to the barbarous Customes of the Irish, or the Popish superstition of Irish and English Irish so as no lesse Cautions were to be obserued for vniting them and keeping them from mixing with the other, then if these newe Colonyes were to be ledd to inhabitt among the barbarous Indians. In which respect caution was thought fitt to be had,

that these newe Colonyes, should not Consist of obstinate
Papists, nor Criminall fugitiues, Cutt purses, and infamous
weomen, or persons rather drawne out to Clense England of ill
members, then to reduce Ireland to Ciuility and true Religion,
but of honest gentlemen and husbandmen to inhabitt the
Country, and honest Cittisens and marchants to inhabitt the
Cittyes, with weomen of good fame, and espetially learned and
honest Preachers and ministers for them both. That the
Cittisens consisting of noble and Plebean Familyes, should
builde and fortifye Cittyes, vpon the riuers and lakes, to be
thorughfayres for the whole kingdome, all other by passages
through woodes and desert places being shutt vp, so as theeues
and malefactors might more easily be apprehended, and all
Catle, being not otherwise to be solde or bough then in the
publike marketts of Cittyes, All theftes and Rapines might
easily be detected and the barbarous people seeing the
Cittisens to liue plentifully vnder good gouernment, and to
growe rich by trades and traffique, might in tyme be allured to
imbrace theire Ciuill manners and profitable industrye. That
the gentlemen inhabiting the adioyning Countryes, should dwell
in Castles of stone, and not keepe there husbandmen vnder
absolute Commaund as Tennants at will, but graunt them
freeholds, Copieholdes, and leases, with obligation to mantayne
horse and Foote, and to rise vp with them for defence of the
Country from theftes and incursions. And in case England was
not able to supply these Colonyes, or the English (as lesse
industrous) were not thought so fitt for this purpose, without
others ioyned with them, then his lordship Judged the
Netherlanders most fitt to be drawne to this worke, as a people
most industrous, peaceable, and subiect to iust commaund, and
abounding with inhabitants, but streaightend by not hauing
large teritoryes. Many other cautions were proiected for the
quality of these Colonies, as that they should not dwell together
in great numbers of one Sapt or name, nor should Consist of
bordering people, vsed to liue like outlawes vpon spoyle, and
one Sept to haue deadly quarrells and hatred (as it were by

inheritance) with an other. That they should be a Free people
like the Flemings, and vsed to liue of themselues like them and
the Italians, not vsed to the absolute Commandes of lordes after
the seruile manner of Ireland, which dependancye makes them
apt to followe theire lords into Rebellion and priuate quarells.
That they should be such, as were not vsed to liue in smoaky
Cotages and Cabines, or to goe naked and in ragged apparrell,
but in Commodious houses and decently attyred, that so they
might not be apt to fall to the Irish manners, but rather to bring
them to ciuility. That they should be planted in remote places
from theire Natiue home, lest in seditions they might easily
drawe theire neighboring frendes and Countrymen to take part
with them. Finally and espetially, that they should be soundly
affected to the Reformed Religion.

Thirdly because his lordship knewe all endeuours would be
in vayne, if Ciuill Magistrates should thincke by fayre meanes
without the sworde to reduce the Irish to due obedience (they
hauing beene Conquered by the sword, and that Maxime being
infallible, that all kingdomes must be preserued by the meanes
by which they were first gayned, and the Irish espetially being
by theire nature plyable to a harde hand, and Jadish when vpon
the least pricking of prouender the bridle is lett loose vnto them)
Therefore it was thought fitt that the Irish should not only
beare no Armes in the pay of the State (which should euer be
committed to the hands of most faithfull Subiects) but should
also haue all priuate Armes taken from them till by Parliament
it might be agreed, what vse of swordes or Peeces were fitt to be
graunted some men by priuiledge for grace and ornament or
for necessary vse, as for fowling and like vses. And howsoeuer
this disarming of the Irish could not well be done during the
Rebellion, when the Counsell of England commaunded it, because
the submitted Irish should thereby haue beene left a pray to the
spoyling of those that were still in Rebellion, yet nothing
seemed more fitt and easy to be done when the Rebellion was
fully appeased, and our Conquering Army houered like Falcons
ouer the heads of any that should dare to resist. And likewise

that lawes of Reformation should be enacted by Parliament, if
either the Irish would consent or could be ouertopped by the
voyces of the new Colonyes and Bishopps, or otherwise should
be imposed by absolute power, as no doubt the king of Spaine
would doe vppon any his Subiects in like case, to whose
subiection the Irish seemed then strongly affected. Fourthly
for the last alledged reason his lordshipp purposed to procure
that the English Army should be continued in some strength,
till Religion were reformed, whereof I shall treate in the last
Chapter of the next Booke, and till the kings Reuenues
Customes and Tributes were established, whereof something
must here be added.

Of old the Customes of exported or imported marchandize,
were very small, the people hauing fewe Commodityes to export,
and desyring not to haué more imported then wynes and such
things for necessity, vppon which things the ancient kings
imposed small or no Customes, in regard the Conquered Irish
were basely poore, and content with any apparrell, yet with
nakednes, and with milke and butter for foode, and for that it
was fitt the English Irish, should haue immunity from such
burthens, thereby to drawe more Inhabitants into that
kingdome. For which reason also the Tolles within land, and
the Rents of the kings lands of Inheritance were of small value,
and both they and the Customes, yea the very Fynes of penall
Statutes, were for rewardes of seruice giuen or lett vppon a
small Rent to the English Irish Cittyes, and lordes of Countryes.
In the last Rebellion the whole Revenues of the kingdome
amounrting to some thirty thousand pounds yearely, were so farr
from defraying the Charge of the Army, as it cost the State of
England one yeare with an other, all Reckonings cast vpp
betweene 200 and 300th thousand pounds yearely aboue the
Reuenue. And the Rebellion being appeased, when the Army
was reduced to 1200 Foote, and some 400 horse, yet the Charge
of these small forces, and the Stipends of Magistrates and
Judges, exceeded the Reuenes some 45 thousand pounds yearely.
But due Courses being taken in this tyme of peace, it was

thought the Reuenues might be much increased, then which
nothing was more necessary.   The Irish Cowes are so stubborne,
as many tymes they will not be milked but by some one woman,
when, how, and by whome they list.   If their Calues be taken
from them, or they otherwise grewe stubborne, the skinnes of
the Calues stuffed with strawe must be sett by them to smell on,
and many fooleries done to please them, or els they will yeilde
no milke.   And the Inhabitants of that tyme were no lesse
froward in their obedience to the State, then their beasts were
to them.   But I would gladly know from them by what right
they challenge more priuiledge then England hath, why they
should not beare the same tributes and Subsidyes that England
beareth, and why so rich a kingdome should be so great a
burthen to the State of England and not rather yeild profitt
aboue the Charge thereof.   One lord of the Countye of Carberie
being in Rebellion mantayned one thousand Rebells against the
State, who after becoming a Subiect, was hardly drawne to
serue the State with thirty foote, at the invasion of the
Spaniards, and yet thought he deserued thankes and reward for
that poore Supply.   I cannot wonder inough, how the lordes of
Ireland can be so blinde in their owne affections as having
mantayned some 15,000 men in Rebellion, they should thinck
much in tyme of peace to pay the Stipends of Magistrates and
Judges, and to mantayne the small Remnant of the English
Army being some 1200 Foote, and vnder 500 horse.   Of old
after the first Conquest, when Vlster was obedient to the State,
that Prouince alone paid 30000 markes yearely into the
Exchequer, and besides, (as many Relations witnes) mantayned
some thousands of Foote for the States seruice, yeilding also
Tymber to build the kings Shipps, and other helpes of great
importance to the state.   No doubt Ireland after the Rebellion
appeased, was in short tyme like to be more rich, and happy in
all aboundance, then euer it had bene, if the Subiects would
delight in the Arts of peace, and the fertility of Ireland yeildeth
not to England, if it had as many, and as industrious
Inhabitants.   In Sommer it hath lesse heat then England,

which proceeding from the reflection of the sunne vppon the earth, is abated by the frequent Boggs and lakes, (which together with rawe or litle rosted meates, cause the Country diseases of Fluxes and Agues fatall to the English) but this defect might be helped by the industry of Husbandmen drayning the grounds, and may hinder the ripening of some fruites, but no way hurtes the Corne, though perhapps it may cause a later Harvest then England hath. Againe in winter by the humiditye of Sea and land, Ireland is lesse subiect to Colde then England, so as the Pastures are greene, and the Gardens full of Rosemary, laurell and sweete hearbes, which the Colde of England often destroyeth. It passeth England in Riuers, and frequent lakes abounding with fish, whereof one lake called the Bande, yieldeth 500li yearely Rent by Fishing. The Hauens from Galloway to Calebeg a third part of the kingdome, are fowerteene in number, whereof some will receiue 200th, some 300th, some 400th great shipps, and only two or three of them are barred, and shallowe, and all these with the other Harbors, Creekes, and Seas, on all sydes of Ireland, abound with plenty of excellent fish, if the Inhabitants were industrious to gett them for foode and traffique.

For the increasing of the kings Customes in tyme by vnsensible degrees, it was thought the Irish were not likely to repyne much thereat, since that burthen greiueth none that are content with natiue Commodityes, and affect not forayne luxuryes, but they haue bene litle vsed to taxes and Tributes vppon their land, and haue euer kicked at the least burthen in that kinde for the seruice of the State, only bearing it chearefully for their owne ends, as to support the Popish Religion, and to mantayne Agents in England, to pleade for that, and other Clamorous greiuances. Howsoeuer the question is not how willingly they will yeilde profitt to the king, but how it may be most commodiously raysed. To which purpose in regard the Wealth of Ireland consists especially in Cattell and victualls, and wanted nothing more then mony, the best Relations of the Irish estate in those tymes of the Rebellion

appeased, thought not so fitt to rayse it by new Compositions
of all Countryes, and increasing the old, as by making Ireland
only to beare the Charge of the Magistrates, and Judges
Stipends, and moreouer, to be (as it were) a nursery for some
Competent English forces, extracting old Soldiers from thence
vppon occasion of seruice, and sending new men to be trayned
vpp in their place.   This done whereas forayne Enemyes
heretofore thought Ireland the weakest place wherein England
might be annoyed, henceforward, they would rather dare to
invade England, then Ireland thus armed.   And the Rents by
Compositions would be a trifle in respect of this profitt of
Sessing soldiers.   By sessing I meane, the allotting of Certayne
numbers to each Citty and shire to be mantayned by them, who
would be as so many Spyes to obserue their Parleyes and
Conspiracyes, and as Garisons in Townes to keepe them in awe,
whether they might be sent in greater or lesse numbers as the
publike seruice required.   Prouided alwayes, that this Sessing
should be to the kings profitt only, not (as it was in the last
Rebellion) for the Captaynes profitt, who tooke all the profitt
thereof without taking a penny lesse pay from the State, or
making any satisfaction to the Subiects, though they had their
hands to charge them.   As this Sessing was thought to be most
profitable to the State, (easing it of the Armyes charge,
espetially for victualls, whereof the publike stores could neuer
be replenished but with farr greater expence then any
Compositions were like to yeilde), so was this kinde of Charge
most easy for the Irish abounding in victualls.   Prouided that
the Soldiers were restrayned from extorting by violence more
then should be due to them, and the due prouision were gathered
by orderly course.   For preuention whereof, and for the Soldiers
safety, they should not lye scattered in the Country, but
together in Garisons, yet not leaving it in the power of the
Irish to starue them, but they fetching in victualls aforehand,
if according to order it were not brought to them.   Prouided
also, that the Soldiers trauelling for any seruice, should in like
sort be restrayned from extortions.   When the Rebellion was

ended, and the English Army in strength, this course was thought easy to be settled, and if at any tyme after, the State should thinck fitter to receiue yearely Rents, it was not doubted but this Course for a tyme would after make the people glad to raise their Compositions, so as the Sessing might be taken away. And by this practise we see that Fraunce hath of late raysed great Tributes, increasing them vppon new burthens of warr, and so making the most seditious to abhorr troubles, and loue peace.

Then it was proiected that Commissioners should be sent ouer out of England, To veiwe such lands, for which small or no rent had long bene payd to the king, vppon false pretence that they lay waste. To rayse the Rents of those vndertakers in Mounster, to whome the Queene having graunted to some 3000, to some more Acres of good land for small Rent, or they having bought it at second hand at so easy a price, as some of them raysed as much profitt in one yeare as payd the Purchase, and they hauing broken all their Couenants with the Queene, not peopling the land with English Tenants, nor having English seruants, but vsing the Irish for both, as seruing vppon base Conditions, and not building their Castles, but suffering the old Castles to goe to ruine, and so in the Rebellion being betrayde by their owne Irish men, and having no English to serue the State, or keepe their owne possessions, were forced vppon the first tumults to quitt their lands, or charge the Queene with warders to keepe their Castles, for which causes, if their estates were not taken from them vppon breach of Couenants, yet at least they deserued to be charged with greater rents. To tye them strictly to the obseruing hereafter of all Couenants for the publike good, vppon payne to forfeite their graunts. To dispose for the kings best profitt all concealed lands giuen to superstitious vses, which were thought of great value. To dispose of spirituall lands and livings by custody to the kings profitt, for a tyme till a learned Clergie might be setled. To rate the Sessing of Soldiers in Vlster where it was thought the people would willingly beare any reasonable burthen, so they might be freed from the great lords Tyranny. To doe the like in other parts of the kingdome, at least for a tyme, since if after yearely Rents were thought more commodious the people would more willingly rayse the Compositions to be freed from this Sessing, and mantayning of Garisons. Lastly to rayse the Customes by degrees, and to consider what priuiledges of Cittyes, or of priuatemen, for that present deseruing litle of the State, were fitt to be cutt of, or restrayned.

By these meanes it was thought no difficult thing in fewe yeares, highly to rayse the kings Reuenues, and to reforme in some good measure the Ciuill and Ecclesiasticall policy. Prouided that these Commissioners being of the best sort, for Nobility, and experience, were after the first Reformation continued still in that imployment, and sent ouer once in fiue yeares, or like space of tyme, to visitt that kingdome especially for administration of Justice, yet by the way (with Arts of peace, and by degrees) for setling and increasing the kings Reuenues, which wee see daily and wisely to haue beene done in England. Thus the Irish bearing Common and equall burthen with the English, should haue no iust cause to complayne and finding Rebellions to increase their burthens, would be taught to loue peace, the English should be eased from bearing the wonted burthen of their seditions; the king should haue meanes in Ireland to reward his magistrates, and seruants in that kingdome. And it was hoped such treasure might in tyme be drawne out of Ireland, as might in some measure repay the great expences, England hath heretofore disbursed to keepe Ireland in peace, without raysing any least profitt from a Conquered kingdome.

The Conclusion.

To conclude as I haue taken the boldnes playnely and truely to giue some light of the doubtfull State of Ireland about the tyme of the last Rebellioun, soe me thinkes noe Irish or English Irish of theise tymes should take offence at any thinge

I haue written if they be Cleere from the yll affeccions wherewith those tymes weare polluted (I meane in generall, since I haue not Concealed that some of them deserued well in those worst tymes), And for all other men I trust that in theire loue to truth and for the vse may be made of this plaine narracion in future tymes they will pardon any rudenes of stile or Errours of Judgment which I may haue incurred: God is my witnes that I envye not to the English Irish any wealth liberty or prerogatiue they may Justly Challenge, nor yet to the meere Irish a gentle and moderatt gouernment, soe the English Irish had the noble and faithfull hartes of theire progenitors towardes the Kinges of England or that lenitye wold make the Irish more obedient which heretofore hath rather puffed them with pride and wanton frowardnes: But as they weare both in those tymes very dissobedient (if not malitious) to the State of England I haue byn bould to say that thinges soe standinge England ought to vse power where reason availeth not, nothinge is soe proper as to rule by force, whome force hath subiected. To keepe the Irish in obedience by Armes who were first conquered by Armes, and to vse the like bridle towardes the English Irish who degenerating became Partners in their Rebellions.   To impose lawes on them by authority for the publike good, whome reason cannot perswade, to make them by consent for their owne good.   To reforme the old Colonyes deformed by their owne faults, and to establish them by planting newe.   And to take the sword out of maddmens hands, for such are they that vse Armes against those that armed them. All Subiects must be kept in duty by loue or feare; Loue were better towards both, and especially the English Irish, but the meere Irish are more plyable to feare, and such of the other as by habitt haue gotten their barbarous affections, must be manacled in the same Chayne with them.   Reformation is necessary; neither of them admitts any. Wee must reforme, and that will gall them, and their pride in those tymes was likely to make them kick.   It remayned that by Constant Counsell and all honest meanes, we should take from such

Subiects all power to wreake their malice. For to vse remidyes
sufficient to prouoke them to anger, and to withhold those that
might suppresse their furye, were great folly.   In a word
nothing is more dangerous then midle Counsells, which England
of old too much practised in Ireland.   To what purpose are good
lawes made, if the people cannot be ledd, or forced to obedience.
A man in those dayes might more easily leade Beares and
lyons, then the Irish.   If Orpheus himselfe could not make
those stones and trees daunce after his Harpe, then Hercules
and Theseus must make them follow their Clubbs.   The
Marshalls must make them feele punishment, whome
Philosophers, and Lawgiuers finde without all feeling of their
publike good.   Lett any man who hath beene serued with Irish
Footemen in sober sadnes tell me the truth, if he haue not
alwayes founde them most obedient (by generall experience)
vnder a hard hand, but stubborne and froward towards their
Masters, as soone as they are well cloathed, and sett on
horseback, for they are all in their opinion, and they all wilbe
gentlemen, which pouerty made them forgett.   This properly
belongs to the meere Irish, but such of the English Irish as are
become of that nature, must be content to be ioyned with them,
till they retorne to English manners and affections. Some of our
old Gouernors wisely obserued this nature of the Irish, and
practised the right Course to bridle it, proclayming their
Comaundes at the point of the sword.   Such was the lord Gray
in the late Queenes Raigne lord Deputy of Ireland, who knew
best of all his Predecessors to bridle this feirce and Clamorous
Nation.   Such was Sir Richard Bingham, though only a
subordinate Gouernor of the Prouince of Connaght, who with a
handfull of Soldiers, and a heauy hand of Justice, taught vs
what Reformation might be wrought this way if it were
constantly and sincerely followed.   But I know not vppon what
grounds of policye the Counsellors of our State in those dayes,
did not approue their actions.   For the Complaynts of the
subdued Irish (which no nation can more skilfully frame to
gayne, or at least tye their Judges, they being alwayes

Clamorous, but in aduersity as abiect Suppliants, as proude
enemyes in prosperity) I say their Complaynts founde such
pittye in the Royall (may I with leaue say womanly) breast of
the late famous Queene, and such fauour with the lordes of her
Counsell, (perhapps desyring the present, rather then durable
peace of that kingdome) as these late Rebells were sent back
comforted for their losses with fayre promises, and the
Magistrates recalled into England, reaped heauy reproofe for
their merited reward.   So as their Successors either terrifyed
by that ill successe, or ambitious to gayne the hartes of the
Irish, (at which the Counsells of the next lord Deputy seemed to
ayme) or vppon vayne hope to reduce that nation to obedience
by lenity, did in all iudiciall causes somuch respect the Irish,
as to that end they spared not to lay vnequall burthens
sometymes on the English : Thus new Magistrates bringing
newe lawes and Counsells wrought that Confusion which they
sought to avoyde.   For one Deputy was sharpe and seuere,
another affable and gentle, whereas in all good gouernments
howsoeuer the magistrates are changed, the face of Justice
should constantly remayne one and the same.   And what
preiudice to the Commonwealth this Course hath of old wrought
in Ireland particularly, experience hath made mainifest.   God
graunt that hereafter wee may at least (according to the lattin
Prouerb) growe wise with the wounded fisherman, and as in the
last rebellion wee were good Epimethei, to discerne (by the
sence of ill accidents) the true Causes thereof so heareafter we
may become prouident Promethei, in diuerting foreknowne
dangers, before they fall heauily vpon vs.

Book III.

___

[This Book on Religion occupies pages 300—460 of the MS. I have omitted the Chapters on Turkey and Italy entirely, and have given the longest extracts from the Chapter on Religion in Germany, about which Moryson writes with much knowledge and sympathy. The long Chapter on Italy has less interest for us to-day than most of Moryson's writings. He was a convinced and earnest Protestant, and cannot miss a chance of making a point against Rome. There is, however, nothing unfamiliar in the attitude of an Elizabethan Englishman towards the Papacy. I had more hesitation in omitting his suggestion for the stamping out of Romanism in Ireland, but his views about that country have, I think, been made sufficiently clear in the first part of this volume.—C. H.]

CHAP: i.

Of Germany touching religion.

Page 300 to page 325 of the MS.

[The following account of the differences between the Lutherans and Calvinists in Saxony (Misnia, Meissen), which " on Luther's first preaching of Reformation with full consent imbraced his doctrine," commences on Page 307 of the MS.]

AT the tyme of my being there the Elector Christian imbracing Caluines Reformation, had for many yeares labored to establish the same, yet not somuch by authority and force, as by Arte, appointing Caluinists Preachers, to perswade and teach the people, and hopeing that they being instructed would them-selues desyre that Reformation, which he thought not safe to impose vpon them by his command. While I liued at Leipzig, a preacher was cast into prison, and for a Mounth fedd with

bread and water, and after banished, for hauing preached that
the Elector was forsworne in seeking to change that Religion
which at his entrance he was bound by oath to mantayne. The
Elector appointed a disputation at Leipzig, but the Lutherans
broke it off by Immodest hissing at the Caluinists. At
Wittenburg a Decon Baptising a Chylde without the Crosse or
exorcisme, the Godfathers and other invited strangers, made a
tumolt, so as some chosen students were Armed, to keepe peace
and appease the vprore. And continually by night lybells were
cast forth by both parties, provoking one another to disputation.
About this tyme the neighbour Princes confederate in the Cause
of Religion, did meete together, and after long conferance about
Religion, in the ende decreed that Caluines doctryne might for
the tyme be tolerated, but that no change should be established
without Common consent, and secondly they decreed that ayde
should be sent to the king of Nauarr in France, yet as voluntary
men, leuyed at the kings charge, the Princes being bound to the
Emperour not to make any warr, vpon payne of leesing theire
Fees. Att this meeting the Marquis of Brandeburg Elector,
whose daughter Christian the Elector of Saxony had marryed,
stoode stiftly for the Lutheran Religion, and was said to haue
obtayned promise of his sonne in lawe, that no alteration should
be made, yet fewe weeckes after the Elector Christian put
Doctor Nicholaus Crellius a Caluinist in the place of his
Lutheran Chancelor resigning it because he sawe his Prince did
not fauor him. And in like sorte he dismissed out of his
intertaynment Melius Superintendant of Witteberg and
Policarpus both Professors of Diuinity and arch-Lutherans, and
putt Pierius a Caluinist Superintendant and Professor in the
place of Melius (who was intertayned by the Duke of Wyneberg
the Electors kinsman, as Policarpus was intertayned by the
Senate of Brunswick and there made Superintendent). But
now when very many Students and Cittisens of Leipzig and
Wittenberg, and many in other Cittyes, seemed well affected to
the Doctryne of Caluin, sodenly the Elector Christian fell sick,
and in the tyme of his sicknes (while I yet liued at Leipzig)

these two verses were by night sett on the dore of the cheife Church in Dresden (where the Electors resyde).

> Calua cohors cessa, funes laqueosque paratos,
> Seu Princeps viuat seu moriatur, habes.
> Bald Caluenists cease, halters you shall haue,
> What ere betyde the Prince, life or the graue.

Shortly after, the Reformation after Caluins Rule being rather prepared then begunn, the Elector dyed, and then my eyes, and eares were witnesses, what threatnings, what reproches, what violent abuses the Lutherans cast vppon the Caluenists, preferring the Papists yea Turkes before them, as their owne printed bookes testify, fuller of reproches then arguments against them. And because the duke of Wyneberg one of the sonnes to the deposed Elector, as next kinsman to the young Elector, was by the Imperiall Lawes to be his Tutor, it seemed the people knowing him to be a Lutheran, thought he would beare with wrongs done to the Caluenists, for they hardly refrayned from laying hands on their bodyes and goods, yea they did not altogether refrayne from that violence. For at Leipzig some houses were spoyled, and Gunderman the superintendant or cheife Minister of the Caluenists, was cast into prison (whome it was thought inough to haue banished) and the Students walking in troopes by night, assembled before his dore, and with ridiculous solemnity, there araigned one in his person, and condemned him of many Capitall Crimes with many fowle reproches, and then like Cryers proclaymed in the streets.

> Lieben heren lasset euch sagen
> der Teuffel hatt rote bart weg getragen.
> Louing Gentlemen to you the truth to say,
> the Diuell hath taken redd beard away.

And within few weekes when they continued to vse such cruelty towards him, as no body was admitted to come to him, no not his wife, his Barber, his Cooke, or any that might doe him seruice, so that his poore wife having many Children whereof some were Infants, fell into such despayre as she hanged herselfe, it was credibly spoken that this poore minister knowing nothing of his wifes death, did the night following desyre his keeper to lett in his wife, knocking at the doore, and well knowne to him by her voyce. The like Cruelty they vsed at Dresden towards Crellius the late Chancelor for, having restored to that dignity Hawboldus ab Einsiedeln the Lutheran chancelor of Seauenty yeares old, whome I said formerly to haue resigned that place, they cast Crellius into Prison, and when he requested to haue the windowe of his prison inlarged, the magistrate commaunded the litle windowe he had to be stopped vpp, denying him the benefitt of light and ayre. The Prince of Anhalt, whose Territory borders vppon Misen, then being a Caluinist was not invited to the Electors Funeralls. And to stirr vpp more hatred against the Caluinists many rumors were diuulged of Gentlemen and Citizens that had bene secretly putt to death, and of others that were appointed to dye for professing the Lutheran Religion, and of straunge persecutions intended against the Lutherans, whereof nothing was manifest, nor credible to be done by a Prince of Germany, yet all was beleeued by the Credulous people. Among these tumults a ridiculous strife fell at Leipzig betweene two Lutheran Ministers suing for Gundermans place for one of them perceiuing that the other should be preferred before him, and seeing the people to flock to him for auricular confession fell first to brawling wordes, and after both going out of the gates fought at Cuffes till they were parted by the Students. It is incredible what hatred the Lutherans shewed against the Caluinists openly professing that they would rather turne Papists then agree with them. When any men kill themselues, the manner is not to bury them in the Church yard (except they liued after the fact so long as to giue signes of Repentance), but that the infamous hangman putting their bodyes on a sledge, should bury them in the ditches of the high way. Thus not many yeares past a Student of Witteberg denyed his degree, for shame hanged himselfe,

and was in like sort buryed. And at Dresden the Dukes
Steward hanging himselfe, his body was cast out of the windowe
with the face turned from heauen to the infamous hangman
(not permitted to enter into the Dukes Court to take the bodye)
and by him was buryed vnder the Gallowes. But howsoeuer
this Custome is not to be reproued, yet in a Case so lamentable,
so deseruing pitty and Compassion, as that before mentioned
of Gundermans wife, my mynde abhorrs to remember, that they
not only denyed her the buriall of a Christian, but that the
young men and Children cast durt and stones at the dead body,
following it with scoffes and reproches, yea that the very
magistrates beheld this sadd spectacle with laughter. At
which, while I seemed to wonder, a Student of that vniuersity,
and borne in that Prouince credibly informed me, that the
Elector Augustus not many yeares before having cast a
Caluinist Preacher into Prison, whome after hard vsage he sett
at liberty, and banished, and he hapning to dye within fewe
dayes, while he prepared to goe into exile, his body lay fower
dayes vnburyed, no Lutheran being founde that would carry his
dead body, which at last was drawne out of the Citty by fower
horses all the boyes, in the sight of the Magistrates, vsing like
behauiour towards the dead Corps.

[The Chapter opens with minute defining of the geographical
limits of the Roman Catholic and Protestant territories, which
may be summed up in the statement that all the secular princes
were Protestants excepting the two most powerful, those of
Bavaria and of the house of Austria, while these and the
dominions of the ecclesiastical princes were Catholic. The
following extracts give Moryson's general observations and
conclusions.—C. H.]

Hence it may appeare how far the vulgar saying is true or
false, that the Empire permitts Freedome to all Religions. For
the Imperiall lawes only permitt the Lutheran confession of
Augsburg. And the Emperour, the Arch Dukes of Austria, and
the Cheife Bishopps remayning Papists, because most of their

Subiects are Lutherans, are forced only to permitt that religion and no other. It is true that I shall in the next Chapter shewe great Confusion of religions to be in the Kingdome of Bohemia, as I haue already shewed the like Confusion to be at Emden the Cheife Citty of East Friseland part of the Empire. But the Duke of Bauaria a Papist permitts no Subiect of any other religion. And the Princes of the reformed religion neither permitt Papists, nor the Lutherans and Caluinists permitt one an other in their Territoryes, but the Prince and people are of one Religion.

.   .   .   .

Thus I retorne to my purpose. The Germans aboue all nations respect their owne Doctors in the Chayre, and their owne Captaines in the Warr, for they despise straungers, by whome they will nether be ledd nor drawne. And indeed they only are the men with whome a Prophett is esteemed in his owne Country. For in their Vniuersityes I haue obserued the Students more willingly to reade the printed bookes of their owne Countrymen and their owne professors, then any other forraine booke whatsoeuer, and so great was the estimation of Luther, as his word was insteede of a thousand witnesses, and like αυτος εφη (he said it) to the disciples of Pithagoras. In all Germany, but especially in the lower his owne natiue Country, all professed his doctrine with obstinacy, yea seemed to woorshipp or vnfitly to reuerence the memory of him, and of Phillipp Melancton, being both dead, for they did putt of their hatts, if either of them were named, and were bold to say in Common speach that Luther was the third Elias. While he yet liued the Students attending him wrote all his wordes, and many of his actions, which after his death they published in print by a booke called his Tishrede (that is tabletalke) which after was corrected, yet men best reputed for piety and learning, and being of his religion both in Saxony and other parts, did not approue the same, as contayning many ridiculous things, namely that Luther had such power ouer the diuell, as he was

obedient to him like a Page. That Phillipp Melancton
desyring to see the Diuell, Luther sent him in the habitt of a
seruant to call him to his Chamber, at whose first sight Phillipp
Melancton fell into a Swounde, as one no lesse inferior to Luther
in Courage then holines. And againe that Luther by chance
casting ouer his sandbox, commaunded the diuell to gather vpp
euery moate thereof. To omitt many follyes of this kinde, it is
certaine that the Students did so much reuerence Luther in his
life tyme, as nothing fell from his mouthe in ieast or earnest,
which some curious yong men did not write, as the sentences of
Seneca, or rather the Precepts of St. Paul. And howsoeuer this
did much further the reformation, yet I haue heard graue and
learned Lutherans confesse, that it much displeased Luther.
Insomuch as they haue a vulgar speach to this day, that Luther
seeing his familiar speeches and actions to be made by others,
as rules of their speech and action, and obseruing a young
scholler at his table to write his wordes (wyth reuerence may I
relate it) he broake winde backward, and bad him add that
braue act to his notes, with that significant (though slouenly)
simboll taxing his foolish Curiosity. Moreouer the Germans
not only of the Comon sort, but of them that are not vnlearned,
giue too much Creditt to predictions (which they call
Prophesyes) of their owne Countrymen. They told me that one
Paul Grobner of Schneburg in lower Germany, not many yeares
dead, left a Prophesye, that as Rodulphus was the first Emperor
of the house of Austria, so Rodulphus then Emperor should be
the last, and then Augustus the peaceable should be chosen
Emperor, in whose tyme he named many Cittyes that should be
destroyed, some by Earthquakes, others by warr. Againe that
one Charles Hartman borne in Germany, did (in the tyme of
the Emperor Charles the fifth) foretell all the actions of the
following Emperors, to that day, which the euent had proued
most true. In generall the Germans seeme to haue singular
credulity towards forraine Prophetts, and Astronomers, but
espetially to their owne. And I remember that while I liued
in Leipzig, one Scotus an Italian, calling himselfe an Astrologer

and doing straunge iugling tricks, but by others reputed a Negromant, roade in a Coache with six horses, and was intertayned and rewarded by great Princes, to cast the Natiuityes of their Children.

The Germans in Lower Germany frequently take iourneyes on the Sabaoth day especially in the tymes of great Marts and Fayres, and make no conscience of keeping the Sabaoth day, further then by presence at the Church seruice, so as in many Lutheran Cittyes, I haue obserued Shopps to be open & wares shewed and sold vppon Sondayes, which they excused as done for the Country peoples sake, who that day of purpose came to the Citty, but neither the act, nor the excuse is approuable.

When they take an oath before the Magistrate, they lay not the hand vppon the Bible, as we doe, but as the Sweitzers lift vpp three fingers, so the Germans lift vp two fingers to heaven. Lett me haue fauour freely to deliuer my opinion, that not only the men, but the women and young people of both kindes, more frequently sweare and Curse in Common speech, then any Nation, except the Italians, who in vices and vertues wilbe singuler aboue others, and if any man thinck this rashly spoken, I pray him to remember, how frequent these wordes are in very boyes and virgins mouthes, bey gott den herrn (by God the Lord), Gotts kranckheit (Gods sicknes), der Tiuel holc dich (the diuell take thee), meiner seale (by my soule) and the like. But the Nationall vice, wherein all sorts offend without any measure, yet daily and hourely is drunckennes, yet myselfe for the space of one yeare and a halfe frequenting their Churches, neuer heard any Preacher speake one worde against it, and no maruel :

> Turpe est Doctori cum culpa redarguat ipsum.
> The teacher needs must be ashamed
> Who for that fault himselfe is blamed.

Yea when men condemned to be broken vppon the Wheele, goe to execution, because the torment is greate, the Preachers having rectifyed their Consciences, then suffer their freinds to drinck with them till they be so druncken, as they seeme to

haue no sence of payne, and for so doing, they alledged the text
of the Prouerbs, advising, to giue strong drink to them that are
to dye; but me thincks it were better to mitigate the torment,
then to permitt that excesse.

To be short the Germans in religion are rather good and
honest then zealous or superstitious. The Churches are in many
places curiously carued on the outsyde, especially the Cathedrall
Churches, being all of free stone, but they are commonly
Couered with tyles, some fewe with brasse, and Copper, growing
in Germany, but neuer or very rarely with leade being a
forraine commodity.

And among the Lutherans their Churches on the insyde were
curiously painted with Images (not defaced at the Reformation)
and fayre Alters standing as they were of old; yet to no vse of
religion. For Luther thought it inough to take the woorshipping
of Images out of their harts, though the beauty of them were
not defaced in the Churches. And in some places, as at Lubeck,
I haue seene all the seates, being faire of Carued Wainscott
to be hung weekely in sommer tyme with boughes of Oake,
seeming rather a pleasant Groue, then a Church. But in
generall they frequented the Churches with great modesty and
piety, and it was reputed a great offence to come late, or to
goe out before the end of diuine seruice. In particular I
commend the Mariners of Germany, who putting to Sea,
continually sing Psalmes, and impose penalties vppon swearing
and Cursing, or so much as naming the diuell, but I cannot
commend them when they are out of danger in the hauen, and
vppon land.

Among the great varietyes of opinions about Religion in
Germany, where not only diuerse sects of Christians liue
together, but the very Jewes are permitted to liue (as at
Franckford vppon the Mœne in Germany, where they haue a
streete to dwell in, not to speake in this place of their scattering
through the kingdome of Bohemia, and a Citty allowed them
to dwell in at Prage) I say in this great variety of religions, the
Germans converse peaceably and freindly together, only the

Jewes howsoeuer they liue in safety, yet are subiect there to all indignityes and reproches, being reuiled by all that meete them in the Streets. Yet in this poynt I speake only of vpper Germany, and the Emperors Court at Prage, where this Confusion is only found, and where the Subiects of the Emperor, of the other Arch Dukes of Austria, and of the Popish Bishopps, are forced to this patience in regard the greater number are Lutherans, and where the Subiects of diuerse Princes meete together at Marts, and like publike assemblyes, whome I neuer obserued to dispute seriously about religion, but only sometymes to passe many quipps, and Jeasts one against the other. For in other parts, especially in lower Germany where each absolute Prince allowes but one Religion in his dominion, they will not heare other doctrine preached without tumult. And as I haue shewed in the particular Electorshipp of Saxony so generally in vpper Germany, and especially in the lower, it is incredible, with what bitter frowardnes yea malicious hatred the Lutherans prosecute the Caluinists, often professing that they would rather torne Papists yea Turkes, then admitt the doctrine of Caluin, whereof no sufficient reason can be yeilded. Only some Philosopher or Statesman rather then diuine, may alledge this reason, that the next degrees of religion are most dangerous to seduce, since no Christian will easily be converted to Judaisme or Turcisme, but mans nature being subiect to variety of disputable opinions not apparently wicked, one sect of Christians may easily be drawne to an other, and most easily to the nearest, in which kinde wee daily see that dissentions are more frequent and bitter among neighbous (aswell in Familyes as Commonwealths), then among those that dwell further of. And that I deseruedly blame the Lutherans for this frowardnes may well appeare, not only by continuall experience, but by their printed bookes, wherein the Lutherans vse vnseemely reproches, and reuilings against the Caluinists.

Among the Lutherans any man may preach with the leaue of the Superintendent (so they call the Cheife Minister in each Citty and Prouince placed as Bishopp ouer the rest) I say any

man with his leaue may preach though he haue not taken
the orders of a Minister or of a Deacon, which orders they giue
to none, but to such as haue a lawfull calling (as they terme
it) namely such as are chosen by some Parish or Congregation to
be their Pastor, and who bring their letters of Commendation
to that end. The ordayning of ministers is done by the hands
of all that haue orders, and (as they say) in place, and after
the manner appointed by Christ and his Apostles, and practised
in the Primitiue Church. He that is to be ordeyned, is first
examined, then he preacheth publiquely at which tyme before
all the Congregation prayers are made for him, then handes are
layd vpon his head and power is giuen him to preach the
Gospell, and to administer the Sacraments. At Wittenberg I
did see Bohemian ministers ordayned, (because they had no
Bishopp in Bohemia), who could nether speake Dutch nor latin,
yet were admitted vppon good testimony of their sufficiency for
that charge by letters from the Congregations which had chosen
them to be their Pastors. The Electorshipp of Saxony had
three Superintendants, whereof he that was resident in the place
did examine the Ministers to be ordayned before all the Clergy
of that place, and not only he but all the rest of the ministers
and Deacons laid their hands on his head at the ordination.
These Deacons vsed to preach, which liberty by leaue was also
giuen to them that had no orders, but theire peculiar charge is
for ease of the ministers to Celebrate mariages, to visite the
sicke, to buyrie the dead, and to heare Confessions before the
receauing of the Sacrament. For the Lutherans retayne
Confession, but not alltogether Popish, not auricular but only
generall not of all particular sinnes, according to the forme,
which followeth in shewing the forme of receauing our lords
supper.

The place of a Superintendant is like to that of a Bishop,
and howsoeuer they haue not the trayne nor habitt of Bishopps,
yet they were much esteemed and in great Authority. In free
Cittyes I haue seene them take place next to the Consull or
Burgomaster, aboue all the other Senators, and in all places

they had great Authority with the Princes or Senates, espetially in matters concerning the Care of the Church committed to theire charge, Nether they nor any minister had any tythes nor Arable or pasture growndes, lest they should thereby be diverted from theire bookes, but aswell in the teritoryes of Princes as in free Cittyes, they had a Competent stipend of mony, for small actes, apparrell, and bookes, and a like proportion of greater prouisions necessary to mantayne theire Family. In some places the Superintendants had not much aboue 150. guldens yearely in mony, besydes convenient prouisions of Corne, beefe and wood for theire Familyes, and such yearely guiftes as theire Parishioners volentarily and freely bestooed on them. Yet in the Free Citty Lubeck (as I was informed) the Superintendent had 1500li. yearely in mony, besydes good proportions of Corne, Beefe and wood, and large guifts of the Cittisens freely bestowed on him, and I thincke no other in Germany had greater Reuennues, though some had more some lesse according to the riches and dignity of the place, and qaulity of the person. At Lubeck he did reade a lecture twise a weeke to all the Clargy, and the Cathedriall Church had fyue ministers, who in Course made three sermons on the Sabboth day, and one each day of the weeke earely in the morning, excepting Wensdaye. In like sort throughout all Germany euery Church had two, three or more Ministers, who distributed the Charge betweene them-selues. And in most places they had a laudable Custome, that on the Sabboth day they had prayers at six of the Clocke in the morning and a shorte Catechising sermon, for Cookes and such seruants as were to attend houshoulde buisinesse. Then from eight of the Clooke forward they had prayers and a Sermon for the Cittisens theire Children and the other seruants that had no buisinesse at home, and it was a shame to come late or goe forth before the end. At one in the afternoone they had prayers and Catechising for the Children and servants, and at three of the Clooke one expounded the Epistle read that day. Yea each morning at six of the Clooke (excepting Wensdayes) they had a Sermon, wherein the Preachers seuerally Continued to expounde such scripture as they had chosen. In all Churches at euery Piller they had Alters, to which from old tyme great Reuenues belonged. In most Cittyes they did not buyrie the dead in Churchyeardes, but in a walled fielde without the Citty, which fielde at Leipzig was called gotts aker (the Aker of God), and there a Cittisen might buy a place of buyriall vnder the Covered Cloysters for himselfe for forty shillings, and for himselfe and his Family for twenty pounde, the Common sorte being freely buyred in the open fielde so inclosed. The sayd Reuenues of Alters and the old Tythes, gathered by the magistrates, did serue to pay the Stipends of the Clargy, and for one idle ignorant Priest of old, each Church had now many learned and industrious teachers, and by the same Reuenues the reperations and all necessityes of the Church were most Carefully supplyed.

Touching the lithurgy or forme of Diuine seruice vsed. The Ministers Lutherans wore Surplices and somtymes Coapes (as when the Sacrament was administred) only in the tyme of prayer and singing, not in the pulpitt. First in the morning on the Sabboth day the poore Children of the Schooles came through the streetes to the Church singing a latine song (as in like sorte they goe singing about the streetes at Dinner tyme the same day, receaving Almes at every doore). These singing boyes serued all the Churches, hauing diuine seruice at diuers howers, and by the way lett mee note, that all or most of the Cittisens Children had the Arte of singing. Before diuine service they had Musicke in a gallery of the Church, of wynde Instruments, namely Organs, Cornetts, Sagbuttes and the like. And by the way note that these musitians, together with trumpeters mantayned in most Cittyes of Germany, vsed to sounde in the Steeples of the Cheefe Churches at Noonne on the Sabboth day, and such dayes of the weecke as the Senators did meete in Counsell. After the sayd Musicke the ministers and singing boyes song a Psalme and some shorte prayers in the lattin tounge. Then the minister in the midest of the Church did reade the Epistle for that day in the vulgar tounge. Then agayne they sunge the song of Zacharias called Benedictus, and short prayers in the lattine Tounge, Then the minister did reade the Gospell in the vulgar tounge, and after in the midest of the Church begane a song in lattin. These and all theire songes were printed together in a booke vulgarly called Geistlich Leyder, that is spirituall songes whereof only some fewe are Dauids Psalmes translated into Dutch verse by Luther, but most of them are songes which wee reade in the Gospell (as that of the blessed virgin and of Zachary or others taken out of the Gospell, about Christs birth, his Passion, & his Resurrection and the like subiectes, all composed by Luther in verse and the Dutch language. At Leipzig, these songes were songe one weeke in the latten another in Dutch tounge, all the people did sing with their hatts on, as also the ministers Preached with theire heads Covered. All did stand on theire feete when the Preacher did reade his Text, and I obserued that in many Churches, as well Lutherans as Caluinests Continually prayed standing not kneeling. After they had songe the Creede, the preacher begines, and in the tyme of the Sermon, all the people turned theire faces towardes the preacher in the body of the Church, but in the tyme of prayer all turned theire faces towards the high Alter in the Chauncell. During the Sermon two officers went about the Church to gather Almes, each hauing an open pursse at the end of a sticke, and a litle bell at the bottome of the purse, which being gently sounded they that were next prepared mony to giue, and if any man did sleepe they vsed gently to passe the bell by his eares, that he might awake to heare the Sermon.

By the way giue mee leaue to note, that the Germans being very industrious, haue fewe beggers in the streets or in the high wayes, excepting lepers, which espetially in vpper Germany, frequently begg by the highwayes with Clappers standing farr off, as also at the Doores of theire hospitalls, hauing a box sett vp into which the passengers cast theire Almes. And in generall the Germans euen of the poorest sorte neuer refused to giue Almes to beggers, hauing small brasse monnyes of litle value which the poorest may giue.

CHAPTER ii.

Of Bohemia touching Religion.

[I quote the following as showing the religious freedom which disappeared during the horrors of the Thirty Years' War.]

GENERALLY in all the kingdome there was great confusion of Religions, so as in the same Citty some were Caluinists, some Lutherans, some Hussites, some Anabaptists, some Picards, some Papists, not only in the Cheefe Citty Prage, and the other Cittyes of Bohemia, as Bodly and Spill, but in Sperona and Graniza Cittyes of Morauia. And as the Jewes haue a peculyar Citty at Prage, so they had freedome throughout all the kingdome. Yea the same confusion was in all villages, and euen in most of the priuate Familyes, among those who liued at one table, and rested in one bed together. For I haue often seene seruants wayte vpon theire masters to the Church dore, and there leaue them to goe to another Church. Yea I haue seene some of the Emperours Guarde stand before his face laughing to see him creepe on his knees to kisse the Crucifix and other Reliques. For the Emperours Trabantoes (or Guarde of Foote) were for the most part of his German Subiectes, whereof I formerly sayd the greatest part to be Lutherans, yet hauing generall freedome of Conscience, so as not long before my being in those partes, the Emperour Rodulphus publishing an edict against Caluinists and all other Religions but only the Papists and Lutherans of the Confession of Augsburg his sub-iectes in Austria raysed a tumult, which he was forced to represse by restoring freedome of Conscience, they boldly denying to doe homage without that Caution, and protesting they would rather be subiect to the Turke permitting that freedome, then be vexed by a Christian Prince for theire Conscience. In which respect, as I sayd of the Emperours subiectes in Germany, so I founde his subiectes in Bohemia more differing in opinions of Religion, yet to converse in strang amity and peace together, without which patience a turbulent spiritt could not liue in those partes. As the buyldings of Germany generally, so the Churches and Mounasteryes particularly are much fayrer and more sumptously built then those of Bohemia, wherein I obserued litle Carued worke, excepting that of the Emperours Courte, and the insydes to haue litle beauty, and for the most parte to be vnclenly kept. The Reuennues of the Clargy in Bohemia were large inough. At Prage I was accquainted with a minister of a neighbour towne, who tolde me he had weekly three Dollers in mony, a mutton, a proportion of beare, linnen for his house, and some like necessaryes out of the publike Treasure, besydes his owne oblations and profitts, by Funeralls, mariages, and Christnings, together with a house, an Orcharde, a garden, and two Vin-yardes. The yearely Reuennewes of the Archbishop of Prage were sayde to be twelue thousand Gold Guldens out of the publike treasure of the Citty, and twenty foure thousand from his owne landes. Bohemia hath only this one Archbishop, whose Seate from the tyme of Hus was long voyde, then three Archbishopps succeeded, and from the death of the third it was agayne voyde, and so remayned at my being there. Likewise Bohemia had one Bishop, but his Seate was voyde from the tyme of Hus to that day. Also Prage had an Vniversity, but in the Hussites warre it was translated to Leipzig in Misen. Touching the Hussites, the Reformation was not generall, for to this day they consent with the Papists in many thinges, and for Ceremonyes, if the Papist be superstitious, surely the Hussites (according to theire ignorant zeale) are rediculous. Since the tyme of Hus, the Bohemians hauing nether Bishop nor Vniversity, the Pastors cannot take orders at home, but the Papists seeke them of neighbour Bishops, the reformed from Superintendants and Vniversityes in Germany neerest to them.

The excesse of the Bohemians in drincking is no lesse then of the Germans, yea greater in respect of the weomen, who drincke almost in as great excesse as the men, wherein the wemen of Germany are most temporate. The Hussites Pristes may not marry. Vpon the outsyde of the dore of the Cathedrall

Church in the cheefe Citty of Prague (for it hath a newe, and an olde Citty, besydes a thirde of the Jewes) they haue ingrauen a sworde and a Challice, in memory that by the sworde they extorted from the Pope liberty to Communicate as well the Cupp or blood as the body of our lord in the holy Eucharist. For whereas the Papists giue not the Cupp to the layety, but only the bread, which they say contaynes the blood in the body, the Hussites giue both kyndes, not only to lay men, but to very Infants, because Christ sayth, suffer litle ones to come vnto mee.   But still they beleeue with the Papists the Corporall eateing of the body and blood of our lord with the mouth by transubstantiation.   But they deny that prayers may be made to Sayntes or before Images.   They sing the Masse in lattin, but they reade the Epistle, the Gospell, the forme of Baptisme and buyriall, in the Bohemian Tounge.   They signe the Baptised Infants with the crosse, and anoynte them on the forehead and on the neck with oyle, and vse exorcisme at the dore of the Church before they admitt the Infant into the Church to be Baptised.   They had no holy water, wherewith the Papists vse to sprinckle men in the Church, and leaue it in a kynde of Funt, at the dore, that they which enter may sprinckle themselues therewith.   The townes and villages were some more Reformed then other, hauing absolute freedome in Religion.   They yealded no power to the Pope to remitt sinnes, nether beleeued they or accknowledged the fyer of Purgatory.   They agreed with the Papists for the number of Sacraments, and the doctryne of Predestination.   They sunge no masses for the dead, but vsed rediculous Ceremonyes in buyriall, as shalbe shewed in the next booke.   They obserued the lawdable Custome of Germany to haue extraordinary prayers and Sermons earely in the morning for Cookes and such seruants as for housholde Dutyes could not come to Church at the ordinary tyme of Diuine seruice.

Touching the Picards and Anabaptists frequent in those partes. Theire profession is not so austere as humble, abiect, and industrious. They liued like bretheren in Colledges with theire wyues and Chilldren, hauing one common purse, to which all that entred gaue theire goods. Each Family had lodgings aparte, and each morning earely all went to theire superiors & tooke theire meate and taske of worke for that day. For they exercised all manuary Artes, except the making of swordes and Instruments to hurte other men. And I haue seene some of these men in theire Jornyes apparreled with a long Coate of Course home spunne Cloth, (which all vse without difference) hauing a staffe in theire handes without any other Armes. If any be expelled the Colledge for vnchastity or blasphemy (as swearing and vngodly speeches) or for like offences, they loose the goods they brought, and they vsed severe disciplyne without any respect of persons. They kept the Feasts of the Annuntiation and of Easter, but they did not obserue the Feast of the Natiuity of our lord.

I was at Prage in lent, where I obserued that the Papists and Hussites did fast and eate fish, but the Lutherans and Caluinists did eate flesh without keepeing any fasts.

CHAPT. iii.

Of the Sweitzers, the Netherlanders, the Danes and the Polonians, touching Religion.

Page 339 MS.

Of the Sweitzers.

ABOUT the tyme of my being in those partes, the Cantons of Sweitzerland, though differing in religion yet by great vnanimity, by mutuall loue, and by inviolable observation of theire leagues, constantly governed theire Commonwealth in the old viger, and it seemed to me a wonderfull effect, ether of theire wise government or theire naturall disposition, or both Concurring, that the men of diuers Religions vsed such patience and Charity one towardes the other, as in many places one Church serued both the Caluinists (as they are termed) and the Papists for the exercise of theire Religion, one staying till the other had finnished theire seruice, and so left the Church to theire vse: and that they were neuer seene to haue any priuate quarrells, much lesse could be drawne to Ciuill warrs for the cause of Religion.

. . . .

Page 341 MS.

At Zurech they had a Treasurer for the Reueneues of the Church, more spetially of the Monnasteryes, who yearely payed the ministers stipendes, repayred the Churches, and distributed large releefe to the poore, and layd vp the rest for publike necessityes, whereby in tymes of famyne the poore haue often beene releeued with Corne, bought beforehand and layd vp by the Treasurer for that purpose. And indeede the Sweitzers in generall, haue spetiall care for the wellordering of Almes, of Schooles, of Monasteryes Rents, and of Hospitalls, chusing Magistrates yearely to governe these Reueneues, and to haue spetiall care of the poore, so as they hauing great Reuenues by the Monasteryes, converted from the releefe of Monkes to better vses, and many large hospitalls, giue to the poore such large Almes, aswell in the Cittyes as in the territoryes, as they should not be forced to begg from dore to dore, or from village to village.

. . . .

Page 342 MS.

Adultryes are punished by the Senate at home, and some-tymes Matrimoniall Causes are determined in the publike assembly of the whole Countrye, wherein of late, since the difference of Religion grewe among them, they haue made a publike decree, that spirituall kindred, which the Cannonists say is contracted in baptisme, shalbe no Impediment to marryage. For a Controversy in this point arising among them, the people vnderstanding that the Pope for mony vsed to giue such persons lycences to marry, made a decree, that if it were lawefull to rich men for mony, it should also be lawfull to the poore without mony. Whereby appeares that the Cantons being Papists, yet obey the Pope no further then they thincke reasonable. In generall all the Cantons, aswell Papists as reformed Joyne together in keepeing festiuall dayes, and walking with soleme Procession ouer the places, wherein theire Ancestors haue fought battayles, wherein the Papists Priests goe first singing after theire manner, followed by the reformed ministers, then by the people in ordor, the cheefe men each leading some honor-able straunger with him, and lastly by the flocke of weomen, and when they come to the place of battayle, the Ensignes stand still at each stone erected for memorye, where all pray vpon theire knees, and at the sixth the history of the fight is recited, the Papists giuing thanckes aswell to the Virgin Mary and to theire tutelar Saynts Fredoline and Hillary, as to God, but the Reformed only to God. In the same place a sermon is made one yeare by a Papist Priest, the next yeare by the reformed minister of Glarona, and so yearely in Course. The sermon ended, they goe forwarde to the eleuenth stone, where they of the reformed Religion goe home, but the Papists goe to the Church, and hauing sung a masse for those that dyed in that fyght, they feast the clargy and strangers at the publicke charge, and after dinner retorne home following theire Priests singing, and theire banner with the Images of the Crucifix.

Page 345 MS.

Of Netherland.

They had fayre larg churches, built of bricke, without any beauty on the insyde, or so much as fayre seates, the weomen bringing stooles, and formes being sett about the Pulpitt in the naked body of the Church. Midleburg a great Citty had but two churches, and other great Cittyes had but one or two Churches, which of old perhaps might suffice, but now since the decay of Antwerp the people are infinitely increased by straungers and the banished men of Flaunders and Brabant, dwelling there for traffique and liberty of Conscience. Yet were these Churches seldome full, for very many Sectaryes, and more marchants prœferring gayne to the dutyes of Religion, seldome came to Church, so as in Leyden a populous Citty, I often obserued at tymes of diuine seruice, much more people to be in the markett place then in the Church.

Page 346 MS.

Assoone as the Preaching minister entred into the Church, I obserued him that did reade prayers to finish them abruptly, as if he brought better thinges, or it were vnseemely that he should attend and ioyne with the rest in the Common Prayers. And after that tyme I obserued in England the same superstitious neglect of Common prayer, and excessiue valuation of Preaching, to haue infected some places among vs.

Pages 348—349 MS.

Of Poland.

Touching the kingdome of Poland, it was first converted to Christianity in the yeare 965. (others write 975.) and when Lúther first preached the reformation of Religion some of the great men in Poland (for the Palatines and gentlemen though subiect to a king yet are absolute lordes hauing power of life and death within theire territoryes) did ioyne with the Princes of Germany in theire protestations for reformation of Religion, but it was more fully reformed in Poland the yeare of our lord 1567. The nation is reputed very superstitious in theire devotions, and I haue seene the Papists among them adore the Crucifix with theire bodyes prostrate on the earth, and when they rose vp not only to signe theire faces and brests but theire very hinder partes with the signe of the Crosse. At Cracovia (vulgarly Crakaw) the cheefe Citty of Poland, they permitted the Stewes as it is permitted in the Cittyes of Italy, and each hore payde weekely eight Grosh to the high marshall of the kingdome. They are great drinckers, and verye quarrellsome in drincke, often breaking into shedding of blood, yea into murthers. No people in the world are so much infected with variety of opinions in Religion. Insomuch as it is proverbially sayd that if any man haue lost his Religion, he may fynde it in Poland, if it be not vanished out of the world. Generally the Jewes swarme in all partes of the kingdome, every great man vsing one or more of them to rayse his rents and profitts, in which kynde they are notable extortioners, and many of the people were thought not to be free from the opinions of theire Religion. The King, the Queene, the great Chancelour Zamosky vpon the confynes of Hungary and the greatest parte generally of the nobility, and of the people retayned the Roman Religion. Among them the Jesuites swarmed, and had many Colledges wherein they brought vp the Children of the nobilitie, no kingdome having more of that order, then Poland had. In the harte of the kingdome many of the nobility were reformed after the doctryne of Caluin, whereof the Palatine of Rava one of the

12 Palatines of the kingdome, was cheefe in name and power. Yea though all Religions had liberty of Conscience, yet that profession only had a Church allowed in the Cheefe Citty of Crakow, which Church notwithstanding some six monthes before my passing that way, was burned and pulled downe by the Papists in the drunken tyme of Shroftide, and then did lye wast, but they were confident to haue the Church and all Domages restored at the next generall assembly of the States. In Prussen, the free Citties Dantzke and Melvin with theire territories were parte Lutherans, part Caluinists, and the Dukdom of Konigsperg (being, as the sayd Citties, tributarye to the kingdome of Poland) was wholy reformed after the doctryne of Luther, but in the part of the Province then subiect to Poland, the Roman Religion and the Reformation of Luther and of Calvin were professed with free libertie, but most of them were Lutherans, as likewise in the Province of Massouia next adioyning and in those partes the Cloysters of monkes and Nonnes still remayned. At my being in those partes, the king and Queene of Poland lying at Dantzke to expect a passage by sea into theire kingdome of Suetia, and there seeing some fayre Images broken downe and cast asyde, requested the guift of them from the Cittisens, and hauing obtayned them, did presently sett them vp and worshipped them in theire sight vpon theire knees. Vpon the confines of Moscovy towardes the North, besydes all the forenamed Religions, many imbraced theire doctryne of the Greeke Church, as vpon the Confines of Tartarye towardes the East, many were infected with diuers superstitions of theire neighbors.

CHAPTER iiii.
Of the Turkes Religion.
Pages 349—368 MS.

CAP. v.
Of the Italians or rather the Romans touching Religion.
Pages 368—444 MS.

CHAPTER vi.

Of Fraunce, England, Scotland and Ireland touching Religion.

Page 449 MS.

Of Fraunce.

THE Reformed Churches followe the rule of Caluins doctryne, of which I haue spoken in the discourse of Germany, Sweitzerland, and Netherland, shewing how it differs from the doctryne of Luther, about the presence of our lord in the Sacrament, and other pointes. I will only add, that it reiects all, euen the most allowable Ceremonyes. of the Roman Church, and all kynde of Pictures and Images in the Church. It alloweth not the name or dignity of lords Bishopps, but in place of them hath superintendants, to whome they giue moderate yearely Pensians, and the Causes of the Bishopps Concistoryes are determined by the Elders, Consisting of some cheefe ministers and lay men. And as the Roman Church blynded the world by the ignorance of the Clargy, so this Reformed Church affectes nothinge more, then to haue a learned & honest Preacher in euery Parish, which is hindred by nothing more then by old Alienations of benefices apropriated by the Roman Church, to Colleges, and Cathedriall Churches. Lastly the reformed are very strict in the Censure of manners, forbidding daunces and restrayning the peoples liberty in sports and conversation. To conclude, great and wise men of that Reformed Church haue freely sayd, that this stricktnes in manners, the taking away all Ceremonyes, and the disallowing of Bishopps, haue greatly hindred the increase of the Reformed Church, which was like ere this tyme to haue prevayled throughout all Fraunce, if in these thinges they had followed in some good measure the Reformation established in England.

.   .   .   .

Page 450 MS.

Of England.

I will only add in generall, that the English were allwayes Religiously affected, and while they were obedient to the Pope, yealded him in proportion more profitt then any other kingdome. That they haue built and founded more Stately and rich Monasteries, Colleges, Vniversities and Cathedriall Churches, then any other nation, yea that the building of many Common Churches (perticularly in Lincolnshyre) cost more then all the houses of the towne. And I may boldly say that England hath more Bells, and of greater price, then any three kingdomes, if not then all the worlde besydes. To which giue me leaue to add the old and laudable Custome of England, to toll a Bell when any one lyeth at the pointe of death, to remember all men to pray for him, as the proper tyme when prayers may avayle him, namely while he yet liueth. To conclude these generall Remembrances, I thincke that nothinge in our age hath more pinched the Papists then our gracious Soueraignes wise invencion of the Oath of Aleagiance, For when they suffered for the Oath of supremacy, they had pretence thereby, as for a point of Religion, to be made Martyrs. But howsoeuer the Pope hath made it an Article of Fayth, that he may depose kings and absolue subiectes from the Oath of Alleagence, yet I thinck fewe learned and godly Papists would be content to suffer for that new and strange Article of Fayth.

·   ·   ·   ·   ·   ·   ·   ·   ·

Pages 453—456 MS.

Of Ireland.

It is most Certayne, that generally all the Papists in Ireland (as allso in England) came ordinarily to the Church seruice of the Protestants, till about the yeare 1572. For about that tyme the Pope first resolued to sett the marke of the Beast vpon the foreheades of his followers, forbidding them to come to our Churches, to ioyne with vs in priuate prayer, or somuch as to

say Amen to our graces at table. From which tyme, though
most of them knewe our Church seruice, and I haue heard many
of them freely confesse that they could except against nothinge
therein, the same being all taken out of the old Roman lythurgy,
only omitting prayers to Saynts, and like superstitions, Which
they that listed might performe at home, yet it was more easy,
for the foresayd reasons, to bring a Beare to the stake, then any
one of them to our Churches. I haue heard some of the most
learned among them alledge other reasons of this generall
obstinacy, namely that after the foresayd tyme, the high
Commissionours calleing many into question, released them
after for mony, and after fewe monthes questioned them
agayne, and in like sort released them, vsing that power
rather to impourish then to reforme them, which first wrought
in theire heartes an hatred of the gouernment, and in tyme a
detestation of our Religion, which they called Vendible. But
wee by experience found many other true reasons of this
obstinacy. As first vicious shamefastnes whereby many that
could not deny the truth of our Religion, yet shamed to leaue
the Roman, which all their frends and kinsmen professed, who
would ever after hate theire persons, and avoyde theire Company.
Agayne the respect of profitt, and meanes to liue Comfortably,
since tradesmen becomming of the Reformed Church, lost the
Custome of all Papists, who would neuer after buye any thinge
of them, and men of other Conditions were not only depriued of
any meanes or releefe they might expect from their frendes, but
were most hated and Molested by them. Yea the Papists
generally were so malitious against theire Countrymen turning
Protestants, as they not only in life maligned them, but vpon
their death bedds and in the hower of death, denyed them
releefe or rest, keeping meate and all thinges they desyred from
them, and the wemen and Children continually pinching and
disquieting them when they would take rest, that they might
thereby force them to turne Papists agayne. So as I haue
knowne a Governour forced to appointe men to keepe a sicke
Protestant from these tormentours, and Priests, and to see all

necessaryes ministred to him. To which I may add, that the Irish could alledge many examples, of men of good Condition and estate, who hauing turned Protestants, were not cherished and incorraged by our cheefe Gouernours, but rather left by them to perish by the former & like meanes. Besydes these thinges swaying the myndes of particular men from vs, many generall abuses corrupted the generall State of the Church in those tymes. First the meere Irish lords kept most of the Ecclessiasticall Benefices in theire handes, leauing nothing to mantayne any Protestant Incumbent sent thither by the State, but rather mantayning with them theire owne Popish ignorant and base Priests. For such were both sortes liuing vnder them, whome they, out of a wicked Custome or tyrannicall rule of their barbarous Brehowne lawe, and Contrary to the receaued lawe of England, continually oppressed, no lesse then their laye vassals, with Impositions at theire pleasure (vulgarly called Cuttings) & like extortions, thincking it no fault but rather a meritorious act to defraude and allso oppresse the Protestant ministers sent among them. Indeede the lawes of England, had in those dayes so litle swaye in theire Countryes, as our Ministers could not safely liue there, where a valiant English Captayne with his Armed Company of Foote could not safely liue without some temporising and applying himselfe to theire humours. So as it was no maruayle they oppressed the clergy vnder them by Cuttinges and extortians no lesse then theire lay vassalls, and kept spirituall liuings in theire handes without mantayning any minister, or doing any Religious duty, as Almes, hospitality and the like. Yea the Court of Faculties in those dayes vsed to dispence with lay persons tho vnqualifyed, to possesse Benefices for the vse of Childrens education, who notwithstanding were trayned vp in Spayne and Flaunders, not in our schooles or vniversities, nether in those dayes was there any Booke of Rates for benefices to the great preiudice of the State and subiectes. Many gentlemen of the English Irish held by inheritaunce Impropriations not indowed with any vicarages. Many held Benefices graunted to them vnder the great Seale

for life or Tearme of yeares (wherof I haue knowne one man
to haue sixteene in one graunt by letters Pattents); Others by
right of Patronage to bestow spirituall liuings, held them in
theire owne handes.   And none of these had any the least care
to prouide Preachers or Readers for these benefices, nether were
they bounde by theire graunts and tenours so to doe.   Yea in the
latter tymes wherof I write, some founde a newe tytle (as newe
vices gett newe names) whereby to hold spirituall liuings,
vsing them no better then the former, namely by Custodium or
keeping dureing pleasure.   It is incredible, but most true, that
the Clergy of those tymes was not wanting to sett forward the
generall corruption of the Irish Church.   Ministers were hardly
founde, so as many great congregations euen among the English
wanted Pastors, and the Bishopps were forced for the most part
to tolerate ignorante persons, men of scandalous life, yea very
Popish readers, rather then Parishes should want not only
diuine seruice but the vse of baptisme, Buiriall, Mariage and
the lords Super.   Which the Papists did often cast in our teeth,
saying it was better to haue the Roman Masse, then no seruice
at all, as in many of our Churches.   Many who came ouer out of
England, if they taught well in pulpitt, gaue ill example in life.
The ministers which Ireland had, were blamed for not caring
how many benefices they had, nor how remote they were one
from the other.   Yea the Bishops were no lesse worthy of blame
in this kynde.   For my selfe knewe one not very learned, nor
much approved for his life, who hauing beene a Fryer, and
turning Protestant had three Bishoprickes, besydes many
benefices of the best.   Both Ministers and Bishops non resident
sent to theire remote liuings only Procters to gather theire
tythes and profitts.   And as the Bishopes abused theire Juris-
diction, accounting it a yearely Rent, so theire Proctors,
espetially in the remote partes of the North, abused it much
more, not shaming to imitate the Priests of the barbarous Irish,
who vsed to take a Cowe of maryed people, and two Cowes of
the vnmaryed yearely, as a penalty of incontinency though no
such fault could be proued against them, and more, (according

to theire pleasure), of those who were indeede guilty, and that
without Citation or Conviction by course of lawe. It is strange
but most true, that our Bishopps, in places where themselues
were residend, did followe the meere Irish lords in extorting
vpon the Clergy vnder them. To which purpose my selfe did
heare a Bishop say, that he desyred not to haue learned
ministers or men of quality in his diocesse because he Could not
make so much profitt of them, as he might of others. Both
Bishopes and ministers did lett long leases of theire landes and
benefices (wherin they were not then restrayned by any lawe)
and so all spirituall liuings were made vncompetent to
mantayne worthy Incumbents. The Churches throughout the
kingdome did threaten ruine, yea in most places not only the
Common but those of fayrest building were fallen to the
grounde. The very Church of Armach famous in old tymes for
the seate of that Archbishopp, Primate of that kingdome, was in
those tymes ruined, and lay more like a stable then a Church.
To which filthynes also all Churches in generall were subiect,
except some fewe kept in cheefe Cittyes for the vse of the
English. The Jesuites and Roman Priests swarmed in all
places, filling the houses of lordes, gentlemen, and espetially
Cittisens, and dominering in them, as they might well doe, for
howsoeuer the men grewe weary of them, they had the wemen
on theire sydes. And these men were the bane not only of the
Commonwealth (as I haue formerly shewed) but more spetially
of the Church, obdurating all the subiects in disobedience to the
English Magistrates, confirming them in superstition and
blynde obedience to the Pope, reducing those that were ready
to fall from them, perverting those that were wavering, and
Cementing the disvnited affections of Rebells. The Children
of lords gentlemen and cheefe Cittisens were for the most part
brought vp in Spayne or Flaunders, for nether Ireland had
Scholemasters of the Reformed Religion, nor would the Irish
then haue sent theire Children to any such.

Booke IIII.

CHAPTER I.

Of the Germans Nature and Manners, strength of body and witt, manuall Artes Sciences Universities language pompe of Ceremonyes, espetialy in Maryages, Child-bearings, Christenings, and Funeralls : as also of theire divers Customes, Sports Exercises, and perticulerly of Hunting Hawking Fouling birding and Fishing.

Nature and Manners.

ALL writers commend the Germans or high Dutch, for Modesty, Integrity, Constancy, Placability, Equity, and for grauity, but somewhat inclyning to the vice of Dullnes. The Conversation of gentlemen is very Austere, full of scowling grauity rather then of disdaynfull pryde, Cittizens are more Courteous, both rude inough in lower Germany, and generally haters of French Complement. Generally they dispise humility in strangers, to whome a bigg looke and good suite of Apparrell add no small respect, For all men eating at one Common table, every Coach man will sett downe before him that putts not the best legg forward, and when I was forced in my Jorney from Stoade to Emden, to disguise myselfe in a poore habitt, I obserued that I spent not a penny lesse for my humility, the poorest paying for his meate at the Common table asmuch as the best, only I saued the guift of drincking mony, which the seruants scorned to demande of me (as I haue shewed in the first booke of the third Parte, and the third Chapter, in the xxth Precept of humility). All the Germans haue one Nationall vice of drunckennes in such excesse (espetially the Saxons), as it staynes all theire nationall vertues, and makes them often offensiue to frends and much more to strangers. But it is a great reproach for any woman to be druncken or to drincke in

any the least excesse (as I haue shewed at large in the third
Parte in the Chapter of the Germans dyett). They are by
nature placable, and farr from malice or treason to theire
enemyes. When they dispute they nether haue nor neede any
moderator, but coldly vrge theire Arguments, and are soone
satisfyed with the Answer. And when they fyght they
nether haue nor neede any to parte them, but themselues will
gently take vp the quarrell. They Chyde rudely more than
they fight, for generall all, but espetially the Saxons, and aboue
all the Coachmen and Common people, are rude in behauiour
and wordes, they will not stay a minute in the Inne nor by the
way, vpon any occasion for a Companion in the Coach, and
when they are heated with drincke, they are apt to giue rude
yea reprochfull wordes, espetially to strangers (whose best
course is to passe them ouer, as not vnderstood). But euen
among themselues this rude speech and drunckennes, and
espetially the small daunger in fighting (where it is a villanny
to thrust, and a small Cutt or slash is the worst can befall them)
Cause many quarrells (as I haue shewed at large in the 23.
Precept of Patience, the third Chapter of the third Parte). The
modesty of the wemen in singular, and the like rarely or no
where founde, and the Modesty of men great. Honest wemen
hold it obscenity onlie to name theire Duggs, muchlesse will
they expose them to sight, and least of all permitt them to be
touched. At Nurenburg in the Common Hostery a bell hanges
vnder the table, which they vse in sport to ring, when any man
comes late to dinner, and when any speake vnfitt speeches,
espetially obscene wordes, wherein theire eares are so nice, as
when a French man setting in theire Company, did reade in a
Duch booke the Answer of the Paynter, that his Pictures were
fayre because he drewe them by day, and his Children foule
because they were gotten in the darke, I obserued the wemen
to blush, and the men also to looke one vpon another, as if
those wordes were flatt Baudery. When the wemen goe out
of dores, they lett theire Coates dagle [sic] in the durt, lest they
may seeme vnmodest in shewing any parte of theire feete or

leggs. And when they goe out of dores, they are reputed harlotts, if they couer not theire faces and theire heades with lynnen Cloth, and theire apparell with a Cloke, and if they carry not in theire handes a litle baskett, as if they went abroade to buy somethinge, tho perhapps they goe only to visite a frend. They kisse none but theire husbands, nor them openly, yea they take it for a great wrong, if a stranger ignorant of their Customes, when he takes his leaue for a great Jorney, should offer to kisse or so much as to touch their handes. Yet I will freely say, that in Oldenburg, Westphalia, and those parts, I obserued wemen of the better sorte more barbarous and prone to vse wanton and filthy speeches. Otherwise, the men (as the wemen) are modest in speeches, and hold it great immodesty to make water in the streetes, and in some places the magistrate will punish any vnshamefastnes in that kynde. The Parcimony of the Germans is singuler, spending sparingly if not basely, in theire apparrell, which is Commonly of Cloth, and playne stuffes, with litle or no lace, neuer imbrodered, and worne by them to the vttermost proofe, euen when it is greasy. So are they in theire feasts; which exceed not foure or fyue dishes, and in theire games or sportes, which they seldome vse and neuer for great wagers. Only they spend prodigally in drincke, wherein sometymes I haue seene one gentleman at one nights lodging in his Inne spend tenn or twenty Dollors. Yet howsoeuer poore men will drincke theire apparell from theire backes, I should thincke it a labour of Hercules, for men of the better sorte to consume any reasonable patrimony therein. Procopius imputes Covetousnes to the Germans, because for gold they expose theire liues to danger, but I thincke not Covetousnes but rather want of meanes to ryott in drincke, makes them Mercenary soldyers. They are aboue all nations constant, in Apparrell, dyett and all thinges. For howsoeuer they changed for the Reformed Religion, when they sawe they had beene deceaued, and came to knowe the truth, yet that is to be attributed rather to theire goodnes, then to Inconstantcy. They are of great integrity, trusty and faythfull in worde and deede.

For they demaund no more of the buyer then the iust price
that he must pay. And if you leaue mony or goods in theire
Stoues (or Common eating places of theire howses) they are as
safe as if they were locked in your chest.   Yea wheras the
Common proverbe is, that the Masters eye makes the horse fatt,
and in all Countryes men vse to see theire horses meated, there
you may safely trust, and they continually doe trust, the
seruants of the Inns to meate theire horses, who will neuer
deceave a Dumb beast.   I never obserued any Nation more
prone to suspition, not for any guiltines of wickednes in
themselues (no nation more hating treason, fraude, and all
dissimulation) but rather out of a Conscience of theire
simplicity, whereby they thincke themselues fitt to be betrayed,
howsoeuer they drincke stoutly, and though they eate slowly yet
by setting long at table Commonly eate to satiety, which two
thinges vse to preuoke venerye, yet no doubt theire Chastitye is
admirable.   Perhapps this fullnes chookes their spirittes, and
makes them dull, and so lesse inclyned to venerye.   But no
doubt the men are very chast, and the wemen not only
exceeding modest, as I formerly sayd, but in my opinion most
chast in the worlde, I knowe not whether out of naturall
inclynation, or out of the seuerity of the lawe, restrayning
nature.   For Adultry is punished with death, and the offenders
in that kynde be rare and seldome or never founde.   Fornication
is punished with mulcts of mony, and with exceeding shame,
and howsoeuer some virgins among them of the baser sorte haue
sometymes bastards, and some of the better sort are content to
vse theire seruice for dry norses, yet they are fewe and dispised.
Tacitus writes that of all barbarous nations (as then the Romans
reputed them) only the Germans had eurey man one wife.
Towardes the German Sea, namely at Hamburg, the Citty
aboundes with harlotts, which vsed to allure strangers, and then
giue Notice to the sergants to apprehend them, and bring them
to the magistrate, who imposed great mulcts of mony vpon
them, with small Creditt to the Magistrate, because those
Mulcts were diuided, betweene the Magistrates imposing

them, the harlotts accusing, and the sargants apprehending the
betrayed malefactors. But if the man offending were marryed,
he was punished with death, to which only the breakers of
wedlocke were subiect, the party vnmaryed being through out
Germany only punished with mony. Also at Augsburg vpon
the Confynes of Italy, infected with the Nationall vice of the
Italyans being most vnchast, I obserued great impunity if not
open liberty of fornication. Munster writes that of old the
Germans were reputed vnfruitfull in generation. Bodine on
the Contrary writes all Northerne men to be most fruitefull, and
calls Germany the shopp of Nations from whence the Armyes
of the Gothes, the Hunns, the Cymbrians, the longebardes, and
Normans, infinite in number, swarmed ouer all Europe. For
howsoeuer they were not all Germans, yet those Armyes were
much increased in theire passage through Germany. But since
drunckennes is a great enemy to generation, and Tacitus writeth
that the Germans had but one wife for one man, when other
barbarous nations had euery man many wiues (which is the
most powerfull meanes of fruitefull Procreation) I knowe no
better reason why the Germans should be fruitfull in generation
aboue other Northerne people, then the singular Chastity of
the men and espetially of the wemen. For naturall reason and
experience teacheth, that wemen Prostituted to the lust of
many, neuer haue Children, at least so long as they remayne
Common. No doubt Germany is very populous, and the wemen
there be very fruitefull, as may appeare, not only by the
foresayd invndation of Armyes, but by daly experience. Botero
a Roman omitting Sweizerland, Netherland, Prussia, and
Liuonia, all which speake the German language, writes that
in the Empire tenne millions of persons were Numbred in his
tyme, and that among the very many Cittyes and fayre townes
of Germany, in one Citty of Augsburg 1705 were Baptised and
1227 were Buryed, in a yeare free from the plague or any
mortality by strange diseases. While my selfe soiourned at
Leipzige a woman had three Chilldren at a birth, and the
hauing of more then one was not thought rare or strange, Yea

they haue a Common saying, which may seeme fabulous, but
in likelyhood came at first from some rare accident in that kynd,
namely that a woman reproching another for hauing many
Children at one birth, and being Cursed by her, had herselfe the
next yeare so many Children, as for shame shee went to drowne
some of them in a Ponde, but being apprehended and punished,
the Children that were saued were commonly called Hunds-
kindren that is Dog whelps, because they so hardly scaped the
fortune of whelpes to be drowned. Whatsoeuer hath beene sayd
or may be sayd of the Germans Nature and manners, it must
allwayes be vnderstood, that vpon the Confynes on all sydes,
theire old naturall goodnes is somewhat infected and altered by
the vices of the bordering Nations. For howsoeuer the inland
Germans are at a worde for all thinges they buy and sell, and
no man will offer lesse then is asked, Yet on the borders of
Fraunce they apply themselues to vse some Art to deceave.
In like sorte within land they are most chast, but vpon the
Confynes of Italy, it is no great Cryme to be acquainted with an
harlott. And indeede generally the borderers of all Nations are
Commonly the worst people, and vse more then others to apply
themselues to the manners of theire neighbours.

Bodies and Witts.

Touching the bodies and witts of the Germans, old writers
say that they cannot beare thirst, nor heate, but are most patient
to endure colde. And Tacitus writes that theire bodyes are
great and strong to resist assaults, but not able to endure labour,
thirst, nor heate : and Pomponius Mæla sayth, theire bodyes are
most patient to endure Colde out of Custome to runne vp and
downe naked in theire shirtes, from Childhood to ripenes of
yeares. For my part I thincke thire disability to beare thirst, is
rather Contracted by Custome then by nature, since theire
bodyes are commonly moyst and Phlegmatick, and only
Custome hath taught them to drincke immoderately. Nether
thincke I them able to endure extreame Colde. For howsoeuer

I haue seene theire Children goe naked in the Stoues, and the seruants carry them into colde roomes and sett them downe naked vpon cold plastered floores, till they had made a bedd or done like buisinesse, and bigger Children often runne out naked to play in the snowe, yet these Children soone retyre into hott stoues, wherein the men also and espetially the wemen Continually sett, till they goe to bedd, or vpon necessity of buisinesse goe abroade. Also the heades and faces of the wemen are muffled with linnen Cloth, and they weare Peticoates and Clokes lyned with furr, and the men also weare Capps and Cassockes Commonly lyned with furr, yea most of them weare great stomachers of wooll or furrs, as large as Artizans Aprons, either because they cannot beare colde, or because they so weaken theire stomackes by drincking, as they are forced thus to cherish them. Bodin writes that Gallen was wont to wonder that some nations vsed to putt theire Children in colde water assoone as they were borne, and the Emperour Julian writes in his Epistle to Antiochus, that the Germans vsed to putt theire newe borne Chilldren into the Riuer Rhene, beleeuing that the Bastards would sincke and perish, but those that were Legitimate would floate aboue the water. I knowe not vpon what superstition they vsed then this barbarous and foolish Custome, but at this day I am sure the water is made luke warme in which they Baptise theire Children, whose whole bodyes they sprinckle with the same. Munster writes that the old Germans brought vp theire Children in great liberty, without tying them to labour, or learning of Artes, and that the Germans layd them downe to sleepe where night ouertooke them, and theire Children were left free to doe what they listed. And Cæsar in his Commentaryes, attribuites the Germans bigg stature and strength to this free education, which Bodin attributes to theire aboundance of moysture and heate. For my part I thincke it rather proceedes from a third cause, namely that wemen are seldome marryed till they be twenty fyue yeares old, which maturity of age cannot but bring strong and large Children. If any marye younger, they repute them more fitt

for bedd and boarde, then to gouerne the huswyfery of the
Family, and my selfe at leipzig obserued, the best sorte of the
Cittizens to thincke it strange, when a virgin of seuentene yeares
age was maryed . No doubt the bodies and all the parts of the
Germans are larg and strong. Among other thinges it would
seeme wonderfull to any of our nation, if they should see what
huge tubbes of water the wemen commonly carry vpon theire
heades (insteede of which tubbs in some places they carry two
pales hanging vpon a wodden yoke putt about theire neckes,
which somewhat easeth the Carryage). They may guesse the
ordinary bignes of the Germans bodies to exceede other nations,
who haue seene the two Monsters of men brought from thence
in our tyme to be shewed in forayne parts (as Monsters) for
mony, wherof one had a Sister in Saxony credibly reported to
be much higher, though otherwise not so great as himselfe.
In England we had experience that these two foresayd Gyants
(as I may call them) would not wrestle or doe like exercises with
our men, for the Germans in generall eating and drincking most
part of the day, and sitting continually, and that in hott stoves,
besydes the naturall bignes of stature, become fatt and puffed
up, but seldome or neuer haue actiue bodyes. Yea theire witts,
not very sharpe or quicke by nature, are by the same
intemperance, and by the hott stoues admitting no ayre, and
stuffing the brayne with grosse vapours, made very dull and
heauy. The greatest wemen are Commonly in Saxony, Oldenburg and West Phallia, but the fayrest, and indeede of excellent
beauty, are those of Hamburg, Lubect, Dantzke, and Melvin
vpon the Sea syde. At Hamburg they haue all yellow heyre,
by washing it weekly with one kynd of lee and drying it in
the sunne. The fayrest within land are those of Suevia and
espetially of Augsburg. Both men and wemen in Styria and
Carinthia vpon the Alpps, haue many of them great wenns in
theire throtes, bigger then theire cheekes, ether by drincking
water running through Mynerlls, or snowe falling into the
waters, for snowe lyes most part of the yeare vpon those
Mountaynes. In Feasts they haue no complement intertayne-

ments, discourse, or mirth, but graue and long orations one after
another, theire short speeches are only 'you are welcome,'
'drincke out all,' 'I drincke to your mastership,' and 'I pledge
your mastership,' and the like : theire Actions of mirth are only
daunsing after theire rude manner, or griping of handes. If
they have Fooles to make them merrye, they wring laughter
from others by obsurdity of acction, as falling and breaking
theire shinnes, and by telling written tales, not by sharpenes
of any witty talke. Indeede they knowe not what a pleasant
Jest is, but will interprett literally after the playne wordes, such
speeches, as by strangers are spoken with sauorye and witty
conceyte, if they were taken in the sence they meane them.

Artes and Sciences.

If any obiect that the Germans are exelent in manuall Artes,
and the liberall Sciences, I think that to be attributed not to
theire sharpenes of witt, but to theire industry, for they vse to
plodd with great diligence vpon their professions, not careing to
be ignorant in all other thinges, contrary to the manner of other
nations, who besydes their profession, affect to haue some
superficiall knowledg in all thinges, for discourse and ostentation of learning. Indeede the Germans are excelent in Manuall
Artes, by that plodding industrye, and famous for the same
among all nations, by which also they bring from them much
mony into Germany. In the tyme of Venceslaus the Emperour
Crowned in the yeare 1376. Bertholdus Niger a German Monke
and a great Chymist, is sayd first to haue invented Gunns and
Gunnpowder. And in the tyme of the Emperour Fredericke the
third, Crowned in the yeare 1440, John Gutenberg a German,
borne at Strasburg, did first invent Printing, which was after
perfected at Mentz. At least these men first made these
inventians knowne to the people of Europe. For the historyes
of China are sayd to wittnes, that of old in the tyme of theire
first king, he was taught the vse of Gunns by a Deuill, and
that of old they had the vse of Printing. The Germans also

make exquisite Clockes, such as that of Strasburg, that of Bazill, and that of Lubecke, described in the first part of this worke, excellent for knowledg of Astronomy, and for manuall Art, which are commonly whole Clockes, that is stricking foure and twenty howres, and begining at night, wherevpon they were called of old the Sonnes of Dis, and were sayd of olde to reken tyme by nights not by dayes, as now to this day takeing theire leaue of frendes, they wish them a thousand good nights. Likewise they haue Artificiall mills, to be driuen with a small quantity of water, conveyed in troughes, and falling directly vpon the wheeles, which they vse in theire Mines, as also for other vses, namely for sawing of boardes, with litle helpe of one workeman to fasten the tree to the Mill, which done it draweth the tree to it being never so great, till it haue sawed out the same, so as for euery boarde they doe but once fasten the tree to the Mill, and neede no more attend it. And they haue Mills vpon the Riuers founded vpon a boate, in which they remoue the Mill at pleasure from one towne and village to another. By Manuall Art they make all labours easy, to be donne with litle helpe and attendance, sauing the charge of workmen and seruants. Wemen in Childebed and sicke persons not able to move for weaknes, haue towells fastened vpon wheeles to the toppes of theire bedds, by which without other helpe they can remoue and turne themselues with ease. They haue Cradles for Children, wherein they shutt them, and support them that they cannot fall, and these moue with wheeles which way soeuer the chyld moues them, so as he learnes to goe of himselfe, while the mother, nurse, and maydes, are free to attend housholde buisinesse. For the Germans so abhorr Idlenesse, as I haue seene young men, rather then they would stand Idle, seriously fall to spining of flax. Theire very Plowghs are driuen vpon wheeles with great ease and small number of Plowmen. All seuerall trades of Artizans, haue theire solem feasts yearely, in publike howses for that purpose, whether they all goe together in the morning, marching through the streetes with affected grauity, and there hauing largly dyned, they spend most part of the afternoone, sometymes in daunsing after musicke, sometymes at the table singing and drincking, and then retorne to theire owne howses, marching through the streetes in like manner as they came thether.   The Artizans worke not, as our English, in open shopps, but in close Parlers or chambers, hauing Stoues or Ovens, which are heated in the winter, so as they are troubled with no cold.   They receave youthes bound prentises for six yeares, to be taught theire trades, during which tyme, they vse them with much lesse severity then our Artizans doe in England.   For they worke with their hatts on, and haue many hollidays, wherein they challeng of Custome to be free from labour, in so much as euery Monday (which they call Sondayes brother) they worke not at all, or very litle at their owne pleasure.   If any man come to buy thinges in theire shops namely shooes and bootes, they neuer rise from theire worke, but the buyer chuseth his owne shooes and Bootes, and putts them on himselfe, and then payes the price they aske at a worde and (as of duty) giues some drincking mony to the workemen. The prentises hauing serued theire yeares, and being Jorneymen, that is working for dayes wages, vse to trauell through the great Cittyes of Germany Fraunce and Italy, mantayning theire expences by theire owne labour, and when they haue gotten mony to beare theire charges by the way, they go to another Citty, and before they retorne home, with singular industry become expert in theire trades.   This custome is more spetially vsed by Taylors, and Barbars (who withall professe surgery) and also by Shooemakers.   And in tyme this custome hath gotten such power, as in the great Cittyes of Germany, these wanderers, with great Confidence enter the houses of the best workmen of theire trade, calling for worke, as if they were in theire masters houses, and liuing there vpon theire labour, till they haue gott mony to trauell further, as or long as they list.

For Sciences : There is not a man among the Common sorte who cannot speake lattin, and hath not some skill in Arithmaticke, and Musicke, The very wemen carry chalke in

theire purses wherewith they will truely and speedily cast any
ordinary reckning.   If any aske Almes, they Commonly begg
singing, and the poore schollers vpon hollydayes goe singing
about the streetes, and receaue some Almes at euery house of
the better sorte, Each Cittye and good towne hath Trumpeters,
who commonly dwell in the steeples of the Churches, with theire
whole Familyes, where they haue a convenient Stoue, and a
lodging Chamber, with a voyd Rome or two, for Pullen and like
necessaryes, on the highest topps of the steeples, where daly at
Noone they sounde Trumpitts, and allwayes serue in steede of
watchmen, hanging out flaggs and diuerse signes, whereby the
Cittizens may knowe what horsemen Footemen, or Coaches
approach to the towne, and more spetially thereby the Innkeeper
hath warning to provide for them and expect theire comming,
whether they also come at dinner tyme to receaue some guift of
the Passengers.   In like sorte many Cittyes mantayne at
publike charge Musitians, vsing Sagbutts, Hoboyes, and such
loude Instruments, which wee call the waytes of Cyttyes, and
these play at the publicke house of the City each day at Noone,
when the Senatours goe to dinner, and at all publike Feasts.
And howsoeuer they be of the Reformed Religion after the rule
of Luther, yet in theire Churches, after the manner of the
Roman Church, they vse to sing laten Hymmnes artificially,
and haue not only Organs, but Cornetts and a Consort of like
loude Instruments, sounding whyle the Queristers sing, and
while the whole Congregation singes Psalmes in the vulgar
tounge, the most part (as I sayd) hauing skill in musicke.   In
all theire Meetinges to drincke, they greately delight in
daunsing, and Musicke, as norishing the present humour of
mirth, and cheering them to drincke more largely.   But as they
delight most in loude musicke, so in still Musicke of Lutes and
like Instruments, they like them better who strike hard vpon
the strings, then those who with a gentile touch make sweeter
Melody, which they thincke fitter for Chambers to invite sleepe,
then for feasts to invite mirth and drincking.   Also they are
much delighted in singing birdes, so as not only those of the

better sort, but the common Artizans haue them in theire Stoues, ether flying loose, and resting vpon branches of Laurell, greene in Winter, and hung vp of purpose, or ells many birdes in a large windowe inclosed within the glasse and a windowe of wyer. And my selfe obserued at Leipzig, that in the fayrest streetes, each house of the better sort had nightingales, which ioyntly made sweete musicke to the passengers.

For the Military Science, they willingly followe Captaynes of theire owne Nation, and would not easily obey strangers. They haue that vertue common with the Sweitzers, that when the warr is donne, they willingly and readily laye downe theire Armes, and fall to the workes of theire former vocations. The same selfe loue makes them preferr theire owne writers, in Philosophy, diuinity, and all Sciences, before any forayne Authors, so as I may say, that if in any nation, surely in Germany, a Prophett is most esteemed in his owne Country. The Phisitians in Germany (as my selfe found by experience being sicke at Leiptzig, and by discourse in other places) are very honest and learned, Contrary to the old rule to take when the disease payneth, because after ease Phisitians are litle regarded, they neuer take any mony till they haue donne the Cure, and if the sicke man dye in theire handes, they expect no rewarde of theire vnsuccessfull labours. Yea when he is recovered, they expect no greater reward then after the rate of Eightene pence the day in English mony, and I haue seene them being offered more, to refuse it and turne it backe to the giuer. Yet doe they visitt the sicke twise each day, with much diligence and compassionate Curtesye, not scorning to handle any sore parte, or to looke vpon any Ordure, to discouer the disease. In like sorte the Apothecaryes, are fewe in Number, and only such as are allowed by the Prince, and they indorse the Phisicke they giue vpon the Phisitians bills, and sell theire druggs at a reasonable rate. And howsoeuer the Germans are naturally more honest, then to sell rotten ware, espetially in this case, where it concerns life, yet to prevent any such fraude, the Phisitians, by an Imperiall lawe and by the decrees of severall

Princes, are required and vse yearely to visitt theire shops, where they fayle not to burne all druggs that are not fitt to be vsed. As in Italy, so in Germany, they haue Emperickes, which professe to haue some spetiall receipts, salues, Oyles, and oyntments, approued for some cures, who beare with them testimonialls vnder the great Seales of Princes and free Cittyes, for the Cures they haue donne, and mounting vpon stalls, or litle skaffolds, in markett places, publish these testimonialls, and preach theire owne skill, shewing pictures of Cures they haue donne, and stonnes they haue cutt out, and Teeth they haue drawne. In Italy I haue knowne some of theme to haue good secretes in this kynde, but there they be many in number, here more ignorant, and much fewer, there they haue a zani or foole, to drawe Company by mirth, that they may better vent theire wares, here they sell with playne bragging. Generally they are no Schollers, but flatt Cheaters, yet will vndertake any Cure whatsoeuer. And as in Italy they are called Monti – banchi, that is Mounters vpon Bankes, so here they are called, Tyriaks- kremer, that is marchants or sellers of Treakle. In Germany they haue Masters of Fence, more singlar in formality of taking vp and laying downe wepons, then in skill of defence and offence, and these are made only in Frankford in the two yearely Marts or Fayres. The doctors of Ciuill lawe in Germany liue in great estimation, the Empire being for the most part gouerned by the Imperiall or Ciuill lawe, though in some partes Prouinciall lawes and Customes are mingled with it. They are Chanecellours to the Emperour, and the Princes, which office is the cheefe in dignity and power vnder them, so as no profession is more studied and followed by young gentlemen and those of the better sort. For those who cannot attayne this highest dignity, yet become Gouernours in Cittyes and Prouinces, besydes that all the Vniversityes labour and giue large stipends to drawe those of greatest fame to be Professors and Readers of the lawe in their Schooles, so as Germany must needes abound with learned men of a profession so well rewarded. Yea the very wiues of these Docters, aswell as themselues, haue large

Priuiledges for weareing of Apparrell and many ornaments, by the Imperiall lawes, first compiled and still expounded by men of that profession. Germany hath some fewe wandring Comeydians, more deseruing pitty then prayse, for the serious parts are dully penned, and worse acted, and the mirth they make is ridiculous, and nothing lesse then witty (as I formerly haue shewed). So as I remember that when some of our cast dispised Stage players came out of England into Germany, and played at Franckford in the tyme of the Mart, hauing nether a Complete number of Actours, nor any good Apparell, nor any ornament of the Stage, yet the Germans, not vnderstanding a worde they sayde, both men and wemen, flocked wonderfully to see theire gesture and Action, rather then heare them, speaking English which they vnderstoode not, and pronowncing peeces and Patches of English playes, which my selfe and some English men there present could not heare without great wearysomenes. Yea my selfe Comming from Franckford in the Company of some cheefe marchants Dutch and Flemish, heard them often bragg of the good markett they had made, only Condoling that they had not the leasure to heare the English players. Touching the Germans education in Schooles : vpon the day of St. Gregorye and no other day of the yeare, the Schoolemaster and Schoolers of the publike Schoole in some Cittyes, march about the streetes in theire best apparrell and Festiuall Pompe, to receaue new Schoolers, whome the parents make ready against that day, to present them as they passe, and enter them into the Schoole. And most rich men keepe also a priuate Schoolemaster in theire howses, for theire Children, only to leade them daly to the publike Schoole, and bring them backe from thence, and to teach them at home such lessons as are giuen them in the publike Schoole, and to teach them good behauiour at home. One thinge I cannot commend in the Germans, that for desyre of vayneglory, being yet without Beardes and of smale knowledge, they make themselues knowne more than praysed, by vntimely Printing of bookes, and very toyes, published in theire names. Young Students who haue

scarce layd theire lipps to taste the sweete fountaynes of the
Sciences, if they can wrest an Elegy out of theire empty brayne,
it must presently be Printed, yea if they can but make a
wrangling disputation in the Vniversity, the questions they
dispute vpon, with the Disputers names, must also be Printed.
Yea very graue men and Docters of the liberall Professions, are
so forward to rush into these Olimpick games, for gayning the
prise from others, as they seeme rather to affect the writing
of many and great, then iudicious and succinct bookes, so as
theire riper yeares and second Counsells (allwayes best) hardly
suffice to correct the errours therof, and change (as the Proverbe
is) quadrangles to round formes, wheras the French and other
Authours, feareing the diuersity of diuers mens Judgments, and
the biting detractions of emulous and envious readers, vse to
polish, and often peruse theire owne writinges, before they dare
committ them to the Presse. And herein the bookes of Caluin
litle or nothing Corrected, haue had great advantage ouer the
bookes of Luther often purged and much altered from theire
first Copies. For it may well be sayd of books corrected
after Printing, that was sayd of the Roman Sensures of
manners: The note may be blotted out, but the spott cannot:
since howsoeuer the Corrected bookes are good and profitable (as
many of the Germans are, being purged of theire drosse), yet
envious readers more obserue the spotts of errours blotted out,
then Socraticall sentences newely added. And no doubt, no
bookes haue more felt the sting of this envie, then those of most
learned and holy Luther. From hence it commeth, that the
Printers of Germany, are so farr from giuing the Authors mony
for theire Copies (which they doe in other Countryes) as feareing
not to vent them with gayne, they dare not adventure to Print
them at theire charge. So as the German Authors vse, ether to
pay a great part of the charge leauing the bookes to the Printer,
or to pay a Crowne for the Printing of each leafe, keeping
the bookes to themselues, which they commonly giue freely to
frendes and strangers, as it were hyring them to vouchsafe the
reading thereof.

Vniuersities.

Germany hath very many vniversityes, for after the decay of the Imperiall and Papull power, besydes those of olde founded vpon priuiledges graunted by them, each absolute Prince, and some free Cittyes (which are very many in Germany) haue founded an vniversity in some cheefe Citty of theire Provinces. It were infinite to discribe them all, therefore I will only discribe at large that of Witteberg, where by the quallity of the rest may be gathered. It was founded in the yeare 1502, some fifteene yeares before Martin Luther and Phillip Melancton began there to teach the Reformation of Religion, and in fewe yeares it became famous, by great Concurse of Students from all parts of Germany. If a Professors place be voyde, the Professor Professors chuse another, who must be approued by the Elector of Saxony theire Prince. The Professors chuse the Deanes of the seuerall facultyes, who haue Authority, each in theire owne faculty, ouer promotions to degrees, allowing of bookes to be Printed, and like things. The Professors and Deanes chuse some twelue Assistants, who haue power to allowe priuate meetings, for lectures and Disputations. All these chosen for life, doe out of their owne number yearely chuse the Rector of the vniversity, and commonly in order, one after the other. But if it happen that any Baron or Prince be Student in the Vniversity, they vse to chuse him Rector for the yeare, and he vseth to chuse for his Prorector or Substitute, him who by order and course should haue otherwise beene Rector that yeare, so as the Baron or Prince hath the honour, and his Substitute the Profitt and administration of the office, to whome also at the yeares end, the Baron or Prince vseth to giue a Present (as a peece of plate) for his paynes in that Substitution. In the Rectors election, the publike Notary of the vniversity takes the Voyces, and himselfe giues his voyce, and then pronounceth him to be chosen. This Rector takes place of the Princes Ambassadors if they passe through the towne, and when he goes abroade he weares a redd veluit hoode vpon his Cloke

(for the Doctors and Students in Germany weare not gownes,
but Clokes, and hatts insteede of Cornard Capps vsed with vs).
The foresayde Senate, of Rector, Professors, Deanes, Assistants
and publike Notary, governe the vniversity, and punish the
Students, in Common faults with pecuniary mulcts, and in
greatest offences with Banishment, who by theire oath are
bounde to obedience vnder payne of periury. This oath my
selfe tooke, contayning these heades : First that I should obey
the Rector, secondly that I should reade and obserue the
Statutes, thirdly that I should obey any lawfull Arest, fourthly
that I should submitt my selfe to banishment if it were imposed
vpon me, fifthly that I should not reveng any wrong by violence.
For my admission I payd the third part of a doller. Only the
Students of Hungary, by the fauour of Phillip Melancton had a
priuiledge not to be called before the Rector, but to haue all
theire causes iudged by an Elder chosen of theire owne nation,
which priuiledge at the tyme of my being theire was suspended,
for a tyme, because they did not duely pay theire Credits and
Hosts. They haue foure Professors of diuinity, wherof some
had foure hundreth, others three hundreth fyfty Guldens of
siluer (each valued at three shillings foure pence English mony)
for theire yearely Stipend. Three Docters and Professors of
Phisicke, had each three hundreth Guldens yearely. Fiue
Doctors and Professors of the Ciuill lawe, had each 250. Guldens
yearely, One Professor of Logicke, and one Professor of the
Mathematicks, one of Historyes, one of Rhetorick, one of the
Hebrewe toung, one of the Sphere, one of Poetry, and one of
Naturall Philosophy, had each of them 250 Guldens yearely
Stipend. And howsoeuer these Stipends are sometymes
increased or deminished, according to the worthines of the
Professor, yet the greatest is neuer aboue six hundreth, the least
not vnder a hundreth Guldens yearely. These Professors reade
continually through out the yeare, without any vacations, as wee
haue in our vniversities, for they reade in the very Dogdayes.
In theire Lectures they doe not insist vpon a worde for
ostentation of learning and elequence, but in a Convenient tyme

soundly and grauely absolue the booke they vndertake to expounde, that the Students may daly goe forwarde to finish theire Studies. This worke they performe exactly and with great diligence, aswell because theire Stipends are sufficient to mantayne them, as because the Prince, hauing a small Teritory to distract him, vseth many tymes to take knowledge of theire diligence, and to punish the negligent, but espetially to satisfye theire Auditors. For the Students of Germany haue litle learning from priuate reading, but take the most part therof vpon trust (or hearesay) from the lectures of these graue Professors who dictate theire Lectures with a slowe and tretable voyce, which they write out word by word, their many penns sounding like a great shower of rayne, and if the Professor vtter any thing so hastily that the Students cannot write it, they knocke vpon the Deskes till he repeate it agayne more tretably. This vniversity had of old 4000 Guldens yearely Reuenue, which the Dukes Electours haue since increased to 20000 Guldens yearely rent, vpon the suppression of Bishoprickes and Monasteryes. Out of this Reuenewe the Professors Stipends are payd, and Certayne poore Schoolers are norishied, which sing in the Electors Chappell, though he be seldome resident there. It hath only two Colleges, the Augustine, and the Bernardine, both formerly Monasteryes, as apeares by the names. They are nether farely built, nor of large extent, nor endowed with any yearely Reuenewe, and such and so fewe are the Colleges of all the vniversities in Germany, where generally only poore Schollers liue in the Colleges, all the other Students lodging and boarding in Cittisens howses. Here in the Augustine College, the foresayde Schollers singing in the Electours Chappell are lodged freely and haue a diett, at the rate of foure siluer Grosh and a halfe for each man by the weeke, and to that table all poore Schollers what soeuer may be admitted, if they will pay that rate weekly, and whatsoeuer is spent aboue that rate is payde out of the publike Reuenew of the vniversity. For howsoeuer the Dyett be simple and sparing, yet that rate will not mantayne it. But fewe and only those that are very poore take the benifitt of this table, because they cannot be lodged in the College. The Duke Electour of Saxony giues in the same College Chambers freely, and the same dyett at his owne charge, to 70 poore Schollers of his owne subiectes, not perpetually so long as they list to stay, but only for so many yeares as are sufficient to absolue theire Studies, and make them fitt to be imployed in the Church and commonwealth which course makes them diligent, lest the time should prevent them before they had finished theire studyes, and the rather because theire mantenance for that tyme is poore and sparing, whereas no doubt the inioying of Fellowships (being a Competent mantenance, and a pleasant easye life) perpetually or during theire owne pleasures in our vniversities, causeth much losse of tyme idle and carelessly spent. Likewise in the foresayd Bernardine College only the Children of the poore Cittizens of Witteberg are mantayned, hauing chambers freely, and like dyett allowed out of the old revenues of that monasterye, Converted to that and like vses of piety. Wee reade not of any degrees in vniversities, before the decree of Gratian published in the yeare 1151 when the Bishops of Rome, desyring to haue theire decretalls and scholasticall diuinity practised in Courts of Justice and in the Church, first began, by the sayd tytles and degrees to allure young men to Study those Professions. After in the Councell of Vienna in the yeare 1311 these degrees were approved, and a lawe made to limitt the Expence in takeing them. Bachilers of Arts, had the name giuen them of Baculus, or Bacillus, that is a staff, deliuered them as an ensigne of freedome. Licentiates of the lawe were so called, of license giuen them to practise, and then to take the highest degree. Docters were so called of teaching. At Paris in Fraunce, the diuines who did reade vpon the sentences of Lombard, were called Doctours, and at Bologna in Italy likewise those who did reade the Ciuill lawe, and when the number of Docters increased, lawes were published for the number of yeares making capeable of that degree, with many like constitutions. A master of Art is so called of the Magi or wise men of Persia, and this title is proper to Philosophers, but at Paris and at Louan the Doctors of diuinity who take vpon them the Censure of Doctrynes, and would be preferred before all other Doctors, are styled Magistri Nostri, that is our Masters. The gentlemen of Germany study the Ciuill lawe, richly rewarded among them, and some become docters thereof, but they dispise all other degrees, and esteme a Master of Art no better then a Pedant. This my selfe founde in Austria, when speaking with a gentleman, and vpon his wonder that I spake the latten toung readily, telling him I was a Master of Arts, I perceaved that after he esteemed me no better then a Scholemaster, or man of like quality, wherevpon I neuer after in Germany confessed my selfe to haue that degree. Att Witteberg the Bachilors and masters of Arts keepe no disputations for those degrees, being only examined by the Professors. But the doctors, besydes examination, dispute once from seuen in the morning to foure in the after noone. The Phisitians and Ciuill lawyers should dispute once in the month, and the Diuines euery third Month publikely, which charge falls vppon the Professors, and the Diuines orderly kepte this Course, but the other hardly disputed once in the yeare. In these disputations helde in the publike Schooles, only Docters and masters answer, but from the Docters to the youngest Students, all in Course vse to appose, and in the end of the disputation they vse a Ceremony to invite all those who are not satisfyed, to propound and vrge theire Arguments agayne. They vse to dispute hauing theire heades covered with their hatts, and haue no Moderator, as wee haue in our Vniversities, but vrging theire Arguments coldly, leaue them in the first or second Motion, as satisfyed with any slight answer. And indeede the Number of the Opponents is so great, as the tyme will not permitt any one man to propound many arguments, or to urge one to the full. Students haue a Custome that some fewe of them, of theire owne free will, with the leaue of the deane of theire faculty, will agree to hold publike declamations and disputations for seuerall dayes, which they make knowne to the rest by Printing the Theses or Questions vpon which they dispute and declame. Philip Melancton was authour of making a Statute, that whosoeuer asked a degree should not be denyed it, which he did vpon a sadd event, of a Scholler in his tyme hanging himselfe for shame, that hauing asked his degree he was refused as vnworthy thereof, whose Sepulcher they shewed mee in the feildes without the Citty, for he that kills himselfe, may not be buyried in any churchyard or place of Christian buyriall. Yet when they take degrees, all are examined for fashion sake, and those that are found lesse worthy, are noted of impudent boldnes, and are only admonished that howsoeuer theire degree in fauour is not denyed them, yet they must after ply theire Studies with more diligence, to repayre theire present unworthines. In giuing degrees, they nether respect the tyme how long, nor the place where the partie Studied, if he be founde worthey for learning. For the examination whereof, two Professors and two Assistants are chosen, but any other that will may allso examine them, and this examination should last three dayes, but the Rector vseth in fauour to craue remission of the third day, and for the other two dayes commonly some priuate frendes, making shewe to examine them, passe the tyme in familliar talke. And one Custome is strange, were it not in Germany, that the Examiner and the Examined, very often, if not at euery question and answer, drincke one to the other, hauing potts sett by them of purpose, which Custome they say once produced a pleasant accident, the Professor and the Student after much drincking falling both asleepe, and the professor first awaked, asked the Student, what is sleepe, who answered with the old verse

> Stulte, quid est somnus, gelidæ nisi Mortis Imago.
> Thou Foole, what may sleepe seeme to thee?
> It cold deaths Image seemes to mee.

Masters and Docters are promoted together, twise euery yeare, namely some fewe dayes before Easter, and a litle after the feast of St. Michael. A Deane Gouerns (or his President) at the Promotion or commencement of Bachilors, but the Vice-

Chancelor is President ouer that of Masters and Docters. But this Vice-Chancelour is not (as with vs in England) cheefe Gouernour of the Vniversity (who is here stylled Rector) but is a peculiar officer, for the tyme of Promotions, chosen and confirmed by the Bishop of Merzburg, and hauing authority from him to Conferr those degrees. And since the suppression of Bishoprickes in those teritoryes of the Saxon Elector, and the Administration of them vsed to be giuen by the Elector to some cheefe gentlemen of the Country, this office of vice-chancelor is Chosen and confirmed by the gentleman on whome the Elector hath bestowed the administration of the Bishoprick of Merzburg, and the office ceaseth when the tyme of each seuerall Promotion is expired. Before which Promotion this Vice-Chancelour takes the names of all that desyre to take those degrees, who must bring to him a Testimoniall from the Professor whose lectures they haue heard for two yeares past, and he that cannot bring that testimoniall must pay aboute seuen Dollors for Completion (as they call it). In like sort the Bachelors must bring this testimoniall to the Deane from a Professor whose Auditors they haue beene for one yeare or in default pay a like some of mony. And this mony for Completion is deuided betweene the Vice-chancelour (for the masters and Doctors) or the Deane (for the Bachilors), and betweene the Rector, the Examiners, and the Bedells. Also they must bring to the Vice-chancelor or Deane, each one his priuate Schoolemaster, to testifye the Course of his life for his studie and manners, from his childhoode to that day. For I haue former sayd, that in Germany the richer sort, sending theire Children to Schoole, keepe a priuate Schoolemaster to attende them to Schoole, and to instruct them at home, which Schoolemaster they send also with them to the vniversities, Commonly giuing him his dyett and some fyfty French Crownes yearely Stipend. If our rich men in England would take this care, and be at this Charge with a priuate Schoolemaster well chosen, theire Children would not leese so much tyme as they doe, espetially in the Vniversities, where our English Parents seldome enquire after the diligence of Tutors, to whome they committ their Chilldren and much lesse giue them such Competent reward for theire paynes. The sayd Vice-chancelour, before the Promotion, reades a publike lecture for six weekes to those who are to take degree. And at the begining of the Promotion or commencement, they giue a publike supper, and call it the supper of the Calendes, and at the end they giue a dinner, and call it the Aristotelian Dinner. The Ceremonyes of taking Degrees are donne with great Pompe of grauity, the takers of them marching to the publike Schooles with torches lighted by day, and many Musitians playing before them, most Commonly with loude instruments. But when I was at Witteburg, they had no Musicke, because the Elector was newly dead. When they come to the Schooles, they fall on their knees, and a Chosen Professor makes an Oration, to the Vice-chancelor for Masters and Docters, or to the Deane for Bachilors, Crauing his fauour to admitt them, and he graunting this request, they are brought vp to him, where a Bedell takes theire Oath, first to be obseruant to theire superiores, secondly to shewe fauour towards the Vniversity, thirdly to promote pure profession of Religion, fourthly to be thanckfull towardes the College of their owne Faculty. The Phisitions giue a peculiar Oath to practise upon knowledg, not with old wiues Receipts, not to destroy any Children in the mothers wombe, nether to giue any deadly poyson or hurtfull medicine to any sicke person. Then they reade the names of the Promoted, and of the Citty where each of them was borne, and they vse to giue Seniority according to theire learning. Yet (by the waye be it sayd) lest it should be disgracefull to be named in the last rancke, they vse in some forrayne Vniversities (namely at Lovan) to reade many conterfeit names in the end, so as the latter true names cannot be publikely knowne. Then the vice chancelor makes an Oration in Prose, or sometymes in Verse, then they who are to commence, or to be promoted, masters and Docters, are willed to ascend into the vper seates, where for the first Ceremony, each of them is placed in a Chayre, as hauing power giuen them to teach out of a Pulpitt, or eleuated seate. Secondly, each one hath a purple capp giuen him as distinguishing him from the vulgar sort, and giuing him more open viewe of the heauens. Thirdly each hath a ring putt on his finger, as marryed to Philosophy, Fourthly each hath an open booke giuen him, as inviting him to reade, and a closed booke, as remembring him to ioyne Contemplation with reading. To the Docters the Vice Chancelor vseth a fifth Ceremony of imbracing them, as receaved into his order. And sixtly each of them, askes some Doctor a question, which he answers presently, which answer is vnderstoode to be vnpremeditated yet Commonly they reade it out of writen hand, by which it appeares that the question was made knowne to them. For indeede the Germans seldome or neuer pronounce any thinge by heart, Justly (as it seemes) distrusting theire memoryes, weakned with Continuall drincking. Lastly the Doctors of the Ciuill lawe in some Vniversities are girded with a Military Belt, as bound to defend the lawe. In Conclusion, one of the Promoted makes an Oration giuing thanckes for himselfe and all his Fellowes, and so the cheefe Professor of diuinity and the Vice chancelor going before all the Promoted Graduates followe in order, up to the high Alter, where they pray vpon theire knees. For the place of these Ceremonyes is the Church wherein for the tyme a place is compassed in with barrs of wood, into which they only are receaved, who are spetially invited by the promoted Graduates and each of them hath a payre of Gloues giuen him, besydes many gloues Cast out of the Circle into the presse of the Studentes, to be snatched by those can gett them. The licentiates of the Ciuill lawe, are only Pronounsed in bare wordes, without any Ceremonyes vsed, yet in Fraunce they are no lesse esteemed then Doctors. All Ceremonyes thus ended, the Promoted Graduates and the Professors, two in a rancke, and bareheaded, retourne from the Church with the same Pompe as they came thether, to the publike house of the Citty, where this and all publike Feasts are kept. At Wettebirg the charge of a Doctors Promotion was

37 golde Guldens, and of a master of Arts eight silluer guldens, and halfe of this mony was deuided, betweene the Rector, the Deane, the Notery, the Examinors, and the Beedells, the other halfe was putt into the Publike Treasure of the Promotions (distinguished from the publike Treasury of the Vniversity) and was Commonly imployed, for Almes, for publike guifts, and for repareing of publike buildings. The Germans despise those who take degrees in Italy, and not without cause, the Italyans themselues proverbially saying: wee take mony, and send an asse in a Doctors habitt into Germany. For In Italy many cheefe Doctors, out of old Custome, and for preheminence aboue ordinary Doctors, obtayne of the Popes to be called and created Counts Palatines, who (among other priuiledges) haue power to create Doctors, giuing them theire Bulla (that is Sealed letters Pattents) to witnesse that they haue this degree, which often in base Couetousnes, they conferr for mony vpon most vnworthy men. And many strangers take this degree from them, not only for want of learning, but for other causes, as namely to escape the oath of Religion which they should take in theire Vniversities at home. In like sort by the Imperiall olde lawe the Notaryes of Germany haue the power (and at this time whereof I write, one Doctor Melissus a German, by the Emperours spetiall graunt had this power) to create Doctors, vnder theire Seales, wherevpon these (as the former) are in reproch called Doctors of the Bulla or seale, and both are dispised in Germany, by the Graduates of the Vniversityes. The vniversityes of Germany, haue no Taxers (or Clarkes of the Markett) for the price of vittles (as our vniversityes haue) because the Students liue in Cittizens houses, and so leaue the care of the Markett to them. Nether haue they any Proctors, who with vs in England (besydes theire superintendancy ouer the Commencements or Promotions, and charg of other things) keepe the night watches, and punish all disorders donne in the night. So as nothinge was more ·frequent at Witteberg, then for Students to goe by night to Harlotts, and being druncke, to walke in the streets with naked swordes, slashing them against

the stones, and making noyse with Clamours. And howsoeuer the Duke Elector, at my beeing there strictly forbadd these disorders (as the Princes of Germany haue leasure to obserue the government of their vniversityes) yet after a small forbearance thereof they retourned to theire former liberty, Notwithstanding the Students at Weiteberg weare no swordes by day, and though at Leipzig, (an Vniversitye not farr distant vnder the same Elector) the Doctors of lawe and Phisicke, and young gentlemen Students there, had the priuiledge to weare swordes by day, yet the Cittizens and theire seruants in both those Vniversityes were not permitted to weare them. When any Maryage is Celebrated at Weiteberg, the Bridegrome, the bryde, and the invited guests, aswell men as wemen, Cittizens as strangers, hauing feasted at home, march in graue pompe to the publike Senate house, with their Musitians, to spend the after-noone there in drincking and dansing, and all Students, though they be not invited and likewise Cittizens, vse to come thether, to beholde their dauncing, and the best sort are commonly invited to Daunce and drincke with them. And the Students are by a spetiall lawe restrayned from any immodesty in those meetings, though generally by nature the Germans are not inclyned to vse any publike insolency towardes weomen. Most of the Students weare litle feathers in theire hatts, and commonly blacke, but the Doctors of the Ciuill lawe through all Germany weare white fethers, euen in the Chambers of Judgment. The Students are gouerned by the Rector, the Cittizens by theire Senate, and the Villages or Country people by the Dukes officer residing there, and if any man be wronged, the accused drawes the Cause to his owne Court, where the accused being founde guilty is punished, but if he be not founde guilty, the Accuser renounceth his Action, and is sent backe to be punished by his owne Magistrate. Thus if a Student be wronged by any Cittizen, or any of the Country, the Rector sendes two or three Professors, to the Senate of the Citty, or to the Dukes officer, to demaund Justice in his name, and the other wronged by any Student, their Magistrate sendes to the

Rector to demaunde Justice in theire names. But all Cappitall offences are determyned by the Senate of the Citty. Yet of old the Vniversyties had such preuileges, as only the Rector iudged Capitall offences Committed by Students, and commonly theire greatest punishment for Murther was banishment, or perpetuall imprisonment. And howsoeuer these preuileges haue beene since lesse regarded, or taken away, yet of late in the vniversity of Konigsberg, a Student hauing killed one of the watch, was only punished with perpetuall imprisonment. But in the publike schoole of Strasburg (being no allowed Vniversity) only the Senate of the Citty iudgeth Students in all Causes. At Witteburg they still retayne the old custome of Salting freshmen, or admitting young Students with ridiculous Ceremonyes, and as wee call them freshmen, so they call them Beiani, and the Ceremony is by them called the deposition of hornes. And for this purpose, they haue a peculiar officer called Depositor, and a Chamber peculiar for those Ceremonyes, where each student salted or admitted, payes six Siluer Guldens. And many in those parts, send theire Chilldren very young, from the Gramer Schooles, to the Vniversity, only to be thus salted or admitted, carrying them backe to the Gramer Schooles agayne, till they be made fitt to Studdy in the vniversity, or perhaps by priuate teaching inabled, to come thether only to take degrees. Some may perhapps be content to knowe the ridiculous Ceremonyes of this office, wherof I will relate a fewe for theire satisfaction. The depositor first comes with a payre of Pinsers, making as if he would pull the horne from theire foreheades. Then he makes them all lye flatt vpon the grownd, with theire faces vpward, stretching those out that are shorter, and making as if he would cutt those that are longer then theire fellowes, hauing first compassed them with a rownde Magicall Circle, and so cast water vpon them till they rise vp, all which tyme a litle bell is rung, and a great noyse made by the beholders. Then he Poseth them in all the sciences, asking them many pleasant questians, As this for one: Canis, ouis, Capra, Millœ Boues. howe many feete. If they answer 4012, he sayth there be but three foote and a halfe in a verse. Agayne, why is there no Vacuity in the worlde, and whatsoeuer they answer, he replyes with his reason, because all things are full of fooles. Then he giues them many precepts no lesse ridiculous, as this, when you sett downe to meate, be sure to haue your hand first in the dish. Then he makes a long Oration to commend this Custome, which he sayth Nazianzen and Bazill testifye to haue beene vsed of old in the Vniversity of Athens, where they vsed, before the Admission of young Students to aske them many Captious and sophisticall questions and to leade them to a Bath with tumultious Clamors and wylde gestures, and to try theire witt and Constancy of mynde with other like inventions, and so at last to receaue them for members of the Vniversitye. And this Custome he proues to be very profitable, trying theire witts and manners, abating pryde in them, and shewing theire modesty or impudencye, and like vertues or vices. In Conclusion he bids them putt off theire filthy garments, which they had putt on of purpose, and putting a litle Salt in theire mouthes, and powring a litle wyne on theire heades, he remembers them, that they are now Ciuill in Apparrell and manners, and haue theire witts sharpened, and theire loue of Knowledge inflamed, and so admitts them Students of the Arts. At the tyme of my liuing at Witteburg 800 Students were numbred there, but many of them liued, who remembred the number to haue exceeded 4000. All other Vniversityes of Germany may be knowne in all points by this discription of Witteberg, but I liued in some other Vniversityes, where I obserued some small differences from it, which I will relate in a word. At Leipzig, not farr distant, and vnder the same Elector of Saxony, one of the Professors of the lawe had 700, and another 500 syluer Guldens for yearely stipend, the Professor of Phisicke 300, the Professor of Diuinity, being also Superintendent in the Church, had as Professor 300 Guldens from the Treasure of the Vniversity, and as Superintendent 700 Guldens from the Treasure of the Citty for yearely Stipend, besydes many Prouisions to helpe him. The Bedell had 300

Guldens yearely stipend. In the Dogdayes the Professors cease
to reade, and those who stand to be Masters of Artes reade for
them, and therevpon are in way of Jeast vulgarly called the
Canicular Professors. Agayne the masters of Arts and the
Bachelors of the Promotion last past, dispute weekely halfe the
yeare following in order as often as it falls to theire course, the
Masters on Satterdayes the Bachelors on Sondayes in the after
noone. Agayne those who desyre to take the degrees of Master
and Bachelors of Artes, are strictly examined for tenne dayes
space, by the Deane of theire faculty and six Professors chosen
of purpose, and the masters are Promoted once yearely in the
month of January, but the bachelors thrise in the yeare. Also
the charge of taking degrees at Leipzig was farr greater then at
Witteberg, the Masters spending about 32 gold guldens, the
licentiates 200 and the Doctors aboue three hundreth. For each
master giues two gold Guldens to each Professor of Philosophy,
and each licentiate and Doctor giues foure gold Guldens to each
Professor of his faculty, and likewise a perticular present of
some ells of Satten or Veluitt, with a quantity of Suger, and
some payres of gloues, besydes the expences of the publike
Feast.

The publike Schoole at Strasburg was not reputed an
vniversity, yet gaue the degrees of Bachelors and masters of
Artes, hauing a publike house for that purpose, and publike
Schooles where learned Professors did reade, namely foure
for diuinity, four for Phisicke, one for Rhetoricke, one for
historyes, one for Astrology, one for Arithmeticke, one for
Politickes, and one for Ethickes, besydes many allowed by the
Professors to reade priuate lectures. And at my being there,
the Students were numbered 1000, wherof 30 were Barrons
and Earles, Students flocking thether from all partes, aswell for
the beauty and strength of the Citty, aswell for the purity of
their language. The vniversity of Heydelberg was founded in
the yeare 1346 by the Palatine Rupertus the second. At my
being there the Students were about 500 in number, and the
Earle of Hanow for honours sake was the Rector, but his Deputy

Rector (after the Custome of Germany aboue mentioned) was doctor Pacius an Italian and famous Doctour of the Ciuill lawe, who had there a large Stipend to be Professor thereof. It had three Colleges which were ruinned monasteryes. In that Colledge called Sapientia, 70 poore Schollers were mantayned, each hauing some 80 Guldens yearely, and they might not goe out of the Collage without leaue, in that called Bursa, 12 poore Schollers were mantayned, each hauing 60 Guldens yearely, and they being of riper yeares, had liberty to goe forth and retorne at pleasure, and many Students of the poorer sort had theire Chambers and dyett there, at theire owne charge. In that of Casimire (so called of the late Palatyne Casimire founder therof) 50 poore Schollers were mantayned, partly by the founders guift partly by the publike treasure of the vniversity. The Rest of the Students liued at theire owne charge in the houses of Professors and Cittisens, as they doe in other Vniser-sityes of Germany.

Language.

Touching the language, the latten Toung (liuing only in writing, not in practise) and the Sclavonian and the German tounges, are reputed the fountaynes of all the most part of the languages in Europe. The Germans (as I formerly sayd) spake the latten readily in discourse, hauing practised the same from their Childhood, but in the vniversityes of England wee write it much more eligantly, and howsoeuer for want of practise, wee never vsing it but in disputations, speake it not so readily, when wee first goe into forayne parts, yet after small practise, we speake it also more readily and eligantly. For I dare boldly say by experience, aswell for the latten as for other languages, that they who learne them, if in the begining they rashly speake them, without long vse of the Grammer and reading of Authours, they take by habitt ill Phrases of speaking, and howsoeuer for the tyme they may speake readily, yet nether knowing truely to write or to reade or to pronounce, they soone forgett what they haue learned. On the Contrary, that they who first learne well to reade and write the tounge, and after beginn to practise it, doe retayne the same for euer, and in processe of tyme, speake and reade it exquisitely. Yet since travelours, who will not spend more tyme in fitting themsellues to serue in the Commonwealth, then in the seruice it selfe, cannot stay so many yeares in forayne partes, as to learne perfectly many languages (which growing from one roote, are in my opinion imposible to be so learned, by any one man, without mingling and mistaking of wordes, as I haue shewed in the third part and in the Chapter of Precepts) I would aduise them, who to make themselues fitt to be imployed as Ambasadours, or in like seruices of the Commonwealth, desyre perfectly to learne one or two languages of most vse, growing from diueres rootes, that they followe the second course abouenamed of learning them, being slowe but of more firme Retention. Likewise I would aduise them who in speedy and short trauell visite many nations, and desyre rather to haue a smak of many tounges, then perfection in anyone, that they mingle both the former courses of learning them, namely to reade the grammer, that they may knowe to vse the right moodes, Tenses, numbers and persons, and to reade some of the purest Authours, that they may learne to write the toung with true Orthography, and espetially bookes of Epistles, being of spetiall vse, and to learne the proper handwriting of the language (if they haue leasure) being no small ornament in the skill of languages, lest they be like Marchants, who desyre no more skill in toungs, then to be vnderstood for traffique, and learning them by roate (I meane by practise without reading) soone forgett them, when they cease to traffique in those parts or be like to wemen and Children, who learning only by roate soone forgett what they haue learned. And secondly I aduise them, when they first beginn to reade, to ioyne therewith the practise of speaking, lest in theire swift passage, by soden leauing of the Country, they should be preuented of hauing tyme of learning to speake the toung, with naturall pronountiation, true accents, and proper Phrases therof, Particularly the language of the Germans hath of old borrowed many wordes of the Greekes (from whome also they tooke the Custome of large drincking and long feasts). Also from the lattin toung of old and to this day they borowe many wordes, but ill dissemble the borowing of them, not otherwise disguising the worde then by adding some leter to the end, as for example, for the latin worde Transferre, they vse Transferirn, and these wordes and the like are only vsed by the learned. The Germans likewise at this day traueling into Fraunce and Italy, bring some wordes from thence, but the Common people very hardly admitt the vse of them. The German language is not fitt for Courtship, but in very love more fitt rudely to commande then sweetly to perswade, it being an Imperious short and rude kynde of speech, and such as would make our Children affrayd to heare it, the very familyer speeches and pronuntiations sounding better in the mouth of Tamberlin, then of a Ciuill man. When the Children come into the house, they salute the mother, ' Grusse dich Fraw,' 'woman health to thee,' when they goe forth, 'Hette dich Mutter,' 'Mother keepe thee well.' They haue many abuses in pronuntiation, as F. for V. so for the worde Venus (the Goddesse of loue), they pronounce Fenus that is usurye. And thus a German in Italy, when he would haue sayd Io ho Veduto sayd (Io ho fututo) il Papa con tutti i Cardinali, insteade of I haue seene, sayd I haue (with leaue be it spoken) buggered, the Pope, with all the Cardinalls. So they pronounce the letter R lightly, or not at all, which in Italy made a foule mistaking betweene a Curtezan and a German, who saying to her Non importa, was vnderstoode as if he had changed the R into T wherevpon shee offered him an Italian Cortesy, abhorred by all the nations on this syde the Alpes, and more spetially by the modest Germans. Likewise the Italians obserue them to pronounce B insteede of P, remembring a like mistaking of a German at Padoa who telling some Italians that he came from the Portello (that is the gate house) was vnderstood by them as if he had sayd he came from the

Bordello (that is the Stewes). The English worde mayde, comes from the Dutch worde Magde, but signifyes with vs an hired woman seruant, or a Virgin, and with them a woman borne a slaue. For the Germans call not those seruants, who attend them for wages, as wee doe, but the man diener, the woman dienerin, of theire attendants. Among other wordes, the English borowe from the Saxon Germans, and vse in a differing sence, the German worde kranck, which with them signifyes sicke or ill disposed, but with vs signifyes healthfull or liuely. In England the Barrons or lordes are called Noblemen vulgarly, and in latin Nobiles, and those of the inferiour nobility are vulgarly called gentlemen, and in latten Generosi, but in Germany the Barrons haue in laten the title of Generosi, and the inferiour sort are in laten called Nobiles, master is the title of English gentlemen, which the Germans and Netherlanders only giue to Artizans. And the title master giuen to the second degree in the vniversityes, is honorable in England, where many gentlemen receaue that degree, but the German gentlemen scorne the degree and title, and are called vulgarly Die Herrn (that is the lords) and in latten Domini which wee translate masters and lordes, but they (as I sayd) take in the last sence. Agayne the Germans contrary to the English preferr the tytle of worshipfull (as belonging in the highest degree of Diuine worship only to God), before the title of honorable. The Germans in the latten tounge speake to men in the third person, as Dominatio vestra intelligat (or Intelligant) that is lett your worshipp (or worshipps) vnderstand, and likewise the Germans speake to one man in the plurall number, as your worships and you, Contrary to the latten tounge, which to God and to Ceasar sayth thy Maiesty, and thou. To conclude the purest language in Germany is that of Leipzig, and all the Prouince of Misen vnder the Electour of Saxony, the next is that of the Palatinate, but espetially the cheefe Citty Heidellberg, and the language of Strasburg is reputed pure in this second degree. In some parts of Garmany the old language of the Vandalls liueth in the mouthes of men at this day, howsoeuer that nation hath long beene scattered, and as it were extinct. For in the villages neere Witteburg, and in the Dukedomes of Pomerarnia, and Meckelburg, and those parts vpon the Baltick Sea, men so commonly speake that Language in the villages, as it is probable that nation of old inhabited those parts, but I haue allso heard the same vsed in villages neere Augsburg, which Citty for distinction from another of the same name, is to this day called **Augsburg of the Vandalls.**

The Ceremonyes.

Touching Ceremonyes, the Germans performe them with great ostentation of pompe, I meane not for any Magnificence or sumptuousness, for the Germans haue no such thing, the very Princes wearing ordinary apparell, hauing no rich furniture in there houses, and requiring litle reverence in the seruice of theire persons. So as at Prage I sawe the Emperour apparreled all in cloth, if not without welts, surely without gardes, or imbrodering, his Rapier hauing ordinarye hilts and a sheath of lether, and when himselfe was in the next Chamber with the dores open, his seruants without any reverence walked by the poore chayre of estate with theire heades couered, yea sometymes leaning vpon it. And I sawe the Archdukes his bretheren serued by a Caruer and Taster, but not vpon the knee, and they allso in the Princes presence layde theire hatts vpon the Chayre of Estate. But I meane for the very great grauity the Germans vse in very small matters, as by the following Ceremonyes shall appeare. First when they visitt one another, they doe not exchang short speeches, but first the visited entertaynes his frend with a long Oration, and ends it with a harty draught of beare or wyne to his welcome, then the visiter answers him with a long Oration and a like Salutation of the Cupp, and so by Course declaming and drincking they passe the tyme till they take theire leaues. When they meete one another in the markett place or streetes, they doe not walke, but stand in a Circle without moving a foote, so long as they talke together. They giue one another not only high titles among meane persons, but many of them, as it were by dossens or wholesale, so as the preface of tytiles is longer then the name of the bragging Soldyer in Plautus which filled foure whole sheetes of paper. In all invitations to Feasts, of maryage or the like, or to attend vpon a Funerall, and in Conference at these Meetinges they vse long Orations which with much teadiousnes they adorne with many old Apothegms of great and learned men. Allwayes they begin with these titles, as for example in the vniversityes, I haue heard Doctours thus invited, ' most Courteous, most learned, most worthy, and also most regardable herr Doctour the Magnificall Colledge of the Ciuill lawyers, in the name of the most adorned Graduates now premoted, invites your worthynes, to the most Ample Auditory &c.' A gentleman in Germany scornes the title of master, as he doth that degree of Arts, and must be saluted vulgarly Herr, in latten Domine, and not without great Epithites ioyned to that title, and contrary to the Custome of England the title of gentleman, in latten generosus, is preferred before that of Noble, and likewise that of worshipfull before that of honorable. In the Feasts of maryage and the like, theire pompe is tedious and two serious, the men walking with a slowe Senatours pace, like so many Images, moved rather by art then nature, and the wemen seeming rather to swimm or slyde away, then to goe a naturall pace. And in taking place at the Feasts, they are Curious not to yeald theire right to another. If two walke together, the best man, not regarding the wall, goes on the right hand of the other, three walking together, the best man goes in the midest, the next on the right hand of both, foure walking together, the best man goes on the right hand the next on the left in the midest, and the third vppermost on the right hand.

Of Maryage.

In many Cittyes and townes of Saxony, they appoint Tuesday or some other of the working dayes for the Celebration

of maryages, thincking Sonday most vnfitt in regard of the
nationall vice of drincking, never more vsed then at these
Feasts. Before the feast a young man well apparrelled and sett
forth with scarffes and Plumes, rides on horsebacke through the
streetes, to invite the Guests, for which purpose he hath a foote
boy Running by him, to lett him knowe that the partyes are
at home, before he light from his horse, who vseth premeditated
speeches, or one speech for all, in the foresayd forme, when he
invites them. And this young Youth with two Brideboyes (or
as I may say brideyouths) attende the Bryde on the maryage
day, Carrying torches before her whersoeuer shee goeth, as likewise two other Bryde youthes, each with a torch in his hand,
solemly leade the Daunces. For assoone as dinner is ended, in
most places they Daunce at the house of the Feast, but in
other places (as at Witteburg and where the house hath no larg
Romes) after dinner is ended the Bridegroome, Bride, and all
the guests march from the house of the Feast to the publike
house of the Senate, with soleme Pompe, and there spende the
afternoone in dauncing and drincking, marching from thence to
supper with like pompe, but without Clockes, which they send
home when they beginn to daunce. To this publike house any
Cittizens men or wemen, or any Students being not invited, may
come to daunce with them, where the men stand in order on one
syde, and the wemen on the other syde of the roome, and the
Brideyouths bring and present the wemen, to the men who are
to daunce with them. But in these Daunces they vse no kynd
of Art, for all that are present, or so many as the Circle of the
Chamber will Contayne, and of all sortes, Doctours, Senatours,
Young men, boyes, and old wemen, young wemen, virgins, and
girles, Daunce all together in a large Circle rounde about the
Chamber. And in the slowe Daunces, which wee call measures,
they doe not followe the musicke, with artificiall motion of the
feete, sometymes forward, sometymes backward, sometymes
sydewayes, as wee doe, but playnly walke about the roome with
grauity inough and to spare, which kynde of dauncing they
iustly call Gang, that is going, likewise in the daunces which

wee call Gallyardes, of the lusty motion, and they call Lauff
that is a leape, they doe not Daunce with measure of paces, and
trickes lowe or lofty, as wee doe, but pleaynly first lift vp on
legg then the other, so leaping about the Roome, with such
force as makes the strongest chambers shake and threaten
falling.   And for other kyndes of daunces they haue none.
Once at a Maryage, where my selfe was invited, I remember the
Bride in dauncing lost her maryage Ring, and a litle after
stumbled and fell, which chances made her frendes very sadd,
or portending some ominous euent.   Sometymes when they
daunce in theire priuate houses, some fewe men and wemen
daunce by course, whyle the other drincke at the Tables, for all
must drincke, or daunce, or leaue the Company.   And for my
selfe sometymes Invited to these Feasts, I confesse, to escape
drincking I was gladd to make one in theire Daunces, which
any stranger might performe without any great teaching.
When a man takes out a woman to daunce, he gently putts her
Arme vnder one of his, and his other vnder her other Arme, and
modestly imbraceth her, and sometymes in lesse solemne
meetinges of more liberty the men in iolity with inarticulate
voyces of Joye will catch the wemen by the middle, and lift
them vp sometymes so high as they shewe more then modesty
allowes, when they daunce the foresayd lauff.   If a woman
refuse to daunce with any man, it beares an action of Iniury,
in so much as a young man giuing a box on the eare to a virgin
that refused to daunce with him, and being accused for the same
before a Judge in the vpper parts of Saxony, the young man
was dismissed, as hauing doune her no wrong, because shee
disgraced him, as a person infamous, and vnworthy to daunce
with her.   The virgins many tymes will intreate the men that
daunce with them, that when they are weary of dauncing, they
will giue them to the handes of some others whome they affect.
For the men being often weary, and the wemen never satisfyed
with motion, the men of Custome present theire wemen to some
others, as a fauour and grace to them.   It seemed to me very
straung, that at the maryage of the richest Cittizens, aswell as of

the poorer, they haue a gathering or presenting of mony by guift to the maryed Couple (which only is vsed by the pourer sorte with vs), and the richer they are the more they haue giuen them, for they invite theire equalls who are able to giue largely, whereas the poore inviting guests of like Condition, many tymes spend almost so much in the Feast, as they receaue by guifts. Myselfe invited to a maryage feast of a Cittisens daughter in Leipzig, thought to be worth more than forty thousand gold guldens, did obserue that the men first in order, and after them the wemen, marched to the Church, whence after the maryage they retourned home in like order, where at the inner gate, the bridegrome stayed to welcome the men, and the bryde to intertayne the wemen. And after Supper all (not one excepted) came to offer their guifts in orderly course, to the Bridegrome sitting at the table accompanyed with some cheefe guests and frendes, whyle the Bryde with the young men and wemen Daunced in another Roome, till it came to theire Course to offer, in which offering I obserued no man to giue lesse then a Doller, which came to a great summe of mony. Yet may not every one that will giue mony, come to these feasts, but only they who are invited. Nether doe these guifts much inrich them, for they invite not only kindred and frends at home and of other Cittyes and townes, but most parte of the Cittizens of theire owne quallity, so as these marriages being frequent, the Continuall charge of them in shorte tyme equalls the guifts themselues Receaved. In some places (as at Heydeberg [sic]) they keepe these Feasts not only in priuate houses but more Commonly in publike Inns, and the lawe restraynes aswell the Number of the guifts, as of the dishes in the Feast (which in other partes by custome is allwayes moderate), so as in publike Inns they invited not more then forty guests, where every man payd tenn Batzen for his dinner (vulgarly Malzeit) and for extraordinary drinncking after the meale (vulgarly Zeick) each man his part ratably, and besydes offered guifts to the Bride-grome and Bride Commonly in mony, for I never obserued any plate to be giuen. And they who keepe these feasts in theire

owne houses, might not provide more then two tables (which
are Commonly square, and not very large) where they payed
nothing for meate or drincke, but only offered guifts of mony.
And in most places they seldome haue aboue six or seuen dishes,
with wyne in aboundance, the meates also being such for the
most parte as invite drincking. Also in many places I haue
seene Cittizens of good quality gather mony of the guests to pay
the Musitions. When the Bride is of another Citty, the
Bridegrome vseth to meete her on the way, well accompanyed
with horsemen, and the bridegrome riding betweene two cheefe
men, whereof the cheefe intertaynes the bride and her company
with a long oration, to which the cheefe of her Company makes
Answer. And being Cittizens, not gentlemen, yet both
Companyes haue trompitts sounding before them. At Leipzig
I obserued a Cittizen Bridegrome, to haue 17. horsemen before
him, followed by himselfe and cheefe frendes in theire Coaches,
with 17 horsemen likewise behinde him. At Witteberg vpon
like occasion, the Dukes cheefe officer, with some horsemen, all
wearing skarffes did ryde before, then followed the bridegrome
being a Doctour, riding betweene two young Barrons then
Students of that vniversity, with 9 horsemen following, and
after fewe myles ryding they mett the Bryde, attended with
9. Coaches and six horsemen whome the eldest Barron
intertayned with a long Oration, answered by the cheefe man in
her Company. Shee had Trumpitts before her, but they
sounded not, because the Duke Elector of Saxony being then
sicke (of which sicknes within fewe dayes after he dyed), the
bridegrome forbore to bring any trumpitts with him. When
the Parents haue agreed vpon the brides portion, and like
transactions, I haue seene them in some places goe to the
Church, there to betroath them, and the bride there to receaue
a Ring from the bridegrome, which shee kept till the maryage
day, when shee gaue it back to him to be marryed therewith,
when they goe to church to be marryed, in many places they
vse torches lighted at noone day, among the Lutherans. The
trompitters goe first, then the bridegrome, ledd betweene two

frendes or cheefe men, then he that invited the guests followes
alone, then the kinsmen, neighbours and invited strangers
Followe in order, two in a rancke the meanest first, and the
best last, then followe the wemen, the litle girles and virgins,
and of them the youngest and meanest first, then followes the
Bride ledd betweene two young men, whome wee call Brideboyes,
only touching her elbowe lightly. But at Witteberg the bride
being of suspected Chastity, I haue seene her led by a Doctor,
that in reverence to him, the Students might forbeare hissing
and laughing at her, and this Doctor did not lay his hand vpon
her elbowe, as the other, but lightly vpon her backe aboue the
wast. Two young men bareheaded, each hauing a garter about
his Arme tyed in true loue knotts, followed the Bride, whome
the maryed wemen did followe in order, the meanest first, and
the best last, but betweene each rancke of the maryed wemen,
the maydes seruants followed, being like poore kichen mades,
and sometymes ill appareled. Assoone as they entred the
Church, the minister mett them neere the dore, and there ioyned
the hands of the betroathed, and putting a ring on the brides
finger, sayd these wordes, That which God hath ioyned lett no
man seperate. Then the Common sort going to theire seates,
only some of the cheefe led the Bridegrome and Bride to the
high Alter, where hauing sayd short prayers, they discended
also to theire seates. And then at Witteburg I haue seene the
invited guests offer theire guifts in the Church to the
bridegrome and bryde, not only of gold and siluer putt into a
Silver Bason, but also Potts and kettles of Brasse, and dishes of
Puter, which were carryed home by their mayde seruants. Then
the Bridegrome and the cheefe men ascended agayne to the
Alter, and going about it, gaue an offering to the Priests or
ministers of the Church. After them the Bride and cheefe
weemen and virgins in like sorte, the best going first, as strangers
in the first place, then the wyues of Doctours, then of Senatours,
then of Cittisens, then the virgins, in like order ascended to the
high Alter, and made the like offering. In the meane tyme all
the Common sort did sett on theire seates, and musicke

Continually sounded aswell of Organs and loude Instruments, as of lutes, and mens voyces. They retourned from the Church with a greater trayne. For the bridegrome was ledd backe by two cheefe men, as a Doctor and a Senatour, followed by the Professors, Senatours, and Cittizens, and many young men who had expected theire Comming in the Church, nowe ioyned to the trayne attending them backe. In like sort the Bride was led by her Father, and besydes the foresayd trayne following in like order, was attended by many virgins, who had attended her comming at Church. When they came home, and in the midest of dinner, and many tymes vpon occation of drincking healths, the bridegrome Bride and guests exchanged many long Orations of Congratulation. At the begining of the feast, the young men and virgins did sett apart at the table, but entrance being once made to Dancing and drincking, they satt mingled each man setting by the woman with whome he daunced. The young men on theire bare heades weare krantzes that is Garlands of Roses, both in winter and Sommer, presented them for a fauour by the bryde at the dore of her house, as wee present gloues, the wemen likewise weare garlandes of Roses, on theire heades, and Chayns about their neckes. And during the Feast, the young men and virgins for tokens of loue exchanged garlandes, and the young men sometymes wore the virgins Chaynes, as also the Bridegrome on the first day of the Feast did weare the Brides Coronet of gold and Pearle on his bare head. The men and wemen, in all meales, but the first, and at the drinckings betweene meales, sett mingled, a man and a woman, but the men only drinck healths, the wemen only in fauour sipping of the Cupp, as it were to helpe the men. Besydes they haue many loue tokens betweene them, as a young man and a virgin take a Comfitt and together bite it in peeces, and the party biting the greater peece is merily punished, Agayne the virgins putt some morsells of bread in some dilicate sawce, which the young men take out, as deliuering theire mistresses out of danger. Agayne sometymes they shewe theire Purses, hauing an obcene meaning in the longest and largest Purse. In some places the tables are made so, as they may turne rounde about both the meate and the Guests, which they doe somtymes for a frolike. Whole barrells of beare and wyne are sett forth, and drawne out in the very roome where they eate, as the Bridegroome intertaynes the men, so the Bride hath two wemen of her neerest kindred to cheere vp the wemen. And as wee giue Marchpanes, so these wemen present them with Rowles baked like dry Fritters, and sett forth with Penons of Cutt paper, in the forme of Apes, Birdes, and like thinges. The Dishes are Commonly fewe and the meates not costly, but they haue allwayes fumed herrings, rawe Beanes, Water Nuttes (as they call them) and breade slised salted and pepered, to prouoke drincking. The Bridegrome and the Bride supp not with the guests, but after supper the Bride Youthes with torches lighted bring them into the Dauncing Roome, where they daunce the first Daunce alone, which doune, the Bridegrome giues the Bride into the handes of some cheefe man to daunce with her, and so goes himselfe to sett with some cheefe men at the Brides table, where the guests in order present theire guifts to him. In the Prouince of Thuringia the bridegrome and Bryde vse to be maryed on Sondyes, but they goe allso to church agayne on Mondayes, marching in the foresayd pompe, but not with the same trayne, being on Monday accompanyed with those who were not invited or could not come the day before. And all the tyme betweene the publike betroathing and the day of the maryage, they liue together both at bed and boarde. In the Province of Marchia vnder the Elector of Brandeburg the maryed Couple, as likewise Children to be Christened, and wemen to be Churched, must haue the blessing of the minister at the dore, before they may enter into the Church. And the maryed, the Christened, and the Churched, must enter at three seuerall dores, appointed for those purposes, And besydes they vse many of the old and superstitious Ceremonyes to this day, though they be of the Reformed Religion according to the rule of Luther.

Funeralls.

Touching Funeralls. They invite Company to attend them, as to Maryages, by a horseman with a laquay runing by him, but the invited haue no feast, only strangers of other Cittyes invited are intertayned by them in theire howses, more spetially at the solemne Funeralls of Princes. They nether toule bells for them when they are dying, nor ringe them when they are dead, so as the dead persons are only made knowne to be dead by the foresayd inviting of Company, and by the Beere vpon which they are to be caryed, being sett at theire dores in the streete the day before they are buryed, and by notice thereof giuen by the Preacher in the Pulpitt, for most dayes of the weeke they haue Sermons and prayers earely in the morning. They are Commonly buryed in Coffinnes, hauing windowes ouer the face of the dead body, to be drawne and shutt agayne, and at Leipzig I obserued the frendes to open this windowe, and cast earth vpon the face of the dead body, and the Saxston after to cast in a greater quantity of earth (as they say) to make the body soonner rott, and then putt the Coffinne in the ground. At Leipzig, as in most places, they are not buryed in Church-yeardes, but they haue for that purpose without the Citty a peece of ground, compassed with a wall, and a litle chappell lying open on the sydes, and a Couered Cloyster round about the wall, which feilde is called vulgarly Gottsacker that is the Aker of God, where the richer sorte purchase a place of buryall for them and theire Family vnder the Couered Cloyster, and the Common sorte arc buryed in the open parte of the feilde. They are Lutherans, Yet the crosse is carryed vpon the Coffinne, and all the Monuments haue paynted or grauen crosses. The body was committed to the grounde with silence, but in many other places the singing boyes of the publike Schooles followe the dead body to the graue, where most Commonly the preacher makes a short Sermon, or rather Oration principally to Commende the life and ende of the dead person, and then the people sing a Psalme while the body is buryed. The men that are cheefe Mournours haue their faces Covered with blacke Sipres hanging downe behynde the neck, and so are ledd and supported by a servant, as likewise the wemen that are cheefe Mournours haue theire faces muffled with white linnen Cloth, being narrowe and hanging downe all the right syde, vulgarly called Schleres. The other men that followe the Herse haue no mourning Clokes nor gownes, vsed by vs in England, but only hattbandes of black Sipres hanging downe behynde, Called Trawerbandes that is mourning bandes, which they were long after the Funerall. In the Pompe the wemen goe first and of them the best and the neerest frendes next to the herse then the cheefe mournours are ledd, then the herse followes, then goe the men, and of them the best and the neerest frendes next to the hearse. In some places I haue seene the husband followe next to the Hearse of his wife, and so the wife to followe the husbands hearse, hauing a poore mayde seruant to carry the trayne of her gowne. When the body is burryed, the wemen stay at the graue, till the men goe into the Church and Compassing the high Alter offer mony to the vse of the ministers, and when they come forth the wemen likewise enter to make the offering, for they hauing small brasse monyes, no body is so poore that offer not somethinge, besydes that they pay aboue a dollour to the Minister for his paynes, and these Ceremonyes being frequent, no doubt the ministers haue great profitt thereby. At the burying of a Student in Witteberg, the Cheefe men of the Vniversity were invited by his frendes with long and graue Orations, as they vse to invite at feasts. And when they carryed the body to the graue, only the singing boyes of the Schoole went singing before the Hearse, which was followed by the Rectour, the Professors, and the Students, in order. For the wemen and virgins came not in Company with the men, but after them in seuerall Companyes, and stood in order a good distance from the graue. In tyme of the buryall the Scholers did sing, and in the end the Deacon did sing out of a booke about some six lynes written in Prose. The invited straungers of other Cittyes, were (as I sayd) intertayned in theire howses, but those of the Citty vse not to haue ether drinckings, or dinners.

Old writers wittnes that the Germans of old vsed no ambition or pride in Funeralls. That they vsed not to cast Odours or garments, but only the Armes of the dead man, into the Funerall fyer, the heathen then vseing to burne the dead bodyes. That for a monument they only raysed a turffe or greene Sodd of the earth. That the wemen only lamented, and the men only with sadnes remembred theire dead frendes, so as they soone forgott to weepe, but long retayned sadnes. But at this day I am sure in the Funeralls of Princes, they burye precious Jewells with them, laying the dead body with the face vncovered some three dayes in the Chappell, to be seene by any who will come to see it, and then inclosing it in Copper to be so layd in the monument. For Germany hath litle leade, and aboundes with Copper, wherewith many Cittyes haue Terretts steeples and whole Churches Covered. Besydes at the Funeralls of Princes they cast among the Multitude great peeces of siluer, Coyned of purpose with inscriptions fitting the dead person and the tyme, myselfe at Fryburg did see the Funerall of Christian Duke and Elector of Saxony, and like wise the Ceremonyes vsed at Dresden where he dyed. First at Dresden the dead body was layde in the Chappell of the Court, with the face open, for two dayes, to be seene of all that would, the body had a velvitt Capp (vulgarly Mitz) on the head with a Costly Jeuell on it and was lapped in a quilted veluitt mantle, things lying by, which should be buryed with him, or hung vp for ornament ouer his Monument, as first to be buryed with him, a golden Chayne about his necke, with a tablett the badge of die gulden Geselshaft, that is the golden fellowship, betweene the Protestant Princes of the Vnion, allso three Ringes on his fingers, a Dyamond, a Turky, and a Ruby, giuen him by his Dutches, also two braceletts of gold about his Armes, a guilded hammer in his right handd, and at his left hand lay diuers things to be hung vp, as his Coate Armour, his Rapier, his Spurrs, and diuers banners. After two dayes the body was

Closed in Copper, with his Armes graven vpon it. And a learned German perceaving me to thincke it strange, that those Jewells should be buryed with him, to satisfye me therein, alledged many Texts of scripture to proue that dead bodyes should be adorned, as Isaiah Chapter 61. Zachary 3. Ecclesiasticus 18. Ephesians 6. saying that these ornaments of the dead did signify Spirituall garments, and the Armes hung vp did signify knighthood in the spirituall war, adding that the Jewells were as safe from leesing or stealing in the vault of the monument, as if they were layd vp in a strong Castle. After fewe dayes the Corpes was attended by the Courtyers, and carryed from Dresden to Fryburg, being a dayes Jorney, and by the way in all villages the Bells were rung, and the ministers with the people came forth to meete it, with Copes, lighted torches, Crosses of wood, and like superstitious Ceremonyes. And at the Castle of Fryburg, the gentlemen of the Bed Chamber tooke the body out of the Coach, and carryed it into the Schloss kirke, that is the Church of the Castle, and there it lay till the day of the Funerall, when it was Carryed thence, and putt into his Monument in the cheefe Church of the Citty after this manner. First a Grafe, that is Earle, carryed the Blutfahne that is bloody Banner, then followed fyfteene great horses, richly harnessed, and ledd by ordinarye Querryes, or groomes, and by each horse was carryed a banner with the Armes of a Family of which the Duke discended, the tenn first being carryed by gentlemen, the fyue last by Earles. Then followed the sixteenth horse richly harnessed, mounted by a gentleman of the Bedd Chamber, all Armed, and representing the Dukes person, and by him an Earle, on foote (as the former) carryed the Hauptfahne that is the head and cheefe Banner, of all the Dukes Armes vnited, and the sayd gentleman mounted had in his right hand a shorte Cudgel, which the Churfirst (that is Prince Electour) of Saxony vseth to carry at the Feast of an Emperours Coronation. After him was carryed first the sworde, and then the Seale of the Electorship. And then, came the Corpes drawne by six horses in an open Charyott all covered with blacks. And

vpon the Charyott hung a table vpon which was written, in
golden letters, and in the lattin toung, to this effect.

> ' The Most &c. Pr: Chr: D.S.
> S.R.I vij. Vir: (that is one of
> the seuen Electours)

Hath here deposed what soeuer was mortall, his Soule immortall
inioyes eternall happines with God.   Thou passenger myndefull
of humayne fraylty, prepare thy selfe soone to followe him
(when thou art called) in the same stepps of true piety, and
Fayth to God, in which he hath gone before thee.'

This table was to be hung vpon his monument.   After the
Corpes followed on foote the Princes invited to the Funerall,
and then the Courtyers, strangers, and Cittizens, in order.   All
the way as the Corpes passed, certayne officers scattered among
the multitude, whole, halfe, and quarters of Dollers, Quoyned
of purpose, with many wordes grauen in the midest, and rounde
about this sentence in lattin, Jacturam ostendet Dies (that is
Tyme will shewe the losse).   Generally the Princes of Germany
doe in like sorte vse to Coyne monyes expressly for Remembrance of any great Act, done by them, or Concerning the
Commonwealth.   As when the Emperor had proscribed the
Duke of Coburg, elldest sonne to John Fredericke late Electour
of Saxony and had giuen authority to Augustus, present Electour
of Saxony by the guift of the Emperour and father to the
Electour Christianus nowe buryed, that he as marshall of the
Empire (indeede as his cheefe enemy for the emullation of the
Electorship which he had gotten from his Father) should make
warr vpon the sayd Duke of Coburg, and when he vpon the sayd
authority, but with his owne forces, and at his owne charge,
had taken and dismanteled Gotha the sayd Dukes strongest
Forte, he at his retorne to Dresden in triumph, did cast like
monyes amonge the people, Coyned of purpose for memory of
that act, whereof my selfe did see many peeces kept by diuers
Cittizens.

Childe bearinges and Christininges.

When a woman is brought to bedd, for the tyme shee lyes in, whosoeuer enters the house, vseth to giue the woman some small guift towardes her paying of the midwife, and the nurse, and for like occasions. The wemen lye in or keepe house some six weekes according to the distance from our lords birth day, to the purification of our lady vpon Candlemas day. They keepe a Feast at the Christning, but none at the Churching, which is donne without Ceremony, only with some wemen her frendes, whome she desyres to accompany her to the Church. When the Childe is to be Baptised, the pompe of going to Church and retorning, is no lesse then that of maryages, formerly discribed. When they come to Church the Chylde with the Godfathers and Godmothers stand before the Deacon or minister attended by the Clarke, at the dore of the Church where the Deacon reades an exorcisme, that is a kynd of Coniuration to driue away the ill Spiritt, which by reason of originall sinne they Imagin to possesse the Chylde till it be baptised. Then they all together enter the inclosure made about the Funt, where the Clarke powres a Cann of hott water into the Funt: Then the midwife layes the chylde starke naked, and the face downewarde, with the navell of the belly vpon the Palme of the Deacons hand, (which by reason the legs and shoulders of the Chylde were of bloody coller, seemed to me no comely thinge to beholde). Then the Godfathers and Godmothers hauing named the Chylde, and promised for it, the Deacon baptising it, powers with his other hand much hott water all ouer the backe of the Chylde presently restored to the handes of the norse, or midwife, who lappes it warme, and so they depart. The Godfather is vulgarly called Geuater, and the Godmother Geuaterine, but they haue no certayne number of them, some hauing more some fewer, and the greatest men haue Commonly most in number so as the Elector Duke of Saxony lately invited a whole Citty to Christen one of his Children, and every Cittisen presented a guift to the Chylde. But commonly these guifts to the Chylde, the midwife or nurses are small, as about an halfe or a whole Doller to a nurse. One thinge is remarkable, that as the Mothers if they be able, Commonly giue sucke to theire Children, so they euer take a Nurse into the house not only for a dry Nurse but euen to giue it sucke, and not one of them will send the Chylde abroade to be nursed out of theire owne houses, yea these theire nurses are not maryed wemen, but commonly harlotts gotten with Childe before they marry, which wee would abhorr, fearing to take an harlott or drunken women to nurse our Chilldren, who might perhaps thereby proue infected with the nurses vices.

Customes.

When the Germans take an Oath before a magistrate, they lay no hand on the booke, as wee doe, but lift two fore fingers vp to heauen, (as the Sweitzers lift vp three fingers, and French men the whole hand).

In the Chapter of the Germans diett, I haue written of many Customes, in publike Inns, and Feastings, wherof I will now remember some fewe. The Innkeepers hange not out any signes or Iuye bushes, but the best Inns are knowne by the Multitude of the Armes, fastned vpon the gate and in the dyning Rome. For the guests, ether at the hosts intreaty, or by theire owne free offer, for Curtesey or for glory, vse to pay for the tricking of theire Armes, and to giue them to the hosts, to be hung vp, as our Ambassadours doe in their Jornyes. So as I haue at one Inn numbred 124. Armes, partly of Princes, Earles, Barrons, and gentlemen, partly of Cittizens (for they also giue Armes after their owne fancyes, but with a Close helmett). The guests eate not in priuate Chambers, but all together in a publike Stoue, at Diuers square tables, where they sett as they come, with smale or no respect of persons. In drincking, for token of loue, they often ioyne handes, with such force as if they would splitt one anothers thumbs from the fingers. And because they eate in Stoues heated in winter tyme, at eateing and spetially at drincking they sett bare headed, and sometymes open theire dubletts to the naked breast. In the Inns of Witteberg, in sommer tyme, I obserued the pages of some gentlemen to stand by them at table with a Fann of Peacokes feathers, to Coole them and to dryue flyes from them: and that the gentlemen often whispered together (which we repute ill manners), and asked the other guests many strang questions, as me in particular, whether I were a gentleman or no, and who was next heyre to the Crowne of England (whereof the English were then by Statute forbidden to speake). And being men neuer before seene of me, it was strang with what what confidence and (as it were) famillarity, they inquired after such secreets of State, and Actions of great persons, as a man would hardly impart, or speake freely of them, to any but inward frendes. If they sett at table farr from the bread, they thincke it ill manners to reach it vpon the poynt of a knife, and call to haue it reached by hand, nether doth any man dipp his meate but only his bread into any sawce, and that not with his fingers, but vpon the poynt of his knife. They Carue no meate to any man, but the very best men will lay or take vpon their trenchers a whole shoulder of mutton, or like Joynt of meate, to Carue themselues, in the meane tyme leaving the dish empty. And they hold it a point of Ciuility and Curtesey to take away the foule treancher of theire guest or frend setting neere them, and to giue him a cleane one, or to lay it in the Charge when they take away. Indeede they haue reason to be Curyous of dipping into sawces, since gentlemen Plebeans and very Coachmen sett at the same table, and vse the same liberty in all thinges. When they are halfe druncke, they will kisse theire next neighbours, sometymes with foming mouthes, allwayes with small sweetnes, and in theire Potts will promise any thinge, and make all bargaynes, but the consent of the sobber wife at home, must be had before any thing be performed. Theire heighest cheereings vp at table, are these. 'Seyt frolich,' be mery : 'Drinckt Auss,'' drincke all out, with some like Courtships, and except a man whope or hallowe, vulgarly called Jouxsen, he is neuer thought to be merye.

Assoone as they haue drunck to any man, they importune to be pledged, which they require also of wemen for fashion sake to kisse the Cupp: But wemen never enter the publike houses where wyne and beare is soulde, and in Feasts at home men seldome or neuer drincke to wemen, only they are permitted to helpe theire husbandes and frendes, in token of loue, by sipping of the Cupp they are to drincke, which also they doe very sparingly. In Saxony they commonly drincke rounde, that euery man may haue his share, and where they drincke to what frende they please, so many glasses are filled and placed about his trencher who is to pledge them, and if he be slowe in that duty, he shall not want calling upon, neither is there any meanes to avoyde this taske, but by taking some occasion to goe out of the Stoue, as to make water, which the most mannerly often doe, (for many sicke not to doe it vnder the table), and to pray the seruant in your absence to take away some of the glasses, or your selfe dexterly to remoue some of them to your next neighbours trenchers. They doe not gulpe downe theire drincke hastely, nether drincke they healthes in great glasses, but only sipp to haue longer pleasure in drincking, and that in small glasses. So as a stranger hath no better defence, then when any man drinckes to him, to beginn another health to him, espetially if he haue a great glasse before him, which euery man feares to drawe vpon himselfe. Generally when they drincke to any man, they rayse theire bodyes from theire seates, in honour to him, Commonly gentlemen when they be- ginne to be merrye, for sporte make theire Pages swell theire Cheekes with winde, which they strike with the Palme of theire hands, to breake the wynde with a noyse, and if they present them a fayre blowe, they giue them Drinckgelt, that is drinck- ing mony, (for so they call all guifts, as if they had no other vse but for drincking). In like sorte they punish there Pages, if they seeme weary in holding the Candle vp aloft, whyle theire masters are on foote to goe to bedd, and are tedious with inter- mixed healths, to take there leaues of the Cupp and one of another. Young men, vpon the day of the yeare bearing theire

owne name, if any such be in the Calender or on the day of
theire birth pay some banckquet or at least the wyne, to the
young wemen in the house where they liue, or ells they vse to
bynde them hand and foote till they performe it. In
Misen vpon the twelfth day after candle light, men disguised
in apparrell like the wise men of the East that came to Christ,
whome they call three kinges, vse to goe about the towne to
theire frendes houses, vpon the day of St. Nicholas they vse to
hide mony, Ringes, Garters Poynts, or like things in places
most frequented by theire kinsfolke, frends, sonnes and
daughters, that they might fynde them (as wee in England present neweyeares guifts) which they call gods guifts vsing also a
proverb vpon the Popes extortions, what God giues that St.
Pether takes away. Vpon Easter Monday, the young men vse
to beat the virginnes with knotted wandes, till they giue them
egges, and the next day the virgins vse them in like sorte, till
they giue them Oranges. In the publike drincking Stoues, of
Inns and priuate houses, they commonly haue a narrowe bed,
with a long Cushion, and a short pillowe, Covered with leather,
in all things but the narrownes like to a standing bed of wood,
only for one to lye vpon, which they call the faulebett, that is
the Idle bed. Wherevpon they lay any man that hath druncke
so much till he falls asleepe. For with them it is no shame
espetially in the lower partes of Germany from Nuremberg to
the Northerne Sea, if they drincke till they vomitt, and make
water vnder the table, and till they sleepe. But some who are
more temporate, and shame not to be overcome in this mastery,
vse to dissemble drunckennes by sleepe to avoyde drunckennes
indeede, or ells to that purpose finde some occasion to withdrawe
themselues out of the Stoue, or steale away, neuer taking leaue
of theire Companyes. For they who meane to sett out till the
last, neuer suffer any to departe so sober, as to take his leaue,
and espetially when they invite guests, they thincke they haue
not performed theire duty towardes them, except they leaue
them sleeping vpon the bedd, Benches, or vnder the Table, or
ells leade them home reeling, stumbling, and scarce able to

stand. Thus they drincke healths till they leese theire owne
health. Yet in the midest of this Common excesse of drincking, my selfe haue bene familiar with some gentlemen (namely
of the Palatinate) generally temperate, and whereof two were
abstemious, neuer drincking wyne, but only water, whose Com-
plexions notwithstanding were as pure sanguen, as can be
imagined. In the great free Cittyes of Germany, they haue
a laudable Custome, when any famous learned men, gentlemen
or lords (be they Germans or strangers) come to the towne, to
present them with some flaggons of wyne from the Senate, if
ether they be of that quallity as the Senatours haue knowledge of theire arryuall, or be made knowne to any Cittizen
that he may giue notice thereof to the officers of the Senate
house. But the honour of this Custome is abated by the abuse.
For as many Flaggons as are sent, so many officers beare them,
who not only expect a rewarde, of a Dollour more or lesse,
according to the quality of the person honored with the present,
but allso to be invited to supper, which in a publike Inn costs
much more then the value of the wyne. Besydes that they
make the present with long tedious orations, and looke to be
answered in the same forme, which is troubelsome espetially to
strangers. In most Cittyes vsing beere for Common drincke,
they haue no Taverns for wyne, but it is solde only at the Senate
house, and the gayne imployed for publike vses. And the
cheefe Senatours and Cittisens only, brewe beere, and that by
course, one after the other, selling it by retayle. At Leipzig
when this brewing came to the course of my host, with whome
I boarded, being a man worth tenn thousand powndes at least,
I obserued that, assoone as he had sett vp a wispe at the doore
(according to the Custome) not only all Cittizens sent thether
for beare, but also great multitudes continually flocked thether
to drincke, at many tables sett vp of purpose, in the lower
roomes, the yearde, and the very Cellers. And I obserued that
they payed for theire drincke before they had it, that theire
purses might teach them moderation, who otherwise knowe
none, espetially the Common sorte. In so much as most of

them being poore, I did see my hosts seruants take theire
Cloathes for pawne, when theire mony was spent, and some of
them to drincke till they had nothing but a shirte to cover
nakednes. In some Cittyes of lowe Germany, I haue seene
Cittizens bidd frendes to dinner, and yet make them pay for it,
as at Luneburg in particular a Senatour invited some of our
Consorts in Coach to dynner, and when they came to goe on our
Jorney after dinner, by there relation they had spent more
(perhaps in large drincking of wyne) then wee had spent in the
publike Inn. Of old the Cittyes lying neere the German Ocian
and Balticke Sea, and hauing large preuiledges of traffique
among themselues and in forayne Countryes, haue beene there
vpon called Hans Stetin, that is free Cittyes. And these haue
an old Custome in euery Citty at the first comming thether of
any marchant stranger, to make him free of the place, which
Ceremony they performe in the publike Inns after this manner.
The eldest marchants take a trencher with salt vpon it, sending
it rounde about the table, that they who are strangers may, by
touching the Salt in manner of an Oath, professe whether they
be hansed that is made free or no, and when anyone Confesseth
that to be his first comming to the Citty, then the oldest
marchant taking vpon him to be his Godfather (as they call it)
askes him whether he will haue grace or Justice, and if he
desyre grace, (as most doe to avoyde the seuerity of Justice),
then he imposeth vpon him halfe or a whole Dollor or more
(according to the quallity of the person) to bestowe on the
Company in wyne, which donne he admitts him free, hauing
first giuen him some aduise or precepts, whereby he may in
shorte tyme recouer more then he hath spent. As namely that
hauing written a letter, he neuer send it away, till he reade it
over agayne, or that when he goes from any Inn, the last thinge
he doth be to looke about the Chamber and the dyning Stoue,
that he leaue nothinge behynd him, Or in Jeast that he preserue
the sweate of the virgins with whome he shall daunce, for each
ounce or pounde wherof he promiseth to pay him a great price.
And it seemes that of old Princes, gentlemen and other

passengers to accomodate themselues to the Company, did
voluntarily submitt to this Custome, for at this day they
chalenge it of them aswell as of marchants, and at extraordinary
rates, so as a gentleman passing through these Cittyes (which
are many) fyndes it no small charge. For besydes they haue
diuers other Customes whereby to impose vpon strangers the
paying of wyne to the Company. As namely if any man putt
not off his hatt in reverence to the Salt as it passeth round
about the table, or if any man keepe his napkin till the Cloth
be taken away, with many other like obseruances. They haue
another Common Custome, which being frequent, is no litle
charge to the passengers, namely guifts which they call drinckgelt, that is drincking mony (as if mony were for no vse but
for drincking). And these being at first free guifts are nowe
challenged of right. The seruants in Inns, though they doe a
passenger no seruice, but only at table, not so much as pulling
off his bootes, and be so rude, as if he call to haue any thinge
reached him, they will readily answer he hath as many handes
and feete as they, and may reach it himselfe, and though they
giue him foule sheetes to his bedd, yet they will challenge of
him this drincking mony as theire due. Yea if he goe away
and forgett to giue it, they will followe him to exact it, as if he
had forgotten to pay for his dyett. Like is the practise of
Artizans in shopps. If a man come to buy shooes or bootes,
himselfe must chuse those that fitt him, and pull them on
himselfe. Yet when he hath payde the master for them (which
must be asmuch as he demaundes, without abating one peny)
the Prentises must haue this drincking mony, and will refuse it
with Scorne and reproches, if it be not ac much as they expect.
Myselfe hauing my horse shodd, and payd the Smith, his
gesellen (that is Prentises) demaunded this drincking mony, and
when I gaue them two Grosh (which is more then foure pence
English mony) they refused it, and extorted more from mee.
In the partes of high Germany, they haue likewise this Custome,
but after a more Ciuill fashion. For in the Inns the men
seruants when you take Coach or horse, will bring you a Cupp

of beare or wyne with reverence, and the mayde seruants (theire partners of this rewarde) will present you a Nosegay of flowers with bending of the body, thereby crauing not exacting this drincking mony. The very Coachmen, who carry themselues very rudely to all passengers, who in the Inns will not stay a minute for any man that is not ready to goe with them, and by the way if any man haue necessary cause to light, will driue on, leauing him behinde if he cannot ouertake the Coach, yet at the end of the Jorney, besydes payment, will extort large drincking mony, as due to them, not of Curtesey but of right. Trumpeters and Musitians, hauing publike stipends of Cittyes, yet because among other dutyes they giue warning to the host of passengers approaching the towne, they vse in those places to putt a trencher abut the table to receaue this drincking mony. But trauelers fynde no Custome of Germany so costly as the Schlaffdrincke, that is sleeping drincke. For after supper the Cloth being taken away, if any passenger doe not presently rise from the table, and by ignorance of the Custome chance but once to sipp of the Cupp, he must pay equall portion with them who drincke all night, though himselfe goe presently to bedd without taking any quantity of this drincke to invite sleepe, which his other Companions take so largly, as often drincking till it be day they haue no tyme left to sleepe. So as a stranger ignorant of this Custome shall in the morning haue to pay, not only for his supper, but perhaps halfe or a whole Dollor, yea sometymes six or seuen Dollors for his companions intemperance, paying equall portion with them. In Saxony the Inns haue a litle bell hanging ouer the table, by ringing wherof they call the seruants to attend, and at Nurenberg in the Inn they haue a bell hanging vnder the table, which they ring in mirth, when any comes late to dinner or supper, and likewise for a Remembrance to any that sweare or speake immodest or vnfitt speeches. Of old the Germans were wonte to end more quarrells with bloodshed then with brawling, but nowe they are much changed in this point. For howsoeuer in Saxony man-slaughter is often committed betweene druncken men, yet in

Saxony when they are sober, and in all other parts generally, a man shall heare many scolde like oysterwyues, without drawing a sworde. And howsoeuer some gentlemen may goe into the feilde to fight, yet the professe never to fight with any purpose to kill, and to that end holde it a villainy to thrust, or stabbe, only striking with the edge of the sworde to Cutt and slash, ayming at opinion of valour by taking or giuing a small scare rather then by victory. So as when the first drop of blood is drawne, they presently vse to shake handes, and he that is wounded payes the wyne to all the rest who are partnors of the quarrell, or beholders of the fight, which is commonly performed so Coldly, as a stranger would thincke them not in ernest but in Jest: he that kills any man is beheaded without fayle, if he be taken, but only sargants may apprehend malifactours, so as with fauor of slowe pursuite many escape by flying. As I formerly sayd in disputations they haue no moderator, but themselues will take easey satisfaction, so in these frayes no man vseth to parte them that fight, and you see that themselues will easily take vp the quarrell, being not very hott in either kynde. But of this point I haue spoken more at large in the first part, namely in the Chapter of Precepts, and perticularly in the precept of Patience: the Custome or lawe of Coaches meeting is strang, giuing the way one to the other of Duty, as they come from the vpper or lower parts of Germany.

The Germans haue a peculiar Custome to that nation, that travelers and strangers liuing in vniuersities, haue a writen booke called Stam-buch (that is a booke of Armes) in which they intreate theire frendes to trick theire Armes, and write a motto signed with theire handes.

The vse of Bathes is frequent in Germany. For most Cittizens of any account haue in theire owne howses a priuate Stoue for bathing, which they vse to heate on Satterday for theire owne family, which euening in most Cittyes the wemen sett at theire dores spreading theyre hayre vpon the brimms of strawe hatts, to drye it in the Sunne, which also maketh the hayre of many very like in Colour, inclyning to yeallowe. They haue also publike Stoues or hott houses in each Citty, which they who haue not priuate Stoues, commonly vse on Satterdayes. And this frequent Sweating is vsed by the men to repayre theire health Crased by immoderate drincking as the wemen vse it for Clenlynes. These publike hott howses are in many Cittyes Common to men and wemen, only couering theire partes of shame, and they are attended by men and wemen seruants to wash and dry them, and sometymes to drawe blood from them by Cooping. But in some Cittyes the men are parted from the wemen with blancketts, where at maryages they vse to invite all the cheefe guests to bath together the day before the maryage, and in some places they vse such liberty that many men bringe harlotts as theire wiues to bathe with them in the same stoue and tubb. They haue also publike bathes of medecinall waters, to which they make great Concourse at the seasons of the yeare, and they vse such liberty as many come thether more for wantonnes and loue, then for Corporall diseaces.

They vse, espetially in the lower parts of Germany to giue one another potions to force loue, and the Apothecaryes haue some druggs, as Spanish flyes and like thinges, which they hold to haue great vertue in like witchcrafts, but I was informed they were vpon great pennalty forbidden to sell them, to any, without knowing the vse they would make of them. And these accidents I thincke to be more frequent, because myselfe haue seene some, as at Leipzig, where three virgins gaue three Aples to three young men, all infected by this art, wherof one vpon the eating of his Aple dyed the next day, and the second also eating his, fell the same day into a Phrensey, and was hardly recovered by the helpe of learned Phisitians, after long sicknes, and the third by good happ, forbearing that day to eate his Aple, was by his frendes mishapp warned to forbeare eating it, and to consume it with fyre that no other man might eate it.

In the same parts of Germany I haue seene some men lay vp theire cleane linnen (as it were to be perfumed) among aples, the smell whereof wee hold unpleasant, yea among Quinces, the

smell wherof wee hold vnholsome, if not infectious. The
Germans doe many tymes change theire names if they haue any
base signification, as the Popes of Rome haue long done by
Custome, arysing at first (as Authours write) from the same
cause. Thus one Bawer (which name signifyeth a Clowne or
tiller of earth) called himselfe Agricola, which in lattin hath
like signification (whose booke wee haue printed vnder that
name). Thus a learned man, and a great helper of Luther in
Reformation of Religion, being called Schwartz Eard, that is
black earth, tooke the name of Melancton hauing the same
Notation in the Greeke toung. And thus in the Dukedome of
Holst (a Prouince of Germany, but now incorporated to the
kingdome of Denmark) a learned gentleman well knowne by
diuers bookes he hath Printed, being called Toppfer, which
signifyes a Potter, changed his name to Chitreus of the same
signification in the greeke toung.

The Germans Cherish Storkes, which builde theire nests
vpon the tops of houses, yea themselues builde large nests of
wood vpon the topes of theire Senate houses, and of ther publike
and priuate houses, to invite them to breede there. These
Birdes only abyde with them in Sommer (except some fewe
which are tame, and haue theire winges Clipt) and when they
goe away towardes winter, they say that they vse to leaue one
of theire young ones, as for the Rent of theire nests, and kill
another as for a sacrifice. The Stoarkes among the Egiptians in
theire Hieroglyphicks, did signify Justice, And the Germans for
opinion of Justice or like cause, thincke the place lucky, where
they builde nests, and say that they neuer build in any
kingdome, but only in Commonwealths, which they repute the
most Just governments. And howsoeuer the Princes of
Germany be absolute in theire owne Territoryes, they hold the
whole Empire to be a Commonwealth. Yet in Italy being no
kingdome, and Consisting as well of Commonwealths as
Principalityes, I remember not to haue seene any Stoarkes,
much less publikely cherished. But I obserued them to be no
lesse cherished in Netherland. And likewise at Bazill among

the Sweitzers, where a Stoarke changing her nest from the Senate house to the Gallows, it was taken for an ill presage.

At the tyme of publike fayres or Marts, after the ringing of a Bell, all Banckrouts and condemned fugitiues may freely abide there, so they be carefull to be gonne before the second ringing of the Bell at the ende of the Martt, For at Leipzig my selfe did see an harlott beheaded because hauing formerly had a finger Cutt off, and beene banished for some Cryme, she was apprehended there after the ringing of the sayd Bell.

In many Cittyes (espetially of Misen and all Saxony) I obserued the lawe to forbid the shooting of Gunnes within the walls of the Citty, And in the same partes as at Dresden, the gates of the Citty were shutt, and the streetes chayned at Dinner tyme, as if it were in tyme of warr, and in most Cittyes they haue Trumpeters, dwelling in the Steeple of the cheefe Church, who daily sounde theire Trumpetts at sett howers, and by hanging out of Flaggs giue notice of Coaches, horsemen, and Footemen, approaching the Citty, and how many they are in number, as is vsed in tyme of warr. In most Cittyes they haue watchmen, which wee call Bellmen, going about to see that no mischance fall by Candle or fyer, and to Cry with a loude voyce the hower of the night, which they doe at Leipzig with wynding a great horne and in these wordes.

Lieben herrn lasset euch sagen, die Zieger hat elfe geschlagen, sehet zu das fewer vnd das light, auff das kein schade geschight. That is Louing Sirs (or Lords) lett me say to you, The Clock eleun hath strucken now, Looke to your fyer and your light, That no mischance befall this night.

When a stranger will enter any Church, to see any monument therein, the Germans vse to take their reward before they open the Dore to shewe it, and in many places they wilbe payd for any seruice, before they doe it. At Dantzke I obserued that generally all the Cittisens and common people, vsed to putt off

theire hatts (as it semed in reverence to Justice), when they
passed by the dore of the Senate house, being the publike Seate
of Justice.   In the States where Religion is Reformed, they all
kept the old style of kalender, but in Austria, Bauaria and the
States of Popish Bishops they followe the newe Style of Pope
Gregory.   The Clockes strike Commonly as ours doe but some
few strike 24 howres, yet both beginn the day at six in the
Euening (as I formerly shewed) and keepe the same course all
the yeare long, not following the Sunne, and so changing the
Noone and all howers of the day, as the sunne changeth his
rising and setting according to the manner of the Clocks in
Italy.

Pastymes and exercises.

Touching Pastymes and exercises, Tacitus writes that the
old Germans when they were most sober, playd at Dice as
seriously as they did workes of calling, with such rash adventure
of gayning and loosing, as for the last hazard they would
adventure theire liberty at a Cast, And Munster himselfe a
German, Confirmes that they vsed to play away theire liberty,
so as they were bound and sold for slaues.   But for my part, so
long as I liued with them, I neuer sawe any in priuate or
publike houses play at dyce, nor yet did I see any tables, or vse
of them, hauing passed through most parts of Germany, though
some sayd that these games were in some places knowne, but
litle vsed.   In Misen and those parts, I haue seene some play
at Cardes, but very seldome and only for wyne, neuer for
mony or any great wager.   And theire Cardes differ much from
ours, being all paynted on the insyde, with a Fagott of short
trunchons in the midest in steede of our Clubbs, and rounde
Circles paynted insteede of our Dymons &c. and the outsyde
drawne thicke with blacke lynes like our latices.   Nether did I
euer see them vsed in the Inns or publike houses, but only in
some priuate houses.   Indeede all theire delight and pastyme,
in my obseruation, seemed to consist in daily drincking, aswell
in priuate as in publike houses, and in long immoderate

daunceings, at publike feasts and most commonly in publike houses. Att Shrostyde I haue seene them runne on horsebacke through the streetes and markett places with Coulestaffes in theire handes, and vsing many trickes to giue one another falls. Likewise in tyme of snowe and great Frosts, they haue sledges, made like a Chayre, on which the dryuer setts, and a lower seate vpon which betweene his legs he many tymes placeth his mistres, and the sledge is drawne with one horse firnished with many litle bells. And vpon these sledges I haue seene many take short Jorneyes ouer the Snowe and yce, but most commonly they ride thus as it were in triumph through the streetes of the Cittyes and townes, and comming to the markett places they vse to wheele often about, with swift and shorte turnings, and great daunger of taking falls, wherein the driuer is much disgraced if his mistres ryding with him should chaunce to fall from the sledge, or not to be carryed gently and with ease. For which sport (according to the vse of other Princes) I obserued the Electour of Saxony to haue a large rome ouer his famous stable hung with many furnitures for these horses, and allmost filled with many Sledges, some covered with veluitt, and like stuffes, layd with lace of gold and silver, some with Cloth of gold, some with guilded leather, and some Sledges made of vntryed siluer, as it was taken out of the Mynes of his owne Province.

The Germans haue a Commendable exercise of shooting at a butt with Crosbowes and Harquebuzes. For which sport the better sorte and their very Princes with them, (if they liued not in free Cittyes) vsed to meete vpon sett dayes once or twise in the weeke, in a publike house for that purpose, where they haue plenty of wyne and beere to sell, for they cannot endure thirst either in worke or sporte. Besydes priuate men make matches of shooting at this publike house, for mony, or more commonly for suppers and drinckings in the same house. The place where they shoote is an open Terras covered ouer the head, the Butt lying open vncovered. Also the cheefe Cittizens make many priuate meetings to this purpose of Feasting vpon

Sondayes, and holy dayes, And howsoeuer the Butt at which they shoote be large, with much earth cast vp behynde it, yet my selfe at Heydelberg [saw] diuers wounded with shaftes and Bulletts sometymes missing the Butt, and then by Casualty hitting them.   Likewise there haue I seene the Prince Electour Pallatine, some tymes to vse this recreation with the Cittizens his Subiects vpon some sett matches made for wagers.   And because drincking is euer intermixed by the Germans, aswell in theire sports as Serious actions, which hateth nothing more then sober beholders (as indeede generally, it is not safe in Germany for sober men to stay in the Company of drinckers, theire Custome being ether to take as many Cupps as the rest haue had before, and so to ioyne with the Company, or ells presently to withdrawe themselues from it), I say for this or some like cause of desyring to be priuate, I obserued that if any man entred the place, besydes the Cittizens shooting and the Courtyers attending the Prince, and strangers of quality . . . . the place was soon cleared of idle beholders.   Likewise the Germans vse like exercise of shooting with Musketts and Crosbowes, out of the Cittyes, and in the open feildes at an Image of some birde sett on the topes of maypolles, where he that hitts the head hath the greatest prise, he that hitts the winge hath the next, and he that hitts the Foote hath the third, these being the parts of most vse, and the hitting of any other part hath a seuerall but lesse reward.   But this kynde of shooting they generally vse only once or twise in the yeare, yet vpon priuate matches they vse it oftner in some places. And in some places the rewardes are the parts of an oxe diuided for that purpose, with different portions of mony which Custome (they say) was of old taken from the Greekes. And in these places of shooting they hang vp Banners for memory of Victoryes.   For the rewardes being deuided and the number of shotts allowed to each man, they haue the most stately banner, who winne the cheefe prises and the greatest number of them.

Touching Hunting and Hawking, Cesar in his Commentaryes writes of many beasts in Germany, to the killers wherof that nation attributed great honour; namely a wylde oxe, hauing the bodye of an hart, with one only horne, and the Alces, [Elks?] hauing a like body with two short hornes, and leges without any ioynt, so as they were taken by Cutting the trees against which they vsed to leane, for the tree falling with the waight of the beast, it lay without power to rise (as some write of the Elephants in like sort taken), and they are like to Bulls, and as big as Elephants, and the Bisontes in the woodes of the high Alpes towardes Italy, so great in body as the skinne of one would couer thirteene men. These beasts, as he reports, were then in the Alpes, and in the great wood called Hircinia Sylua dayes is in great part wasted, and these beasts so destroyed, as none of them are founde. But in the Alpes, the same wood and other wodes of Germany, they haue to this day Beares, wylde oxen, Bubuli, a deformed kynde of Oxen, Wolues, and wyld Boares, in the killing whereof they glory much. Only the Alpes yealde some fallowe Deare, which are not found in any other parte of Germany, but in all parts they haue great stoare of Hares. And through all Germany the Princes haue great heardes of Hartes or redd Deare, not in Parkes, but freely lodging by Heardes in theire woodes. In most parts of the Empire all Hunting is forbidden, to any but absolute Princes in theire owne teritoryes (except the Hunting of the foresayd hurtfull beasts). Only in some parts the Hunting of Hares is permitted to gentlemen, as in Saxony, where the Elector buying of the gentlemen the olde right they had in the hartes of the woodes, and the hunting of them, only left to them, and no other of inferiour sorte, the liberty of Hunting hares. Which notwithstanding they vse only with gray howndes, for I neuer sawe them followe that sporte with the sent of slowe houndes. And it is a great fauour for a gentleman to giue an hare to his host or any inferiour frend. My selfe knewe an English marchant of good quality, who hauing a grayhound and by chance fynding and killing a hare, betweene Stoade and Hamburg, was imprisoned by the gentleman lord of the Soyle, and was glad to pay his three hundreth Dollours to escape greater punish-

ment. Christian the Electour of Saxony was without measure
delighted in hunting, and was little beloued of his subiects,
because with regall immunity he suffered his wylde beasts to
spoyle theire groundes. For towards Harvest the Country
people were forced to watch all night, that they might, with
whistlings and Clamours, driue the Redd Deare out of theire
Corne and viniyardes, for which notwithstanding they moued
not one foote, as hauing founde by experience that they
durst not hurte them, who might not to that purpose keepe a
dogg, except one of his feete were lamed. And indeede through
all Germany it seemes the beasts knowe this theire preuiledge.
For my selfe haue in Coaches passed by heardes of Redd Deare,
which lying by our Wheeles, would not stirr, though wee made
a noyse, and presented our peeces to them, as if they had
knowne we durst not shoote or hurte them. In the Electorship
of Saxony, and some other partes, if any man hunte and kill
a Redd Deare, a wylde Boore or a Goate, yea when they spoyle
his corne, he dyes for it by the lawe. In other partes the putting
out of his eyes is helde a myld punishment, as likewise that
punishment which I obserued in the Palatynate, where to
mitigate the rigour of the lawe, he is bounde to weare the
Hornes about his necke, so long as he liueth, at least when he
goeth out of his house, (whereof my selfe did see one example).
Yea the subiects of Austria may not take very Sparrowes without leaue from the lord of the Soyle. All men may hunt other
hurtfull beasts take and kill them, yea they are invited by
rewardes to doe it. The woodes on all sydes abounde with
wolues, which about the Natiuity of Christ, when the males and
females vse to Coople, and the grounde is commonly Covered
with snowe, keepe together in great multitudes, and passengers
see many trackes of theire footing, and at this tyme the Country
people tye theire Bitches to trees, that the wolues may ingender
with them, which bring a kynde of Dogg not great but most
fearce, and excelent to hunt the wolues. And whyle the wolues
thus flocke together a passenger going alone and without Armes,
espetially wemen venturing to passe the woodes, are sometymes

deuowred by them, besydes theire frequent deuowring of Cattle, for which cause he that kills a wolfe hath in some places tenne Dollors, in others mor or lesse for his rewarde, as likewise they that kill a Puttock or kyte by shooting haue a Dollor for rewarde, but the wolues for most part of the yeare lye hid in the thickest vnaccessable places of the woodes, and are seldome seene neere the high way, or in open feilde.   In the woodes of Thuringia and the vper partes of Germany many of the inhabitants haue the heades of wolues, and the heades and skinnes of Beares which themselues haue killed, fastened at theire gates, as a memory of that braue act.   Yea the Princes and theire Courtyers, mounted vpon good horses, and armed with a shorte sworde, and a sharpe forked speare, doe many tymes hunt Beares, wounding them often and lightly with theire speares, and then flying, while others persue till at last they fall downe wounded and wearyed, and then the Courtyers keeping them downe with theire speares, the Prince hath the honour to pull out the Beares hart with his speare, forked for that purpose. But it seemes they number not wilde Boares among hurtfull beasts, for in many places, they are reserued for the Princes game. Of these they haue great stoare, lying in the thickest of the woodes, and seldome doeing hurt to passengers, if they meete them not when they haue young Pigs.   And they are hunted by horsemen with speares, and with doggs brought out of Ireland and Denmarke, and when the horseman strikes them with his speare, he flyes, and they followe him, till another strikes them, to whome they presently turne, leauing the persuite of the former, and so they are wearyed, till at last the doggs fasten vpon them, and so they are killed by the huntsmen.   The Princes Hunte Redd Deare and Harts seldome, and only at sett tymes of the yeare, and then they rather murther then hunte them.   For the Clownes driue whole heardes of them into the Toyles, Compassing a great Circuite of grounde, wherein they shoote at them with gonnes and Crosbowes, and when they are fallen, kill them with shorte swordes, by hundreths at a tyme, which doune the Prince sendes some

fewe of them to be distributed among the gentlemen of the
Country, and the Senatours of the Cittyes, and the rest he
sendes to his Castles, to be powdred with salte (as they likewise
vse the Boares they take) and here with he feedes his Family as
wee doe with powdred Beefe, by which Continuall feeding vpon
redd deare and wylde Boares, no meate growes so irksome to
them as this venison. In all Germany I neuer sawe any man
Carry a hawke vpon his fist, much lesse any company Hawking
in the fielde, nor yet Hunting after houndes. For Fishing they
haue great stoare of fresh fish in Riuers and Pondes, and in
the mouth of the Riuer Elbe neere Hamburg and Stoade, they
catch so many Salmons and Sturgens, as they transporte great
quantity therof to forrayne parts, and feede theire seruants so
plentifully with them, as they abhorr that meate, and condition
with theire masters how many tymes in the weeke they should
feede therewith.

CHAPTER II.

Of Sweitzland touching the heades of the first Chapter.

Nature and Manners.

THE Sweitzers are by nature, education, and much more by rewarde, giuen to the military life. For they are borne in the high mountaynes called the Alpes, and mountanous people are Commonly Robustius, apt to suffer labor, Colde, hunger, and thirst, lovers of liberty, and naturally indued with rude boldnes, And for theire education, they are trayned vp from Childehoode in exercises of Armes, theire Festiualls, solemnityes, sportes, and exercises, tending therevnto. But espetially, in the last ages, they haue beene allured to be mercenary Soldyers, by ample rewardes, and stipends both in peace and warr, from the kings of Fraunce and Spayne, and from the Bishop of Rome, and by the manner of theire warfare, wherein they neuer come to danger but in the day of a battayle, which Princes vse not to hazard without great aduantage or necessity, so as they long inioye theire pay and the spoyle of Countryes, and seldome come to fyght for it (as I haue shewed at larg in the former discourse of that Commonwelth). And they haue that property with the Germans, at the end of any warr to retorne to theire trades of peace, nothinge Corrupted with the license of theire former Military life. For nature, education, and poverty of theire private estates, make them hate Idlenes, so as the men will milke Cowes rather then be Idle, whervpon also the Germans in scorne call them Cowmilkers. Besydes that the Justice of the land is so severe, as they haue no theeues nor Robbers among them, so as those mountaynes are more safe to Carry plenty of gold, then any other Country I knowe, and riche marchants come and goe safely to and from the Marts, without any Convoye, which they ordinarilly haue in Germany. They are reputed to be Hospitable by nature, and as the land lyes betweene Italy, Fraunce, and Germany, so all straungers

passe and liue there with safety and good vsage. Likewise they
are reputed charitable to the poore, not only releeuing them in
hospitalls, buylt for them in all Cittyes, with officers Carefully
to ouersee theire vseage, but also by mony and vittles
distributed among the poore of the townes and Country, by
officers chosen of purpose. They are Certaynely louers of
Justice, as appeares by theire lawes, and by theire leagues,
aswell betweene themselues at home, as those they make with
forrayne Princes, for a tyme or perpetuall. And they are so
famous for equity at home, as many strangers dwelling neere
them haue often committed theire Controuersyes both publike
and priuate to be determined by them. And nothing more
then this Justice and equity, and the Constancy thereof, among
other good effects, worketh one strang thing, namely that they
being military men and (as I may say) rude inhabiters of
mountaynes, and not free from continuall excesse in drincking,
yet haue fewe priuate quarrells that come to any sheeding of
blood. For in all parts they haue magistrates chosen of
purpose, who with Constancy and severity, according to theire
lawes (which are excelent in that kynde) repayre all men really
and fully in the least Iniuryes doune to them by worde or
deede. And if any come to blowes, all that stand by are bound
to parte them, and to remember them of the sayd lawes, to
which remembrance if they shewe the least contempt, by
Continuing the quarrell in worde or deede, they are sure not to
escape seuere punishment, according to the quality of theire
offence. Theire publike Feasts, and priuate meetings of
Cittizens with theire wyues to make merrye, are commonly
keept in publike houses, which haue yardes to walke in, and one
great tree or more to shadowe them in sommer, in the branches
whereof Commonly they haue a Roome built, contayning two or
three tables, with fresh water brought vp with spouts to wash
theire hands and drincking glasses. And by Custome the
magistrates and cheefe men of each Citty, towne, and society,
haue theire tables in these houses, which they allso frequent,
whereby all disorders and excesses are avoyded. In these

meetings they seldome or neuer haue any musicke (nether haue they many or skillfull musitians) for they delight more in discourse, and to haue the old men relate the braue Actions they haue seene, in the Commonwealth, and in the warr, at home and a broade, and such as theire forefathers tolde them. They haue plenty of milke, Butter, and hony, but flesh in lesse plenty, and want not daynties, as Venison, Birdes, and plenty of good fishes, in lakes and Rivers. But they vse no excesse of meate in these meetings, where the Feast is ended with two dishes of flesh at each table, and some other trifles. Of old they reputed him infamous that was drunken at these meetinges, and vsed great modesty and temperance in them, and the modesty and temperance in meates and behauiour are in good sorte retayned to this day, and drunckennes restrayned by the presence of magistrates and cheefe men, but as the inhabitants of vper Germany vse lesse excesse in drincke then those of the lower parts, Yet often and foully offend theirein, so the Sweitzers being of the same language, Communicate with them the same vice. And I thincke, Josias Sembler, who hath written a Compleate discourse of that Commonwealth, as he wittneseth theire frugality & temperance of old, when they liued vpon the fruites of theire owne land, and kept themselues at home, so truely confesseth that the decrease of those vertues, and increase of the Contrary vices first began when they gaue themselues to serue as mercinary Soldyers out of theire owne Country, and aswell the Corporations as the cheefe Captaynes and leaders began to receaue not only pay for the tyme of warr, but yearely and perpetuall stipends in tyme of peace, from forrayne Kings and States. Himselfe for drunckennes in particular, acknowledgeth that they are not free from it, nether is it now reputed so disgracefull, as he would haue it seeme to haue beene of old, yet he alledgeth a Common Custome among them at this day, to punish drunckards with forbidding them wyne for a yeare, and then restoring them to the vse of it, vpon promise of future temperance, which seemes notwithstanding to be litle putt in execution, or only against those who are most noted for Continuall and enormous excesses, and ill behauiours therein. For my experience thereof, I founde no such examples of dead drunckennes and shamefull effectes thereof, as I did many in Saxony, but I sawe great and frequent excesses therein. And indeede the inhabitants of those mountaynes, which for the greatest parte of the yeare are Couered ouer with deepe and harde Snowe, being much restrayned from exercises abroade, haue no smale invitation to spend the tyme in drincking, according to the delight they take therein.

Bodyes and Witts.

The Sweitzers (as commonly all Inhabitants of greate mountaynes) haue large bodyes by nature and free education, and strong and active by exercyses, which the Sweitzers vse both in military traynings and frequent Hunting of wylde beasts. For which reasons theire bodies are more Actiue, and they haue more viuacity of spiritt and witt, then most parte of the German nations. In Sweitzerland as in the next partes of vper Germany (perhapps by drincking the waters of the Alpes running through minoralls) they haue many lepers which begg with Clappers of woode standing farr off by the high way and haue spittle houses built of purpose for them.

Manuall Arts Sciences Vniversityes and Language.

Yet are they not so excellent, as the Germans are by singular industry, in Manuall Arts. Yea the Germans in my opinion excell them in Sciences, by continuall plodding vpon one profession alone, as well as by multitude of Vniversities and learned men. Sembler confesseth that of old both before and after they were settled in the liberty they nowe haue, and so freed from all subiection to the Princes of Austria, they were not much giuen to the studdyes of Learning, only hauing some rude Poetts who writt theire warrs and victoryes in vnpolished rymes, yet had they of old two Schooles of learning in the monastery of St. Gallus, and in the Colledge of Churr, which

haue beene long since decayed.   But Pope Pius the second
formerly called Aeneas Syluius, did institute an vniversity at
Bazell, which hath yealded many famous learned men, being
founded by him with great preuiledges, in a fruitefull Country,
and a very wholesome ayre, for which cause and more to honour
that Citty, he also helde a generall Councell in the same.   They
haue also a famous Schoole at Zurech, which is no vniversity,
yet hath yealded many learned men, espetially in the profession
of diuinity, as likewise a Schoole at Berne, and an other at
Lausana, And for bookes, the Stationers at Bazell, at Zurech,
and at Geneua, haue shopps so well firnished with them, as
they yealde not therein to any in Germany.   To speake
somthinge more largly of Bazell.   It was founded by the sayd
Pope in the yeare 1459. in nothing more famous then in the
great Confluence of strangers, so as yearely some 50. Doctours
haue taken degree therein.   At my being there they had only
two Colledges, In the vpper lived 11. Students mantayned by
the Citty, in the lower 6. Students mantayned by particular
men, and each had a Steward or housekeeper, all the rest of the
Students liuing in the Citty.   I obserued that the Batchelors
of Arts were promoted vpon the tenth of may, and was informed
that the vniversity hath only a breefe Coppy of the priuileges
(which they call vidimus), hauing delivered the originall therof
to the Senatours of the Citty, for which cause all Controversyes
of Students, espetially if they fall betweene them and Cittizens,
are brought before the Senate.   In a Controuersy betweene two
Students at my being there, one of them was Committed by the
Professors, and being within fewe dayes inlarged, first tooke
his Oath no way to revenge his Imprisonment.   I found there
two Professors of Diuinity, James Gryneus (who also did reade
the lecture of historyes at tenn of the Clocke in the morning)
and Brundmuller, which two did reade in the publike Schooles
each second day by turnes, at three of the clocke in the after
noone, and each had yearely for his stipend two hundredth
Guldens, 24. sackes of Corne, and 12. Saumes or horselodes of
wyne.   The Professors of the Ciuill lawe were Samuell Gryneus,

who did reade vpon the Digesta, and Guther, who did reade
vpon the Codex, and Isellius, who did reade vpon the Institutions, and each had for yearely stipend 100. French Crownes,
and 40 sackes of Corne.　The Professors of Phisicke were,
Platerus, who did reade vpon his owne practise, and Stapanus,
who did reade Gallen De Diff: Sympt: and Bauchinus who did
reade vpon the Anatomy, and they two first had each for yearely
stipend 150. Guldens. 20. Sackes of Corne (I meane wheate,
Commonly called bread Corne) and tenne Sackes of Oates, and
the third had yearely 100 Dollors, and 24 Sackes of Corne.　The
Professors of naturall Philosophy, of Ethickes, two of Rhetorick,
two of Logick, one of the Greeke, an other of the Hebrewe
toung, and one of the Mathematicks, had each for yearely
stipend 100. Dollours, and 24 sackes of Corne.　He that tooke
the degree of Batchelour payde for his examination and to the
publike treasure 48. Batzen, and for the Feast according to the
number of the Graduates, as they being 4. each one payde 54.
Batzen, to the Beadle each one payde 4 Batzen, and to the
Printer for Printing the questions of disputation, each one
payde 20. Batzen.　They disputed weekely by turnes vpon
Thursdayes.　He that tooke the degree of Master of Arts, payde
for his examining each one 6. Guldens and 6. Batzen and for his
first dinner or Feast called Bona Noua (good newes) made to
the examiners, each one payde 24. Batzen, and for his second
dinner to the Professors he payde eight pownde and 4. Batzen
(that is 6 Guldens and tenn Batzen) and to the Beedle halfe a
Franck, and to the Printer 20. Batzen, and besydes each one
payde for his extraordinary guests for each of them 6. Batzen.
They disputed and declaymed weekely by turnes vpon Satterday, but if a stranger take that degree he answers in disputation
once extraordinarily, all the Professors and Graduates apposing,
as they generally vse in all disputations.　They that tooke the
degree of Doctor in Diuinity or Ciuill lawe, payde for examining
21. Guldens, but the Phisitians payde only 19 Guldens.　Each
payde for a dinner to the examiners at the graunting of the
degree called Bona Noua, some 5. Guldens, to the Notarye one

Gulden, and to the Beadle one Gulden, and for the Doctorall Feast 12. Guldens, besydes paying for extraordinary guests, if one take the degree alone, but if they be many they spend lesse, according to the rate, For this degree they answered once in disputation, or did reade two lectures. But ordinarily the Professors of Diuinity did answer monthly in disputation : sometymes the Professors of Phisicke did holde like disputations but of free will for exercyse of the Students. To conclude, all the Students liued in the howses of Professors and Cittizens, but if any woulde liue in the foresayd Colledges for poore Schollers, the Steward vsed to giue them Chambers, as many as he had voyde, and a Convenient Dyet at his owne table, for a reasonable rate. The language of the Sweitzers is the same with the German which also is more purely spoken vpon the Confynes of Sweitzerland, namely in the Teritoryes of Strassburg and the Palatinate, then in any other part of Germany, Misen only excepted. Of olde they thought the Studdy of the latten Toung and of the liberall sciences, not vsefull to military men, as they were, but only to appertayne to such as were Priests or had taken some orders in the Church. But since the founding of the vniversity at Bazill, and in our tyme, that nation had and hath many learned men, both Professors of sciences more spetially of Diuinity, as also Linguists. Yea men of all sortes, though vnlearned, and wanting the latten toung, yet by profession of mercinary Armes, haue skill in the French, Italian, and Spanish languages, and are conversant in reading olde and modern Historyes, which in our age are commonly translated into the French, and theire owne vulgar language, many of the States men and cheefe leaders in the warr, hauing well firnished libriaryes of these and other bookes written or translated in theire vulgar toung of late tyme.

Ceremonyes, spettially Mariages Children Christininges and Funeralls.

Most of theire Ceremonyes and feastiuall Pompes, haue some tast of theire military Profession. As for Marryages, the Brides ar brought home with Companyes of Pikemen, and with shott, and with Drumms and Trumpitts, and the more shott and Pikes shee hath to conduct and meete her, the more honour shee is thought to receave. And in these pompes and like Feasts, these Soldyers march after the beating of the Drumme, and with all Military Ensignes. Yea the young men and boyes from eight yeares old, vpward, often Joyne with them in these Military marches, and so without any trayning they vse themselues to the military marches and comely bearing of theire Armes. Yet are the Soldyers also yearely mustered, euen in tymes of greatest peace, Commonly at the dedications of Churches, or dayes of publike Marts, or yearely at the entring of newe magistrates. In all solemnityes, of marryages, and the like, they march in the Cittyes with as much order and gravity as the Germans, only as they all haue a mixed profession of marchants and Soldyers, so the men at these meetinges, and continually in the Cittyes, weare rownde blacke Capps of woll, with Clokes and Rapyers. And in all Feasts they are more temperate then the Germans, in meates, mirth, and espetially drincking.

For the Customes of Childebearing, Christninges and Funeralls, I must passe them ouer by reason I made short stay in that Dominion. Only I will say that as in language and manners they differ litle from the inhabitants of vpper Germany, so I thincke they are not vnlike to them in these particular Customes.

Customes.

Among theire Customes, they vse laudable order in quenching fyers, happning in theire townes and Cittyes. For howsoeuer all people flocke to resist this common mischeefe, yet nothing is there doune without order and overseeres. First aswell for the approaching of enemyes, as for preventing and quenching these fyers, they haue watchmen in the Steeples, and at the gates, and others that walke about the Citty proclayming the howers of the night, and looking that no hurte be doune by Candles and fyers, and also Armed Cittizens keepinge the watch in diuers streetes. Besydes that they haue spetiall officers to commaund and direct the people how to quench the fyers, and to appointe some to preserue the goods of them that are in danger. And to preuent tumults in the Citty, or assaultes of enemyes, when these fyers happen presently the whole Citty takes Armes, and some goe to the gates and walls, which haue that office by former order, and are chosen men out of all Tribes or Companyes, others keepe the Citty, being alwayes diuided into parts, wherof each hath his owne Captayne and Banner to the which they repayre. And the Consulls and Senatours also drawe to the publike house of Counsell, to Consulte and provide for all accidents. At Zuricke, actiue young men are yearely chosen, with a Senatour to leade them, that they may giue helpe to the Country, if any such fyers happen there, likewise in some places they haue officers chosen to ouersee the Ouens and Chimnyes that they be safe from Danger of fyer.

They may not sell or morgage any houses or landes to strangers, but only to them that dwell in the same teritory or Region.

Vpon the dayes when theire Auncesters gott any famous victoryes, they goe in solemne processions to the place of the Battayle, the Prists or ministers singing hymnes or Psalmes before them, and the Senatours with a multitude of men wemen and Children following them, and in some Conveniant place neere that feilde, haue a publike feast before they retourne home.

Bastardes may not beare publike offices, nor sett in Courts of Judgment. For howsoeuer they are not authors of theire vnlawfull birth, and many of them haue proved exelent men, yet to preserue the dignity of marryage, they thincke fitt that acts of lust should be punished with some note of disgrace. And in some places Cittizens discended of strangers haue no parte in the publike Counsells, in other places they may be of the great Senate, but not of the lesser, after they haue liued twenty yeares with them, and so in tyme haue all priviledges of Cittizens.

In publike assemblyes for chusing of magistrates, where the people giue voyces, they giue consent by lifting vp one hande, and the number of them is taken by officers of purpose. And when they take an Oath before Magistrates, they lift vp three fingers, as the Germans lift vp two, And the French men one whole hand.

They esteeme (with the Germans) the building of Storkes with them to be a luckey presage, and at Bazell they thought the accident ominious, when a Storke remoued her nest from the Senate house to the gallous.

By my Jorney from Padoa to the Grizons being Protestants I founde that they vse to write after the old style, not after the newe of Pope Gregory, nether did I obserue any change of Style in my passage through the Catholike Cantons.

Sports, exercises, Hunting, Hawking and Fishinge.

Touching sportes, exercises, Hunting, Hawking and Fishing. In my passage through Sweitzerland, I did neuer see any one to play at dyce, Cardes, or Tables. In generall the Sweitzers are military by nature, as bred among heigh mountaynes, and of old were forced by necessity to frequent vse of Armes, against tyrannous governours, and ambitious neighbours. And so all theire Ceremonyes Sportes and exercises, haue some relation to the warr. To make them good and ready shott, they vse shooting with gunnes and Crossbowes at a marke, for a Continuall exercise and recreation, as the Germans doe, giuing rewardes to them that shoote best at publike meetinges, so as from verye childehoode they practise the vse of gunnes, since the tyme that the vse thereof was brought into the warrs of Europe. Theire Ceremonyes tast of the warr. At maryages (as I formerly sayd) the Brides are brought home by companyes of Pikes and shott, following theire Banners and Coulers, with a military march beaten by Drumms. For they serue not on horsebacke with trumpitts, that seruice being of small o rno vse in that mountanous Country. And the very young men and Chilldren, at those and like Festiuall tymes, vse to carry harquebuzes, Pikes,

and Halbardes, and so march after theire Drummes and
Banners, though some of them seeme not of strength to beare
those Armes.   Besydes that they haue generall musters yearely
taken before the magistrates.   Also theire exercises tende to
make them Actiue in the warrs, as running, leaping, Casting of
stones, wrastling, and fensinge with all kyndes of weapons, most
of these exercises hauing publike rewardes propounded to the
good performance of them.   And as they haue great Lakes, and
Rivers of violent Course, so they vse very Fishing to military
endes, being generally more skilfull in the Art of swymming,
then any other nation.   To the same ende the very Country
people, when they haue doune theire worke, or haue any tyme of
recreation, exercise themselues in Hunting, wherein they Clime
Mountaynes and Craggy Rockes, to followe theire game, as
wylde Goates, and Beares, and many tymes wolues and Beares,
which they feare not to incounter, because it is a great honour
to kill them and fasten theire heades and skinnes vpon the Posts
of theire dores, besydes a publike rewarde giuen them from
the magistrates, for which reasons also the cheefe men among
them often adventure themselues, not only in Hunting generally, but euen in the danger of assayling these fierce beasts.
Hunting among them is free for all men, they hauing fewe
gentlemen, whome they almost rooted out in the warr they
made at first to gayne theire liberty.   Nether haue they much
game but only in the heighest mountaynes and Alpes for in other
places they destroye all wylde beasts, lest they shoulde spoyle
theire growndes, which commonly are narrowe feildes, or
mountaneous pastures and in some places barren, but made
fruitfull by industrye.   In like manner all sortes of men haue
freedome to fish, in all Riuers, Brookes and lakes, being in the
Teritoryes of theire perticular Cantons or Commonwealths.   And
like freedome they haue to Hawke, and take all kyndes of Birdes
by netts and like Arts, but I remember not to haue seene any
Hawkes among them, and the greatest part of the Country is
not commodious for theire flying, being very full of great and
thicke woodes.

CHAPTER III.

Of the vnited Provinces of Netherland touching all the subiectes of the first Chapter.

Nature and Manners.

FOR the Vnited Provinces of Netherland, touching theire Nature and Manners. They are a iust people, and will not Cozen a Chylde, or a stranger, in changing a peece of gold, nor in the price or quality of thinges they buy. For equall courses among themselues, I will giue one instance, small for the subiect, but significant to proue theire generall Inclination. The very wagonners if they meete other wagonns in the morning whyle theire horses are fresh, vse to giue them the way, but if they meete any in the afternoone, comming from neerer bating places when their horses beginne to be weary, they keepe their way, by a generall Custome among them, that they who haue gonne more then hafe the way, shall keepe it against all that haue gonne lesse parte of the Jorney. And as they loue equality in all things, so they naturally kick against any great eminency among them, as may be proved by many instances, and euen that before named. For as they haue fewe gentlemen among them in Holland or Zeland, hauing of old rooted out the Nobility, so I obserued, that when our Wagoner hauing gone more then halfe the way, yet gaue the way to a gentlemans waggon, all the Passengers were very angry with him, saying he had no right to take the way. To which purpose they haue a Comon saying, " if he be rich lett him dyne twise, and weare two gownes, for one serues mee," in that kynde comming neere the Italians pride, to liue of themselues, and not to borrowe, or to eate at the table of others, to make them slauish to greatnes or riches. They are generally frugall, in dyett, Apparrell and all expences, as I haue formerly shewed in the Chapters treating thereof. In manners they were of old rude, and are so to this day in some measure, and the Hollanders haue of old beene vulgarly called Plumpe, that is blunt or rude. Yet since their last long warr in which they haue intertayned English and French Soldyers and leaders, they are much refyned in manners by their conversation, as also of poore Countryes they are become very rich, even by warr, and vnder great taxces to mantayne it, which commonly destroy all other nations at least for the tyme of warr. And this may seeme strange, if wee consider not withall that they haue still kept the warr vpon the frontyers, by fortifyed places, so as the enemyes liued vpon theire owne Country, and haue by theire Navall power kept traffique by Sea free to themselues, and shutt vp to theire enemyes, by which meanes theire enemyes on the Contrary, of most florishing States haue growne poore. So as the Vnited Provinces may say with the Athenian "Perijssem nisi Perijssem, I had bene vndone, if I had not beene vndone," since theire misery hath turned to theire good. In this point of manners I speake not of Brabant and Flanders, which people therein are free from the French levity and from the German gravity or morosity, being of a midle and good temper betweene them. In Conversation the wemen may seeme vnchast, but are not so, as I will shewe by Instances in theire Customes and Pastymes. For vallour they are bolde in drincking quarrells, which often arise among them, and then they drawe theire knives, and agree one with the other whether they will Stecken, or Schneiden, that is stabb or Cutt, (a strang Contreriety of agreement in discord) which done they fyght accordingly. And howsoeuer these knives are long, small, and sharpe, pearcing in to the body more then any dager or Stiletto, yet they who fight with knives are lesse punished then if they should fyght with daggers and Swordes, as my selfe haue seene by experience. And to prouoke these quarrells, they vse base ignominious raylings, and horrible oathes. Most of them are borne by the Sea, and vpon waters, and so by nature are bold Seamen in tempests, and as the Bataui or Hollanders were reputed braue Soldyers when they serued the Roman Emperours, so nowe (espetially warmed with drincke) they fight bloodely at Sea, but theire warrs vpon land are made with expence of strangers blood, espetially of the English, the nature people hauing done litle therein, howsoeuer theire his toryes take the honour to themselues, which the English and other strangers haue iustly deserued.

Bodyes and Witts.

Touching theire bodies, the men, by free edvcation, haue large and strong bodies, and much more actiue then the Germans, by vsing more exercise, and by drincking lesse (For howsoeuer theire excesse in drincking be no lesse, yet it is not so frequent and continuall, as among the Saxons) and also they are more quick spirited, by vsing fyers in Chimnyes and not being dulled with hott Stoaues. They are very populous, so as Botero, the Roman reckons the people of Netherland in the 17 Prouinces to be three millions of persons, and Guicciardine writes that they haue 208 walled townes, 150. priuiledged places, and 6300. villages with Church and steeple, but as these Vnited parts are seated in the midest of Seaes and waters, and vse excesse in drincking so they are Comonly of flegmaticke com- plections, and begett more femalls then males, and for this reason, or because great part of the men is commonly abroade at Sea, I am sure in all meetings the number of wemen and girles doth farr overtop the number of men and boyes, at least fiue to one. The wemen of Flaunders and Brabant are very fayre, and theire discent attyre and white linnen setts forth their beauty; I cannot say that the Hollanders are generally beautifull, though they haue the ornament of white linnen, but either my eyes deceaued me, or the wemen of Dort lying vpon the inland Sea that beates vpon Brabant, and the wemen of Zeland, are much fayrer then the rest.

For witt, they seeme a very simple people, when my selfe with some English gentlemen passed through North Holland and Freeseland, the people gazed vpon vs, and touched our apparrell, as if they had neuer seene a stranger, and when wee bought necessaryes at Amsterodam, the boyes followed vs, be-holding and handling our apparell, and what soeuer wee bought, asking why and to what vse we bought it. But howsoeuer they seeme, no doubt the men are indeede most Crafty espetially in traffique, eating vp all nations therein, by frugallity, industry, and subtilety, as likewise in Coynes, hauing no siluer, but drawing it from all nations in plenty, and making profitt of forrayne Coynes, by raysing and decrying them at pleasure, and indeede are most witty in all meanes to growe rich, as the experience of our age hath taught vs, wherein we haue also founde them expert men in State matters, to proue most wise and iuditious, though most of them are of Mechanicall educa-tion.

Manuall Artes Sciences Vniversityes and Language.

Tuching Manuall Arts, they are a people more industrious then the Germans, and excell them in all Arts and trades. For howsoeuer, I must confesse that the Germans of Nurenberg in those parts are esteemed the best workmen for Clookes and some like thinges, yet in generall they are not to be compared to the Netherlanders, who make infinite proportians of hangings for houses, and like furniture for them, and the best and richest of them wrought with gold and silke, which are named Arras, of the towne where the best sorte are made, and are exported into many kingdomes of Europe, as also they make diuers stuffes for wearing, and Cloathes aswell wollen as espetially linnen whereof they exporte great quantity, and Fyner then any other parte of Europe yealdeth. Yea for other Manuall trades they are most industrious and skilfull workemen. And it is worth the observa-tion, that the richest amongst them cause their Children to be taught some arte or trade, whereby they may gayne theire bread in the tymes of warr, or banishment, or of like adversityes. The tradesmen take no Prentises bound for yeares, but they who will learne any trade, giue them mony to be taught it at their shops, taking their meate and lodging at theire owne home. And those who meane to professe any trade, when they haue learned it at home, goe (according to the Custome of the Germans) to other Cittyes at home, and forrayne Countryes abroade, most famous for excelent workemen in those trades, that of them they may learne to excell in them. Only as English travelars fynde no such Barbars in any place, as they haue at home, so in these Vnited Provinces, they are not to be Commended, for skill or handsomnes in that trade, besydes that they wash mens beardes in dreggs of beare, before they shaue them with the Raysour, as ours doe with hott water and seete balls.

For Sciences, they haue and of old had many learned men in all Professions wherof some are knowne by theire writings, as Ralphe Agricola of Freeseland, and Erasmus borne at Roterodame in Holland. But for Commedians, they litle practise that Arte, and are the poorest Actours that can be imagined, as my selfe did see when the Citty of Getrudenberg being taken by them from the Spanyards, they made bonsfyers and publikely at Leyden represented that action in a play, so rudely as the poore Artizans of England would haue both penned and acted it much better. So as at the same tyme when some cast Players of England came into those partes, the people not vnderstanding what they sayd, only for theire Action followed them with wonderfull Concourse, yea many young virgines fell in loue with some of the players, and followed them from Citty to Citty, till the magistrates were forced to forbid them to play any more.

For Vniversities, I will not speake of the famous Vniversity Lovan in Flanders, which before the Ciuill warrs had sixteene thousand Students, and is nowe decayed, nor yet of that at Doway, now florishing, only I will say that the glory of them was and is in the learned Professors, which of old were drawne thether from all parts, by large Stipends, but now are commonly Jesuites (except the Professors of lawe and Phisicke), for they gladly ingrosse Childrens and young mens education and instruction, as well in Diuinity as in the liberall Artes (the growndes of all learning). For these Vniversityes haue not many Colleges fayrely built, and founded with large Rents, to mantayne Schollers, and large for all the Students to liue in them and not in the towne, as our Vniversityes haue in England.   But after the manner of Germany, haue publike schooles wherein the Professors reade, and one or two Colleges for poore schollers, most of the other Students liuing in the towne.   The like may be sayd of the vniversityes in the vnited Provinces, whereof that of Froniker in Frieseland, was founded of old, and being decayed was of late restored, yet florished not greatly ether in learned Professors or in the number of Students. The Vniversity of Leyden in Holland was founded in the begining of the Ciuill warrs, to keepe Students from going to the vniversityes of Flanders.   At my being there it had many learned Professors.   John Heurnius Professor of Phisicke did reade Hypocrates at eight of the Clocke in the morning, and had for stipend 800 Flemish Guldens yearely.   And as in Germany so here all Professors dictate theire Lectures, and the Students write them worde by worde.   At the same hower in other Schooles, Thomas Sosius did reade a booke of the Ciuill lawe, with like stipend, And Lucas Trelcatius did reade the Common places of Diuinity with stipend of 600 Guldens yearely for his Lecture, and 300 Guldens for his preaching in the Church.   At nyne of the Clocke Gerard Tuning did reade the Institutions of the Ciuill lawe, with stipend of 300 Guldens yearely.   Peter Paw did reade the Anatomy, with stipend of 500 Guldens.   And Henry Bredius did reade Tullyes Oratour, with stipend of 200 Guldens.   At tenne of the Clocke Fraunces Ivnivs a famous Diuine did expound the Prophett Isaiah, with stipend of 1200 Guldens yearely. At one of the Clocke in the after noone, James Anthony Trutius did reade Aristotiles Phisickes.   At eleuen of the Clocke Paulus Merula did reade, by turnes each second day, the historyes of Eutropius and Suetonius, with stipend of 400 Guldens yearely, At one of the Clocke in the after noone, James Ramsey did reade the logicke lecture, with stipend of 400 Guldens yearely.   At two Everard Branchorst did reade the Pandects of the Ciuill lawe.   And Gerard Bontius Professor of Phisicke did reade Paulus Aeginita.   And Frances Rapheling the Professor of the Hebrewe toung did reade vpon the Sections

out of the Prophetts, each hauing 400. Guldens yearely Stipend.
At three of the Clocke Two other Professors did reade, Corne-
lious Gratius the Ciuill lawe, and Bonaventura Vulcanvs the
Greeke toung, each hauing 400. Guldens yearely. At foure of
the Clocke Rodulphus Swellius did reade one day vpon the
naturall historye of Plinny, and the next day the Mathematikes,
hauing 300. Guldens yearely stipend. All these Professors had
houses allowed to each of them by the States, excepting two,
who had the Rents of some land allowed to provide them houses.
Some poore Schollers were mantayned in a ruinous College (as
they are no better ouer all Germany) each hauing 30. Flemish
Poundes yearely stipend, who had theire dyett yearely at the
vper table for 150 at the lower table for 100 Flemish Guldens,
and two of each Citty were admitted into this College, and they
all studdyed Diuinity, but were mantayned in the College no
longer then six yeares, in which tyme they must take the degree
of theire Profession, and then beginn to practise it, if they be
fitt for the same. In each Citty they haue an Hospitall to
bring vp poore Orphants, whereof the best witts are sent vnto
the vniversity, the other putt to trades. At Leyden all the
Students liued in the houses of Cittizens. The Prince of Orange
when he tooke vpon him the defence of these Provinces in the
begining of the Ciuill warrs, did founde this Vniversity, and
kept to himselfe and his heyres the power to name the Rector.
At my being there, vpon the first of February, the Professors
Chose three men at Leyden, and sent them with theire letters
to the Hage, where Count Mavritz the sayd Princes Sonne
appointed one of them to be Rector, who was settled in his office
for the yeare following vpon the eighth of February, when the
Statutes and Customes were publikely read before the Students,
who within three dayes entred theire names with the Rectour,
and otherwise were no more to be accounted in the nomber of
Students. But the States pay the Professors Stipends, out of
Rents allowed to that vse. Each Student hath yearely 80.
Stoupes of wyne allowed free from assise or tax, and six vessells
of Beare at two shillings sixpence starling the vessell lesse then

the ordinary price the Cittizens pay, and they with whome they dyett, take this allowance in theire names and right, besydes that the Professors and Students are free from all other taxes and tributes.   The Rectour Judged the Controversyes betweene Students and Cittizens.   The vniversity had three chosen Protectours amonge the States, whereof one at that tyme was Janus Douza a learned man well knowne by his writinges. And when a Professors place is voyde, the Professors having chosen a worthey man at home or abroade, these Protectours invite him to supply that place.   But the States must approue him, who also allott and pay his Stipend.   And howsoeuer at my being there this Vniversity newly founded had not 400. Students, yet the States drawing thether most learned Professors, it was hoped that in shorte tyme it would greatly florish. The Professors doe not reade aboue 30 weekes in the yeare, hauing long vacations, as vpon the 3. of Occtober they Cease to reade for 15. dayes, because that day Leyden was besegged by the Spaniardes, in memory whereof they haue publike playes poorely representing the Actions and Crueltyes of that seige. The Diuines disput twise in the weeke, other Professions haue no sett dayes, but dispute often vpon private agreements, made knowne by Printing the questions and setting them vpon the gates of the Schooles, donne by them that answer to the end all Students who list, may provide to appose and reply against them.   And this they doe for Commendable exercise, without any reproofe to make ostentation of theire learning.   In Promotions of degrees, each Graduate payes 30. Guldens to the Treasurer of the Vniversity, at my being there a frende of myne commenced Doctour of the Ciuill lawe, who besydes his feast payde about eight pound starling to the Doctours of his Profession, and some fewe Gulldens to the Bedells and besydes payde for the publike testimoniall of his degree which he tooke alone for they vse no sett tymes for this Ceremony, but one or more are promoted whensoeuer they craue that fauour. Nether vse they at these tymes the Germans Pompe and gravity in marching through the streetes, only the Bedell, without any

Mace and with his head covered, went before the Rectour, who with some Professors and Studients, partly in gownes partly in Cloakes, all weareing hatts (for I neuer sawe any cornerd Capps worne by Graduates in any vniversity beyonde the Seas) Conducted the young Doctor to the publike Schooles, where he hauing made his Oration, a Doctor of that faculty did reade the graunt of power to create Doctors. And then, first he called the party promoted to sett in his Chayre, as giving him power to teach, secondly he made him sett downe by him, to shewe the necessity of Conference and Counsell in doubtfull matters, thirdly he gaue him an open booke in his hand, to shewe that he must not Judge after his owne opinions but after the written lawe, fourthly a booke Closed, to shewe that he must haue wisdome to Judge of right and equity in cases not expressly defyned by the lawe, fyftly he put on his head a Cap of scarlett as the badge of his degree, Sixtly a gold Ringe on his finger, the token of his dignity, and seuenthly the old Doctour shaked the young Doctor by the hand, as welcomming him to be of theire nomber, which in other places I haue seene figured by imbracing and kissing him vpon the Cheeke. This done, the young Doctor by a shorte oration gaue thanckes, and so was ledd backe to the Rectors house, in the same order he was brought to the Schooles. His dinner or Feast was kept in a publike Inne, to which he invited the Professors and such guests as himselfe pleased to haue, for I obserued some cheefe Burgers to be present at the Creation in the Schooles, who were not invited to dinner. The language of the Netherlanders is a Dialect of the German toung, but sweetned with the leuity of the French toung, which most of the inhabitants by education learne to speake as naturally as the vulgar, besydes that many of them speake the English, Italyan, and other languages of nations with whome they traffique, as there is almost no place in the worlde where they trade not. As the Saxons and lower partes of Germany (excepting Misen) speake more rudely then the vpper partes and the Sweitzers, so the Netherlanders so much assert the sweetnes and alacrity of the French toung, as

they preferr it before theire owne, and delight more to speake
the French toung, then theire owne vulgar language, which
they pronounce much more gently then the Germans, omitting
many of the Consonants and dipthonges which they vse. As I
haue formerly sayde that the Germans toung borrowes many
wordes of the Greeke, so I say also of the Flemish or Netherlanders language. And Marchantius in his history of Flanders
the 25 page of the first booke, setteth downe many particular
wordes apparently derived from the Greekes. But howsoeuer
he produceth Authours to proue that the Flemish toung was
knowne and spoken in some partes of Turky and of the West
Indyes, though it is not vnprobable that a banished man or
marchant (espetially of the Flemings whereof some are founde
in many and most remote partes of the worlde) may carry his
language, and perhapps spreade it in his owne family and
discent among some nations farr distant, yet I never obserued
the Flemish toung to be vsed in forayne partes, but only by
those of theire owne nation, and I am sure that themselues at
home spake the French toung, as vulgarly and naturally as
their owne. And it standes with reason, that they who are very
industrous in traffique, and hauing litle of theire owne to
export, (except lynnen) doe trade most with the Commodityes
of other nations, should themselues learne many languages,
whereas other Nations haue not the same reason to learne the
Flemish tounge. And by reason of the Flemings generall skill
in strang languages, strangers may passe and trade among them
though they cannot speake a worde of the vulgar toung. As
wee giue the title of master only to gentlemen, and those of that
degree in our Vniversityes, so I obserued In the Vnited Provinces, that a tradsman and espetially a Barbar was vulgerly
saluted Meister. In so much as in the beginning of the Ciuill
warr, when our English forces came into Holland, and the best
sorte being richly apparrelled were saluted masters, the Common
people at theire first enterance tooke them for tradsmen, and
wondred they should be so brave in apparell. Though those
of the vnited Provinces were then rude in manners, yet their

language then had, and still hath, a very amorous Phrase in Vulgar speeches, Commonly answring one another, Wat sag you Mein Shaff, or mein kinde, or Mein Vatter, or Mein Moure, that is, what say you my lamb, or my Chylde, or my Father, or my Mother, Yea they salute old men, with the title of brother and Childe, and salute young men and maydes with the title of Father and mother. Freyen signifyes to wooe, and therevpon they call Bachelors Fryern, and young virgins Freysters.

Ceremonyes Pompes Marryage Funeralls Christnings Childebed.

Touching Ceremonyes, Pompes, Maryages, Funeralls, Christnings, and Childebedd. No people of Europe in my opinion vseth lesse Ceremonyes and Pompous shewes or marchings, in festiuall solemnityes, then those of the Vnited Provinces, doing all such thinges without any ostentation, yea with great simplicity and nakednes.

For marryages, the wemen in Netherland, Contrary to the Custome of the Germans, were married very young, so as not long before my being in those partes, a girle of twelue yeares age, at Harlam, had a Chylde by her husband. They vse to wooe long, some yeare two or more before they marye, and in that tyme they haue strange liberty of Conversation together, yet with vncredible honesty for the most parte, conversing together by day and by night, and slyding on the yce to remote townes to feast and lodge there all night. Yea some that are betroathed make long voyages, as to the East Indies, before they be maryed, and in all voyages where the master of the shipp is a wooer, they hang a garland of Roses on the topp of the mayne mast. The frendes of the marryed Coople, vse to present them with meate for the feast, and the guests are invited a day before, and agayne invited some hower before they goe to church, or before the dinner. For they goe to Church more priuately then in Germany, without marching through the streetes in any Pompe, or with great Company, some-where only going to

Church with nyne, other where with three of theire neerest
frendes and strangers of other townes. I haue seene some
maryed without a ringe, only Joyning handes insteede thereof.
Som maryed at tenne in the morning, and theire dinner begane
at two, and ended at six of the Clocke in the after noone, hauing
no supper, or the tables taken away, but going to daunce in
other Roomes, and retorning to the table to drincke, when they
pleased. Others maryed at three in the after noone, and supped
from six to twelue. And after the meales, strangers vsed to
come in to the daunceing. The second day of the marryage they
invited neere frendes of the towne, only to supper and dauncing,
and the third day in like sorte they invited neighbours and
ordinary frendes. Some day or two before the maryage, and
agayne some day or two after the maryage, the young men
and virgins were invited, to daunce after supper, when theire
Fathers, mothers, and all other were gonne to bedd, where they
daunced all night, and at the twilight in the morning, they
daunced about some of the next streetes, and so taking theire
leaues went home.

For Funeralls, they vse small or no pompe in them, nether
remember I in those Prouinces to haue seene any monumentes,
or so much as graue stones for the memory of the dead, except
one Monnument at Delph, erected to the memory of the Prince
of Orange, which was the poorest that ever my eyes behealde,
espetially for so famous a Prince, and one that merited so much
of the Vnited Provinces. Some gentlemen and others of the
best sorte dying, had theire Armes sett vpon theire doores for
a yeare following, and the widowe so long kept her house, no
man for halfe a yeare entering her Chamber, nor any speech
being made to her till the yeare was ended for any second
maryage.

The wemen are sayd to be delliuerd ordinaryly of theire
Children with much more ease then those of other nations,
(excepting onely the Irish) but ill Conceptions are frequent
among them, and very paynefull in the delivery. Of these
monsters I harde incredible reports, from very Credible persons,

which modesty forbides mee to write, espetially since the
Curious may easily be informed thereof by many English who
haue liued long in that Country. Only I will say that some
of them haue beene of such vivacity and nimblenes in leaping,
as the wemen had much adowe to kill & destroy them, and that
some attribute these frequent effects to the peoples grosse
feeding, and liuing much vpon waters.

For Baptisme, the minister in the Pulpitt hauing read the
vseuall wordes, the Deacon standing belowe, pronounced a
blessing to the Chyld, and sprinckled it with water. The Boyes
haue two Godfathers and two Godmothers, and so haue the
girles, whereas our boyes haue but one Godmother and two
godfathers and our girles but one godfather and two godmothers. And howsoeuer ordinarily they haue no more but
two, yet some (as with vs) haue a greater number, being a
thinge at pleasure; most commonly the mothers nurse theire
Children themselues. Guifts are giuen both to the Children
and to the Norses according to theire qualityes, but neuer
great in value so farr as I obserued.

For a womans lying in Childebed. If shee haue a boy, the
ringe of her dore is all Covered with tape or linnen Cloth (and
in some places vndersett with a small sticke) and over the ringe
a face cloath is fastned. If it be a girle, the ring is but halfe
covered, and is not vndersett, but hath also a facecloth, and as
many Children as shee hath, so many facecloathes they fasten
aboue the ringe of the doore, which are richly wrought, or
playne & Course, according to the quality of the Parents. They
lye a month in Childbed (as our wemen vse in England) and
then are Churched, the minister prayinge with them, and when
the dutyes are payde to him, they retourne home and Feast
together.

Customes Exercises Pastymes particularly of Hunting Hawking Birding and Fishing.

Among their Customes, some seemed very strange to me.
My selfe landing at Dockam in Friesland, after a great tempast

at Sea, incountred this recreation in the Inn. There were
newly aryved young gentle wemen of spetiall worth and
beauty, who supped not priuately in theire Chambers, according
to the Custome of England, but at the publike table for all
passengers, and after supper wee retyred to the fyer, where
formes were sett round about it, and Flagons of Beare sett to
warme at the fyer, (as they Commonly drincke warme beare)
and if a man druncke to a woman, he carryed her the Cupp, and
kissed her, and a woman drincking to a man, caryed the Cupp
to him, and kissed him not so much as bending his head to
meete her, And so with fayre discourse wee passed two howers
before wee retyred to our Chambers. This is the generall
Custome in all Fresland, so as some husbandes haue quarrelled
with men, for not kissing theire wyues and daughters at the
deliuery of the Cupp to them, as if they thought them not
worthy of that Curtesy, or dispised them, as poore, foule, or
reputed infamous. But nothing is more strang, then that this
Custome though performed in much mirth and cheerefullnes
yet is free from the least suspition of vnchastity. Agayne it is
generally obserued that as the wemen of these Provinces
overtopp the men in number (which I formerly shewed) so they
commonly rule theire famylyes. In the morning they giue
theire husbandes drincking mony in their pursses, who goe
abroade to be merry where they list, leaving theire wyues to
keepe the shop and sell all thinges. And nothing is more
frequent, then to see the girles to insult and domineere (with
reproofes and nicknames) ouer theire brothers, though ellder
then they be, and this they doe from the first vse of speech, as
if they were borne to rule ouer the malles. Yea many wemen
goe by Sea to traffique at Hamburg for marchantdize, whyle
theire husbandes stay at home. At Leyden young wenches of
12 or 13. yeares age, after 9 of the Clocke in the morning,
shamed not ordinarily to doe those necessityes of nature in the
open and fayre streetes, which our wemen will not be seene to
doe in private houses. In the same Citty I haue seene men
milke Cowes, and carry the milke in two payles fastned to a

wooden yoke before them, which they wore about theire neckes.
The wemen, vpon their bedds head insteed of a pillowe, haue a
shorte hard Coushen, litle and vneasy to rest vpon, so as they
say it is rather for a secret vse, then for rest of their heades.

The colde of winter is very sharpe in these Provinces, lying
open to the Sea Northward, without any shelter of hills or
woodes, for which cause some wemen of the best sorte wore
breeches, of lynnen or silke stuffes, to keepe them warme, but
commonly the wemen sett with fyer vnder them, in passetts
namely litle pans of Coales within a case of woode boared
through with many hole on the topp, which remedy spotting
the body is lesse convenient then wearing of breeches.   And
these Passets they not only vse at home, but in the Churches,
and in theire Jorneyes by Shipp and by waggon. So as my
selfe passing in a waggon stroaded thicke with strawe to keepe
our feete warme sawe a young woman in great distresse, who
vsing this passett, and therewith setting the strawe on fyer
vnder her and that setting fyer on her Cloathes, was forced to
vse the vndecent helpe of men, and yet hardly escaped the
burning of her body.

They strawe the paued floures of theire howses with Sand,
to keepe them Cleaner, but the dirty shooes of them that enter,
Clodding the Sand, they seeme to foule theire howses themselues, for feare other should foule them.

Holland and Zeland are devided from Brabant and Flanders,
as likewise Zeland is devided into Ilandes and from Holland, by
an Arme of the Sea within land. In like sorte Holland on the
other syde is diuided from Freesland, and that from the
Empire, by two other Armes of the Sea. And many Riuers
falling into these Calme Seas, with a gentile Course, in
Countryes lying lowe and playne, haue giuen the inhabitants
commodity to Cutt frequent ditches, not only to make passages
by water from towne to towne, but also to compasse their
pastures and meadowes with ditches full of water, either
standing or very gently moving. And the colde is so extreme
in these partes, as most parte of winter these ditches of water

are Continually frozene. So as the Virgins in winter tyme are most braue in apparell, and haue most Jollity of meetinges with young men. For they both daly walke into the fieldes next the townes, and vpon the broadest waters slyde together vpon the yce. To which purpose they putt vpon theire shooes Pattens of wood, with a long sharpe Iron in the bottome to Cutt the yce, Continually mooving and frigging theire feete vp and downe, forwardes, or in Circle, which motion mee thought was not very modest for wemen, but if they stand still they are sure to fall, and those that are vnskillfull thereby take many and sometymes dangerous falls. Commonly some two or foure hundreth will slyde together vpon ane peece of yce, seeming not able to beare them, yet vse makes them bolde to venture, though sometymes it giues dangerous Crackes. A man and a woman, holding a handcherker betweene them, slyde together, and sometymes many Couples in like sort holding handkerchees slyde together a breast as many as the bredth of the yce will beare. And in like sort many men laying theire handes on a Coulestaffe slyde abreast together. Also the frost for great part of winter is so great, as sometymes for a month or more, the foresayde Armes of the Sea wilbe so Frozen, as men passe ouer them, either slyding vpon the sayd Pattens, or vpon a sledge drawne with a horse, and in the midd wayes, vpon divers passages, men keepe boothes wherein they haue a pann of Coales to warme the passengers, with drincke and meate to refresh them. They vse to lay great wagers vpon each first breaking of the Ice, and at those tymes many rash venturers are cast away. At Delph a man had 300. Guldens for venturing to slyde ouer the towne ditch one Christmas day, when the Ice began to breake. At Amsterodam one had tenne pounde sterling to venture over the Teye, and the first venturer ouer the Armes of Sea, after a frost beginns to breake, hath ordinaryly two Dollours rewarde, and a Gulden for drincking mony. The wemen of these parts giue great liberty to theire daughters. Sometymes by chance they slyde on the yce till the gates of the Citty be locked, and the young men feast them at Inns in the Subbarbs, all the night, or till they please to take rest. Sometymes the young men and virgins agree to slyde on the yce, or to be drawne with horses vpon sledges to Cittyes 10. 20. or more myles distant, and there feast all night, and this they doe without all suspition of vnchastity, the hostesses being carefull to lodge and oversee the wemen. In like sorte the mothers of good fame permitt theire daughters at home, after themselues goe to bedd, to sett vp with young men all or most part of the night, banqueting and talking together, yea with leaue and without leaue to walke abroade with young men in the streetes by night. And this they doe out of a Customed liberty, without preiudice to theire fame, wheras the Italian wemen strictly kept thincke it folly to omitt any opportunity they can gett to doe ill.

As the Germans, so this people, vse to builde nests for Storkes, and repute them lucky birdes hanting only free Commonwealths, as best obseruers of Justice. At Leyden (and so I thincke in other Cittyes) If the Cry for fyer be raysed, he that owes the house payes six Gulldens for penalty, and the night watch men of townes and Cittyes goe about the streetes making a noyse with wooden Clappers, as ours doe with litle bells, and at Leyden by night a Trompett in the steeple is sounded each hower, when the Clocke strikes.

The kennells of the streete are not in the midest, as Commonly with vs, but are made on each syde of the streete one, neere the houses, the Pauement on each syde rising to the midest of the streete, which is highest, and the cheefe place of dignity for walking, the next being the right hand of the midest, and the third the left hand, and so in order, according to the number that walkes together.

The Bishopricke of Vtrecht, and the Prouince of Gellderland, keepe the old Callender, but Holand obserues the newe of Pope Gregory, so as if a man goe from Holland to Vtrecht or Gellderland vpon the fourtenth of December, and retorne into Holland vpon the 24. of December, he shall keepe no Christmas day that yeare, and if a man come from Vtrecht or Gellderland to Leyden, the fourteenth of December, and retorne backe to those parts the 24. of December, he shall keepe two Christmas dayes in one yeare, Contrarye to our English proverb, inviting to mirth because Christmas comes but once a yeare.

Since the tyme of the warr, all passengers entring into Cittyes and Forts, leaue theire swordes and weapons with the Soldyers at the place where they keepe guarde, and the next day when they goe forth there receave them agayne.

I haue formerly sayd, that the wagonours, while their horses be fresh, namely before they haue gone halfe way to the next bayting place, giue the way to all waggons they meete, but after they haue gone more then halfe the way, in like sorte take the way of all they meete. At the dayes of old victoryes or theire Progenitours great Actions, they keepe Feasts, and in triumph make bonfyers, and represent the Action in playes poorely acted by Artizans.

Pastymes Exercises Huntinge Hawkinge Birding Fishing.

For Pastymes and exercises. I haue formerly spoken of theire daly Pastime and exercise all the tyme of winter, in slyding vpon yce with Iron in theire wooden Pattens, and of theire making Jorneys, for pleasure and necessety, vpon a sledge drawne over the Ice with one horse. Now I will only add that this motion of slyding vpon the Ice is very swift, some say after one 100th myles in the day, but I am sure it is vullgarly spoken, that when Leyden was besidged by the Spaniardes, who helde guardes of Soldyers on both sydes the narrowe waters leading to the towne, which at that tyme were frozen, messengers slyding on these Pattens daely passed through the sayd guardes with letters to and from the towne, and so swiftly, as the Spaniardes sometymes seeing them, and making thicke shott against them on both sydes of the water, yet could not hinder theire Continuall passing. Likewise in Jorneyes by sledges, they often passe from Leyden to Harlam and backe agayne in one day, which is tenn Fleemish myles and requireth tenn howers to be runne by waggon, laying another waggon and fresh horses in the midd way. They haue a Common Pastyme and exercise to dryue a litle ball through the feildes and vpon the Ice, with a sticke of wood turning in at the lowe end, like the basting ladells we vse in kichens, saue that they are not made hollowe but are rounde in the end, and this sporte I haue seene frequently vsed not only by boyes and young men, but by men of 40. yeares age and vpward. They haue in all Cittyes publike houses, with a larg yeard and garden, vulgarly called Dooles, (whereof Amsterodam had three) in which houses the Cittizens meete both men and wemen to drincke and eate, and in the large yardes the men exercise shooting with the long bowe and Crosse bowe. For these very sportes the Cittisens are devided into brotherhoods, and putt vnder ensignes, and many of the cheefe brothers haue their Pictures in these houses. They shoote at a Parratt of wood, and he that wins the Prise, is called the king of the Parratt.

For hunting Hawking and Birding, Marchantius writing of Flanders, which Province hath giuen the name of Flemings to all the Netherlanders of the seuenteen Provinces, setts downe the lawes of Hunting and Hawking in the leafe 107. and 108 and shewes that Hunting of Hares, and takeing of many Foules, as Partriges, Phesants, and the like, are appropriated to gentlemen. But I thincke he writes this of Flanders, Brabant, and the partes within land, for in the vnited Provinces lying vpon the Sea, the gentlemen of Holand and Zealand are almost rooted out, though in West Fressland and the other Provinces many gentlemen still remayne. And in Holland Zealand and Freesland all the feildes are compassed with frequent ditches of water, and with Armes of the Sea, so as they are not fitt for Hunting with dogs, or flying of Hawkes. Holland and Zealand haue some stoore of Partridges and like land Foule, which I haue seen sold to any that would buy them, by vulger men who tooke them by other ordinary meanes. And Freesland hath very great stoore of Sea foule, which (for ought I could heare) were taken by ordinary meanes, and solde by vulgar men without reserved priviledges. Nether did I euer see any vse of

Hunting dogs, or Hawkes in these Provinces though most parte of the Hawkes, brought from Norway and those parts into England and Fraunce, commonly passe through Freesland Holland, and Zealand.

For Fishing. They cannot but haue plenty of fish, lying vpon the ocion, and divers Armes of the Sea breaking into the land, and dwelling among frequent ditches of waters, and some great lakes, made by the Rivers, of Rheine in diuers branches, and of Mosa, and Mosella, where they gently fall towardes the Sea, or rather ende in standing waters. So as they haue plenty of all Sea fish, and in the Arme of the Sea entring betweene Zealand and Holand vp to Brabant, and in the River of Mosa, they take great plenty of Salmons, one towne of Bredaw for fishing there, paying yearely 4000. poundes to Count Mauritz lord of the towne. For fresh water fish, as the lakes and ditches are frequent, so haue they plenty of fish, and being industrious, they take more fish at Sea vpon the Coasts of England then wee doe, espetially the kyndes that are dryed and salted, as ling and herrings, both sortes fresh and salt they commonly dresse after one manner but [the latter] more swimming in buter, and (as the Germans) love to see the Fresh fish liuing, not prising that which is dead.

CHAPTER IIII.

Of Denmarke touching all the heades of the first Chapter.

[I omit entirely the Chapter on Denmark, Page of MS. 532—539, and the Chapter on Bohemia, Page 539—545.   In the latter Moryson describes the deserted state of the Prague University.   Charles V. took away its privileges, and the students flocked to the new German Universities, especially Leipzig.   Moryson saw six ruined Colleges "as one called the Kings, another the Queens, the third the College of Nations, which three had but 24 students in them."—C.H.]

CHAPTER V.

Of Bohemia, touching all the heades of the first Chapter.

CHAPTER VI.

Of Poland touching all the heades of the first Chapter.

Nature and Manners.

THE Polonians, espetially the cheefe part of them lying vpon the East syde of Germany, are discended if not of the same nations with the Bohemians, yet of neere bordering people (as I haue formerly shewed in the precedent Chapter and shall haue present occasion more largly to shewe, treating of the Polonian language) And though the Bohemians are as it were incorporated into the Empire of Germany, by hauing their king one of the Electours, and the Emperours for many ages hauing beene their kings, so as in nature and manners they are much conformed to the Germans, yet to this day they and the Polonians are in many thinges of like disposition. For the Polonians exceede the Bohemians in putting of hatts, with like salutations, and in all Curteous affability, saue that they seeme to doe it more out of pryde, seldome vseing Curtesy to any who doe not first honour them. In like sorte they exceede the Bohemians in giuing large titles of honour one to the other, as experience teacheth, and (if we may beleeve the Germans, who litle loue that nation) the inferiour sorte giue the title of Genade (that is Grace) to very Coachmen. The Bohemians (as I haue shewed) are a valyant nation by nature, but this valour is much tempered by the placability and moderation they haue Contracted from the Germans. But the Polonians besydes that they are naturally valyent, are more subiect to sudden passions, and out of pride apte to take small thinges in worde or deede for scornes and iniuryes, and so prone to quarrells, wherein they will assayle with any disparity or advantage of number. For

younger brothers gentlemen seruing or following the great
lords and gentlemen of Countryes (who are absolute lords with
power of life and death, all the people of the Country being
their slaues) they cleaue together like burrs in all quarrells.
Yet can I not say this proceedes from any base mynde, hauing
seene them apt to quarrell who had great disaduentage, as in
many other places, so at Dantzke, where the kings guard being
fewe in number, and lodged in the Subarbes, not admitted into
the Citty, yet a German Porter hapening to rush vpon one of
them, and after the blowe bidding him take heede, he had not
the patience to forbeare the Porter, but with his shorte sworde
almost cutt off his Arme, and thereby drewe the whole Citty
into Armes, against him and his fellowes.   But besyde the
Polonians bolde Courag, other thinges make them very prone
to quarrells and murthers, namely the excesse of drincking in
all sortes high and lowe, and the priviledges which great men
haue, particularly that a gentleman cannot be Condemned but
by a publike Parlament helde but once in three yeares, and by
voyces of gentlemen Commonly partiall one to the other, as also
the vse of gentlemen to beare out theire seruants and slaues in
all disorders, to their vttermost power.   So as the Germans say,
that in Poland they care no more to kill a man then a dogg.
The Country people, when they fyght, hold it more valour to
receaue a wounde without feare, then by skill to defende the
body, and commonly he that strikes bids his adversarye to
take heede to his head, or any other parte he meanes to strike,
who presently defendes that part and no other, for they use
not to falsifye theire wordes therein.   The Germans write the
Polonians to be inhospitable (I thincke for the respect of
quarrells) and flattering (I thincke in respect of the foresayd
Curtesey), and great drinckers (as in deede generally they are).
When I behelde the king to com by water, in a poore boate from
Crakaw to Dantzke, and the small provisions for him, his
Queene and Courtyers, of a fewe bottles of wyne, and a small
quantity of vittles, I Judged the Polonians to be very frugall,
but after by experience founde them rather prodigall, aswell

in Poland where they are generally bountifull as more spetially in Italy, where I obserued the sonnes of Castellandes (that is keepers of Castles for life) to spend theire whole patrimony in liuing aboue theire degree.   For they are great Travelars espetially into Italy and the Vniversityes of Germany, and howsoeuer the foresayd defects in nature and manners may generally be imputed to them, yet these travelers are very Curteous espetially to strangers and complete gentlemen in behauiour and many noble vertues, and perticularly free from that quarelsome disposition which is iustly imputed to the vulger sorte of gentlemen.

Bodyes and Witts.

The Polonians are Commonly tall of stature with bigg and strong limbes by reason of free education, and the loose garments they generally weare, and haue actiue bodyes, quick witts and great viuacity of spiritt, but exercise both the Abilityes of bodyes and myndes most in horsemanship.

Manuall Artes Sciences Vniversityes Language.

For Manuall Artes.   They are not industrious in them the Plebeans being borne slaues, who cannot exercise Trades to theire owne profitt but only for theire lordes vse, and the Cittisens liuing with traffick by wholesayle or retayling.   So as they haue fewe of Manuall Trades, and those only shooemakers and Taylors for dayly necessity.   All are Cookes for dressing theire owne meate, very gentlemen hauing skill to dresse theire owne Fish, in preparing wherof they are curious, and most vulgar men make theire owne shooes and all the apparrell they weare.

For sciences, there is not a ragged boy, nor a smith that shooes your horse, but he can speake latten readily the most corruptly of all I euer hard.   Their lawyers are well studyed in the Ciuill lawes, but I could not heare of any famous for skill in Phisicke or any profession of the liberall Sciences, nether haue we any or very fewe famouš Authors or writers of that nation, so farr as I suddenly remember theire gentlemen being for the most parte military men.

Vniversityes.

Touching Vniversityes, the Polonians haue one in the cheefe Citty Crakaw, but it hath only two Colleges nothinge lesse then fayrely built, called the great and the litle College, in which some fewe poore schollers were mantayned, and the Professors in them haue theire dyett and Schooles for reading of lectures they being all Pristes and so vnmaryed. The rest of the Students liue in Cittisens howses, but indeede there is small Concurse thether of Polonians themselues, much lesse of strangers. For the Polonian gentlemen commonly haue theire education in the great Cittyes and Vniversityes of Germany, Sweitzerland, Italy and Fraunce. In that vast kingdome they haue other Vniversities which in my cursory iourny I did not see as Vilna in Lituania and (as I heard) Gnesna.

Language.

Touching the Polonian language, I haue formerly sayd that the Bohemians descende from the Dalmations, and that they with the people of Illyris and other bordering Provinces, are by olde writers called Slavonians, which name is nowe proper to one Province lying with Dalmatia vpon the Gulfe of Venice; likewise I haue sayd, that the Polonians are by olde writers called Sarmations of which name some were in Asia called also Sythians, and other were of Europe, from whome the inhabitants of great Polonia seeme to me to haue theire originall, as the inhabitants of lesser Poland (in which lyes the Cheefe Citty and seate of the king) bordering vpon Bohemia and the Easterne partes of Germany, and likewise the Bohemians are discended from the foresayd old Dalmations or bordering nations, which of old by a common name are called Sclavonians.

For the historyes of Germany recorde, that about the yeare 550, two young Princes Lechus and his brother, to avoyde sedition at home, did leade out a great Colony of the sayd people, whereof parte with Lechus planted themselues in a Country of thick woodes after called Poland of the playne grownd, and the other brother with the rest seated themselues in Bohemia and Morauia. In a worde, the Bohemians, Morauians, Polonians, Lituanes, Moscovites, and Russians (as Munster a German writeth) haue one language, which some call the Sclavonian others the old Vandalls tounge, but differing some more some lesse in theire seuerall Dialects, and pronvntiations. The Polonians write theire wordes allmost all with Consonants, but must needes pronovnce them with Vowells, and howsoeuer so many Consonants cause asperity and distortion of the mouth in speaking, yet the gentlemen at this day pronovnce theire wordes gently vsing the consonants rather in theire penns then in theire speech. A learned stranger who had long liued in that king-dome, assured mee that the Polonians haue six letters more then wee, commonly vsed in theire speech, but I then forgatt to learne what these letters were. Diabolo (that is Devill) is as frequent in the mouthes of Polonian gentlemen, (who commonly living much in Italy haue from thence drawne this worde) as Catso is with the Italians, Futre with the French, and Das Dich Gott to the Germans, vpon all disdaines or passions. All the Polonians, yea very smithes and like Artizans, can speake the lattin tounge, and that roundly, but most falsly, for quantity of sillables, and for all the rules of Gramer. To this kingdome of Poland partayned of old many Provinces of Germany, then and at this day vseing the german toung, which nowe of long tyme haue beene divided from that Crowne, by warr, and con-tracts of maryages, namely the Provinces of Silesia, and Lusatia. (incorporated nowe to the kingdome of Bohemia) and Pomerania and Meckelburg hauing theire owne Dukes to this day and incorporated to the Empire of Germany.

Ceremonyes perticularly of maryages Funeralls Childe-bearinges and Christeninges.

Touching Ceremonyes, the Polonians vse litle reverence to theire king, much lesse to the chayre and Cloth of estate and regall ensignes in the Kinges absence, nether knowe they what it is to kneele on theire knees to the king.   Only when he eates, all people and strangers haue free accesse to see him, and when he drinckes all men in the roome putt of theire hatts, and the very Queene and ladyes rise vp in reverence.   Among the pompes and Cerimonyes of the Crowne, the generall meeting of all the Gentlemen vpon the Kinges death to chuse a newe king, is performed with great magnificence.   The meeting for this Election and Coronation is commonly neere Crakaw, and lasts some six weekes, all the Gentlemen lying in Tents like an Army taking vp some tenn myles compasse, and hauing a great Tent for the generall meetinges, and all this tyme nether the King nor the kingdome are charged with the expences of this multitude, but the cheefe Gentlemen (vpon whome the rest depend) haue theire owne provisions for them and their followers.

Maryage.

For maryages, I obserued at Crakaw, that the Bridegrome and Bride dined at the publike house of the Senate, and from thence after dinner marched orderly with theire frendes to theire dwelling house, with trumpitts sounding before them. In my shorte abode there I could not well knowe theire Ceremonyes and Customes, only I vnderstood by discourse; that the maryed partyes were betrothed before the tyme of maryage, and then were wedded with a Ring, and that they kept sumptuous Feasts, consisting most in plenty of Drinck, and therein more chargable because they haue Spanish wyne at a deare rate as farr fetched (vsing no French wynes, nor hauing any wyne growing, but vpon the frontyers in Hungary very good wyne but the Caryage by land making it deare, and in Austria, which is a sharpe and small wyne, besydes that they vse much spices, which are imported from remoted places and so very deare; that they haue also sumptuous banquets of sweete preserues.

Funeralls.

That in theire Funeralls, the dead are caryed to Church with a great Company to attend them, but they haue no such Doles to the poore, Drinckings, Dynners or banquets as wee vse. That they haue great Bells, but neuer towle them whyle the sick lye dying, who are only prayed for in the Church, only at the buiryall these Bells (hanging commonly in Churchyardes vncouered) are towled and iangled, neuer rung out or answering one the other in musicall tunes, nether vse they any knells after the tyme that the body is buiryed.

Childebearinge and Christenings.

That wemen lye in Childbed some six weekes after the distance betweene Christmas and the Feast of our ladyes Purification called Candlemas. And wheu they are Churched, they take some neighbors to accompany them, but the Priest vseth no Rite or Cerimony to the woman in the Church, nether keepe they any Feast at home. That the Common sort both male and female haue two Godfathers and two Godmothers, but gentlemen often haue twenty more or lesse, taking it for an honour to haue many. That they giue some halfe Doler to the nurse, and some Ducat or a peece of Plate to the Childe, as they are able, but never in such excesse or frequency of that charge, as by abuse of late is practised in England. That the mothers not being able to nurse their Children, take Nurses into their houses, but neuer send them out of dores to be nursed. And that they keepe a great Feast at the Christning of their Chilldren.

Customes.

Touching Customes. They haue a strange Custome, seeming to me ridiculous, because it is Contrary to nature, whereas Art is not commended but in the imitation of nature, namely that, as they take great pride in adorning the furniture of theire horses, so they paynt theire maynes, tayles, and the very bottomes of the bellyes most subiect to durt, with a Carnation Coulour, which nature neuer gaue to any horse.

Whereas the Germans forbidd shooting of peeces within many of theire Cittyes, at Crakaw in the cheefe Citty of Poland, they not only discharge peeces within the walls, but ordinarily walke with Pistolls charged, which is a dangerous Custome for a Nation so much giuen to quarrells, by nature, and for Common excesse in drincking.

The Polonians write not after the old style of all nations, but after the newe stile or Kalender of Pope Gregorye lately alltered.

They vse whole Clockes, striking 24 howers which beginn to strike one, when the sunne ryseth, and so the noone alters each month as the sunne varyeth the rising, in which sort allso the Clockes of Italy followe the Sunne.

Pastymes Exercises Hunting Hawkeing Birding and Fishinge.

For Pastymes and exercises. Though drincking swallowes vp most Pastymes and exercises, where it is a nationall vice, yet the Polonians being excessive Drinckers, doe also play very much at dyce and Cardes, and the gentlemen for deepe hazard of much mony, as two or three hundreth Guldens at a tyme, and they play much at Tables, Commonly Tick Tack and lurch, but never at Irish, whereof they haue no skill, Horsmanship is theire cheefe exercise, wherein they excell, as allso they are practised in other military exercises.

Hunting and Hawking.

For Hunting, and Hawking, thy sometymes vse these exercises, but not ordinarily, and howsoeuer some vse them more some lesse, yet are they farr from making it a whole dayes worke, yea the Continuall workes of dayes monthes and yeares, as very many great men in England doe.

As once in Bohemia so one in Poland, neere Crakaw, I did once meete a gentleman with his followers Hawking in the feildes, and never ells, as I traueled, did in any place see any exercise ether of Hunting or Hawking, which so frequently offers it selfe to passengers neere the high wayes of England.

Birding and Fishing.

For Birding (or fouling) and for fishing, my abode was so small in that kingdome, as I could make no observations fitt to be related. Only for Fishing, the situation within land barrs them from hauinge Sea fishes, but they haue greate plenty of Fishe in Riuers, Pondes, and lakes, and are generally noted by all strangers, to dresse them Curiously and with great Cost, the gentlemen not disdayning this Cookery with theire owne hands, but in any case they will see the Fish aliue, and otherwise will not eate it, but leaue it for the poore.

CHAPTER VII.

Of Turkey touching all the heades of the first Chapter.

[Moryson's personal impressions of Turkey have been so well put forth in the first Chapter of this volume that there is little freshness or brightness left for this later and rather laborious Chapter. Much of it is sheer repetition, and I have decided to omit the whole of it. It extends from Page 551 of the MS. to Page 579.—C.H.]

Booke V.

CHAPTER I.

Of the Italyans Nature and Manners, Bodyes and Witts, Manuall Artes, sciences, Vniuersities, language, Cerimonyes, particularly in Mariages, Childbearings, Christnings, and Funeralls as also of their diuers Customes, Pastimes, Exercises, particularly of theire hunting, hawking, Fouling, Burding, and Fishing.

Nature and Manners.

In the first booke and the second Chapter of the thired Part of this worke, among the proverbyall speeches of the Cittyes and Provinces of Italy, many thinges are formerly written, which may giue light to this discourse, but I omitt them here, to avoyde tediousnes, referring the reader to that place, who desyres to peruse them.   Now being to write of the Italyans, the Conquerers of the world, I will beginne with valour.   And therein I will lay this maxime for my grounde, that pryde and vayne glory may produce Actions of bestially boldnes, but no man can haue true fortitude in ventering his life, who is not well resolued of the happy being of his soule after death. Therefore as the old Romans Religion taught morall vertues and espetially fortitude in ventering life for theire Country to be the ready way to their Elizan feildes, so no men trode more warely and Constantly in those stepps, being in generall exemplary for posterity to imitate them therein. Yet I confesse that I doe not fully beleeue all the relations their historyes haue made of the old Roman fortitude, which were they never so false, yet nether the Conquered durst obiect the falshood against the Conquerers, nor coulde the contrary historyes of barbarous enemyes haue gotten Creditt against the Romans most eloquent and learned in those tymes, and I rather suspect

the same, because all travellers into Italy fynd at this day how
they did rayse hills to mountaynes, brookes to Riuers, and small
things to be reputed famous Monuments, and why may wee not
thincke they magnifyed in like sorte the Roman Actions aboue
the due proportion. Why should wee beleeue Liuy more in the
Actions of Curtius, of Manlius, of the Fabij, and like worthy
men, then in the sweating of stones, Nodding of Images, and
like supperstitious Miracles. And since he putt Orations into
the mouthes of dead men who neuer spake them liuing, why
might he not impute braue actions to dead men who neuer did
them liuinge, or at least did them not in such high measure.
And if I graunt all his relations to be true, yet remember that
braue Actions may be imputed to true fortitude which proceede
from pride and vayne glory, more proper to the nature of the
old Romans, and of all Italians to this day, then any other
nation. Further I will boldly say that the Romans Conquered
the worlde not so much by fortitude, as other meanes. For
when learning in all sciences and espetially eloquence were
founde in Asia, the Empires of the worlde followed them. When
the Grecians had learning and eloquence, they allso had the
Empire of the world, and when they became barbarous, then
the Romans hauing learned from them all sciences and
powerfull eloquence, they drewe therewith the Empire to
themselues, and no doubt they gott this Empire espetially by
witty Art and pollicy, and by their true vertues, of Justice,
Temperance, and the like, subduing all mens hearts to them,
or at least by ostentation of these vertues. So they subdued the
Grecians by pretence to defende theire libertyes. So they
subdued the Galles by norishing and assisting the factions of
the Sequani and Hedui. So they subdued barbarous nations by
feeding their factions and helping the weaker. In like sorte
they long mantayned this Empire by Constancy in theire
Actions, and provident wisdome to keepe what they had gott,
which vertues are helde proper to men borne in that Clyme.
They gott and strengthned this Empire by making the Roman
tounge Common to all nations conquered by them, and by

the fame of theire Justice, but espetially by making the most
noble of the Conquered free of their Citty, and very Senatours
of Rome, wherby they were made partners of farr greater power
and honour at Rome, then they had lost at home. As also by
planting and transporting of Colonyes. But touching fortitude,
I graunt that the old Romans were more valient then the other
Italians whome they Conquered by their owne power, as to
this day the Souldyers of Romagna and Marchia are the best in
Italy, yet I will boldly say that much fame was attributed to the
Romans which duely belonged to the famous legions of the
Brittans and the Bataui, and to other barbarous legions who
were all made free of the Citty of Rome, and gladly tooke to
themselues the name of Romans and whome the Romans vsed
in their greatest Actions, and the subdueing of other nations
to them. The Barbarous Invndations of the Normans, Goathes,
Vandalles & Hunnes, and Lombardes, had the name of the
nation first mouuing them, and the same had also the reputation
of all Victoryes. Yet no doubt their Armyes in great parte
consisted of great Multitudes and the most resolute men of other
nations, ioyning with them as they passed through their
Countryes. So the Romans were the leaders and cheefe men in
their Armyes, and had the honour of all victoryes in which
notwithstanding they were assisted with forayne legions who
being reputed Romans and vsing the Romayne disciplyne, were
the cheefe causes of their good successes. To conclude this
point it will appeare that to conquer the world, the Romans in
their wisdome and policy made more vse of forrayne fortitude
then their owne, if wee consider how in the declining of that
Empire, they hauing the same vertues, and being only forsaken
of their forayne assistants, and so standing vpon their owne
valour and strength, haue bene euer since troden vnder the
feete by forayne nations. Did not the foresayde Invndations of
barbarous people overflowe and conquer all Italy without any
memorable resistance, or one braue battle fought by them in
defence of their Country, which they so much loue and esteeme.
Did not the French and after the German Emperours for many

ages keepe them vnder, and giue them lawes without any
memorable resistance made by them with the sworde, tho by
other practises they often anoyd those Emperours, haue not the
Italians had small or no part in the warrs of Europe from that
tyme to this day, and that litle which they haue done in that
kynde, haue they not done it more by forayne forces hyred for
their mony, then by theire owne. And why should wee not
beleeue that the old Romans conquered the world more by
strength of their witt art and policy, then by the force of
Armyes, since wee see the Roman Bishopes, without force of
their owne Armes, but only by forayne Armes vsed to their
assistance, and by trickes of witt and spirituall bugbeares, haue
more subiected the world to them, then euer the old Romans
coulde doe by theire owne, or by forayne swordes assisting them.

Now I will speake of the Italians in our tyme, wherein I
pray you remember my former maxime, that braue actions of
boldnes may proceede from pride and vayne glory, but no man
can with true corrage putt his life in hazarde, who is not perswaded of the goodnes of his cause, and of his sowles well being
after death. When the Popes of old raysed Armyes by the
preaching of the Crosse, that is by his full pardon of sinnes and
freedome from Purgatory graunted to all Soldyers dying in that
quarrell, no doubt they fought with more corage, because they
thought the cause good, and their sowles assured of eternall
happines. But the truth is that as of old when the Popes were
apposed by forayne kings, the Italyans haue then beene obserued
most to vphold them, for the dignity and wealth of Italy, and
when they were most honored abroade, the most to dispise them,
as litle fearing their spirituall thuntherbolts, so in these
dayes, the Italyans haue small confidence in these papall pardons and spirituall promises, and somuch loue their owne earth,
as they will not giue the seene and felt pleasures it yealdes
them, for the vnseene and vnfelt ioyes of heaven, hauing a
Common Prouerb, Qui c' ha buon' pan' et boun' Vino, chi sa se
ci n' ha in Paradiso, I Frati ne ciarlano, ma sanno nulla—that
is, here is good bread and good wyne, who knowes if any such

be in Paradice, the Fryers prate therof but knowe nothing. And indeede they are so diffident in all their spirituall hopes, as they feare nothing so much as death, according to their proverb, Ogni Tormento piu presto che la Morte, that is, all torment rather then death. Then how can these men haue true valor. In their nature they are most impatient of any the least reproch or iniury, but the common sort reveng them by fighting at Cuffes (being allowed no vse of weapons). And the greater men by treasonable murthers. The Popes howesoeuer they vse to kindle fyer in forayne kingdomes, yet haue allwayes beene carefull to keepe it from Italy, lest it might happen to scorch the solder of their triple Crownes, and the Italyans seldome serue in forayne warrs, yet if I graunt that some fewe Italyans of late tymes haue proued famous in Naples and Netherland, and done great Actions in those seruices, notwithstanding fewe particulars cannot proue a generall assertion, and why may not those braue actions proceede from pryde and vayne glory, to which the Italyans aboue all Nations are subiect, rather then from the vertue of true fortitude. For in like sorte and for the same cause, the Italyans sometymes make most sumptious feasts yet are not thereby reputed liberall or bountifull, being generally in their nature frugall, and in this particular expence sordidly base. Nothing is more proper to pride then to circomvent enemyes for revenge of wronges by treason and vpon all disadvantages, yet this is so bredd in the bone of the Italyans, as it will neuer out of their nature. Also it is a manifest token of cowardise to vse no measure in reveng, as fynding no safety but in the death of him who hath in any small measure wronged them, wherevpon it is proverbyally sayd, that it is better to fall into the handes of a valiant then of a proude enemy, yet this kynde of Reueng is generally most proper to the Italyans nature. For Combatts or single fighting, being equall tryalls of honour by the sworde, the Councell of Trent hath severely forbidden them, and not only the fighters but the very beholders are punished with the most seuere Censures of the Church, instituted at first to represse

most haynous sinnes. And this priuate revenge was most iustly
forbidden, if the same Act had prouided to repayre temporall
honour, without which our corrupt nature cannot be subdued to
Christian patience in bearing wrongs. But the Italyans being
still as impatient as euer to beare the least Iniurye, and hauing
gotten this fayre pretence to avoyde equall Combatts (which in
their nature they litle loued and seldome practised before) from
that tyme haue exercised all revenges vpon all advantages, of
nombers, of weapons, and of places, with many followers and
most deadly weapons assayling their enemyes, though vnarmed
and alone yea naked in bed and perhapps sleeping. Nether is
any reuenge lesse then death (except towardes Harlotts whome
they are content to mangle and marke in the face) for the dead
bite not, but the liuing may agayne revenge the wronge offered
them. Or if sometymes' one man perhapps challenging another to single fight, they doe it after a childish and ridiculous
manner. My selfe at Syenna sawe two gentlemen fall at
defiance in the streete, who hauing each his sworde and
Gauntlett, yet agreed to goe home and take more Compleate
Armes, and then to retourne to fyght, not in the fielde, but
(forsooth) in the markett place, whether after an howers space
these Champions retorned, armed as the Proverbe is, Fin' alle
stinche et al' buco del culo: that is to the very skinne bones,
and the shamefull part behinde, and there they slashed a blowe
or two with the peoples great applause of their Corrage, because
their faces were not Armed, but presently the sargants (whome
they could not but expect) came to parte the fray, and Carry
them 'to the governour. Then for many dayes, till the
governours could take vp the quarrell, these gentlemen with
some hundreths of Armed followers, after a Thrasonicall manner
walked the streetes, one of the Companyes walking neere the
Easterne, the other at the Westerne gate of the Citty, to avoyde
meeting; at last the Governour hauing called certayne Bravoes
from Milan for that purpose, discussing all points of honour,
made peace betweene them. These Bravoes are a generation of
swaggerours, abounding in Lombardy, who daily weare some

thirty poundes weight of Iron to Arme their bodyes for defence, and are to be hyred for mony to fyght with any man, and to doe any murther, yea stand vpon their Creditts and honestyes (forsooth) in performing these wicked actions. My selfe and some worthy gentlemen in England knowe it to be true, that one of them hyred to kill a gentleman in Genoa, tooke him alone in his Closett, where bidding him prepare to dye, and the gentleman vnderstanding by whome he was hyred to kill him, and for what mony, gaue him a farr greater price to kill him that hyred him, which he also tooke with promise to effect it, but the gentleman thinking thus to escape, he answered that it lay vpon his creditt to kill him, hauing receaved mony and promised to doe it, but he might dye Comforted, that his enemy should not long outliue him. So he killed him, and within fewe dayes his aduersary also. Are not these murtherers honest men of their worde. These Bravoes are most subtille disputers in pointes of honour, and will cutt an hayre in giuing euery man his due. As indeede the Italyans generally can excellently dispute of honour and like vertues. But as it was sayde that the Athenians knewe good, but the Lacedemonians did it, so I may say that the Italyans knowe but the Transalpines doe actions of honour. Behold what the Fathers of Trent haue donne by forbidding Combatts, which hath produced willfull Murthers. Beholde howe the Italyans effect these murthers, not by their owne but by their followers swordes. For as each Harlott among them hath a Bravo to defend her from wrong, so almost each gentleman hath at least one Bravo to depend vpon him and execute his revenges. To conclude if an Italyan be wronged, he is very likely to take revenge, and that very deepe beyond the quallity of the offence, but he will neuer fight vpon equall tearmes with his Adversarye, and whether this basenes be naturall (as to men abounding and transported with worldly pleasures), or by custome and practise be growen into a second nature, surely it is much increased not only by the decree of the Councell of Trent, but also by the government of all Princes, seuerely punishing all quarrells, and (in imitation of Numa

Pompilius) by superstition somuch allaying military courage in the people, as they haue altogether extinguished it. And because they oppresse their subiectes so as they dare not trust them, and therefore in all their warrs are only confident in their treasure, by which they hyre forayne soldyers, they make their subiectes yet more dasterdly by forbidding them the ordinarye vse of any weapons, but only in Jorneys by the high way, wherein also they must depose them into the hands of the Guarde at the gate of euery Citty, which prouing troublesome, and costly in the paying those who carry them to the Inne (and deliuer them to the host to be keept till they take horse) they seldome weare any weapons in Jorneyes. This vse of Armes is forbidden in all partes vnder the payne of fyfty Crownes or some like penalty. In the Popes state they who weare a sworde by the high waye, yet may not in any place weare a dagger, as fitt to doe suddayne muscheefe, for which cause at Lucca a man may not carry a knife except it be blunted at the point. And in all places for the same cause, Pistolls and all shorte weapons easye to be hidd are strictly forbidden. In the State of Florence, most safe from theeues and murtherers, some are permitted in the Citty by espetiall leaue to weare swordes, but no man may carry other defensiue Armes, as Coates of male, litle headpeeces and Gauntlets, which all may weare in Lumbardy, where murthers also abound. And generally a long peece or Muskett may not be carryed except the locke be taken fro mthe stocke. So as the common sorte not vsed to carry weapons are afrayd of a swordes pointe as of Joues thunderbolte. They who haue license to Cary swordes in the Cittyes, yet must not weare them when the euening beginns to be darke, or at any tyme going abroade in the night. At Padoa a stranger ignorantly discharging a Pistoll at his windowe by night, was carryed to the Podesta, and deepely fynned.

By this Nature, or practise growing to a second nature, the Italyans aboue all other nations, most practise revenge by treasons, and espetially are skillfull in making and giuing poysons. For which treasons the Italians are so warye,

espetially hauing a quarrell, as they will not goe abroade nor
yet open their doores to any knocking by night, or somuch as
putt their head out of a windowe to speake with him that
knockes. For poysons the Italians skill in making and putting
them to vse hath beene long since tryed, to the perishing of
kings and Emperours by those deadly potions giuen to them in
the very Chalice mingled with the very precious blood of our
Redeemer. Insomuch as Rodulphus of Habspurg the first
Emperour of the house of Austria among the Germans, first
refused to enter Italy with an Army, for the Receaving of the
Imperiall Crowne at Rome, as other Emperours had formerly
donne, hauing obserued many of them to haue perished by
poyson, and other treasons closely carryed, with the breaking
of their whole Armyes, and for his so doing borowed the Foxes
reason, being affrayde to visitt the lyon in his Denn as other
beasts did.

> Because their stepps forwarne my deadly wrack
> all tending towards thee, none turned back.

In our tyme, it seemes the Art of Poysoning is reputed in
Italy worthy of Princes practise. For I could name a Prince
among them, who hauing composed an exquisite poyson and
counterpoyson, made proofe of them both vpon condemned men
giuing the poyson to all, and the Counterpoyson only to some
condemned for lesse Crymes, till he had found out the working
of both to a minute of tyme, vpon diuers complections and ages
of men. The history of Pope Alexander the sixth, and the
Duke his sonne (for that Pope first avowed and publikely
accknowledged his Chilldren, which other Popes vse to call their
Nephewes and Neeces) hauing prepared poyson for two
Cardinalls they had invited to dyne with them in a garden, and
themselues by the providence of God being poysoned with the
same poyson they had prepared for the Cardinalls: and the
history of a late Dutches of Italy, hauing prepared poyson for a
Cardinall her husbands brother, and therewith by the same
providence of God destroying her husband, and vpon dispayre

of the accident her selfe voluntarily taking the same, are
historyes pleasant to reade, and of good vse to obserue, but I
will not inlarge them here, because in this worke I haue
formerly related the last of them falling in our age, and both
are otherwise famously knowne in historyes and the mouthes of
liuing men.

The Italians haue beene of old, and still are, very factious,
and apt to take partes in priuate murthers and publike seditions.
Of old when the Popes began to pull downe the Emperours who
had exalted them, all Italy was deuided and rent in peeces by
the faction of the Guelphs and Gibellines one holding with the
Emperour the other with the Pope. And in late tymes it hath
also beene generally devided into the faction of Spayne and
Fraunce. Also some particuler Cittyes haue beene noted to be
more spetially adicted to these generall factions, and continually
to domesticall factions among themselues. Genoa is a great
free Citty and hath great Familyes, and hath euer beene subiect
to be rent in peeces with domesticall seditions, more spetially by
the faction of the Adorni and the Fregosi. The Citty Pistoica
is nowe subiect to the Duke of Florence, but hath the name
of the Plague from the seditious soldyers and followers of the
Roman Catiline who infected with the Plague, first inhabited it.
And they left a posterity adicted aboue all others to seditious
Factions, by which the Citty hath suffered many calamityes,
more spetially by two Factions, first of Neri and the Bianchi,
and after of the Cancellieri and the Panzodici. In generall
these names of factions haue beene extinguished in processe of
tyme, but to this day the Familyes vnder other names retayne
the old hatred, and are very suspitious one of the other, and
ready to offer mutuall iniuryes. Also generally these factions
were of old distinguished by diuers fashions of wearing the
hatt, of drincking on diuers sydes of the Cupp, and the like, and
by diuers signes worne, vpon the most visible partes of the
body, and in diuers fashions, and vpon contrary sides of the
body. Nether are these distinctions altogether left to this day,
so as the Duke of Florence a litle before my being there, did

by a seuere Edict forbidd the Pistoians vpon no lesse then payne
of death, to weare Roses or any of the vsed signes, as provoking
and stirring vp myndes of seditious men to the old factions.

The Italyans in all their Councells are close, secrett, crafty,
and the greatest dissemblers in the world, wherof I could giue
nomberlesse instances, but take one for a taste, of Fraunces
Duke of Milan, who by his Ambassadors aduised the French
king Lewis the eleuenth, that being ouerlayde with many
enemyes at once, he should vpon any Conditions make peace
with all but the greatest, and turne all his forces vpon him who
being overcome, he might easily fynde occasions to single out
the rest and subdue them one after another. Thus the Italyans
being by nature false dissemblers in their owne actions, are also
most distrustfull of others with whome they deale or converse,
thincking that no man is so foolish to deale playnly, and to
meane as he speakes, For which cause the Pope and the Princes
of Italy neuer take Italyans for the guarde of their bodyes, but
onely Sweitzers or Germans which nations they repute faithfully
minded, free from treasons, and strong of body to appose Treason
attempted by others, and to execute for them any buisines
requiring trust, and a dull brayne not searching into the Justnes
of proceeding, but doeing what they are commanded. For
which cause also the Bakers of bread in most partes of
Lombardy, as hauing meanes to betray men by poyson, are not
Italyans, but Commonly Germans.

For fleshly lusts, the very Turkes (whose carnall Religion
alloweth them) are not somuch transported therewith, as the
Italyans are (in their restraynt of Ciuill lawes and the dreadfull
lawe of God). A man of these Northerly partes can hardly
beleeue without the testimony of his owne eyes and eares, how
chastity is laughed at among them, and hissed out of all good
company, or howe desperate adventures they will make to
atchiue disordinate desyre in these kyndes. As the Germans
louing drinck themselues, are so tender hearted to their horses
that they hinder them not from drincking whensoeuer they putt
downe their heades for that purpose, though the waters scarcely

couer their shooes, so the Italyans are so farr from keeping
their horses from mares, as in Lombardy where both commonly
stand in one stable, the Ostlers (as my selfe founde by
experience) will by night vntye gentlemens horses to make
themselues sporte with their Couering of Mares.   In Italy
marryage is indeede a yoke, and that not easy, but so grevious,
as bretheren no where better agreeing, yet contend among
themselues to be free from marryage, and he that of free will
or by perswasion will take a wife to continue their posterity,
shalbe sure to haue his wife and her honour as much respected
by the rest, as if shee were their owne wife or sister, besyde
their liberall contribution to mantayne her, so as themselues
may be free to take the pleasure of wemen at large.   By which
liberty (if men only respect this world) they liue more happily
then other nations.   For in those frugall Commonwealths the
vnmaryed liue at a small rate of expences, and they make small
conscience of fornication, esteemed a small sinne and easily
remitted by Confessors.   Whereas other nations will liue at any
charge to be maryed, and will labour and suffer wants yea begg
with a wife, rather then haue the stinge of Conscience and
infamy by horing.   The wemen of honour in Italy, I meane
wiues and virgins, are much sooner inflamed with loue, be it
lawfull or vnlawfull, then the wemen of other nations.   For
being locked vp at home, and covered with vayles when they
goe abroade, and kept from any conversation with men, and
being wooed by dumb signes, as walking twise a day by their
howses kissing of the Posts therof, and like fopperies, they are
more stirred vp with the sight and much more with the
flattering and dissembling speeches of men, and more credulous
in flattering their owne desyres, by thincking the sayd poore
actions of woeing to be signes of true loue, then the wemen
of other nations hauing free conversation with men.   In
generall the men of all sortes are Caryed with fierce affections
to forbidden lusts, and to those most which are most forbidden,
most kept from them, and with greatest cost and danger to be
obtayned.   And because they are barred not only the speech

and conversation but the least sight of their loue (all which are allowed men of other nations) they are carryed rather with a blynde rage of passion and a strong Imagination of their owne brayne, then with true contemplation of Vertues, or the power of beauty, to adore them as Images, rather then loue them as wemen. And as nowe they spare no cost, and will runne great dangers to obtayne their lustfull desyres, so would they persue them to very madnes, had they not the most naturall remedy of this passion ready at hand to allay their desyres, namely Harlotts, whome they call Curtizans, hauing beauty and youth and whatsoeuer they can imagine in their mistres, besydes the pleasure of change more to delight them, so driuing out loue with loue, as one nayle with another. This makes them litle reguard their wiues beauty or manners, and to marry for Dowry, Parrentage, and procreation wemen vnknowne and allmost vnseene, resoluing Cauar' i capriccij d' Amore, that is to satisfye the humours of loue (be they of conversation, of beauty, or of disordinate lusts in the diuers and some beastiall kyndes of inioying that pleasure) by the freedome of the Stewes. While Curtizans walke and ride in Coaches at liberty, and freely saluted and honored by all men passing by them, theire wiues and virgins are locked vp at home, watched by their wemen attending them abroade, haue their faces covered with a vaile not to be seene, and it is death by priuate reveng for any man to salute them or make the least shewe of loue to them; if it be perceaued by any of the kindred, who will not fayle to kill him (for their revenge is neuer lesse then death). In regarde of this ieloseye, that the young wemen may not be defyled, nor the olde wemen their keepers hyred to be bawdes to them, no wemen goe to markett, but only men, and the most rich disdayne not to buye all necessaryes for their owne Familyes, in which fewe haue any men or at least they come not neere the wemen. Yet for all this care, the Italyans many tymes weare the fatall hornes they somuch detest, because wemen thus kept from men, thincke it simpliscity to loose anye oportunity offered, though it be with the meanest seruant, and because there want not men

as watchfull to betray their Chastity, as their husbandes are
to keepe it, but espetially because snares are layde for them in
the very Churches, and more spetially in the Nonneryes, whether
they cannot deny their wiues and daughters to repare vpon
festiuall dayes of Devotion. The cheefe cause of most
desprate quarrells is for wemen, wherevpon, and because suites
at lawe are of great charge and trouble, they haue a proverb :
l' Amor', vna Quistion' et vn' Piatto, fanno vn' sauio : that is
being in loue, hauing a quarrell, and following a suite at lawe,
make a wise man. To which purpose they haue also another
proverb : chi l' Asini caccia, chi Donne mena : Non l' mai senza
guai et pena.

> Whoso driues Asses, or leades in his trayne
> Wemen shall never want great woe and payne.

For asses must be continually pricked with goades by the
driuer, and wemen cause many quarrells to the leader of them.
In Italy as Adultry seldome or never falls within the
punishment of the lawe, because the Italyans nature carryes
them to such an high degree of priuate revenge as the lawe
cannot inflict greater (which private revenge by murther vpon
iust groundes of ielosye is Commonly taken secretely, and if
knowne, yet wincked at and favored by the Magistrate, in his
owne nature approuing aswell the revenge as the secrecy therof,
for avoyding shame) so fornication in Italy is not a sinne
wincked at, but rather may be called an allowed trade. For
Princes & States raise great tributes from it. At Naples each
poore Curtizan payes to the Prince two Carlines the mounth,
besydes greater extortians vpon those that are fayre, and hauing
great and many louers growe proude in apparrell, and rich in
purse, and the nomber of harlotts was thought to exceed sixty
thousand. At Venice the tribute to the State from Cortizans
was thought to exceede three hundreth thousand Crownes
yearely. And the Popes holines made no lesse gayne from this
fayre trade at Rome. In some Cittyes Cortizans are
distinguished from other wemen by habites, as at Sienna they

weare yellowe vailes, others wearing white or black. In some
Cityes their lodging is restrayned to one or more streetes, called
Il Chiasso that is the Stewes, as at Florence, where they may
not dwell among honest wemen, but may be driven away by the
neighbours. In some Cittyes they are forbidden to weare rich
apparrell and diuers ornaments, but in these cases it is inough
to corrupt the sargants by brybes, that they be not accused. In
Venice they are free to dwell in any house they can hyre, and
in any streete whatsoeuer, and to weare what they list. In
generall they are courted and honored of all men, so as Princes
in their owne Cittyes disdayne not to visite them priuately, to
salute them passing in the streetes, and in the tyme of Carnovall
publikely to grace them by flinging egs filled with rosewater
at their windowes, where they stand to be seene. Yea they
haue at Florence a peculiar Court of iustice, called the Court
of honesty, where Judges clad in purple giue them right against
those who pay them not for the vse of their bodyes, or any way
defraude them. Each Cortizan hath Commonly her louer
whome she mantaynes, her Balordo or Gull who principally
mantaynes her, besydes her Customers at large, and her Bravo
to fight her quarrells. If any Cortizan haue a Chylde, the
father takes the males, but shee keepes the females to mantayne
her when shee is olde, for such dwell with and vnder their
mothers. The richer sorte dwell in fayre hired howses, and
haue their owne servants, but the Common sorte lodge with
Baudes called Ruffians, to whome in Venice they pay of their
gayne the fifth parte, as foure Solz in twenty, paying besydes
for their beds, linnen, and feasting, and when they are past
gayning much, they are turned out to begg or turne baudes or
seruants. And for reliefe of this misery, they haue Nonneryes,
where many of them are admitted, and called the converted
sisters. Both honest and dishonest wemen are Lisciate fin' alla
fossa, that is paynted to the very graue. The Italyans loue fatt
and tall wemen, and for those causes the Venetian wemen are
sayd to be Belle di bellito, bianche di calcina, grasse di straccie,
alte di legni o zoccole, that is fayre with paynting, white with

chalke, fatt with raggs (or stuffed linnen) and high with wood
or Pantofles (which many weare a foote or more deepe).
The Italians howsoeuer by nature they are revengfull for open
and knowne wronges, yet by naturall disposition to wisdome
and grauity, they are not inclyned to contentions and verball
brawlings or falling out with their accquaintance, vpon slight
occasions, except perhaps some ielosye about wemen fall
betweene them. And particularly for brothers, as many of
them liue in fratellanza, that is in brotherhood, without
deviding their Patrymony but imploying it in Common, so
many brothers liue in one family or house throughout all Italy,
without any household Jarres, frequent among all other nations
espetially among bretheren. Indeede Commonly one of them
only is marryed, so as they are free from the cause of contention
otherwhere frequently arysing from diuerse wemen of equall
degree liuing in one house. But this concorde of bretheren in
Italy, hauing all goodes, all ioyes and sorrowes, all Curtesyes
and wrongs common to them all, is a rare example and worthy
of Imitation.

The Italians by nature loue to liue of their owne, and scorne
to liue vpon other mens trenchers and bounty, most disdayning
vn' scroccator d' i Pasti, that is a shifter for meales. In
somuch as the Country being very populous (Contayning in that
narrow land about nyne millions of people as Botero writes) and
this pride being naturall to the meanest as to the greatest, and
the small disorders being punished with slauish service in
Gallyes, or with shame which their nature no lesse abhorrs, the
meaner sorte, to gayne their bread, will doe much seruice for a
litle peece of monye, and the Common people by nature
exorbitant in all thinges, are restrayned and kept in good order,
and beggers are very rare among them, those that are in
extreame miserye being relieued in hospitalls, yea their pryde
somuch abhorrs begging, as the poorest will not take Almes
except it be putt into their windowes, in which case they
accknowledg it only from God, howsoeuer they knowe it
mediately to come from the charity of the Parish or of good

neighbours.   Only the Inkeepers are permitted by all Princes (some more some lesse) to extorte without measure vpon all passengers, because they pay vnsupportable rents to them.

Touching particular Cittyes.   The Bresscians are helde the posterity of Frenchmen, and together with the next Citty Bergamo haue beene sometymes vnder the power of the French, where the wemen insteede of vayles weare scarffes neere the French fashion, and haue somwhat of the French liberty, in Conversation, at the table and in daunsing, and in salutations as they passe the streetes, which other Italyans in generall would not permitt.   Yet in the very heart of Italy at Masso, they haue somwhat of the French liberty, and more spetially at Sienna (in the last Age commaunded for a tyme by a French garryson) where also men vnmasked and the wemen haue publike meeteings for daunsing, with some freedome of Conversation, whereas in other partes these daunses are only vsed in the Carnouall, where the men are masked and haue no liberty of discourse with wemen.   Likewise at Genoa bordering vpon Fraunce, and for a short tyme governed by a French garryson, the wemen haue almost asmuch liberty as the foresayd wemen of Bresseia, for conversation at the table and in discourse, and for salutations in the streetes, and of that Citty it is proverbyally sayde Montagni senza legni, Mar' senza Pesci, huomini senza fede, Donne senza Vergogna, Genoa superba, that is, mountaynes without woodes (as are all in Liguria), Sea without Fish, (that Coast hauing none), men without Faith (not regarding their worde where they are not bounde by writting), wemen without shame (for the foresayde French liberty), Genoa the proude (theire cheefe marchants being Princes and their houses stately built).   The Citty of Florence hath the name of Florishing like a flower, being most swetely seated, and indeede the Dukedome of Tuscanye, and the State of Sienna vnder the same Duke, are more commodious for dwelling, espetially for strangers abroade, for the pleasure of the Country, and ayre, the puriety of language, the good government making it free from murthers, and the high wayes

most safe from theeues, though men travile by night, and
espetially for the disposition of the inhabitants.   For the
Florintines are reputed Courteous, modest, graue, wise, and
excelent in many vertues.   Likewise the Cittizens of the free
Citty Lucca are reputed Courteous, verye modest, good, and
reall in all affayres.   The Cittizens and inhabitants of Marchia
and of Romagna, as they are the best Soldyers, so are they the
worst disposed people of all Italy, so as the proverb sayth, that
Marchia can furnish all Italy with swaggerers and murtherers.

Touching the manners of the Italians.   They are for the
out syde by natures guift excellently composed.   By sweetnes
of language, and singular Art in seasoning their talke and
behauiour with great ostentation of Courtesy, they make their
Conuersation sweete and pleasing to all men, easily gayning the
good will of those with whome they liue.   But no trust is to be
reposed in their wordes, the flattering tounge hauing small
accquaintance with a sincere heart, espetially among the
Italyans, who will offer Curtesyes freely, and presse the
acceptance vehemently, only to squeese out Complement on both
sydes, they neither meaning to performe them, nor yet dareing
to accept them, because in that case they would repute the
Acceptar ignorant and vnciuill, for euer after avoiding his
Conversation as burthensome to them.   And indeede in these
fayre speeches which wee call courting, they so transcend all
golden mediocrity, as they are reputed the Authors of all flattery
spread through all our transalpine nations, espetially in salutations by worde of mouth, and Epistles, forced with Hiperbolicall
protestations and more then due titles to all degrees.   For in
Italy vostra Signoria that is your mastershipp or worship is
giuen to Plebeans, molto magnifico that is very magnificall is
giuen to Cittizens, Illustro Signor that is Illustrous Sir is giuen
to ordinary gentlemen, and the title of Altezza that is highnes
is giuen to lords of a Citty or smale territoryes (as many are in
Italy hauing absolute power of life and death) yea the
gentlemen of Venice proude aboue all others, wilbe called in
ordinary salutations Clarissimi that is most bright or famous,

and challenge this title peculiar to themselues, not communi-
cable to any other gentlemen whatsoeuer, so as if a man say
that a Clarissimo without name did or sade this or that, he is
vnderstood to say that a gentleman of Venice did or sayd it.
The Neapolitans as they are reputed most Curteous in wordes,
so are they in worde and deede as proude as the Venetians who
vse small or no curtesy in wordes, wherevpon Annibal' Caro a
very eloquent Secretary writes to a frende at Naples; Ancora
che Stiate a Napoli, non vi do delle Signorie that is; Tho you
liue at Naples I giue no titles of worship. As the
Italians in generall are of sweete Conversation, so they
are respectfull to all men of all degrees (the meanest
hauing pryde to revenge), but familiar to fewe or none. They
are affable at the first sight, but no long accquaintance can
make them famillier, much lesse rude in behauiour, as some
other nations are, who being familiar yea perhaps litle or not at
all acquainted, will presently call men by nicknames, yea being
their superiours, as Tom, Jack, Will, Dic, and the like, yea will
leape vpon their frendes shoulders, and if they wilbe merye,
presently fling Coushions, stooles, yea Custardes or whatsoeuer
is next hand, one at anothers head, and thereby many tymes fall
from sport to earnest quarrals. This kinde of familiarity
Italians hate above all others, and thincke it a manifest signe
of a barren witt, falling to such sporte for want of ability to
discourse, wherof they Commonly say, touch me with your
toung not with your hand. And haue a Proverbe, Giogo di
mani, giogo di Villani, that is, the sport of handes is the sport
of Clownes. And another, Giogo di mani dispiace fin' a gli
pedocchi, that is, the sport of handes displeaseth to the very
lice. If an Itályan be in conference with you in a Chamber
or in the streete and an other man goethe or passeth by, who is
of greater quallity then your selfe, and with whome he hath
greater buisinesse then with you, yet will he not leaue you
sodenly to goe to him, till first he haue excused himselfe and
desyred your leaue, lest he should seeme in any sorte to vnder-
value your Company. Most of their howses are built with a

gallerye in the middest, and Chambers on each syde, and such
are the Chambers hyred by men of diuers sortes and nations,
where an Italian hauing his Chamber doore open, and one of
another Chamber walking in the gallerye, will not shutt his
doore as it were in his teeth to exclude him, but rather salute
him and stay till he be gone; much lesse will he shutt his dore
at the heeles of any man going out, as if he were gladd to be
ridd of him. And indeede in those publike houses they seldome
shutt their dores by day lest they should seeme to doe or haue
any thinge they would be loath should be seene. So as my selfe
walking with an Italian in a gallerye where two English
gentlemen entring their chamber shutt the dore close after
them, he asked me if the younger were not a woman in mans
apparrell, and gaue the shutting of their dore for a reason of
his suspition. So nise are they euen in the smalest points of
behauiour, wherof I will add only one Instance more. That the
Italians saluting in the streetes putt off their hatts a good
distance before they meete, but much longer after they are past
one another, lest ether party looking backe and seeing the other
couered, should thincke he obserued his eye more then his
person. Thus Tacitus sayth truely, The more things are fayned
which men doe, the more they doe them. To conclude, as the
Italians in generall are of exquisite behauiour, so I haue seene
many of them in some particular things, very vnmanerly, as in
frequent vseing beastly wordes as Interiections of Exclamation
or Admiration, namely Coglioni, Catzo, Potta, signifying the
priuy parts of men and wemen, and the like. But I lesse
wonder at this because blasphemous oathes and rotten talke are
among their nationall vices, and they can hardly seeke to please
men in those thinges wherein they feare not to offende God.
Agayne it is not rare, espetially at Venice and Padoa, to see an
Italyan setting on the Closestoole and talking with his Chamber
fellowes while they are eating. Agayne the Italians by venery
and the heate of the Clyme haue not only faynt bodyes and
weake ioyntes, so as in Jorneyes they will not walke downe a
hill, but also for the same causes are much trobled with the

Itch at least, and they wearing Commonly breches loose at the knees, I haue seene many of good sorte scratch their thighs when they were ready to sett downe to meate, not somuch as washing their handes after it.   Agayne at Naples, not only the Prisoners (as I formerly sayd) but men of good sorte, taking me and my companions for frenchmen, rudely mocked vs as wee passed the streetes.   For they hate the french their old lordes, and no lesse the Spaniardes who presently gouerne them, being a people neither knowing howe to obey nor able to mantayne their freedome.

Bodies and Witts.

Touching the Italians bodyes, they are generally of person tall, and leane, and of a browne and pale complection.   Only many of the Venetians bordering vpon the Germans (the marchants and gentlemen wherof haue frequent and great concurse and abode in that Citty), and being borne at the foote of the Alpes, and in the midest of litle lakes made by the Sea (the inhabitants of which mountaynes and borders of the Sea are commonly noted to be more fayre then others) are not so pale as other Italyans, but for great parte of a more sanguine complexion. Whatsoeuer they weare aboute their body, they desyre to haue it rather commodious and easy then fyne and rich, as falling bands rather then Rooffes, Caps of taffety rather then hatts, and all garments light and easy to be changed. But espetially in Jornyes, wherein they will not disease themselues by lighting to ease their horses, somuch as goeing downe a hill, their bootes are of thicke leather, and so large as vntying the stringes they fling them off without helpe of handes, their hatts, Clokes, and bases are Commonly of Spanish Felt thicke as a boarde, and not to be pearced with rayne.   And vpon their saddles they fasten soft cushions of leather, laughing at the Englishmen who vse Cushions in the howse but ride vpon Northern saddles as hard as boardes. To conclude, their bodies are faynt by the Clyme, and many of them much more faynt

and diseased by intemperance of lusts, but they are neate &
clenly about their bodyes, not enduring a sweaty shirte without
present changing, and their wemen say they are not only more
clenly but of sweeter complexion and more free from Goutish
Sauour, then the nations beyond the Alpes.

They haue by nature and vertue of the Clyme vnder which
they are borne, sharpe and deepe reaching or searching witts,
but lesse refyned by Art then those of some other Countryes.
For they thincke themselues to haue somuch vnderstanding,
and their Country to yealde somuch sweetenes, fruitfullnes, and
such Monuments of Arts and fabricks, as they seldome or never
travaile into forayne kingdomes, but driuen by some necessity,
ether to Followe the warrs, or to traffique abroad : This opinion
that Italy doth afforde what can be seene or knowne in the
world, makes them only haue homebred wisdome, and the
prowde conceete of their owne witts, and their addiction to
pleasure, make them at home and in their owne Vniversities
lesse laborious and studious to gayne knowledge, which point I
shall more explayne in the following discourse of Sciences.
For these reasons, strangers comming into Italy, fynde
ordinarily litle singularity in the gentlemen, but rather wonder
at the naturall witt of the Country people and vulgar Artisans,
in discourseing strangely of naturall thinges and the very
historyes and matters of State falling out in their owne tyme.
Whereas gentlemen of other nations, brought vp in schooles and
Vniversityes, & hauing seene forrayne kingdomes and Courtes,
not only excell other gentlemen of their owne nation wanting
that breeding, but are much respected abroad, and by the very
Italians, for their knowledge, experience, and behauiour. Yet
I confesse the Italians taxe these strangers for Curyosity, and
some in scorne will shewe toyes for antiquityes, as heades lately
carved in stone or brasse for the heades of old Emperours, and
the like, wherein they mistake the endes of travailers, being to
see many Cittyes, diuers manners of men, and to obserue good
things for imitation, ill thinges to avoyde them, and beholding
these Antiquities onely by the waye and as it were for recreation.

And if any deserue the blame of Curious[i]ty by inquiring after these monewments, it should rather be imputed to the fault of lying historyes extolling them too much then to any errour in them. The Italyans witt in generall tendes to extremes, and it may welbe sayd of them as of Brutus, Quod vult nimis vult, what he willes he willes too much. For a woman kept and lockt vp from them, what will they not adventure, but the ende is ill. In a Feast what will they not spende, not of bounty, which generally they haue not, but of vayne glory and pride which are naturall to them. And as it was sayde of the Athenians for their witt, Si boni optimi, Si mali pessimi, If they be good they are best, if they be ill they are worst, so it may be sayd of the Italians searching witts, they are not extended so much to the superlatiue degree of goodnes, as to the extremes on both sydes, namely in Religion to superstition, or to Atheisme. Among all the Cittyes and Provinces of Italy, Toscany, and more spetially the Citty and State of Florence therein contayned, is noted to yealde men of stronge memorye, and excelent witt to fynde out and to improve sciences and Artes, men most ingenious and fitt for affayres, and skillfull in sciences Arts and traffique. The Citty and state of Florence hath yealded most famous men, as Dante, Petrarcha, Boccacio, for Poets: Nicolo Machiauelli the politition, Vespuccio sent by the king of Portugall to discouer the West Indyes, Accursio the Jurist, Andrea Sansouino of great learning and experience. Francesco Guicciardini the worthy Historyographer, Pietro Aretino of excellent witt if he had well imployed it, and Michael' Angelo Bonaritio, most famous for the Arts of Paynting, Sculpture, and Architecture, with many other for breuity omitted.

Artes sciences Vniversityes Language.

Touching Manuall Artes, those that are most vulgar trades, as Taylores and the like vsed about the body, I cannot commend for any singularity, because indeede the Italyans affect no

Curyous workes of these kyndes, only respecting ease and commodity therein. But for paynting, sculpture or Carving in brasse and stone, and for Architecture, they haue beene of olde and still are most skillfull Masters, and whatsoeuer the Flemings or any nations on this syde the Alpes can doe in these Artes, they haue learnt it from them. In all three the Florintyne Michael Angillo of the last age was most famous, and much respected by all the Princes and States of Italy desyring to haue masterpeeces of his worke, which made him also vse great presumption and boldnes towardes them. Being to paynt the Popes private Chappell in his Pallace, he would not vndertake it till the Pope by oath promised him, that nether he nor any of the Cardinalls shoulde come in to see his worke, till it was finished, and after fynding by the Popes discourse with him, that he by the perswasion of some Cardinalls had come in by a backe doore of the vestery, and had seene his worke, he being then in hand to paynt Hell, did for this breach of Faith make the pictures of the Pope and those Cardinalls so liuely among the Deuills, as they were easily knowne, till by perswasion and intreaty he defaced them. Agayne being to make a Crucifix for the Pope he hyred a Fachino that is a Porter to be fastned to a crosse, and when he came to giue life to the passion, he gaue the Porter a deadly stroake with a penknife and during the Agonies of his death, made a rare Crucifix, and no lesse rare monument of his wickednes.* For which the Pope could not but for a tyme banish him from Rome, in which tyme he was intertayned by the Duke of Vrbin. And when the Pope called him backe to Rome, the Dutchesse of Vrbin sending to him for the Pictures of many Saynts, he in scorne of her indiscretion to intreate so great a worke of so rare a workeman, was sayd to haue written vnto her, that the taske her highnes had imposed vpon him could not soddenly be donne, but in the meane tyme he had sent her the Father of all the Saynts, which oppened was the preuy parte of a man liuely

---

* This venerable tale has been attached to many artists—I am sorry that Moryson should have believed it of Michael Angelo. (C.H.)

paynted. The Italians, and espetially the Venetians, excell in
the Art of setting Jewells, and making Cabinetts, tables and
mountings, of Christall, corall, Jasper, and other precious
stones, and curious worke of Caruing. The Italians, and
espetially the Venetians excell in making lutes, Organs, and
other Instruments of musicke.

And as Italy hath yealded many rare workemen in these
Artes of paynting, Caruing in stone and brasse, Architecture,
setting of Jewells composing these Cabinetts tables and mountings and makeing of Instruments so the Princes and States of
Italy are Curious in gathering and preseruing the rare peeces
of these workemen, but espetially the Venetians, which Citty
aboundes with infinite rare Monuments of these kyndes, aswell
in publike Pallaces and Churches, as in the priuate houses of
gentlemen, who for Curtesy, or their owne glory, are as willing
to shewe them to strangers, as they can be to see them. The
free Citty of Lucca being of old subdued by tyrants, the best
and richest Cittizens left the Citty, till the liberty therof was
regayned, which they hold to this day. And they liuing then
in other Cittyes of Italy, taught them the Art of weauing silke,
wherein the Italyans excell, but espetially the Venetians and
Florintines, with whome most of the exiled men liued, and the
Florintines also learned of them the Art of making flowers &
curious workes like Imbroderies vpon silke stuffes, wherein to
this day they are most skillfull. The Venetians make the best
Treakell, which is transported throughout all Europe, and about
the first of November, at which tyme they make it, those
Artizans haue a Feast, wherein they weare feathers, and haue
Trumpitts continually sounding, and during the tyme of this
worke all the shops about Rialto resounde with the blowing
thereof. The Wemen in Italy are Curious workers with the
needle, of whome other Nations have learned to make the laces
commonly called Cuttworkes. And the Nunnes, more spetially
at Sienna, Rauena, and Mantua, vsed to worke Curious flowers
in silke, which our wemen of late haue worne on their heades,
and at my being there they made most of the sweetemeates
which the Apothecaryes soulde.

Touching Sciences and Vniversityes, howsoeuer learning in generall came first from Asia to Greece, from thence to Rome, and so to the Nations vnder that Empire, and that Rome long kept this glory in the freedome of that State, and then most when in the tyme of Augustus, about the birth of our Lord that Empire most florished, And howsoeuer (no doubt) the Italyans naturally haue strong witts to search into the depth of all sciences, yet within fewe hundreths of yeares, by the invndations and invasions of barbarous Nations, that Westerne Empire in Italy being destroyed, learning also was withal much defaced in Italy, and in the ages following, by the Popes norishing of Ignorance as fitt to advance his vsurped power, Italy lost the glory of learning, wherein other Northerly and Westerne nations generally overtope them to this day. In the tyme of this ignorance, most of the bookes printed by Italians, haue beene of historyes, of Poetry, with like Studies of humanity, of pleasant discourses, and straynes of witt, as commending ignorance aboue knowledge, the asse aboue all beasts, the nettle aboue all hearbs, and like subiectes, in which kyndes of Studyes most of the gentlemen who affect any learning (which are no great nomber) doe for the most parte exercise themselues to this day. To which Studyes I will add the Art of Musick, wherein the Italians, and espetially the Venetians, haue in all tymes excelled, and most at this day, not in light tunnes and hard striking of the stringes, (which they dislike), nor in companyes of wandering fidlers, (wherof they haue none or very fewe single men of small skill) but in Consortes of graue soleme Musicke, sometymes running so sweetely with softe touching of the stringes, as may seeme to rauish the hearers spiritt from his body, which musike they vse at many priuate and publike meetings, but espetially in their churches, where they ioyne with it winde Instruments, and most pleasant voyces of boyes and men, being indeede such excellent Musicke as cannot but stirr vp devotian in the hearers. For the nature of musick being not to provoke newe but to eleuate present affections, and the greatest or best sorte Comming to Church for deuotion, such

Musick cannot but increase the same.   Only the Popes Chappell
hath no instruments of musicke, but only most excelent voyces
of men and boyes.   Also in the sayd tyme of ignorance, and to
this day, Italy being most governed by the Imperiall and Papall
lawes and both much swaying in all Christian Kingdomes, the
Italyans for the great rewarde thereof much following those
Studyes, their Vniversities haue yealded and still yealde many
famous men for the knowledge of these lawes.   But the studye
of Diuinity hath long tyme throughout all Italy beene altogether
exiled from the Vniversities into Monnasteryes, where by the
sloath and ignorance of Fryers it long tyme rusted, till the
Reformation of Religion awaked them, since which tyme they
and spetially the Dominican and Franciscan Fryers, and more
espetially the newe order of the Jesuites, haue Preached
diligently, saying and writting as much, as strong witts can
say or write to mantayne a bad cause.   The Vniversities of
Sienna and Salernam of old, and espetially of Padoa aswell of
old as to this day, haue yealded famous Phisitians, who in
Italy are also Shirgians and many of them growe rich, for all
that haue any small meanes, will in sicknes haue their helpe,
because they are not prowde but will looke vpon any ordure and
handle any sore, but espetially because they are carefull for
their Patients, visite them diligently, and take litle fees which
make heauy purses.   They visite twise each day the poorest
Patient, and not only in Italy but also in Germany and
Fraunce, they expect no greater fee then the value of eightyne
pence English for a visite.   Only the Italyans and French take
ready monye, whereas the Germans are not payde untill the
ende of the sicknes, when if the party be dead they haue
nothinge, if he recover they are payde after that rate, and will
refuse more if it be offered them.   The Italyans as well as the
Germans carefully visite the Apothecaryes shops, and burne all
druggs that are not sounde.   But Italy hath a generation of
Emperiks, who frequently and by swarmes goe from Citty to
Citty, and haunt their Markett places.   They are called
Montibanchi of mounting banckes or litle scaffolds and also

Ciarletani of prating. They proclame their wares vpon these scaffolds, and to drawe concourse of people, they haue a Zani or Foole with a Visard on his face, and sometymes a woman, to make Comicall sporte. The people cast their handkerchers with mony to them, and they cast them backe with wares tyed in them, which some buy for vse, others only to haue more sporte from the foole, for one man proclaymes his wares and sells them, the other makes sporte to the beholders, by turnes one after the other. The wares they sell are commonly distilled waters, and diuers oyntments for burning Aches and stitches, and the like, but espetially for the Itch and scabbs, more vendible then the rest. Some carry Serpents about them, and sell remedyes for their stinging, which they call the grace of St. Paule, because the Viper could not hurt him. Other sell Angelica of Misnia at twelue pence English the ounce, naming (as I thincke) a remote Country to make the price greater, for otherwise that colde Country shoulde not yealde excelent herbes. Many of them haue some very good secretts, but generally they are all cheaters. The like Emprikes vulgarly called Tireakse-kremer, that is Marchants of Trekle, goe about Germany, but nothinge so frequently, and neuer with any foole to make sporte, rather carrying the grauity of great Doctours. For they ride in Coaches, and cary about them Testimonialls vnder great Seales, and pictures of strange Cures they haue donne, and great stones they haue Cutt from men. Some of them are good to Cure some one infirmity, but they professe to Cure all, and are Commonly dull Cheaters. Italy hath many Vniuersities, whereof two are most famous, that of Padoa the cheefe, and of Bologna the next. The Vniuersity of Bologna is the most auntient, first built (as their recorde sayth) by the Emperour Theodosious the younger, and long florished vnder that State (sometymes free, sometymes vnder priuate Princes) and hath many previleges from the Popes to whom at last in the tyme of Pope Alexander the sixth it became subiect. By many Inscriptions in the Princes Pallace and the publike Schooles, it accknowledgeth Pope Pius the fourth for a spetiall Benefactor, where also many thinges are written in memorye and honour of the great Jvrest Baldus. The Popes long tyme haue indowed the same with great stipends for Professors, but espetially for those of the Imperiall and Papall lawes, and for a cheefe Professor of Historyes, of whome many learned men haue beene vpholders of the Papall power and lawe, against the Emperours. Yet I would desyre no better wittnes against the Papall vsurpation, then Sigonius the Popes stipendiary Professor of historyes in this Vniversity. Now because many other Vniversities in Italy and those partes, haue beene instituted after the forme of this in Bologna, I will write something thereof, as breefely as I can possibly contract it.

As I haue formerly sayd of the Vniversities in Germany, so I must say of Bologna, and generally of the vniversityes of Italy, that they are generally well founded for stipendes of professors, some large and very rich, all competent to mantayne them, so as they may giue themselues wholy to the studyes of their professions and reade diligently orderly and breefely, for the best profitt of their hearers, and quicke dispatch in the Course of their studyes, but each Vniversity hath commonly but one or two Coleges, both for schooles of the Professors, and for Chambers to lodge some poore schollers, who are fewe, poorely mantayned, and for no longer tyme then sufficeth to finish their studyes, all the rest of their schollars (Consisting most of forayne nations, and the lesse nomber of their owne natiues) liuing at their owne Charge in Cittizens houses, whereas in our famous Vniversityes of England, the Cheefe professors haue small stipends, so as they cannot attend that worke for seeking other meanes to mantayne them. And the inferiour publike readers are chosen yearely among young men, who hauing trifling stipends for that one yeare, reade more for ostentation of their owne learning then for the profitt of the hearers. So as our schollers gett theire learning, not by hearesay from the Professors as in forayne Vniversities, but by priuate studye in their Colleges: But each of our Vniversities hath more then twenty Colleges, Stately built, and richely endowed with Rents to mantayne many Schollers and Fellowes, yet this aboundance hath his mischeefe, in that the Fellowes hauing liberty to keepe theire Fellowships till death, and they being a sufficient mantenance, which some cannot easely gett abroad, wee may complayne with St. Barnard, that wee haue old men in the schooles and young men in the Pulpitts. For the Fellowes often keeping their places long, young men who cannot be preferred to them, are forced to practise abroad before they be well founded in their professions. Also our schollers, being all natiues and fewe or no forayners, liue in the Colleges not in the townes, and so are more orderly governed and instructed by theire priuate Tutours or Teachers.

Bologna hath a fayre College wherein the professors reade, hauing 17. Superiour and tenne inferiour Schooles. And it hath chosen men, who haue power to make newe Statutes or alter the old.

1. This one Vniversity indeede hath two Academies, one of the nations beyonde the mountaynes, the other of those on that syde the Alpes, and each hath a Rector yearely chosen, who by Statute must be a Clarke or Cler[g]y man, and vnmaryed, and one that hath liued there fyue yeares, and who is 25. yeares old, and able to beare the expences of an honorable office. If it can be proued by fyue wittnesses that any man by himselfe or by any frend makes meanes to be chosen Rectour, he must pay 50. Lyers and his procuring frend 30. No scholler may without leaue goe from the vniversity within two monthes of this election.

2. The Rector Vltramontane (that is of the nations beyond the Alpes) must be chosen by the former yeares Rectour, and by the newe Counselors, with as many assistants, vpon the first of May. And the Citramontane (that is of the nations on that syde the mountaynes) vpon the feast of the holy Crosse in the same monthe. No man may be Rectour twise without a generall consent of all. The Vltramontane must be chosen the first yeare out of the french, the Burgundians and the Savoyans &c. the second yeare out of the Castellans, the Portugalls, the

Navarreans, the Aragonians &c. the third yeare among the Germans, the Hungaryans, the Polonians, the Bohemians or the English, or the Fleminges, and each three yeares other Nations partners of that election followe in order.

3. The Citramontane must be chosen the first yeare of the Romans. The second of the Tuscans, the third of the Lombardes. Both are chosen of sworne men by schedules cast into a box, and if the voyces be equall, the Doctours sway the Election, and if they also be equall, then they are chosen by the voyces of all the Students.

4. In the Rectours Courtes, Causes of fyue powndes must be iudged within fyftene dayes, of tenne powndes within twenty dayes, and all Causes aboue that some within two monthes .

5. Students must be iudged by their Rector, and if one be thought partiall, the cause may be referred to the other.

6. If any strife be betweene one beyonde the Mountaynes, and an other on that syde, it must be iudged by the Rectours, And if they differ, then foure chosen men on each part determyne it.

7. Halfe the penaltyes or Fynes goe to the Rectour, and halfe to the Vniversity, and if a Rectour forbeare to impose any Fynes, he is punished at the ende of the yeare by the Syndici (or Judges).

8. These Judges are two of each Rectoursship, and they must Condemne or absolue each Rectour within one month after his yeare is ended.

9. The Stationers are Chosen by three Citramontans, and three Vltramontans.

10. The Vltramontans chuse 19. Counselers, and the Citramontans chuse also 19 (wherof 8. must be Romans, six Tuscans, and fyue Lombards.

11. Officers may not be absent aboue a mounth.

12. Newe Students must giue their names with in tenne dayes.

13. Each one must haue a gowne long to the foote.

14. Each payes 12. lires for Matriculation.

15. The Statutes may not be changed but from 20. to 20 yeares.

16. The Citramontans chuse 19. and the Vltramontans 19. Counsellors who appoint the readers of the lawe among the Competitours for lectures, namely one yeare 4 Vltramontane Jurists and two Citramontane, the other yeare 2. Vltramontane and 4 Citramountane. And when they demaunde their Stipends, they take oath that they did reade diligently. And no extraordinary lecture is permitted without leaue of the Rectour.

17. The Ciuill laweryers must study 8. yeares, and the Cannonists 5. yeares, before they be made Doctours, and they must be examined priuately and publikely.

18. Two Taxers are chosen to taxe the Students lodgings, and see that they pay not more then in former yeares, and not to suffer the richer sort by paying more, to putt the poorer from their lodgings. And these taxers are to be fyned if they take any bribe.

19. If any Student be killed or wounded in his lodging, that house and tenn nex adioyning loose the previlege of lodging Students for tenn yeares following.

20. He is guilty of Periury, who comes not to the Funerall of any deceased Student.

21. The Vltramontans and Citramontans are each governed by their owne Statutes.

22. Each weeke a Doctour disputes in order, or should so doe by Statute, but they only dispute on Sundayes, not to hinder the lectures (a godly Consideration forsoth) but if any Doctour hath beene a Reader of a lecture 24 yeares, he is not tyed to dispute.

23. The foresayde vi Professors or lecturers of the lawe, mentioned in the Statute, 16. to avoyde discord among the Counsellours who chuse them, are to be chosen, not by voyces but by lott.

24. Whosoeuer suies for a Lecture, must haue beene

Matriculated three monthes before at least, for otherwise he is
not Capable of it.

25. Poore Schoolers haue their degrees free without any
payment, at the intercession of their Rectour.

The second Vniversity of Italy for Antiquity is that of Pauia
in Lombardy, instituted by the French Emperor, when the
Westerne Empire was renewed, namely Charles the great, after
he had subdued the Kingdome and the last King of the
Lombards, which Vniversity is now much decayed.

The third for antiquity, but cheefe for dignity, is the famous
Vniversity of Padoa. The German Emperour Frederick the
second, iustly offended with the Cittizens of Bologna, transferred
the priuileges of that Vniversity to Padoa about the yeare 1222.
It began to florish when it was confirmed and indowed with
priuileges by Pope Vrban the sixth, about the yeare 1260. It
was governed (as that of Bologna) by two Rectors, and after some
yeares hauing the Statutes corrected by the Statutes of Bologna
and after hauing the names of the Rectours changed from
Vltramontane and Citramontane, to be called one of the Jurists
the other of the Artes, yet so that they were chosen equally each
second yeare of the sayd nations beyonde or on that syde the
mountaynes. But the State of Venice about the yeare 1405.
subduing Padoa, and holding it subiect to this day, did amplify
the Vniversity with priuileges and many ornaments, continually
giuing charge to their governour, to mantayne these priuileges
and dignityes of the Vniversity, and to keepe the Schoollers
from tumults among themselues. The members of the Vniversity are these.

1. The two Rectors, one ouer the Jurists, the other ouer the
Artists, one yeare of the Vltramontans, the other of the
Citramontans, chosen the one the tenth the other the xvth of
August, by all the Students devided into their Nations, and in
the presence of the Governour (to avoyde all tumults) and in
solemnity presented to the Governour within three dayes.

2. The Vicar is Counseller and assistant to the Rector, who
nameth and chuseth him.

3. The Substitute is one whome the Rectour may appoint in his absence for eight Dayes.

4. The Vice Rector is chosen by the Vniversity, When the Rectour is forced to be absent aboue a moneth.

5. The Sapiens or wisemen yearely chosen foure dayes after the Rectors, for each one, to be his Legate for the yeare, are chosen by the Rector and Counsellers in the presence of the Gouernor.

6. The Counsellers 22 for the Jurists and 12. for the Artists, each nation chusing their Counseller.

7. The foure Syndici or Judges are yearely chosen to censure the Actes of the Rector and his ministers after his yeare is ended, whose office expires after xxij dayes.

8. The congregation is one of the Counsellers who supplyes the Bedells place to call them to Metings, where the Rector is a party, in which case the Bedel is suspected as sworne to him.

9. The Messarius or Steward keepes the publike accounts.

10. The Notary keepes the Statutes, the priuileges and publike Instruments.

11. They haue a library keeper.

12. The Professors or Doctors are also members of the Vniversity. Wherof some reade publikely (as the professors) others practise their art but reade not. In the Cannon lawe the ordinary readers are two in the morning, which reade the first and second booke of decretalls, and towe in the after noone, who reade the other bookes of the same. And in the Ciuill lawe the ordinary Readers are two in the morning, wherof the first reades the Codex, the second the olde digests, and two in the afternone, who reade the newe digests and the Institutions. Besydes Doctors, who are extraordinary Readers in both the lawes. And these, as the following Readers, Dictate, so as euery worde they speake may be writen by the Students, and they resolue and end this Reading, in due tyme for the profitt of the hearers. Agayne in Phisick, the ordinary Professors are two for Theory, who reade the first yeare Auicenna, the second Hippocrates, the third Galen, and two for practise, who reade

the first yeare Auicenna of Agues, and the other two yeares
Rasis ad Almansorem, besydes a Professor of Chirurgey, and
foure extraordinary Readers, two for Theory, and two for
practise. In naturall Philosophy, two ordinary Professors in
three yeares reade diuers bookes of Aristotle, and as many
extraordinary reade the same bookes, at diuers tymes; Diuinity
hath two Professors, the one a Scotist, the other a Thomist.
Two Professors reade the Metaphysicks, the one a Scotist, the
other a Thomist, one Professor reades the Ethicks, and another
the Mathematikes. Lastly the Professors of Logicke in the
morning reade Priora Analytica, and Posteriora, in the afternoone the Topicks and Elenches. The Jurists and the Artists
being the two bodyes making one Vniversity, haue each their
owne Treasurey, each in their house giuen them of old, and the
Treasure consists of the rents of lands giuen them by diuers
Benefactours from tyme to tyme, and of the yearely Matricula-
tions of newe Students, and of mony payde by those who take
any degree, and of Fynes imposed on Students for disorders, and
of like casualtyes, out of which treasure each pay the Stipends
of their Professors and like thinges. But the poore Students in
their Coleges are mantayned by priuate liberallity. The
Congregations of all the Students (in the publike Pallace of the
governour for Elections, and of the cheefe members of each
Rectorship in the schooles) or in the Rectors house (for their
affayres) are called together by the Bedells voyce, or most
commonly by papers sett vpon posts. The Vniversity hath
great priuileges as in perticular, all Students haue Immunity
from tributes during life through the State of Venice. In all
meetings the Rector of Jurists has the third place, and
the Rectour of the Artists the fourth, only the gouernour and
the Bishop hauing place before them. The Rector of the
Artists in his owne meetinges hath place aboue the Rectour of
the Jurists, who generally takes place of him. Each Rectour
in pomps hath a mace of siluer caryed before him by his Bedle,
and after his yeare ended hath two voyces in all elections, and
if he liue tenn yeare after his Rectorshipp in Padoa, he is a

Senator of the Citty, and by the Dukes graunt hath knightly
dignity in the Citty of Venice. For breuity I will omitt the
Indemnaty of Students from the publike magistrates Justice,
and many other priuileges. They who suie for degrees, may
obtayne them at any tyme of the yeare, but first they lay downe
the mony they haue to pay, into the hands of the Bedle, then
they are examined publikely by the Doctors and the Bishop, so
as the lectures be not hindred thereby, and they who are
reiected leese the mony they layd downe, and the approued are
led with pompe to their houses, and for the degree they haue
the publike seale. Indeede fewe or none are reiected, many
vnworthy men obtayning degres for mony, so as themselues
haue a vulgar speech, wee take mony and send the Asse into
Germany. The Students who are subiectes to the State of
Venice, may not take degree any where but at Padoa. Each
yeare two of the poore Schollers haue the degree of Doctor
freely giuen them without paying any mony vnder the Jurests
(one of the Cannon, the other of the Ciuill lawe) and likewise
two vnder the Artists (the one in Philosophy master of Artes,
the other in Phisick Docter, or both in ether). He that takes
degree in Philosophy, must haue studyed fyue yeares, and in
Phisicke first he must study three yeares, and then before he
practiseth himselfe, he must for one yeare follow the old
Doctors, only to see and obserue their practise, who comming
to a Patient, first aske the opinion of these young Doctors
before they deliuer their owne, wherby the young men cannot
but profitt very much. As also that from Aprell to September,
in a Curious garden of Simples they follow the Professors
discoursing to them the natures thereof. These Professors of
Phisick reade from Occtober to Aprill yearely vpon diuers
Anatomyes of all kyndes of bodyes, men, Children, and very
Embrioes.

And this Vniversity hath beene and still is no lesse famous
for learned and experienced Physitians, then Bologna hath
beene for great Professors in the Cannon and Ciuill Lawes.
And for the foresayd causes many English gentlemen prise the

Phisitians of Padoa, hauing such meanes to excell others, but
that hinders not Ignorant men corruptly to procure the
Doctours degree, which in that sorte may easily be obtayned.
Therefore I would rather prise him, who hauing studyed some
yeares in Padoa, should then retorne to take his degree in our
Vniversityes at home, where it cannot be stolen or bought by an
vnworthy man. Besydes no place is better then Padoa for the
Studye of the Mathematicks, wherof, besydes the publike, many
priuate teachers may here be founde, and ther want not
Students to Consorte and ioyne together, if neede be, to hyre
these priuate teachers. Also it is an excelent place to learne
and practise the Art of Musicke and playing vpon any
Instrument. And thereby excelent teachers to manage great
horses, which they kepe also of their owne in stables and yeardes
fitted to that purpose. And Padoa affordeth also most skillfull
masters and teachers to Fence. So as the desyre to learne these
vertues and qualityes, drawes many natiue and forrayne
gentlemen to spend some tyme in this vniversity. Only the
Privilege freeing Students from the publike Justice (to be tryed
and punished only by the Rectours Courtes of Justice, the
extreame punishment wherof is expulsion and banishment) or at
least the feare of the schollers raysing in Armes if a Student
should be apprehended by the officers of Justice, (giuing the
greatest malefactours opportunity to eskape by flyght) causeth
more harme then good to this vnoiversity. By reason whereof
vnlawfull assemblyes of Schollers by night and their being
Armed also with weapons forbidden both by day and night,
are very frequent, and many murthers are committed, not only
of enemyes but sometymes of strangers mistaken for enemyes,
and of others falling into suddayne quarrells (commonly about
wemen).

Italy hath diuers other Vniversities, as in Ferrara one,
instituted by the Dukes therof, who built a fayre Colege or
schooles wherein the Professors reade (which Citty with the
whole Dukedome, for want of heyres males, is now subiect to the
Popes of Rome). Pisa of old a free Citty and State of Tuscany

hath long beene and now is subiect to the Dukes of Florence, and it hath an Vniversity, wherein the Duke mantaynes 48. Professors with Stipends according to their worthines, from 50. Crownes yearely upwarde. At my being their, Doctour Poppone the cheefe Professor for the Cannon and Ciuill Lawes, had a 1000. Crownes yearely, and Mercurialis the cheefe Professor of Phisicke had 1700 Crownes, and Jacobo Mazone reader of Phylosophy had 700. Crownes yearely, and a Fryer of St. Anthonyes order Reader of Deuinity had 200 Crownes yearely. Besydes the Duke in the one only Colledge of Sapience, mantayned 44. poore Schollers, to whome for a lymited tyme to finish their Studyes, he allowed Chambers in the Colege, with a small portion of bread and wyne and ounces of flesh by the day, the rest of the Students liuing in Cittizens houses at theire owne charge. Also Sienna or old a free State of Tuscany, now subiect to the Dukes of Florence, hath an Vniversity not much frequented. For at my being there, it had not aboue 200. Students, and one only Collage, wherein the Professors did reade, and 24. poore schoolers had chambers freely, whereof 4 were Germans, and these poore schollers paying each 60. Crownes, had for certayne yeares to finish their Studye, a portion of bread and wyne and eight ounces of flesh each meale; and if any offended against the Statutes, they were punished with losse of dinners and suppers, which was no small affliction in theire poore allowance, and when their tyme came to be Doctours, they were to leaue the Colledge for others to succede. The Professors had some 30. some 50. some a 100. Crownes yearely Stipend. The Rector had power to promote three Doctours yearely without paying any Mony. They giue degrees at any tyme of the yeare when Schollers suie for them. A German at my being there Promoted Doctour, was led from the College with foure trumpitts sounding before him to the Bishops house, who gaue him a writing for this degree, and the next day being examyned priuately by fyue Doctours, he was made Doctor with the ordinary Ceremonyes, and with the sound of trumpitts, and after a Doctors Oration to him, and his retorne

of thanckes, all was concluded with a Dinner he gaue to the
Professors. For breuity I will omitt the Vniversityes in the
Kingdome of Naples. And lastly I will remember one laudable
Custome of all these Vniversityes, for Students to make priuate
Academies of a Certayne number of them agreeing to meete
twise or thrise in the weeke for priuate disputations and
exercises of theire perticular Studdyes and Professions.

Touching the Italyan language, the roote of it is the Lattin
tounge, to which espetially the Roman language at this day
hath neerer affinity then the speech of any other Province in
Italy, all which haue beene more corrupted by the barbarous
people invading the Roman Empire, and subduing Italy.
Besydes that the Italyans haue most Authours translated into
vulgar tounge, and most of their owne write in the same, for
which cause and for the long tyme required to learne the Lattin
tounge fewe endevour to attayne it. The neerenes of the
Italyan to the latten makes fewe of them write the latten and
much lesse speake it purely, and without corruption of many
words. For I haue formerly shewed in the third Part of this
worke, and the Chapter of precepts, howsoeuer many will vawnt
to speake many languages perfectly, and they who haue lesse
skill in them most easily beleeue it, yet for my part I thincke
it is very difficult, if not impossible, to speake two or more
languages derived from one roote with purity and perfection
and without many corrupt mixtures. As for example the
French, Spanish and Italyan tounges being derived from the
Lattin, who hath not hard many French men in speaking Lattin
mingle wordes of their owne toung, and for Spanish, the Oration
of the Duke of Alua to the Schollers of Lovan hath priuilegios
and many other Spanish wordes vsed for Lattin, and for Italian
my selfe hauing beene scarce two monthes in Italy, in writing
two Lattin verses mistooke for Lattin two Italyan wordes of the
same signification, namely mando and remando insteede of
Mitto and Remitto. Thus the Neapolitan language is most
corrupted with the Spanish, by soldyers of that nation
governing them. Thus the Province of Calabria in that

Kingdome, hauing beene of old much inhabited by the Greekes bordering vpon them, by mixture of their wordes, haue the most corrupt language of all Italy. And thus the Citty and territory of Bergamo bordering vpon France and diuers nations of the Alpes, haue the most corrupt tounge of all Lombardy. Among diuers propertyes giuen to seuerall languages by a Prouerbiall speech attributed to the Emperour Charles the fyfth, the Italian is sayd to be most proper for making of loue. And indeede no language in the world hath a more sweete pronuntiation, or more insinuating and pearcing accents, wordes, and Phrases, espetially in the passages of loue, to which the Italians can best giue life by gestures and actions, where that expression is allowed them. Generally the Tuscans are reputed to speake the best Italian, and of them, some holde the inhabitants of Lucca to haue the purest language, being free from many offensiue accents vsed by the other Toscanes. The most vulgar opinion is, that the Citty and teritory of Sienna speakes the purest language of Toscany, and of all Italy, whether many strangers resorte espetially for that cause. But as Florence is the cheefe Citty of Tuscany, and yealdes most excelent witts, so they drawe this reputation to that Citty, where learned gentlemen haue instituted a priuate Academy among themselues, of chosen men called the Protectours of the Tuscan language, and the Academye of the Crusca, so called Metaphorically of sifting of bad wordes from the good, as branne is sifted from meale by the boulting Cloath and siue, and this Academye hath lately published a Dictionary vulgarly called Diceria, Contayning the purest words of the language, collected out of approued Authors. Lastly many learned and great men defend the Court language of Rome to be the best of all Italy, as more mixt, and seruing it selfe of all wordes and Phrases in other languages, which most significantly and most breefely expresse the speakers meaning, wherein giue me leaue to say, that they are confuted, who traduce the English tounge to be like a beggers patched Cloke, which they should rather compayre to a Posey of sweetest flowers, because by the sayd meanes, it hath beene in late ages excellently refyned and made perfitt for ready and breefe deliuery both in prose and verse.

Ceremonyes　Maryages　Childbearinges　Christninges Funeralls and diuers Customes.

Touching Ceremonyes, the Italians are full of them in their priuate actions, but farr exceede in publike Pompes of State, and processions of Religion.　For the Pope, the humble seruant of seruants, I will giue you a tast with what pompe he passeth the streetes of Rome, by one example which my selfe sawe, and haue formerly related, yet must agayne mention here, because it fitts the purpose.　First many of the Popes footemen marched, attending an empty litter, lyned with Crimson velvett, and caryed by two white mules.　Then followed on foote the Sweitzers of the Popes guarde.　Next rode some 400. gentlemen of Rome brauely mounted.　Next rode some 20. of the Popes Chamberlayns and cheefe officers, cloathed in gownes of violett Cloth, and carying white staues long and thicke in their hands, Followed by the Cardinalls cheefe seruants on horsebacke, carrying their lords hatts of Red Velvett.　Next rode the Cardinalls (as many as were then in Rome) vpon mules, with rich foote Cloathes.　Then came white mules and hacknyes with rich footeclothes, as many as the Pope had sett yeares, they being of the yearely tribuite for Naples.　Next came the Pope with his triple Crowne, riding in a litter open like a Chayre, and drawne by white hackneyes, hauing a rich Canopy over his head, carryed by six men in Crimson veluitt gownes, and on each syde of him rode an officer in like habitt, hauing a Fann of Peacokes tayles or like Fethers, wherewith the one kept the sunne from the Popes face, the other making wynde to Coole his holynes.　Before the Pope rode the master of the Ceremonyes, Crying downe, downe, that the people might kneele to receaue the Popes benediction, made with the signe of the Crosse.　After the Pope, Rode the Arch Bishops, the Bishops, Abbotts, and cheefe officers, followed by their serfants, and sometymes the reere of the trayne is closed vp with the Popes

troope of light horsemen well mounted and Armed. Thus the
Pope rode from his Pallice to St. Maryes Church, where arived,
he was taken from his litter, and seated in a Redd vellvett
Chayre, without touching the grounde with his feete, and so
carryed on the shoulders of those who bare the Canopy, not
only into the Church, but into the vestry, and there placed some
stepps from the grownde, where a rope and certayne Robes were
putt vpon him, which done he was in like sorte carryed on mens
shoulders to his throne on the other syde of the Church, neere
to the Alter vpon which masse was to be song in his presence, at
which tymes he that singes the masse brings the hostia to the
Pope, by his handes to be elevated that the people may addore
it. And because they holde it to be the very body and blood
of Christ after the Consecration, I expected the Pope would
haue decended some stepes of his throne at least, and haue
bended his knee at least when he receaved it, but he did nether,
only rising from his seate to lift it vp to the people. After the
masse the people came in thronge to kisse the Popes Pantofle.
And thus his pryde exceedes that of the Turkish Emperour, in
his Canopy, his fanns, his carrying on shoulders without
touching the grounde, and the kissing of his Pantofle, and his
making the people kneele to receaue his blessing. For the great
Turke lightes from his horse at the dore of the moschee or
Church, and goes on foote to his seate, nether permitts he any
to kneele before him, but only to bende the body and to goe
forth from his presence with their faces still towardes him. It
were tedious to relate the Ceremonyes of State, when the Pope
setts in his Conclaue, when he Creates Cardinalls, and when he
sings Masse himselfe, with one Cardinall seruing him as
Deacon, and another as subdeacon. In all which the greatest
part of adoration is to the Popes person, the Cardinalls kissing
his vesture, the Bishops his knee, and all others his Pantofell,
and many lowe Reverences being made to him. But I could
neuer see heare nor reade, that the Pope himselfe falles vpon
his knees, or so much as bendes them in any diuine worship.
The Roman Catholikes will say that the Pope prayed at the

tyme of the Sea fight against the Turkes at Lepanto many howers by the Clocke with his windowe open (whereof I beleeve that if he prayed the window was open) and that he prayes and kneeles when he is a priuate Auditor and when himselfe sayth not masse. But now another sung the Masse, and he only eleuated the Hostia (as they say he doth allwayes when he is present) and methinckes he should most kneele when he sayth masse himselfe, but I am sure I neuer sawe him kneele or shewe like reverence to God, but often sawe him receaue from all sortes of men both kneeling and the kissing of his pantofle. Innumerable are the Ceremonyes of Religion through all Italy, in sprincklings of holy water, hallowing of Churches, Chappells, Alters, and Bells, in Baptising of Bells, in Processions vpon the Saynts festiuall dayes, at the Churches dedicated to them, wherein the Prists with lighted tapers, with banners, and singing, and Trumpitts, carye the Saynts Images about the Church and parish to be adored by the people. And in all Churches vpon all Sondayes and festifall dayes they haue consortes of excelent musicke, both lowde and still Instruments and voyces, and they clothe the Images with fresh Robes, and sett forth Images, called the lay mens bookes, to expresse the history of the Gospell for that day, as vpon the day of Palmes the Image of Christ riding vpon an asse with a branch of Palmes in his hand, and vpon Easter day the Image of Christ sett vpon the Alter attyred in carnation satten like a younge Cupid, with like expressions of his death vpon good fryday, and his buyriall with funerall processions. In all Churches, besydes the solemne masse song alowde, they haue many masses mumbled in the same Church, and often at the same tyme; vpon many other Alters, wherein the Priests vse only dumb signes, and movings of their lipps, without speaking a worde, in both which, and in all which, the Crossings, bowings, turnings of the body to the Alter, and from it to the people, the liftings vp of the handes, head, and eyes, and all gestures for euery worde of the masse, are prescribed to the Priests by written rules, made familiar to all of them by continuall Custome. The

Ceremonyes of State and Processions of Religion in the Citty
of Venice, are frequent and performed with great pompe, in
both which they passe all States not only of Italy, but of the
whole worlde (if you except the Popes carying on mens
shoulders and his like Adorations, which neuer any other
Potentate by Ciuill or spirituall power assumed to himselfe, no
not the Persion Emperours, more famous for pryde then all
other vices and vertues). First for pompes of State, the Duke
and the Signory haue of old by diuers lawes and at diuers tymes
Instituted publike Andate in Trionfo, that is walkes in triumph,
some in memory of victoryes obtayned, or publike dangers
escaped, or of publike benefactours, some for rites of the
Church, and diuers devotians, and some by vowes. They are
called walkes, because they are performed on foote by land, and
in the triumpfall Barke (called Bucentoro as Capable of 200.
men) when they must passe by water, never riding on horse
backe, since the Citty being buylt within lakes vpon litle
Ilands, distant on all sydes some foure or fiue myles from firme
land, the Importing of horses is troublesome, besydes that the
streetes are very narrow, so as since the Citty grewe populous
and fully built, it is a rare thinge to see a horse brought thether.
In these walkes first 8. standards are carryed, then followe six
siluer Trompitts, then march two by two the Dukes officers,
whome the Romans called Cryers, being all 50. in nomber,
attyred in Turchine gownes, with the Cognizance of St. Marke
in mettall vpon one sleeue, and Red Caps vpon their heades.
Then follow the waytes of the Citty, and the Drumms, attyred
in Red, sounding and beating all the way. Then followe the
Dukes sheilde bearers two by two, attyred in gownes of black
velvett, then another officer of the Duke bearing in his hand
a taper of white wax in a Siluer Candlesticke, with six Chanons
following and three parish Priests. Then follow the Dukes
Castaldi, then the Secretaryes (and the Dukes Chaplayne)
attyred in Robes of Crimson veluitt, then the Dukes two
Chancelours, then the great Chancelour of the State, attyred
in Crimson with larg ducall sleeues, Then follow two sheilde

bearers, the one on the right hand carrying the Dukes Seate, the other on the left hand Carying the Dukes Cushion of Cloth of gold.   Then followes the Duke in his Robes, with an hoode of powdred Ermines vpon his shoulders, a Scudiero carying his ombrella betweene him and the sunne, and two men beareing vp the trayne of his Robe, and vpon each syde of the Duke march the legate and Ambàssadours, of the Pope, Kings, and Princes.   Next after the Duke Followes a gentleman, carying the Dukes Ensigne of State, then the Dukes six Counselors, then the Procuratours of St. Marke two by two, then the three heades of the Counsell of forty, then the three heades of the Counsell of tenne, then the Censors.   And after these Magistrates, followe 60. of the Cheefe Senatours, and 60 inferiour (whose turne it is from six to six moneth to attend the Prince in these publike walkes of triumph).   These Walkes in triumph are yearely tenn in number.   The first is to the Church of our lady Maria Formosa, vpon the evening of the Purification of our Lady, which feast falls yearely on the second of February.   And it was instituted vpon this occasion.   The Cittizens of old were wont to espouse their virgines, and to pay their dowryes before the Bishop in the Church of St. Peter, vpon 31th of January yearely.   Which Pyratts knowing and hiding themselues in that Iland in the yeare 943. came Armed vpon them, and having killed many, tooke away the spouses, and the dowryes ; but the Artizans espetially of this St. Maryes Parish, vpon the outcrye taking Armes, and following them in Barques, overtooke them the same day while they were deuiding the spoyle, and defeating them, recovered the Virgins and dowryes, for which seruice being required to demaund what recompence they would haue, they required nothing but the establishing by a lawe of this walke in the foresayd triumph, to their said parish Church, at the sayd Feast of our Lady yearely, bynding themselues to send the Duke two hatts for feare it should rayne that day, and to giue him and his Company two Flagons of malmsye to drincke.   The second walke is to the Church of St. Zachary vpon Easter day, instituted vpon holy reliques and

great Pardens of sinne sent and graunted by Pope Benidicke
the third, to all that should visite the sayd reliques deposed in
that Church vpon the sayd day. The third walke is vpon the
8th day after Easter, to the Church of St. Geminiano Instituted
in memory of a Duke inlarging that part of the markett place
of St. Marke or vpon pennance imposed by a Pope. The fourth
walke is to the Church of St. Marke vpon the 25th of Aprill, the
Feast day of that Saynt. Whose body being brought to Venice
in the moneth of January in the yeare 828, this Church was built
where the Church of Saynt Theodour stoode, who till that tyme
was the Tutelar Saynt of the State, but now the Senate ordayned
St. Marke to be the Protector thereof, and his new built Church
to be the Dukes golden Chappell, where the sayde Feast is
yearely solemnized, as the greatest of all the rest, and in
greatest triumph, the Duke that day Feasting the Senate with
great magnificence. The fifth walke is to the two Castles,
instituted vpon this occasion. Pope Alexander the third chased
from Rome by the German Emperour Frederick (nicknamed
Barbarossa) after he had liued vnregarded in Fraunce, came to
Venice about the yeare 1176, and there liued disguised in the
habitt of a poore Priest, till he was knowne by a French man,
who had seene him in Fraunce, and made him knowne to the
Duke and State of Venice, wherevpon they came to adore the
Pope, and attyre him in Pontificall Robes, and mantayned and
supported him for Pope, which caused the Emperour to send his
sonne Otho to make warr vpon the Venetians by Sea, whome
they overcame in a Navall fight, and tooke Otho himselfe
prisoner, by which accident the Emperour was induced to make
peace with Alexander the third, and come to Venice there to
Asknowlege and adore him for Pope. Nowe this Pope in
thanckfullnes, gaue to the Duke and State an hallowed taper
of white wax (which vseth to be lighted when the Pope himselfe
sings Masse) and also a sworde hallowed, and eight Banners of
diuers Collers, and six siluer Trumpitts all to be caryed before
the Duke (as I haue formerly shewed) in all his pompes of
triumph. And because the Venetians obtayned the sayd victory

against Otho vpon the Ascension daye, the Pope confirmed to that State as wone by sword, the absolute Commande of that Sea, nowe called the Gulfe of Venice, giuing the Duke a gold ringe, with which he should espouse the Sea to that State yearely vpon the Ascention day, the Senate then by lawe establishing this yearely Walke, which is the greatest solemnity of the yeare, concurring with a great fayer yearely, lasting 15. dayes, and with a perpetuall Indulgence or Pardon from the Pope, beginning in the Church of St. Marke vpon Ascention even. Thus the Duke yearely vpon the Ascension day marcheth in the foresayd Pompe from his publike Pallace to the great Channell, and at a bridge neere the Arsenall, he with his trayne enters the Ducall Barque called Bucentoro (as Conteyning two hundreth persons, which is a litle Gally rowed with oares, hauing a large Chamber built ouer it of wood, with seates rounde about it, all guilded, and for the tyme adorned with rich hangings within, and rich Carpetts within and without, besyde the sayd Banners, Siluer trompitts, and other ensignes of State) hauing two smale Gallyes going before to tow it on if perhaps the Sea or wynde be contrary, and being attended by the exquisite musicke of St. Marke, and with a strange nomber of Gondole wherein the Cittizens and strangers passe to see the pompe, which being thus sett forwarde, the Patriarke meetes the Duke in the midd way, and fastening his Barque to the Bucentoro, they passe to the two Castles, the Patriarke present-ing to the Duke and Senatours three siluer Basons full of most sweete and rare flowers, and when they come a litle beyonde the Castles, the Duke casts a golde ringe into the Sea, saying wee espowse thee as a signe of our perpetuall dominion ouer thee, as the husband hath ouer the wife, or in like wordes to that purpose, according to the sayd Popes institution. Then the Patriarke blesseth the Sea against Shipwrackes, and to be as a Church yearde hallowed to the bodyes dying therein. And so the Duke retornes to the two Castles, and dismounting heares masse at the Church of St. Nicolas, which done he retornes in like manner to his Pallace, where the Senatours of that trayne

dyne with him. The sixth walke is to the Church of St. Vito,
vpon the 15th of June, in memory of the States liberty
preserued in the yeare 1310. vpon that 15th day of June, from
the vsurping tyranny of Baiamonto Tierpoli, a rich ambitious
Cittyzen, the Pompe whereof is the greater because it is
accompanyed with a solemne Procession of Religion.   And
in generall the pompe of these Processions consists in
Companyes of Prists and Fryers of Religious Orders, carrying
with them the Crosse and banners of the Images of Saynts, and
singing all the way they march, as likewise in the attendance
of the bretheren of the Schooles, espetially of the six great
Schooles, marching in like sorte with their banners and Images.
And these Schooles are Fraternityes of gentlemen and cheefe
Cittizens, vnited in one body, and each hauing their schoole or
hall or Pallace proper to them, and not only inriched with
lybraryes and precious antiquities, but of old endowed with
lands of great yearely Reuenues, besyde their treasure, daly
increasing by legacyes, which the dying bretheren giue in their
last wills and testaments, all which they imploy in workes of
piety and pittye, as in the adorning of Alters, and in freely
giuing dowryes to poore virgins (with great magnificence) and
in like workes.

The seuenth Walke is to the Church of St. Marina vpon the
17th of July, the feast of that Saynt, instituted to heare Masse
and giue thanckes because on that day and by medeation of
that Saynt, they recovered Padoa and all their State of firme
land, which they had vtterly lost by the league of Cambray,
(which Pope Julio the second made with the Emperour Maximilian and the King of Fraunce, all Combyned against the
State of Venice).

The eighth Walke in triumph, is to the Church of our Redeemer, vpon the third Sonday in July, instituted in the yeare
1576, when the Citty, being wasted by a fearce pestilence, vpon
a vowe made by the whole Senate to our Redeemer, was by
his goodnes in shorte tyme cleared from this mortall infection,
and so this yearely walke was established by lawe of devotion
of theire thanckfullnes.

The nynth walke in Triumph, is to the Church of Sta Giustina vpon the vijth of October the Feast day of that Saynt, and this walke was Instituted by a lawe in the yeare 1571, for memory of the famous nauall victory obtayned at that tyme by the Combyned nauall forces of the Venetians the Pope and the King of Spayne against the great Turkes powerfull Nauye, and to giue yearely thanckes to God for the same victory, giuen them at the intercession of Sta Giustina.

The tenth and the last walke in Triumph, is to the Church of St. George the greater, on Christmas day after dinner to heare Vesper, and the next morning being the day of St. Stephen to heare masse, instituted some say in the yeare 1109, others say 1179, some say in memory of St. Stephens body then brought vpon that day to the Citty, others say in memory of a Duke who then left to the State by his last will and testament the inheritance of Certayne landes lying in the same Iland of St. George.

The Duke hath also two walkes in Triumph, but only on the euenings of feasts not on the feasts dayes, both to St. Markes Church, one vpon the euening of his feast, the other on the euening of the ascention day.

Also the Duke hath many other walkes but not in Triumph, (that is without the foresayde Pompe and trayne) because most of them are to the Church of St. Marke ioyning close to the publike Pallice in which the Duke resydes. And hereof foure are principall, as instituted by the Senate.

The first is to our Ladyes Church vpon our ladyes feast day in March, instituted because the first foundation of the Citty was layde as vpon that day of the yeare, when the Goathes came first into Italy.

The second is vpon the feast day of St. Isider being the 16th of Aprill, in the Chappell of that St. within the Church of St. Marke, instituted by the Senate in memory of a Duke executed for conspiring against the liberty of the State in the yeare 1348. wherein the Duke is accompanyed with a Religious Procession, of the Clergy, the orders of Fryers, and the foresayd

Schooles, and 12 lighted tapers are caryed in memory of that
Dukes Funerall. And because the Duke and the Procession
passe betweene two marble pillers wanting only timber layd
acrosse to make a payre of Gallowes, it is also thought a remembrance to the present Duke to Contayne himselfe within the
boundes of his limited dignity.

The third is to the Church of St. Marke vpon the feast of
Corpus Domini on the 20th of June. This feast was instituted
first by Pope Vrban the 4th, in the yeare 1264. vpon a Miracle
at Bolsena, where a Priest hauing Consecrated the hostia, and
doubting still that it was not the body of Christ, the same shedd
forth much blood (if you will beleeue a lye, or at least a lying
Miracle) and this walke was instituted at Venice in the
yeare 1407, with a Procession as aforesayde, but with greater
pompe, the Patriark singing Masse and after carying in Procession the hostia within a Tabernacle, and the Priests weareing
their richest vestments, and all men their best attyre, besydes
that much plate and many Reliques are caryed about in that
Procession, performed as they say with much humility, but it
may better be sayd with grosse Idolatry. And of old on this
day a Gally was appointed for transporting Pilgrims to Jerusalem, and each Senatour tooke a Pilgrim to walke with him
in the sayd Procession, but at this day fewe Pilgrims passing,
the sayd Gally is no more provided for them.

The fourth walke without Triumph, is to the Church of
St. Marke the 25 of June, Instituted by the Senate in the yeare
1094. vpon this occasion. The body of St. Marke being of old
deposed in this Church, and all memory being lost of the place
where it was layd, the Duke and the Senate in the sayde yeare
moved by deuotion and greefe, required the Patriark that vpon
the sayde day he would publish a solemne Fast and devote
Procession, to pray vnto God that he would reveale the place
where the blessed Euangelists body was layd, which donne, after
the singing of the Masse and publike prayers, the Marbles of a
Pillar, in the sight of the Duke and Senatours, Claue asunder,
and St. Markes Coffin by litle and litle thrusting out it selfe, at

last appeared playnely to the vewe of all the people. It is worth
the marking, that in the former ages when the Reliques of dead
Saynts were not worshipped, all memory was lost where the
bodye of St. Marke was layde, and that this Miracle is written
to fall at the tyme when the blynd Ignorance and superstitious
devotion of the Roman Religion was highly increased in the
Westerne Church.

Moreover the Duke with the Senate makes some 22. publike
Walkes without Triumph to the Church of St. Marke, whereof
that vpon Christmas Even is the most solemne, when the Vesper
is song with most exquisite musicke both of Instruments and
voyses, and also a Masse is song before midnight by old priuilege from the Bishops of Rome, for otherwise Masses are not
sayd but in the morning and by Priests who are fasting and
haue not yett either eaten or druncke. And it is most strange
to see the Church. so full of lights both within and without,
from the topp to the botome, as a man would thincke it all on
fyer. For they have 1500. small lights, each of a pounde
weight, and 60 great lights each of 12 pounds weight, and
all these are of wax as white as snowe, the yellowe being
not esteemed by them, besydes all the ordinary lampes
burning, and the waxlights and torches vpon the high Alter,
and the great nomber of torches caryed before the Duke and
Senatours when they goe from the Church. Nether is it lesse
strange to see all these Candles and torches lighted in a moment
by foure men at the foure corners of a Crosse, giuing light to
flax, which conveyeth light by lynes to all the said candles and
torches. At which tyme also they haue a most solemne Procession with the assistance of the foresayd schooles, Fryers of
Religious orders, and parish Priests. And by the way note,
that these Priests are to this day chosen by the lay Parishioners,
hauing howses and landes in the Parish, and are only confirmed
by the Patriarke of Venice.

The State of Venice vseth also great pompe in publike
Feasts, some common to the whole Citty, some peculiar to
Familyes and Parishes, Some are yearely. As when of olde

they defeated and tooke prisonour the Patriarke of Aqualegia, the Senate Instituted by lawe and vpon great penalty the yearely feast of Fatt Thursday (being called Giouedi grasso vulgarly, and falling on the Thursday before Lent). And vpon that day the Duke and the Senators sitt in a gallery of the publike Pallice lying vppon the markett place of St. Marke, in which a Bull is killed before them, by cutting off his head at one blowe, with a two handed sworde made very sharpe and heauy for that purpose. This done of old they had a Castle of wood built in a large Chamber of the Pallace, which the Senatours Armed with tronchions did assault and take, but this Ceremony in after ages seeming ridiculous boyes play, hath long beene out of vse. Also they vsed of olde to kill 12 Porkes, and send peeces therof to the Senatours; but this Ceremony also hath long tyme beene out of vse. But to this day they tye Bulls in Ropes helde by men, chasing them through the streetes, which being very narrowe they Cry Guarda il toro, that is take heede of the Bull, lest any passenger should be gored by them. Allways Vnderstande that the feastes are Celebrated more with outwarde pompe and Ceremony then with larg provisions and proportions of wyne and meate. Some Feasts are Casuall. And thus the State hath many tymes stately intertayned Popes, Kinges, and Princes, of which kynde the intertaynment of the French king Henry the thirde in the yeare 1574, is most fresh in memorye and was performed with great pompe and publike expence, when this King retorned that way from Poland into Fraunce, assoone as he came to the Confynes of this State, he was daly mett and attended by the gouernours of the places wher he passed, and by the troopes of horse and foote Companyes on the firme land, and daly saluted for his welcome by vollyes of small shott, and from all Forts and Castles by peales of great Ordinance; when he came to the water syde, he was mett by many Senatours comming with great Nomber of Gondele or small boates, which use to be covered with blacke Cloth, but were then richly covered with Cloath of golde and Imbrotheryes,

espetially those brought for the King and his trayne. Thus
passing, before he came to the Citty he was mett with a guarde
of Soldyers in boates, and many young gentlemen of the
greatest familyes sent to attend his person, and was saluted
with peales of great Ordinance from diuers Castles and from
many Gallyes and Shipps lying in the Porte. And so he passed
with loude soundes of Drumms and trumpitts to the Pallace of
Foscarini where he was lodged, because it had a fayre prospect
both wayes vpon the great Channell. Daly he was attended
by Senatours and the Duke with the Bucintoro, to invite &
conduct him to Banquitts, wherein he was intertayned with
some French liberty. For one day at a banquitt in the great
Chamber, where the generall Counsell of the Duke Senatours
and gentlemen vseth to assemble, two hundreth [and] forty
Virgins were invited to attend the King, who satt all on one
syde, all attyred in white with rich Jewells. The King entring
and drawing neere to them bareheaded, they all rose, and as
he passed and saluted them, they made lowe Reuerence to him,
and after the banquitt and tables remoued, the Frenchmen and
other gentlemen tooke them all to daunse the measures, and
after daunsing of some Gallyardes, all departed, the Duke and
Senatours in the Bucintoro conducting and attending the King
to the Pallace where he lodged. Also the King was conducted
to see all the rare things in the Citty, and intertayned with
diuers other pastymes, as two partyes one keeping the other
assayling bridges, built within sight of his lodging, which
sporte they often vse at other tymes with no other weapons
then Armes and fists, and sometymes fall from Jeast to earnest,
at dry blowes, and flinging one another into the water. In
like sorte the King was attended and feasted at his departure
till he came to the Confynes of that State lying towardes
France, with great magnificence and expence of that State, in
testimony of loue to Fraunce.

Maryages.

They keepe also soleme Feasts at the maryage of the Duke,

which seldome happens, by reason they are olde before they are chosen, but the Duchesse is allwayes Crowned with great solemnity and feasting. At which tyme (as also at the Maryages betweene persons of great familyes) Tylting and like military exercises are proclamed for many dayes, and to them whome the Judges thincke to haue best deserued therin, the cheefe prise Commonly is some rich peece of Cloath or stuffe, with like honorable guifts allotted by the Senate or by the Patrons of the feast.

Ceremonyes in Generall.

For Ceremonyes in generall (besydes that I haue formerly sayd) the Italyans giue high and exessiue tytles one to another, in their salutations by worde & writing, and haue beene the Authors to spreade this flattery through all these parts of the worlde. The title of Count seemes not much respected by them, for they are not absolute Princes. I haue seene at Sienna a Countesse walke in the Streete ledd by a man seruant, her young daughter going before her, and two men seruants going before her, hauing only one mayde seruant following all, not attyred like a gentlewoman, but like a poore Chamber mayde and this Countesse to take an ordinary place in the body of the Church. Gentlewemen and others most commonly goe leaning with one hand vpon olde wemens shoulders, and the reason why they goe thus Ledd or leaning, is because they weare high Startups or Pantofills of wood, so as they cannot goe without helpe.

Maryages.

Touching Ceremonyes of Maryages. Howsoeuer I haue sayd that in Venice persons of great Familyes are marryed with Feasts and tiltings, yet generally the Italians are Jelious, and delight not to shewe the beauty of their brydes. Of olde in the Provinces of the State of Venice, historyes write that they were wont to mary their virgins at the outcrye, namely to him that would giue most for them, and by the mony giuen for the fayrest, raysed dowryes for them that were ill fauored, and so deformed as they founde none would giue mony for them. After the Citty of Venice was built, and the Cittizens became Christians I haue formerly shewed (vpon the first walke of the Duke and Senate in triumph to the Church of St. Mary the faire, instituted in the yeare 943.) that the Virgins vpon 31 of January came all to the Church of St. Peter, each bringing her dowry in a portable box (for in those ages the dowryes were small) where the Patriarke after the Masse made a Sermon of maryage, which done and the Patriarkes blessing giuen to the maryed, the young men there attending with their Parents and neerest kinsmen, tooke the virgins they liked with their dowryes, and caryed them to their houses. In latter ages the maryages of the gentry are concluded betweene the Parents before the Virgin is once seene by her husband; then they are brought into the Court of the publike Pallace, where in the presence of many Senatours and gentlemen, the Parents publish the affinity, and the young Cuple hauing touched handes together the Parents invite the guests against a day appointed, at which day the guests comming to the house of the Virgins Parents, and being sett downe, the Virgin is brought to them, with her hayre wauing loose, but tyed in the Crowne with threds of golde, and being all attired in white, of old custome. There the wordes and Ceremonyes of the espowsall being performed, she is led about the roome with the sounde of Drumms, Trumpitts, and other musicall Instruments, going in a Comely measure of daunsing, and often bending the body to the guests as shee passeth, and so being seene of them all, retyres into her Chamber. Then shee discendes agayne accompanied with many gentlewemen, and enters a Gondola where shee setting in a litle throne adorned, and the rest following her in other Gondole or boates, shee passeth by water to visite the Nunneryes where shee hath any kinswemen. Then the feast is Celebrated with great ioye, and plentifull Prouisions, but limited by the lawes according to the nomber of the guests, which many tymes and Commonly are some 100th persons. After fewe dayes the young maryed wemen visite the Bride. The Bridesgrome and bride were wont to visitt the Duke, to make him wittnes of the maryage; but of late tymes that Custome is left, and the maryage with the Indentures of Contract is regestred in a publike office. Through all Italy ingenerall, the espowsall or betrothinge with the Ring, is made priuately, the bride being never seene by the Bridsgrome before that day, and that performed, they lye together in bedd, and some dayes or monthes after at best leasure, the Parents and neerest kindred on both sydes meete together, and going to a masse in pompe, keepe that day among themselues the maryage feast in a priuate manner and with no great expence.

Childbearing.

Touching Childebearing. In Venice, the Children of gentlemen, and the tymes of their birth, are registred in the foresayd publike office, in which maryages are registred, and the howses of gentlewemen brought to bed, and espetially the Chambers wherein they lye, are richly sett forth with costly hangings, with Tables and Cabinetts of mother of pearle, and pearles and Jasper, and other precious stones, and with curious workes of Paynters, and Carving, in brasse, gold, and siluer, and like Jewells, in which permanent riches the Italyans and espetially the Venetians greatly delight and abounde. And they were wont to make such large expence in confections to entertayne visitours, as the Senate hath beene forced by lawes to lymitt that excesse. Generally in Italy, and more spetially in the State of the Duke of Toscany, the mothers nurse not their owne Children, but send them forth (as in England) to be nursed in the Country, thincking the open ayre of the Country more healthfull for them and they lye in a moneth (as our wemen doe). When a woman is Churched the Priest meetes her at the Church dore, where he sayth some exorcismes or prayers, and then he takes her by the vper garment (shee laying holde on his stoale) and leading her to the body of the Church, there sayth some latin prayers (as their prayers are all in Latin) whence shee departs, but vseth to make no feast to her frends and neighbours.

Christninges.

Touching Christnings: The Citty of Venice differs from all other in Italy vpon firme land, in some thinges. They were wont to spend excessiuely in confections, till that expence was restrayned by lawes. The gentlemen haue not two godfathers as other where, but sometymes 150. And because that spirituall kindred (as they call it) hinders maryage in the Roman Church, the lawe forbids them to be gentlemen of Venice, and the Priest when he powers water on the Childes head, is bounde to aske and looke that none of them be gentlemen of Venice. And these godfathers are at no charge of guifts, except some at pleasure will cast mony on the Alter for the Priest, but the Chyldes father presents each of them with a marchpane. And this Ceremony is done for boyes, no woman being present, but one that caryes the Chylde. Here and in all Italy, and generally through out the Roman Church, the Prist meetes the Chylde at the Church dore, and exorciseth it with holy water and Crossings (a kynde of Coniuration they vse to expell the Deuill, or originall sinne, or I know not what) and that donne, the Chylde is permitted to enter the Church, and at the Funt is baptised in the name of the Father, sonne, and holy ghost, in the lattin tounge (as all diuine seruice is sayd) hauing water powred on the head with many Crossinges). In other partes of Italy, more spetially in the State of the great Duke of Toscany, the godfathers and godmothers present guifts both to the Childe and nurse (as wee doe, but not in that excesse which of late hath crept in among vs in England) according to the quality of the person. And they vse likewise both to make Festiuall Dynners and banquets. Only the Childe, be it male or female, hath but one Godfather and one Godmother, besydes the Father who vseth also to promise for his Chylde.

Funeralls.

Touching Funeralls. When the Duke of Venice is dead, his body attyred in Ducall habitt is layd forth in a large publike roome of the publike Pallice, and 20. Senatours are chosen to attend and sett about the body in Scarlett Robes, for three dayes; after which he is buyred with solemnity. Assoone as he is dead, the vj Counselors (wherof the eldest is Viceduke till another be chosen) and three heades of the Counsell of 40, enter the publike Pallace, and come no more forth till a newe Duke be chosen. At the Dukes death there is no more change in the State then if a priuate gentleman were dead, only in the Citty all lawe causes cease till a newe Duke be chosen, because the Judges are imployed in that buisines. After the Duke is buiryed, the great generall Counsell the first day chuseth fyue Counselours, and three Inquisitours to examyne the life of the late Duke, and they are bounde to present all errours therof to the great Counsell, which for great errours sometymes imposeth Fynes vpon the hayres. Thus of late Duke Loredan, otherwise of singular goodnes and wisdome, being founde to haue liued more sparingly then that his dignity required, was by the great Counsell Fyned 1500. Ducates, which his hayres payd. The great Counsell vpon the second day, after an Oration in prayse or disprayse of the late Duke, begins the Election of a new. In the Church of St. Marke none are buryed, but Cardinalls, the Popes legattes, Forayne Princes, and the Generalls of the State for horse and foote, whose Funeralls are attended by the Duke and Senatours, and performed at the publike charge of the State. The euening before the buyriall, the body is brought into the Church, and layd vnder a Canopy, with many wax lightes burning about it, and so it lyes to be seene of all men till the next day at Vesper, when the seruice for the dead is songe, and then the body is carryed about with a solemne procession, and after buryed. The Dukes are buryed in what churches themselues appoint, and the bodyes are caryed thether by night. In Venice ordinary Funeralls are per-

formed with more Ceremony then vpon firme land. The first
day the body is layd foorth in the house till two howers within
night, when the Priests and frendes of the dead attend the
body to the Church, where it is sett downe with two lighted
torches at the head, and two at the feete, and the next day the
seruice for the dead is song, and the body carryed in procession,
and then layd in the graue. The Funerall is not counted
honorable in Venice that costs not some 400 Ducates, and the
pompe of the foresayd Procession takes vp long way in the
streetes, and is very great, tho the Duke and Senatours be not
allwayes present, in regard of the rich Vestures, Crosses, and
Banners of Images, which are Patron Saynts to the Clergy, the
Fryers, and the Fraternityes of Schooles. In the midst of this
Funerall pompe, the dead body is carryed by eight men, and
the body is richly apparreled and covered with a Cloth of golde,
and followed by the Children and Kinsmen and seruants of
the dead person, all Mourning in black gownes with their
heades covered. For the rest of the followers only those of the
fraternity to which the dead person belongs, haue their heads
covered. The wemen mournours, as at Venice so through all
Italy, weare over their forehead a French bongrace Couered
with black Cipres, which also covers the head and hangs ouer
the shoulders, and vpon a blacke gowne they weare a peece of
white Cloath, one or two handfulls broade, hanging about
their neckes and so downe the forepartes to theire feete. As in
Venice so through all Italy, they are not buryed in seuerall
graues digged of purpose, as commonly with vs, but in Caues
or vaults, either private to their Familyes, or common to the
people. And they are buryed in their Apparrell, and haue their
faces open till the Cave be opened, at which tyme theire faces
are covered with linnen, and the bodyes are cast into the Cave,
which is presently made vp very close, because as some of the
dead bodyes are consumed, so others are more or lesse rotten,
as they haue beene longer or latter buryed, from the stincke
whereof they feare infection. In the Citty of Pisa they haue
a large and very fayre Churchyarde, with many fayre marble

Pillers, for a Common buryall place, called Campo Santo that
is the holy fielde, because the German Emperour Frederick
Barbarossa returning from Jerusalem with his Ships ballasted
with earth of the holy land, layd the same there, and they say
that the bodyes buyried vnder that earth are consumed within
two or very fewe dayes. Generally In Italy (more spetially in
Tuscany) they giue Doles of bread wyne and mony to the poore,
but they make nether Dynners nor Banquets to those who
are invited to attend the body. They neuer toll any Bell for
any lying at the point of death, but after the buiryall (when
they thincke prayers auayle the dead no lesse then while they
liued) they ring a knell with one great Bell (for the Churches
seldome haue more) or with the Santsbell where they haue none
greater.

Customes.

Touching diuers Customes, I haue formerly sayde that the
Italians are proverbyally taxed with madnes twise in the yeare,
namely of deuotion in the tyme of lent (whereof I haue allready
spoken in the discourse of Religion) and of licentious life in the
tyme of Carnauall from Christmas feast to Ashwensday (so
called of biding farewell to flesh) aswell for eating flesh as for
carnall lusts with wemen (since then the old and most deuoute
leaue or at least frequent not much the Company of Curtizans).
This Carnauall is a most licentious tyme, wherein men and
wemen walke the streetes in Companyes all the afternoones,
and sometymes (espetially towardes the end of that tyme) also
in the mornings, excepting only fryday in the after noone,
hauing their faces masked, and the men in wemens, wemen in
mens apparrell at theire pleasure. And very matrons towardes
the end of the tyme walke the streetes thus masked, but allwayes
in wemens apparrell and in the Company of their husbands.
They thus walke vp and downe the markett places, and some
companyes leade musicke with them and table to place some
Instruments in the markett places, where they play excelent
musicke. All this tyme, the Curtizans are so taken up as they

must hyre them beforehande who will haue their Company to walke and feast with them. By day they that are masked may weare no weapon, espetially, no pockett weapons, which are forbidden at all tymes. But in the nights of this tyme it is dangerous to walke the streetes, wherein Companyes of swaggerours walke armed, often committing murthers and horrible outrages. All this tyme many houses keepe publike meeteinges for dansing, where all that are masked may freely enter, and dance with wemen there assembled and he that danseth at the ende of his danse payes the musitians an ordinary rate of small mony. Yea the very houses of noblemen and gentlemen, vpon occasions of meetings to danse with wemen and virgins of honour, are open for any masked persons to enter and beholde them. At Genoa all the yeare long they haue weekely a publike meeting for dansinge, and in other Cittyes (as Sienna) many like meetings, not only for the vulgar, but also for the Nobility and Gentry. At Rome and Naples in the tyme of Carauall they haue many races of horses runne for prises, and likewise of Buffoli (which are beasts like oxen, but bigger and deformed with galled backes, and wanting hayre in many partes of their body, whose flesh is not eaten, but their skinnes are good to make lether, and the best vse of them is for drawing). Also at Rome the Jewes runne naked a miles race within the walls for prises, with many like sportes.

As the Italians liue licentiously, so they giue, or at least cannot forbid the people to vse like liberty in taxing their faultes by libells, espetially diuulged in the foresayd tyme of Carnouall, and more espetially at Rome, where vpon two Images, the one called Pasquin, (being of stone, yet hauing the Armes and leggs Cutt off, as in a revenge for libeling, and beinge sett vpright against the wall of a Pallice in the Cornour of a streete nere the Markett place Navona) the other called Marforio, (being of great stature, and of marble, layde downe in length with a lowe toomb vnder it, vpon parte of the mount Capitoline:) I say vpon these two Images, (famously knowne not only in Italy but to all strangers affecting knoledge of forayne matters) all the sayd lybells at Rome are fastened, commonly in forme of a dylogue Marforious asking the question, and Passqui answring from which Custome the worde Passqui is vulgarly taken for a libell.

The gentlemen seldome feasting one another, except it be vpon rare occasions, and those rather particular to some fewe Familyes, then generall to all, as vpon affinity contracted by maryage, yet to preserue loue and acquaintance among them, daily haue generall meetinges in the markett places, and priuate in gardens, and to the same ende, as also because in many Cittyes they are the cheefe marchants, they kepe the generall meetinges no lesse strictly then the marchants of our partes keepe their daily meeteinges at the exchange, espetially at Venice, where the gentlemen daly meete, with the marchants, before noone at Rialto, where they stand by themselues, and towardes euening in the markett place of St. Marke, where they walke together.   As the Italyans loue ease in all thinges and commodity rather then pride, wearing their apparrell large, and in Journeyes hauing their bootes wyde, their hatts and Clokes of thicke felte, and softe Cushions vpon their hard Sadles, and never lighting from their horses (by reason of the hott Clyme and the fayntnes of their bodyes Commonly in some measure diseased through naturall incontinency) So vpon the foresayd reasons, they haue commodityes for easey passages in the streetes of their Cittyes.   In Venice they may passe to all partes of the Citty by water in commodious boates, aswell as by land.   In Genoa they haue in diuers places attending Porters, with Chayres to carry passengers whether they will, which Chayres are called Seggioli, and haue Curtaynes to drawe before and on each syde, so as the passenger may see all going by him, but is seene of none, and they are caryed by two Porters one behind, the other before, by two round and thick Coulestaues, and the gentlemen haue also litters, both vsefull in that Citty seated on sydes of Mountaynes, but they vse no Coaches because the streetes are narrowe and for most part steepe.   In Naples also in great part seated vpon a mountaynes syde and top they haue like Seggioli for passengers. In Rome they haue Coaches and horses with Footeclothes standing in certayne places ready vpon all occasions to be hyred, and commonly they ryde one in the saddle and another behinde vpon the Footecloth. In the playne Country, as Lombardy, for Jornyes they vse Coaches, commonly drawne with litle horses, but I haue seene a lady in depth of winter and durty wayes to haue her Coach drawne by Oxen, and in hilly or mountanous Countryes they ryde vpon Mules, Asses, and horses Commonly of litle stature.

As, through all Italy priuate men plowe and plant their grownds to the very doores of theire houses, (which haue no such wastyardes about them as euery Farmers house hath with vs) and also plant with trees and vines the very forrowes of theire land in the open fieldes, so particularly in the States of the Duke of Florence, the very ditches of the high wayes and also of walled townes and Castles, as belonging to the Duke, are to his vse planted with Mulbery trees, for feeding of silke wormes (wherof they keepe infinite Nombers) with the leaues therof, which the Duke sells to his people, and if any one be founde to pull the leaues or breake the branches, he shalbe deepely Fynned.

They are carefull to avoyde infection of the plague, and to that purpose in euery Citty haue magistrates for health. So as in tymes of danger when any Citty in or neere Italy is infected, travelers cannot passe by land, except they bring a bolletino or certificate of their health from the place whence they come, and otherwise must make la quarantana or tryall of forty dayes for their health, in a lazaretto or hospitall for that purpose. But by Sea generally both the men and all the goods of the shipp, except they can make cleare proofe of health in the partes whence they came, must make the sayd tryall of forty dayes, espetially Shipps comming from Constantinople which is seldome free from infection. And this they vse not only for health, but as a mistery of traffique, by which they knowe the quality of all marchants, and of all goodes, before they be admitted to Free traffique in the Cittyes.

The richest and noblest gentlemen scorne not to buy their owne meate in the marketts, whose prouision is so small, as commonly they carry it themselues in handkerchers, hauing allwayes prouision at home of wyne, oyle, and bread, but if they neede a Porter, there stand boyes ready with basketts by whome they send their provisions to their howses, going themselues about their buisines, for these boyes being well knowne, they neuer fayle to deliuer them safely.

Sicke persons vse much to drincke the milke of Goates, and in diuers Cittyes Droves of Goates are driuen through the streetes, to be milked at theire doores, that they may drincke the milke when it is warme.

The Italians beginne the day after the Sunne is sett as wee doe at midnight, hauing whole Clockes stricking twenty-foure howers, as our halfe clockes only strike twelue, so as, not to be weary with telling the clocke, a man had neede of a stoole and a Cushion to sett at ease. The first hower after the Sunne is sett, strikes one, the Noone or midday varyeth daily as the Sunne doth his setting, for when the Sunne setteth at eight in the euening, the next Noone is when the Clocke strikes sixteene, and when the Sunne setts at seuen, the next noone is when the Clocke strikes seuenteene, and so it differs for the rest of the howers and minutes. They followe the newe style of Pope Gregory, going tenne dayes before the old style vsed with vs, so as when they write the first of January, wee write the 23th of the former month December. Our Almanakes write that Florence, Sienna, and Pisa, begin the yeare as wee doe vpon the 25th of March, but all other Italians begine the yeare at the feast of our Lords Circumcision, being the first of January after their style, which is with vs the 23th of the former month December.

And they call their first of January Newyeares day, but they are farr from our Custome of Newyeares guifts vpon that day, holding to the Contrary, that it is vnlucky to pay or send anything out of doores that day, and that it is a good hansell of the newe yeare to receave mony, or any goods in to the house vpon that day.

The Italians saluting one another, crosse the right hand ouer the breast laying it vpon the heart, as the Turkes to the Contrary crosse the left hand. Both Italians and Turkes in saluting bend the head and body very lowe, onely the Turkes neuer vncouer theire heades, wheras the Italyans lowely putt of their hatts, and stand still bareheaded a good space to the greater person saluted, that if he chance to looke backe he may see their respect to him, or if they be equalls, both goe forward but vncovered for a litle tyme after they parte. The Italians if they salute neerer, giue a light touch in manner of imbracing, but the gentlemen of Venice salute one another with a kisse vpon the cheeke. At Venice I obserued that young Virgins of the Nobility passing the streete, and hauing their Faces couered with a Vayle like a Nett, so as they might see and be seene tho not fully, gentlemen for a Curtesy would stop their way, standing still before them as amazed at their beauty, and they tooke pryde to declyne asyde with a smyle and light blushing. In the Cittyes vpon land the highest place is to goe next the wall, but in Venice most of the streetes are narrow for two to walke, and the kennells are on each syde next the houses, and there the right hand is the highest place, as in larger streetes and Marketplaces raysed in the midst and declining to the kennels on each syde, the greatest man goes in the midst, and the next on the right hand, the third on the left hand of him who goes in the midst, and so for the rest, the right hand being still preferred to the left.

At Table it were discurtesy to carue Salt, (which the Goate loues, by which name they note Lust and call Cuckolds) as also to carue Braynes (as imputing folly or want of brayne to him to whome they carue).

In the hott Clyme of Italy, wemen in cold wether putt pans with fyer vnder them, as they vse in the most frosen Countryes of Netherland. And I wondered to see Husbandmen in that warme Country to house their Ewes in Stables at Lambing tyme, since ours are left in the open field, which I thinck they doe out of too much indulgency to them as hauing fewe Cattle in those partes.

In Italy I haue seene Companyes of wandring Tawny people like to our Gypsyes, whome they vulgarly call Singari, and they also tell Fortunes.

The Harlotts called Cortisane commonly weare dobletts and Breches vnder their wemens gownes, yea I haue seene some of them (as at Paduoa) goe in the Company of young men to the Tennis-Court in mens Apparrell and Racketts in their handes, most commonly wearing doblets and Hose of Carnation Satten, with gold buttons from the Chinne round to the wast behinde, and silke stockings, and great Garters with gold lace both of the same colour. And I mett a Dutches carryed in a horse litter to Rome, whose gentlewemen and ladyes of honour rode astryde vpon ordinary hackney horses, in dobletts and breeches of the sayd stuff fashion and colour. But all these had their heades attyred like wemen. And I obserued them to be thus apparrelled at ordinary tymes of the yeare, besydes the foresayde liberty of Carnauall, when men and wemen masked walke the streetes at pleasure in mens or wemens apparrell.

As in tyme of Carnauall walking the streetes by night is most dangerous, espetially in Lombardy, so at all tymes of the yeare and in all partes of Italy it is vnsafe to walke the streetes by night. In Florence I obserued, that the gentlemen in Companies walked by nights in the streetes, with Rapyers, and close lanthornes, I meane halfe light, halfe darke, carrying the light syde towardes them, to see the way, and the darke syde from them, to be vnseene of others, and if one company happened to meete with another, they turned their light syde of theire lanthorns towardes the faces of those they mett, to knowe them, and to keepe themselues vnseene behynde the darke sydes, and except they were accquainted frendes they seldome mett without some braule, or tumult at the least.

Pastymes Exercises Hawkeing Hunting Fowling Birding and Fishinge.

Touching Pastymes and exercises. In gentlemens or Cittizens howses I neuer sawe any playing at dice, Cardes, or Tables, nether doe I remember to haue seene any Tables in Italy, but at Cardes and dyce I haue seene many play, not in priuate houses, but vpon the stalls of shopps, and broade stones in publike places, and they who played were sometymes shopkeepers and men of Reasonable quality, but Commonly of the baser sorte. At Naples they haue a flatt stone in the markett place upon the harbour, where such men play at dyce, and will venture to loose theire very liberty. For governours of Galleyes standing by, vse to lend them mony, which they repay if they winne, otherwise loosing are carryed away to rowe as slaues in the Galleyes, till they be redeemed, which seldome happens, because hauing scant dyet, and being trusted for foode in the Gallyes, their debt daly groweth vpon them. In Venice and 25. Myles from the Citty, the lawe forbids dycing, and like games, vpon great penaltyes, except it be in publike Innes or at Feasts of great maryages, or vnder the two great Pillers in the markett place of St. Marke, which pillers being erected by a Lombard, the Senate, besydes his rewarde in monye, graunted him this priuilege for gamsters, to play freely and without penalty vnder the sayd Pillers. In the publike Inne kept by a German in Venice, whether most strangers of the best quality resorte, I haue seene young gentlemen of Italy play franckly with strangers at dyce, but generally in Italy this gamming is forbidden, in some places more strictly then others, and to be a Common gammster is disgracefull, nether are these games vsed in priuate houses to wast whole dayes and nights for pastyme, as in our partes. They haue a game commonly vsed by the Fachini that is Porters, and sometymes by horsemen as they ryde in the high waye, wherein they name a number vnder tenne, and sodenly as they name it cast out some of their fingers, or all fyue, and he winnes, whose nomber hitts the nomber of the fingers cast out by both at one instant. In the tyme of Carnauall all Cittyes vse to haue publike Comedies acted by Cittizens, and in Florence they had a house where all the yeare long a Comedy was played by professed players once in the weeke and no more, and the partes of wemen were played by wemen, and the cheefe Actours had not their parts fully penned, but spake much extempory or vpon agreement betweene themselues, espetially the wemen, whose speeches were full of wantonnes, though not grosse baudry (which the Italians like, but neede no such provocation) and their playes were of Amorous matters, Neuer of historyes, much lesse of tragedies, which the Italyans nature too much affects to imitate and surpasse. And one Lucinia a woman player, was so liked of the Florintines, as when shee dyed they made her a monument with an Epitaphe. Also not only in Carnauall but all the yeare long, all the Markett places of great Cittyes are full of Monte-bankes, or Ciarlatanes, who stand vpon tables like stages, and to sell their oyles, waters, and salues, drawe the people about them by musicke and pleasant discourse like Comedies, hauing a woman and a masked foole to acte these partes with them. In tyme of Carnauall espetially, and also at other tymes, they haue publike dances of gayne, in howses standing open and free to enter, where for each danse the man payes twopence to the musicke and to the house : and at Geno[a] the best sorte haue a publike meeteing for dansing once each weeke, as likewise at Syenna where strangers may freely enter and are intertayned with much curtesey, by the gentlemen and gentlewomen, after the French liberty in both Cittyes. In generall the Italians loue not to be excluded from musicke or Comedyes (excepting the playhouse at Florence where men payde for entrance) and therefore at these meetinges the doores are commonly left open. In the tyme of Carnauall and at publike Feasts of great maryages (besydes the liberty of men and wemen in the Carnauall to walke the streetes disguised and masked), they haue Tiltings, Runnings with lances against a Post Armed like a man at all peeces, Diuers races, of men, horses, and other

beasts, with diuers like sportes.   For Festiuall dayes the
Celebration of them consists, in the kitchen for fasting and
feasting, and in the Church for visiting the shrynes of Saynts
and making offerings, and in the peoples Processions ouer the
precincts of each Saynts parish, with Images caryed and Priests
singing before them, but many of them besydes haue temporall
Jollytyes, as at the feast of St. Martin, to haue a stuble Goose
rosted, and the boyes singing in the streetes in Italian, long
liue St. Martin with his cupp of wyne and his goose rost, giue
me a bitt my host, and the cause of this Ceremony is, that St.
Martin is writen to haue hidden himselfe among a floocke of
Geese, from the people that would make him Bishop.   Also at
the feast of St. Luke, because he is sett fourth by the picture of
an Oxe with hornes (as St. Mathew by an Angel, St. Marke by
a lyon, and St. John by an Eagle) therefore the people esteeme
him the Patron of Cuckolds, and because they holde he was a
Paynter and paynted most of our Ladyes Pictures, the paynters
also take him for their Patron, and make Feasts vpon his day.
Such vses they make of the Saynts Pictures which they call lay
mens bookes.   But the worst vse they make of feasts, is that
the Chastity of wemen is not more corrupted by any meanes,
then at these meetings of feasts, vpon pretence of holynes,
which vayle is so safe, as the Jelious Italians can hardly preuent
this mischeefe.   Vpon diuerse other dayes of the yeare they
vse like Jolyties, as vpon the first of May being at Sienna I
obserued them to erect maypooles, according to our vse, and
the boyes and girles dauncing about it at the sounde of a
Bagpipe, layde holde on passengers to begg mony of them, as
wee vse vpon the Monday after Easter.   Many goe about with
basketts selling wiggs and diuerse kyndes of delicate sweete and
pleasant bread in small proportians, and they commonly stand
at the Cellers where Muskadyne and sweet wynes are solde, and
as our Costermongers sometyme[s] sell Apples at best betrust
[*sic*], so they sell this bread Alla tenuta, that is he paying
on whome they lay holde, but they allwayes lay holde on him
who is most stranger, neuer on him who bringes the Company
to them.

Touching exercises. At Padoa the Schollers haue Tennice Courtes, but the Italyans faynt bodyes, espetially in the heate of that Clyme, loue not such styrring exercises, which are vsed most by strangers resorting thether. And it was vulgarly sayde, that when they purposed to builde Tennice Courtes at Venice, the Curtizans paying much tribute made suite to the Contrary, lest it shoulde hinder their trading, which at Venice is insteede of all exercises. For if you call for a boate, and say you will goe a spasso that is for recreation, howsoeuer you meane to take the ayre vpon the water, he will presently carry you to some Curtezans house, who will best pay him for bringing her Customers, as if there were no other recreation but only with wemen. The Venetians seldome or neuer come on horsbacke, and vulgar Jeasts are raysed on them for ignorance of ryding, as of one who would hyre one horse to carye as many as came with him in his boate, and of another who ready to take horse, asked how the wynde stoode, as thincking he could no more ride then sayle against the wynde, with many like Jeasts. But the Neapolitans are excellent horsemen, and much vse that exercise. And at Naples I haue seene gentlemen play in the playne with a little ball and a sticke like a basting ladle, to driue it before them, which sporte the Hollanders much vse vpon the yce in Winter. Generally all Italyans much vse the exercyse of Ballon, which is somewhat violent, they play in their shirtes, hauing braces on the right Armes with knobbs of wood, with which they tosse a ball one to the other, as great as our foote ball, but somewhat lighter. At Venice for exercise and sporte the young men assaulte and defende bridges, and goe to Cuffes at first in Jeast, but often prouing earnest, yet no further then hand blowes.

Touching Hunting, Hawking, fowling, birding, and Fishing. The fieldes of Italy are in greate parte like gardens or Orchardes, wherein all wylde beasts are destroyed, nether can men persuie their game without great domage to other men, and for the same reason they are vnfitt for the flying of Hawkes. For my part, in my passage through Italy I sawe not one Hawke carryed on the fist or setting on the pearch, nor any Howndes or Spaniells, neither are these sportes vsed in most parts of Italy, only in the teritory of Rome where the fieldes are more wylde, and in some part of the State of Sienna, they say that Hunting is free for all men, euen in other mens growndes, and when two Companyes followe one wylde beast, it belongs to them that first followed or hurte it, though another take it, so they desist not to persuie it. And the Duke of Florence hath a wood in a desert parte of that State, where he keepes wylde Boares for his owne Hunting, but I neuer heard of any fallowe or read Deare, much lesse Beares or like wylde beasts to be in any part of Italy. The Venetians say, that in Histria parte of that State lying on the North syde of the Gulfe, The people are much delighted with Hawking, Hunting and Fishing, and that in the lakes neere the Citty, many delight to persue in small boates a kynd of litle fish but delicate to eate, taken by hitting it with a little forked Instrument. They haue litle or no Sea fowle, but only at Venice, and there in no great plenty. But as the Italyans spetially delight in gardens, Conduites of fresh water, fountaynes, and building of fayre Pallaces with many Chimnies seldome smoking, and adorning richly the Chappells which belong to their particular Famillyes. So the[y] exceedingly delight in Birding, to which purpose many gentlemen haue curious Vccellami Boschetti and Ragnarij, that is plottes of grownde and thicke rowes of trees fitted and planted for Birding. Among many Vccellami which I haue seene I will discribe one, belonging to a Florintyne gentleman named Bondelmonte, lying neere St. Casciano. Vpon a hill somwhat large but not very high, and of easy asscent, this place of delight was planted, where first vpon the rising of the hill vpon one syde was a litle howse built, hauing a pleasant prospect, on the one syde towardes the lower groundes fitt for the sporte of Birding, on the other syde towardes the hill. At the one end this howse had a Beddstead fitted with Cushions of lether, and being narrowe it had a Cubbard which drawne out inlarged it for a bedfellowe if neede were. The rest of the house coulde not well receaue aboue six persons. The insyde was curiously paynted, but with Lasciuious pictures of naked wemen with diuers postures to wanton daliance. It had a litle table hunge vp against the wall, vnder which was a most obscene picture of a Satyre and a naked woman. And neere it was a Cubbard, wherein the gentleman had Pasta Reale, Ciambelini, and like delicate kindes of bread, with other Junketts, and a bottle of white Muskadyne, to intertayne his Mistres or other frendes. From this house on both sydes and rounde about the hill, were planted hedges and Arbours in forme of a fortresse, the lowe hedges being like Battlements, and the Arbours like towers and Bullwarkes, all which were hunge with lymed twiggs, and in the Arbours were Cages of diuers birdes, with Sparowe Hawkes and Owles tyed neere them, whose least stirring made the birdes Cry, which made flying birdes come and fall vpon the lymed twiggs. Vpon the greene plott before the house, and within the hedges, diuers netts were spread, and liuing birdes tyed to stickes, and within the house satt the gentleman governing all this sporte, by diuerse ropes lifting vp the stickes and birdes, which fluttering and Chirpping made flying birdes fall among them, and with other ropes drawing the netts when any birdes fell within their Compasse. The same gentleman not farr of had a thickett of lawrell and other trees, very high and thicke on both sydes, and in the midst open like a glade, where hauing a great nett at the one ende, they came from the other end, with talking and light striking of the trees, driuing the birdes before them into the nett, which others presently lett fall. These thicketts are Common in the States of the Duke of Florence, and these and like Arts of birding are much vsed through out Italy. And in some places I haue seene them catch birdes in the ayre, as fishes are caught in the waters, by baytes and hookes, fastned to a peece of Corcke, which by long thredes they lett hang from high walls and high windowes and terretts, and therewith, moued to and fro by the wynde, they catch birdes swallowing the bates and hookes.

The Ligustick Sea yealdes no fish at all, as I haue formerly related the proverb attributing to Genoa a Sea Voyde of fish, Mountaynes wanting woodes, with like strang propertyes. But the gulfe of Venice yealdes Sea fish, wherewith the Citty of Venice hath the marketts furnished in good plenty, as I haue formerly shewed in the third part of this worke and the Chapter of Italyan dyett, wherein I haue also shewed that Italy hath some great lakes and Riuers yealding some quantity of fresh water fish, and very many litle brookes yealding some small fishes and no great quantity of them, whereof the cheefe lakes and places of fishing are appropriated to Princes and States in whose dominions they are. But generally I obserued no Citty but only Venice to be all the Yeare well serued with fish, and that other Cittyes within land in the very tyme of lent, haue small quantity of fish or none at all, and those marketts which are furnished with some quantity, (as in Bologna) yet haue them dead before they can be brought to them. And howsoeuer the dull sporte of fishing may seeme agreeable to the Italyans nature, inclyned to sad meditations, yet I neuer founde any gentlemen or Cittisens delighting in that recreation.

CHAPTER II.

Of the French mens Nature, and manners, Bodyes and witts, Manuall Artes, Sciences, Vniversityes, languages, Ceremonyes, particularly in maryages, Childbearings, Christnings and Funeralls, as also of theire diuers Customes, Pastimes, Exercises, particularly of theire Hunting, Hawking, Birding, and Fishinge.

[Moryson is never satisfactory when writing about France, and the only passage I quote from this Chapter, which extends from Page 635 to Page 646 of the MS. is one on Page 641, in which our author takes the opportunity of praising Oxford and Cambridge.—C.H.]

. . . Fraunce hath many Vniversityes, some more spetially famous for each of the sayd professions. But the Vniversity of Paris is cheefe and most famous for all the professions. The two famous vniversityes of England (I may boldly say) excell all other in the worlde by many degrees, I meane not in the learning of Professors and Students, wherein some nations and many particular men may perhaps challeng preheminence, nor meane I in the florishing of all professions, whereof some, as namely the studdy of Ciuill and Cannon lawes, may seeme more to florish in other partes where the professors of them are better rewarded, but I meane in the magnificall foundation of them. For whereas generally the Vniversityes beyonde the Seas haue only one or two Coleges, wherein the Professors reade and some fewe poore Students are mantayned for a short tyme the rest of the Students liuing in the towne. The famous Vniversities of England haue each of them (besydes the publike schooles & libraryes) many Coleges, towardes or about the nomber of twenty, and those stately built of free stone, with very convenient Chambers to lodge not only the Students mantayned by the founders, but all other Students whatsoeuer

comming thether to liue at their owne charge, who haue both
lodging and dyet at a reasonable rate within the Colleges,
mantayning officers for that purpose.   As also they haue
publike lectures, and disputations, and exercises for all students
from the lowest to the highest.   And these Colleges are richly
endowed by the founders with lands, the yearely Rents whereof
mantayne in the greatest one hundreth or more schollers till
they take degree of Master of Arts, and some 50 or 60 Fellowes
of diuerse Professions during life, or till they can gett preferment in the Commonwealth, and the least of them in like sorte
mantaynes some 30 or forty poore schollers and some dosen or
sixteene Felowes, some professing the Ciuill lawe, some
Phisicke, and the greatest part diuinity.   The Vniuersity at
Paris in Fraunce of all other in the world commeth neerest to
the sayd famous Vniuersities of England as indeede it was first
founded in imitation of them, by foure Monkes, who hauing
beene in Oxford the Schollers of Beda,* an English man (so
famous for learning as antiquity hath giuen him the style of
Reuerent) did in the tyme of the French Emperour Charles the
great, beginne to teach at Paris, and moved the French to
founde that Vniuersity.   It may seeme ill planted in the Cheefe
City of the kingdome and so neere the kings Court, both apt to
withdrawe schollers from their Studyes to other Courses of life,
or to dissolute manners, but the vniuersity is a seuerall Part
of the Citty closed with gates, in which compasse all the
Students reside, who liue not in the Colleges.   And these
Colleges were of old foureteene in nomber, and I nether heare
nor reade that the nomber hath beene incrased in late ages. . . .

---

   * The Venerable Bede at Oxford! I feel that it is rather unkind to
Moryson to quote this passage.—C.H.

CHAPTER III.

Of England touching nature, and manners, Bodyes and witts, manuall Artes, Sciences, Vniversityes, language, Ceremonyes, particularly in mariages, Childbearinges, Christnings, and Funeralls, as also of diuers Customes, Pastymes, Exercises, particularly of Hunting, Hawkeing, Fowling, Birding, and Fishing.

THIS discourse (as the former, of the Commonwealth of England, and also of Religion) I will referr to the intended treatise of England and Scotland vpon these subiectes, more exactly to be written, to avoyde the imputation of ignorance in affayres at home, while I assert knowledge of Forrayne States.

Yet in the meane tyme till that treatise be compiled I desyre leaue for strangers sake, breefly to note some singularities of England in these poyntes. And first for the satisfaction of strangers, who say that old writers haue taxed the old Brittayns to haue beene Cruell and inhospitable by nature towards strangers, and that to this day they fynde by experience the English to be insolent and rude towards them. For the old brittons cruelty and inhospitality, generally the most barbarous people are most cruell, but in the tyme of Cesar, himselfe wittneseth that the inhabitants of Kent were most curteous and full of humanity, and as shortly after they imbraced Christian Religion in the primitiue Church, and had then famous Vniversityes, before France had any, (that of Paris being founded in the modell and Imitation of them) so no doubt they were farr from Barbarisme. And since the Saxons gaue the name of England to this Iland, and since the Normans did Conquer it, I did neuer reade history, through the long and victorious warrs they made in Fraunce & other kingdoms, which euer taxed them of Cruelty, but rather recorde many examples wherein they vsed singuler mercy and humanity towardes the Conquered, and all such as they tooke prisoners. Yea in our tyme, during the raigne of Elizabeth late Queene of famous memory, in her renounned victoryes, wee remember and our enemyes cannot but wittnes with vs, singular mercy and humanity to haue beene vsed towardes all Captiues and prisoners, more spetially in the nauall victory of the yeare 1588. And at the seige of Kinsale in Ireland, in both which it is notoriously knowne that singular mercy was vsed to all Prisoners, and that many Captiues of the best sorte liued in as good if not better condition then they did at home, & gayned by theire Captiuity, being released without ransome or paying any thinge for theire expences, which burthen, besydes the bounty of presents, they sustayned to whome they were Captiues by the lawe of warr.

Now for the Imputation of strangers that the English are inhospitable towardes them, and to this day apt to vse insolent wronges towardes them. Strangers commonly arryue at Grauesende, inhabited by people who haue beene themselues in forrayne parts, and are apt to vse like extortions to them, as perhapps themselues haue receaued abroade. And indeede generally that towne giues such ill intertaynment to the very English, as fewe men of the better sorte will lodge there, but vpon necessity. From thence strangers are directed to like hosts at London, where they may be ill vsed for expences, and there perhapps are sometyme arronged by the insolency of the baser sorte of Prentisces, seruing men Dray men, and like people, which presuming vpon theire nombers doe many like insolences to English gentlemen and laydies. Besydes I cannot deny, that the Cittizens of London and of lesse Cittyes, haue had and may haue a spleane against strangers for growing rich among them by traffique vsed to theire preiudice. But if a stranger will chuse an honest guide, and converse with the better sorte, he shall fynde singular Curtesy, out of naturall disposition from lords, from the gentry, from all schoolers, and not only verball but reall in being made welcome to their houses and tables, bearing all respects to them rather aboue then vnder theire degrees. For as the English, contrary to the

Custome of all nations, giue the higher place and way to wemen though of lower degree then themselues, out of a noble mynde to giue honour and support to weakenes, so giue they like respect to strangers, espetially to military men and Doctours of liberall professions, (as indeede they generally preferr schollers both strangers and natiues) yea they are naturally so inclyned to beare respect and good opinion towardes strangers, as this vertue exceeding meane declyneth to vice, in preferring and more esteeming strangers aswell Phisitians as other like professors, then their owne Countrymen, as more learned and skillfull then they are, which makes the English also so much travayle in forrayne parts, and so much esteeme theire owne Countrymen being travelers, wisely iudging that the experience of Vlisses could not but add much to his other naturall vertues, and this all experienced strangers doe confesse, but they vnthanckfully misconceaue the cause, attributing that excessiue curtesy to the simplisity of the English, which truely belongs to the nobility of their myndes, as may appeare by the foresayd respect to wemen, and espetially in that this curtesy towardes strangers aboundes most in the most noble and learned men, farthest from simpliscity. Yet I confesse that also very husband men and Country people in England espetially, within land (for they on the Sea coasts haue daly exasperations against borderinge strangers) I say within land, are naturally curteous and kynde towardes strangers, espetially when by their guide or their owne language, they can make themselues in some weake measure vnderstoode whence and who they are.

Agayne it is a singularity in the nature of the English, that they are strangly adicted to all kyndes of pleasure aboue all other nations. This of old was Justly attributed to Idlenes, when the multitude of monasteryes and the great traynes and large howse keepinges of lords and gentlemen were nurseryes of theefes and Idle persons, so as wee were serued for the most parte by strangers in all manuall trades. But since the putting downe of monasteryes and of these great traynes and large

howse keepings howsoeuer I cannot deny that, out of this
naturall adiction to pleasure (or idlenes if you will so call it)
and out of naturall boldenes lesse to feare death then want, more
persons are executed in England for stealing and Roberyes by
the high way, then in many vast kingdomes abroad, yet doe not
these offences so much abounde as in those former tymes, and
for manuall trades, wee are now almost altogether serued by
natiues, who for necessity to eate theire owne breade, are in
good measure growne industrious Artizens.   But for the poynt
of pleasures, the English from the lordes to very husbandmen,
haue generally more fayre and more large Gardens and
Orchardes, then any other nation.   All Cittyes, Townes and
villages swarme with Companyes of Musicians and Fidlers,
which are rare in other Kingdomes.   The Citty of London alone
hath foure or fiue Companyes of players with their peculiar
Theaters Capable of many thousands, wherein they all play
euery day in the weeke but Sunday, with most strang concourse
of people, besydes many strange toyes and fances exposed by
signes to be seene in priuate houses, to which and to many
musterings and other frequent spectacles, the people flocke in
great nombers, being naturally more newe-fangled then the
Athenians to heare newes and gaze vpon euery toye, as there
be, in my opinion, more Playes in London then in all the partes
of the worlde I haue seene, so doe these players or Comedians
excell all other in the worlde.   Whereof I haue seene some
stragling broken Companyes that passed into Netherland and
Germany, followed by the people from one towne to another,
though they vnderstoode not their wordes, only to see theire
action, yea marchants at Fayres bragged more to haue seene
them, then of the good marketts they made.   Not to speake of
frequent spectacles in London exhibited to the people by
Fencers, by walkers on Ropes, and like men of actiuity, nor of
frequent Companyes of Archers shooting in all the fieldes, nor
of Saynts dayes, which the people not keeping (at least most
of them, or with any deuotion) for Church seruice, yet keepe for
recreation of walking and gaming.   What shall I say of

daunsing with Curious and rurall musicke, frequently vsed by
the better sort, and vpon all hollydayes by country people
daunsing about the Maypooles with bagpipes or other Fidlers,
besydes the iollityes of certain seasons of the yeare, of setting
vp maypooles daunsing the morris with hobby horses, bringing
home the lady of the harvest, and like Plebean sportes in all
which vanityes no nation commeth any thing neere the English.
What shall I say of playing at Cardes and dice, frequently vsed
by all sortes, rather as a trade then as recreation, for which all
strangers much blame vs.   As the English are by nature
amorous, so doe they aboue other nations assert and followe the
pleasant Study of Poetry, and therein haue in good measure
attayned excellency.   To conclude with Hawking and Hunting.
No nation so Frequently vseth these sports as the English.   No
nation of greater compasse, alloweth such great proportions of
lands for Parkes to impale Fallowe and Red deare.   And as
England hath plenty of Red deere, so I will boldly say that it,
perhaps one shyre of it, hath more Fallowe deere then all
the Continent of the worlde that I haue seene, And for the
Parkes of Fallowe deere lately planted in Denmarke Brabant
and Holland, they haue beene stored in our Age out of England
by the late Queens fauour.   No Nation followeth these
pastimes and exercises on horse backe and on Foote, so
frequently and paynfully in any measure of Comparison.
England yealdes excelent sparrow hawkes, and Ireland hawkes
of diuers kyndes, but espetially excellent Goshawkes, and
gentlemen with great charge procure plenty of the best hawkes
from forrayne partes.   Not only gentlemen but yeomen
frequently hunt the hayre, not only with grayhownds but
hownds, in keeping wherof for that purpose diuers yeomen
ioyne together, for England wants not Acteons eaten vp by
their owne dogs.   And for all these sportes and other vses,
England hath without comparison greater nomber and better
dogs, then any other Nation, as Mastiues for keeping the
howse, rough water dogs for the Duck, grayhounds for the
hayre, diuers kyndes of hounds for all huntings, and Spanyels

for hawking, and bloodhounds to track stolen Deere or other thinges, and litle dogs for wemens pleasure, and all these beautifull and good, and some most rare, as the sayd bloodhoundes, and Tumblers for Couyes, and setting doges to catch Partriges by the nett (which sport notwithstanding is vnlawfull).

Agayne the Nature of the English is very singular aboue other Nations in liberality and bounty of Presents, gifts and rewardes, if it be not rather prodegality or folly, as when gentlemen and great men will paye more then is due, in small thinges because they will not stand to change mony, in greater because they will not stand to examine Reconings, but rather would seeme negligent in spending, and in all voluntary rewardes assert bounty aboue their quality and meanes, as I coulde shewe by many instances. The vniversityes of England are most famous, wherein no kingdome can compayre with it by many degrees, as I haue shewed in the discourse of the Vniversities in Germany, and also in France.

London hath foure singularities aboue all other Cittyes, as the Monuments of Westminster, the Goldsmithes rowe in Cheepsyde, the Exchange for marchants meeting, and the Bridge ouer Thames. And generally no kingdome may compare with England for Churches, espetially the supmtuous and large building and the number of Cathedrall Churches. Not to speake of famous antiquities throughout all England excellently described by our famous Antiquary Mr. Camden.

England hath great magnificence in the Feasts and Ceremonyes of the Kings Coronation, but is singular aboue all other kingdomes or Cittyes, in the yeerely Feast of St. George, and the particular feasts of installing each knight of the Garter, and in the yearely triumphes and Pagents of the Citty of London when the newe Maiour takes his oath, and espetially in the Tables of the Maiour & espetially Sheriffes of London, all the yeare open to intertayne all men of quality, natiues and strangers, who may freely resorte to them.

England hath the best Barbers, and the most commodious Innes of all the world besydes.

The English language is very copious of wordes and
expressions of any thinge to be spoken, and being mixed is
therefore more and not lesse to be esteemed, as I haue shewed
in the former discourse of the Italian tounge.

Touching Customs, England keepes the old kalander,
beginnes the day at midnight, and the yeare vpon the 25th of
March.   But to my purpose of only naming singulari-
tyes.   Strangers blame two Customes of the English First that
a man telling of a tale or speaking to others at table, if any
of them drincke, wilbe silent till they haue druncke, which may
be good manners if the speech demand or require a present
answer, but otherwise is needeles, his drincking not hindring
his hearing, and if any ill manners be, it is rather in him that
drinckes and so deserues no such respect.   Secondly that wee
putt off hatts too often at table, with offence of shedding loose
haires and the like, and too litle at other meetings as at
Ordinaryes, where some, as in a place of equall expence, will
enter without any salutation, & generally thincke it needlesse
towards familiar frends, and base towardes vnknowne men.
England excells all other Countryes in the goodnes and nomber
of ambling naggs and Geldings and no other nation hath so
many and easy Padds to ryde vpon, nor in any measure Chayres
and stooles so frequently bombasted and richly adorned.   But
strangers seeing most of our gentlemen ride vpon hard northerne
saddles, wonder they shoulde vse them abroad, who desyre to
sett so soft at home.   The Custome for each parish to keepe a
Register of all Children Christned, whereby any man may proue
his age (being a thinge important for many cases of lawe and
otherwise) was first begonne in England in the tyme of King
Henry the Eighth, and the Romans hauing borowed it of vs,
call it the Custome of England, but I knowe no other Country
that vseth it.   England hath three very olde and very laudable
Customes, vsed in no other Kingdome that I knowe.   First for
Children at morning and euening to aske their Parents blessing,
and extraordinarily their Godfathers when they meete them.
Secondly that all malefactours are followed from village to

village by publike officers with Hue and Cry. Thirdly that
when any man is at the point of death, a great bell is towled,
to warne all men to pray for him while he yet liueth, and when
the party is dead, by a nomber of seuerall stroakes at the bell,
notice is giuen whether the party dead be a man woman or
Chylde, and then the bell is rounge out. As likewise at the
buryall all the bells of the Church for some howers are runge
out. Touching bells England hath many singularities, as in
the generall greatnes of them, some one (as that of
Lincolne Minster) requiring the helpe of many men to toule it,
and some dossen or twenty men to ringe it out. Also in the
incredible nomber of them, so as I may boldly say England hath
more bell mettall then all the Contenent of Europe and that
part of Asia which I haue seene. Besydes that most Churches
of England haue each of them three, fyue, or seuen bells of
differing bignes, which men commonly ringe out in musicall
tunes for recreation, which I neuer obserued to be donne in any
other Country. For Turky hath no bells at all, the Priests
calling them to the Moschees by the voyce, as our Falconours
call hawkes to the lure. The French haue some great bells,
which they ringe not out but only toule them for seuerall
Masses and purposes. And the Italian Churches haue for the
most part litle bells which wee call Saynts bells. Only Venice
hath some great bells, whereof they brought the greatest out
of England after the destroying of our Monasteries.

These singularities remembered in a shorte meditation, shall
suffice, referring the rest to the intended full discourse vpon all
the heades of this Chapter.

CHAPTER IIII.

Of Scotland touching nature and manners, Bodyes and Witts, Manuall Arts Sciences, Vniversities, language, Ceremonyes, particularly in Maryages, Childbearinges, Christnings, and Funeralls, and also of theire diuers Customes, Pastimes Exercises, particularly of their Hunting, Hawking, Fowling, Birding and Fishinge.

This discourse also (as the former of England) I will referr to the intended tretise of England and Scotland upon the foresayd subjects more exactly to be written.

CHAPT. V.

Of Ireland, touching nature, and manners, etc.

[I give two extracts from this Chapter. Moryson always writes well about Ireland, but frequently repeats what he has written before. The Chapter extends from Page 653 to Page 664 of the MS.—C. H.].

Nature Manners Bodies and Witts.

IN this Chapter I will speake of the Meere Irish. Only I will say for the English Irish that they may be knowne by the description of our English at home. But as horses Cowes and sheepe transported out of England into Ireland, doe each race and breeding declyne worse and worse, till in fewe yeares they nothing differ from the races and breeds of the Irish horses and Cattle. So the posterities of the English planted in Ireland, doe each discent, growe more and more Irish, in nature manners and customes, so as wee founde in the last Rebellion diuers of the most ancient English Familyes planted of old in Ireland, to be turned as rude and barbarous as any of the meere Irish lords. Partly because the manners and Customes of the meere

Irish giue great liberty to all mens liues, and absolute power
to great men ouer the inferiors, both which men naturaly affect.
Partly because the meere Irish of old overtopped the English
Irish in nomber, and nothing is more naturall yea necessary,
then for the lesse Nomber to accommodate it selfe to the
greater. And espetially because the English are naturally
inclyned to apply themselues to the manners and Customes of
any forrayne nations with whome they liue and Converse,
whereas the meere Irish by nature haue singular and obstinate
pertinacity in retayning their old manners and Customes, so
as they could neuer be drawne, by the lawes gentile government, and free conversation of the English, to any Ciuility in
manners, or reformation in Religion.

Now to retorne to the meere Irish. The lords or rather
cheefes of Countryes (for most of them are not lords from any
graunts of our kings, which English titles indeede they dispise),
prefix O or Mac before their names, in token of greatnes, being
absolut tyrants ouer their people, themselues eating vpon them
and making them feede their kerne or footemen, and their
horsemen. Also they, and gentlemen vnder them, before their
names putt nicknames, giuen them from the Colour of their
haire, from lameness, stuttering, diseases, or villanous inclinations, which they disdayne not, being otherwise most impatient
of Reproch, though indeede they take it rather for a grace to
be reputed actiue in any Villany, espetially Cruelty and theft.
But it is strange howe contrary they are to themselues, for in
apparrell, meate, Fashions, and Customes, they are most base
and abiect, yet are they by nature proude and disdaynefull of
reproch. In fighting they will runne away and turne agayne
to fight, because they thincke it no shame to runne away, and
to make vse of the advantage they haue in swift running, yet
haue they great Corage, in fighting, and I haue seene many
of them suffer death with as constant resolution as euer Romans
did. To conclude this point they knowe not truely what honour
is, but according to their knowledge no men more desyre it,
affecting extreamely to be Celebrated by their Poetts or rather

Rimers, and fearing more then death to haue a Ryme made in their disgrace & infamye. So as these Rymers, pestilent members in that commonwealth, by animating all sortes by their Rymes, to licentious liuing, to lawlesse and rebellious actions are somuch regarded by them, as they grow very rich, the very wemen, when they are young and new Marryed or brought to bed, for feare of Rymes, giuing them the best Apparrell and ornaments they haue.

The Irish are by nature very factious, all of a Sept or name liuing together, and cleeuing close one to another in all quarrells and actions whatsoeuer, in which kynde they willingly suffer great men to eate vpon them, and take whatsoeuer they haue, proverbyally saying defend mee and spende Mee, but this defence must be in all cawses, Just or vniust, for they are not content to be protected from wronge, except they may be borne out to doe wronge.

They are by nature extreamely giuen to Idlenes. The Sea Coasts and harbors abounde with fish, but the fishermen must be beaten out, before they will goe to their Boats. Theft is not infamous but rather commendable among them so as the greatest men affect to haue the best theeues to attend vpon them, and if any man reproue them, they answer that they doe as their fathers did, and it is infamy for gentlemen and swordsmen to liue by labour and Manuall trades. Yea they will not be perswaded that theft displeaseth God, because he giues the pray into their handes, and if he be displeased, they say yet he is mercyfull and will pardon them for vsing meanes to liue. This Idlenes makes them also slouenly and sluttish in their howses and apparrell, so as vpon euery hill they lye lowsing themselues, as formerly in the discourse of the Commonwealth. I haue remembered foure verses, of four beasts that plague Ireland namely, lyse vpon their bodyes, Ratts in theire howses, wollues in their fieldes and swarmes of Romish Prists tyranising ouer their Consciences. This Idlenes also makes them to loue liberty aboue all thinges, and likewise naturally to delight in musick, so as the Irish Harpers are excelent, and their solemne musicke is much liked of strangers, and the wemen of some partes of Mounster, as they weare Turkish heades and are thought to haue come first out of those partes so they haue pleasant tunes of Moresco Danses.

They are by nature very Clamorous, vpon euery small occasion raysing the hobou (that is a dolefull outcrye) which they take one from anothers mouthe till they putt the whole towne in tumult. And their complaynts to magistrates are commonly strayned to the higest points of Calamity, sometyes in hyperbolicall tearmes, as many vpon small violences offered them, haue Petitioned to the lord Deputy for Justice against men for murthering them while they stoode before him sounde and not so much as wounded.

In the late Rebellion wee founde the Munster men to betray the Earl of Desmond their cheefe leader into our handes, for their owne Pardons and rewardes of mony. But howesoeuer the State by publike Proclamation did sett a great reward vpon the head of Tyrone, to any should bring his head, and a greater to any should bring him aliue, yet the northern men cold not be induced by any rewardes of mony or Pardons for theire owne estates and liues, to betray him, no not when themselues were driuen to greatest misery, and he forced to hyde his head in the woodes without any forces, and only was Followed by some fewe of his most trusty vassalls. In like sort by experience we reputed the Northern men of better nature and disposition to peace, to Ciuill government, and Reformation of Religion, then the Mounster men at that tyme Rebells. For howsoeuer the Northern men followed their lordes with all their hartes, and powers in rebellious and vnlawfull actions, yet they did it because they liued by them, and had feeling of their power ready at hand to doe them good or hurt, and had formerly no knowledge of the kings power and Justice but farr off and not ready to supporte and protect them in theire obedience, whereas the Mounster men had long liued happily vnder the Protection of the State and English lawes, Yea when they warrs were ended, and the English Judges went their Circuites through all,

Ireland, the Northerne people more obediently and more joyfully then any other receaved the English lawes, and government to protect them from the oppression of great lords and their swordsmen. And howsoeuer the Northerne men were generally Papists, yet wee considered that they must be so or of no Religion, hauing not formerly beene taught any other, whereas the Rebells of other partes, by long conversation with the English, and liuing amonge them, had formerly had great opportunity to be well instructed in Religion and Ciuill manners.

It is an old saying,

Rustica gens optima flens, pessima ridens.

The Country Clownes are best when they doe weepe,

and worst when they in plenty laugh and sleepe.

And this saying may more truely be spoken of the Irish then any other nation. For nothing more brings them to obedience then pouerty, and heretofore they neuer had plenty but presently they rushed into Rebellion. For particular experience, lett them wittnes who haue kepte Irish footemen, if euer they could bring any of them on foote agayne, whome once they had sett on horsbacke, and if they haue not had better seruice from them whome they kepte most bare in apparrell or mony, and most subiect to correction, then from those the kept most bountifully and vsed most freely and gently.

. . . .

The bodyes of men and wemen are large for bignes and stature, because they are brought vp in liberty and with loose apparrell, but generally the very men are obserued to haue litle and ladylike hands and feete, and the greatest part of the wemen are nasty with fowle lynnen, and haue very great Dugges, some so big as they giue their Children suck ouer theire shoulders. The the wemen generally are not straight laced, perhapps for feare to hurt the sweetenes of breath, and the greatest part are not laced at all. Also the Irish are generally obserued to be fruitfull in generation, as at Dublin in the tyme of the last warr, it was generally knowne for truth, that one of the Segers, while she lodged in the house of Mres Arglas, bare fyue Children at one birth, and we all knowe an Alldermans wife that bare three at a birth, with many like examples.

For the witts of the Irish, they themselues bragg that Ireland yealdes not a naturall foole, which bragg I haue hard diuers men confirme, neuer any to contridict. My honored lord the late Earle of Deuonshyre, till his dying day kept an Irishman in fooles Apparrell, and Commonly called his lordships foole, but wee found him to haue craft of humoring euery man to attayne his owne endes, and to haue nothing of a naturall foole. But for the Irish generally they are subtill temporisers, and because they haue beene vsed to frequent change of Governours, if they cannot atayne their owne endes, they labour by all shifting deuises to delay their adversaryes preuayling against them, till a newe governour be sent, as crafty Davus in the Comedy, thincking he had donne well to putt off his young masters maryage but for one day, hoping that some newe impediments might therein arise. They are Crafty to obserue their governours humours, and to present to them at their first comming causes of Justice formerly determined against them, from whome if they can gett (while they are yet vnpractised in the affayres) any new decree contrary or differing from the old, they will not cease to make new trouble to their adversaryes. Yea many getting the governours hand to their Petitions, though nothing to their fauour, yet haue made such vse of it with their adversaryes at home, as if it had beene an absolute graunt of their requests. If they can fasten vpon their gouernours any brybe (which is allwayes Cowes), they hold them as slaues for euer. And if they will not be corrupted, but execute Justice against them, then are they most Clamorous in Complaynts to the supreame magistrate, or to the State in England, and when the inferiour governours are called to Dublin, or the Lord Deputy recalled into England, they fly after them with open throtes to lode them with false Callumnies, espetially if these governours happen to be in any disgrace with the State, or haue any greate enemyes at home glad to backe theire Complayntes.

CHAPTER VI.

A generall and brife discourse of the Jewes and Greekes.

[I print all that Moryson says of the Jews but omit most of what he records of the Greeks, as not being very interesting. —C. H.]

THE Jewes are a nation incredibly dispised among all Christians, and of the Turkes also, and were dispersed throughout the face of the world, saue that they haue beene long banished out of some Christian Kingdomes, as England Fraunce, and Netherland, where notwithstanding they lurke disguised, though they be not allowed any habitation by the State. And where they are allowed to dwell, they liue vpon vsury and selling of Fripery wares, as Brokers, therein permitted by Christian Princes for priuate gayne to vse horrible extortions vpon their subiectes, but are not allowed to buy any lands, howses, or stable inheritances, nether haue they any Coyne of their owne, but vse the Coynes of Princes where they liue. The tenn Tribes of the kingdome of Israell, were long since carryed Captiue and dispersed in the furthest East, and are not knowne where they liue, hauing no commerce with the Jewes knowne to vs.

Touching those of the kingdome they had at Jerusalem, they are thought to be mingled in theire trybes and familyes, but the generall opinion is, that those of the Tribe of Judah liue in Turky, and those of the Trybe of Beniamyn liue in Italy, Germany, and Poland. They are a miserable nation and most miserable in that they cannot see the cause thereof, being the curse of the blood of their Messiah, which they tooke vpon themselues and their Children, whose comming they still expect, saying it is thus long deferred for their sinnes, but they looke for his comming from the East before and towardes the end of the world. At Prage vnder the Emperour of Germany they are allowed a litle Citty to dwell in, with gates whereof they keepe the keyes, and walled rounde about for theire safety. The Emperour also allowes them to dwell in two Cittyes of Silesia, and diuers villages of Moravia, being Provinces of the kingdome of Bohemia. In Germany they haue only a streete allowed them to dwell in at Francfort, (famous yor the yearely Marts). In Poland, at Crakaw they haue a litle Citty, wherein were about 700 Familyes, which payde yearely to the king 500 Guldens, besyde the tribute vpon occasions imposed of a Gulden for each head, and their obligation to lend the king mony vpon his occasions. They haue also habitation in other Townes of Poland, and myselfe passed a village only inhabited by Jewes. Besydes the great men there intertayne Jewes to be their Balyes, to order and gather their Rents, finding them very vsefull in all seruices of profitt, and wherein witt is required. Generally in Poland they liue in equall right with Christians, for king Casimire the great hauing a Jewe to his Concubyne (which he was not permitted to marry) gaue them great priuileges, and this among the rest, that the lawe might not proceede against a Jewe in any action but vpon the testimony of Jewes. But in Bohemia and Germany, the Jewes vnder the Emperour, liued in great oppression and basely contemned by the people being Christians. In Italy likewise the Jewes liue in no respect no not the most learned or richest of them, but in less contempt of the people, and the Princes who extort vpon their owne subiectes, doe also for gayne admitt the Jewes into their Cittyes, and permitt them to vse horrible extortion vpon their subjectes, in the lending of mony, and in selling or letting out by the day or weeke vpon vse both mens and wemens apparrell and furnitures for horses, and all kyndes of Fripery wares. Thus at Venice they haue a Court yearde closed with gates and capable of great Nombers, wherein they dwell. At Rome they haue whole streetes allowed for their habitation, and liue there in great nomber, paying their tribute to the Pope at Shrostyde, when they are allowed to shewe publike games. They are allowed to liue in all Cittyes of Italy and haue greater priuileges in Piemont then in other partes, but in all these places they are tyed to weare a Redd or Yellowe Capp, or more commonly a litle bonett or hatt.

Only in Mantua they haue more priuileges then the Christian Citizens, keeping the cheefe shops in the very markett places, and hardly to be knowne from Christians, being only tyed to weare a litle snipp of yellowe lace vpon the left syde of their Clokes, which some weare on the insyde of their Clockes, or so, as (they being foulded vnder the left arme) the marke cannot be discerned. In Turky they liue vpon the Sea Coasts, and in Citties of greatest traffique, and commonly haue the offices to gather the Emperours tribuites. As likewise among Christians they liue in Cittyes hauing greatest Concourse of marchants. For not one of them liveth vpon any manuall trade, but growe rich by their witts, or rather fraudes in extortions, wherein also many Christians and Turkes fynde their imployment and seruice very vsefull and profitable to them. In Turky they are not seene in any townes within the Continent, but only in theire Jorneyes from one Citty of traffique to another, much lesse are they seene at Jerusalem which is a desert Citty for the habitation of religious men, but hath no traffique of Marchants.

When I passed through Bohemia I founde at Prage the foresayd litle Citty inclosed, and hauing gates to be shutt vp, allowed to the Jewes for habitation, where free liberty of all Religions being permitted, I had oportunity (without Communicating with them so much as in the least outward reverence of standing bareheaded) not only to beholde the diuers Ceremonyes, of the Hussites, the Lutherans, the Papists, and the singular Jesuites, but also to haue free speech with the Jewes, and to enter their Synogoges at the tyme of diuine seruice. Some 500 Jewes dwelt in this litle Citty, that Nomber being often increased or deminish[ed] as they haue occasion to passe from one Citty to another for traffique. The lawe byndes the men to weare red hatts or bonetts, and the wemen a garment of the same Coller, neere blood, to witnesse their guiltinesse of Christs blood, but with mony they gett some dispensation from this lawe, yet so as the men are knowne by apparant markes in their hatts, and the wemen by their lynnen and handes dyed (after the manner in Turky) with a Coller like saffron. Thus in all places the Jewes long seruitude and wonderfull scattering is exposed to all Christians for a fearefull spectikle, and to themselues for a dayly remembrance of Gods Curse layd vpon them. At Prage they haue the priuilege of Cittizens, but they buye it and continue it with great payments of mony, aswell imposed on them by the Pope, as by free guift of large sommes to the Emperour, and firnishing him with mony vpon all occasions. Besydes they liue in exceeding contempt, hearing nothinge but reproches from the people, and vsed by them more like doggs then men, which for gayne they beare, though they might goe into Italy where they liue in better fashion, and where the Deuill himselfe bringing stoore of mony may be welcome and reuerenced.

At Prage many Familyes of Jewes liued packed together in one litle house, which makes not only their howses but their streetes to be very filthy, and theire Citty to be like a Dunghill. Also they feede continually vpon Onyons and Garlike, so as he had neede first to breake his fast, and haue some good Oder in his hand, who will enter their Citty or haue Conference with any of them. They eate not the hinder partes of any beast in Remembrance of Jacobs lamed thigh, so as at home and in their Jornyes they kill and dresse their owne meate. In this their Citty they haue Authority yearely to chuse foure Judges among themselues, to rule them and Judge causes betweene them, but in Cases betweene a Jewe and Christian they are determined by the Christian magistrate. The Authority of the cheefe Rabby or Priest is very great among them. They punish Adultry by standing vp to the Chinn in water a whole day. Theft with restitution and recompence of dommages, but Murther was vnhard of among themselues. They had no slaues bought with mony or so borne, but after the manner of Christians the poore serued the rich for yearely wages. Only the richer sort made wills or testiments in writting, others made verball testaments, and if any dyed without them, their male Chilldren deuided theire goodes, and were bound to provide for their sisters, which were allowed no dowryes. They tooke such oppressiue usury, as it seemed wonderfull the magistrate would suffer them so to devoure Christians; vpon a pawne of gold or siluer they tooke a fourth part, and vpon a pawne of Apparrell or stuffe they tooke halfe the principall for vse, and neuer lent without pawnes, Yea wheras the lawe of Germany allowes but fyue in the hundreth for a yeare, many Christians were so wicked as to extort the former vse in the name of Jewes, agreeing with a poore Jewe to bring them the pawnes and the mony when it was repayd, and then giueing the Jewe some part of the vse, did retayne the rest for themselues. At my being at Prage the Jewes had no Maryages, abstaining from them for seuen weekes in which they Celebrated the memorye of a great Rabby dead of old, and after abstayning from them for another feast in memory of the lawe giuen to Moses. But the Jewes and Christians related to me that the Bryde among them vsed to sett in the Synogog vnder a rich cloth of State, and to giue her Fayth to her husband in the hands of the Rabby, confirming it by taking a Ringe, and to spende the rest of the day in feasting and daunsing, with the doores open for all Jewes or Christians that would enter, permitting imbraces but no kisses whyle they daunsed. They admitted diuorce for Barrennes, and many like causes, euen the smalest where both partyes consented. The Virgins maryed at 11 or 12 yeares and the young men at 15 or 16 yeares age to avoyde fornication, and if they had no Children the first or second yeare, there was no loue but continuall reproches betweene themselues and their Parents.

Touching Funeralls. Vpon each fryday being the evening of their Sabboth, the Jewes in Turky vse to lye and beate themselues vpon the Tombes of their dead frends. In generall from the tyme of our lord's death we fynde the Jewes to haue daily more and more declyned to superstitions and perticularly in this point of mourning for the dead, and keeping Feasts and Ceremonyes in memory of them. So as they are now come to

keepe a booke of the Names of all dead persons, and thrise each
yeare to reade publikely in the Synagoge the names of all such
as haue dyed within the compasse of the yeare, and to pray
vnto God that he will receave them into Paradise. Yea contrary to the rules of mourning in the scriptures, vpon the death
of a frend, they are now come to rende their garments, for a
day or two not to eate in the house, but abroade, to abstayne
from eating flesh or drincking wyne, except it be vpon the
Sabboth day, not to wash or anoynte themselues for seuen dayes,
nor yet to lye with theire wyues, and to followe the dead body
to the graue barefooted, and for seuen nightes to leaue a lampe
lighted at home, vpon a Foolish opinion that the soule doth so
long retorne to the house to seeke the body, and finally (as I
sayd) weekely vpon Fryday to lye and beate themselues vpon
the Sepulcheres of the dead. At Prage the Jewes washed the
dead body, and wrapt it in linnen, and buryed it the same day
before the sunne sett, calling the people to the Funerall by the
voyce of a Cryer passing through all the streetes. The body
being brought to the graue, the boyes did reade songes written
vpon the wall of the Churchyeard, bewayling the mortall condition of men, and confessing death to be the most iust punishment of sinne, which ended the body was putt in the graue
without any further Ceremony but only the laying of a greene
Sodd vnder the head. Then they retorned to the sayd wall
reading another song, praying God for Abrahams Isackes and
Jacobs sake, not to permitt the diuill to kill men, and recom-
mendinge to those Patriarkes in vehement wordes the afflicted
State of their Posterity.

Touching Religion I obserued that at Prage, aswell at the
doores of theire priuate houses as of theire Synagoges, they had
a prayer clossed vp within the Posts or walles, that God would
protect their going out and comming in, which places of the
Posts or walls they kissed so oft as they entred or went forth.
Also the Jewes did weare about them the tenn Commandments
written in a long shred of parchment, which they wore aboute
theire heades stiched vp vpon the insyde of the Crownes of

theire hatts, and also foulded about their left armes. In the
Porch of the Synogoge before they entred, they sayd some
prayers, and also washed their hands, hauing basons of water
and towells layde there for that purpose, which was their inward
and outwarde preperation before they entred. The Synagoges
had no bells, but the people were called together by the voyce
of a Cryer passing through all the streetes. Each synogoge
had some 20 or 30 Rabbyes, with some 400 Dollers allowed to
each of them for yearely stipend, but of these one was supreme,
who hauing a greater stipend, had care of educating their
Children, and of preaching, which he did with his head covered,
sometymes in the language of the Germans, sometymes in the
Hebrewe toung. The whole Congregation did singe altogether,
each man hauing imbrodred linnen cast about his shoulders
with knotted fringes to the nomber of the Commandements
(which I take to be their Philacteryes), so as the Rabby could
not be knowne from the rest, but by his standing at the Alter.
Their singing was in a hollow tone, very lowe at the first,
but rysing by degrees, and sometymes stretched to flatt roring,
and the people in singing answered the Rabby, and some tymes
bowed their heades lowe, shaking their hinder partes, with many
ridiculous tones and gestures. Their diuine seruice (saue that
they dispise the newe testament) is not vnlike ours, for it consists of Psalmes, and two lessons, one out of the lawe, the second
out of the Prophetts (which last a boye reades, they lesse esteeming them then the lawe). In the midst of the Synogog they
had a litle rounde building open in the vper parte where the
lawe was layd vp, which was foulded like a Rowle betweene two
Joillers of siluer. And this lawe was in the morning opened
and lifted vp to be shewed to the people, all men first offering
mony to the Treasurye, with great emulation to haue the
honour to shewe it by giuing most. And while it was shewed
all the people often turned their bodyes rounde, with diuers mad
gestures, and at last fell to weeping and flatt roring, yet so as
it appeared an outwarde Ceremony rather then inwarde passion
or devotion. In prayers they neuer kneeled but only bended

forward, and neuer putt off their hatts in there devotions or in entring or going out of the Synogoge. Vpon the Saboth day being Satterday, diuine seruice continued from morning to night, but diuers companyes went out to eate or sleepe or refresh themselues at their pleasure, and in shorte space re-torned agayne. But that day no Jewe dressed any meate, nor bought or souled, nor would Receaue any mony though it were a desperate debt, nor yet pay any mony for any gayne. They had lampes burning by day in the Synogoge, to the honour of God only, and these were very fewe. The wemen came not into the Synogoge among men, but vnder the same Roof had their owne Synogoge and a doore to enter it, hauing windowes or narrowe Cleftes in the wall to heare the men singing, but them-selues only did reade or mumble with a lowe voyce, and were otherwise silent.

The Jewes beleeue the Resurrection of the dead. They deny the Trenity of persons in the deity, and holde no eternall damnation, but that in prossesse of tyme the most wicked, yea the very Deuills after long repentance and punishment shalbe saued, and hell abolished, and all the Creatures restored to the state in which they were first Created. They whip themselues in the Synagoges, but more gently then the Papists, being con-tent to weare out the rods vpon the stones; hauing broken the lawe, they come to the Rabby to impose punishment on them, but make no particular confession of the Fact. They keepe duly all their old Feasts, and Fastinges, yet fast not at nights but only at noone, and are very Charitable in workes of Pitty more spetially in ransoming Captiue Jewes.

They keepe the feast of Easter the 14th day of theire first month from the Creation of the Sunn and moone, only for eight dayes eating vnleuened bread, for they hold it vnlawfull to kill a Paschall lambe or to offer any sacrifice but only at Jerusalem.

At Prage they Circumcised their Children vpon the eighth day, and this Circumcision they vse to the dead as to the liuing, but thincke it not necessary to Saluation, (as at their first com-ming out of Egipt they were not Circumcised in the

wildernes for forty yeares), the Covenant standing firme without
the seale therof when it cannot be had. My selfe did see the
Ceremonyes therof in this manner when the Chylde came neere
to the Synagog, they raysed a clamour in the Hebrewe
tounge; Blessed is he that commeth in the name of the lord.
At the dore, the wemen not permited to enter, deliuered the
Childe to the Father, who caryed it to the Alter, and then was
a generall offering made with great emulation who shoulde
carry the box of powder, who the Salt, who the knife, as in
England wee offer who shall haue the Brides gloues. Then the
Chyldes linnen Clothes being opened, the Rabby cutt off his
prepuce, and (with leaue be it related for clearing of the
Ceremony) did with his mouth sucke the blood of his priuy part,
and after drawing and spitting out of much blood, sprinckled
a red powder vpon the wounde. The prepuce he had at the
first cutting cast into a guilt syluer bowle full of wyne, wherof
the Rabby the Father and the Godfather did drincke, sprinck-
ling some drops into the Chyldes mouth. Then the prepuce or
foreskinne was taken out, and putt into a box of salt to be
buryed after in the Churchyearde. The Father helde the
Chylde all this tyme in his Armes, and together with the God
Father testifyed that it was the seede of Abraham, and so gaue
the name to it. This donne the Father carying the Chylde
backe to the doore of the Synagog, there deliuered it to the
Nurse and wemen expecting it. The daughters without vsing
any Ceremony insteede of Circumcision, haue names giuen
them by their parents at dinner or supper vpon the eighth
day among frends called to the Feast, after the singing of a
Psalme.

Of the Greekes.

Now Touching the Grecians somthing must be very breefly
sayd of them, before I come to my much wished Peryod of this
discourse, because I passed through many Prouinces and Iles
inhabited by them. The Empire and kingdome of the Greekes

from all antiquity famous (and continuing of great power till the Turkes invaded Europe and tooke Constantinople), from that tyme hath beene vtterly abolished, and the people haue beene troden vnderfeete. Of them some liue as in exile (at Naples, in Apullia, in Calabria, at Rome, and in the Citty of Venice) hauing nether land nor coyne of their owne. Others liue subiect to the State of Venice in their owne land, and inioying Inheritances of land, but vse the Coyne of that State, (as in the Ilands of Corfu, Cephalonia the greater and the lesser, of Zante, and of Candia). But the greatest part liue in the Ilands and Continent of Greece vpon their owne land, yet possessing not one foote thereof by inheritance, but liuing as most base slaues to the Turkish tyranny and vsing theire Coynes, inioying only liberty of Conscience in Religion, and Churches to meete in for that purpose, vnder Capitall punishment if they perswade any to become Christians, or speake a worde against Mahomett, but otherwise disarmed and vsed like borne slaues, so oppressed by the Rapyne of the Turkes as they cannot inioye the goodes they gett by the sweate of theire browes, the Corne they sowe, nor the wyne they plant, yea not the Children they begett, since (as I haue formerly shewed in the Turkes Commonwealth) every third yeare their most ingenious and strong Children are taken for tribute, and brought vp by the Emperour in Turkish Religion to serue in his warrs, where they proue the greatest haters and persecuters of all Christians and of theire owne parents and kindred. Yea the Greekes are more dispised by the Turkes then any other Christians, because they lost their liberty and Kingdome basely and Cowardly, making small or no resistance against the Turkes Conquest. . . . . . It seemed strange to mee that the Pope should tolerate the Greekes to haue Churches in Italy and Rome it selfe, calling them only scismatikes, whereas they stand condemned for heritikes in the highest Article of Fayth touching the Trenity, and yet is so farr from suffering Protestants to haue Churches vnder him, as he will not lett them liue where he hath power to kill them if they be knowne to be Protestants.

To conclude, besyde the Nation of the Greekes the great Empire of the Moscouites professeth their Religion. And so I gladly ende this discourse and worke.

> All glory be to God the Father
> the sonne the holy Ghost for euer.
> Amen.

14° Junij 1626: Imprimatur.   Tho: Wilson.

INDEX

Compiled by Elena Tanasescu